World Military Aviation

aircraft, air forces,
weaponry, insignia

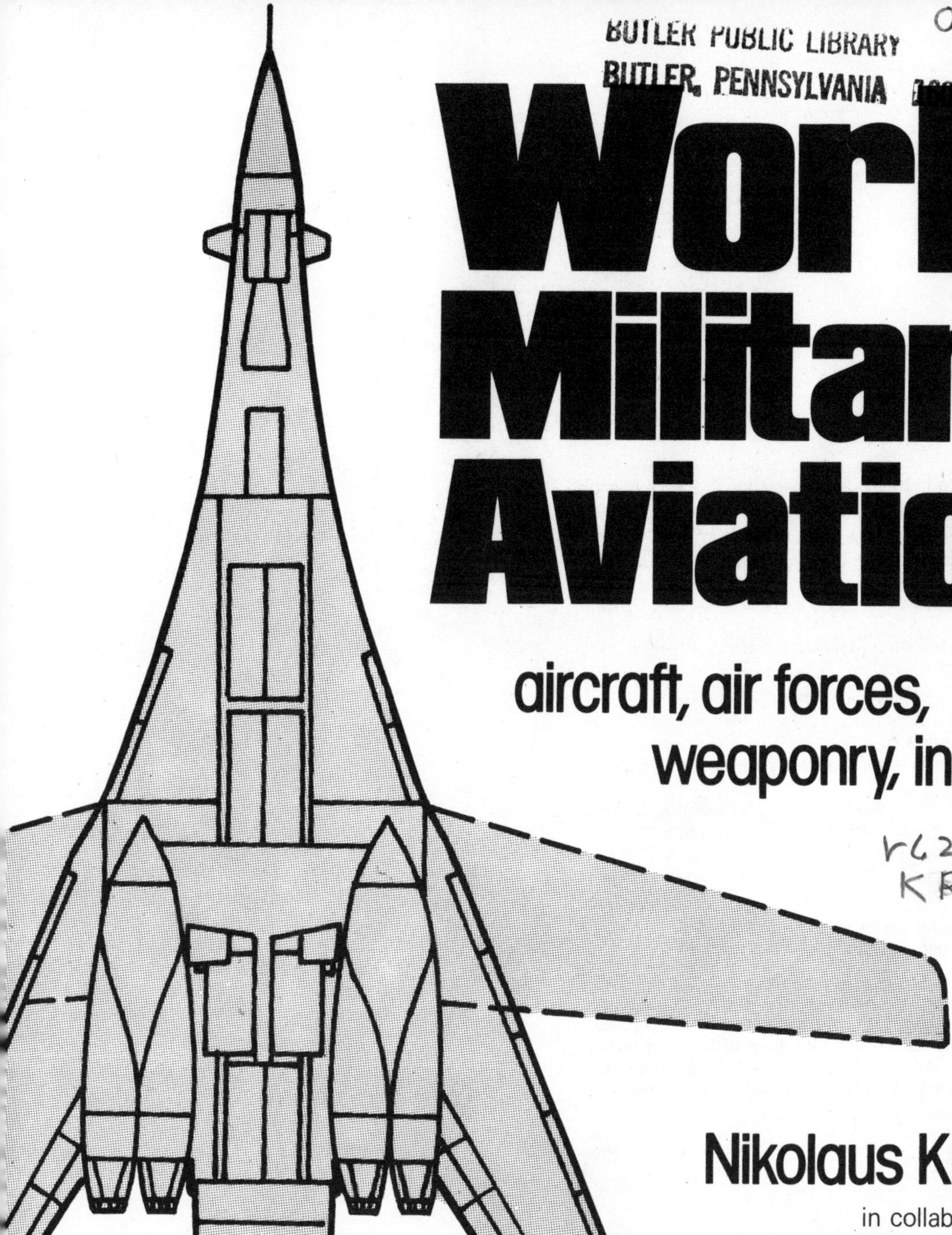

World Military Aviation

aircraft, air forces, weaponry, insignia

Nikolaus Krivinyi

in collaboration with
Franz Kosar and Johann Kroupa
Illustrated by Franz Gruber
Translated by Elke C Weal

ARCO PUBLISHING COMPANY, INC
New York

Published by Arco Publishing Company, Inc 219 Park Avenue South, New York, N.Y. 10003

Library of Congress Cataloging in Publication Data:
Krivinyi, Nikolaus
  World military aviation.
  'Updated and revised from Taschenbuch der Luftflotten.'
  Includes index.
  1. Air forces. 2. Airplanes, Military. 3. Aeronautics, Military.
I. Kosar, Franz. II. Kroupa, Johann. III. Taschenbuch der
Luftflotten. IV. Title.
UG632.K69 1977 623.7'46'09047 77–6639
ISBN 0–668–04348–2

The publishers wish to acknowledge the invaluable assistance of Michael J. Gething in the preparation of this edition.

Title-page illustration: the Rockwell B–1A heavy strategic bomber (see page 182). Compare this to the Soviet Tupolev Tu–26 (Backfire–B) illustrated on the front of the book jacket and on page 212. The cancellation of the B–1A project was announced by President Carter shortly before this book went to press.

Layout by A. A. Evans.
Printed in Great Britain by Cox & Wyman Ltd, Fakenham, England.

Contents

Preface, 7
Glossary, 8
Insignia, 9

Air forces, 17
Abu Dhabi, 17
Afghanistan, 17
Albania, 17
Algeria, 18
Angola, 18
Arab Emirates, United:
  see United Arab
  Emirates, 68
Argentina, 18
Australia, 19
Austria, 20
Bahrain, 21
Bangladesh, 21
Belgium, 21
Bolivia, 21
Brazil, 22
Brunei, 23
Bulgaria, 23
Burma, 23
Cambodia, 24
Cameroun, 24
Canada, 24
Central African Republic,
  25
Ceylon: see Sri Lanka,
  62
Chad, 25
Chile, 25

China (People's Republic),
  26
China, Republic of: see
  Taiwan, 64
Colombia, 27
Congo (Brazzaville), 27
Congo (Kinshasa): see
  Zaire, 75
Costa Rica, 27
Cuba, 27
Cyprus, 28
Czechoslovakia, 28
Dahomey, 28
Denmark, 28
Dominican Republic, 29
Dubai, 29
Ecuador, 29
Egypt (UAR), 30
Eire, 30
El Salvador, 31
Ethiopia, 31
Finland, 31
France, 32
Gabon, 33
Germany, East (DDR), 34
Germany, West (Federal
  Republic), 34
Ghana, 35
Great Britain, 35
Greece, 37
Guatemala, 38
Guinea, 38
Guyana, 38

Haiti, 38
Honduras, 38
Hong Kong, 39
Hungary, 39
Iceland, 39
India, 39
Indonesia, 40
Iran (Persia), 41
Iraq, 42
Ireland: see Eire, 30
Israel, 43
Italy, 43
Ivory Coast, 44
Jamaica, 45
Japan, 45
Jordan, 46
Kenya, 46
Korea (North), 47
Korea (South), 47
Kuwait, 47
Laos, 48
Lebanon, 48
Liberia, 48
Libya, 48
Madagascar (Malagasy),
  49
Malawi, 49
Malaysia, 49
Mali, 50
Malta, 50
Mauritania, 50
Mexico, 50
Mongolia, 51

Morocco, 51
Mozambique, 51
Nepal, 51
Netherlands, 52
New Guinea: see
  Papua–New Guinea, 55
New Zealand, 52
Nicaragua, 53
Niger, 53
Nigeria, 53
Norway, 53
Oman, 54
Pakistan, 54
Panama, 55
Papua–New Guinea, 55
Paraguay, 55
Peru, 55
Philippines, 56
Poland, 57
Portugal, 57
Qatar, 58
Rhodesia, 58
Romania, 58
Rwanda, 59
Saudi Arabia, 59
Senegal, 59
Sierra Leone, 59
Singapore, 60
Somali, 60
South Africa, 60
South Yemen (People's
  Democratic Republic),
  61

Soviet Union: see USSR,
  72
Spain, 61
Sri Lanka (Ceylon), 62
Sudan, 63
Sweden, 63
Switzerland, 64
Syria, 64
Taiwan (Republic of
  China), 64
Tanzania, 65
Thailand, 65
Togo, 66
Trinidad and Tobago, 66
Tunisia, 66
Turkey, 67
Uganda, 68
United Arab Emirates,
  68
United Arab Republic: see
  Egypt, 30
United States of America,
  68
Upper Volta, 72
Uruguay, 72
USSR, 72
Venezuela, 73
Vietnam, 74
Yemen Arab Republic
  (North), 74
Yugoslavia, 74
Zaire, 75
Zambia, 75

Aircraft, 77
Argentina, 78
Australia, 78
Brazil, 79
Canada, 80
China (People's Republic),
  84
Czechoslovakia, 85
France, 87
Germany, West (Federal
  Republic), 99
Great Britain, 101
India, 116
Israel, 118
Italy, 118
Japan, 123
Netherlands, 126
New Zealand, 127
Poland, 127
Spain, 128
Sweden, 131
Switzerland, 134
Taiwan (Republic of
  China), 135
United States of America,
  136
USSR, 191
Yugoslavia, 216

Weaponry, 219
Index to Aircraft section,
  227

Preface

In recent years, there have been several significant changes and developments in the air forces of the world. The fourth Arab–Israeli War of October 1973 demonstrated, among other things, that the importance of electronic warfare has sharply increased. Only after the Americans had flown-in ECM equipment and anti-missile devices did the Israeli fighter aircraft begin to be effective against Arab gun emplacements and tank squadrons. In this conflict, there was also an ample demonstration of the global supportive role of the United States Military Airlift Command. (The Soviet Union, on the other hand, managed but few, inadequate airlifts for the Arabs.)

Soviet air power, meanwhile, has been considerably strengthened by the introduction of more sophisticated aircraft, such as the swing-wing fighter SU–17 (Fitter–C), SU–19 (Fencer) and MiG–23 (Flogger), as well as the Tupolev 'Backfire' strategic bomber and the Mi–24 (Hind) attack helicopter. At sea, the first Soviet aircraft carrier, *Kiev*, is now operational, with a complement of Yak–36 (Forger) VTOL aircraft. Together with the overall improvement in avionics, this all adds up to a perceptible shift in the balance of power in favour of the USSR.

In order to re-equip the depleted NATO forces in Europe, and to provide a viable substitute for the ageing F104G Starfighter, Belgium, Denmark, the Netherlands and Norway have ordered the American F–16 fighter, while Germany, Great Britain and Italy are going ahead with their MRCA Tornado. (A decision is still awaited concerning the purchase of AWACS.)

The United States, besides being the only member of NATO to have significantly increased the number of its aircraft in Europe, is also bringing into service a number of new aircraft – most notably the F–15 and F–16 fighter/strike-fighters and the armoured low-altitude Fairchild A–10A ground-attack aircraft. New transports, tankers and the B–1 swing-wing strategic bomber are also being developed, and electronic techniques and anti-missile devices improved. Tank warfare remains one of the United States' major problems, although a number of anti-tank helicopters have now been introduced. To counteract the threat posed by the growing Soviet naval forces, the US Navy has acquired F–14A Tomcats, F–18 Hornets, S–3A Vikings and various helicopter types.

In Asia, Africa and Latin America, air forces are increasingly being re-equipped with modern, up-to-date units: Iran has purchased the American F–14, Libya has the Soviet MiG–23 (Flogger); while Oman and Ecuador are taking the Anglo–French Jaguar. This sort of expensive equipment, however, can only be maintained with help from abroad.

Glossary

Air Force Section

(?) information uncertain; – no information available.

Squadrons: Total given includes fighter, strike-fighter, ground-attack, bomber, reconnaissance, maritime-reconnaissance and ASW, transport and helicopter squadrons, but NOT liaison and AOP squadrons nor training squadrons.

Operational aircraft: These include fighters, strike fighters, ground-attack aircraft, bombers, reconnaissance and ECM aircraft, maritime-reconnaissance and ASW aircraft plus transports, but NOT liaison and AOP aircraft nor trainers. Army aviation is the only exception: Here, liaison and AOP aircraft are also classed as 'operational aircraft' – as their role differs from those of the Air Forces and Naval Air Arms.

Helicopters: Include all helicopters, regardless of operational function, i.e. also armed and attack-helicopters.

Aircraft Section

Weight empty: The combined weight of airframe, power plant(s) and standard equipment. The different interpretations of standard equipment by individual nations can result in differing figures.

Normal take-off weight: Encompasses empty weight plus load, the latter comprising crew, fuel, lubricants and payload.

Maximum take-off weight: The highest permissible take-off weight dependent upon runway conditions, local authorities and/or flight characteristics.

Maximum speed: The highest speed it is possible to achieve in horizontal flight for a limited period, under ideal conditions and at a fixed height above ground level.

Maximum cruising speed: Highest possible speed over longer periods. Not to be confused with economical cruising speed for maximum range.

Patrol speed: Quoted mainly for maritime aircraft as optimum search speed.

Radius of action (often referred to as penetration range): The distance an aircraft can fly in any one direction, dependent upon its returning to base.

Range: The distance an aircraft can fly at the optimum cruising speed for any given weight *with* a fixed payload fuel capacity (inc auxiliary tanks) without refuelling.

Ferry range: The distance an aircraft can fly at the optimum cruising speed for any given weight *without* payload at the most favourable altitude and with maximum fuel capacity (inc auxiliary tanks) without refuelling.

Initial rate of climb: The maximum rate of climb near ground level, generally in relation to normal take-off weight.

Service ceiling: Generally taken as the height at which rate of climb drops to 1.64ft/sec (0.5m/sec).

Hovering ceiling: The maximum height at which a helicopter can remain stationary in both horizontal and vertical planes. Because of ground-effect this ceiling is dependent upon the height of the machine above ground level.

Static thrust (st): The static thrust of its turbojet engines is given in lb (kg) without/with afterburning.

Abbreviations

AAM	Air-to-air missile
AOP	Aerial observation post
ARM	Anti-radar missile
ASM	Air-to-surface missile
ASR	Air-sea rescue
ASW	Anti-submarine warfare
AWACS	Airborne warning and control system
ECM	Electronic counter-measures
ft/sec	feet per second
hp	horse-power
kg	kilograms
m	metres
mhp	miles per hour
m/sec	metres per second
rpg	rounds per gun
s/l	sea-level
sq ft	square feet
sq m	square metres
st	static thrust
STOL	Short take-off and lift/landing
VTOL	Vertical take-off and lift/landing
w.m.p.	with maximum payload

Insignia

Abu Dhabi

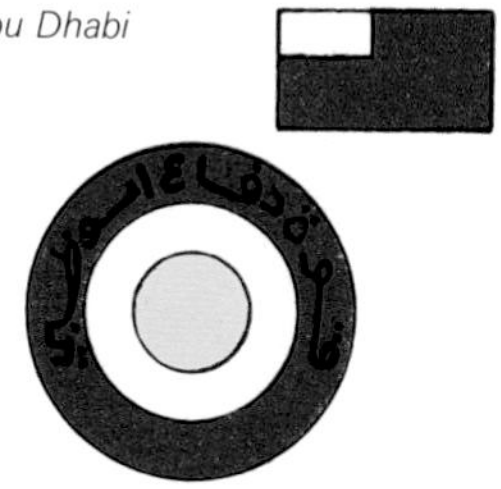

Afghanistan (no fin flash)

Albania

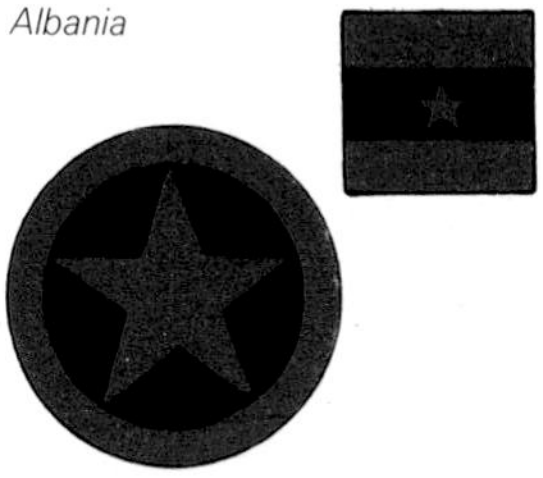

Algeria

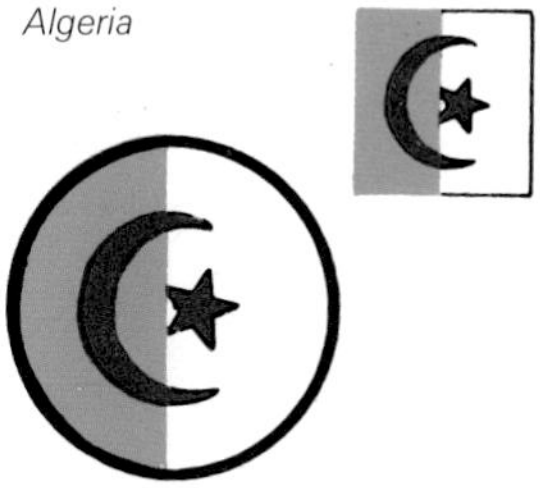

Argentine

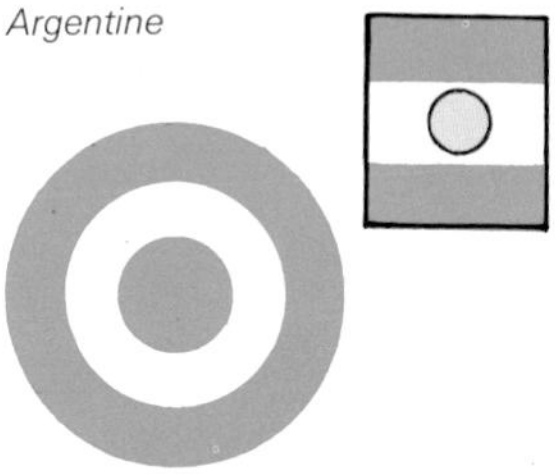

Argentinian Navy

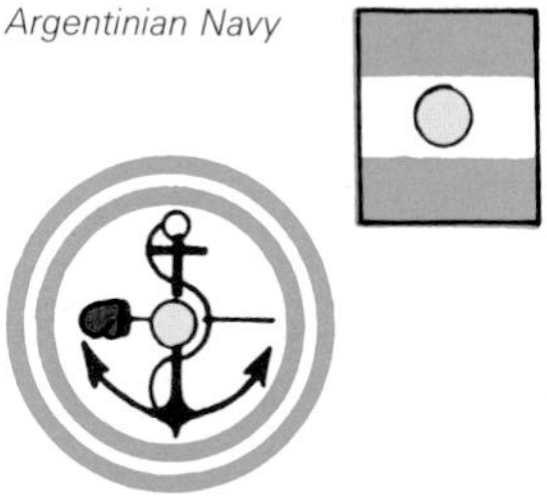

Australia

Austria (no fin·flash)

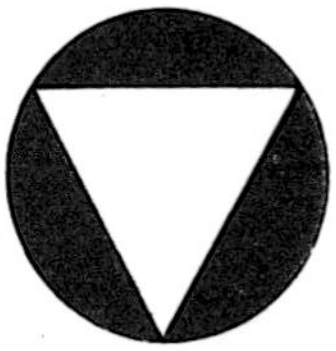

Bangladesh

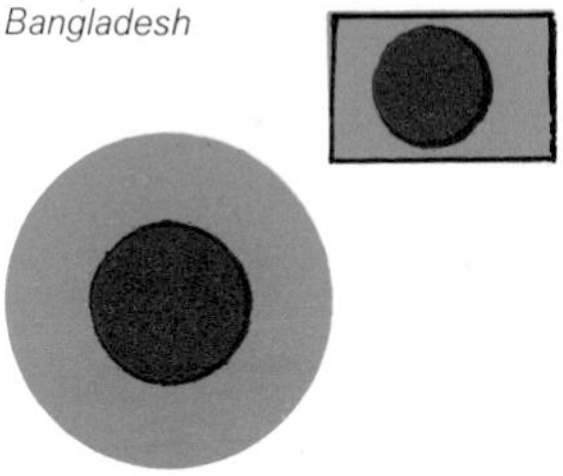

Barbados (no fin flash)

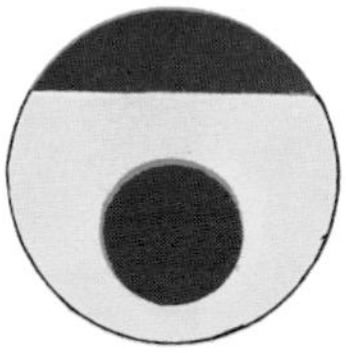

Belgium

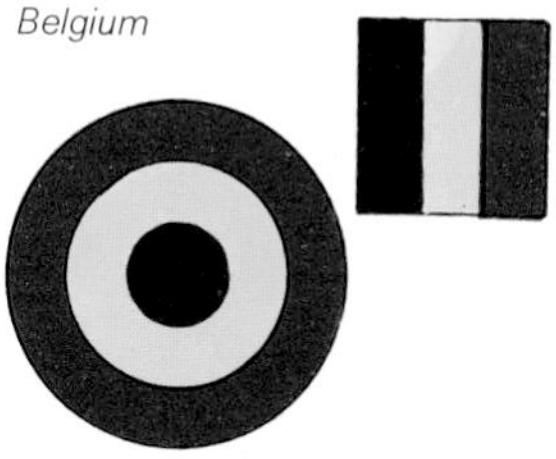

Bolivia

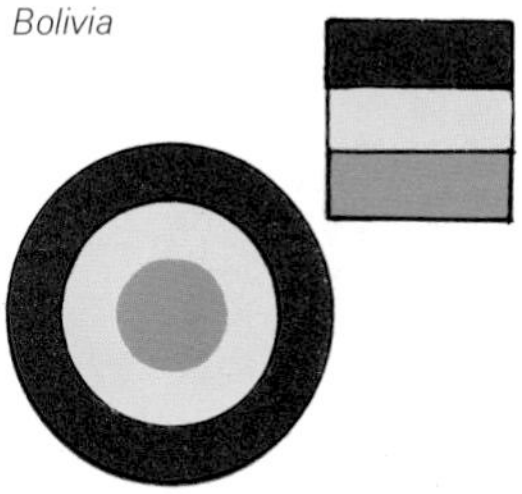

Brazil

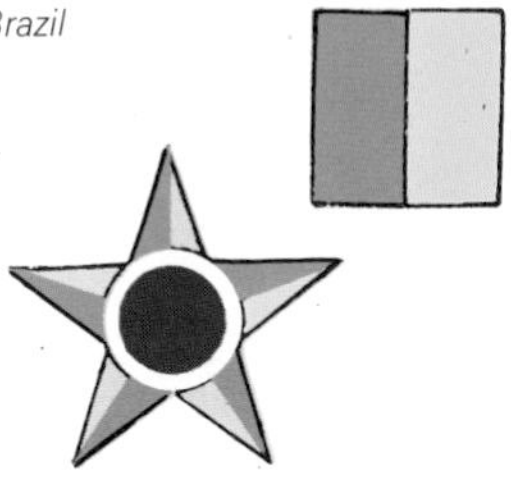

Brazilian Navy
(no fin flash)

Brunei (no fin flash)

Bulgaria

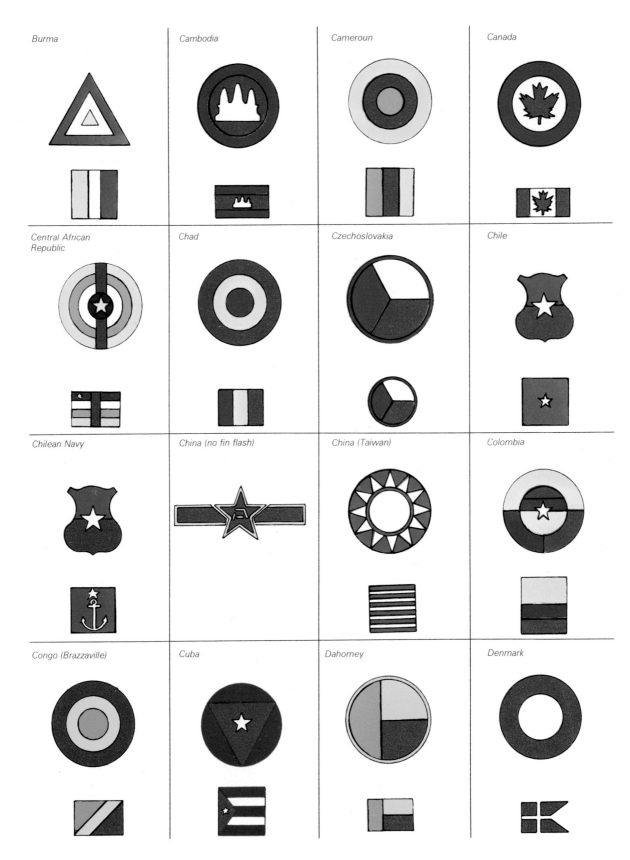

Burma

Cambodia

Cameroun

Canada

Central African
Republic

Chad

Czechoslovakia

Chile

Chilean Navy

China (no fin flash)

China (Taiwan)

Colombia

Congo (Brazzaville)

Cuba

Dahomey

Denmark

Dominican Republic

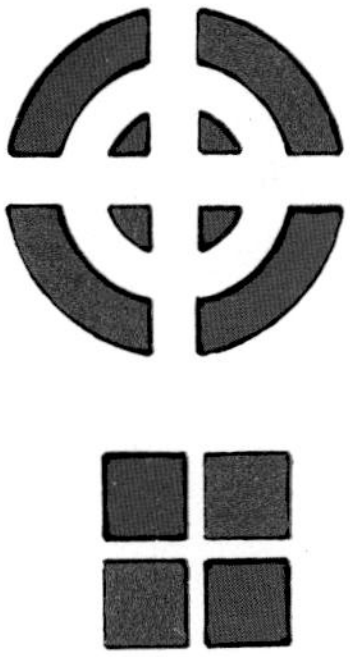

Ecuador

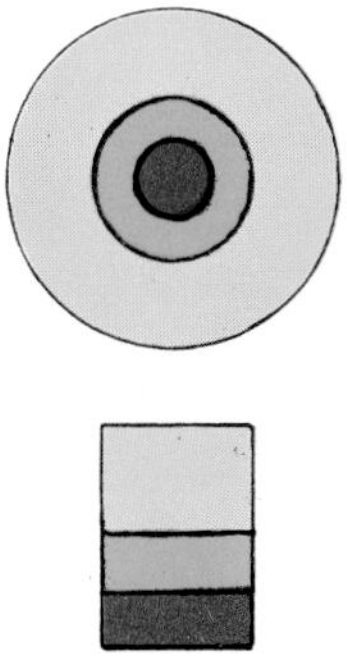

Egypt

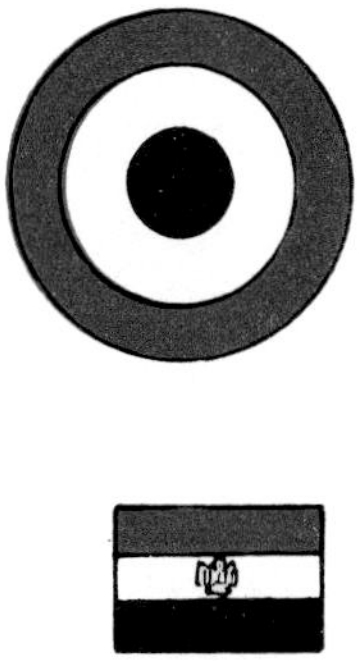

Eire (no fin flash)

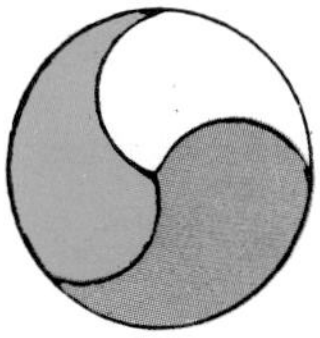

El Salvador

Ethiopia (no fin flash)

Finland (no fin flash)

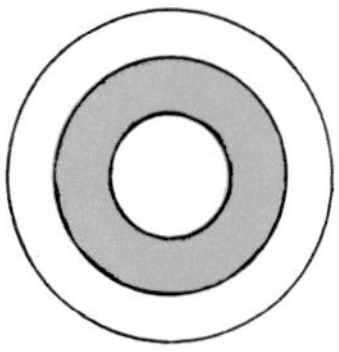

France

French Navy
(no fin flash)

Gabon

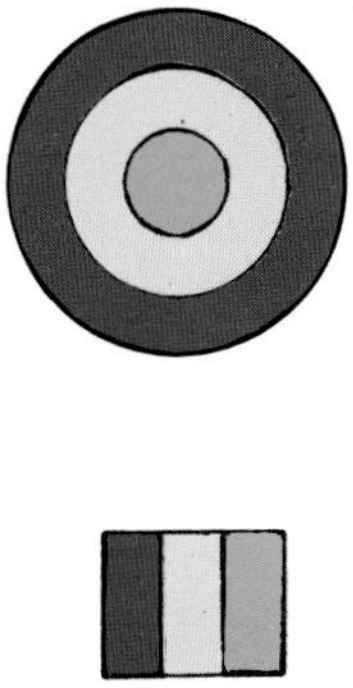

Germany (West)

Germany (East)

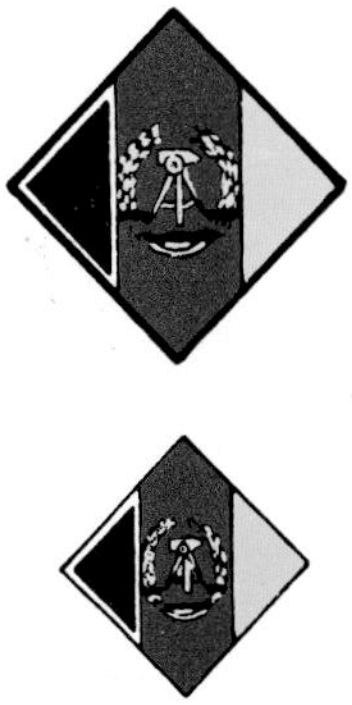

Ghana

Great Britain

Great Britain
(camouflage pattern)

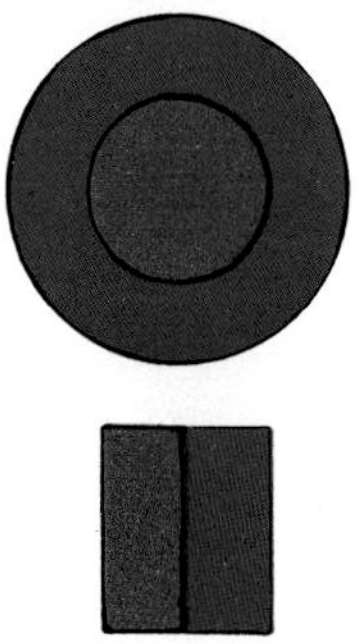

Greece

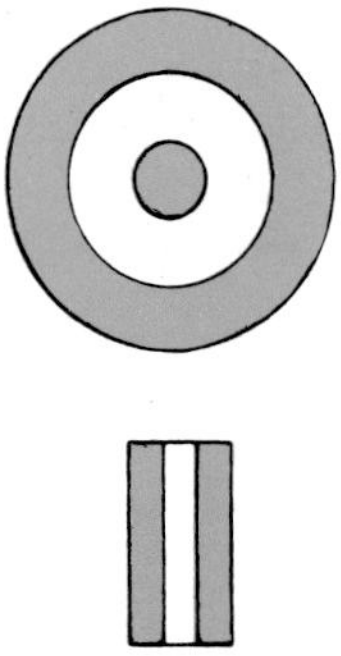

Guatemala

Guinea (no fin flash)

Guyana (no fin flash)

Haiti (no fin flash)

Honduras

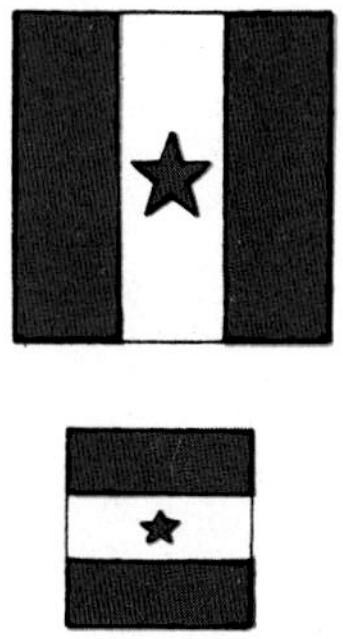

Hungary

India

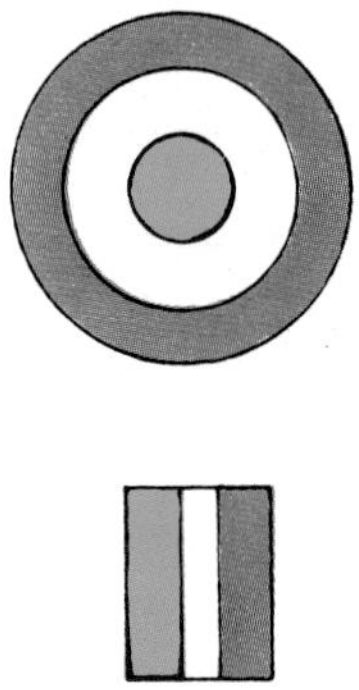

Indonesia

Indonesian Navy

Indonesian Army

Iran

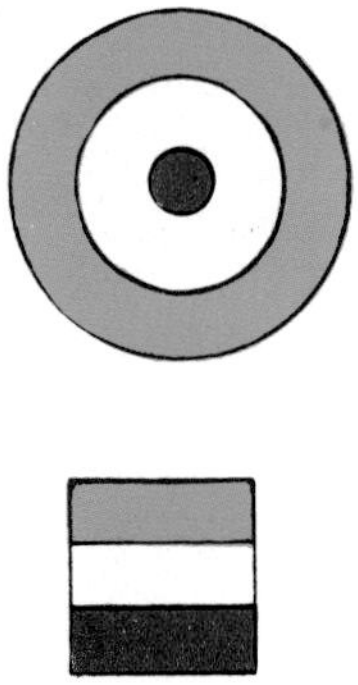

Iraq

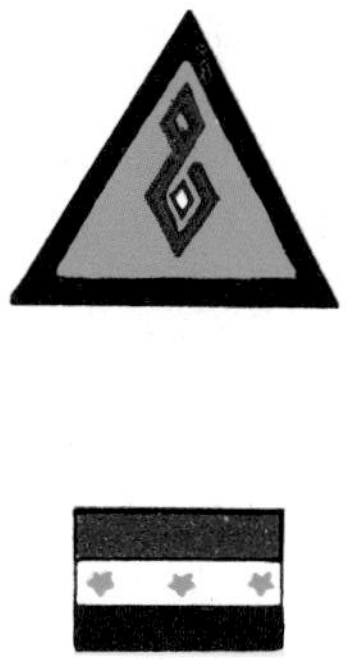

Israel (no fin flash)

Italy (no fin flash)

Ivory Coast

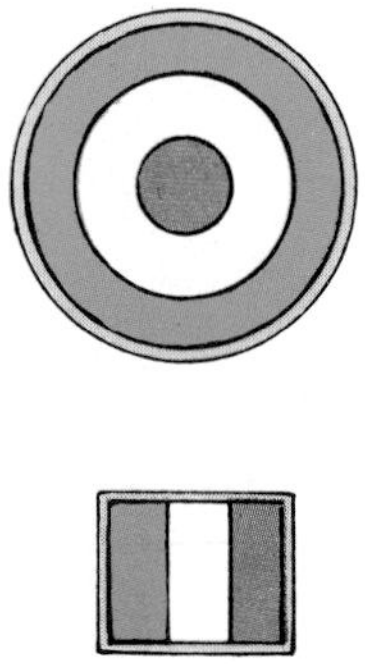

Jamaica

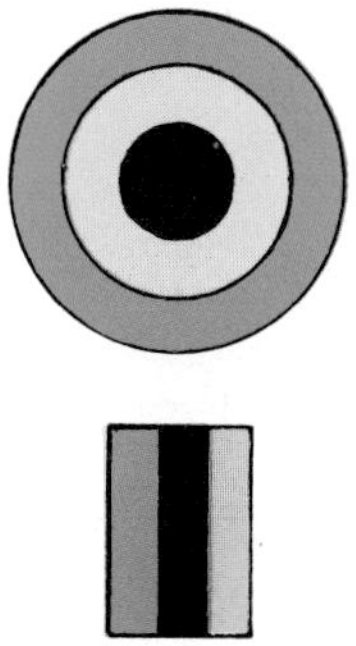

| Japan (no fin flash) | Jordan | Kenya | Korea (North) (no fin flash) |

Japan (no fin flash)

Jordan

Kenya

Korea (North)
(no fin flash)

Korea (South)
(no fin flash)

Kuwait

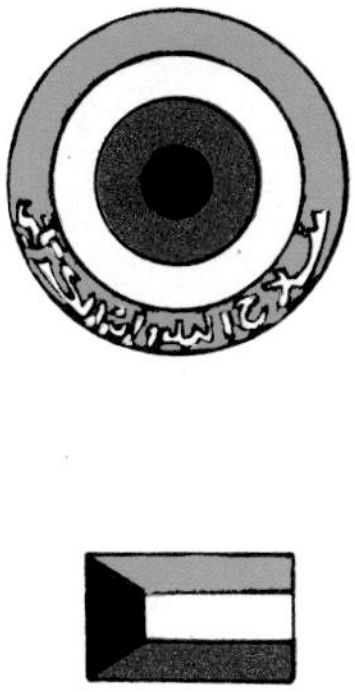

Laos

Lebanon

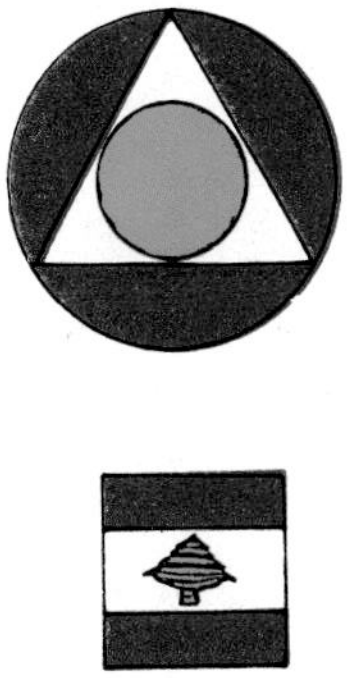

Libya

Madagascar

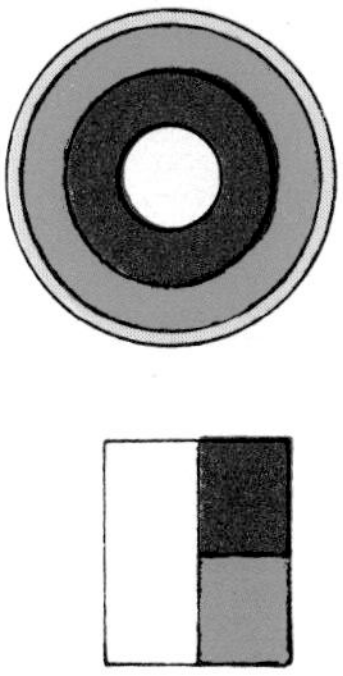

Malaysia

Mali

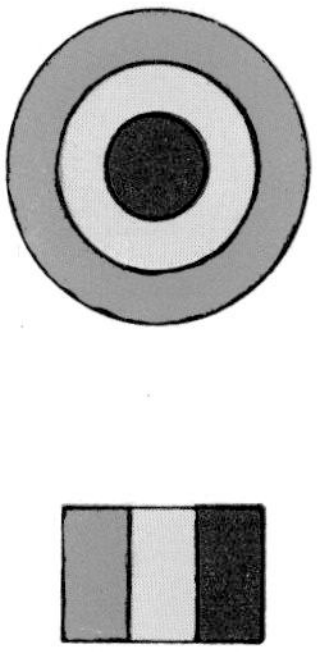

Mauretania

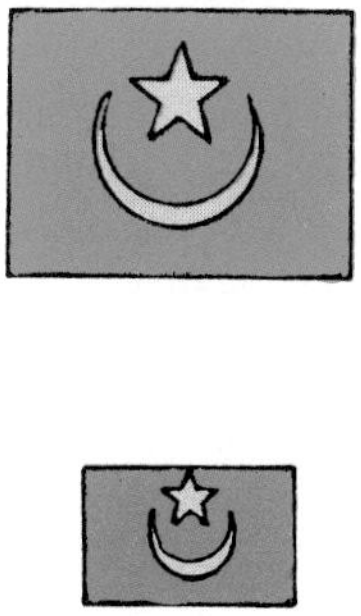

Mexico

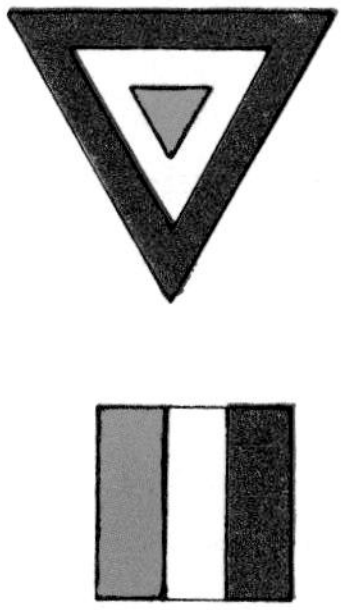

Mongolia (no fin flash)

Morocco

Nepal

Netherlands (no fin flash)

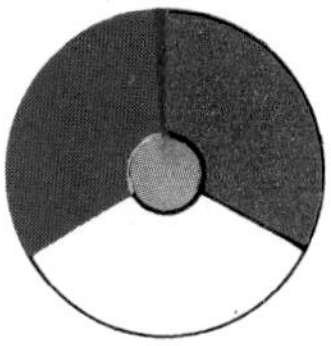

New Zealand

Nicaragua

Niger

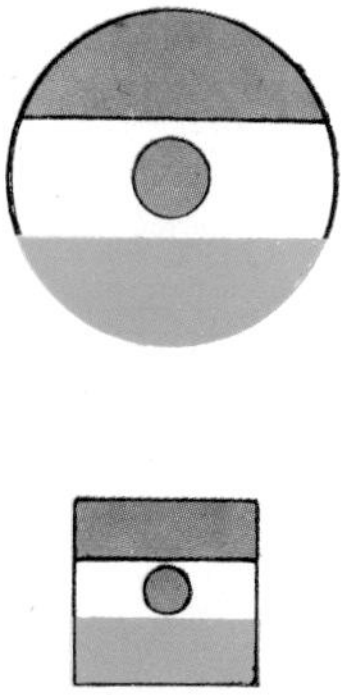

Nigeria

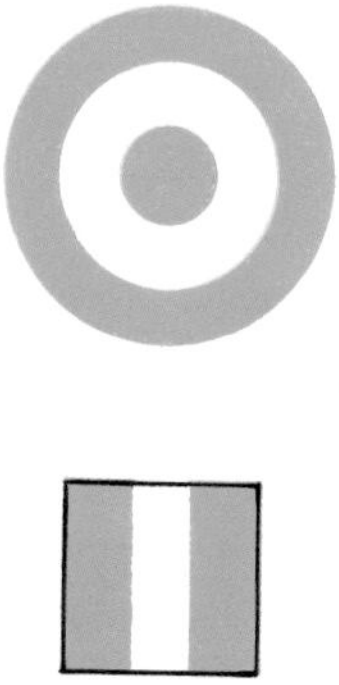

Norway (no fin flash)

Oman

Pakistan

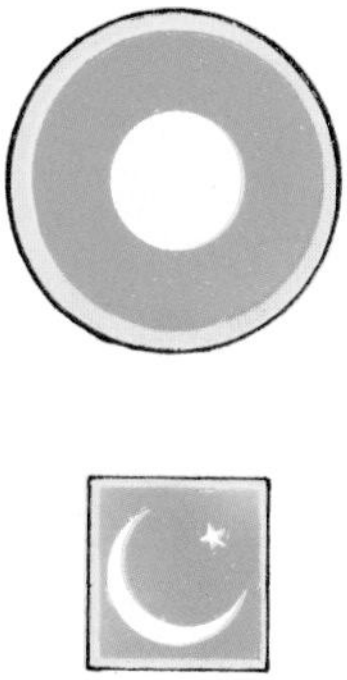

Panama

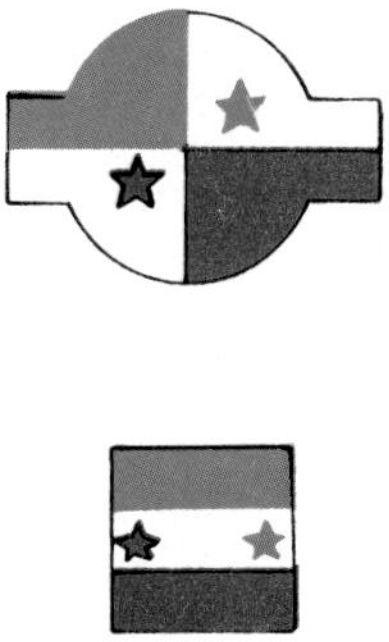

Paraguay

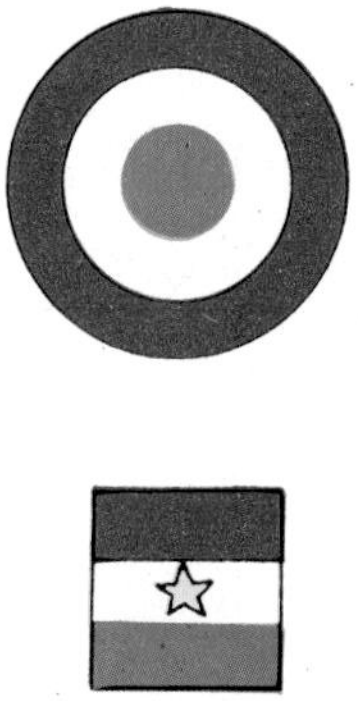

Peru

Philippines (no fin flash)

Poland

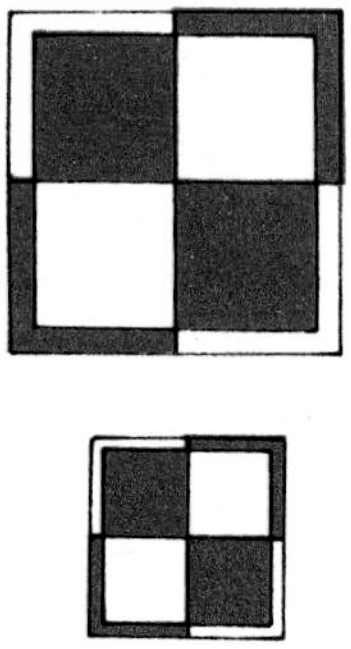

Portugal

Qatar

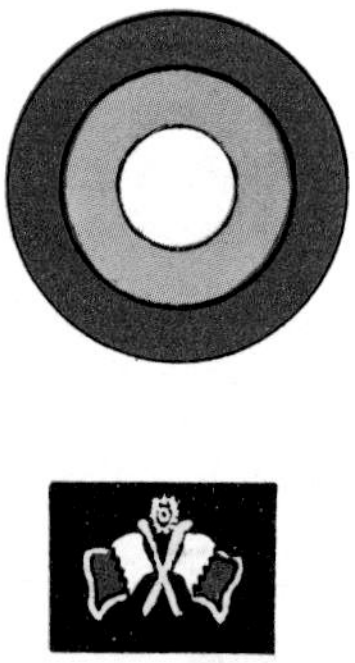

Rhodesia	Romania	Ruanda (no fin flash)	Saudi Arabia

Senegal	Singapore (no fin flash)	Somalia	South Africa

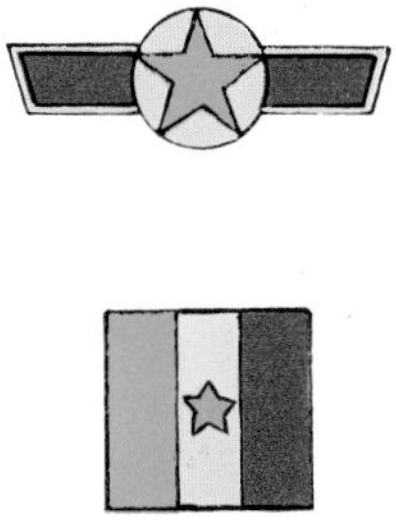

Spain	Sri Lanka (Ceylon)	Sudan	Sweden (no fin flash)

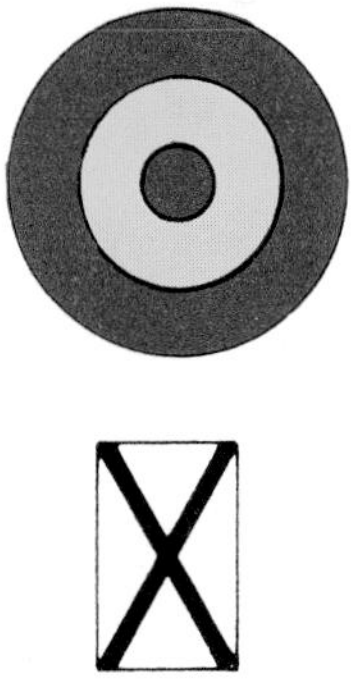

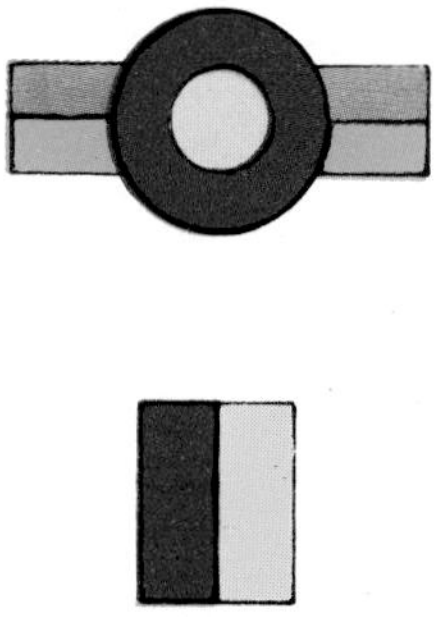

Switzerland	Syria	Tanzania	Thailand

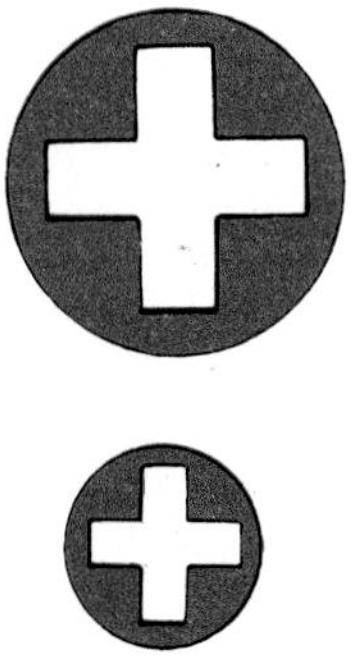

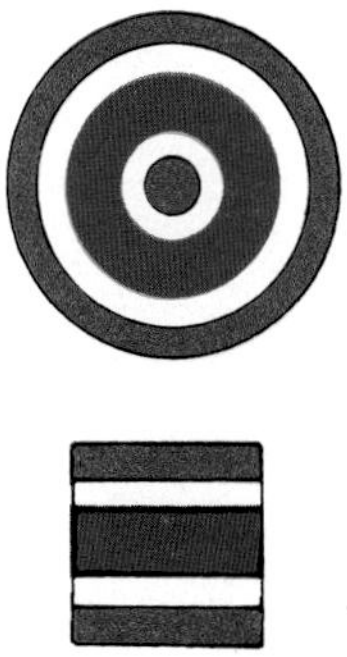

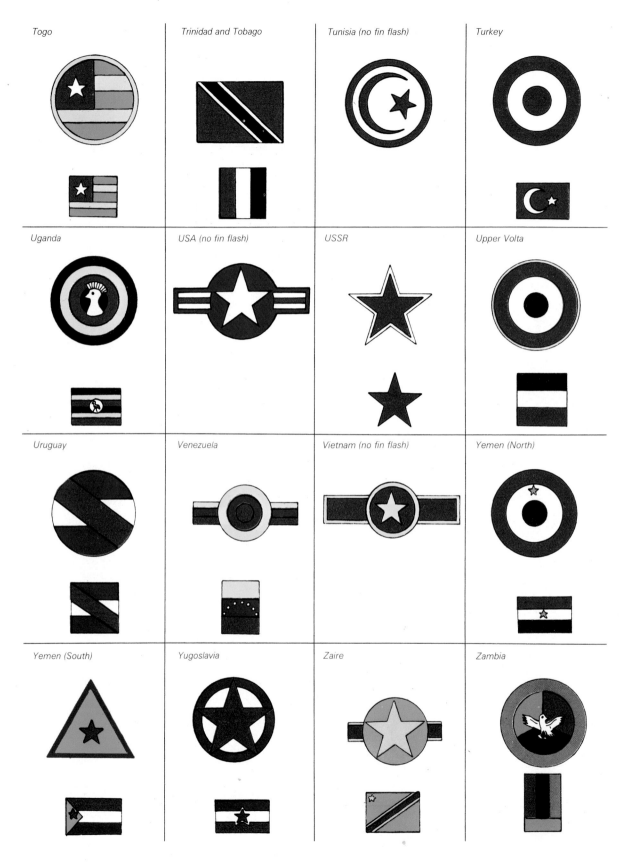

Togo	Trinidad and Tobago	Tunisia (no fin flash)	Turkey
Uganda	USA (no fin flash)	USSR	Upper Volta
Uruguay	Venezuela	Vietnam (no fin flash)	Yemen (North)
Yemen (South)	Yugoslavia	Zaire	Zambia

Air forces

Abu Dhabi
Air force (Air Wing Abu Dhabi Defence Forces)
men 1,200.
squadrons 4.
operational aircraft 36.
helicopters 12.
Organization
1 strike-fighter squadron with Mirage 5–AD and 5–RAD.
1 strike-fighter squadron with Hunter FGA.76.
1 transport squadron with DHC–4 and BN–2.
1 helicopter squadron with Alouette III and S.A.330.
Major bases
Abu Dhabi, Sharjah.
Military training aid from
Great Britain, Pakistan.
Equipment
Fighters and strike-fighters:
10 Dassault Mirage 5–AD.
2 Dassault Mirage 5–DAD.
8 Hawker Hunter FGA.76.
2 Hawker Hunter T.77.
Reconnaissance aircraft:
2 Mirage 5–RAD.
Transports:
12 BAC VC10.
4 Britten-Norman BN–2.
4 de Havilland Canada DHC–4.
2 Lockheed C–130H.
Helicopters:
7 Aérospatiale Alouette III.
5 Aérospatiale S.A.330.
Programme
On order: 14 Dassault Mirage 5–AD strike-fighters, 3 Mirage 5–RAD reconnaissance aircraft and 1 Mirage 5–DAD strike-trainer, delivery 1977–78. Phasing out of Hawker Hunter strike-fighters.
Army 8,600 men.
Navy 200 men.

Afghanistan
Air force
men 6,000.
squadrons 12.
operational aircraft 125.
helicopters 24.
Organization
3 fighter squadrons with MiG–21.
3 strike-fighter squadrons with MiG–17F.
2 strike-fighter squadrons with Su–7.
1 bomber squadron with Il–28.
2 transport squadrons with Il–14.
1 helicopter squadron with Mi–4.
1 helicopter squadron with Mi–8.
– trainer squadrons with Yak–11 and Yak–18.
Fighter and strike-fighter squadrons each with 10–12 aircraft.
Major bases
Herat, Jalalabad, Kandahar, Mazar-i-Sharif, Pagram, Sherpur, Shindand.
Military training aid from
Soviet Union.
Equipment
Fighters and strike-fighters:
25 Mikoyan MiG–17F.
40 Mikoyan MiG–21 and MiG–21U.
24 Sukhoi Su–7.
Bombers:
10 Ilyushin Il–28.
Transports:
10 Antonov An–2.
15 Ilyushin Il–14.
2 Ilyushin Il–18.
Helicopters:
6 Mil Mi–1.
12 Mil Mi–4.
6 Mil Mi–8.
Trainers:
approx 40 aircraft, inc Yakovlev Yak–11 and Yak–18, Mikoyan MiG–15UTI.
Programme
Replacement of further Mikoyan MiG–17 by Mikoyan MiG–21 and Sukhoi Su–7 strike-fighters.
Army 80,000 men.
Army aviation
The Air Force is a component part of the Army.

Albania
Air force
men 4,000.
squadrons 9.
operational aircraft 70.
helicopters 20.
Organization
1 fighter squadron with F–8 (MiG–21).
2 fighter squadrons with F–6 (MiG–19).
2 strike-fighter squadrons with F–4 (MiG–17F).
1 strike-fighter squadron with MiG–15.
1 transport squadron with An–2 and Il–14.
2 helicopter squadrons with Mi–1 and Mi–4.
Fighter and strike-fighter squadrons each with 10–12 aircraft.
Major bases
Berat/Kucove, Durazzo/Shiyak, Tirana, Valcona.

Military training aid from
China (People's Republic).
Equipment
Fighters and strike-fighters:
10 Mikoyan MiG–15.
20 Shenyang F–4 (MiG–17F).
20 Shenyang F–6 (MiG–19).
15 Shenyang F–8 (MiG–21).
Transports:
3 Antonov An–2.
3 Ilyushin Il–14.
Helicopters:
approx 20 Mil Mi–1 and Mi–4.
Trainers:
Yakovlev Yak–11 and Yak–18, Mikoyan MiG–15UTI.
Programme
Replacement of Mikoyan MiG–15 and Shenyang F–4
(MiG–17) strike-fighters by Shenyang F–8 (MiG–21).
Army 30,000 men.
Navy 3,000 men.

Algeria
Air force (Al Quwwat Aljawwiya Aljaza)
men 4,500.
squadrons 17.
operational aircraft 150.
helicopters 60.
Organization
3 fighter squadrons with MiG–21F.
3 strike-fighter squadrons with MiG–17F and PF.
2 strike-fighter squadrons with Su–7BM.
2 bomber squadrons with Il–28.
1 transport squadron with An–12 and Il–18.
1 transport squadron with F.27.
3 helicopter squadrons with Mi–4.
1 helicopter squadron with S.A.330.
2 trainer squadrons with C.M.170.
Fighter, strike-fighter and bomber squadrons each with
10–12 aircraft.
Major bases
Algiers, Biskra, Boufarak, Dar-el-Beider, Maison Blanche,
Marine, Mers-el-Kebir, Oran, Oukar, Paul-Cazelles,
Sidi-bel-Abbès.
Military training aid from
Egypt (UAR), France, Soviet Union.
Equipment
Fighters and strike-fighters:
45 Mikoyan MiG–17F and PF.
40 Mikoyan MiG–21F and MiG–21U.
20 Sukhoi Su–7BM.
Bombers:
20 Ilyushin Il–28.
Maritime-reconnaissance:
2 Canadair CL–215.
Transports:
8 Antonov An–12.
6 Fokker-VFW F.27.
some Ilyushin Il–14.
3 Ilyushin Il–18.
Helicopters:
5 Aérospatiale S.A.330.
6 Hughes 269A.
some Mil Mi–1.
40 Mil Mi–4.
5 Mil Mi–8.
Trainers:
approx 55 aircraft, inc Yakovlev Yak–11, Yakovlev Yak–18, 26
Potez-Air Fouga C.M.170.

Programme
Replacement of Ilyushin Il–28 bombers by Mikoyan MiG–21
and Sukhoi Su–7 fighters and strike-fighters.
Army 55,000 men.
Navy 3,500 men.

Angola
Air force (FAPA)
men 1,500(?).
squadrons –.
operational aircraft –.
helicopters –.
Organization
1 strike-fighter squadron with MiG–21.
1 strike-fighter squadron with MiG–17.
Military training aid from
Cuba, Soviet Union.
Equipment
Fighters and strike-fighters:
some Mikoyan MiG–17.
8(15?) Mikoyan MiG–21.
Liaison aircraft:
2 Pilatus PC–6B–1/H–2.
Transports:
2 Nord N.2501.
Trainers:
2 Mikoyan MiG–15UTI.
Army 27,000(?) men.
Navy 300(?) men.

Arab Emirates, United: see United Arab Emirates

Argentina
Air force (Fuerza Aérea Argentina)
men 21,000.
squadrons 12.
operational aircraft 170.
helicopters 36.
Organization
1 fighter squadron with Mirage IIIEA.
1 strike-fighter squadron with A–4P.
1 strike-fighter squadron with A–4F.
2 ground-attack squadrons with I.A.58.
1 bomber squadron with Canberra B.62.
1 transport squadron with F.27.
1 transport squadron with C–130E and DC–6.
1 transport squadron with C–47.
1 transport squadron with DHC–6.
1 helicopter squadron with OH–6A.
1 helicopter squadron with UH–IH.
– trainer squadrons with T–34B.
– trainer squadrons with M.S.760.
Ground-attack squadrons each with 12 aircraft.
Major bases
Chamical, Comodore, Rivadavia, El Palomar, El Plumerillo,
Mar del Plata, Mendoza, Moron, Paraná, Reconquista, Rio
Gallegos, Santa Fé, Tandil, Villa Reynolds.
Military training aid from
United States(?).
Equipment
Fighters and strike-fighters:
10 Dassault Mirage IIIEA.
2 Dassault Mirage IIIDA.
25 McDonnell Douglas A–4P.
15 McDonnell Douglas A–4F.
some North American F–86F.
Ground-attack aircraft:
30 FMA I.A.58.

Bombers:
9 English Electric Canberra B.62.
2 English Electric Canberra T.64.
Transports:
6 Beechcraft C–45.
1 Boeing 707–320B.
4 Canadair CC–106.
some de Havilland Dove(?).
4 de Havilland Canada DHC–6.
6 Douglas C–47.
1 Douglas C–118.
2 Douglas DC–6.
3 Fiat G.222.
10 FMA I.A.50.
9 Fokker-VFW F.27.
3 Fokker-VFW F.28.
1 Hawker Siddeley H.S.748.
4 Lockheed C–130E.
3(5?) Lockheed C–130H.
Liaison and reconnaissance aircraft:
approx 35 aircraft, inc Beechcraft Bonanza, Cessna 182,
  Cessna 320 and 3(?) de Havilland Canada DHC–2.
Helicopters:
6 Aérospatiale S.A.315B.
3 Bell 47G.
1 Bell 47J.
6 Bell UH–1H.
12 Hughes OH–6A.
2 Hughes 500M.
4(?) Sikorsky S–58T.
2 Sikorsky S–61NR.
Trainers:
25 Beechcraft T–34B.
25 FMA I.A.35.
Programme
Replacement of Morane-Saulnier M.S.700 trainers by 8(24?)
  Aermacchi MB.326K ground-attack aircraft. Purchase of
  further 50 FMA I.A.58 Pucará ground-attack aircraft planned.
Army 83,500 men.
Army aviation (Comando de Aviación Ejército)
– men.
– squadrons.
39(?) operational aircraft.
28 helicopters.
Equipment
Helicopters:
20 Bell UH–1H.
2 Bell 212.
6 Fairchild-Hiller FH–1100.
Liaison and AOP aircraft:
1 Beechcraft King Air.
5 Cessna 207 Turbo-Skywagon.
2 Cessna 310.
5 Cessna T–41D.
10 Cessna U–17A.
4(?) Piper Apache.
5 Piper L–21A.
Transports:
2 de Havilland Canada DHC–6.
1 Rockwell Sabreliner.
14(?) Rockwell (North American) Shrike Commander.
Programme
Purchase of further helicopters (and 5 Rockwell Turbo
  Commander 690A transports).
Navy 33,000 men.
1 aircraft carrier.
Naval aviation (Comando de Aviación Naval)
3,000 men.
9 squadrons.

75 operational aircraft.
19 helicopters.
Organization
1 strike-fighter squadron with A–4Q.
1 ground-attack squadron with MB.326GB.
1 ground-attack squadron with T–28D.
1 maritime-reconnaissance and ASW squadron with SP–2H.
1 maritime-reconnaissance and ASW squadron with S–2A.
2 transport squadrons with L–188, C–47 and C–54.
1 helicopter squadron with Bell 47 and Alouette III.
1 helicopter squadron with S–61D.
Major bases
Commandante Espora, Ezeiza, Puerto Belgrano, Punta de
  Indio, Trelew, Ushaia.
Equipment
Fighters and strike-fighters:
15 McDonnell Douglas A–4Q.
Ground-attack aircraft:
8(?) Aermacchi MB.326GB.
20 North American T–28D Fennec.
Maritime-reconnaissance and ASW aircraft:
3 Grumman HU–16B.
6 Grumman S–2A.
4(3?) Lockheed SP–2H.
Transports:
approx 20(?) aircraft, inc Beechcraft C–45.
1 de Havilland Canada DHC–6.
some (8?) Douglas C–47.
2 Douglas C–54D.
1 FMA I.A.50.
1 Hawker Siddeley H.S.125–400.
3 Lockheed L–188.
Liaison and AOP aircraft:
2 Beechcraft Super King Air 200.
2 de Havilland Canada DHC–2.
1(3?) Fairchild-Hiller (Pilatus) PC–6A.
Helicopters:
9(?) Aérospatiale Alouette III.
6(10?) Bell 47D, G and J.
4 Sikorsky S–61D–4.
Trainers:
approx 20 aircraft, inc 12(?) North American T–6G, some
  North American T–28A.
Coastguard (Prefectura Nacional Maritima)
8,000 men.
Transports:
5 Short Skyvan 3M.
Helicopters:
1 Bell 47G.
2 Bell 47J.
6 Hughes 500M.
Aircraft factories
FMA (Fabrica Militar de Aviones), known as DINFIA in period
  1957–68.

Australia
Air force (Royal Australian Air Force, RAAF)
men 21,500.
squadrons 16.
operational aircraft 225.
helicopters 44.
Organization
2 strike-fighter squadrons with Mirage IIIOA.
1 strike-fighter squadron with Mirage IIIOF.
2 strike-fighter squadrons with F–111C.
1 reconnaissance squadron with Canberra B.20.
1 maritime-reconnaissance and ASW squadron with P–3B.
1 maritime-reconnaissance and ASW squadron with SP–2H.

2 transport squadrons with DHC–4.
1 transport squadron with C–130A.
1 transport squadron with C–130E.
1 transport squadron with BAC 1–11, Falcon 20, H.S.748 and C–47.
1 helicopter squadron with UH–1B and UH–1D.
1 helicopter squadron with UH–1H.
1 helicopter squadron with CH–47C.
– trainer squadrons with CT–4.
– trainer squadrons with MB.326H.

Major bases
Amberley, Brisbane, Edinburgh, Darwin, East Sale, Fairbarn, Learmouth, Pearce, Richmond, Townsville, Williamstown.

Equipment
Fighters and strike-fighters:
30 Dassault (Commonwealth CA–29) Mirage IIIOF.
40 Dassault Mirage IIIOA.
15 Dassault Mirage IIID.
24 General Dynamics F–111C.
Bombers:
some English Electric Canberra B.20.
Reconnaissance aircraft:
8 English Electric Canberra B.20.
Maritime-reconnaissance and ASW aircraft:
10 Lockheed SP–2H.
9 Lockheed P–3B.
Transports:
2 BAC 1–11.
3 Dassault Falcon 20.
3 de Havilland Canada DHC–3.
22 de Havilland Canada DHC–4.
18(?) Douglas C–47.
2 Hawker Siddeley H.S.748C.2.
12 Lockheed C–130A.
12 Lockheed C–130E.
Helicopters:
15 Bell UH–1B.
2(?) Bell UH–1D.
15(?) Bell UH–1H.
12 Boeing-Vertol CH–47C.
Trainers:
75 Aermacchi MB.326H.
some (8?) Commonwealth CA–25 Winjeel.
8 Hawker Siddeley H.S.748T.2.
37 NZAI CT–4.
A number of machines have been mothballed, inc 23 Dassault Mirage IIIOA and Mirage IIIOF, 6 General Dynamics F–111C, 10 Aermacchi MB.326H, Boeing-Vertol CH–47C and some de Havilland Vampire T.35(?).

Programme
Replacement of Lockheed SP–2H maritime-reconnaissance and ASW aircraft by 10 Lockheed P–3C (delivery from 1977), and of Lockheed C–130A transports by 12 Lockheed C–130H (delivery 1978). Seeking replacements for Dassault Mirage IIIO strike-fighters and Aermacchi MB.326H trainers.

Army 31,000 men.

Army aviation (Australian Army Aviation Corps)
800(?) men.
3 squadrons.
23 operational aircraft.
48 helicopters.

Organization
2(3?) helicopter squadrons with OH–58B and Bell 47G.
1 transport squadron with Nomad.

Equipment
Helicopters:
18 Bell 47G–3.
30 Bell OH–58B.

Liaison and reconnaissance aircraft:
12 Pilatus PC–6A.
Transports:
11 GAF Nomad N22.

Programme
Replacement of Bell 47G–3 helicopters by further 23 Bell OH–58B.

Navy 16,200 men.
1 aircraft carrier.

Naval aviation (Royal Australian Navy, Fleet Air Arm)
1,400 men.
5 squadrons.
30 operational aircraft.
19 helicopters.

Organization
1 strike-fighter squadron with A–4G.
2 maritime-reconnaissance and ASW squadrons with S–2E.
1 helicopter squadron with UH–1B.
1 helicopter squadron with Sea King Mk. 50.
1 trainer squadron with MB.326H, A–4G and TA–4G.

Equipment
Fighters and strike-fighters:
13 McDonnell Douglas A–4G.
4 McDonnell Douglas TA–4G.
Maritime-reconnaissance and ASW aircraft:
1 Grumman S–2E.
Transports:
2 Hawker Siddeley H.S.748.
Helicopters:
2 Bell OH–58B.
7 Bell UH–1B.
10 Westland Sea King Mk. 50.
Trainers:
7 Aermacchi MB.326H.

Programme
Replacement of 12 burnt-out Grumman S–2E maritime-reconnaissance and ASW aircraft by 12 modernized S–2 from American stock.

Aircraft factories
CA (Commonwealth Aircraft Corporation), GAF (Government Aircraft Factories).

Austria
Air force (Österreichische Luftstreitkrafte)
men 3,000.
squadrons 7.
operational aircraft 28.
helicopters 73.

Organization
1 transport squadron with Skyvan 3M and PC–6B–2.
1 helicopter squadron with AB.206A.
1 helicopter squadron with OH–58B.
2 helicopter squadrons with Alouette III.
2 helicopter squadrons with AB.204B.
1 trainer squadron with Saab 91D.
3 trainer squadrons with Saab 105OE.
The Saab 1050E trainer squadrons are also to be used in the ground-attack role.

Major bases
Graz-Thalerhof, Langenlebarn, Linz-Hörsching, Zeltweg.

Military training aid from
Sweden.

Equipment
Transports:
2 Short Skyvan 3M.
Liaison and AOP aircraft:
13 Cessna O–1A and E.
1 de Havilland Canada DHC–2.
12 Pilatus PC–6B–2.

Helicopters:
Aérospatiale Alouette III.
22 Agusta-Bell AB.204B.
13 Agusta-Bell AB.206A.
12 Bell OH–58B.
2 Sikorsky S–65OE.
Trainers:
15 Saab 91D.
36 Saab 105OE.
Programme
Formation of 1 fighter squadron (with 24 Northrop F–5E or
12 Dassault Mirage F1?). Phasing out of Cessna O–1 and de
Havilland Canada DHC–2 liaison and AOP aircraft from 1977.
Replacement of Short Skyvan 3M transports by 4 IAI Arava
under consideration.
Army 27,000 men.

Bahrain
Air force
Police (Security) force only with 2 Westland Scout
helicopters.

Bangladesh
Air force (Biman Bahini)
men 2,500.
squadrons 3.
operational aircraft 17.
helicopters 9.
Organization
1 strike-fighter squadron with MiG–21F.
1 transport squadron with An–24 and An–26.
1 helicopter squadron with Alouette III and Mi–8.
Bases
Chittagong, Comilla, Tezgaon (Dacca), Jessore.
Military training aid from
India, Soviet Union.
Equipment
Fighters and strike-fighters:
7(9?) Mikoyan MiG–21F.
2 Mikoyan MiG–21U.
Transports:
4 de Havilland Canada DHC–3(?).
1 Antonov An–24.
3(?) Antonov An–26.
Liaison and AOP aircraft:
some aircraft, type unknown.
Helicopters:
4 Aérospatiale Alouette III.
3(?) Mil Mi–8.
2 Westland Wessex HU.5.
Army 30,000 men.
Navy 500 men.

Belgium
Air force (Force Aérienne Belge/Belgische Luchtmacht)
men 20,000.
squadrons 11.
operational aircraft 206.
helicopters 8.
Organization
2 fighter squadrons with F–104G.
2 strike-fighter squadrons with F–104G.
3 strike-fighter squadrons with Mirage 5-BA.
1 reconnaissance squadron with Mirage 5–BR.
1 transport squadron with C–130H.
1 transport squadron with H.S.748 and Boeing 727–29QC.
1 helicopter squadron with S–58C and H–34A.
– trainer squadrons with SF.260MB.
2 trainer squadrons with C.M.170 and T–33A.

Fighter, strike-fighter and reconnaissance squadrons each
with 18 aircraft.
Major bases
Beauvechain, Bierset, Florennes, Kleine Brogel, Melsbroek.
Equipment
Fighters and strike-fighters:
55 Dassault Mirage 5–BA.
45 Dassault Mirage 5–BD.
75 Lockheed F–104G.
9 Lockheed TF–104G.
Reconnaissance aircraft:
24 Dassault Mirage 5–BR.
Transport:
3 Boeing 727–29QC.
2 Dassault Falcon 20.
3 Hawker Siddeley H.S.748.
12 Lockheed C–130H.
6 Swearingen Merlin IIIA.
Helicopters:
4 Sikorsky H–34A.
4 Sikorsky S–58C.
Trainers:
12(?) Lockheed T–33A.
35 Potez-Air Fouga C.M.170.
35 SIAI–Marchetti SF.260MB.
Programme
Replacement of Lockheed F–104G fighters and strike-fighters
by 102 General Dynamics F–16 from 1979, and of Potez-Air
Fouga C.M.170 trainers by 33 Dassault-Breguet/Dornier
Alphajet from 1978.
Army 62,700 men.
Army aviation (Aviation Légère de la Force Terrestre)
– men.
4 squadrons.
18 operational aircraft.
70 helicopters.
Organization
4 helicopter squadrons with Alouette II.
Equipment
Helicopters:
70 Aérospatiale Alouette II.
1 Aérospatiale S.A.330.
Transports:
12 Britten-Norman BN–2A.
Liaison and AOP aircraft:
some Dornier Do–27D.
Navy 4,200 men.
Naval aviation
8 helicopters.
3 Aérospatiale Alouette III.
2 Westland Sea King Mk.48.
Aircraft factories
Fairey SABCA (Société Anonyme Belge de Constructions
Aéronautiques).

Bolivia
Air force (Fuerza Aérea Boliviana)
men 3,000.
squadrons 5.
operational aircraft 50.
helicopters 12.
Organization
1 strike-fighter squadron with F–86F and T–33A–N.
1 ground-attack squadron with EMB–326GB and F–51D.
2 transport squadrons with C–47 and Convair 440.
1 liaison squadron with Cessna 185.
1 helicopter squadron with Hughes 500M.
1 trainer squadron with T–6G and T–28A.

1 trainer squadron with S.11.
1 trainer squadron with T–23.
Bases
Charana, Colcapina, El Tejar, El Trompillo, La Florida, La Paz,
Puerta Suarez, Santa Cruz.
Military training aid from
United States.
Equipment
Fighters and strike-fighters:
3(4?) North American F–86F.
Ground-attack aircraft:
18 Embraer EMB–326GB (Aermacchi MB.326GB).
some 10(?) North American F–51D.
Transports:
some Beechcraft C–45.
4 Convair 440.
10 Douglas C–47.
2 Douglas C–54(?).
1 Douglas DC–6B(?).
5 IAI Arava.
Liaison and AOP aircraft:
2 Beechcraft King Air.
3 Cessna 172.
8 Cessna 185.
2 Cessna Turbo Centurion.
7 Cessna U–206.
some Cessna 310.
1 Cessna 402.
1 Cessna 414.
1 Cessna 421.
1 Fairchild-Hiller Porter.
1 Gates Learjet 25B.
Helicopters:
12 Hughes 500M.
Trainers:
18 Aerotec T–23.
some Cessna T–41D.
8 Fokker S.11
12 Lockheed T–33A–N.
12 North American T–6G.
4 North American T–28A.
Programme
1 Lockheed C–130H transport on order, delivery 1978.
Army 21,000 men.

Brazil
Air force (Fôrça Aérea Brasileira)
men 35,000.
squadrons 26.
operational aircraft 340.
helicopters 85.
Organization
1 strike-fighter squadron with Mirage IIIEBR.
2 strike-fighter squadrons with F–5E.
6 ground-attack squadrons with AT–26 (MB.326GB).
1 maritime-reconnaisance squadron with HU–16A.
1 maritime-reconnaissance and ASW squadron with S–2A,
S–2E and CS2F–1.
6 transport squadrons with C–95.
2(3?) transport squadrons with DHC–5.
1 transport squadron with H.S.748.
1 transport squadron with C–130E and C–130H.
1 transport squadron with Boeing 737-200 and H.S.125.
6 liaison squadrons with C–42/L–42 and O–1E.
1 helicopter squadron with UH–1D and Bell 206A.
2 helicopter squadrons with UH–1H.
– trainer squadrons with T–23 and T–25.
– trainer squadrons with T–37C.

– helicopter trainer squadrons with Bell 47J.
Ground-attack squadrons each with 16 aircraft.
Major bases
Belém, Brasilia-Anápolis, Campo dos Alfonços, Campo
Grande, Canoas, Cumbica, Florianopólis, Fortaleza, Galeaõ,
Guaratinguetà, Manaus, Natal, Pirassununga, Porto Alegre,
Recife, Rio de Janeiro, Salvador, Santa Cruz, Santos, Saõ
José dos Campos, Saõ Paulo.
Military training aid from
United States.
Equipment
Fighters and strike-fighters:
12 Dassault Mirage IIIEBR.
4 Dassault Mirage IIIDBR.
33 Northrop F–5E.
6 Northrop F–5B.
Ground-attack aircraft:
105 Embraer-Aermacchi AT–26 Xavante (MB.326GB).
Reconnaissance and ECM aircraft:
3 Douglas EC–47.
2 Hawker Siddeley H.S.125.
Maritime-reconnaissance and ASW aircraft:
6 Convair PBY–5A.
12 Grumman HU–16A.
5 Grumman S–2A and CS2F–1.
8 Grumman S–2E.
6 Lockheed P–2E.
Transports:
2 Boeing 737–200.
21 de Havilland Canada DHC–5.
80 Embraer C–95 Bandeirante.
8 Hawker Siddeley H.S.125.
12 Hawker Siddeley H.S.748.
7 Lockheed C–130E.
3 Lockheed RC–130E.
3 Lockheed C–130H.
2 Lockheed KC–130H.
Liaison and AOP aircraft:
approx 125 aircraft, inc Cessna O–1E, 110 Neiva C–42 and
L–42, 5 Pilatus PC–6.
Helicopters:
10 Bell 47G.
24(?) Bell 47J.
10 Bell 206A.
12 Bell UH–1D.
24(36?) Bell UH–1H.
5 Bell SH–1D.
Trainers:
approx 260 aircraft, inc
100(?) Aerotec T–23, 8 Beechcraft TC–45T, 25(?) Cessna
T–37C, 125 Neiva T–25.
The Dassault Mirage IIIEBR fighters and Lockheed P–2E
maritime-reconnaissance aircraft have been grounded for
maintenance reasons.
Programme
40 further Embraer-Aermacchi AT–26 Xavante ground-attack
aircraft have been ordered. Replacement of Lockheed P–2E
maritime-reconnaissance aircraft by 16 Embraer EMB–111
from 1978. Purchase of 6 IAI Arava transports under
consideration(?).
Army 170,000 men.
Navy 49,500 men.
1 aircraft carrier.
Naval aviation (Fôrça Aéronatale)
– men.
3 squadrons.
– operational aircraft and 32 helicopters.
Organization
1 ASW squadron with SH–3D and SH–34J.

1 helicopter squadron with Whirlwind 3.
1 helicopter squadron with Bell 206B.
1 helicopter trainer squadron with Bell 206B.
Equipment
Helicopters:
18 Bell 206B.
6 Sikorsky SH–3D.
3 Westland Wasp AS.1.
5 Westland Whirlwind 3.
The shipboard ASW squadron with S–2A, S–2E and CS2F–1 is subordinated to the Air Force.
Programme
30 Aérospatiale S.A.341 helicopters (delivery from 1976) and 9 Westland WG.13 Lynx helicopters (delivery from 1977) on order.
Aircraft factories
Aérotec, Embraer (Emprêza Brasileira de Aéronautica SA), Neiva.

Brunei
Air force
Part of the Army.
Army – men.
Army aviation (Askar Melaya Diraja Brunei)
– men.
2 squadrons.
1 operational aircraft.
10 helicopters.
Organization
1 helicopter squadron with Bell 205A and Bell 212.
1 helicopter squadron with Bell 206A.
Equipment
Transport:
1 Hawker Siddeley H.S.748.
Helicopters:
2 Bell 205A.
4 Bell 206A.
2 Bell 212.

Bulgaria
Air force
men 22,000.
squadrons 21.
operational aircraft 200.
helicopters 40.
Organization
6 fighter squadrons with MiG–21.
3 fighter squadrons with MiG–17F and PF.
4(6?) strike-fighter squadrons with MiG–17.
2 reconnaissance squadrons with MiG–17 and Il–28R.
1 transport squadron with An–2.
1 transport squadron with Il–14.
1 transport squadron with An–12 and Il–18.
3 helicopter squadrons with Mi–4 and Mi–8.
– trainer squadrons with Yak–11 and Yak–18.
– trainer squadrons with L–29 and MiG–15UTI.
Fighter, strike-fighter and reconnaissance squadrons each with 10–12 aircraft.
Major bases
Balchik, Burgas, Ignatiev, Karlovo, Plovdiv, Sofia, Tolbuchin, Yambol.
Military training aid from
Soviet Union.
Equipment
Fighters and strike-fighters:
80 Mikoyan MiG–17F and PF.
75 Mikoyan MiG–21 and MiG–21U.
Reconnaissance aircraft:
some Ilyushin Il–28R.
15 Mikoyan MiG–17.

Transports:
8 Antonov An–2.
some Antonov An–12.
10 Ilyushin Il–12 and Il–14.
4 Ilyushin Il–18.
some Lisunov Li–2.
1 Tupolev Tu–134.
Liaison and AOP aircraft:
some L–60 and PZL–104.
Helicopters:
10 Mil Mi–1.
20 Mil Mi–4.
10 Mil Mi–8.
Trainers:
approx 80 aircraft, inc Aero L–29, Yakovlev Yak–11 and Yak–18, Mikoyan MiG–15UTI.
Programme
Re-equipment of Mikoyan MiG–17 strike-fighter squadrons with Mikoyan MiG–21, replacement of Mil Mi–4 helicopters by Mil Mi–8.
Army 120,000 men.
Navy 10,000 men.
Naval aviation
Helicopters:
2 Mil Mi–1.
6 Mil Mi–4.

Burma
Air force (Union of Burma Air Force)
men 7,000.
squadrons 6.
operational aircraft 24.
helicopters 27.
Organization
1 strike-fighter squadron with F–86F.
1 transport squadron with DHC–3.
1 transport squadron with C–47.
1 liaison squadron with U–17A.
1 helicopter squadron with Bell 47G.
1 helicopter squadron with Alouette III.
1 helicopter squadron with HH–43B.
1 helicopter squadron with Bell 47G.
– trainer squadrons with DHC–1 and Provost T.53.
1 trainer squadron with T–33 and Vampire T.55.
Major bases
Hmawbi, Kengtung, Mandalay, Meiktila, Mingaladon (Rangoon), Myitkyina.
Military training aid from
United States.
Equipment
Fighters and strike-fighters:
8 North American F–86F.
Transports:
4 Beechcraft C–45.
6 de Havilland Canada DHC–3.
6 Douglas C–47.
Liaison and AOP aircraft:
10 Cessna U–17A.
4 Pilatus PC–6B
Helicopters:
10 Aérospatiale Alouette III.
9 Kaman HH–43B.
5 Kawasaki-Bell 47G.
3 Kawasaki-Vertol KV–107.
Trainers:
some de Havilland Canada DHC–1.
3 de Havilland Vampire F.55.
some Hunting Provost T.53.

3 Lockheed T–33.
10 SIAI-Marchetti SF.260.
Army 145,000 men.
Navy 7,000 men.

Cambodia
Air force
men –.
squadrons –.
operational aircraft –.
helicopters –.
Bases
Battambang, Pochentong (Pnom Penh), Seam Reap.
Military training aid from
Vietnam, Soviet Union(?), China(?).
Equipment
Ground-attack aircraft:
10(?) North American T–28D.
Night ground-support aircraft:
8(?) Helio AU–24A Stallion.
Transports:
25(?) Fairchild C–123B.
some de Havilland Canada DHC–3.
15(?) Douglas C–47.
Liaison and AOP aircraft:
30(?) Cessna O–1.
Helicopters:
18(?) Bell UH–1D and UH–1H.
Trainers:
some Cessna T–37B and T–37C(?).
10(?) Cessna T–41D.
It is questionable how many of these ex-Cambodian AF
machines, captured in April 1975 by the present régime, can
be made operational.
Programme
Reactivation of Air Force with Soviet and Chinese
equipment(?).
Army 75,000(?) men.
Navy 2,500(?) men.

Cameroun
Air force
men 300.
squadrons –.
operational aircraft 5.
helicopters 4.
Organization
–.
Base
Bangui.
Military aid from
France.
Equipment
Transports:
2 Dornier Do–28B.
1(2?) de Havilland Canada DHC–4.
2 Hawker Siddeley H.S.748.
Liaison and AOP aircraft:
1 Beechcraft Queen Air.
Helicopters:
2 Aérospatiale Alouette II.
1 Aérospatiale Alouette III.
1 Aérospatiale S.A.330.
Trainers:
4 Potez-Air Fouga C.M.170.
Programme
2 Lockheed C–130H transports on order, delivery 1978.
Army 4,000 men.
Navy 300 men.

Canada
Air force
men 34,000.
squadrons 14.
operational aircraft 320.
helicopters 24.
Organization
3 fighter squadrons with F–101B.
3 strike-fighter squadrons with CF–104.
2 strike-fighter squadrons with CF–5A.
1 ECM squadron with CF–100 and T–33A–N.
2 transport squadrons with C–130E and C–130H.
1 transport squadron with Falcon 20.
1 transport squadron with DHC–6.
1 transport squadron with Boeing 707–320C.
– trainer squadrons with Musketeer.
– trainer squadrons with CL–41.
1 trainer squadron with TF–101B and T–33A–N.
2 strike-trainer squadrons with CF–5A and CF–5D.
1 strike-trainer squadron with CF–104.
Fighter, strike-fighter and reconnaissance squadrons each
with 16–18 aircraft.
Major bases
Bagotville, Calgary, Chatham, Cold Lake, Comox, Edmonton,
Gagetown, Halifax, Montreal, Moose Jaw, Namao, North
Bay, Ottawa, Petawawa, Portage la Prairie, Rivers, St.
Hubert, Toronto, Trenton, Uplands, Valcartier, Winnipeg.
Equipment
Fighters and strike-fighters:
14 Canadair CF–100.
65 Canadair CF–104 (F–104G).
25 Canadair CF–104D (RF–104G).
60 Canadair CF–5A (Northrop F–5A).
40 Canadair CF–5D (Northrop F–5B).
44 McDonnell F–101B.
6 McDonnell TF–101B.
some CF–104 and CF–5 have been mothballed.
Transports:
5 Boeing 707–320C.
7 Convair C–131B.
7 Dassault Falcon 20.
7(13?) de Havilland Canada DHC–4.
7 de Havilland Canada DHC–6.
some Douglas C–47.
19 Lockheed C–130E.
5 Lockheed C–130H.
Helicopters:
6 Boeing-Vertol CH–113.
18 Bell OH–58A.
Trainers:
25 Beechcraft Musketeer Sport.
158 Canadair CL–41A.
25(?) Canadair T–33A–N.
58 CL–41A have been mothballed.
Programme
Replacement of McDonnell F–101 fighters, Canadair CF–5
(Northrop F–5) and Canadair CF–104 (F–104G) strike-fighters
by McDonnell F–15 or General Dynamics F–16. Dassault
Falcon 20 and Douglas C–47 transports to be phased out.
Army 28,000 men.
Army aviation
– men.
13 squadrons.
41 operational aircraft.
110 helicopters.
Organization
4 helicopter squadrons with UH–1N and OH–58A.
1 helicopter squadron with OH–58A.
1 helicopter squadron with CH–47C.

1 transport squadron with DHC–5.
6 transport squadrons with DHC–3.
Equipment
Helicopters:
47 Bell OH–58A.
some Bell UH–1H.
50(30?) Bell UH–1N.
7 Boeing-Vertol CH–47C.
Transports:
30 de Havilland Canada DHC–3.
14 de Havilland Canada DHC–5.
Navy 14,000 men.
Naval aviation
– men.
8 squadrons.
1 operational aircraft.
30 helicopters.
Organization
3(4?) maritime-reconnaissance and ASW squadrons with
  CL–28.
2 maritime-reconnaissance and ASW squadrons with S–2A.
3 ASW squadrons with SH–3A.
1 trainer squadron with CL–28.
Equipment
Maritime-reconnaissance and ASW aircraft:
26 Canadair CL–28.
16 de Havilland Canada Grumman S–2A (14 additional aircraft
  have been mothballed).
9 Grumman HU–16B.
Helicopters:
30(35?) Sikorsky SH–3A.
Programme
Replacement of Canadair CL–28 maritime-reconnaissance
  and ASW aircraft by 18 Lockheed P–3C (delivery 1979–80).
Aircraft factories
Canadair, de Havilland Canada (DHC).

Central African Republic
Air force (Force Aérienne Centrafricaine)
men 150.
squadrons 1.
operational aircraft 5.
helicopters 5(?).
Organization
1 transport squadron with C–47.
Base
Bangui.
Military training aid from
France.
Equipment
Transports:
1 Dassault Falcon 20.
3(12?) Douglas C–47.
1 Douglas DC–4.
Liaison and AOP aircraft:
8 Aermacchi AL.60C5.
3 Max Holste M.H.1521M.
Helicopters:
1 Aérospatiale Alouette II.
some Sikorsky H–34.
Army 1,000 men.

Ceylon: see **Sri Lanka**

Chad
Air force (Escadrille Tchadienne)
men 300.
squadrons 2.
operational aircraft 19.

helicopters 10.
Organization
1 ground-attack squadron with A–1D.
1 transport squadron with C–47.
Base
N'Djamena (Fort Lamy).
Military training aid from
France.
Equipment
Ground-attack aircraft:
9 Douglas A–1D.
Transports:
9 Douglas C–47.
1 Douglas DC–4.
Liaison and AOP aircraft:
2 Max Holste M.H.1521M.
4 Reims-Cessna F.337.
Helicopters:
approx 10(15?) machines inc Aérospatiale Alouette II,
  Aérospatiale Alouette III, Sikorsky H–34.
Army 4,000 men.

Chile
Air force (Fuerza Aérea de Chile)
men 12,000.
squadrons 15.
operational aircraft 135.
helicopters 36.
Organization
2 strike-fighter squadrons with Hunter FGA.71 and FR.10.
1 strike-fighter squadron with F–5E.
1 ground-attack squadron with A–37B.
1 bomber squadron with B–26.
1 maritime-reconnaissance and ASW squadron with HU–16B
  and SP–2H.
2 transport squadrons with C–47.
1 transport squadron with Beechcraft 99A.
1 transport squadron with DHC–6.
1 transport squadron with C–118, DC–6B and C–130H.
1 Liaison squadron with Cessna 180.
1 helicopter squadron with Bell 47G and UH–12E.
1 helicopter squadron with S.A.316.
1 helicopter squadron with UH–1D and UH–1H.
1 helicopter squadron with S–55T.
– trainer squadrons with T–25 and T–34.
– trainer squadrons with T–37B and T–37C.
1 trainer squadron with Vampire T.55 and Sea Vampire T.22.
1 trainer squadron with T–33A.
Major bases
Antofagasta, Bahia, Catalina, Balmaceda, Chamiza, Cerro
  Moreno, El Bosque, Iquique, Los Cerillos, Los Cóndores,
  Maquehue, Punta Arenas, Puerto Montt, Quintero.
Military training aid from
United States.
Equipment
Fighters and strike-fighters:
18(24?) Hawker Hunter FGA.71.
2(4?) Hawker Hunter T.72.
15 Northrop F–5E.
3 Northrop F–5F.
Ground-attack aircraft:
16 Cessna A–37B.
Bombers:
10 Douglas B–26.
Reconnaissance aircraft:
4 Hawker Hunter FR.10.
Maritime-reconnaissance and ASW aircraft:
5 Grumman HU–16B.
4 Lockheed SP–2H.

Transports:
some Beechcraft C–45.
9 Beechcraft 99A.
6(11?) de Havilland Canada DHC–6.
25 Douglas C–47.
4 Douglas C–118.
5 Douglas DC–6B.
2 Lockheed C–130H.
Liaison and AOP aircraft:
5 Beechcraft Twin Bonanza.
10 Cessna 180.
4 Cessna O–1.
Helicopters:
5 Aérospatiale S.A.316.
7 Bell 47G.
10 Bell UH–1D.
2 Bell UH–1H.
6 Hiller UH–12E.
6 Sikorsky S–55T.
Trainers:
30(36?) Beechcraft T–34.
28 Cessna T–37B and T–37C.
6 de Havilland Sea Vampire T.22.
5 de Havilland Vampire T.55.
8 Lockheed T–33A.
some North American T–6G(?).
10 Neiva T–25.

Programme
Hawker Hunter strike-fighters, strike-trainers and
reconnaissance aircraft to be phased out from 1977–78.
Formation of a second ground-attack squadron with 18
Cessna A–37B(?). Planned order for 8 further Neiva T–25
trainers.

Army 40,000 men.

Army aviation
1 liaison and AOP squadron with 6 aircraft (type unknown).
1 helicopter squadron with S.A.330.
approx 15 helicopters, inc 9 Aérospatiale S.A.330, 2 Bell
206A, 3 Bell UH–1H.

Navy men 21,800.

Naval aviation (Aviaçon Naval)
500 men.
2 squadrons.
11 operational aircraft.
10 helicopters.

Organization
1 maritime-reconnaissance squadron with PBY–5A.
1 transport squadron with C–45 and C–47.

Equipment
Maritime-reconnaissance and ASW aircraft:
3 Convair PBY–5A.
Transports:
5 Beechcraft C–45.
3 Douglas C–47.
Helicopters:
4(14?) Bell 47G.
4 Bell 206A.
2 Bell UH–1D.
Trainers:
6 Beechcraft T–34.
some (5?) Beechcraft D–18.

Programme
Acquisition of (12?) new maritime-reconnaissance aircraft
planned. Replacement of Beechcraft C–45 and Douglas
C–47 transports by 3 Embraer C–95 Bandeirante.

China
Air force (Chung-Kuo Zhen Min Tsie-Fang Tsun Pu-tai)
men 220,000.

squadrons approx 350(?).
operational aircraft 3,450(?).
helicopters 300.

Organization
120(?) fighter squadrons with F–6 (MiG–19) and F–9.
150(?) strike-fighter squadrons with F–4 (MiG–17F), F–8
(MiG–21) and F–2 (MiG–15).
20(?) bomber squadrons with Il–28 and Tu–16.
– transport squadrons with An–2 and Fongshu 2.
– transport squadrons with Il–14 and Il–18.
– helicopter squadrons with Mi–1 and Mi–4.
– trainer squadrons with Yak–11 and Yak–18.
– trainer squadrons with MiG–14UTI.

Major bases
Canton, Changsha, Chengchow, Chienchiao, Futshau,
Hsincheng, Hungchiao, Kunming, Kwangchan, Lhasa,
Liencheng, Luchiao, Nanhai, Nanking, Peking, Pingtau,
Shenyang, Sian, Tenghai, Tsaochiao, Wuhan.

Equipment
Fighters and strike-fighters:
100 Shenyang F–2 (MiG–15).
1,400 Shenyang F–4 (MiG–17F).
1,000 Shenyang F–6 (MiG–19).
75(50?) Shenyang F–8 (MiG–21).
200(300?) Shenyang F–9.
Bombers:
150(300?) Ilyushin Il–28.
some Tupolev Tu–4.
60(100?) Tupolev Tu–16.
Maritime-reconnaissance and ASW aircraft:
Beriev Be–6.
Transports:
approx 400 aircraft, inc Antonov An–2, Fongshu 2, 50 Ilyushin
Il–14, Ilyushin Il–18, Lisunov Li–2.
Helicopters:
approx 300 machines, inc Mil Mi–1, Mil Mi–4, 13
Aérospatiale S.A.312.
Trainers:
Yakovlev Yak–11.
Yakovlev Yak–18.
300 Mikoyan MiG–15UTI.

Army 2,700,000 men.

Navy 230,000 men.

Naval aviation
30,000 men.
– squadrons.
500 operational aircraft.
50 helicopters.

Organization
– fighter squadrons with F–6 (MiG–19) and F–9.
– strike-fighter squadrons with F–4 (MiG–17F) and F–2
(MiG–15).
– bomber squadrons with Il–28.
– helicopter squadrons with Mi–4.

Equipment
Fighters and strike-fighters:
80 Shenyang F–2 (MiG–15).
200 Shenyang F–4 (MiG–17F).
100 Shenyang F–6 (MiG–19).
some Shenyang F–9
Bombers:
100 Ilyushin Il–28.
Helicopters:
approx 50 machines, inc Mil Mi–1, Mil Mi–4.
Trainers:
approx 120 aircraft.

Aircraft factories
Fongshu, Shenyang.

China, Republic of: see Taiwan

Colombia
Air force (Fuerza Aérea Colombiana)
men 6,300.
squadrons 8.
operational aircraft 61.
helicopters 50.
Organization
1 strike-fighter squadron with Mirage 5–COA.
1 strike-fighter squadron with F–86F and CL–13B.
1 maritime-reconnaissance squadron with PBY–5A.
1 transport squadron with C–47.
1 transport squadron with C–54 and C–130.
1 liaison squadron with DHC–2.
1 liaison squadron with PC–6 and PC–6A.
1 helicopter squadron with OH–6A.
1 helicopter squadron with HH–43B.
1 helicopter squadron with UH–1B.
– trainer squadrons with T–6G, T–34A and T–41D.
1 trainer squadron with T–37C.
Major bases
Baranquilla, Bogotá, Cali, Melgar, Palanquero.
Military training aid from
United States.
Equipment
Fighters and strike-fighters:
4 Canadair CL–13B Sabre Mk.6.
14 Dassault Mirage 5–COA.
2 Dassault Mirage 5–COD.
6 North American F–86F.
Reconnaissance aircraft:
2 Dassault Mirage 5–COR.
Maritime-reconnaissance aircraft:
4 Convair PBY–5A.
Transports:
3 Beechcraft C–45H.
4 de Havilland Canada DHC–3.
6 Douglas C–47.
3(10?) Douglas C–54.
1 Fokker-VFW F.28.
3 Hawker Siddeley H.S.748.
2 Lockheed C–130B.
2 Lockheed C–130E.
5 Rockwell Commander.
Liaison and AOP aircraft:
7 de Havilland Canada DHC–2.
6 Pilatus PC–6 and PC–6A.
Helicopters:
15 Bell 47D, G and J.
1 Bell 212.
6 Bell UH–1B.
4 Hiller OH–23G.
12 Hughes OH–6A.
6 Hughes TH–55A.
6 Kaman HH–43B.
Trainers:
some Beechcraft T–34A.
10 Cessna T–37C.
30 Cessna T–41D.
4(10?) Lockheed T–33A.
some North American T–6G(?).
Army 50,000 men.
Navy 8,000 men.

Congo (Brazzaville)
Air force
men 300.
squadrons 1.
operational aircraft 9(?).
helicopters 4.

Organization
1 transport squadron with An–24 and Il–14.
Base
Brazzaville.
Military training aid from
France, Soviet Union.
Foreign air forces in Congo (Brazzaville)
1 strike-fighter squadron with 8(?) Mikoyan MiG–21 (flown by Algerian, Cuban and Russian volunteers?). Additional Soviet aircraft deliveries, possibly for use in Angola.
Equipment
Transports:
2 Antonov An–24.
1 Douglas C–47.
1 Fokker-VFW F.28.
5(?) Ilyushin Il–14.
Liaison and AOP aircraft:
3 Max Holste M.H.1521M.
Helicopters:
3 Aérospatiale Alouette II.
1 Aérospatiale Alouette III.
Army 3,000 men.
Navy 200 men.

Congo (Kinshasa): see **Zaire**

Costa Rica
Air force
Component part of Army.
Army 1,200 men.
Army aviation
3 Cessna U–17A liaison aircraft.
1 Beechcraft C–45 transport.

Cuba
Air force (Fuerza Aérea Revolucionaria)
men 20,000(?).
squadrons 22.
operational aircraft 210.
helicopters 50.
Organization
6 fighter squadrons with MiG–21.
2 fighter squadrons with MiG–19.
4 strike-fighter squadrons with MiG–17F and PF.
1 strike-fighter squadron with MiG–15.
2 transport squadrons with Il–14.
1 transport squadron with An–24.
2 helicopter squadrons with Mi–4.
1 helicopter squadron with Mi–8.
– trainer squadrons with Zlin 226 and Zlin 336.
– trainer squadrons with MiG–15UTI.
Fighter and strike-fighter squadrons each with 10–12 aircraft.
Major bases
Camaguey, Havanna, Holquin, Santiago de Cuba.
Military training aid from
Soviet Union.
Equipment
Fighters and strike-fighters:
10 Mikoyan MiG–15.
45 Mikoyan MiG–17F and PF.
20 Mikoyan MiG–19.
90 Mikoyan MiG–21 and MiG–21U.
Transports:
approx 45(50?) aircraft, inc Antonov An–2, Antonov An–12, Antonov An–24 and Ilyushin Il–14.
Helicopters:
20 Mil Mi–1.
20 Mil Mi–4.
10 Mil Mi–8.

Trainers:
approx 100 aircraft, inc 25 Mikoyan MiG–15UTI and 60 Zlin
 226 and Zlin 336.
Army 90,000 men.
Navy 7,000 men.
Naval aviation
some (10?) Mil Mi–4 helicopters.

Cyprus
Air force (Cyprus National Guard, Air Wing)
men –.
squadrons –.
helicopters 2.
Bases
Akrotiri, Dhekelia, Larnaka(?).
Military training aid from
Greece, Turkey.
Foreign air forces in Cyprus
1 helicopter squadron with Whirlwind HAR.10, plus Turkish
 helicopters and liaison aircraft in Turkish-controlled northern
 sector of island.
Equipment
Helicopters:
1 Agusta-Bell AB.47J.
1 Fairchild-Hiller FH–1100.
Army 20,000(?).
Navy – men.

Czechoslovakia
Air force (Československé vojenské Letectvo)
men 42,000.
squadrons –.
operational aircraft 500.
helicopters 100.
Organization
18 fighter squadrons with MiG–21.
12 strike-fighter squadrons with Su–7.
6 reconnaissance squadrons with MiG–21R.
– transport squadrons with An–2.
– transport squadrons with Il–14.
– helicopter squadrons with Mi–4.
– helicopter squadrons with Mi–8.
– trainer squadrons with Zlin 226 and Zlin 336.
– trainer squadrons with L–29.
Fighter, strike-fighter and reconnaissance squadrons each
 with 10–12 aircraft.
Major bases
Barca, Bechyně, Brunn (Brno), Čakovice, Časlav, České,
 Budějovice (Bohemian = Budweis), Choceň, Dobřany, Eger
 (Cheb), Ivanka/Slovakia, Kbely near Prague, Klecany,
 Kunovice, Letnany, Lučenec/Slovakia, Milovice, Mimon,
 Mosnov, Muchovo, Otrokovice, Pardubitz (Pardubice),
 Pieštany/Slovakia, Pilsen (Plzeň), Poprad/Slovakia, Prerau,
 Preschau, Pressburg (Bratislava), Ruzyně near Prague, Saaz
 (Žatec), Sliač, Spisska-Nova Ves.
Military training aid from
Soviet Union.
Foreign air forces in Czechoslovakia
approx 400 Soviet fighters, strike-fighters and reconnaissance
 aircraft.
Equipment
Fighters and strike-fighters:
20(?) Mikoyan MiG–17F and PF.
200 Mikoyan MiG–21 and MiG–21U.
150 Sukhoi Su–7 and Su–7U.
Bombers:
some Ilyushin Il–28 and Il–28U.
Reconnaissance aircraft:
70 Mikoyan MiG–21R.

Transports:
approx 50 aircraft, inc Antonov An–2, Antonov An–24,
 Ilyushin Il–14, Lisunov Li–2, Tupolev Tu–134.
Liaison and AOP aircraft:
L–60, LET L–200 Morava, PZL–104, Zlin Z–43.
Helicopters:
approx 100(90?) machines, inc Mil Mi–1, Mil Mi–4, Mil
 Mi–8, WSK/Mil Mi–2.
Trainers:
approx 100(90?) machines, inc Mil Mi–1, Mil Mi–4, Mil Mi–8,
 WSK/Mil Mi–2.
Programme
Partial replacement of Sukhoi Su–7 by Sukhoi Su–20 (and
 Mikoyan MiG–23?) from 1975–76? Replacement of Aero
 L–29 trainers by 100 Aero L–39 from 1975–76.
Army 155,000 men.
Aircraft factories
Aero, Letov, Zlin.

Dahomey
Air force (Force Aérienne du Dahomey)
men 150.
squadrons –.
operational aircraft 2.
helicopter 1.
Organization
–.
Base
Porto Novo.
Military training aid from
France.
Equipment
Transports:
1 Aero Commander 500B.
1 Douglas C–47.
Liaison and AOP aircraft:
1 Cessna 337.
2 Max Holste M.H.1521M.
Helicopter:
1 Aérospatiale Alouette II.
Army 2,000 men.
Navy 100 men.

Denmark
Air force (Kongelige Danske Flyvevåben)
men 7,100.
squadrons 8.
operational aircraft 150.
helicopters 8.
Organization
2 fighter squadrons with F–104G.
2 strike-fighter squadrons with F–100D.
1 strike-fighter squadron with Saab 35XD.
1 reconnaissance squadron with Saab 35XD.
1 transport squadron with C–130H.
1 helicopter squadron with S–61A.
1 trainer squadron with Supporter.
Fighter and strike-fighter squadrons each with 20 aircraft,
 reconnaissance squadron with 16 aircraft.
Major bases
Aalborg, Karup, Kastrup, Odense, Skrydstrup, Tirstrip,
 Verløse, Vandel.
Military training aid from
United States.
Equipment
Fighters and strike-fighters:
36 Lockheed F–104G.
9 Lockheed TF–104G.
28 North American F–100D.

12 North American F–100F.
20 Saab 35XD.
10 Saab 35XT.
ECM aircraft:
8 Lockheed T–33A.
20 Saab 35XD.
Transports:
some (6?) Douglas C–47.
2 Douglas C–54D.
3 Lockheed C–130H.
Helicopters:
8 Sikorsky S–61A.
Trainers:
7 Lockheed T–33A.
24 Saab Supporter.
Programme
Replacement of Lockheed F–104G fighters by 48 General
  Dynamics F–16 from 1979. Phasing out of Douglas C–47
  and C–54D transports and of de Havilland Canada DHC–1
  trainers.
Army 21,500 men.
Army aviation (Haerens Flyvetjeneste)
1 squadron with 12 Hughes 500M helicopters.
2 Piper L–18C liaison aircraft.
Programme
Replacement of Piper L–18C liaison aircraft by (8?) Saab
  Supporter.
Navy 5,800 men.
Naval aviation (Sovaernets Flyvevaesen)
8 Aérospatiale Alouette III helicopters.

Dominican Republic
Air force (Aviación Militar Dominicana)
men 3,000.
squadrons 5.
operational aircraft 38.
helicopters 12.
Organization
1 strike-fighter squadron with Vampire Mk.1 and Mk.50.
1 ground-attack squadron with F–51D.
1 bomber squadron with B–26K.
1 transport squadron with C–46 and C–47.
1 helicopter squadron with Hughes 500M.
– trainer squadrons with T–28D and T–41D.
Bases
Azua, Barahona, La Romana, La Vega, Monte Christi, Puerto
  Plata, Saibo, San Isidor, Santiago, Santo Domingo.
Military training aid from
United States.
Equipment
Fighters and strike-fighters:
7(?) de Havilland Vampire Mk.1 and Mk.50.
Ground-attack aircraft:
15 North American F–51D.
Bombers:
3 Douglas B–26K.
Maritime-reconnaissance and ASW aircraft:
2 Convair PBY–5A.
Transports:
1 Aera Commander.
5 Curtiss C–46.
5 Douglas C–47.
Liaison and AOP aircraft:
3 de Havilland Canada DHC–2.
Helicopters:
2 Aérospatiale Alouette II.
1 Aérospatiale Alouette III.
7 Hughes 500M.

2 Sikorsky UH–19.
Trainers:
approx 15 aircraft, inc some Beechcraft T–11.
4 Cessna T–41D.
1 Morane-Saulnier M.S.893A Rallye.
6 North American T–28D.
Army 9,000 men.
Army aviation
3 Cessna 170 liaison aircraft.
Navy 3,800 men.

Dubai
Air force
Part of the Army.
Army
1,500 men.
Army aviation (Dubai Defence Force Air Wing)
– men.
2 squadrons.
6 operational aircraft.
8 helicopters.
Organization
1 ground-attack squadron with MB.326KD.
1 helicopter squadron with Bell 205A and Bell 212.
Base
–.
Equipment
Ground-attack aircraft:
3 Aermacchi MB.326KD.
1 Aermacchi MB.326L.
1 SIAI-Marchetti SF.260WD.
Transports:
1 Aeritalia G.222.
Liaison and AOP aircraft:
1 Cessna 182N.
Helicopters:
2 Bell 205A–1.
3 Bell 206A.
3 Bell 212.
Programme
Acquisition of 4 further Aermacchi MB.326KD.

Ecuador
Air force (Fuerza Aérea Ecuatoriana)
men 3,500.
squadrons 7.
operational aircraft 59.
helicopters 16.
Organization
1 strike-fighter squadron with Jaguar S(E).1.
1 ground-attack squadron with BAC 167.
1 bomber squadron with Canberra B.6.
1 transport squadron with C–47.
1 transport squadron with H.S.748 and DC–6B.
1 helicopter squadron with Alouette III.
1 helicopter squadron with S.A.315B.
– trainer squadrons with T–28A and T–41A.
1 trainer squadron with T–33.
Bases
Latacunga, Loja, Manta, Quito, Riobamba, Salinas.
Military training aid from
United States(?).
Equipment
Fighter and strike-fighters:
10 SEPECAT Jaguar S(E).1.
2 SEPECAT Jaguar T(E).2.
Ground-attack aircraft:
16 BAC 167 Strikemaster Mk.89.

Bombers:
5 English Electric Canberra B.6.
Transports:
6 Beechcraft C–45.
2 de Havilland Canada DHC–5D.
8 Douglas C–47.
2 Douglas DC–6B.
4 Hawker Siddeley H.S.748.
4 Lockheed L–188 Electra.
Liaison and AOP aircraft:
8 Cessna 172F.
1 Gates Learjet 24D.
2 Gates Learjet 25B.
Helicopters:
6 Aérospatiale Alouette III.
4 Aérospatiale S.A.315B.
2 Aérospatiale S.A.330.
3 Bell 47G.
1 Fairchild-Hiller FH–1100.
Trainers:
24 Cessna 150.
16 Cessna T–41A.
5 Lockheed T–33A.
8 North American T–28A.
Programme
On order: 24 IAI Kfir C2 strike-fighters, 14 Beechcraft T–34C and 12 SIAI–Marchetti SF.260 trainers. Replacement of Douglas C–47 transports by 3 de Havilland Canada DHC–6 from 1976. (12?) Beechcraft T–34C trainers on order.
Army 15,000.
Army aviation
— men.
1 squadron.
14 operational aircraft.
Organization
1 transport squadron with Arava.
Equipment
Liaison and AOP aircraft:
1 Cessna 172G.
1(3?) Cessna 185D.
2 Fairchild-Hiller Porter.
Transports:
9(6?) IAI Arava.
1 Short Skyvan 3M.
Navy 3,800 men.
Naval aviation (Aviacion Naval Ecuatorianas)
5 operational aircraft (and 2 helicopters?).
Helicopters:
2 Aérospatiale Alouette III(?).
Liaison aircraft:
2 Cessna R. 172.
1 Cessna 177.
1 Cessna T. 337.
Transports:
1 IAI Arava.

Egypt (UAR)
Air force (Al Quwwat Aljawwiya Ilmisriya)
men 28,000.
squadrons 51(?).
operational aircraft 580.
helicopters 145.
Organization
2 fighter squadrons with MiG–235.
9 fighter squadrons with MiG–21.
12 strike-fighter squadrons with Su–7.
4 strike-fighter squadrons with MiG–17F and PF.
2 strike-fighter squadrons with Mirage IIISDE.

3 strike-fighter squadrons with MiG–27.
2 bomber and reconnaissance squadrons with Tu–16.
4 transport squadrons with Il–14.
2 transport squadrons with An–12.
2(?) helicopter squadrons with Mi–4.
6(?) helicopter squadrons with Mi–8.
2 helicopter squadrons with Commando Mk.1 and Mk.2.
1 helicopter squadron with Sea King Mk.47.
– trainer squadrons with Yak–11, Yak–18 and Zlin 226.
– trainer squadrons with L–29.
Fighter and strike-fighter squadrons each with 10–12 aircraft.
Major bases
Abu Sueir, Alexandria, Almaza, Assuan, Beni Sueif, Bilbeis, Cabrit, Cairo-West, El Mansura, El Minya, Fayid, Gamil, Heliopolis, Heluan, Hurghada, Inchas, Luxor, Ras Banas.
Military training aid from
China(?), Soviet Union(?).
Equipment
Fighters and strike-fighters:
30 Dassault Mirage IIISDE.
4 Dassault Mirage IIISDD.
40 Mikoyan MiG–17.
45(?) Mikoyan MiG–19.
180 Mikoyan MiG–21.
20 Mikoyan MiG–21U.
20 Mikoyan MiG–23S.
some Mikoyan MiG–23U.
30 Mikoyan MiG–27.
120 Sukhoi Su–7.
Bombers:
18(25?) Tupolev Tu–16D and Tu16G.
Transports:
19 Antonov An–12.
6 Lockheed C–130H.
some (5?) Antonov An–26.
1 Boeing 707–366C.
1 Dassault Falcon 20.
40(?) Ilyushin Il–14.
Helicopters:
some Mil Mi–1.
20(35?) Mil Mi–4.
15 Mil Mi–6.
70 Mil Mi–8.
1 Sikorsky S–61.
5 Westland Commando Mk.1.
23 Westland Commando Mk.2.
6 Westland Sea King Mk.47.
Trainers:
approx 150 (200?) aircraft, inc Aero L–29, Gomhoureya (Bücker Bestmann), 30 Hispano HA–200, Yakovlev Yak–11, Yakovlev Yak–18, Zlin 226.
Some of the fighters, strike-fighters and bombers, as well as the Mil Mi–6 helicopters, have been grounded due to lack of pilots and spares. The Hispano HA–200 trainers have been mothballed.
Programme
244 Dassault Mirage F1 fighters and strike-fighters, 42 Aérospatiale S.A.341 helicopters (for army?), 250 Westland WG.13 Lynx helicopters, and 200 Hawker Siddeley trainers and light ground-attack aircraft on order. Replacement of Antonov An–12 and further 14 Lockheed C–130 transports planned.
Army 282,000 men.
Navy 17,500 men.
Aircraft factories
Helwan Aircraft Factory.

Eire
Air force (Irish Army Air Corps)

men 600.
squadrons 1.
operational aircraft 2.
helicopters 8.
Organization
1 liaison squadron with FR.172H.
1 helicopter squadron with Alouette III.
1 trainer squadron with C.M.170–2.
Bases
Baldonnel, Gormanston.
Equipment
Transports:
2 de Havilland Dove.
Liaison and AOP aircraft:
8 Reims-Cessna FR.172H.
Helicopters:
8 Aérospatiale Alouette III.
Trainers:
some de Havilland Canada DHC–1.
3(4?) Hunting Provost T.51 and T.53.
6 Potez-Air Fouga C.M.170–2.
Programme
Formation of 1 trainer squadron with 10 SIAI-Marchetti
SF.260W from 1976–77. Purchase of 4 Short Skyvan 3M
transports under consideration. Phasing out of Hunting
Provost T.51 and T.53.
Army 11,000 men.
Navy 450 men.

El Salvador
Air force (Fuerza Aérea Salvadoreña)
men 1,000.
squadrons 2.
operational aircraft 29.
helicopters 1.
Organization
1 strike-fighter squadron with Ouragan.
1 transport squadron with C–47.
1 trainer squadron with T–6G and T–34.
1 trainer squadron with C.M.170.
Base
Ilopango.
Military training aid from
United States.
Equipment
Fighters and strike-fighters:
18 Dassault Ouragan.
Transports:
6 Douglas C–47.
1 Douglas DC–4.
1 IAI Arava.
Liaison and AOP aircraft:
3 Cessna 180.
1 Cessna 182.
1 Cessna 185.
Helicopter:
1 Fairchild-Hiller FH–1100.
Trainers:
approx 15 aircraft; some Beechcraft T–34, 10(?) North
American T–6G.
6 Potez-Air Fouga C.M.170.
Programme
Acquisition of further (18?) IAI Arava transports.
Army 4,000 men.
Navy 130 men.

Ethiopia
Air force men 2,300.
squadrons 8.

operational aircraft 55.
helicopters 12.
Organization
1 strike-fighter squadron with F–5A.
1 strike-fighter squadron with F–86F.
1 ground-attack squadron with T–28D.
1 bomber squadron with Canberra B.52.
1 transport squadron with C–47 and C–54.
1 transport squadron with C–119K.
1 helicopter squadron with Alouette III.
1 helicopter squadron with AB.204B.
1 trainer squadron with Saab 91B and C.
1 trainer squadron with T–28A.
1 trainer squadron with T–33.
Major bases
Asmar, Bishiftu, Debre Zeit, Harar, Jijiga.
Military training aid from
United States.
Equipment
Fighters and strike-fighters:
some North American F–86F.
7 Northrop F–5A.
2 Northrop F–5B.
8 Northrop F–5E.
Ground-attack aircraft:
6 North American T–28D.
Bombers:
4 English Electric Canberra B.52.
Transports:
2 de Havilland Dove.
2 Dornier Do–28D.
6(12?) Douglas C–47.
2 Douglas C–54.
2 Fairchild C–119G.
10 Fairchild C–119K.
1 Ilyushin Il–14.
Helicopters:
5 Aérospatiale Alouette III.
5 Agusta Bell AB.204B.
2 Mil Mi–8.
Trainers:
10 Lockheed T–33.
15 North American T–28A.
20 Saab 91B and C.
Programme
14 Northrop F–5E strike-fighters, 2 Northrop F–5F strike
trainers, 12 Cessna A–37B ground-attack aircraft and 15
Cessna 310 liaison aircraft on order.
Army 40,000 men.
Army aviation
1 helicopter squadron with UH–1H.
Helicopters:
6 Bell UH–1H.
Navy 1,500 men.

Finland
Air force (Suomen Ilmavoimat)
men 3,000.
squadrons 5.
operational aircraft 63.
helicopters 11.
Organization
2 fighter squadrons with MiG–21F.
1 strike-fighter squadron with Saab 35XS.
1 ground-attack squadron with C.M.170.
1 transport squadron with C–47.
1 trainer squadron with Saab 91D.
– trainer squadrons with C.M.170.
Fighter and strike-fighter squadrons each with 12 aircraft.

Major bases
Kuopio, Luonetjärvi, Pori, Rovaniemi, Utti.
Military training aid from
Soviet Union.
Equipment
Fighters and strike-fighters:
18 Mikoyan MiG–21F.
2 Mikoyan MiG–21US.
6 Saab 35BS.
3 Saab 35C.
12 Saab 35XS.
Ground-attack aircraft:
12 armed Potez-Air Fouga C.M.170.
Bombers:
2 Ilyushin Il–28(?).
Transports:
8 Douglas C–47.
Liaison and AOP aircraft:
1 Cessna 402.
5 Piper PA–28R Cherokee Arrow.
Helicopters:
1 Aérospatiale Alouette II(?).
1 Agusta-Bell AB.206A.
1(2?) Hughes 500.
3 Mil Mi–4.
5 Mil Mi–8.
Trainers:
3 Mikoyan MiG–15UTI.
30(?) Potez-Air Fouga C.M.170.
20 Saab 91D.
Programme
Purchase of further 15 Saab 35 strike-fighters? Replacement
  of Potez-Air Fouga C.M.170 trainers by (50?) Hawker
  Siddeley Hawk, and of Saab 91D trainers by Finnish
  developed Velmer Leko–70 (30 from 1978?).
Army 30,300 men.
Navy 3,000 men.

France
Air force (Armée de l'Air)
men 102,000.
squadrons 58.
operational aircraft 900.
helicopters 110.
Organization
3 fighter squadrons with Mirage IIIC.
6 fighter squadrons with Mirage F1.
2 fighter squadrons with Super Mystère B2.
8 strike-fighter squadrons with Mirage IIIE.
2 strike-fighter squadrons with Mirage 5–F.
1 strike-fighter squadron with Mirage IIIB.
1 strike-fighter squadron with F–100D.
6 strike-fighter squadrons with Jaguar A.
6 bomber squadrons with Mirage IVA.
3 reconnaissance squadrons with Mirage IIIR and IIIRD.
1 ECM squadron with N.2501.
3 transport squadrons with C.160F.
4 transport squadrons with N.2501.
3 tanker squadrons with KC–135F.
2 transport squadrons with DC–6 and N.262.
1 transport squadron with N.262 and Falcon 20.
1 transport squadron with DC–6B and DC–8.
5 helicopter squadrons with Alouette II, Alouette III and
  S.A.330.
– trainer squadrons with C.M.170 and T–33A.
– trainer squadrons with M.S.760.
1 strike-fighter trainer squadron with Jaguar E.
1 bomber-trainer squadron with Vautour IIB.

Fighter and strike-fighter squadrons each with 12–16, and
  reconnaissance squadrons each with 18 aircraft.
Major bases
Aix-en-Provence, Avord, Bordeaux, Bretigny, Cambrai,
  Chartres, Cognac, Colmar, Creil, Dijon, Etampes, Istres, Le
  Bourget, Limoges, Luxeuil, Metz, Mont-de-Marsan,
  Nancy-Ochey, Nîmes, Orange, Orléans-Bricy, Reims, St.
  Dizier, Strasbourg, Toul-Rosières, Toulouse, Tours,
  Villacoublay.
Equipment
Fighters and strike-fighters:
50 Dassault Mirage IIIC.
135 Dassault Mirage IIIE.
44 Dassault Mirage IIIB.
48 Dassault Mirage 5–F.
100 Dassault Mirage F1.
some Dassault Mystère IVA.
25 Dassault Super Mystère B2.
140 SEPECAT Jaguar A and Jaguar E.
Bombers:
45 Dassault Mirage IVA.
20(?) Sud Aviation S.O.4050 Vautour IIB.
Reconnaissance and ECM aircraft:
60 Dassault Mirage IIIR and IIIRD.
4 Dassault Mirage IVA.
1 Douglas DC–8.
8 Nord N.2501.
Transports:
5 Aérospatiale N.262A.
18 Aérospatiale N.262C.
1 Aérospatiale S.E.210 Caravelle III.
11 Boeing KC–135F.
some (20?) Dassault M.D.315 Flamant(?).
2 Dassault Falcon 10.
9 Dassault Falcon 20.
6(9?) Douglas DC–6B.
4 Douglas DC–8F.
100(170?) Nord N.2501.
48 Transall C.160F.
Liaison and AOP aircraft:
approx 70 aircraft;
2 Cessna 310K.
2 Cessna 310L.
8 Cessna 310N.
12 Cessna 411.
40 Max Holste M.H.1521M.
2 Piper PA–31.
some SOCATA Rallye 180GT.
Helicopters:
40 Aérospatiale Alouette II.
50(90?) Aérospatiale Alouette III.
1 Aérospatiale S.A.321.
20 Aérospatiale S.A.330.
Trainers:
approx 450(?) aircraft;
26 CAARP CAP–10.
1 Dassault Falcon 20.
100(150?) Lockheed T–33A.
some Morane-Saulnier M.S.733.
25 Morane-Saulnier M.S.760.
300(?) Potez-Air Fouga C.M.170 and C.M.170–2.
Programme
Mirage IIIC and Super Mystère B2 fighter squadrons to be
  disbanded from 1977/78. Three additional Mirage F1 fighter
  squadrons to be formed by 1980 (total 135 machines
  delivered or on order). Three additional Jaguar A
  strike-fighter squadrons to be formed by 1979 (total
  170–200 machines delivered or on order). Replacement of
  Douglas DC–6B transports by 3 Aérospatiale Caravelle IIR.

Replacement of Lockheed T–33A, Morane-Saulnier
M.S.760, Potez-Air Fouga C.M.170 and C.M.170–2 trainers
by 200 Dassault-Breguet/Dornier Alphajet from 1977.

Army 328,000 men.
Army aviation (Aviation légère de l'Armée de Terre, ALAT)
3,700 men.
33(?) squadrons.
100 operational aircraft.
500 helicopters.
Organization
15(?) helicopter squadrons with Alouette II and S.A.341.
8 helicopter squadrons with Alouette III.
10 helicopter squadrons with S.A.330.
helicopter squadrons each with 10 machines.
Equipment
Helicopters:
180(195?) Aérospatiale Alouette II.
80 Aérospatiale Alouette III.
140 Aérospatiale S.A.330.
100 Aérospatiale S.A.341.
Liaison and AOP aircraft:
approx 100 aircraft;
60 Cessna O–1.
30 Max Holste M.H.1521M.
10 Piper L–18.
Trainers:
85(?) Nord 3202.
Programme
Partial replacement of Aérospatiale Alouette II helicopters by
Aérospatiale S.A.341 (60 additional S.A.341 delivered or on
order).

Navy 68,000 men.
2 aircraft carriers.
1 helicopter cruiser.
Naval aviation (Aéronautique Navale-L'Aéronvale)
12,000 men.
19 squadrons.
212 operational aircraft.
85 helicopters.
Organization
2 fighter squadrons with F–8E(FN).
2(3?) strike-fighter squadrons with Etendard IV–M.
1 reconnaissance squadrons with Etendard IV–P.
4 maritime-reconnaissance and ASW squadrons with
  Br.1150.
2 maritime-reconnaissance and ASW squadrons with
  Br.1050.
2 maritime-reconnaissance and ASW squadrons with P–2H.
2 transport squadrons with N.262A and PA–31.
2 helicopter squadrons with Alouette II and III.
1 helicopter squadron with Alouette III.
1 helicopter squadron with S.A.321.
1 helicopter squadron with S.A.330.
2 trainer squadrons with Rallye and M.S.760.
1 strike-fighter trainer squadrons with C.M.175 and Etendard
  IV–M.
1 trainer squadron with N.262A.
Bases
Landivisiau, Lann-Bihoué, Lanvéoc-Poulmic, Lorient,
  Nîmes-Garons, St. Mandrier, St. Raphael.
Equipment
Fighters and strike-fighters:
42 Dassault Etendard IV–M.
32 Vought F–8E(FN).
Reconnaissance aircraft:
12 Dassault Etendard IV–P.
Maritime-reconnaissance and ASW aircraft:
40 Breguet Br.1050.
37 Breguet Br.1150.

15 Lockheed P–2H.
12 Canadair CL–215.
Transports:
21 Aérospatiale N.262.
1 Douglas DC–6B.
Liaison aircraft:
10 Piper PA–31.
Helicopters:
20 Aérospatiale Alouette II.
25 Aérospatiale Alouette III.
15 Aérospatiale S.A.321.
9 Aérospatiale S.A.330.
16(12?) Sikorsky SH–34J.
Trainers:
2 Dassault Falcon 10.
12 Morane-Saulnier M.S.760.
16(27?) Potez–Air Fouga C.M.175.
10 SOCATA Rallye 100 Sport.
6 SOCATA Rallye 100 ST.
Programme
Replacement of Dassault Etendard strike-fighters and
  reconnaissance aircraft by 60(80?) Dassault Super Etendard
  from 1976–77. Partial replacement of Aérospatiale Alouette
  II and Alouette III helicopters by 18 Aérospatiale-Westland
  Lynx from 1976–77. 6 additional Dassault Falcon 10 MER
  radar-trainers on order. Purchase of additional (8?)
  Aérospatiale-Westland Lynx helicopters under consideration.
Aircraft factories
Aérospatiale (Société Nationale Industrielle Aérospatiale –
  S.N.I.A.S., formed in 1970 by the merger of Sud-Aviation
  and Nord-Aviation. Sud-Aviation has taken over
  Morane-Saulnier in 1966 and Potez in 1967). Breguet
  (combined with Dassault since 1971). Dassault/Breguet
  (Avions Marcel, Dassault/Breguet Aviation). Max Holste.
  Nord-Aviation, see Aérospatiale. Potez-Air Fouga, see
  Aérospatiale. Sud-Aviation, see Aérospatiale.

Gabon
Air force (Force Aérienne Gabonnaise)
men 200(?).
squadrons –.
operational aircraft 10.
helicopters 7.
Organization
–.
Base
Libreville.
Military training aid from
France.
Equipment
Transports:
2 Aérospatiale N.262C.
1 Dassault Falcon 20.
2 Fokker-VFW F.28.
1 Grumman Gulfstream II.
1 Lockheed L–100–20.
1 Lockheed L–100–30.
2 NAMC YS–11A.
Liaison and OAP aircraft:
2 Reims-Cessna F.337.
Helicopters:
4 Aérospatiale Alouette III.
3 Aérospatiale S.A.330.
Programme
Formation of strike-fighter squadron with 3 Dassault Mirage
  5G plus 2 Mirage 5RG reconnaissance aircraft.
Army 800 men.
Navy 100 men.

Germany, East (DDR)

Air force
men 30,000.
squadrons 25.
operational aircraft 280.
helicopters 60.

Organization
18 fighter squadrons with MiG–21.
1 transport squadron with Il–14.
2 transport squadrons with An–2 and An–14.
4(6?) helicopter squadrons with Mi–4 and Mi–8.
– trainer squadrons with Yak–11, Yak–18 and Zlin 226.
– trainer squadrons with L–29 and MiG–15UTI.
Fighter and strike-fighter squadrons each with 10–12 aircraft.

Major bases
East German: Bautzen, Bergen, Brandenburg-Briest, Cottbus, Dessau, Drewitz, Janschwalde-Ost, Jocksdorf, Kamenz, Marxwalde (earlier Neuhardenberg), Neubrandenburg, Peenemünde, Prenzlau, Preschen, Rothenburg, Strausberg-Eggersdorf.
Soviet: Altenburg, Alt-Lonnewitz, Brusin, Finow, Finsterwalde, Fürstenwalde, Gross-Dölln, Grossenhain, Jüterbog, Köthen, Merseburg, Neuruppin, Oranienburg, Parchim, Puetznitz, Rechlin-Lärz, Stendal, Spremberg, Welzow, Werneuchen, Wittenberge, Wittstock, Wünsdorf-Zossen(?), Zerbst.

Military training aid from
Soviet Union.

Foreign air forces in East Germany
approx 800(920?) Soviet operational aircraft (680 fighters, strike-fighters, reconnaissance aircraft and light bombers plus 120 transports) and 160 Soviet helicopters plus 1 ECM squadron with Il–14.

Equipment
Fighters and strike-fighters:
approx 210 Mikoyan MiG–21.
30 Mikoyan MiG–21U.
Transports:
approx 40(35?) aircraft;
20 Antonov AN–2 and Antonov An–14.
some Antonov An–24 and An–26.
10 Ilyushin Il–14M.
1–2 Ilyushin Il–18.
some Li–2(?).
1–2 Tupolev Tu–124.
1–2 Tupolev Tu–134.
Liaison and AOP aircraft:
some Yakovlev Yak–12, L–60, PZL–104 and Zlin Z–43.
Helicopters:
approx 60(85?) machines, inc Mil Mi–1, Mil Mi–2, Mil Mi–4 and Mil Mi–8.
Trainers:
approx 100(120?) aircraft, inc Aero L–29, Mikoyan MiG–15UTI, Yakovlev Yak–11, Yakovlev Yak–18, Zlin 226.

Programme
Replacement of older trainers by 100 Aero L–39 from 1976.
Army 98,000 men.
Navy 17,000 men.

Naval aviation
1 helicopter squadron with Mil Mi–4 helicopters.
8(10?) Mil Mi–4.

Germany, West (Federal Republic)

Air force (Deutsche Luftwaffe)
men 111,000.
squadrons 35.
operational aircraft 1,200.
helicopters 105.

Organization
8 fighter squadrons with F–4F.
8 strike-fighter squadrons with F–104G.
5 strike-fighter squadrons with G.91R.3.
4 reconnaissance squadrons with RF–4E.
6 transport squadrons with C.160D.
4 helicopter squadrons with UH–1D.
1 trainer squadron with T–37B and T–38A.
Fighter and reconnaissance squadrons each with 15 aircraft, strike-fighter squadrons (F–104G) each with 15–18 aircraft, strike-fighter squadrons (G.91) each with 21 aircraft.

Bases
German: Ahlhorn, Bremgarten, Büchel, Celle, Fürstenfeldbruck, Hohn, Husum, Jever, Lager Lechfeld, Landsberg, Leck, Leipheim, Manching/Ingolstadt, Memmingen, Neubiberg, Neuburg/Donau, Nörvenich, Oldenburg, Pferdsfeld, Rheine-Hopsten, Sobernheim, Wittmundhaven.
American: Bitburg, Hahn, Ramstein, Rhein-Main (Frankfurt), Spangdahlem, Zweibrücken.
British: Brüggen, Gütersloh, Lahrbruch, Wildenrath.
Canadian: Baden- Söllingen, Lahr.

Military training aid from
United States.

Foreign air forces in Germany
19 American squadrons:
3 fighter squadrons with F–15A.
8 strike-fighter squadrons with F–4C, F–4D and F–4E.
2 reconnaissance squadrons with RF–4C.
1 reconnaissance squadron with OV–10A.
1 special-duties squadron with EC–135, C–130A and B.
1 transport squadron with C–130E.
1 AOP squadron with O–2A.
1 helicopter squadron with CH–53C.
14 British squadrons:
2 fighter squadrons with Phantom FGR.2(F–4M).
2 fighter squadrons with Lightning F.2A.
3 strike-fighter squadrons with Jaguar GR.1.
3 strike-fighter squadrons with Harrier GR.1 and GR.3.
2 bomber squadrons with Buccaneer S.2B.
1 reconnaissance squadron with Jaguar.
1 transport and liaison squadron with Pembroke C.1 and Devon C.2.
1 helicopter squadron with Wessex HC.2.
1 helicopter squadron with Gazelle AH.1 (S.A.341B).
4 Canadian squadrons:
3 strike-fighter squadrons with CF–104.
1 helicopter squadron with OH–58A.

Equipment
Fighters and strike-fighters:
190 Fiat G.91R.3.
50 Fiat G.91T.3.
375 Lockheed F–104G.
100 Lockheed TF–104G.
173 McDonnell Douglas F–4F.
Reconnaissance and ECM aircraft:
5 MBB–HFB 320.
85 McDonnell Douglas RF–4E.
18 Rockwell North American OV–10C (also as target-tugs).
Transports:
4 Boeing 707–320C.
101 Dornier Do–28D.
3 Lockheed JetStar.
8 MBB–HFB 320.
76 Transall C.160D.
3 VFW-Fokker 614.
6(8?) MBB–HFB 33.
Liaison and AOP aircraft:
some Dornier Do–27.

Helicopters:
105(125?) Bell UH–1D.
Trainers:
47 Cessna T–37B.
45 Northrop T–38A.
Programme
10 additional McDonnell Douglas F–4F fighters on order
  (delivery 1976–77). Replacement of Fiat G.91R.3
  strike-fighters by 200 Dassault-Breguet/Dornier Alphajet
  trainer/ground-attack aircraft from 1978, and of Lockheed
  F–104G strike-fighters by 200 Panavia MRCA Tornado from
  1978. Phasing out of Lockheed JetStar transports.
Army 345,000 men.
Army aviation (Heeresflieger)
9,000 men.
28 squadrons.
6(?) operational aircraft.
540 helicopters.
Organization
15 helicopter squadrons with Alouette II.
7 helicopter squadrons with UH–1D.
6 helicopter squadrons with CH–53DG.
Equipment
Helicopters:
230 Aérospatiale Alouette II.
200 Bell UH–1D.
110 Sikorsky CH–53DG.
Liaison and AOP aircraft:
some (6?) Dornier Do–27.
Programme
Replacement of Aérospatiale Alouette II helicopters by 227
  MBB BO–105 from 1979–82. Acquisition of 212 MBB
  BO–105 PAH anti-tank helicopters from 1979.
Navy 39,000 men.
Naval aviation (Marineflieger)
6,000 men.
7 squadrons.
160 operational aircraft.
30(?) helicopters.
Organization
3 strike-fighter squadrons with F–104G.
1 reconnaissance squadron with RF–104G.
2 maritime-reconnaissance and ASW squadrons with
  Br.1150.
1(2?) helicopter squadrons with Sea King Mk.41.
Strike-fighter and reconnaissance squadrons each with 18
  aircraft, maritime-reconnaissance and ASW squadrons each
  with 9 aircraft.
Bases
Eggebek, Jagel, Kiel-Holtenau, Nordholz.
Equipment
Fighters and strike-fighters:
85(95?) Lockheed F–104G.
10 Lockheed TF–104G.
Reconnaissance aircraft:
25 Lockheed RF–104G.
Maritime-reconnaissance and ASW aircraft:
13 Fairey Gannet AEW.3.
20 Breguet Br.1150.
3 Fairey Gannet COD.4.
Transports:
20 Dornier Do–28D.
Helicopters:
some Sikorsky SH–34G.
21 Westland-Sikorsky Sea King Mk.41.
Trainers:
5 Fairey Gannet T.5.
Programme
Replacement of Lockheed F–104G strike-fighters and

RF–104G reconnaissance aircraft by 122 Panavia MRCA
Tornado from 1978. Replacement of Breguet Br.1150
maritime-reconnaissance and ASW aircraft by 15 Lockheed
S–3A from 1978 under consideration.
Aircraft factories
Dornier, MBB (Messerschmitt-Bölkow-Blohm), VFW
(Vereinigte Flugtechnische Werke)-Fokker.

Ghana
Air force
men 1,400.
squadrons 5.
operational aircraft 33.
helicopters 9.
Organization
1 ground-attack squadron with MB.326F and MB.326K.
1 transport squadron with BN–2A.
1 transport squadron with Skyvan 3M.
1 transport squadron with F.27.
1 helicopter squadron with Alouette III and Bell 212.
1 trainer squadron with Bulldog.
Bases
Accra, Kumasi, Tamale, Takoradi.
Military training aid from
Great Britain.
Equipment
Ground-attack aircraft:
6 Aérmacchi MB.326F.
6 Aérmacchi MB.326 K.
Transports:
8 Britten-Norman BN–2A.
5 Fokker-VFW F.27 Mk.400M.
1 Fokker-VFW F.27 Mk.600.
1 Hawker Siddeley H.S.125.
6 Short Skyvan 3M.
Liaison and AOP aircraft:
1 Cessna 337.
Helicopters:
4 Aérospatiale Alouette III.
2 Bell 212.
3 Hughes 269(?).
Trainers:
12 Scottish Aviation Bulldog.
Army 13,000 men.
Navy 1,200 men.

Great Britain
Air force (Royal Air Force, RAF)
men 91,000.
squadrons 65.
operational aircraft 775.
helicopters 145.
Organization
7 fighter squadrons with Phantom FGR.2 (F–4M).
1 fighter squadron with Phantom FG.1 (F–4K).
2 fighter squadrons with Lightning F.3 and F.6.
6 strike-fighter squadrons with Jaguar GR.1.
3 strike-fighter squadrons with Hunter F.6 and T.7.
5 bomber squadrons with Buccaneer S.2B and S.2A.
7 bomber squadrons with Vulcan B.2.
2 reconnaissance squadrons with Jaguar.
1 reconnaissance squadron with Vulcan SR.2.
2 reconnaissance squadrons with Canberra PR.7 and PR.9.
1 ECM squadron with Canberra B.15, B.16, E.15 and T.17.
1 ECM squadron with Canberra B.6 and Nimrod R.1.
1 ECM squadron with Andover and Argosy E.1.
5 maritime-reconnaissance and ASW squadrons with Nimrod
  MR.1.
1 maritime-reconnaissance squadron with Shackleton AEW.2.

2 tanker squadrons with Victor K.2.
4(5?) transport squadrons with Hercules C.1 (C–130K).
1 transport squadron with VC10.
3 transport squadrons with Devon C.2, Pembroke C.1,
  H.S.125 and Whirlwind HAR.10.
2 helicopter squadrons with Whirlwind HAR.10.
2 helicopter squadrons with Puma HC.1 (S.A.330).
3 helicopter squadrons with Wessex HC.2.
16 trainer squadrons with Bulldog T.1.
– trainer squadrons with Jet Provost T.3, T.4 and T.5.
– trainer squadrons with Gnat T.1 and Hawk T.1.
3 trainer squadrons with Canberra T.4, TT.18 and T.19.
Fighter, strike-fighter, bomber and reconnaissance
  squadrons, each with 8–12 aircraft, maritime-
  reconnaissance squadrons, each with 6–8 aircraft.

Major bases
British: Abingdon, Bawtry, Benson, Binbrook, Brampton,
  Brawdy, Brize Norton, Chivenor, Coltishall, Coningsby,
  Finningley, Honington, High Wycombe, Kinloss, Leuchars,
  Linton-on-Ouse, Lossiemouth, Lyneham, Marham, Northolt,
  Odiham, Scampton, Stanmore, St. Mawgan, Upavon,
  Waddington, West Raynham, Wittering, Wyton, Yeovilton.
American: Alconbury, Bentwaters, Greenham Common,
  Lakenheath, Mildenhall, Sculthorpe, Upper Heyford,
  Wethersfield, Woodbridge.

Foreign air forces in Great Britain
17 American squadrons:
3 strike-fighter squadrons with F–4D and F–4E.
3 strike-fighter squadrons with F–111E.
4 strike-fighter squadrons with F–111F.
1 fighter squadron with F–5E.
1 reconnaissance squadron with RF–4C.
1 electronic-reconnaissance squadron with RC–135C. D and U.
1 special-duties squadron with EC–135H and J.
1 transport squadron with C–130E.
1 tanker squadron with KC–135A.
1 air-rescue squadron with HH–53C, HC–130H and N.

Equipment
Fighters and strike-fighters:
30(?) BAC Lightning F.3 and F.6, 15(?) BAC Lightning T.4 and
  T.5.
48(70?) Hawker Hunter F.6, FGA.9, FR.10, T.7 and T.7A.
80 Hawker Siddeley Harrier GR.1 and GR.3.
13 Hawker Siddeley T.2.
20 McDonnell Douglas Phantom FG.1 (F–4K).
110 McDonnell Douglas Phantom FGR.2 (F–4M).
100 SEPECAT Jaguar GR.1 and T.2.
Bombers:
25 English Electric Canberra B.2, B.6, B.15 and B.16.
100(?) Hawker Siddeley Buccaneer S.2A and S.2B.
50 Hawker Siddeley Vulcan B.2.
Reconnaissance and ECM aircraft:
25 English Electric Canberra PR.7, PR.9 and E.15.
10 Hawker Siddeley Andover C.1.
9(?) Hawker Siddeley Argosy E.1.
8 (10?) Hawker Siddeley Vulcan SR.2.
3 Hawker Siddeley Nimrod R.1.
Maritime-reconnaissance and ASW aircraft:
12 Avro Shackleton AEW.2.
some Avro Shackleton MR.2 and MR.3.
38 Hawker Siddeley Nimrod MR.1.
Transports:
14 BAC (Hunting) Pembroke C.1.
9 BAC VC10.
some de Havilland Devon C.2.
25 Handley Page Victor K.2.
some Hawker Siddeley Andover C.1 and CC.2.
4 Hawker Siddeley H.S.125 CC.1.
2 Hawker Siddeley H.S.125 CC.2.

48 Lockheed Hercules C.1 (C–130K).
Helicopters:
approx 145 machines;
36 Aérospatiale Puma HC.1 (S.A.330).
14 Aérospatiale Gazelle HT.3 and HCC.4 (S.A.341D).
60 Westland Wessex HC.2 and HCC.4.
35 Westland Whirlwind HAR.10 and HCC.10.
Trainers:
approx 400 (450?) aircraft, inc:
179 BAC Jet Provost T.3, T.3A, T.5 and T.5A.
– English Electric Canberra T.4, T.17, TT.18 and T.19.
49 Hawker Siddeley Dominie T.1.
52 Hawker Siddeley Gnat T.1.
– Hawker Siddeley Hawk T.1.
132 Scottish Aviation Bulldog T.1.
8 Scottish Aviation Jetstream T.1.
In addition to the above the RAF has approx 100 or more
  mothballed aircraft in reserve, inc:
Transports:
13 Lockheed Hercules C.1 (C–130K).
2 BAC VC10.
30(35?) Hawker Siddeley Argosy C.1.
15(?) Hawker Siddeley Andover C.1.
5 Scottish Aviation Jetstream T.1.

Programme
Formation of 5 additional Jaguar GR.1 strike-fighter
  squadrons (total 165 delivered or on order) and 2 additional
  Jaguar T.2 strike-fighter squadrons (total 35 delivered or on
  order). Replacement of McDonnell Douglas Phantom FG.1
  and FGR.2 fighters, and of Hawker Siddeley Buccaneer S.2
  and Vulcan B.2 bombers, by 385 Panavia MRCA Tornado
  (220 fighters, strike-fighters and reconnaissance models,
  165 bombers) from 1978–79. Replacement of BAC Jet
  Provost T.3, T.4 and T.5, and of Hawker Siddeley Gnat T.1
  trainers by 175 Hawker Siddeley Hawk T.1 trainer and light
  ground-attack aircraft from 1976–80. On order: 15 Westland
  Sea King HAR.3 helicopters. Reduction of personnel strength
  to 79,000 by 1978.

Army 172,000.

Army aviation (Army Air Corps)
– men.
17 squadrons.
20 operational aircraft.
280 helicopters.

Organization
5 helicopter squadrons with Sioux AH.1.
11 helicopter squadrons with Scout AH.1.
Gazelle AH.1 (S.A.341B).
1 helicopter squadron with Scout AH.1 and Sioux AH.1
  squadrons each with 12 aircraft.

Equipment
Helicopters:
some Aérospatiale Alouette II.
60 Aérospatiale Gazelle AH.1 (S.A.341B).
80 Westland Scout AH.1.
105 Westland Sioux AH.1.
30 Westland WG.13 Lynx AH.1.
Liaison and AOP aircraft:
20 de Havilland Canada DHC–2.
Trainers:
20 de Havilland Canada DHC–1(?).

Programme
Replacement of Westland Scout AH.1 helicopters by
  Westland WG.13 Lynx AH.1 (approx 140 delivered or on
  order), and of Westland Sioux AH.1 by Aérospatiale Gazelle
  AH.1 (S.A.341B) (13 delivered or on order).

Navy 75,000 men.
1 aircraft carrier.
1 helicopter carrier.

Navy aviation (Fleet Air Arm, FAA)
— men.
12 squadrons.
65 operational aircraft.
205 helicopters.
Organization
1 fighter squadron with Phantom FG.1 (F—4K).
1 bomber squadron with Buccaneer S.2C and S.2D.
1 maritime-reconnaissance and ASW squadron with Gannet
  AEW.3.
1 transport squadron with Heron, Sea Devon C.20 and
  Wessex HU.5.
2 helicopter squadrons with Wessex HU.5.
5 helicopter squadrons with Sea King HAS.1.
1 helicopter squadron with Wasp HAS.1.
1 trainer squadron with Jetstream T.1.
6 helicopter training squadrons with Wessex HAS.1, HAS.3
  and HU.5, Sea King HAS.1, Wasp HAS.1 and Gazelle HT.2.
Fighter and bomber squadron each with 12 aircraft.
Bases
Culdrose, Lee-on-Solent, Portland, Prestwick, Yeovilton.
Equipment
Fighters and strike-fighters:
12 McDonnell Douglas Phantom FG.1 (F—4K).
Bombers:
14 Hawker Siddeley Buccaneer S.2C and S.2D.
Maritime-reconnaissance and ASW aircraft:
15 Fairey Gannet AEW.3.
Transports:
4 de Havilland Heron.
10(13?) de Havilland Sea Devon C.20.
2 Hawker Siddeley H.S.125 CC.1.
some Hunting Sea Prince C.1 and C.2.
Liaison and observation aircraft:
some Fairey Gannet COD.4.
Helicopters:
6 Aérospatiale Gazelle AH.1.
23 Aérospatiale Gazelle HT.2 (S.A.341C).
55 Westland Sea King HAS.1.
some Westland Sioux AH.1.
25(?) Westland Wasp HAS.1.
60 Westland Wessex HAS.1, HAS.3 and HU.5.
30(35?) Westland WG.13 Lynx HAS.2.
Trainers:
approx 60 aircraft, inc:
9 de Havilland Canada DHC—1.
10 English Electric Canberra T.4, T.22 and TT.18.
2 Hawker Hunter PR.11.
some Hunting Sea Prince T.1.
12 Scottish Aviation Jetstream T.1.
Programme
On order: 3 helicopter cruisers (commissioning from
  1980—81), 25 Hawker Siddeley Sea Harrier FRS.1 strike
  fighters (delivery from 1979), 13 Westland Sea King Mk.2
  helicopters (delivery from 1976). Phasing out of Westland
  Sioux AH.1 and Wasp HAS.1 helicopters.
Aircraft factories
BAC (British Aircraft Corporation), Fairey (Britten-Norman),
  Hawker Siddeley, Scottish Aviation, Short, Westland.
  Planned amalgamation as British Aerospace Corporation
  from 1977.

Greece
Air force (Elliniki Vassiliki Aeroporia)
men 23,000.
squadrons 22.
operational aircraft 320.
helicopters 45.

Organization
2 fighter squadrons with Mirage F1CG.
2 strike-fighter squadrons with F—104G.
2 strike-fighter squadrons with F—4E.
4 strike-fighter squadrons with F—5A.
3 strike-fighter squadrons with A—7H.
1 reconnaissance squadron with RF—5A.
1 maritime-reconnaissance and ASW squadron with
  HU—16B.
2 transport squadrons with N.2501D.
1 transport squadron with C—130H.
1 helicopter squadron with Bell 47G.
1 helicopter squadron with AB.205.
1 helicopter squadron with UH—1H.
1 trainer squadron with T—41A.
1 trainer squadron with T—37B.
3 trainer squadrons with T—2E and T—33A—N.
Fighter, strike-fighter and reconnaissance squadrons each
  with 16—18 aircraft.
Major bases
Andravidha, Araxos, Athens, Eleusis, Larissa, Nea Ankhialos,
  Soloniki, Sedes, Suda (Crete), Tanagra, Tatoi.
Military training aid
United States.
Foreign air forces in Greece
1 American ASW squadron with P—3 in Crete and sometimes
  1 American strike-fighter squadron with F—4.
Equipment
Fighters and strike-fighters:
some Convair F—102A and TF—102A.
40 Dassault Mirage F1CG.
30 Lockheed F—104G.
4 Lockheed TF—104G.
60 Northrop F—5A.
8 Northrop F—5B.
60 Vought A—7H.
38 McDonnell Douglas F—4F.
Reconnaissance aircraft:
14 Northrop RF—5A.
Maritime-reconnaissance and ASW aircraft:
5 Canadair Cl—215.
8 Grumman HU—16B.
Transports:
some Douglas C—47.
1 Grumman Gulfstream 1.
6(8?) Lockheed C—130H.
30 Nord N.2501D.
Helicopters:
some Agusta-Bell AB.204.
6(12?) Agusta-Bell AB.205.
6 Agusta-Bell AB.206.
10 Bell 47G.
14 Bell UH—1H.
Trainers:
approx 130 aircraft, inc 35(?) Canadair (Lockheed) T—33A—N,
  15 Cessna T—37B, 21 Cessna T—41A, and T—41D, 33(?)
  Lockheed T—33A, 40 Rockwell (North American) T—2E.
Programme
Formation of 1 reconnaissance squadron by mid 1977 with 8
  McDonnell Douglas RF—4E.
Army 120,000 men.
Army aviation (Aeroporia Stratou)
— men.
— squadrons.
30(?) operational aircraft.
55(?) helicopters.
Equipment
Helicopters:
5 Bell 47G.

40(?) Agusta-Bell AB.204B and Agusta-Bell AB.205.
10 Bell Uh–1D.
Liaison and OAP aircraft:
15(?) Cessna U–17A.
15(?) Piper L–21.
Transports:
2 Rockwell (North American) Commander 680FL.
Programme
Replacement of Bell 47G helicopters by additional
  Agusta-Bell AB.205.
Navy 18,000 men.

Guatemala
Air force (Fuerza Aérea de Guatemala)
men 1,000.
squadrons 3.
operational aircraft 25.
helicopters 10.
Organization
1 ground-attack squadron with A–37B.
1 transport squadron with C–47.
1 helicopter squadron with UH–1D.
1 trainer squadron with T–6G.
1 trainer squadron with T–37C and T–33A.
Bases
La Aurora (Guatemala City), Puerto Barrios, Puerto San Jose.
Military training aid from
United States.
Equipment
Ground-attack aircraft:
8 Cessna A–37B.
Transports:
6(10?) Douglas C–47.
1 Douglas C–54.
1 Douglas DC–6B.
7(10?) IAI Arava.
1 Rockwell (North American) Turbo Commander 680.
1 Rockwell (North American) Turbo Commander 690.
Liaison and AOP aircraft:
6 Cessna 170.
1 Cessna 172K.
3 Cessna 180H.
1 Cessna 182K.
2 Cessna U–206C.
Helicopters:
6 Bell UH–1D.
1 Hiller OH–23G.
3 Sikorsky H–19.
Trainers:
3 Cessna T–37C.
5 Lockheed T–33A.
7 North American T–6G.
Army 9,000 men.
Navy 300 men.

Guinea
Air force (Force Aérienne de Guinée)
men 300.
squadrons 1.
operational aircraft 18.
helicopters 1.
Organization
1 strike-fighter squadron with MiG–17F.
1 trainer squadron with Yak–18.
Base
Conakry.
Military training aid from
Soviet Union.

Foreign air forces in Guinea
some Soviet Tu–16 and Tu–20 bombers and reconnaissance
  aircraft.
Equipment
Fighters and strike-fighters:
8(5?) Mikoyan MiG–17F.
Transports:
4 Antonov An–14.
4 Ilyushin Il–14.
2 Ilyushin Il–18.
Helicopters:
1 Bell 47G.
Trainers:
some (3?) Aero L–29.
7 Yakovlev Yak–18.
2 Mikoyan MiG–15UTI.
Army 5,000 men.
Navy 350 men.

Guyana
Army 2,000 men.
Army aviation (Guyana Defence Force Air Wing)
2 Britten-Norman BN–2A transports.
2 Helio H–295 Super Courier liaison aircraft.
2 Hughes 269 helicopters.

Haiti
Air force (Corps d'Aviation d'Haïti)
men 250.
squadrons 3.
operational aircraft 9.
helicopters 7.
Organization
1 ground-attack squadron with F–51D.
1 transport squadron with C–45 and C–47.
1 liaison and ground-attack squadron with Cessna 337.
1 helicopter squadron with H–34 and Sikorsky S–55.
Base
Bowen Field (Port-au-Prince).
Equipment
Ground-attack aircraft:
4(6?) North American F–51D.
Transports:
2 Beechcraft C–45.
3 Douglas C–45.
Liaison and AOP aircraft:
1 Cessna 310.
6 Cessna 337.
Helicopter:
3 Sikorsky S–55.
4(2?) Sikorsky H–34.
Trainers:
2(3?) North American T–6G.
2(3?) North American T–28A.
Army 5,000 men.
Navy 250 men.

Honduras
Air force (Fuerza Aérea Hondureña)
men 1,200.
squadrons 3.
operational aircraft 20.
helicopters 2.
Organization
1 strike-fighter squadron with Super Mystère B2.
1 ground-attack squadron with F4U.
1 transport squadron with C–47.
– trainer squadrons with T–28D, T–41D and T–33A.

Bases
San Pedro Sula, Toncontin.
Military training aid from
United States.
Equipment
Fighters and strike-fighters:
8 Dassault Super Mystère B2.
Ground-attack aircraft:
6 Vought F4U–4, F4U–5 and F4U–5N.
Transports:
some Beechcraft C–45.
6 Douglas C–47.
2 Douglas C–54.
Liaison and AOP aircraft:
some (4?) Cessna 180 and Cessna 185.
Helicopters:
2 Sikorsky H–19.
Trainers:
5 Cessna T–41D.
3 Lockheed T–33A.
4 North American T–28D.
Army 5,000 men.
Navy 40 men.

Hong Kong
Air force (Royal Hong Kong Auxiliary Air Force)
men 130.
squadrons –.
operational aircraft 1.
helicopters 3.
Bases
Sek Kong, Kai Tak.
Military training aid from
Great Britain.
Foreign air forces in Hong Kong
1 British helicopter squadron with 8 Wessex HC.2.
Equipment
Transports:
1 Britten-Norman BN–2A.
Helicopters:
3 Aérospatiale Alouette III.
Trainers:
2 Beechcraft Musketeer.
3 NZAI Airtrainer CT–4.
Army – men.
Navy – men.

Hungary
Air force (Magyar Légierö)
men 12,000.
squadrons 14.
operational aircraft 140.
helicopters 25.
Organization
6 fighter squadrons with MiG–21.
3 strike-fighter squadrons with Su–7.
1 transport squadron with An–2.
1 transport squadron with Il–14 and Li–2.
2 helicopter squadrons with Mi–4 and Mi–1.
1 helicopter squadron with Mi–8.
– trainer squadrons with Yak–11 and Yak–18.
– trainer squadrons with L–29 and MiG–15UTI.
Fighter and strike-fighter squadrons each with 10–12 aircraft.
Major bases
Hungarian: Budapest, Debrecen, Estergom, Kaposvàr,
Kiskunfélegyháza, Miskolc, Nyiregyháza, Pécs, Szeged,
Szolnok.
Soviet: Dombovàr, Gyor (Raab), Papa, Székesfehérvàr
(Stuhlweissenburg), Szombathely (Steinamanger), Tököl.

Military training aid from
Soviet Union.
Foreign air forces in Hungary
approx 250(200?) Soviet fighters, strike-fighters and
reconnaissance aircraft.
Equipment
Fighters and strike-fighters:
some Mikoyan MiG–17F and PF.
70 Mikoyan MiG–21 and MiG–21U.
35 Sukhoi Su–7 and Su–7U.
Transports:
approx 30 aircraft:
10 Antonov An–2.
some Antonov An–24.
some Lisunov Li–2.
10 Ilyushin Il–14.
Liaison and AOP aircraft:
approx 15 aircraft, inc 1 Reims-Cessna F.337.
Helicopters:
approx 25 machines, inc Mil Mi–1, Mil Mi–4, Mil Mi–8, WSK
SM–2.
Trainers:
approx 50(?) aircraft, inc Aero L–29, Mikoyan MiG–15UTI,
Yakovlev Yak–11, Yakovlev Yak–18.
Army 90,000 men.
Navy 500 men.

Iceland
No national armed forces.
Coastguard (Lanhelgisgaezlan)
2 Fokker-VFW F.27 Mk.200 transport.
3 helicopters: 2 Bell 47J, 1 Sikorsky S–62C.
Foreign air forces in Iceland
1 American fighter squadron with F–4, some P–3C
maritime-reconnaissance and ASW aircraft, and EC–121H.
ECM-aircraft at Keflavik.

India
Air force (Bharatiya Vayu Sena)
men 98,000.
squadrons 62.
operational aircraft 900.
helicopters 260.
Organization
8 fighter squadrons with Gnat.
13 fighter squadrons with MiG–21FL and MiG–21M.
4 strike-fighter squadrons with Hunter F.56.
4 strike-fighter squadrons with Su–7.
3 strike-fighter squadrons with HF–24.
1 bomber squadron with Canberra B.(I)58 and B.66.
1 maritime-reconnaissance squadron with Canberra PB.57.
2 transport squadrons with An–12.
3 transport squadrons with C–119G.
2 transport squadrons with DHC–3.
1 transport squadron with DHC–4.
1 transport squadron with Tu–124 and H.S.748.
3 transport squadrons with C–47.
5(7?) helicopter squadrons with Alouette III.
6 helicopter squadrons with Mi–4.
3 helicopter squadrons with Mi–8.
– trainer squadrons with HT–2.
– trainer squadrons with HJT–16.
1 bomber trainer squadron with Canberra T.4.
1 strike trainer squadron with Hunter T.66 and F.56.
1 helicopter trainer squadron with Alouette III.
1 transport trainer squadron with H.S.748 and C–47.
Fighter and strike-fighter squadrons each with 12–18 aircraft.
Major bases
Adilabad, Agartala, Agra, Ahmedabad, Akola, Alir, Allahabad,

Ambala, Amritsar, Arkonam, Asansol, Aurangabad,
Bangalore, Baroda, Barrackpore, Belgaum, Benares, Bhawi,
Bhopal, Bhubaneshwar, Bhuj, Bidar, Bikaner, Bilaspur,
Calcutta, Chakalia, Cochin, Dum Dum, Ferozepore, Gaya,
Gorakpur, Gurgaon, Gwalior, Hyderabad, Iharsuguda, Imphal,
Jaipur, Jammu, Jamnagar, Jodhpur, Jubbulpore, Kalaikunda,
Kanpur, Kolar, Kumbhirgram, Lalitpur, Lucknow, Madras,
Madura, Manipur Road, Mohanbari, Nagpur, Palam, Pali,
Poona, Raichur, Raipur, Rajah Mundry, Rampurhat, Ranchi,
Saharanpur, Santa Cruz, Satna, Srinagar, Tamaram, Tanjore,
Tezpur, Tiruchirappalli, Trivandrum, Utterlai, Vijayawada,
Visakhapatnam, Warangal.

Military training aid from
Soviet Union.
Equipment
Fighters and strike-fighters:
some HAL Ajit.
60 HAL HF–24.
80 Hawker Hunter F.56 and T.66.
160 Hawker Siddeley Gnat.
220 Mikoyan MiG–21 and MiG–21U.
75 Sukhoi Su–7 and Su–7U.
Bombers:
55 English Electric Canberra B.(I)58.
8 English Electric Canberra B.66.
10 English Electric Canberra T.4.
2 English Electric Canberra T.67.
Reconnaissance aircraft:
8 English Electric Canberra PR.57.
Transports:
32 Antonov An–12.
25 de Havilland Canada DHC–3.
15 de Havilland Canada DHC–4.
50 Douglas C–47.
40 Fairchild C–119G.
45 Hawker Siddeley H.S.748.
6(12?) Ilyushin Il–14.
3 Tupolev Tu–124.
Helicopters:
150 Aérospatiale Alouette III and S.A.315B.
75 Mil Mi–4.
35 Mil Mi–8.
1 Sikorsky S–62A.
Trainers:
approx 150 aircraft, inc 65 HAL HJT–16, 10 HAL HT–2.
Programme
On order: further (130?) Mikoyan MiG–21MF and 100 HAL
  Ajit fighters and strike-fighters, Aérospatiale Alouette III and
  S.A.315B helicopters, plus 50 WSK TS–11 trainers.
  Replacement of Hawker Hunter and Sukhoi Su–7
  strike-fighters, and of de Havilland Canada DHC–4, Fairchild
  C–119G and Ilyushin Il–14 transports (by 80 de Havilland
  Canada DHC–5?) from 1976(?). Replacement of HAL HT–2
  trainers by HPT–32 from 1979.
Army 825,000.
Army aviation
– men.
– squadrons.
15(?) operational aircraft.
50(?) helicopters.
Organization
– helicopter squadrons with Alouette III.
– helicopter squadrons with S.A.315B.
Equipment
Helicopters:
30 Aérospatiale Alouette III and S.A.315.
20(?) Mil Mi–8.
Liaison and AOP aircraft:
some Auster AOP.9 and HAL HAOP–27.

Navy 30,000 men.
1 aircraft carrier.
Naval aviation
1,500 men.
7 squadrons.
38 operational aircraft.
36 helicopters.
Organization
1 strike-fighter squadron with Sea Hawk FGA.6, Mk.100 and
  Mk.101.
1 ASW squadron with Br.1050.
1 maritime-reconnaissance and ASW squadron with L.10496.
2 helicopter squadrons with Alouette III.
2 helicopter squadrons with Sea King Mk.42.
1 trainer squadron with HJT–16.
1 trainer squadron with Hughes 300 and Alouette III.
Equipment
Fighters and strike-fighters:
18(?) Armstrong Whitworth Sea Hawk FGA.6, Mk.100 and
  Mk.101.
Maritime-reconnaissance and ASW aircraft:
3(4?) Lockheed L.1049G Super Constellation.
11 Breguet Br.1050.
Transports:
5 Britten-Norman Defender.
2 de Havilland Devon.
Helicopters:
2 Aérospatiale Alouette II.
18 Aérospatiale Alouette III.
4 Hughes 300.
12 Westland Sea King Mk.42.
Trainers:
4 de Havilland Vampire T.55.
7 HAL HJT–16.
15 HAL HT–2.
Programme
Replacement of Armstrong Whitworth Sea Hawk
  strike-fighters by McDonnell Douglas A–4?. Acquisition of 4
  Ilyushin Il–38 maritime-reconnaissance and ASW aircraft
  (delivery from 1977) and phasing out of Breguet Br.1050.
Aircraft factories
HAL (Hindustan Aeronautics Ltd.).

Indonesia
Air force (Tentara Nasional Indonesia-Angkatan Udara,
  TNI-AU)
men 28,000.
squadrons 9.
operational aircraft 80.
helicopters 27.
Organization
1 strike-fighter squadron with CA–27 (F–86F).
1 ground-attack squadron with F–51D.
1 ground-attack squadron with OV–10F.
1 transport squadron with DHC–3.
1 transport squadron with C–47.
1 transport squadron with F.27.
1 transport squadron with C–130B.
2 helicopter squadrons with Bell 204B and UH–34D.
6(?) trainer squadrons with Airtourer T.6 Musketeer and
  T–34.
1 trainer squadron with T–33A.
3 helicopter squadrons with Mi–4 and Mi–6.
Of the strike-fighter and ground-attack squadrons only the
  ground-attack squadron with F–51D are operational. All
  others are grounded due to lack of spares.
Bases
Amboina, Balikpapan, Denpasar, Djakarta, Husein (Bandung),
  Lombok, Medan, Palembang, Semerang.

Military training aid from
Australia, United States.
Equipment
Fighters and strike-fighters:
16 Commonwealth CA–27 Sabre Mk.32 (F–86F).
Ground-attack aircraft:
11 North American F–51D.
12 Rockwell (North American) OV–10F.
Transports:
6 CASA C.212.
7 de Havilland Canada DHC–3.
some Douglas C–47.
8 Fokker–VFW F.27 Mk.400.
8 Lockheed C–130B.
1 Lockheed JetStar.
3 Lockheed L–1049G Super Constellation.
1 Short Skyvan 3M.
Liaison and AOP aircraft:
2 Beechcraft King Air A–100.
1 Beechcraft Super King Air.
1 Cessna 310.
5 Cessna 401A.
2 Cessna 402A.
5 Cessna T207 Turbo Skywagon.
50(?) PZL–104 Wilga.
Helicopters:
4 Aérospatiale Alouette III.
3 Bell 47G.
5(2?) Bell 204B.
1 Sikorsky S–61A.
12(4?) Sikorsky UH–34D.
Trainers:
approx 60 aircraft, inc 21 Beechcraft T–34, Beechcraft
  Musketeer, 20(?) Lockheed T–33A, some NZAI Airtourer
  T.6. In addition, the Indonesian Air Force has a number of
  Soviet aircraft which have been grounded due to lack of
  spares; these include:
Fighters and strike-fighters:
15 Mikoyan MiG–17F and PF.
20(?) Mikoyan MiG–19.
15 Mikoyan MiG–21.
Bombers:
10 Ilyushin Il–28.
22 Tupolev Tu–16.
Transports:
6 Antonov An–12.
10 Ilyushin Il–14.
Helicopters:
16 Mil Mi–4.
6 Mil Mi–6.
Programme
4 additional Rockwell (North American) OV–10F
  ground-attack aircraft on order, delivery 1977. The
  acquisition of 16 Vought A–7 strike-fighters is under
  consideration.
Army
140,000 men.
Army aviation (Angkatan Darat Republik Indonesia)
some (6?) Aérospatiale Alouette III helicopters.
Navy
30,000 men.
Naval aviation (Angkatan Laut Republik Indonesia)
1,000(?) men.
1 squadron.
20 operational aircraft.
9 helicopters.
Organization
1 maritime-reconnaissance and ASW squadron with HU–16D
  and Nomad.

Equipment
Helicopters:
3 Aérospatiale Alouette II.
3 Aérospatiale Alouette III.
3(4?) Bell 47G.
Maritime-reconnaissance and ASW aircraft:
6 GAF Nomad.
5 Grumman HU–16D.
Transports:
6 Douglas C–47.
3 Rockwell Courser Commander.
Aircraft factories
Lipnur (Lembarga Industri Penerbangan Nurtanio).

Iran (Persia)
Air force (Nirou Havai Shahanshahiyé Irân)
men 60,000.
squadrons 35.
operational aircraft 570.
helicopters 44.
Organization
2 fighter squadrons with F–4D.
2 fighter squadrons with F–14A.
10 strike-fighter squadrons with F–4E.
10 strike-fighter squadrons with F–5E and F–5A.
1 reconnaissance squadron with RE–5A.
1 reconnaissance squadron with RF–4E.
1 transport squadron with F.27M.
2 transport squadrons with C–130E.
2 transport squadrons with C–130H.
1 transport squadron with Boeing 747F.
1 tanker squadron with Boeing 707–320C.
1 helicopter squadron with AB.206A.
1 helicopter squadron with S.A.321.
– trainer squadrons with Bonanza.
– trainer squadrons with T–41D.
– trainer squadrons with T–33A.
Fighter, strike-fighter and reconnaissance squadrons each
  with 16–20 aircraft.
Major bases
Abu Musa, Ahwaz, Bandar Abbas, Bushihre, Chah Bahar,
  Doshan-Tappeh, Eshafan, Galeh-Marghi, Ishafan, Khatami,
  Kish, Mashbad, Mehrabad, Schiras, Täbris, Teheran.
Military training aid from
United States, Italy.
Equipment
Fighters and strike-fighters:
30 McDonnell Douglas F–4D.
175 McDonnell Douglas F–4E.
30 Grumman F–14A.
20(?) Northrop F–5A.
20 Northrop F–5B.
140 Northrop F–5E.
28 Northrop F–5F.
Reconnaissance aircraft:
12 McDonnell Douglas RF–4E.
12(?) Northrop RF–5A.
Transports:
12 Boeing 707–320C.
11 Boeing 747F.
4 Dassault Falcon 20.
10 Fokker-VFW F.27M.
4 Fokker-VFW Mk.600.
15 Lockheed C–130E.
40 Lockheed C–130H.
3 Rockwell Turbo Commander 681B.
1 Rockwell Turbo Commander 690A.
Liaison and AOP aircraft:
1 Beechcraft Super King Air.

2 Cessna O–2A.
5 de Havilland Canada DHC–2.
Helicopters:
16 Aérospatiale S.A.321.
10 Agusta-Bell AB.206A.
5 Agusta-Bell AB.212.
2 Agusta (Meridionali)-Boeing-Vertol CH–47C.
2 Agusta-Sikorsky AS–61A–4.
9 Kaman HH–43B.
Trainers:
45 Beechcraft Bonanza F32C, F33A and F33C.
30 Cessna T–41D.
Lockheed T–33.
Programme
A further 50 Grumman F–14A fighters for 3 squadrons are on
  order, delivery 1977–78. Formation of 10 additional fighter
  squadrons with 160 General Dynamics F–16 planned from
  1979. 39 Bell 214C helicopters on order, delivery 1977–78.
Army 175,000 men.
Army aviation (Gordan Havanirouz)
8,000 men.
– squadrons.
64 operational aircraft.
375 helicopters.
Organization
– helicopter squadrons with AH–1J.
– helicopter squadrons with AB.205.
– helicopter squadrons with AB.206A.
– helicopter squadrons with Bell 214A.
1 helicopter squadron with CH–47C.
1 helicopter squadron with HH–43B.
– liaison and AOP squadrons with Cessna 185.
Equipment
Helicopters:
45 Agusta-Bell AB.205.
20 Agusta-Bell AB.206A.
14 Agusta (Meridionali)-Boeing-Vertol CH–47C.
approx 140 Bell 214A.
approx 150 Bell AH–1J.
8 Kaman HH–43B.
Liaison and AOP aircraft:
45 Cessna 185.
6 Cessna 310.
10 Cessna O–2A.
Transports:
3 Rockwell Turbo Commander 690.
Programme
Establishment increase to 14,000 men and 800 helicopters
  by 1978–79. Bell AH–1J (total 202) as well as Bell 214A and
  Bell 214C helicopters are currently being delivered. Further
  22 Agusta (Meridionali)-Boeing-Vertol CH–47C helicopters
  and 2 Fokker-VFW F.27 transports on order, delivery 1977.
Navy 15,000 men.
Naval aviation
– men.
3 squadrons.
13 operational aircraft.
35 helicopters.
Organization
1 maritime-reconnaissance and ASW squadron with P–3F.
1 ASW squadron with SH–3D.
1 transport squadron with F.27.
Equipment
Maritime-reconnaissance and ASW aircraft.
6 Lockheed P–3F.
Transports:
2 Fokker-VFW F.27 Mk.400M.
2 Fokker-VFW F.27 Mk.600.
3 Rockwell Turbo Commander 690.

Helicopters:
4 Agusta-Bell AB.205.
11 Agusta-Bell AB.206A.
6 Agusta-Bell AB.212.
10 Agusta-Sikorsky SH–3D.
4 Sikorsky S–65A.
Programme
6 Sikorsky RH–53D helicopters and 3 Lockheed P–3C(?)
  maritime-reconnaissance and ASW aircraft on order. The
  purchase of 5–10 Grumman E–2C early warning and
  maritime-patrol aircraft is under consideration.
Aircraft factories
Iran Aircraft Industries – under construction.

Iraq
Air force
men 114,000.
squadrons 26.
operational aircraft 250.
helicopters 84.
Organization
5 fighter squadrons with MiG–21.
3 strike-fighter squadrons with MiG–17F and PF.
3 strike-fighter squadrons with MiG–27.
3 strike-fighter squadrons with Su–7.
1 strike-fighter squadron with Hunter F.6 and FGA.59.
1 bomber squadron with Tu–16.
1 transport squadron with An–2.
1 transport squadron with An–12.
1 transport squadron with An–26.
2 helicopter squadrons with Mi–4.
2 helicopter squadrons with Mi–8.
2 helicopter squadrons with Alouette III.
1 helicopter squadron with S.A.321H.
– trainer squadrons with Yak–11 and Yak–18.
– trainer squadrons with L–29 and MiG–15UTI.
Major bases
Al Qurna, Basra, Habbaniya, Hurriyah, Kirkuk, Mossul
  Raschid, Shaiba.
Military training aid from
Soviet Union.
Equipment
Fighters and strike-fighters:
20 Hawker Hunter F.6, FGA.59 and T.69.
30 Mikoyan MiG–17F and PF.
60(90?) Mikoyan MiG–21.
30 Mikoyan MiG–27.
50 Sukhoi Su–7.
Bombers:
some Ilyushin Il–28.
7 Tupolev Tu–16.
Reconnaissance aircraft:
2 Britten-Norman BN–2A.
2 de Havilland Heron(?).
Transports:
12 Antonov An–2.
6 Antonov An–12.
10 Antonov An–24 and An–26.
some Ilyushin Il–14.
2 Tupolev Tu–124.
Helicopters:
4 Mil Mi–1.
20 Mil Mi–4.
30 Mil Mi–8.
20 Aérospatiale Alouette III.
10 Aérospatiale S.A.321H.
Trainers:
approx 30(50?) aircraft, inc Aero L–29, Mikoyan MiG–15UTI,
  Yakovlev Yak–11 and Yakovlev Yak–18.

Programme
Purchase of (50?) Dassault Mirage F.1 strike-fighters, 2
  Lockheed L–100–30 transports, and (40?) Aérospatiale
  S.A.342 helicopters is planned. Replacement of Aero L–29
  and Mikoyan MiG–15UTI trainers by Aero L–39 (from
  1977?).
Army 95,000 men.
Navy 2,500 men.

Ireland: see Eire

Israel
Air force (Heil Avir le Israel)
men 16,000 (20,000 after mobilization).
squadrons 30.
operational aircraft 670.
helicopters 100.
Organization
1 fighter squadron with F–15A.
3 fighter squadrons with Kfir and Mirage IIICJ.
6 strike-fighter squadrons with F–4E.
6 strike-fighter squadrons with A–4E, A–4H and A–4N.
1 reconnaissance squadron with RF–4E.
2 transport squadrons with N.2501.
1 transport squadron with C–47.
1 transport squadron with KC–97G and Stratocruiser.
2 transport squadrons with C–130E and C–130H.
2 helicopter squadrons with Bell 205.
2 helicopter squadrons with UH–1D.
1 helicopter squadron with S.A.321.
1 helicopter squadrons with CH–53D and HH–53C.
1 helicopter squadron with CH–47C.
– trainer squadrons with C.M.170.
Bases
Bir Giggafa, Bir Thamada, Ekron, El Arish, Gebel, Libni, Haifa,
  Hatzerim, Hatzor, Jerusalem, Lod, Lydda(?), Ramat David,
  Tel Aviv.
Military training aid from
United States(?).
Equipment
Fighters and strike-fighters:
25 Dassault Mirage IIICJ.
3 Dassault Mirage IIIBJ.
some (6?) Dassault Mystère IVA.
some (5?) Dassault Super Mystère B2.
50(100?) IAI Kfir.
200 McDonnell Douglas A–4E, A–4H and A–4N.
25 McDonnell Douglas TA–4H.
200 McDonnell Douglas F–4E.
25 McDonnell Douglas F–15A.
Reconnaissance and ECM aircraft:
15 McDonnell Douglas RF–4E.
some Grumman EV–1.
some(6?) Sud Aviation S.O.4050, Vautour IIA and Vautour IIN.
Transports:
5 Boeing 707–131C and 707–320C.
10(12?) Boeing KC–97G and Stratocruiser.
4(10?) Britten-Norman BN–2A.
15(10?) Dornier Do–28.
10 Douglas C–47.
14 IAI Arava.
21 Lockheed C–130E and C–130H.
2 Lockheed KC–130H.
20 Nord N.2501.
Liaison and AOP aircraft:
approx 40 aircraft:
12 Beechcraft Queen Air.
10 Cessna U206C Turbo Skywagon.
5 Dornier Do–27.

2 IAI Westwind.
2 Pilatus PC–6B.
8 Piper L–18C.
Helicopters:
5 Aérospatiale Alouette II.
9 Aérospatiale S.A.321K.
some (5?) Bell 206A.
6 Bell AH–1G.
20 Bell 205.
some Bell 206A.
25 Bell UH–1D.
8 Boeing-Vertol CH–47C.
15(12?) Sikorsky CH–53D.
some (6?) Sikorsky HH–53C.
Trainers:
65 Potez-Air Fouga C.M.170.
Programme
On order: 50(100?) IAI Kfir fighters, 6 McDonnell Douglas
  RF–4E reconnaissance aircraft (delivery 1977), 4 Grumman
  E–2C early-warning aircraft (delivery 1977–78), and 12
  Sikorsky CH–3C helicopters. Replacement of McDonnell
  Douglas A–4 and F–4 strike-fighters by further McDonnell
  Douglas F–15 fighters and 200 General Dynamics F–16(?)
  strike-fighters from 1980–81.
Army
135,000 men (375,000 after mobilization).
Navy
5,000 men (7,000 after mobilization).
Aircraft factories
IAI (Israel Aircraft Industries).

Italy
Air force (Aeronautica Militare Italiana, AMI)
men 70,000.
squadrons 40(?).
operational aircraft 620.
helicopters 160.
Organization
7 fighter squadrons with F–104S.
2 strike-fighter squadrons with F–104G.
4 strike-fighter squadrons with G.91R.1.
4 strike-fighter squadrons with G.91Y.
3 reconnaissance squadrons with RF–104G.
1 ECM squadron with PD–808.
1 ECM squadron with F.27, EC–119 and EC–47.
2 transport squadrons with G.222, C–119G and C–119J.
1 transport squadron with C–130H.
1 transport squadron with C–47, Convair 440.
4 liaison squadrons with S.208M, P.166M and AB.204B.
2 helicopter squadrons with AB.47J and AB.204B.
4(?) helicopter squadrons with AB.204B.
4(?) helicopter squadrons with AB.206A.
1 trainer squadron with T–6G.
3 trainer squadrons with MB.326 and MB.326G.
3 strike trainer squadrons with G.91T.1.
1 trainer squadron with P.166M and C–47.
1 helicopter trainer squadron with AB.47G, AB.47J and
  AB.204B.
Fighter, strike-fighter and reconnaissance squadrons each
  with 15–18 aircraft.
Major bases
Aviano, Brindisi, Cameri, Cervia, Ciampino, Decimomannu
  (Sardinia), Ghedi, Gioia del Colle, Grazzanise, Grosseto,
  Istrana/Treviso, Pisa, Rimini, San Giorgio de Cervia,
  Sigonella (Sicily), Treviso, Villafranca.
Foreign air forces in Italy
2 American squadrons: 1 strike-fighter squadron with F–4
  and 1 maritime-reconnaissance and ASW squadron with
  P–3 (in Sicily).

Equipment
Fighters and strike-fighters:
70 Fiat G.91R.1.
50(75?) Fiat G.91T.1.
65 Fiat G.91Y.
30 Lockheed F–104G.
180 Lockheed F–104S.
20 Lockheed TF–104G.
Reconnaissance and ECM aircraft:
2 Douglas EC–47.
3 Fairchild EC–119J.
2 Fokker-VFW F.27.
1 Lockheed EC–130H.
45 Lockheed RF–104G.
8(15?) Piaggio PD–808.
Transports:
44 Aeritalia G.222.
some Beechcraft C–45.
4 Convair 440.
Douglas C–47.
15 Fairchild C–119G and J.
13 Lockheed C–130H.
2 McDonnell Douglas DC–9–30.
1 McDonnell Douglas DC–9–32.
50 Piaggio P.166M.
Liaison and AOP aircraft:
40 SIAI-Marchetti S.208M.
10 Piaggio PD–808.
Helicopters:
50(90?) Agusta-Bell AB.47G and J.
50(40?) Agusta-Bell AB.204B.
3(?) Agusta-Bell AB.205.
50 Agusta-Bell AB.206A.
8 Agusta (Meridionali)-Boeing-Vertol CH–47C.
2 Agusta-Sikorsky S–61.
Trainers:
approx 220 aircraft, inc 130 Aermacchi MB.326 and
MB.326G.
20(?) Lockheed T–33, some North American T–6G, 15
Piaggio P.148, 25 SIAI-Marchetti SF.260.
Programme
Part replacement of Lockheed F–104G and F–104S fighters
and strike-fighters by 100 Panavia MRCA Tornado from
1978–83. Phasing out of Fairchild C–119G and C–119J
transports, and of Piaggio P.148 trainers. Introduction of
Aermacchi MB.399 trainers and light ground-attack aircraft
from 1977–78(?).
Army 306,000 men.
Army aviation (Aviazione Leggera dell Esercito)
– men.
21(25?) squadrons.
150 operational aircraft.
220 helicopters.
Organization
– helicopter squadrons with AB.47G and AB.47J.
– helicopter squadrons with AB.206A.
– helicopter squadrons with AB.204B.
– helicopter squadrons with AB.205.
– helicopter squadrons with CH.47C.
– liaison and AOP squadrons with SM.1019.
– liaison and AOP squadrons with L–18C and L–21B.
– squadrons each with 10-18 aircraft.
Equipment
Helicopters:
5 Agusta-Bell A.109 Hirundo.
80(?) Agusta-Bell AB.47G and J.
50 Agusta-Bell AB.204B.
30 Agusta-Bell AB.205.
130 Agusta-Bell AB.206A.

26 Agusta (Meridionali)-Boeing-Vertol CH–47C.
Liaison and AOP aircraft:
approx 150 aircraft:
some Cessna O–1E.
20 Aeritalia-Aermacchi AM.3C.
20(?) Piper L–18C and L–21B.
100 SIAI-Marchetti SM.1019.
Programme
Phasing out of Cessna O–1E, Piper L–18C and L–21B liaison
aircraft.
Navy 44,500 men.
1 helicopter cruiser.
Naval aviation (Aviazione per la Marina, Marinavia)
2,000 men.
9 squadrons.
40 operational aircraft.
80 helicopters.
Organization
3 maritime-reconnaissance and ASW squadrons with Br.1150
and S–2F.
1 maritime-reconnaissance squadron with HU–16A.
2 ASW squadrons with SH–3D.
2 ASW squadrons with AB.204B and AB.212AS.
1 helicopter squadron with AB.204B.
Major bases
Cagliari, Catania, Naples, Trapani.
Equipment
Maritime-reconnaissance and ASW aircraft:
18 Breguet Br.1150.
12(11?) Grumman HU–16A.
10(?) Grumman S–2F.
Helicopters:
28 Agusta-Bell AB.204B.
13 Agusta-Bell AB.212AS.
24 Agusta-Sikorsky SH–3D.
15(20?) Agusta-Sikorsky HH–3F.
Programme
Phasing out of Grumman UH–16A maritime-reconnaissance
aircraft. Replacement of Agusta-Bell AB.204B helicopters by
further 16 Agusta-Bell AB.212AS by 1977.
Aircraft factories
Aerfer-Industrie Aerospaziali Meridionali, Aeritalia, Aermacchi
(Aeronautica Macchi), Agusta (Construzioni Aeronautiche
Giovanni Agusta), Fiat, Piaggio, SIAI-Marchetti.

Ivory Coast
Air force (Force Aérienne de la Côte d'Ivoire)
men 300.
squadrons –.
operational aircraft 8.
helicopters 8.
Organization
–.
Base
Port Bouet (Abidjan).
Military training aid from
France.
Equipment
Transports:
1 Aero Commander 500B.
1 Dassault Falcon 20.
2 Douglas C–47.
2 Fokker-VFW F.27.
1(2?) Fokker-VFW F.28.
1 Grumman Gulfstream II.
Liaison and AOP aircraft:
2 Reims-Cessna F.337.
4 Max Holste M.H.1521M.

Helicopters:
2 Aérospatiale Alouette II.
3 Aérospatiale Alouette III.
3 Aérospatiale S.A.330.
Trainers:
2 Cessna 150(?).
Programme
Formation of strike-fighter squadrons.
Army 3,700 men.
Navy 200 men.

Jamaica
Air force (Jamaica Defence Force Air Wing)
men 250.
squadrons –.
operational aircraft 2.
helicopters 6.
Organization
–.
Base
Up Park Camp (Kingston).
Military training aid from
Great Britain.
Equipment
Transport:
1 Britten-Norman BN–2A.
1 de Havilland Canada DHC–6.
Liaison and AOP aircraft:
3 Beechcraft 60 Duke.
1 Beechcraft King Air.
1(2?) Cessna 185.
Helicopters:
2 Bell 47G.
1(3?) Bell 206A.
3 Bell 212.
Army 1,000 men.
Navy 50 men.

Japan
Air force (Koku Jietai)
men 42,000.
squadrons 21.
operational aircraft 600.
helicopters 27.
Organization
5 fighter squadrons with F–4EJ.
5 fighter squadrons with F–104J.
4 strike-fighter squadrons with F–86F.
1 ground-attack squadron with F–1.
1 reconnaissance squadron with RF–4EJ.
2 transport squadrons with C–1.
1 transport squadron with YS–11.
1 helicopter squadron with KV–107.
1 helicopter squadron with S–62A.
4 trainer squadrons with T–34.
3(?) trainer squadrons with T–1 and T–33A.
2 strike-trainer squadrons with T–2.
1 ECM trainer squadron with C–46 and T–33.
Fighter and strike-fighter squadrons each with 18–25 aircraft.
Bases
Ashiya, Boufu, Chitose, Gifu, Hamamatsu, Hayakuri, Iruma,
  Kadena (Okinawa), Komaki, Komatsu, Matsushima, Miho,
  Misawa, Naha (Okinawa), Niigata, Nyutabaru, Shizuharma,
  Tachikawa, Tsuiki.
Military training aid from
United States.
Foreign air forces in Japan
11 American squadrons in Japan: 1 fighter squadron with

F–14A, 6 strike-fighter squadrons with F–4, 1 bomber
  squadron with A–6, 1 reconnaissance squadron with RF–4C,
  1 ECM squadron, 1 maritime-reconnaissance and ASW
  squadron with P–3C.
6 American squadrons on Okinawa: 3 strike-fighter
  squadrons with A–7D and 3 transport squadrons with
  C–130.
Equipment
Fighters and strike-fighters:
170 Lockheed F–104J.
18 Lockheed F–104DJ.
125 McDonnell Douglas F–4EJ.
180 North American F–86F.
Ground-attack aircraft:
26 Mitsubishi F–1.
Reconnaissance aircraft:
14 McDonnell Douglas RF–4EJ.
Transports:
28 Kawasaki C–1.
15(18?) Mitsubishi MU–2E.
4 Mitsubishi MU–2J.
8 Mitsubishi MU–2K.
12 NAMC YS–11.
Liaison and AOP aircraft:
5 Beechcraft Queen Air.
Helicopters:
20 Kawasaki-Vertol KV–197.
7 Mitsubishi-Sikorsky S–62A.
Trainers:
approx 300 aircraft, inc 80 Fuji-Beechcraft T–34, 50 Fuji T–1,
  150(?) Lockheed T–33A, 42 Mitsubishi T–2A.
Programme
Further 14 McDonnell Douglas F–4EJ fighters on order.
  Replacement of Lockheed F–104J fighters by 109
  McDonnell Douglas F–15 and 14 McDonnell Douglas TF–15
  strike trainers from 1981 planned (5 squadrons). On order: 4
  Mitsubishi Mu–2S transports, 8 Kawasaki-Vertol Kv–107
  helicopters, 60 Fuji KM–2B trainers (replacement for
  Fuji-Beechcraft T–34 from 1976–77).
Army 180,000 men.
Army aviation
– men.
24(?) squadrons.
70 operational aircraft.
340 helicopters.
Organization
– liaison squadrons with LM–1 and LM–2.
– liaison squadrons with O–1A and O–1E.
– helicopter squadrons with OH–6J and Bell 47G.
– helicopter squadrons with UH–1B and UH–1H.
– helicopter squadrons with KV–107.
1 trainer squadron with T–34.
Major bases
Akeno, Asahikawa, Iwanuma, Kamimachi, Kasumigauru,
  Kasuminome, Kisarazu, Medachigahara, Obihiro, Okadama,
  Tachikawa, Takaasohara, Yao.
Equipment
Helicopters:
70 Fuji-Bell UH–1B.
55 Fuji-Bell UH–1H.
10(30?) Kawasaki-Bell 47G.
110 Kawasaki-Hughes OH–6J.
38 Kawasaki–Hughes TH–55.
58 Kawasaki-Vertol KV–107.
Liaison and AOP aircraft:
approx 40 Cessna O–1A and O–1E.
23 Fuji LM–1 and LM–2.
Transports:
8 Mitsubishi MU–2C and MU–2K.

Trainers:
9 Fuji-Beechcraft T–34.
Programme
Further Fuji-Bell UH–1H and Kawasaki-Hughes OH–6J
helicopters on order. Phasing out of Kawasaki-Bell 47G
helicopters and Cessna O–1 and Fuji LM–1 and LM–2
liaison aircraft. Seeking an anti-tank helicopter.
Navy 39,000 men.
Naval aviation
2,200 men.
13 squadrons.
121 operational aircraft.
81 helicopters.
Organization
4 maritime-reconnaissance and ASW squadrons with P–2J
and P–2H.
2 maritime-reconnaissance and ASW squadrons with S–2F.
1 maritime-reconnaissance and ASW squadron with PS–1.
1 transport squadron with YS–11.
3(4?) ASW squadrons with SH–3A.
1 helicopter squadron with KV–107.
1 helicopter squadron with S–62A.
– trainer squadrons with T–34 and KM–2.
Bases
Atsugi, Hachinoe, Iwakumi, Kanoya, Komatsujima, Ohminato,
Oomura, Ozuki, Shimofusa, Tateyama, Tokushima,
Utsunomiya.
Equipment
Maritime-reconnaissance and ASW aircraft:
22 Grumman S–2F.
20 Kawasaki-Lockheed SP–2H.
50 Kawasaki P–2J.
16 Shin Meiwa PS–1.
3 Shin Meiwa SS–2.
Transports:
10 NAMC YS–11.
Liaison and AOP aircraft:
12 Beechcraft Queen Air B65.
4(6?) Beechcraft King Air C90.
Helicopters:
6 Kawasaki-Hughes OH–6J.
11 Kawasaki-Vertol KV–107.
9 Mitsubishi-Sikorsky S–62A.
55 Mitsubishi-Sikorsky SH–3A.
Trainers:
12 Fuji-Beechcraft T–34.
30 Fuji KM–2.
Programme
Further 36 maritime-reconnaissance and ASW aircraft on
order (30 Kawasaki P–2J, 6 Shin Meiwa PS–1), plus 24
Mitsubishi-Sikorsky SH–3A helicopters, delivery by 1980.
Phasing out of Kawasaki-Lockheed SP–2H maritime-
reconnaissance and ASW aircraft, replacement by 34
Lockheed P–3C(?). Purchase of 15 Grumman E–2C
early-warning and maritime-patrol aircraft under
consideration.
Aircraft factories
Fuji (Fuji Heavy Industries Ltd.), Kawasaki (Kawasaki Aircraft
Co. Ltd.), Mitsubishi (Mitsubishi Heavy Industries Ltd.),
NAMC (Nihon Aeroplane Manufacturing Co.), Shin Meiwa.

Jordan
Air force (Al Quwwat Aljawwiya Amalakiya Alurduniya)
men 4,600.
squadrons 6.
operational aircraft 87.
helicopters 16.
Organization
1 fighter squadron with F–5E.

1 fighter squadron with F–104A.
2 strike-fighter squadrons with F–5A.
1 transport squadron with C–119K and C–130B.
1 helicopter squadron with Alouette III.
1 trainer squadron with Bulldog.
1 trainer squadron with T–37B.
Major bases
King Abdullah (Amman), Aquaba, King Hussein (Mafraq),
Prince Hassan (H–5).
Military training aid from
United States, Iran.
Equipment
Fighters and strike-fighters:
18 Lockheed F–104A.
2 Lockheed F–104B.
30 Northrop F–5A.
4 Northrop F–5B.
22 Northrop F–5F.
Transports:
1 Boeing 727.
4 CASA C.212A.
1 Dassault Falcon 20.
1 de Havilland Dove(?).
4 Lockheed C–130B.
Helicopters:
16 Aérospatiale Alouette III.
Trainers:
12 Cessna T–37B.
8 Scottish Aviation Bulldog.
Programme
On order: further 22 Northrop F–5E strike-fighters, 2
Northrop F–5E strike trainers and 4 Sikorsky S–76
helicopters, delivery 1978.
Army 70,000 men.
Navy 250 men.

Kenya
Air force
men 700.
squadrons 3.
operational aircraft 15.
helicopters 5.
Organization
1 fighter squadron with Hunter FGA.9.
1 ground-attack squadron with BAC 167.
1 transport squadron with DHC–4.
1 liaison squadron with DHC–2.
1 trainer squadron with Bulldog.
Bases
Eastleigh (Nairobi), Mombasa, Nanyuki.
Military training aid from
Great Britain.
Equipment
Fighters and strike-fighters:
4 Hawker Hunter FGA.9.
Ground-attack aircraft:
5 BAC 167 Strikemaster Mk.87.
Transports:
6 de Havilland Canada DHC–4.
Liaison and AOP aircraft:
7 de Havilland Canada DHC–2.
2 Piper PA–31 Navajo.
Helicopters:
3 Aérospatiale Alouette II.
2 Bell 47G.
Trainers:
14 Scottish Aviation Bulldog.
Programme
Formation of 1 strike-fighter squadron with 10 Northrop F–5E

and 2 F–5F. Further 9 Scottish Aviation Bulldog trainers on order.
Army 6,500 men.
Navy 350 men.

Korea (North)
Air force
men 40,000.
squadrons 30.
operational aircraft 390.
helicopters 35.
Organization
9 fighter squadrons with MiG–21.
9 strike-fighter squadrons with MiG–17F and PF.
3 strike-fighter squadrons with Su–7.
2 bomber squadrons with Il–28.
1 reconnaissance squadron with Il–28R.
2 transport squadrons with Il–10 and Il–14.
1 transport squadron with Li–2.
2 helicopter squadrons with Mi–4.
1 helicopter squadron with Mi–8.
– trainer squadrons with Yak–11 and Yak–18.
– trainer squadrons with MiG–15UTI.
Fighter, strike-fighter and bomber squadrons each with 12–15 aircraft.
Major bases
Pyöng-ni, Pyöngyang, Pyöngyang-East, Saamcham, Sinuiju, Sunan, Taechon, Uijū, Wonsan.
Military training aid from
Soviet Union, China(?).
Equipment
Fighters and strike-fighters:
20(?) Mikoyan MiG–15.
130 Mikoyan MiG–17F and PF.
130 Mikoyan MiG–21 and MiG–21U.
30 Sukhoi Su–7 and Su–7U.
Bombers:
Ilyushin Il–28 and Il–28U.
Reconnaissance aircraft:
10 Ilyushin Il–28R.
Transports:
approx 40(50?) aircraft, inc Antonov An–2, Antonov An–24, Ilyushin Il–12, Ilyushin Il–14, 4 Ilyushin Il–18, some Lisunov Li–2, 1 Tupolev Tu–154B.
some PZL–104 liaison and AOP aircraft.
Helicopters:
some Mil Mi–1.
20 Mil Mi–4.
10 Mil Mi–8.
Trainers:
approx 70 aircraft, inc Yakovlev Yak–11 and Yak–18 plus Mikoyan MiG–15UTI.
Programme
Replacement of Mikoyan MiG–17 strike-fighters by Sukhoi Su–7.
Army 400,000 men.
Navy 17,000 men.

Korea (South)
Air force (Republic of Korea Air Force)
men 25,000.
squadrons 18.
operational aircraft 320.
helicopters 15.
Organization
2 fighter squadrons with F–4D.
2 fighter squadrons with F–4E.
7 strike-fighter squadrons with F–5A and F–5E.
1 ground-attack squadron with OV–10G.

2 transport squadrons with C–46 and C–47.
1 transport squadron with C–123K.
1 transport squadron with C–54.
– liaison squadrons with O–1 and U–17A.
1 helicopter squadron with UH–1D.
1 helicopter squadron with UH–19.
– trainer squadrons with T–28A.
– trainer squadrons with T–33A.
– trainer squadrons with T–41.
Fighter and strike-fighter squadrons each with 18–25 aircraft.
Major bases
Chinhae, Chongju, Chunchon, Hoengsong, Kananung, Kimpo, Kunsan, Osan, Pohang, Pusan, Pyong-teak, Saechon, Seoul, Suwon, Taegu.
Military training aid from
United States.
Foreign air forces in Korea (South)
3 American strike-fighter squadrons with F–4.
Equipment
Fighters and strike-fighters:
36 McDonnell Douglas F–4D.
36 McDonnell Douglas F–4E.
30 Northrop F–5A and some (3?) F–5B.
120 Northrop F–5E.
9 Northrop F–5F.
Ground-attack aircraft:
24 Rockwell OV–10G.
Transports:
20(?) Curtiss-Wright C–46.
some Douglas C–47.
10(12?) Douglas C–54.
12(?) Fairchild C–123K.
2 Hawker Siddeley H.S.748.
some Rockwell Aero Commander 520 and 560F(?).
Liaison and AOP aircraft:
Cessna O–1, Cessna U–17A and 1–2 Beechcraft U–21A.
Helicopters:
2 Bell 212.
5 Bell UH–1D.
2 Kawasaki KH–4.
6 Sikorsky UH–19.
Trainers:
approx 90 aircraft, inc 20 Cessna T–41D, 20 Lockheed T–33A, 20 North American T–28A, 4 Pazmany PL–2.
Programme
100 Hughes 500M–D Defender-attack helicopters on order, delivery from 1977.
Army 560,000 men.
Navy 20,000 men.
Marines 20,000 men.
Aircraft factories
Under construction.

Kuwait
Air force (Kuwait Air Force)
men 2,000.
squadrons 8.
operational aircraft 70.
helicopters 36.
Organization
1 fighter squadron with Mirage F 1CK.
2 strike-fighter squadrons with A–4KU.
1 strike-fighter squadron with FGA.57.
1 ground-attack squadron with BAC 167.
1 helicopter squadron with AB.204B and AB.205.
1 helicopter squadron with S.A.342.
1 helicopter squadron with S.A.330.
Base
Kuwait.

Military training aid from
Great Britain.
Equipment
Fighters and strike-fighters:
18 Dassault Mirage F 1CK.
2 Dassault Mirage F 1BK.
4 Hawker Hunter FGA.57.
2(5?) Hawker Hunter T.67.
30 McDonnell Douglas A–4KU.
6 McDonnell Douglas TA–4KU.
Ground-attack aircraft:
11 BAC 167 Strikemaster Mk.83.
Transports:
2 de Havilland Canada DHC–4.
2 Lockheed L–100–20.
2 McDonnell Douglas DC–9CF.
Helicopters:
10 Aérospatiale S.A.330.
20 Aérospatiale S.A.342.
2 Agusta-Bell 204B.
4 Agusta-Bell AB.205.
Programme
Phasing out of Hawker Hunter FGA.57 strike-fighters.
Army 8,000 men.
Navy 200 men.

Laos
Air force
men 2,000.
squadrons 8(?).
operational aircraft 80(?).
helicopters 30(?).
Organization
3 ground-attack squadrons with T–28D.
1 night ground-support squadron with AC–47.
2 transport squadrons with C–47 and An–24.
2 helicopter squadrons with UH–34D.
Major bases
Chieng Khouang, Savannakhet, Pakse, Vientiane.
Military training aid from
Vietnam, Soviet Union(?).
Equipment
Ground-attack aircraft:
50 North American T–28D.
Night ground-support aircraft:
10 Douglas AC–47.
Transports:
6 Antonov An–24.
15(?) Douglas C–47.
Liaison and AOP aircraft:
some Cessna O–1.
4 Cessna U–17A.
1 de Havilland Canada DHC–2.
Helicopters:
some Bell UH–1D.
some Mil Mi–8.
20(?) Sikorsky UH–34D.
Trainers:
approx 20 aircraft, inc 6 Cessna T–41B.
It is not certain how many of these aircraft are still in service.
Programme
Re-arming with Soviet equipment.
Army 50,000 men.
Navy 500 men.

Lebanon
Air force (Force Aérienne Libanaise)
men 1,000.
squadrons 4.

operational aircraft 28.
helicopters 22.
Organization
1 fighter squadron with Mirage IIIEL.
1 strike-fighter squadron with Hunter F.6, F.70 and FGA.9.
1 helicopter squadron with Alouette II and Alouette III.
1 helicopter squadron with AB.212.
1 trainer squadron with Bulldog.
1 trainer squadron with C.M.170–2.
Bases
Beirut, Rayak, Tripoli.
Military training aid from
France.
Equipment
Fighters and strike-fighters:
10 Dassault Mirage IIIEL.
1 Dassault Mirage IIIBL.
4 Hawker Hunter F.6.
6 Hawker Hunter F.70.
4 Hawker Hunter FGA.9.
2 Hawker Hunter T.69.
Transports:
1 de Havilland Dove.
Helicopters:
3 Aérospatiale Alouette II.
5 Aérospatiale Alouette III.
6 Agusta-Bell AB.212.
Trainers:
3(?) de Havilland Canada DHC–1.
7 Potez-Air Fouga C.M.170–2.
6 Scottish Aviation Bulldog.
Due to Civil War it is not certain how many of these aircraft are still in existence. 4 Dassault Mirage IIIEL fighters and the Mirage IIIBL have been mothballed.
Army 14,000 men.
Navy 300 men.

Liberia
Air force
men 150(?).
operational aircraft 2.
Organization
–.
Base
Monrovia.
Equipment
2 Douglas C–47 transports.
4 liaison aircraft: 2 Cessna 172, 1 Cessna 185, 1 Cessna 207.
Army 4,800 men.
Navy 200 men.

Libya
Air force (Al Quwwat Aljawwiya Al Libiyya)
men 5,000.
squadrons 12.
operational aircraft 102.
helicopters 33(?).
Organization
1 fighter squadron with MiG–23S.
2 fighter squadrons with Mirage 5–DE.
4 strike-fighter squadrons with Mirage 5–D.
1 bomber squadron with Tu–22.
1 transport squadron with C–47.
1 transport squadron with C–130E.
1 helicopter squadron with Alouette III.
1 helicopter squadron with S.A.321.
1 helicopter squadron with CH–47C.
1 trainer squadron with C.M.170.
1 strike-trainer squadron with Mirage 5–DD.

Bases
Benina (Benghazi), El Adem, El Awai, Okba Ben Ben Nafi (Wheelus, Tripoli).
Military training aid from
Pakistan, Soviet Union.
Equipment
Fighters and strike-fighters:
50 Dassault Mirage 5–D.
10 Dassault Mirage 5–DD.
30 Dassault Mirage 5–DE.
12(30?) Mikoyan MiG–23S.
Bombers:
12 Tupolev Tu–22.
Reconnaissance aircraft:
10 Dassault Mirage 5–DR.
Transports:
1(2?) Dassault Falcon 20.
9 Douglas C–47.
8 Lockheed C–130E.
Helicopters:
1 Agusta-Bell AB.212.
10(24) Agusta (Meridionali)-Boeing-Vertol CH–47C.
1 Agusta-Sikorsky A5–61A–4.
3 Aérospatiale Alouette II.
10 Aérospatiale Alouette III.
8 Aérospatiale S.A.321.
Trainers:
3 Lockheed T–33A.
some Potez-Air Fouga C.M.170.
12(?) Soko G–2A–E Galeb.
The majority of fighters, strike-fighters and reconnaissance aircraft have been grounded due to lack of pilots.
Programme
On order: 16 Dassault Mirage F1A strike-fighters, 16 Dassault Mirage F1E fighters, 6 Dassault Mirage F1B strike-trainers and 12 Mil Mi–8 helicopters.
Army 25,000 men.
Army aviation
Helicopters:
4 Aérospatiale Alouette III.
3(6?) Agusta-Bell AB.47G.
5 Agusta-Bell AB.206A.
Navy 2,000 men.

Madagascar (Malagasy)
Air force (Armée de L'Air Malgache)
men 200.
squadron 1.
operational aircraft 7.
helicopters 4.
Organization
1 transport squadron with C–47.
Bases
Diego-Suarez, Ivato (Tananarive).
Military training aid from
France.
Equipment
Transports:
1 Britten-Norman Defender.
5 Douglas C–47.
1 Douglas C–54D.
Liaison and AOP aircraft:
4 Cessna 172 M.
1 Piper Aztec D.
3 Reims-Cessna F.337.
Helicopters:
1 Aérospatiale Alouette II.
2 Aérospatiale Alouette III.
1 Bell 47G.

Army 4,000.
Navy 500 men.

Malawi
Air force
men (100?).
squadron 1.
operational aircraft 6.
Organization
1 transport squadron with C–47 and Pembroke.
Base
Blantyre(?).
Military training aid from
Great Britain.
Equipment
Transports:
4 Douglas C–47.
2 Hunting Pembroke.
Army 1,500 men.

Malaysia
Air force (Tentera Udara Diraja Malaysia)
men 5,300.
squadrons 10.
operational aircraft 70.
helicopters 50.
Organization
1 fighter squadron with F–5E.
1 strike-fighter squadron with CA–27.
2 transport squadrons with DHC–4.
1 transport squadron with Dove and Heron.
1 transport squadron with C–130H.
1 liaison squadron with Cessna 402B.
2 helicopter squadrons with Alouette III.
2 helicopter squadrons with S–61A–4.
2 trainer squadrons with CL–41G.
1 trainer squadron with Bulldog.
Bases
Alor Star, Butterworth, Kuala Lumpur, Kuantan, Kuching, Labuan.
Military training aid from
Australia, Great Britain, Pakistan.
Foreign air forces in Malaysia
2 Australian strike-fighter squadrons with Mirage IIIO.
4 Australian C–47 transports.
Equipment
Fighters and strike-fighters:
16 Commonwealth CA–27 Sabre Mk.32 (F–86F).
14 Northrop F–5E.
2 Northrop F–5B.
Transports:
5 de Havilland Dove.
2 de Havilland Heron.
14 de Havilland Canada DHC–4.
7 Handley Page Herald 401.
2 Hawker Siddeley H.S.125.
6 Lockheed C–130H.
Liaison and AOP aircraft:
12 Cessna 402B.
Helicopters:
25 Aérospatiale Alouette III.
6 Bell 47G.
5 Bell 206B.
14 Sikorsky S–61A–4.
Trainers:
17 Canadair CL–41G.
12 Scottish Aviation Bulldog.

Programme
Phasing out of Handley Page Herald 401 transports. Some
  Agusta-Bell AB.212 helicopters on order.
Army 51,000 men.
Navy 4,800 men.

Mali
Air force (Force Aérienne du Mali)
men 200.
squadrons –.
operational aircraft 4.
helicopters 2.
Organization
–.
Base
Bamako.
Military training aid from
Soviet Union.
Equipment
Fighters and strike-fighters:
3 Mikoyan MiG–17F.
Transports:
2 Antonov An–2.
2 Douglas C–47.
Helicopters:
2 Mil Mi–4.
Trainers:
some Yakovlev Yak–12 and Yakovlev Yak–18, 1 Mikoyan
  MiG–15UTI.
Army 4,000 men.
Navy 50 men.

Malta
Air force
men 250.
squadrons –.
helicopters 5.
Organization
–.
Bases
Hal Far, Luqa, Takali.
Military training aid from
Germany, Great Britain.
Foreign air forces in Malta
2 British squadrons: 1 reconnaissance squadron with
  Canberra P.R.7 and P.R.9, 1 maritime-reconnaissance and
  ASW squadron with Nimrod MR.1.
Squadrons to be recalled from 1977–79.
Equipment
Helicopters:
4 Bell 47G.
1 Agusta-Bell 206A.
Army
1,250 men.
Army aviation
2(3?) Dornier Do–27 liaison aircraft.
Navy 500 men.

Mauritania
Air force (Force Aérienne de la République Islamique de la
  Mauritanie)
men 100.
squadrons –.
operational aircraft 8.
Organization
–.
Base
Nouakchott.
Military training aid from
France.

Equipment
Transports:
1 Britten-Norman BN–2A.
2 Britten-Norman Defender.
2(4?) Douglas C–47.
2 Short Skyvan 3M.
Liaison and AOP aircraft:
1 Aermacchi AL.60.
2 Max Holste M.H.1521M.
1 Reims-Cessna F.337.
Army 1,400 men.
Navy 100 men.

Mexico
Air force (Fuerza Aérea Mexicana)
men 6,000.
squadrons 7.
operational aircraft 41.
helicopters 40.
Organization
1 strike-fighter squadron with Vampire F.3.
1 transport squadron with Arava.
1 transport squadron with C–47.
1 transport squadron with C–54.
1 liaison squadron with LASA–60.
1 liaison squadron with Bonanza.
1 helicopter squadron with Bell 47G.
1 helicopter squadron with Bell 206A.
1 helicopter squadron with Bell 205.
3 trainer squadrons with T–6G and Musketeer Sport.
2 trainer squadrons with T–28A.
1 trainer squadron with T–33A.
1 trainer squadron with T–34A.
Bases
Cozumel, El Cipres, Guadalajara, Ixtepec, Pie de la Cuesta,
  Puebla, Santa Lucia.
Military training aid from
United States.
Equipment
Fighters and strike-fighters:
10 de Havilland Vampire F.3.
3 de Havilland Vampire T.11.
Transports:
5 Beechcraft C–45.
3 Britten-Norman BN–2A.
6 Douglas C–47.
5 Douglas C–54.
2 Douglas C–118A.
5(10?) IAI–201 Arava.
1 Lockheed JetStar.
1 Mitsubishi MU–2J.
Liaison and AOP aircraft:
20 Beechcraft Bonanza F33C.
18 Lockheed-Azcarate LASA–60.
Helicopters:
6 Aérospatiale Alouette III.
3 Aérospatiale S.A.330.
14 Bell 47G.
10 Bell 205.
5 Bell 206A.
1 Bell 212.
1 Hiller OH–23G.
Trainers:
20 Beechcraft Musketeer Sport.
15 Beechcraft T–11.
10 Beechcraft T–34A.
15 Lockheed T–33A.
45(30?) North American T–6G.
30 North American T–28A.

Programme
Replacement of de Havilland Vampire F.3 strike-fighters. 5
  further IAI Arava transports on order.
Army 65,000 men.
Navy 11,500 men.
Naval aviation (Armada de Mexico, Departemento de
  Aeronautica)
340 men.
– squadrons.
9(?) operational aircraft.
6 helicopters.
Organization
–.
Base
Balbuena.
Equipment
Maritime-reconnaissance and ASW aircraft:
some (5?) Convair PBY–5A.
4 Grumman HU–16B.
Liaison aircraft:
1 Gates Learjet 24D.
Helicopters:
4 Aérospatiale Alouette II.
1 Bell 47G.
4 Bell 47J.

Mongolia
Air force (part of the army)
men 2,000.
squadrons 1.
operational aircraft 40.
helicopters 10.
Organization
1 strike-fighter squadron with MiG–15.
Major bases
Sayn Shanda, Ulan Bator.
Military training aid from
Soviet Union.
Foreign air forces in Mongolia
several Soviet fighter, strike-fighter and reconnaissance
  squadrons.
Equipment
Fighters and strike-fighters:
10 Mikoyan MiG–15.
Transports:
approx 30 aircraft, inc Antonov An–2, Antonov An–24,
  Ilyushin Il–12, Ilyushin Il–14, Tupolev Tu–104.
Liaison and AOP aircraft:
some PZL–104.
Helicopters:
approx 10 aircraft, inc Mil Mi–1 and Mil Mi–4.
Trainers:
approx 30 aircraft, inc Mikoyan MiG–15UTI, Yakovlev Yak–11
  and Yakovlev Yak–18.
Army 28,000 men.

Morocco
Air force (Al Quwwat Aljawwiya Almalakiya Marakishiya)
men 4,000.
squadrons 7.
operational aircraft 65.
helicopters 80.
Organization
1 strike-fighter squadron with F–5A.
1 transport squadron with C–119G and C–47.
1 transport squadron with C–130H.
2 helicopter squadrons with AB.205.
2 helicopter squadrons with S.A.330.
1 trainer squadron with T–28D.

2 trainer squadrons with C.M.170.
– trainer squadrons with T–6G.
Bases
Kénitra, Marrakesh, Meknes, Nouasseur, Salé (Rabat).
Military training aid from
United States.
Equipment
Fighters and strike-fighters:
12 Mikoyan MiG–17F.
17 Northrop F–5A.
3 Northrop F–5B.
Bombers:
2 Ilyushin Il–28.
Reconnaissance aircraft:
2 Northrop RF–5A.
Transports:
some (10?) Douglas C–47.
8(16?) Fairchild C–119G.
12 Lockheed C–130H.
1 Dornier Do–28D.
Liaison and AOP aircraft:
6 Beechcraft King Air A100.
2 Beechcraft Twin Bonanza.
1 Cessna 141.
Helicopters:
4 Aérospatiale Alouette II.
20 Agusta-Bell AB.205.
some (8?) Agusta-Bell AB.206A.
5 Agusta-Bell AB.212.
4 Bell 47G.
40 Aérospatiale S.A.330.
Trainers:
2 Mikoyan MiG–15UTI.
35 North American T–6G.
25 North American T–28D.
20 Potez-Air Fouga C.M.170.
2(28?) SIAI-Marchetti SF.260M.
The Soviet aircraft (Il–28, MiG–15UTI, MiG–17) have been
  mothballed.
Programme
On order: 25 Dassault Mirage F1 fighters (delivery from
  1980), 12 Beechcraft T–34C trainers (delivery from 1977)
  and 120 Rockwell T–2 trainers.
Army 55,00 men.
Army aviation
3 Aérospatiale Alouette III helicopters(?).
Navy 2,000 men.

Mozambique
Air force
men –.
squadrons –.
operational aircraft 10.
helicopters –.
Organization
1 transport squadron with N.2501.
Military training aid from
Portugal; Soviet Union.
Equipment
Transports:
2 Douglas C–47.
8 Nord N.2501.
Helicopters:
2 Aérospatiale Alouette III.
Army 8,000(?) men.
Navy – men.

Nepal
Air force (part of the army)
men 100.

squadrons –.
operational aircraft 6.
helicopters 5.
Organization
–.
Base
Katmandu.
Military training aid from
Great Britain.
Equipment
Transports:
3 de Havilland Canada DHC–3.
1 Hawker Siddeley H.S.748.
2 Short Skyvan 3M.
Helicopter:
3(?) Aérospatiale Alouette III.
2 Aérospatiale S.A.330J.
Army 20,000 men.

Netherlands
Air force (Koninklijke Nederlandse Luchtmacht)
men 19,000.
squadrons 9.
operational aircraft 209.
Organization
2 fighter squadrons with F–104G.
2 strike-fighter squadrons with F–104G.
3 strike-fighter squadrons with NF–5A.
1 reconnaissance squadron with RF–104G.
1 transport squadron with F.27M and F.27.
1 strike-trainer squadron with NF–5B.
Fighter, strike-fighter and reconnaissance squadrons each
  with 18 aircraft.
Major bases
Eindhoven, Gilze Rijen, Leeuwarden, Soesterberg, Twente,
  Valkenburg, Volkel.
Military training aid from
Canada.
Foreign air forces in the Netherlands
1 American fighter squadron with F–4E (re-equipment with
  E–15 planned for 1976–77).
Equipment
Fighters and strike-fighters:
80 Lockheed F–104G.
16 Lockheed TF–104G.
68 Canadair (Northrop) NF–5A.
28 Canadair (Northrop) NF–5B.
Reconnaissance aircraft:
18 Lockheed RF–104G.
Transports:
6 Fokker-VFW F.27M.
3 Fokker-VFW F.27.
Trainers:
some (10?) Fokker S.11.
Programme
Replacement of Lockheed F–104G fighters and strike-fighters
  by 84 General Dynamics F–16 from 1979.
Army 75,000 men.
Army aviation (Groep Lichte Vliegtuigen)
– men.
3 squadrons.
24 operational aircraft.
90 helicopters.
Organization
3 helicopter squadrons with Alouette III and BO–105.
Equipment
Helicopters:
60 Aérospatiale Alouette III.
30 MBB BO–105.

Navy
18,500 men.
Naval aviation (Marine Luchtvaartdienst)
1,500 men.
4 squadrons.
19 operational aircraft.
25 helicopters.
Organization
1 maritime-reconnaissance and ASW squadron with SP–2H.
1 maritime-reconnaissance and ASW squadron with Br.1150.
1 helicopter squadron with Wasp and Lynx.
1 trainer squadron with Lynx and AB.204B.
Bases
DeKooy, Valkenburg.
Equipment
Maritime-reconnaissance and ASW aircraft:
8 Breguet Br.1150.
11 Lockheed SP–2H.
Helicopters:
6 Agusta-Bell AB.204B.
11 Westland Wasp.
8 Westland WG.13 Lynx.
Trainers:
some Fokker S.11.
3 Fokker-VFW F.27M.
Programme
Replacement of Lockheed SP–2H maritime-reconnaissance
  and ASW aircraft, and of Agusta-Bell AB.204B and Westland
  Wasp helicopters, by 13 Lockheed P–3C and 8 further
  Westland WG.13 Lynx respectively.
Aircraft factories
Fokker (N.V. Koninklijke Nederlandse Vliegtuigen-fabriek
  Fokker) – amalgamated with German VFW concern.

New Guinea: see Papua–New Guinea

New Zealand
Air force (Royal New Zealand Air Force, RNZAF)
men 4,200.
squadrons 6.
operational aircraft 56.
helicopters 19.
Organization
1 strike-fighter squadron with A–4K.
1 ground-attack squadron with BAC 167.
1 maritime-reconnaissance and ASW squadron with P–3B.
1 transport squadron with C–130H.
1 transport squadron with Andover C.1.
1 helicopter squadron with Bell 47G, UH–1D and UH–1H.
– trainer squadrons with CT–4, Airtourer and Devon C.1.
Bases
Hobsonville, Ohakea, Whenuapai, Wigram.
Equipment
Fighters and strike-fighters:
9 McDonnell Douglas A–4K.
4 McDonnell Douglas TA–4K.
Ground-attack aircraft:
16 BAC 167 Strikemaster Mk.88.
Maritime-reconnaissance and ASW aircraft:
5 Lockheed P–3B.
Transports:
6 de Havilland Devon C.1.
1 Fokker-VFW F.27.
10 Hawker Siddeley Andover C.1.
5 Lockheed C–130H.
Helicopters:
6(8?) Bell 47G.
4 Bell UH–1D.
9 Bell UH–1H.

Trainers:
4 NZAI Airtourer T.6.
11(13?) NZAI CT–4 Airtrainer.
Army 5,500 men.
Navy 2,800 men.
Naval aviation
2 Westland Wasp helicopters.
Aircraft factories
NZAI (New Zealand Aerospace Industries) – until 1973 AESL
 (Aero Services Ltd.).

Nicaragua
Air force (Fuerza Aérea de Nicaragua)
men 1,500.
squadrons 3.
operational aircraft 24.
helicopters 9.
Organization
1 ground-attack squadron with F–51D(?).
1 bomber squadron with B–26.
1 transport squadron with C–45 and C–47.
1 trainer squadron with T–28A.
1 trainer squadron with T–33A.
Bases
Managua, Puerto Cabezas.
Military training aid from
United States.
Equipment
Ground-attack aircraft:
12(?) North American F–51D(?).
Bombers:
4 Douglas B–26K.
Transports:
4 Beechcraft C–45.
3 Douglas C–47.
1 IAI Arava.
Liaison and AOP aircraft:
10 Cessna 180.
Helicopters:
2 Hughes 269.
4 Hughes 500M.
3 Sikorsky CH–34A.
Trainers:
6 Lockheed T–33A.
4 North American T–6G.
6 North American T–28A.
Programme
Phasing out of North American F–51D ground-attack aircraft.
Army 5,400 men.
Army aviation
2 Cessna U–17A liaison aircraft.
Navy 200 men.

Niger
Air force (Force Aérienne de Niger)
men 150.
squadrons –.
operational aircraft 7.
Organization
–.
Base
Niamey.
Military training aid from
France.
Equipment
Transports:
1 Rockwell Commander 500B.
1 Douglas C–47.

1 Douglas C–54B.
4 Nord N.2501.
Liaison and AOP aircraft:
1 Cessna 337D.
1 Reims-Cessna F.337.
Army 2,000 men.

Nigeria
Air force
men 3,000.
squadrons 6.
operational aircraft 49.
helicopters 7.
Organization
1 fighter squadron with MiG–21.
1 strike-fighter squadron with MiG–17F.
1 transport squadron with Do–28.
1 transport squadron with F.27.
1 transport squadron with C.130H.
1 helicopter squadron with BO–105 and Whirlwind.
1 trainer squadron with Bulldog.
1 trainer squadron with L–29.
Bases
Kano, Lagos.
Military training aid from
Great Britain(?), Soviet Union(?).
Equipment
Fighters and strike-fighters:
4 Mikoyan MiG–15(?).
8 Mikoyan MiG–17F.
10(12?) Mikoyan MiG–21.
Bombers:
3 Ilyushin Il–28.
Transports:
4 Dornier Do–28A and B.
4 Dornier Do–28D.
3(7?) Douglas C–47.
6 Fokker-VFW F.27.
1 Fokker-VFW F.28.
6 Lockheed C–130H.
Liaison and AOP aircraft:
some Dornier Do–27.
2 Piper PA–31P Navajo.
1 Piper PA–31–350 Navajo Chieftain.
Helicopters:
4 MBB BO–105.
2 Westland Whirlwind 2.
1 Westland Whirlwind 3.
Trainers:
8 Aero L–29.
2 Mikoyan MiG–15UTI.
20 Scottish Aviation Bulldog.
Programme
3 further Fokker-VFW F.27 transports on order.
Army 80,000 men.
Navy 2,500 men.

Norway
Air force (Kongelige Norske Flyvåpen)
men 9,000.
squadrons 12.
operational aircraft 137.
helicopters 40.
Organization
2 fighter squadrons with F–104G.
3(4?) strike-fighter squadrons with F–5A.
1 reconnaissance squadron with RF–5A.
1 maritime-reconnaissance and ASW squadron with P–3B.
1 transport squadron with C–130H.

1 transport squadron with DHC–6.
2 helicopter squadrons with AB.204B.
1 helicopter squadron with Sea King Mk.43.
1 trainer squadron with Saab 91B.
1 trainer squadron with T–33A.
Fighter and strike-fighter squadrons each with 16 aircraft,
  reconnaissance squadron with 12 aircraft.

Major bases
Banak, Bardufoss, Bodø, Gardermoen, Ørlandet, Rygge, Sola.

Military training aid from
United States.

Equipment
Fighters and strike-fighters:
35 Lockheed F–104G.
2 Lockheed TF–104G.
50 Northrop F–5A.
20 Northrop F–5B.
Reconnaissance aircraft:
13 Northrop RF–5A.
Maritime-reconnaissance and ASW aircraft:
5 Lockheed P–3B.
Transports:
2 Dassault Falcon 20.
4 de Havilland Canada DHC–6.
6 Lockheed C–130H.
Liaison and AOP aircraft:
approx 20 aircraft, inc Cessna O–1E and Piper L–18C.
Helicopters:
30 Agusta-Bell AB.204B.
10 Westland Sea King Mk.43.
Trainers:
15 Lockheed T–33A.
20 Saab 91B.

Programme
Replacement of Lockheed F–104G fighters by 72 General
  Dynamics F–16 from 1979. Replacement of Agusta-Bell
  AB.204B helicopters by 40 Westland WG.13 Lynx.
Army 18,000 men.
Navy 8,000 men.

Oman

Air force (Sultan of Oman's Air Force)
men 1,000.
squadrons 7.
operational aircraft 90.
helicopters 24.

Organization
1 strike-fighter squadron with Jaguar S(O).1.
1 strike-fighter squadron with Hunter FGA.9 and FGA.73.
1 ground-attack squadron with BAC 167.
1 transport squadron with Skyvan 3M and DHC–4.
1 transport squadron with Defender.
1 transport squadron with BAC 1–11 and Viscount.
1 helicopter squadron with AB.205.

Bases
Azaiba, Bait-al-Falaj (Muscat), Salalah, Seeb.

Military training aid from
Great Britain.

Foreign air forces in Oman
some Iranian helicopter squadrons with AB.205.

Equipment
Fighters and strike-fighters:
27 Hawker Hunter FGA.9, FGA.73 and T.66B.
10 SEPECAT Jaguar S(O).1.
2 SEPECAT Jaguar T(O).2.
Ground-attack aircraft:
20 BAC 167 Strikemaster Mk.82.
Transports:
3 BAC 1–11 Srs.475.

1 BAC VC 10.
8 Britten-Norman Defender.
1 Dassault Falcon 20.
15 Short Skyvan 3M.
3 Vickers Viscount 800.
Liaison and AOP aircraft:
2 Pilatus PC–6B.
Helicopters:
20 Agusta-Bell AB.205.
3 Agusta-Bell 206.
1 Agusta-Bell AB.212.
Only 12 Hawker Hunter FGA.9 and FGA.73 strike-fighters are
  in service, the majority of the Hunters have been
  mothballed.

Programme:
5 Bell 214A helicopters on order.
Army 13,000 men.
Navy 200 men.

Pakistan

Air force
men 17,000.
squadrons 17.
operational aircraft 210.
helicopters 17.

Organization
4 fighter squadrons with F–6 (MiG–19).
1 fighter squadron with Mirage IIIEP.
2 strike-fighter squadrons with Mirage 5–PD.
4 strike-fighter squadrons with F–86F.
1 bomber squadron with B–57B.
1 reconnaissance squadron with Mirage IIIRP, RT–33A and
  RB–57.
1 maritime-reconnaissance and ASW squadron with Br.1150.
1 transport squadron with C–47.
1 transport squadron with C–130B and C–130E.
1 helicopter squadron with Alouette III.
3 trainer squadrons with Supporter.
– trainer squadrons with T–37B and T–37A.
Fighter and strike-fighter squadrons each with 14–16 aircraft.

Major bases
Chaklala, Chitral, Drigh Road, Gilgit, Kohat, Korangi, Lahore,
  Malir, Masroor (Karachi), Mauripur, Miranshah, Peshawar,
  Risalpur, Samundri, Sargodha, Shorkot Road.

Military training aid from
China, United States.

Equipment
Fighters and strike-fighters:
17 Dassault Mirage IIIEP.
3 Dassault Mirage IIIDP.
2 Dassault Mirage 5–PA.
25 Dassault Mirage 5–PD.
55 North American F–86F and Canadair CL–13B Sabre 6.
60(80?) Shenyang F–6 (MiG–19).
Bombers:
10 Martin B–57B.
Reconnaissance aircraft:
3 Dassault Mirage IIIRP.
4 Lockheed RT–33A.
2 Martin RB–57.
Maritime-reconnaissance and ASW aircraft:
3 Breguet Br.1150.
4 Grumman HU–16A.
Transports:
1 Rockwell Commander 680E.
1 Dassault Falcon 20.
6 Douglas C–47.
1 Fokker-VFW F.27.
8 Lockheed C–130B.

3(2?) Lockheed C–130E.
2 Lockheed L–382.
Liaison and AOP aircraft:
1 Beechcraft Super King Air.
1 Beechcraft Travel Air.
1 Beechcraft Twin Bonanza.
10(?) de Havilland Canada DHC–2.
Helicopters:
12 Aérospatiale Alouette III.
1 Aérospatiale S.A.330.
4 Kaman HH–43B.
Trainers:
approx 85 aircraft, inc 20 Cessna T–37B, 12 Lockheed
   T–33A, some North American T–6G, 45 Saab Supporter.
Programme
Replacement of Lockheed RT–33A and Martin RB–57
   reconnaissance aircraft by 10 further Dassault Mirage IIIRP,
   delivery 1977; licence-production of Cessna T–41D liaison
   and AOP aircraft and of Hughes 500M helicopter.
Army 365,000 men.
Army aviation
– men.
– squadrons.
50 operational aircraft.
42 helicopters.
Equipment
Helicopters:
15(20?) Aérospatiale Alouette III.
15(?) Bell 47G.
12 Mil Mi–8.
Liaison and AOP aircraft:
approx 50 aircraft, inc Beechcraft Twin Bonanza, Cessna 172,
   40(?) Cessna O–1A and O–1E, Cessna Skymaster, some de
   Havilland Canada DHC–2.
Navy 10,000 men.
Naval aviation
– men.
1 squadron.
10 helicopters.
Organization
1 helicopter squadron with Sea King Mk.45.
Equipment
Helicopters:
4 Aérospatiale Alouette III.
6 Westland Sea King Mk.45.
Aircraft factories
Under construction.

Panama
Air force (Fuerza Aérea Panamena)
men 200.
squadrons –.
operational aircraft 10.
helicopters 12.
Organization
–.
Bases
Albrook, France Field, Howard AFB, Tocumen (Panama City).
Military training aid from
United States.
Foreign air forces in Panama
some American trainer squadrons.
Equipment
Transports:
1 Britten-Norman BN–2A.
3 de Havilland Canada DHC–3.
1 de Havilland Canada DHC–6.
3(4?) Douglas C–47.
1 IAI Westwind.
1 Lockheed L–188.

Liaison and AOP aircraft:
4(6?) Cessna U–17A.
Helicopters:
7 Bell UH–1B.
3 Bell UH–1H.
1 Bell UH–1N.
1 Fairchild-Hiller FH–1100.
Army 4,700 men.
Navy 50 men.

Papua–New Guinea
Air force (Papua and New Guinea Air Force)
men –.
squadrons 1.
operational aircraft 4.
Organization
1 transport squadron with C–47.
Base
Port Moresby.
Military training aid from
Australia, New Zealand.
Equipment
Transports:
4 Douglas C–47.
Programme
Formation of further transport and liaison squadrons.
Army – men.
Navy – men.

Paraguay
Air force (Fuerza Aérea del Paraguay)
men 1,000.
squadrons 3.
operational aircraft 19.
helicopters 12.
Organization
1 transport squadron with C–47 and C–54.
1 transport squadron with DC–6B.
1 helicopter squadron with Bell 47G.
1 trainer squadron with S.11 and T–23.
1 trainer squadron with T–6G.
Base
Campo Grande (Asunción).
Military training aid from
United States, Brazil.
Equipment
Transports:
1 de Havilland Canada DHC–3.
1 de Havilland Canada DHC–6.
10(?) Douglas C–47.
2 Douglas C–54.
5 Douglas DC–6B.
Liaison and AOP aircraft:
some Cessna 185.
Helicopters:
9(14?) Bell 47G.
3 Hiller OH–23G.
Trainers:
8 Aerotec T–23.
8 Fokker S.11.
6 North American T–6G.
Army 10,500 men.
Navy 2,000 men.
Naval aviation
4 Cessna U206 liaison aircraft.
2 North American T–6G trainers.

Peru
Air force (Fuerza Aérea del Perú)

men 9,000.
squadrons 15.
operational aircraft 140.
helicopters 60.
Organization
1 fighter squadron with Mirage 5–P.
1 strike-fighter squadron with F–86F.
1 strike-fighter squadron with Hunter F.52.
2 ground-attack squadrons with A–37B.
2 bomber squadrons with Canberra B.(I)68, B.72 and B.(I)78.
1 maritime-reconnaissance and ASW squadron with Hu–16B.
1 transport squadron with DHC–5.
1 transport squadron with DHC–6.
1 transport squadron with C–130E.
– liaison squadrons with Queen Air A80.
1 liaison squadron with Cessna 185 and PC–6A.
1 helicopter squadron with Alouette III.
1 helicopter squadron with UH–1D.
1 helicopter squadron with UH–1H.
1 helicopter squadron with Bell 212.
1 trainer squadron with T–33A.
– trainer squadrons with T–37B.
– trainer squadrons with T–41A.

Bases
Ancon, Arequipa, Chiclayo, Cusco, Iquitos, Las Palmas, Lima, Pisco, Talava, Trujillo.
Military training aid from
United States.
Equipment
Fighters and strike-fighters:
14 Dassault Mirage 5–P.
2 Dassault Mirage 5–DP.
10(?) Hawker Hunter F.52.
2 Hawker Hunter T.62.
10(?) North American F–86F.
Ground-attack aircraft:
24 Cessna A–37B.
Bombers:
11 English Electric Canberra B.(I)68.
18 English Electric Canberra B.72 and B.(I) 78.
2 English Electric Canberra T.74.
Maritime-reconnaissance and ASW aircraft:
4 Grumman HU–16B.
Transports:
16 de Havilland Canada DHC–5.
8 de Havilland Canada DHC–6.
3 Fokker-VFW F.28 Mk.1000.
4 Lockheed C–130E.
2 Lockheed L–100–20.
plus some Douglas C–47 and Douglas C–54.
Liaison and AOP aircraft:
approx 35 aircraft, inc Beechcraft T–42A, 18 Beechcraft Queen Air A80, some (5?) Cessna 185, 2 Gates Learjet 25B, 6(12?) Pilatus PC–6A.
Helicopters:
12 Aérospatiale Alouette III.
some Bell 47G.
16 Bell 212.
9 Bell UH–1D.
12 Bell UH–1H.
4 Mil Mi–8.
Trainers:
5 Beechcraft T–34.
20(26?) Cessna T–37B.
19 Cessna T–41A.
8(?) Lockheed T–33A.
15 North American T–6G.
Programme
Replacement of obsolescent Hawker Hunter F.52 and North

American F–86F strike-fighters by 36 Sukhoi Su–22. Replacement of Douglas C–47 and Douglas C–54 transports by 3 Lockheed L–100–20. Purchase of 14 further Mil Mi–8 helicopters under consideration.
Army 39,000 men.
Army aviation
8 Bell 47G helicopters.
2 Helio Courier liaison and AOP aircraft.
2 GAF Nomad transports.
Navy 8,000 men.
Naval aviation (Servicio Aéronavale)
9(?) Grumman S–2E maritime-reconnaissance aircraft.
30 helicopters.
2 Aérospatiale Alouette III.
2 Bell 47G.
some Bell 206A and 206B.
some Bell UH–1D and UH–1H.
Programme
2 Fokker F.27 maritime-reconnaissance aircraft on order. Acquisition of 6–8 Agusta-Bell AB.212AS helicopters under consideration.

Philippines
Air force (Philippine Air Force, Hukbong Himpapawidng Pilipinas)
men 14,000.
squadrons 11.
operational aircraft 109.
helicopters 38.
Organization
2 strike-fighter squadrons with F–86F.
1 strike-fighter squadron with F–5A.
1 ground-attack squadron with S.F.260WP.
1 night ground-support squadron with AC–47.
1 transport squadron with Nomad.
1 transport squadron with C–47.
1 transport squadron with C–123K.
1 transport squadron with L–100–20 and YS–11.
1 helicopter squadron with UH–1D.
1 helicopter squadron with UH–1H.
2 trainer squadrons with SF.260MP and T–34.
1 trainer squadron with T–28D and T–28A.
Bases
Batangas, Cebu, Clark Field, Florida Blanca, Legaspi, Lipa, Manila, San Fernando, San Jose, Sibuyan, Tacloban, Zamboanga.
Military training aid from
United States.
Foreign air forces in the Philippines
6 American squadrons: 3 strike-fighter squadrons with F–4, 3 transport squadrons with C–130.
Equipment
Fighters and strike-fighters:
20 North American F–86F.
14 Northrop F–5A.
2 Northrop F–5B.
Ground-attack aircraft:
16 SIAI-Marchetti SF.260WP.
Night ground-support aircraft:
12 Douglas AC–47.
Maritime-reconnaissance and ASW aircraft:
4 Grumman HU–16.
Transports:
10 Douglas C–47.
10 Fokker-VFW F.27.
12 GAF Nomad.
4 Lockheed L–100–20.
4 NAMC YS–11.
1 Rockwell Commander 520(?).

Helicopters:
12 Bell UH–1D.
16 Bell UH–1H.
8 Fairchild-Hiller FH–1100.
2 Mitsubishi-Sikorsky S–62A.
Trainers:
some Cessna T–41D.
20 Fuji-Beechcraft T–34.
some Lockheed T–33A.
10 North American T–28A.
16 North American T–28D.
30 SIAI-Marchetti SF.260M.
Programme
38 MBB BO–105 helicopters on order. Replacement of North
  American F–86F strike-fighters by 11 Northrop F–5E.
Army 39,000 men.
Navy 14,000 men.
Naval aviation
some Britten-Norman BN–2A transports.
Aircraft factories
Philippine Aerospace Development Corporation under
  construction.

Poland
Air force (Polskie Wojska Lotnicze, PWL)
men 56,000.
squadrons 74.
operational aircraft 665.
helicopters 120.
Organization
30 fighter squadrons with MiG–21.
12 strike-fighter squadrons with Su–7B.
3 strike-fighter squadrons with MiG–17F (LIM–6).
3 strike-fighter squadrons with Su–20.
6 reconnaissance squadrons with MiG–21R and Il–28R.
4 transport squadrons with An–2, An–12, An–24 and Il–14.
6 helicopter squadrons with Mi–4 and Mi–8.
– trainer squadrons with Yak–11 and Yak–18.
– trainer squadrons with MiG–15UTI and TS–11.
Fighter, strike-fighter and reconnaissance squadrons each
  with 10–12 aircraft.
Major bases
Allenstein (Olsztyn), Breslau, Brieg, Bromberg (Bydgoszez)?,
  Danzig, Deblin, Elbing (Elblag), Graudenz (Grudziadz),
  Hohensalza (Inowtoclaw), Hirschberg (Jelenia Gora),
  Kolberg, Krakau, Krosno, Kutno, Liegnitz, Lublin, Mielce,
  Ohlau, Posen, Radom, Rastenburg, Rzeszow, Schrode
  (Sroda), Siedlce, Stettin, Stolp (Slupsk), Swidnik, Thorn
  (Torun), Warsaw.
Military training aid from
Soviet Union.
Foreign air forces in Poland
approx 250 Soviet fighters, strike-fighters and reconnaissance
  aircraft.
Equipment
Fighters and strike-fighters:
35 Mikoyan MiG–17F (LIM–6).
350 (300?) Mikoyan MiG–21 and MiG–21U.
35 Sukhoi Su–20.
130 Sukhoi Su–7B.
Reconnaissance aircraft:
20 Ilyushin Il–28R and Il–28U.
50 Mikoyan MiG–21R.
Transports:
approx 45(50?) aircraft, inc Antonov An–2, Antonov An–12,
  Antonov An–24, Ilyushin Il–12, Ilyushin Il–14, Ilyushin Il–18,
  Lisunov Li–2, 1 Tupolev Tu–134, Yakovlev Yak–40.
Liaison and AOP aircraft:
PZL–104.

Helicopters:
approx 120 machines, inc Mil Mi–1, Mil Mi–2, Mil Mi–4, Mil
  Mi–8, WSK SM–1, WSK SM–2.
Trainers:
approx 200 aircraft, inc Mikoyan MiG–15UTI, WSK TS–11,
  Yakovlev Yak–11, Yakovlev Yak–18.
Programme
Replacement of Mikoyan MiG–17 strike-fighters by Sukhoi
  SU–7B (or Sukhoi Su–20?).
Army 210,000 men.
Navy 25,000 men.
Naval aviation (Lotnictwo Marynarki Wojennej)
– men.
6 squadrons.
45 operational aircraft.
20 helicopters.
Organization
3 strike-fighter squadrons with MiG–17F (LIM–6).
1 bomber and reconnaissance squadron with Il–28 and
  Il–28R.
1 helicopter squadron with Mi–2.
1 helicopter squadron with Mi–8.
Equipment
Fighters and strike-fighters:
35 Mikoyan MiG–17F (LIM–6).
Bombers and reconnaissance aircraft:
10 Ilyushin Il–28, Il–28R and Il–28U.
Helicopters:
approx 20 machines, inc Mil Mi–2, Mil Mi–4 and Mil Mi–8.
Trainers:
some Mikoyan MiG–15UTI and Yakovlev Yak–11.
Aircraft factories
PZL (Polskie Zaklady Lotnicze), WSK (Wytwornia Sprzetu
  Komunikacyjnego).

Portugal
Air force (Força Aérea Portuguesa)
men 18,500.
squadrons 9.
operational aircraft 125.
helicopters 45.
Organization
1 fighter squadron with F–86F(?).
2(3?) strike-fighter squadrons with G.91R.3 and R.4.
1 maritime-reconnaissance and ASW squadron with P–2E.
2 transport squadrons with C.212.
2 transport squadrons with N.2501.
1 transport squadron with DC–6.
– liaison squadrons with Do–27.
– helicopter squadrons with Alouette III.
3 trainer squadrons with T–6G.
– trainer squadron with T–33A.
– trainer squadron with T–37C.
Fighter and strike-fighter squadrons each with 16–18 aircraft.
Bases
Alverca, Aviero, Jacinto, Lisbon-Portela, Monte Real, Montijo,
  Ota, Porto, Sintra, Tancos.
Foreign air forces in Portugal
1 American rescue squadron with HC–130H in the Azores.
Equipment
Fighters and strike-fighters:
30 Fiat G.91R.3 and R.4.
6 Fiat G.91 T.3.
18(?) North American F–86F.
Maritime-reconnaissance and ASW aircraft:
8(10?) Lockheed P–2E.
Transports:
2 Boeing 707–320C.
24 CASA C.212.

some Douglas C–47.
10 Douglas DC–6A and B.
20 Nord N.2501.
Liaison and AOP aircraft:
2 Cessna 185.
10 Dornier Do–27.
4 Piper PA–32 Cherokee.
30(?) Reims-Cessna F.337.
Helicopters:
2 Aérospatiale Alouette II.
approx 35 Aérospatiale Alouette III.
10 Aérospatiale S.A.330.
Trainers:
25 Cessna T–37C.
some de Havilland Canada DHC–1.
12 Lockheed T–33.
20 North American T–6G.
Programme
2 Lockheed C–130H. transports on order, delivery 1977.
  Phasing out of 16 older transports (Boeing 707–320C,
  Douglas DC–6 and approx 10 Nord N.2501).
Army 120,000 men (reduction to 26,000 men planned).
Navy 19,000 men.
Aircraft factories
OGMA (Oficinas Gerais de Material Aeronáutico).

Qatar
Air force (Qatar Emiri Air Force)
men 250(?).
squadrons 1.
operational aircraft 5.
helicopters 8.
Organization
1 strike-fighter squadron with Hunter FGA.78.
Base
Doha.
Military training aid from
Great Britain.
Equipment
Fighters and strike-fighters:
3 Hawker Hunter FGA.78.
1 Hawker Hunter T.79.
Transports:
1 Britten-Norman BN–2A.
Helicopters:
2 Aérospatiale S.A.341B.
4 Westland Commando.
2 Westland Whirlwind 3.
Programme
3 Westland W.G.13 Lynx helicopters on order.
Army 1,600 men.
Navy 200 men.

Rhodesia
Air force (Rhodesian Air Force)
men 1,200.
squadrons 5.
operational aircraft 48(50?).
helicopters 35(?).
Organization
1 strike-fighter squadron with Hunter FGA.57.
1 strike-fighter squadron with Vampire FB.9.
1 bomber squadron with Canberra B.2.
1 transport squadron with C–47 and DC–4M.
1 liaison squadron with AL.60.
1 helicopter squadron with Alouette III.
1 trainer squadron with Provost T.52.
1 trainer squadron with Vampire T.55.

Bases
New Sarum (Salisbury), Thornhill (Gwelo).
Equipment
Fighters and strike-fighters:
6(?) Dassault Mirage IIIBZ (on loan from South Africa?).
7 de Havilland Vampire FB.9.
12 Hawker Hunter FGA.57.
2 Hawker Hunter T.52.
Ground-attack aircraft:
some Aermacchi MB.326K and M(?).
Bombers:
9 English Electric Canberra B.2.
2 English Electric Canberra T.4.
Transports:
2 Britten-Norman BN–2A.
4 Douglas C–47.
4 Douglas DC–4M(?).
Liaison and AOP aircraft:
7 Aermacchi AL.60.
1 Beechcraft Baron.
some Cessna 185.
Helicopters:
35(?) Aérospatiale Alouette III.
Trainers:
8 de Havilland Vampire T.55.
12 Hunting Provost T.52.
Army 4,500 men.

Romania
Air force (Fortele Aériene ale Republicii Socialiste România)
men 22,000.
squadrons 26.
operational aircraft 220.
helicopters 75.
Organization
9(?) fighter squadrons with MiG–21.
6 strike-fighter squadrons with Su–7 and MiG–17F and PF.
1 reconnaissance squadron with Il–28.
2 transport squadrons with Il–12, Il–14 and Li–2.
1 transport squadron with An–24.
5 helicopter squadrons with Alouette III.
1 helicopter squadron with Mi–4.
1 helicopter squadron with Mi–8.
– trainer squadrons with Yak–11 and Yak–18.
– trainer squadrons with L–29 and MiG–15UTI.
Fighter, strike-fighter and reconnaissance squadrons each
  with 10–12 aircraft, transport and helicopter squadrons each
  with 8–10 aircraft.
Bases
Arad, Bacău, Baneasa, Buzău, Calarasi, Craiova, Galatz,
  Grosswardein (Oradea Mare), Jassy, Klausenburg (Cluj),
  Konstanza, Kronstadt (Braşov), Mamaia, Mediasch,
  Neppendorf (Turnişor), Otopeni, Popeşti-Leordeni, Sathmar
  (Satu Mare), Tecuci, Temesvár (Timisoara), Zilştea.
Military training aid from
Soviet Union.
Equipment
Fighters and strike-fighters:
40 Mikoyan MiG–17F and PF.
100(80?) Mikoyan MiG–21F and MF, plus MiG–21U.
35 Sukhoi Su–7 and Su–7U.
Reconnaissance aircraft:
10 Ilyushin Il–28.
Transports:
approx 35 aircraft, inc 10 Antonov An–2, 10 Antonov An–24
  and An–26, some Ilyushin Il–2, 6 Ilyushin Il–14, 1 Ilyushin
  Il–18, some Lisunov Li–2.
Liaison and AOP aircraft:
some LET L–200 Morava and some L–60.

Helicopters:
45 Aérospatiale Alouette III.
some Mil Mi–1.
10 Mil Mi–4.
12 Mil Mi–8.
some WSK SM–2.
Trainers:
approx 100 (120?) aircraft, inc Aero L–29, Mikoyan
  MiG–15UTI, Yakovlev Yak–11, Yakovlev Yak–18.
Programme
Introduction of the joint Yugoslav-Romanian Orao (Jurom)
  light trainer and ground-attack aircraft from 1978?
Army 145,000 men.
Navy 9,000 men.
Naval aviation
4 Mil Mi–4 (?) helicopters.
Aircraft factories
IRMA (Intreprinderea de Reparat Material Aeronautic).

Rwanda
Air force
men 150.
squadrons –.
operational aircraft 3.
helicopters 2.
Organization
–.
Base
Kigali.
Military training aid from
Belgium.
Equipment
Transports:
1 Britten-Norman BN–2A.
2 Douglas C–47.
Liaison and AOP aircraft:
3 Aeritalia-Aermacchi AM.3C.
Helicopters:
2 Aérospatiale Alouette III.
Trainers:
3 Potez-Air Fouga C.M.170.
Programme
Purchase of 3 Potez-Air Fouga C.M.170 trainers.
Army 3,600 men.

Saudi Arabia
Air force (Al Quwwat Aljawwiya Assu'udiya)
men 5,500.
squadrons 13.
operational aircraft 260.
helicopters 77.
Organization
2 fighter squadrons with Lightning F.53.
4(6?) strike-fighter squadrons with F–5E.
2 ground-attack squadrons with BAC 167.
1 transport squadron with C–130E.
2 transport squadrons with C–130H.
2 helicopter squadrons with AB.205 and AB.206A.
1 trainer squadron with Cessna 172 and T–41A.
1 strike-trainer squadron with F–5B.
Bases
Dhahran, Jedda, Khamis Mushayt, Ridyadh, Tabuk, Taif.
Military training aid from
Great Britain, United States, Pakistan.
Equipment
Fighters and strike-fighters:
2 BAC Lightning F.52.

32 BAC Lightning F.53.
2 BAC Lightning T.54.
3 BAC Lightning T.55.
34 Dassault Mirage IIISDE.
4 Dassault Mirage IIISDD.
20 Northrop F–5B.
70 Northrop F–5E.
20 Northrop F–5F.
Ground-attack aircraft:
35 BAC 167 Strikemaster Mk.80 and Mk.80A.
Transports:
1 Boeing 707–320C.
11 Lockheed C–130E.
20(24?) Lockheed C–130H.
4 Lockheed KC–130H.
2 Lockheed JetStar.
Liaison and AOP aircraft:
1 Beechcraft Super King Air.
1 Cessna 310K.
1 Cessna 421.
Helicopters:
6 Aérospatiale Alouette III.
25 Agusta-Bell AB.205.
16 Agusta-Bell AB.206A.
24 Westland Commando Mk.1 and Mk.2.
6 Westland Sea King.
Trainers:
6 Cessna 172 and T–41A.
The Dassault Mirage IIISDE strike-fighters and Westland
  Commando and Westland Sea King helicopters are to be
  handed over to Egypt.
Programme
400(?) Bell AH–1G attack helicopters are currently being
  delivered.
Army 40,000 men.
Navy 1,500 men.

Senegal
Air force (Armée de l'Air du Sénégal)
men 200.
squadrons 1.
operational aircraft 6.
helicopters 5.
Organization
1 transport squadron with C–47.
Base
Yoff (Dakar).
Military training aid from
France.
Equipment
Transports:
4(6?) Douglas C–47.
2 Fokker-VFW F.27–400M.
Liaison and AOP aircraft:
4 Max Holste M.H.1521M.
1 Reims-Cessna F.337.
Helicopters:
2 Aérospatiale Alouette II.
1 Aérospatiale S.A.341.
2 Agusta-Bell AB.47G.
Army 5,500 men.
Navy 200 men.

Sierra Leone
Air force
men 50(?).
squadrons –.
helicopters 2.

Organization

–.

Base

Freetown.

Military training aid from

Great Britain, Sweden.

Equipment

Helicopters:

2 Hughes 269A.

Trainers:

2(4?) Saab Safari.

Army 1,850 men.

Navy 100 men.

Singapore

Air force (Singapore Air Defence Command)

men 3,000.

squadrons 7.

operational aircraft 109.

helicopters 7.

Organization

2 strike-fighter squadrons with A–4S.

1 strike-fighter squadron with Hunter Mk.74 and Hunter FR.74.

1 strike-fighter squadron with Hunter Mk.74B.

1 ground-attack squadron with BAC 167.

1 transport squadron with Skyvan 3M.

1 helicopter squadron with Alouette III.

1 trainer squadron with SF.260MS.

Bases

Changi, Seletar, Tengah.

Military training aid from

Australia, Great Britain.

Equipment

Fighters and strike-fighters:

10 Hawker Hunter Mk.74.

20 Hawker Hunter Mk.74B.

2 Hawker Hunter T.75.

5 Hawker Hunter T.75A.

40 McDonnell Douglas A–4S.

3 McDonnell Douglas TA–4S.

Ground-attack aircraft:

4 BAC 167 Strikemaster Mk.81.

15 BAC 167 Strikemaster Mk.84.

Reconnaissance aircraft:

4 Hawker Hunter FR.74.

Transports:

6(8?) Short Skyvan 3M.

Helicopters:

7 Aérospatiale Alouette III.

Trainers:

6 NZAI Airtourer T.6.

14 SIAI-Marchetti SF.260MS.

Programme

Replacement of Hawker Hunter strike-fighters by 21 Northrop F–5E and F–5F.

Army 23,000 men.

Navy 2,000 men.

Somali

Air force (Dayuuradaha Xooga Dalka Somaliyeed)

men 2,500.

squadrons 6.

operational aircraft 60.

helicopters 10.

Organization

2 strike-fighter squadrons with MiG–15 and MiG–17F.

1 strike-fighter squadron with MiG–21.

1 bomber squadron with Il–28.

1 transport squadron with An–2 and An–24.

1 helicopter squadron with Mi–4 and Mi–8.

Bases

Berbera, Hargeisa, Mogadisho.

Military training aid from

Soviet Union.

Equipment

Fighters and strike-fighters:

12 Mikoyan MiG–15.

20 Mikoyan MiG–17F.

4 Mikoyan MiG–19.

10 Mikoyan MiG–21.

Bombers:

3(10?) Ilyushin Il–28.

Transports:

3 Antonov An–2.

3 Antonov An–24.

2 Dornier Do–28D.

3 Douglas C–47.

Liaison and AOP aircraft:

1 Helio Courier.

Helicopters:

approx 10–12 machines, inc Mil Mi–2, Mil Mi–4 and Mil Mi–8.

Trainers:

20(?) Yakovlev Yak–11 and Yakovlev Yak–18.

7(?) Mikoyan MiG–15UTI.

3 Piaggio P.148.

Army 17,000 men.

Navy 300 men.

South Africa

Air force (Suid-Afrikaanse Lugmag, South African Air Force, SAAF)

men 8,500.

squadrons 20.

operational aircraft 253.

helicopters 80.

Organization

1 fighter squadron with Mirage IIICZ.

1 fighter squadron with Mirage F1CZ.

2 strike-fighter squadrons with Mirage IIIEZ.

2 strike-fighter squadrons with Mirage F1AZ.

1 strike-fighter squadron with Sabre Mk.6.

1 ground-attack squadron with MB.326K.

1 bomber squadron with Canberra B.(I)12.

1 bomber squadron with Buccaneer S.50.

1 maritime-reconnaissance and ASW squadron with Shackleton MR.3.

1 maritime-reconnaissance squadron with P.166S.

1 transport squadron with C–47.

1 transport squadron with C–47 and DC–4.

1 transport squadron with C–47 and H.S.125.

1 transport squadron with C.160Z and C–130B.

2 liaison squadrons with AM.3C.

1 liaison squadron with Cessna 185.

2 helicopter squadrons with Alouette III.

1 helicopter squadron with S.A.321L.

1 helicopter squadron with S.A.330.

6 trainer squadrons with MB.326M.

Major bases

Bloemspruit, Dunnottar, Durban, Grand Central, Langebaanweg, Malan (Cape Town), Pietersberg, Port Elizabeth, Potchefstroom, Waterkloof, Ysterplaat, Youngsfield, Zwartkop.

Equipment

Fighters and strike-fighters:

18 Canadair CL–13B Sabre Mk.6.

16 Dassault Mirage IIICZ.
34 Dassault Mirage IIIEZ.
3 Dassault Mirage IIIBZ.
4 Dassault Mirage IIIDZ.
32 Dassault Mirage F1AZ.
16 Dassault Mirage F1CZ.
20 de Havilland Vampire FB.5 and FB.9.
Ground-attack aircraft:
20 Aermacchi MB.326K.
Bombers:
6 English Electric Canberra B.(I)12.
3 English Electric Canberra T.4.
10 Hawker Siddeley Buccaneer S.50.
Reconnaissance aircraft:
4 Dassault Mirage IIIRZ.
Maritime-reconnaissance and ASW aircraft:
7 Avro Shackleton MR.3.
18 Piaggio P.166S.
Transports:
25 Douglas C–47.
5 Douglas DC–4.
4(7?) Hawker Siddeley H.S.125.
7 Lockheed C–130B.
7 Swearingen Merlin NA.
9 Transall C.160Z.
1 Vickers Viscount 781.
Liaison and AOP aircraft:
40 Aeritalia-Aermacchi AM.3C.
16 Cessna 185.
Helicopters:
5 Aérospatiale Alouette II.
40 Aérospatiale Alouette III.
15 Aérospatiale S.A.321L.
20 Aérospatiale S.A.330.
Trainers:
160 Aermacchi MB.326M.
20 de Havilland Vampire T.11 and T.55.
80 North American T–6G.
The de Havilland FB.5 and FB.9 strike-fighters and North
  American T–6G trainers have been mothballed as reserve
  equipment.
Programme
Formation of further ground-attack squadrons with Aermacchi
  MB.326K (approx 50 aircraft delivered or on order, further
  (50?) planned). 2 further Piaggio P.166S
  maritime-reconnaissance aircraft on order.
Army 38,000 men.
Navy 4,000 men.
Naval aviation
11 Westland Wasp helicopters.
Programme
8 further Westland Wasp helicopters on order.
Aircraft factories
Atlas (Atlas Aircraft Corporation of South Africa).

South Yemen (People's Democratic Republic)
Air force
men 1,500.
squadrons 4.
operational aircraft 15.
helicopters 12.
Organization
1 strike-fighter squadron with MiG–17F.
1 bomber squadron with Il–28.
1 transport squadron with An–24.
1 helicopter squadron with Mi–4 and Mi–8.
Base
Khormaksar (Aden).

Military training aid from
Soviet Union.
Equipment
Fighters and strike-fighters:
9(15?) Mikoyan MiG–17F.
Transports:
3(6?) Ilyushin Il–28.
3(4?) Antonov An–24.
Liaison and AOP aircraft:
some de Havilland Canada DHC–2(?).
Helicopters:
4 Mil Mi–4.
8 Mil Mi–8.
Trainers:
8 BAC 145 Jet Provost T.52.
2 Mikoyan MiG–15UTI.
The BAC 145 trainers are at present not in service.
Programme
Formation of 1 fighter squadron with 12 Mikoyan MiG–21.
Army 15,000 men.
Navy 300 men.

Soviet Union: see **USSR**

Spain
Air force (Ejército del Aire Español)
men 35,000.
squadrons 17.
operational aircraft 305(?).
helicopters 30.
Organization
2 fighter squadrons with F–4C(S).
2 fighter squadrons with Mirage IIIEE.
1 fighter squadron with Mirage F1CE.
1 strike-fighter squadron with SF–5A.
1 ground-attack squadron with HA–220.
1 reconnaissance squadron with SF–5A.
1 maritime-reconnaissance and ASW squadron with HU–16B
  and P–3A.
2 transport squadrons with C–47 and C.212.
1 transport squadron with DHC–4.
1 transport squadron with C–54.
1 transport squadron with C.207.
1 transport squadron with C–130E.
1 tanker squadron with KC–97L and KC–130H.
1 liaison squadron with Do–27 and O–1E.
1 liaison squadron with King Air.
1 liaison squadron with Bonanza F33.
1 helicopter squadron with Bell 47.
6(?) trainer squadrons with I–115, T–34 and Bonanza.
3 trainer squadrons with HA–200.
1 trainer squadron with T–33A.
2 strike-trainer squadrons with SF–5B.
Fighter and strike-fighter squadrons each with 12–14 aircraft.
Major bases
Albacete, Badajoz, Getafe, Los Llanos, Los Rodeos,
  Madrid/Torrejón, Malaga, Matacan/Salamanca, Rota/Jerez,
  Sanjurio/Valenzuela, Sevilla/Morón, Valencia/Manises,
  Valladolid/Villanubla, Zaragoza.
Military training aid from
United States.
Foreign air forces in Spain
5 American squadrons: 2 strike-fighter squadrons with F–4. 1
  electronic-reconnaissance squadron with RC–135C, D and
  U. 1 transport squadron with C–130. 1 air-rescue squadron
  with HC–130H and CH–3E.

Equipment

Fighters and strike-fighters:
18 CASA SF–5A (Northrop F–5A).
38 CASA SF–5B (Northrop F–5B).
22 Dassault Mirage IIIEE.
6 Dassault Mirage IIIDE.
15 Dassault Mirage F1CE.
34 McDonnell Douglas F–4C(S).
Ground-attack aircraft:
24 Hispano HA–220.
Reconnaissance aircraft:
18 CASA SF–5A (Northrop RF–5A).
Maritime-reconnaissance and ASW aircraft:
4 Grumman HU–16A.
7 Grumman HU–16B.
3 Lockheed P–3B.
Transports:
3 Boeing KC–97L.
10 Canadair CL–215.
20 CASA C.207.
40 CASA C.212.
4 Convair 440.
1 Dassault Falcon 20.
12 de Havilland Canada DHC–4.
15(?) Douglas C–47.
10(?) Douglas C–54.
4 Lockheed C–130H.
3 Lockheed KC–130H.
Liaison and AOP aircraft:
approx 60 aircraft, inc 6 Beechcraft Baron B55, 6 Beechcraft
   King Air C90, 2 Beechcraft King Air A100, 10 Cessna O–1E,
   30 Dornier Do–27, 6 Piper PA–23 Aztec.
Helicopters:
3 Aérospatiale S.A.330.
4 Agusta-Bell AB.205.
15 Bell 47D and G.
3 Bell UH–1H.
some(?) MBB BO–105.
Trainers:
approx 200 aircraft, inc 12(?) AISA I–115, 25 Beechcraft
   T–34, 12 Beechcraft Bonanza F33C, 25 CASA 113E (Bücker
   bü–131), 50 Hispano HA–200, 50(?) Lockheed T–33A.

Programme
Formation of 2 fighter squadrons with 42 McDonnell Douglas
F–4E. On order: 9 additional Dassault Mirage F1CE fighters,
4 Aérospatiale S.A. 330 helicopters and 50 CASA (MBB)
Flamingo trainers. Replacement of Douglas C–47 transports
by 40 CASA C.212. Phasing out of Boeing KC–97L tankers
and of Douglas C–54 transports from 1976.

Army 210,000 men.

Army aviation (Fuerzas Aeromobiles del Ejército de Tierra,
   FAMET)
– men.
5 squadrons.
20 operational aircraft.
55 helicopters.

Organization
2 helicopter squadrons with AB–47G and AB.206A.
1 helicopter squadron with UH–1B.
1 helicopter squadron with UH–1H.
1 helicopter squadron with CH–47C.

Equipment
Helicopters:
7 Agusta-Bell AB.47G.
16 Agusta-Bell AB.206A.
6 Bell 47G.
6 Bell UH–1B.
14 Bell UH–1H.
6 Boeing-Vertol CH–47C.

Liaison and AOP aircraft:
approx 20 aircraft, inc Cessna O–1E and Dornier Do–27.

Programme
3 further Boeing-Vertol CH–47C helicopters on order, delivery
   1977–78.

Navy 44,000 men.
1 helicopter carrier.

Naval aviation (Arma Aérea de la Armada Española)
– men.
6 squadrons.
8 operational aircraft.
50 helicopters.

Organization
1 strike-fighter squadron with AV–8A.
3 ASW squadrons with AB.204, AB.212AS, Hughes 500ASW
   and SH–3D.
1 helicopter squadron with Bell 47G and AB.47G.
1 helicopter squadron with AH–1G.

Bases
A Bajera (El Ferrol), Cartagena, Rota.

Equipment
Fighters and strike-fighters:
6 Hawker Siddeley AV–8A (Harrier Mk.50).
2 Hawker Siddeley TAV–8A (Harrier Mk.51).
Liaison aircraft:
2 Piper PA–24.
2 Piper PA–30.
Helicopters:
4 Agusta-Bell AB.204B.
7 Agusta-Bell AB.212AS.
11 Bell 47G and Agusta-Bell AB.47G.
6 Bell AH–1G.
11(18?) Hughes 500ASW.
11 Sikorsky SH–3D.

Programme
On order: 12 further Bell AH–1G attack helicopters and 12
   Sikorsky SH–3D helicopters. Acquisition of further (16?)
   Hawker Siddeley AV–8A (Harrier Mk.50) strike-fighters?
   Construction of a Sea Control Ship (SCS) planned,
   commissioning from 1979(?).

Aircraft factories
AISA (Aeronautica Industrial, S.A.), CASA (Construcciones
   Aeronauticas S.A.), Hispano (La Hispano-Aviación, S.A.),
   amalgamated with CASA since 1972.

Sri Lanka (Ceylon)
Air force (Sri Lanka Air Force)
men 2,100.
squadrons 4.
operational aircraft 12.
helicopters 13.

Organization
1 strike-fighter squadron with MiG–17F.
1 transport squadron with Dove and Heron.
1 helicopter squadron with Bell 47G.
1 helicopter squadron with Bell 206A.
1 trainer squadron with DHC–1.
1 trainer squadron with BAC 145.

Bases
Banderanaike (Ratmalana/Colombo), China Bay, Katunayake.

Military training aid from
Great Britain, Soviet Union.

Equipment
Fighters and strike-fighters:
5 Mikoyan MiG–17F.
Transports:
1 Convair 440.
4 de Havilland Dove.
2 de Havilland Heron.

Liaison and AOP aircraft:
5 Cessna 150.
4 Cessna 337.
Helicopters:
6 Bell 47G.
7 Bell 206A.
Trainers:
9 de Havilland Canada DHC–1.
6 BAC 145 Jet Provost T.51.
1 Mikoyan MiG–15UTI.
The Mikoyan MiG–17F strike-fighters are not in service due to lack of pilots.
Army 8,500 men.
Navy 2,200 men.

Sudan
Air force (Silakh Al-Jawwiya As-Sudan)
men 2,500.
squadrons 4.
operational aircraft 51.
helicopters 10.
Organization
1 fighter squadron with MiG–21.
1 strike-fighter squadron with F–4 (MiG–17F).
1 transport squadron with An–12 and An–24.
1 transport squadron with An–2.
1 helicopter squadron with Mi–4 and Mi–8.
Bases
Juba, Khartoum, Malakal, Port Sudan.
Military training aid from
China, Soviet Union.
Equipment
Fighters and strike-fighters:
18 Mikoyan MiG–21 and MiG–21U.
15 Shenyang F–4 (MiG–17F).
Transports:
6 Antonov An–12.
5 Antonov An–24.
1 de Havilland Canada DHC–6 Srs.300.
3(?) Fokker-VFW F.27M.
Liaison and AOP aircraft:
some Pilatus PC–6A.
Helicopters:
total of 10 Mil Mi–4 and Mil Mi–8.
Trainers:
3 BAC 145 Jet Provost T.51.
4 BAC 145 Jet Provost T.52.
5 BAC 145 Jet Provost T.55.
The trainers have been mothballed.
Army 42,000 men.
Navy 600 men.

Sweden
Air force (Flygvåpnet)
men 13,000 (50,000 after mobilization).
squadrons 31.
operational aircraft 540.
helicopters 17.
Organization
4 fighter squadrons with Saab 35D.
13 fighter squadrons with Saab 35F.
2 strike-fighter squadrons with Saab 32A.
4 strike-fighter squadrons with Saab 37.
2 reconnaissance squadrons with Saab 32C.
3 reconnaissance squadrons with Saab 35E.
1 reconnaissance squadron with Saab 37.
1 transport squadron with C–47 and C–130E.
1 liaison squadron with Saab 91 and Saab 195.
1 helicopter squadron with BV–107.
– trainer squadrons with Bulldog.
6 trainer squadrons with Saab 105.
1 strike-trainer squadron with Saab 37.
Fighter, strike-fighter and reconnaissance squadrons each with 12–15 aircraft.
Major bases
Arhoga, Ängelholm, Barkarby, Berga, Boden, Göteborg, Hagarnas, Halmstad, Kallinge, Kalmar, Karlsborg, Linköping, Ljungbyhed, Luleå, Malmaslätt, Norrköping, Nyköping, Östersund, Rönneby, Söderhamn, Såtenäs, Torslanda, Tullinge, Uppsala, Västerås.
Equipment
Fighters and strike-fighters:
40 Saab 32A.
approx 300 Saab 35A, B, C, D and F.
100 Saab 37.
Reconnaissance and ECM aircraft:
2 Gates Learjet 24.
30 Saab 32C.
42 Saab 35E.
15 Saab 37.
Transports:
3 Aérospatiale S.E.210 Caravelle.
7 Douglas C–47.
2 Lockheed C–130E.
1 Lockheed C–130H.
Helicopters:
1 Aérospatiale Alouette II.
6(?) Agusta-Bell AB.204B.
10 Boeing-Vertol BV–107.
Trainers:
some Saab 91B and C.
110 Saab 105A.
20 Saab 105B.
55 Scottish Aviation Bulldog.
Programme
Replacement of Saab 35 fighters by Saab 37 from 1978–79 (150–200 aircraft planned, 30 of which already on order). Replacement of Saab 32A strike-fighter by Saab 37 (a total of 150 Saab 37 strike-fighters and 25 Saab 37 strike-trainers delivered or on order). Replacement of Saab 32C reconnaissance aircraft by Saab 37. Number of fighter squadrons to be reduced from 17 to 10 by 1982.
Army
56,000 men (600,000 after mobilization).
Army aviation
– men.
– squadrons.
25 operational aircraft.
32 helicopters.
Organization
1 helicopter squadron with AB.204B.
2 helicopter squadrons with AB.206A.
– liaison and AOP squadrons with Bulldog.
Equipment
Helicopters:
12 Agusta-Bell AB.204B.
20 Agusta-Bell AB.206A.
Liaison and AOP aircraft:
5 Dornier Do–27A–4.
20 Scottish Aviation Bulldog.
Navy
15,000 men (50,000 after mobilization).
Naval aviation
– men.
2 squadrons.
27 helicopters.
Organization
2 helicopter squadrons with Alouette II and Vertol 107.

Equipment
Helicopters:
7 Aérospatiale Alouette II.
10 Agusta-Bell AB.206B.
3 Boeing-Vertol BV–107.
7 Kawasaki-Vertol KV–107.
Aircraft factories
Saab (Svenska Aeroplan A.B.).

Switzerland
Air force (Schweizerische Flugwaffe)
men 9,000 (46,000 after mobilization).
squadrons 7.
operational aircraft 315.
helicopters 100.
Organization
2 fighter squadrons with Mirage IIIS.
7 strike-fighter squadrons with Hunter Mk.58 and Mk.58A.
9 strike-fighter squadrons with Venom FB.50.
1 reconnaissance squadron with Mirage IIIRS.
1 transport squadron with Ju–52/3m.
7 helicopter squadrons with Alouette II and Alouette IIIS.
– trainer squadrons with P–2 and P–3.
– trainer squadrons with Vampire T.55.
Fighter, strike-fighter and reconnaissance squadrons each
   with 12–15 aircraft.
Major bases
Alpnach, Buochs, Dübendorf, Emmen, Interlaken, Magadino,
   Meiringen, Payerne, Sion.
Equipment
Fighters and strike-fighters:
2 Dassault Mirage IIIB.
1 Dassault Mirage IIIC.
35 Dassault Mirage IIIS.
120 de Havilland Venom FB.50.
80 Hawker Hunter Mk.58.
50 Hawker Hunter Mk.58A.
8 Hawker Hunter T.68.
Reconnaissance aircraft:
16 Dassault Mirage IIIRS.
Transports:
3 Junkers Ju–52/3m.
Liaison and AOP aircraft:
3 Beechcraft Twin Bonanza.
6 Dornier Do–27H–2.
6 Pilatus PC–6A–1 and H–2.
Helicopters:
25 Aérospatiale Alouette II.
75 Aérospatiale Alouette III.
Trainers:
30 de Havilland Vampire T.55.
25 Pilatus P–2.
70 Pilatus P–3.
Programme
For the formation of 4 fighter squadrons, 66 Northrop F–5E
   fighters and 6F–5F strike trainers have been ordered,
   delivery 1978/79–81. Disbanding further Venom FB.50
   strike-fighter squadrons.
Army 33,500 men (54,000 after mobilization).
Aircraft factories
Eidgenössisches Flugzeugwerk Emmen (F & W), FFA (Flug
   und Fahrzeugwerke Altenrhein), Pilatus Flugzeugwerke.

Syria
Air force (Al Quwwat al-Jawwija al Arabia as-Suriya)
men 10,000.
squadrons 26.
operational aircraft 350(?).
helicopters 56.

Organization
9 fighter squadrons with MiG–21 and MiG–19.
3 strike-fighter squadrons with MiG–17F and PF.
3 strike-fighter squadrons with Su–7.
3 strike-fighter squadrons with MiG–27.
1 bomber and reconnaissance squadron with Il–28 and
   Il–28R.
1 transport squadron with C–47.
1 transport squadron with Il–14.
1 transport squadron with An–12.
1 helicopter squadron with Mi–4.
2 helicopter squadrons with Mi–8.
1 helicopter squadron with Ka–25.
– trainer squadrons with Yak–11 and Yak–18.
– trainer squadrons with L–29.
– trainer squadrons with MiG–15UTI.
Fighter and strike-fighter squadrons each with 10–12 aircraft.
Major bases
Aleppo, Chliye, Damascus-Mezze, Dumeyr, El Rasafa, Hama,
   Mari Rhiyal, Palmyra, Sahl es Sahra, Saigal, Tango Four.
Military training aid from
Soviet Union, Cuba, Korea (North).
Foreign air forces in Syria
1 Soviet reconnaissance squadron with MiG–25R(?).
Equipment
Fighters and strike-fighters:
40(70?) Mikoyan MiG–17F and PF.
200 (over 250?) Mikoyan MiG–19 and MiG–21.
40(?) Mikoyan MiG–27.
40(60?) Sukhoi Su–7.
Bombers and reconnaissance aircraft:
10(?) Ilyushin Il–28 and Il–28R.
Transports:
3(6?) Antonov An–12.
6 Douglas C–47.
8(6?) Ilyushin Il–14.
4(?) Ilyushin Il–18.
Liaison and AOP aircraft:
2 Piper PA–350 Navajo.
Helicopters:
4 Mil Mi–2.
8 Mil Mi–4.
35 Mil Mi–8.
9 Kamov Ka–25(?).
Trainers:
approx 40 aircraft, inc Aero L–29, Yakovlev Yak–11 and
   Yakovlev Yak–18, Mikoyan MiG–15UTI.
Some fighters and strike-fighters have been grounded due to
   lack of pilots.
Programme
Replacement of Mikoyan MiG–17 strike-fighters by Mikoyan
   MiG–21. Acquisition of 15 (up to 40?) Aérospatiale
   S.A.321(?) helicopters. 2 Lockheed L–100–30 transports on
   order. Purchase of 60 helicopters from Agusta, Italy,
   planned: 24 A.109 Hirundo, 12 SH–3D Sea King, 12
   AB.212AS, 6 S–61A–4, 6 AB.212 SAR.
Army 135,000 men.
Navy 2,500 men.

Taiwan (Republic of China)
Air force (Chung-Kuo Kung Chuan)
men 82,000.
squadrons 24.
operational aircraft 365.
helicopters 66.
Organization
3 fighter squadrons with F–104G.
2 fighter squadrons with F–5A.
3 fighter squadrons with F–5E.

4 strike-fighter squadrons with F–100D.
1 reconnaissance squadron with RF–104G.
1 maritime-reconnaissance and ASW squadron with Hu–16B.
2 transport squadrons with C–47.
2 transport squadrons with C–119G.
1 transport squadron with C–46.
1 transport squadron with C–123K.
1 helicopter squadron with Hughes 500M.
4 helicopter squadrons with UH–1H.
– trainer squadrons with PL–1B.
– trainer squadrons with T–28A and T–6G(?).
– trainer squadrons with T–38A and T–33A.
Fighter and strike-fighter squadrons each with 18–25 aircraft.

Major bases
Chiai, Hsinchu, Kung K'uang, Ping tung, T'ai-chung, T'ai-nan,
  Taipei, Tao-yuan.

Military training aid from
United States.

Equipment
Fighters and strike-fighters:
some Lockheed F–104A(?).
63 Lockheed F–104G and TF–104G.
90 North American F–100D and F–100F.
35 Northrop F–5A and F–5B.
60 Northrop F–5E.
Reconnaissance aircraft:
7 Lockheed RF–104G.
Maritime-reconnaissance and ASW aircraft:
10(?) Grumman HU–16B.
Transports:
1 Boeing 720B.
20 Curtiss-Wright C–46.
25 Douglas C–47.
1–2 Douglas DC–6.
35 Fairchild C–119G.
10 Fairchild C–123K.
Helicopters:
6 Hughes 500M.
60 Bell UH–1H.
Trainers:
approx 100(120?) aircraft, inc 40 Pazmany/CAF PL–1B, some
  Lockheed T–33A, North American T–6G, North American
  T–28A, 30(?) Northrop T–38A.

Programme
Replacement of North American F–100 strike-fighters by
  further 60(120?) Northrop F–5E.

Army 340,000 men.

Army aviation
50 Bell UH–1H helicopters.
2 Kawasaki KH–4 helicopters.
10 Pazmany/CAF PL–1B trainers.

Navy 37,000 men.

Naval aviation
1 maritime-reconnaissance and ASW squadron with 9
  Grumman S–2A.

Marines 35,000 men.

Aircraft factories
AIDC/CAF (Aero-Industry Development Center, Chinese Air
  Force).

Tanzania
Air force (Jeshi la Wanachi la Tanzania)
men 1,000.
squadrons 3.
operational aircraft 40(?).
helicopters 4.

Organization
1 fighter squadron with F–8 (MiG–21).
1 strike-fighter squadron with F–6 (MiG–19).
1 transport squadron with DHC–4.
1 trainer squadron with Cherokee.

Bases
Arusha, Mbeya, Mikymi (Dar-es-Salaam), Moshi, Tabora,
  Zanzibar.

Military training aid from
China.

Equipment
Fighters and strike-fighters:
some Shenyang F–4 (MiG–17F)(?).
12 Shenyang F–6 (MiG–19).
10(12?) Shenyang F–8 (MiG–21).
Transports:
1 Antonov An–2.
8 de Havilland Canada DHC–4.
1 Hawker Siddeley H.S.748.
Liaison and AOP aircraft:
6 Cessna 310Q.
5 Piper PA–28–140 Cherokee.
Helicopters:
2 Agusta-Bell AB.206A.
2 Bell 47G.

Programme
Formation of second strike-fighter squadron with Shenyang
  F–4 (MiG–19). 8 de Havilland Canada DHC–4 transports and
  some Soko G–2 Galeb trainers on order.

Army 13,000 men.
Navy 600 men.

Thailand
Air force
men 42,000.
squadrons 14.
operational aircraft 185.
helicopters 94.

Organization
1 fighter squadron with F–5E.
1 strike-fighter squadron with F–5A.
2 ground-attack squadrons with T–28D.
2 ground-attack squadrons with OV–10C.
2 night ground-support squadrons with AU–23A.
1 reconnaissance squadron with RF–5A.
1 transport squadron with C–47.
1 transport squadron with C–123B.
3 helicopter squadrons with UH–1H.
1 helicopter squadron with CH–34C.
2 trainer squadrons with CT–4.
1 trainer squadron with SF.260MT.
1 trainer squadron with T–37B.
Fighter and strike-fighter squadrons each with 16 aircraft.

Major bases
Bangkok, Don Muang, Kokekathion, Khorat, Nakhon Phanom,
  Nam Phong, Nongkai, Prachuab, Sattahip, Takhli, Ubon,
  Udon Thani, Utapao.

Military training aid from
United States.

Equipment
Fighters and strike-fighters:
some North American F–86F(?).
13 Northrop F–5E.
3 Northrop F–5F.
12 Northrop F–5A.
2 Northrop F–5B.
Ground-attack aircraft:
30 North American T–28D.
30 Rockwell (North American) OV–10C.
Night ground-support aircraft:
some Douglas AC–47.
30 Fairchild AU–23A Peacemaker.

Reconnaissance aircraft:
4 Northrop RF–5A.
2 Lockheed RT–33A.
Transports:
5 Beechcraft C–45.
1 Britten-Norman BN–2A.
20 Douglas C–47.
2 Douglas C–54.
13 Fairchild C–123B.
2 Hawker Siddeley H.S.748.
Liaison and AOP aircraft:
approx 20(?) aircraft, inc Cessna O–1, Helio U–10A and Piper
  L–18C.
Helicopters:
50(22?) Bell UH–1H.
4 Boeing-Vertol CH–47C.
16 Kawasaki KH–4.
4 Kawasaki-Vertol KV–107.
20 Sikorsky CH–34C.
Trainers:
approx 55 aircraft, inc 8(12?) Cessna T–37B, 6 Lockheed
  T–33A, 24 NZAI Airtourer CT–4, NZAI Airtrainer T.6, 2
  Pazmany PL–2, 12 SIAI-Marchetti SF.260MT.
Also in Thailand are approx 70 aircraft of the former South
  Vietnamese and approx 90 aircraft of the former Cambodian
  Air Force, inc:
Ground-attack aircraft:
11 Douglas A–1E and G.
50 North American T–28D.
Night ground-support aircraft:
15 Douglas AC–47.
3 Fairchild AC–119.
3 Helio AU–24H Stallion.
ECM aircraft:
2 Douglas EC–47.
Transports:
8 Douglas C–47.
10 Fairchild C–123B.
6 de Havilland Canada DHC–4.
Liaison and AOP aircraft:
15 Cessna 0–1.
14 Cessna U–17.
Helicopters:
25 Bell UH–1B, D and H.
Trainers:
1 Cessna T–41D.
Programme
Replacement of North American F–86F strike-fighters by
  Vought A–7 or Fairchild A–10A?
Army and Border Guard
135,000 men.
Army aviation
– men.
4 squadrons.
20(?) operational aircraft.
71 helicopters.
Organization
1 helicopter squadron with UH–1B and UH–1D.
2 helicopter squadrons with UH–1H.
1 helicopter squadron with FH–1100.
Equipment
Night ground-support aircraft:
5 Fairchild AU–23A Peacemaker.
Helicopters:
10 Bell UH–1B.
10 Bell UH–1D.
25 Bell UH–1H.
3 Bell 206A.
16 Fairchild Hiller FH–1100.

6 Hiller OH–23G.
1 Mitsubishi-Sikorsky S–62A.
Liaison and AOP aircraft:
2 de Havilland Canada DHC–4.
some Dornier Do–28D.
3 Short Skyvan 3M.
Navy 27,000 men.
Naval aviation
– men.
1 squadron.
7 operational aircraft.
Organization
1 maritime-reconnaisance and ASW squadron with HU–16B
  and S–2F.
Equipment
Maritime-reconnaissance and ASW aircraft:
2 Grumman HU–16B.
5 Grumman S–2F.

Togo
Air force (Force Aérienne Togolaise)
men 130.
squadrons –.
operational aircraft 8.
helicopters 3.
Organization
1 trainer squadron with C.M.170.
Base
Lomé.
Military training aid from
France.
Equipment
Ground-attack aircraft:
3 Embraer-Aermacchi AT–26 Xavante (MB.326GB).
Transports:
2 de Havilland Canada DHC–5D.
2 Douglas C–47.
1 Fokker-VFW F.28 Mk.1000.
Liaison and AOP aircraft:
1 Cessna 337D.
1 Max Holste M.H.1521M.
1 Reims-Cessna F.337.
Helicopters:
2 Aérospatiale Alouette II.
1 Aérospatiale S.A.330.
Trainers:
5 Potez-Air Fouga C.M.170.
Army 1,500 men.
Navy 200 men.

Trinidad and Tobago
Air force (Trinidad and Tobago Defence Force)
1 Cessna 337 liaison aircraft.
1 Aérospatiale S.A.341G helicopter.

Tunisia
Air force (Armée de l'Air Tunisienne)
men 1,500.
squadrons 3.
operational aircraft 25.
helicopters 15.
Organization
1 strike-fighter squadron with F–86F.
1 ground-attack squadron with SF.260W.
1 helicopter squadron with Alouette II and III.
1 trainer squadron with MB.326B.
1 trainer squadron with Saab 91D.

Major bases
Bizerta, El Aouina (Tunis), Monastir.
Military training aid from
United States.
Equipment
Fighters and strike-fighters:
10 North American F–86F.
Ground-attack aircraft:
12 SIAI-Marchetti SF.260W.
Transports:
3 Dassault M.D.315.
Helicopters:
8 Aérospatiale Alouette II.
6 Aérospatiale Alouette III.
1 Aérospatiale S.A.330.
Trainers:
8 Aermacchi MB.326B.
12 Saab 91D.
Programme
Replacement of North American F–86F strike-fighters by 10
   Northrop F–5E and 2 Northrop F–5F strike trainers.
   Replacement of Dassault M.D.315 transports by 3 Fiat
   G.222 planned.
Army 20,000 men.
Navy 1,500 men.

Turkey
Air force (Türk Hava Kuvvetleri, THK)
men 48,000.
squadrons 24.
operational aircraft 360.
helicopters 30.
Organization
2 fighter squadrons with F–104S.
2 fighter squadrons with F–102A.
5 strike-fighter squadrons with F–5A.
2 strike-fighter squadrons with F–5E.
3 strike-fighter squadrons with F–100D and F.
2 strike-fighter squadrons with F–104G.
2 strike-fighter squadrons with F–4E.
2 reconnaissance squadrons with RF–5A.
2 transport squadrons with C.160D and C–47.
1 transport squadron with C–47 and Viscount.
1 transport squadron with C–130E.
– trainer squadrons with T–34B and T–41D.
– trainer squadrons with T–37C and T–33A.
Fighter, strike-fighter and reconnaissance squadrons each
   with 18–25 aircraft.
Major bases
Adana, Balikeshir, Bandirma, Batman, Cigli (Izmir), Diyarbakir,
   Erkilet, Ermac, Eskisehir, Etimesgut, Gaziemir, Incirlik, Ismir,
   Karamürsel, Konya, Malatya, Merzifon, Murted, Yesilkoy.
Military training aid from
United States.
Foreign air forces in Turkey
1 American strike-fighter squadron with F–4.
Equipment
Fighters and strike-fighters:
30 Convair F–102A.
3 Convair TF–102A.
33 Lockheed F–104G.
4 Lockheed TF–104G.
40 Lockheed F–104S.
40 McDonnell Douglas F–4E.
75 North American F–100D and F–100F.
85(90?) Northrop F–5A.
12 Northrop F–5B.
40 Northrop F–5E.

Reconnaissance aircraft:
36 Northrop RF–5A.
Transports:
6 Beechcraft C–45.
2 Britten-Norman BN–2A.
5(?) Dornier Do–28.
10 Douglas C–47.
8 Lockheed C–130E.
20 Transall C.160D.
3 Vickers Viscount 794.
Liaison and AOP aircraft:
3 Cessna 421B.
some Piper L–18C.
Helicopters:
approx 30 machines, inc Agusta-Bell AB.204B, 10
   Agusta-Bell AB.206A and 10(?) Bell UH–1H.
Trainers:
20 Beechcraft T–34B.
5 Beechcraft T–42A.
20 Cessna T–37C.
12(19?) Cessna T–41D.
30 Lockheed T–33A.
15 MBB–223 Flamingo.
Programme
Replacement of North American F–100 strike-fighters by 80
   Northrop F–5E and 40 further McDonnell Douglas F–4E.
   Formation of 1 reconnaissance squadron with 8 McDonnell
   Douglas RF–4E. Acquisition of 40(60?) Dassault
   Breguet/Dornier Alphajet trainers and ground-attack aircraft.
   Purchase planned of 30 further McDonnell Douglas F–4E
   fighters, 20 North American F–100F strike-trainers, 72
   helicopters (36 Bell UH–1B, 36 Bell UH–1H) and 20 Cessna
   T–37 trainers. Under consideration is the purchase of 20
   further Lockheed F–104S fighters and the replacement of
   Convair F–102A fighters and Lockheed F–104G
   strike-fighters by over 100 General Dynamics F–16 from
   1981.
Army 365,000 men.
Army aviation (Kara Ordusu Havaciligi)
– men.
– squadrons.
45 operational aircraft.
60 helicopters.
Equipment
Helicopters:
some Bell 47G.
20 Agusta-Bell AB.204B.
40 Agusta-Bell AB.206A.
some Bell UH–1D.
Liaison and AOP aircraft:
18 Cessna U–17.
some de Havilland Canada DHC–2.
15 Dornier Do–27.
some Piper L–18B and C.
Transports:
2 Dornier Do–28D.
Programme
56 Agusta-Bell AB.205 helicopters on order.
Navy
40,000 men.
Naval aviation (Donanma Havaciligi)
– men.
2 squadrons.
22 operational aircraft.
10(?) helicopters.
Organization
1(2?) maritime-reconnaissance and ASW squadron(s) with
   S–2E and S–2D.
1 helicopter squadron with AB.205 and AB.212AS.

Bases
Antalya, Ismir, Karamürsel, Sinope.
Equipment
Maritime-reconnaissance and ASW aircraft:
8 Grumman S–2D.
12 Grumman S–2E.
2 Grumman TS–2A.
Helicopters:
3 Agusta-Bell AB.205.
some Agusta-Bell AB.212AS.
Aircraft factories
Turkish Aircraft Industries (TUSAS) under construction.

Uganda
Air force
men 1,000.
squadrons 4.
operational aircraft 25.
helicopters 13.
Organization
1 fighter squadron with MiG–21.
1 strike-fighter squadron with MiG–17F.
1 transport squadron with C–47.
1 helicopter squadron with AB.205 and AB.206A.
1 trainer squadron with C.M.170.
Bases
Arua, Entebbe, Gulu, Kampala, Nakasongola.
Military training aid from
Czechoslovakia, Libya(?), Soviet Union.
Equipment
Fighters and strike-fighters:
5 Mikoyan MiG–17F.
12 Mikoyan MiG–21.
Transports:
1 de Havilland Canada DHC–4.
1 de Havilland Canada DHC–6.
5 Douglas C–47.
1 IAI Commodore Jet 123.
Liaison and AOP aircraft:
4 Cessna 180.
1 Piper Aztec.
5 Piper L–18.
Helicopters:
6 Agusta-Bell AB.205.
4 Agusta-Bell AB.206A.
1 Bell 212.
2 Westland Scout(?).
Trainers:
5 Aero L–29.
2 Mikoyan MiG–15UTI.
4 Piaggio P.149D.
6(8?) Potez-Air Fouga C.M.170.
The 11 Mikoyan strike-fighters (4 MiG–17, 7 MiG–21)
  destroyed during the Israeli commando raid on Entebbe on
  3 July 1976, have reportedly been replenished from Iraqi
  stocks.
Programme
Formation of further fighter and strike-fighter squadrons with
  MiG–21.
Army 20,000 men.
Navy 200 men.

United Arab Emirates
Loose confederation of states comprising Abu Dhabi, Shajah,
Ajman, Fujairah, Ras-al-Khaimah and Umm al-Qaiwan.
Air force (Union Air Force)
In being since 1975.
helicopters 7.

Organization
–.
Equipment
Helicopters:
3 Agusta-Bell AB.206A.
4 Agusta-Bell AB.212.
Programme
4 Bell 205A–1 helicopters on order.
Army – men.

United States of America
Air force (United States Air Force, USAF)
men 590,000.
squadrons over 210.
operational aircraft 5,000.
helicopters 250.
Organization
1 fighter squadron with F–5E.
5 fighter squadrons with F–15A.
6 fighter squadrons with F–106A.
38 strike-fighter squadrons with F–4C, D and E.
15 strike-fighter squadrons with F–111E and F.
12(10?) strike-fighter squadrons with A–7D and A–10A.
3 night ground-support and special-duties squadrons with
  AC–130H, C–130 and CH–53.
21 bomber squadrons with B–52D, F, G and H.
4 bomber squadrons with FB–111A.
1 reconnaissance squadron with SR–71.
1 reconnaissance squadron with U–2.
9 reconnaissance squadrons with RF–4C.
11 reconnaissance and ECM squadrons with DC–130,
  EC–135, O–2A, OV–10 and RC–135.
13 transport squadrons with C–141A.
4 transport squadrons with C–5A.
15 transport squadrons with C–130E, H and B.
3 transport squadrons with C–9A, C–135 and helicopters.
2 transport squadrons with VC–137 and VC–140.
33 tanker squadrons with KC–135A.
– helicopter squadrons with HH–3E, HH–53B and C.
– helicopter squadrons with UH–1F, H and N.
– helicopter squadrons with CH–3E.
– trainer squadrons with T–41 and T–37.
– trainer squadrons with T–38A.
– fighter-trainer squadrons with F–5E.
– trainer squadrons with T–43A and T–29.
As part of America's foreign alliance commitments, a number
  of squadrons are permanently based overseas.
Fighter, strike-fighter and reconnaissance squadrons each
  with 18–25, bomber squadrons each with 15, transport
  squadrons each with 16, and tanker squadrons each with
  15–20 aircraft.
Major bases
Atlus AFB(= Air Force Base)/Okla., Andrew AFB/Md.,
Atlantic City/N.J., Baltimore/Md., Barksdale AFB/La., Beale
AFB/Calif., Bergstrom AFB/Tex., Blytheville AFB/Ark.,
Cannon AFB/N. Mex., Carswell AFB/Tex., Castle AFB/Calif.,
Davis-Monthan AFB/Ariz., Dyess AFB/Tex., Edwards
AFB/Calif., Eglin AFB/Fla., Eielson AFB/Alaska, Elmendorf
AFB/Alaska, Ellsworth AFB/S. Dak., England AFB/La.,
Fairchild AFB/Wash., George AFB/Calif., Grand Forks
AFB/N. Dak., Griffiss AFB/N.Y., Grissom AFB/Ind.,
Hanscom AFB/Mass., Hickam AFB/Hawaii, Holloman
AFB/N.Mex., Homestead AFB/Fla., Hurtlburt Field/Fla.,
Kineloe AFB/Mich., Kirtland AFB/N. Mex., Langley AFB/Va.,
Little Rock AFB/Ark., Loring AFB/Maine, Luke AFB/Ariz.,
Malstrom AFB/Mont., March AFB/Calif., Mather AFB/Calif.,
McConnell AFB/Kans., McDill AFB/Fla., Minot AFB/N. Dak.,
Mountain Home AFB/Idaho, Myrtle Beach AFB/S.C., Nellis
AFB/Nev., Offutt AFB/Neb., Pease AFB/N.H., Plattsburg

AFB/N.Y., Pope AFB/N.C., Richards-Gebaur AFB/Mo., Rickenbacker AFB/Ohio, Robins AFB/Ga., Sawyer AFB/Mich., Sewart AFB/Tenn., Seymour Johnson AFB/N.C., Shaw AFB/S.C., Travis AFB/Calif., Vandenberg AFB/Calif., F. E. Warren AFB/Wyo., Whitemen AFB/Mo., Wright-Patterson AFB/Ohio, Wurtsmith AFB/Mich.

Equipment
Fighters and strike-fighters:
approx 2,400 aircraft, inc 120 Convair F–106A and B; 50 Fairchild A–10A; 370 General Dynamics F–111A, D, E and F; 1,340 McDonnell Douglas F–4C, D and E; over 150 McDonnell Douglas F–15A; 30(72?) Northrop F–5E; 290 Vought A–7D.

Ground-attack and night ground-support aircraft:
approx 100 aircraft, inc 6 Cessna A–37B, Douglas AC–47, 10 Lockheed AC–130H.

Bombers:
100 Boeing B–52D.
172 Boeing B–52G.
97 Boeing B–52H.
69 General Dynamics FB–111A.

Reconnaissance and ECM aircraft:
approx 500 aircraft, inc Boeing E–3A, 6 Boeing E–4A, 45(?) Boeing EC–135 and RC–135, Douglas EB–66, Douglas EC–47, Lockheed EC–121, 12 Lockheed SR–71, 20(?) Lockheed U–2, 19 Lockheed WC–130, 16 Martin EB–57 and RB–57, 270 McDonnell Douglas RF–4C, 90 North American OV–10, 45 Republic F–105G.

Transports:
approx 1,550 aircraft, inc Aero U–4A, 16 Boeing C–135, 569 Boeing KC–135A, 55 KC–135Q, 5 Boeing VC–137, Douglas C–47, Douglas C–54, 76 Lockheed C–5A, Lockheed C–121, 285 Lockheed C–130E and H, 11(?) Lockheed C–140A and VC–140, 274 Lockheed C–141A, 30 McDonnell Douglas C–9A, 3 McDonnell Douglas VC–9C.

Liaison and AOP aircraft:
approx 200(?) aircraft, inc 30 Beechcraft C–12, Beechcraft U–8F, Cessna O–1, 95 Cessna O–2A, Cessna U–3A and B, Helio U–10A, B and D.

Helicopters:
approx 250 machines, inc Bell UH–1F, UH–1H and UH–1N, some Kaman HH–43F, Sikorsky CH–3E and CH–53C, Sikorsky HH–3E, Sikorsky HH–53B and HH–53C.

Trainers:
approx 1,800 aircraft, inc Beechcraft T–34, Beechcraft T–42A, 19 Boeing T–43A, 710 Cessna T–37, 65 Cessna T–41, Lockheed T–33, North American T–28, 840 Northrop T–38a.
In addition, the American Air Force also holds approx 2,500 mothballed aircraft in reserve, inc

Fighters and strike-fighters:
Convair F–102A and TF–102A, 12 General Dynamics F–111A, Lockheed F–104A, McDonnell F–101B and CF–101B, North American F–100.

Ground-attack and night ground-support aircraft:
Douglas AC–47, Fairchild AC–119.

Bombers:
Boeing B–52, Douglas B–66, 9 General Dynamics FB–111A, Martin B–57.

Reconnaissance aircraft:
Lockheed EC–121, Lockheed SR–71, Lockheed U–2, McDonnell RF–101.

Maritime-reconnaissance and ASW aircraft:
Grumman HU–16.

Transports:
Boeing C–97, Boeing KC–135A, Douglas C–47, Douglas C–54, Douglas C–118, Fairchild C–119, Fairchild C–123, Lockheed C–121.

Liaison and AOP aircraft:
Cessna O–1, Cessna U–3, Helio U–10.

Trainers:
300 Lockheed T–33A.

Programme
Formation of further fighter and strike-fighter squadrons with McDonnell Douglas F–15 and General Dynamics F–16 (in all, 729 F–15 and 650 F–16 delivered or on order). Re-equipment of further strike-fighter and ground-attack squadrons with Fairchild A–10A (in all, 733 delivered or on order). Replacement of Boeing B–52 bombers by 244 Rockwell B–1 from 1978. Replacement of older transports, helicopters and trainers by newer types.

Air National Guard (ANG)
95,000 men.
89 squadrons.
1,600(?) operational aircraft.
30(?) helicopters.

Organization
1 fighter squadron with F–101F.
6 fighter squadrons with F–106A.
2 strike-fighter squadrons with F–4C.
17(18?) strike-fighter squadrons with F–100D and F.
4 strike-fighter squadrons with F–105B, D and F.
6 strike-fighter squadrons with A–7D.
2 ground-attack squadrons with A–37B.
7 reconnaissance squadrons with RF–4C.
2 reconnaissance squadrons with RF–101C.
2 reconnaissance and ECM squadrons with EB–57B and E.
1 ECM squadron with EC–121S.
7 AOP squadrons with O–2A.
15 transport squadrons with C–130A, B and E.
1 transport squadron with C–123J.
1 transport squadron with C–7A and B.
8 tanker squadrons with KC–97L.
5 tanker squadrons with KC–135A.
2 rescue squadrons with HC–130H and P and with HH–3E.

Programme
Disbanding of McDonnell F–101F fighter squadrons. Replacement of Republic F–105 strike-fighters by McDonnell Douglas F–4, of McDonnell RF–101C reconnaissance aircraft by McDonnell Douglas RF–4C, and of Boeing KC–97L tankers by Boeing KC–135A.

Air Force Reserve (AFRES)
57,000 men.
38(53) squadrons.
450 operational aircraft.
50 helicopters.

Organization
3 strike-fighter squadrons with F–105D.
4 ground-attack squadrons with A–37B.
1 night ground-support squadron with AC–130A.
1 ECM squadron with EC–121T.
18 transport squadrons with C–130A, B and E.
2 transport squadrons with HC–130H.
4 transport squadrons with C–123K.
2 transport squadrons with C–7A.
2 helicopter squadrons with HH–1H.
1 helicopter squadron with CH–3E.
In addition the USAF Reserve has sufficient personnel for the immediate equipping of 17 further operational transport squadrons with C–5A and C–141A.

Programme
Re-equipment of Republic F–105D strike-fighter squadrons with McDonnell Douglas F–4.

Army 784,000 men.

Army aviation (United States Army Aviation)
– men.
200(?) squadrons.
800(950?) operational aircraft.
8,300 helicopters.

Organization
– reconnaissance squadrons with OV–1, OV–10 and RU–21.
– helicopter squadrons with AH–1G, AH–1Q and AH–1S.
– helicopter squadrons with OH–6A and OH–58A.
– helicopter squadrons with UH–1.
– helicopter squadrons with CH–47 and CH–54.
– liaison and AOP squadrons with O–1, DHC–2 and U–7.
– liaison and AOP squadrons with U–8, U–21 and U–25.
– transport squadrons with DHC–3.
– trainer squadrons with T–41B and T–42A.
– helicopter trainer squadrons with TH–55A and TH–13S.

Equipment
Reconnaissance and ECM aircraft:
Beechcraft RU–21A, B, C, D, E, F and J, 200(?) Grumman
OV–1A, B, C and D, 100(?) Rockwell (North American)
OV–10.

Helicopters:
approx 8,300 machines, inc 750 Bell AH–1G, AH–1Q and
AH–1S, 150 Bell OH–13G, H, S and TH–13S, 4,000 Bell
UH–1B, C, D and H, 1,900 Bell OH–58A, 420 Boeing-Vertol
CH–47A, B and C, 400 Hughes OH–6A, 600 Hughes
TH–55A, 75 Sikorsky CH–54A and B.

Transports:
approx 100 aircraft, inc some Rockwell (North American)
U–9C and UH–9D and Beechcraft C–45, 70(?) de Havilland
Canada DHC–3 (U–1A), 2 de Havilland Canada DHC–6
(UV–18A), 15(?) Douglas C–47.

Liaison and AOP aircraft:
approx 350(500?) aircraft, inc U–21A and F, Beechcraft U–8D
and F, 20 Beechcraft U–25A, Cessna O–1, 2 de Havilland
Canada DHC–2 (U–6A), Piper U–7A and B.

Trainers:
50(60?) Beechcraft T–42A, 200(250?) Cessna T–41B.

Programme
Replacement of Bell AH–1 attack helicopters by 472 Hughes
AH–64 from 1981. Replacement of Bell UH–1 helicopters by
Boeing UH–61A or Sikorsky UH–60A.

Navy 536,000 men.
13 aircraft carriers.
8 helicopter carriers.

Naval aviation (United States Naval Aviation)
– men.
144 squadrons.
5,000 operational aircraft.
1,160 helicopters.

Organization
18 fighter squadrons with F–4J and N.
7 fighter squadrons with F–14A.
27 strike-fighter squadrons with A–7B, C and E.
13 bomber squadrons with A–6A and E.
8 reconnaissance squadrons with RA–5C.
4 reconnaissance and ECM squadrons with RA–3B,
EC–121M, WP–3A, EA–3B and EC–130Q.
4 ECM squadrons with EA–5B.
24(26?) maritime-reconnaissance and ASW squadrons with
P–3B, and P–3C.
8 maritime-reconnaissance and ASW squadrons with S–3A.
2 maritime-reconnaissance and ASW squadrons with S–2E
and S–2G.
6 transport squadrons with C–2A, C–118B, C–130F, C–131F
and VC–118.
4 tanker squadrons with KA–6D.
10 helicopter squadrons with SH–3D, G and H.
2 helicopter squadrons with RH–53D.
7(9?) helicopter squadrons with SH–2F, HH–2D, CH–46D and
SH–3.
9 trainer squadrons with T–2, T–28 and T–34.
9 trainer squadrons with TA–4J and TS–2A.
1 trainer squadron with T–29B.

1 helicopter trainer squadron with TH–1L and Th–57A.
Fighter and bomber squadrons each with 12, strike-fighter
squadrons each with 14, reconnaissance squadrons each
with 5–6, ECM squadrons each with 10–15, and
maritime-reconnaissance and ASW squadrons each with
9–10 aircraft.

Major bases
NAS Almeda/Cal. (NAS = Naval Air Station), NAS Barbers
Point/Hawaii, NAS Brunswick/Me., NAS Cecil Field/Fla.,
NAS China Lake/Cal., NAS Corpus Christi/Tex., NAS
Jacksonville/Fla., NAS Key West/Fla., NAS Lakehurst/N.J.,
NAS Lemoore/Cal., NAS Miramar/Cal., NAS Moffett
Field/Cal., NAS Norfolk/Va., NAS North Island/Cal., NAS
Oceana/Va., NAS Patuxent River/Md., NAS Pensacola/Fla.,
NAS Point Mugu/Cal., NAS Whidbey Island/Calif.

Equipment
Fighters and strike-fighters:
approx 1,550 aircraft, inc 250 Grumman F–14A, 100(?)
McDonnell Douglas A–4F, L and M, 120(?) McDonnell
Douglas TA–4J, 580 McDonnell Douglas F–4J and N, 520
Vought A–7B, C, E and TA–7C, 100(?) Vought F–8H, J, K
and L.

Bombers:
approx 500 aircraft, inc 100(?) Douglas A–3B, EA–3B, KA–3B
and EKA–3B, 300 Grumman A–6A, C and E, 42 Grumman
EA–6B, 40(60?) Grumman KA–6D.

Reconnaissance and ECM aircraft:
approx 250 aircraft, inc 40 Grumman E–2B and C, Lockheed
C–130Q, 12 Lockheed EP–3E and WP–3A, Lockheed
EC–121K and M, Lockheed WC–121N, Rockwell (North
American) OV–10A, Rockwell (North American) RA–5C,
Vought RF–8G.

Maritime-reconnaissance and ASW aircraft:
approx 400 aircraft, 30 Grumman S–2E and G, 240 Lockheed
P–3B and C, 100 Lockheed S–3A.

Transports:
approx 300 aircraft, inc Convair C–131, Douglas C–47 and
C–117, 30 Douglas C–118 and VC–118, some Grumman
C–1A, 12 Grumman C–2A, Lockheed C–130, 12 McDonnell
Douglas C–9B, 14 Rockwell (North American) Sabre 40 and
60.

Liaison and AOP aircraft:
20 Piper U–11A.

Helicopters:
approx 1,160 machines, inc Bell TH–1L, Bell TH–57A, 100(?)
Bell UH–1K, L and N, 350(?) Boeing-Vertol CH–46D, E and F
plus UH–46D, 20(?) Kaman UH–43C, 30(?) Kaman UH–2C,
50(?) Kaman HH–2C and D, 20 Kaman SH–2D, 75 Kaman
SH–2F, 30 Sikorsky RH–3D, 270 Sikorsky SH–3A, D, G
and H.

Trainers:
approx 1,100 aircraft, inc Beechcraft T–34, Beechcraft
TC–45(?), Convair T–29, Grumman TC–4C, Grumman
TS–2A, Rockwell (North American) T–2B and C, 41 Rockwell
(North American) T–39D and CT–39E.
In addition, United States Naval aviation holds over approx
1,200(1,500?) mothballed aircraft in reserve, inc:

Fighters and strike-fighters:
McDonnell Douglas A–4, McDonnell Douglas F–4B, Vought
F–8.

Bombers:
Douglas A–3.

Reconnaissance aircraft:
Grumman E–1, Lockheed EC–121 and WC–121, McDonnell
Douglas RF–4B, Rockwell (North American) RA–5C, Vought
RF–8.

Maritime-reconnaissance and ASW aircraft:
Grumman HU–16, Grumman S–2, 150(?) Lockheed P–2 and
SP–2.

Transports:
Beechcraft C–45, Douglas C–47, Douglas C–54, Douglas C–117D, Grumman C–1A, Lockheed C–121.
Helicopters:
Bell UH–1, Sikorsky H–34(?).
Trainers:
Beechcraft T–34, Convair T–29, Grumman TF–9J, Lockheed T–1A, Lockheed T–33B, Rockwell (North American) T–2B.

Programme:
Formation of 11 further fighter squadrons with Grumman F–14A (a total of 301 delivered or on order). Introduction of the new McDonnell Douglas/Northrop F–18 fighter and strike-fighter currently being developed (185 fighters and 345 strike-fighters planned from 1980). Phasing out of McDonnell Douglas F–4 fighters and Vought A–7 strike-fighters. Acquisition of 336 McDonnell Douglas AV–8B strike-fighters (further development of Hawker Siddeley Harrier Mk.50) from 1981 under consideration. Replacement of Grumman TS–2A and TS–2B trainers by 61 Beechcraft T–44A from 1977–79.

Naval Air Reserve (NAR)
– men.
36 squadrons.
350 operational aircraft.
80 helicopters.

Organization
2 fighter squadrons with F–4B.
2 fighter squadrons with F–8J.
6 strike-fighter squadrons with A–7A and A–7B.
2 reconnaissance squadrons with RF–8G.
2 maritime-reconnaissance squadrons with E–1B and E–2.
10 maritime-reconnaissance and ASW squadrons with P–34.
2 maritime-reconnaissance and ASW squadrons with SP–2H.
2 transport squadrons with C–9B.
2 tanker squadrons with KA–3B.
3 helicopter squadrons with SH–3A and SH–3G.
1 helicopter squadron with HH–3.
2 helicopter squadrons with HH–1K.

Marine Corps 196,000 men.

Marine Corps Aviation
34,000 men.
59 squadrons.
580 operational aircraft.
480 helicopters.

Organization
12 strike-fighter squadrons with F–4B, F–4J and F–4N.
5 strike-fighter squadrons with A–4M.
3 strike-fighter squadrons with AV–8A.
5 bomber squadrons with A–6A and A–6E.
3 reconnaissance squadrons with EA–6A and RF–4B.
3 reconnaissance and ground-attack squadrons with OV–10A and OV–10D.
3 transport squadrons with KC–130F.
3 helicopter squadrons with AH–1J.
6 helicopter squadrons with UH–1E and UH–1N.
9 helicopter squadrons with CH–46E and CH–46F.
6 helicopter squadrons with CH–53A and CH–53D.
1 strike-trainer squadron with AV–8A, TAV–8A and TA–4F.
2 strike-trainer squadrons with TA–4F.
1 strike-trainer squadron with A–4M.
Fighter, bomber and transport squadrons each with 12, strike-fighter squadrons each with 16–20, and reconnaissance squadrons each with 14 aircraft; helicopter squadrons each with 18–21 machines

Major bases
MCAS (Marine Corps Air Station) Beaufort/S.C., MCAS Cherry Point/N.C., MCAS El Toro/Cal., MCAS Kanoehe/Hawaii, MCAS New River/N.C., MCAS Quantico/Va., MCAS Santa Ana/Cal., MCAS Yuma/Ariz.

Equipment
Fighters and strike-fighters:
90(60?) Hawker Siddeley AV–8A (Harrier Mk.50), 8 Hawker Siddeley TAV–8A (Harrier Mk.51), 110 McDonnell Douglas A–4M, 30 McDonnell Douglas TA–4F, 144 McDonnell Douglas F–4B, F–3J and F–4N.
Bombers:
60 Grumman A–6A and A–6E.
Reconnaissance aircraft:
21(23?) Grumman EA–6A, 21 McDonnell Douglas RF–4B, 36 North American OV–10A and OV–10D.
Transports:
20 Douglas C–117D, 36 Lockheed KC–130F, 2 McDonnell Douglas C–9B.
Helicopters:
80 Bell AH–1J, 126 Bell UH–1E and UH–1N, 162 Boeing-Vertol CH–46D and CH–46F, 108 Sikorsky CH–53A and CH–53D.
Trainers:
13 Rockwell T–2B.

Programme
Re-equipping 4 McDonnell Douglas F–4 strike-fighter squadrons with McDonnell Douglas F–18 (270 planned) from 1980. Acquisiton of 20 Lockheed KC–130R transports. Formation of further helicopter squadrons with Bell AH–1J (30 on order, further 40 planned), Bell AH–1T (57 attack helicopters on order, delivery 1978/79). Replacement of Sikorsky CH–53A and CH–53D helicopters by Sikorsky CH–53E.

Marine Corps Aviation Reserve
– men.
14 squadrons.
150(?) operational aircraft.
95(?) helicopters.

Organization
2 fighter squadrons with F–4B.
5 strike-fighter squadrons with A–4C, A–4E and A–4L.
1 reconnaissance and ground-attack squadron with OV–10A.
1 transport squadron with KC–130R.
1 helicopter squadron with AH–1G.
1 helicopter squadron with UH–1E.
2 helicopter squadrons with CH–46D.
1 helicopter squadron with CH–53A.

Coastguard 36,700 men.

Coastguard aviation
2,500 men.
– squadrons.
55 operational aircraft.
111 helicopters.

Organization
–.

Equipment
Maritime-reconnaissance aircraft:
34(41?) Grumman HU–16E.
Transports:
1 Grumman VC–4A, 1 Grumman VC–11A, 12 Lockheed HC–130B, 7 Lockheed HC–130H.
Helicopters:
50(?) Sikorsky HH–3F, 60(?) Sikorsky HH–52A.

Programme
Replacement of Grumman HU–16E maritime-reconnaissance aircraft by 41 Dassault Falcon 20G.

Aircraft factories
Beechcraft, Bell, Boeing, Boeing-Vertol, Cessna, Douglas (now merged with McDonnell), Fairchild Hiller, General Dynamics (Convair), Grumman, Helio, Hiller, Hughes, Kaman, Lockheed, McDonnell Douglas, Northrop, Piper, Rockwell International (earlier North American Rockwell), Sikorsky, Vought (earlier Ling Temco Vought, LTV).

Upper Volta

Air force (Force Aérienne de Haute–Volta)
men 50.
squadrons –.
operational aircraft 5.
Organization
–

Base
Quagadougou.
Military training aid from
France.
Equipment
Transports:
2 Aérospatiale N.262.
2 Douglas C–47.
1 Rockwell Commander 500B.
Liaison and AOP aircraft:
2 Max Holste M.H.1521M.
1 Reims-Cessna F.337.
Army 2,000 men

Uruguay

Air force (Fuerza Aérea Uruguaya)
men 2,000.
squadrons 3.
operational aircraft 30.
helicopters 4.
Organization
1 strike-fighter squadron with F–80C.
1 transport squadron with C–47.
1 transport squadron with F.27M.
1 liaison squadron with U–17A.
1 trainer squadron with T–6G and T–41D.
1 trainer squadron with T–33A.
Bases
Carrasco, Laguna del Sauce, Melilla.
Equipment
Fighters and strike-fighters:
6 Lockheed F–80C(?)
Transports:
2 Beechcraft Queen Air A–65.
12 Douglas C–47.
5 Embraer Bandeirante.
3 Fairchild Hiller FH–227B.
2 Fokker-VFW F.27M.
Liaison and AOP aircraft:
2 Cessna 182D Skylane.
6(10?) Cessna U–17A.
Helicopters:
2 Bell UH–1H.
2 Hiller OH–23F.
Trainers:
6 Cessna T–41D.
6 Lockheed T–33A.
10(20?) North American T–6G.
Army 16,000 men.
Navy 2,500 men.
Naval aviation (Aviacion Naval)
Maritime-reconnaissance and ASW aircraft:
3 Grumman S–2A.
3 Beechcraft C–45 transports.
2 Bell 47G helicopters.
3 Sikorsky SH–341 helicopters.
1 Beechcraft T–34B trainer.
3 North American T–6G trainers.

USSR

Air force (Voenno-Vozdushnye Sily, VVS)
men 550,000.
squadrons –
operational aircraft 10,500.
helicopters 2,000.
Organization
– fighter squadrons with MiG–17, MiG–19 and MiG–21.
– fighter squadrons with Su–9, Su–15 and MiG–25.
– fighter squadrons with Yak–25, Yak–28P and Tu–28.
– strike-fighter squadrons with MiG–17, MiG–21 and MiG–23.
– strike-fighter squadrons with Su–7, Su–17 and Su–19.
– bomber squadrons with Il–28 and Yak–28.
– bomber squadrons with Tu–20 and M–4.
– bomber squadrons with Tu–16 and Tu–22.
– bomber squadrons with Backfire.
– reconnaissance squadrons with Il–28R and Yak–28.
– reconnaissance squadrons with Tu–20.
– ECM squadrons with Il–14.
– transport squadrons with An–2 and An–28.
– transport squadrons with An–24, An–26 and Il–14.
– transport squadrons with An–12 and Il–18.
– transport squadrons with An–22 and Il–76.
– helicopter squadrons with Mi–1, Mi–2 and Mi–3.
– helicopter squadrons with Mi–6 and Mi–10.
– helicopter squadrons with Mi–24.
– trainer squadrons with Yak–11 and Yak–18.
– trainer squadrons with L–29, L–39 and MiG–15UTI.
Fighter, strike-fighter and reconnaissance squadrons each with 10–12, bomber squadrons each with 9 aircraft.
Bases
approx 500 airfields, inc approx 300 in European (Western) Russia and nearly 90 in northern latitudes.
Equipment
Fighters and strike-fighters:
approx 7,000(6,500?) aircraft, inc 1,000 Mikoyan MiG–17, and MiG–19, 2,200(?) Mikoyan MiG–21 and MiG–21U, 1,000 Mikoyan MiG–23, 400 Mikoyan MiG–25, 500 Sukhoi Su–7 and Su–7U, 750 Sukhoi Su–9 and Su–9U, 500 Sukhoi Su–15, Sukhoi Su–17, Sukhoi Su–19, Tupolev Tu–28, Yakovlev Yak–25, 300(?) Yakovlev Yak–28.
Bombers:
approx 1,500(1,800?) aircraft, inc Ilyushin Il–28 and Il–28U, 85 Myasischev M–4, 150 Tupolev Tu–16, 10 Tupolev Tu–20, 300 Tupolev Tu–22, 85 Tupolev Backfire, Yakovlev Yak 28 and Yak–28U.
Reconnaissance and ECM aircraft:
approx 300(500?) aircraft, inc Ilyushin Il–14, Ilyushin Il–28R, Tupolev Tu–20 and Tu–126, Yakovlev Yak–28.
Transports:
approx 1,700 aircraft, inc Antonov An–2, An–8, 400 Antonov An–12, 40 Antonov An–22, 300 An–24 and An–26, An–28, 200 Ilyushin Il–14, 400 Ilyushin Il–18, 20(?) Ilyushin Il–76, Lisunov Li–2. In addition there are approx 400 aircraft of the national airline Aeroflot available for military employment. These include Tupolev Tu–114, Tu–124, Tu–134, Tu–144, Tu–154 and Ilyushin Il–62.
Liaison and AOP aircraft:
approx 300(?) aircraft, inc Yakovlev Yak–12 and PZL–104.
Helicopters:
approx 2,000 machines, inc 500 Mil Mi–2 and Mi–3, Mil Mi–4, over 1,000 Mi–6, Mi–8 and Mi–10, Mil Mi–24. Of these, approx 1,200 are subordinated to the Shock Armies.
Trainers:
approx 4,500 aircraft, inc Aero L–29 and L–39, Mikoyan MiG–15UTI, Yakovlev Yak–11 and Yak–18.

Programme
Phasing out of Yakovlev Yak–25 and Tupolev Tu–28 fighters and of Ilyushin Il–28 bombers. Replacement of Mikoyan MiG–17 and MiG–19 fighters and strike-fighters by Mikoyan MiG–23 and MiG–25 and Sukhoi Su–17. Replacement of

Tupolev Tu–16 and Tu–22 bombers by Tupolev Backfire. Formation of further transport squadrons with Antonov An–22 and Ilyushin Il–76, and of further helicopter squadrons with Mil Mi–24.

Army 2,200,000 men.
Army aviation
approx 1,200 of the 2,000 Air Force helicopters are available to the Shock (assault) Armies.
Navy 500,000 men.
1 aircraft carrier.
2 helicopter carriers.
Naval aviation (Aiatsija-Voenno Morskovo Flota, AVMF)
80,000 men.
– squadrons.
780 operational aircraft.
250 helicopters.

Organization
– strike-fighter squadrons with Yak–36.
– bomber squadrons with Backfire.
– bomber squadrons with Tu–16 and Tu–22.
– bomber squadrons with Yak–28.
– reconnaissance squadrons with Tu–16.
– reconnaissance squadrons with Tu–20.
– maritime-reconnaissance and ASW squadrons with Be–6 and Be–12.
– maritime-reconnaissance and ASW squadrons with Il–38.
– helicopter squadrons with Ka–18, Ka–20 and Ka–25.
– helicopter squadrons with Mi–4 and Mi–8.

Equipment
Fighters and strike-fighters:
40(?) Yakovlev Yak–36.
Bombers:
some Ilyushin Il–28T.
180(280?) Tupolev Tu–16.
50 Tupolev Tu–22.
20(?) Tupolev Backfire.
40 Yakovlev Yak–28.
Reconnaissance and ECM aircraft:
90 Tupolev Tu–16.
50 Tupolev Tu–20.
Maritime-reconnaissance and ASW aircraft:
100 Beriev Be–12.
55(100?) Ilyushin Il–38.
Transports:
approx 150(200?) aircraft, inc Antonov An–12, An–24 and An–26, Ilyushin Il–14 and Il–18, Lisunov Li–2.
Helicopters:
approx 250 machines, inc Kamov Ka–15, Kamov Ka–18, Kamov Ka–20, Kamov Ka–25, 10 Mil Mi–4 and Mi–8.
Trainers:
approx 150 aircraft.

Programme
Second aircraft carrier commissioning 1978–79. The introduction of Yakovlev Yak–36 'Forger' V/STOL strike and reconnaissance fighter from 1976–77.

Missile troops
350,000 men.

Aircraft factories
Antonov (An), Beriev (Be), Ilyushin (Il), Kamov (Ka), Mikoyan-Gurevich (MiG), Mil (Mi), Myasichev, Sukhoi (Su), Tupolev (Tu), Yakovlev (Yak).

Venezuela
Air force (Fuerzas Aéreas Venezolanas)
men 8,000.
squadrons 10.
operational aircraft 135.
helicopters 33.

Organization
1 fighter squadron with F–86K.
1 strike-fighter squadron with Mirage IIIEV and Mirage 5–V.
1 strike-fighter squadron with CF–5A.
1 ground-attack squadron with OV–10E.
2 bomber squadrons with Canberra B.82 and B.(I)88.
1 transport squadron with C–123B.
1 transport squadron with C–130H, C–47 and C–54.
1 helicopter squadron with Alouette III.
1 helicopter squadron with UH–1D and UH–1H.
2 trainer squadrons with T–34.
2 trainer squadrons with T–2D.

Bases
Barcelona (Anzoátegui), Barquisimeto, Boca de Rio/Maracay, Caracas, Palo Negro.

Military training aid from
United States.

Equipment
Fighters and strike-fighters:
15 Canadair CF–5A.
2 Canadair CF–5D.
9 Dassault Mirage IIIEV.
4 Dassault Mirage 5–V.
2 Dassault Mirage 5–DV.
20 North American F–86K.
Ground-attack aircraft:
16 Rockwell (North American) OV–10E.
Bombers:
15 English Electric B.82.
8 English Electric Canberra B.(I)88.
2 English Electric Canberra T.84.
Reconnaissance aircraft:
2 English Electric Canberra PR.83.
Transports:
1 Boeing 737–200S.
approx 15 Douglas C–47.
3 Douglas C–54.
12 Fairchild C–123B.
1 Hawker Siddeley H.S.748.
5 Lockheed C–130H.
Liaison and AOP aircraft:
6 Beechcraft Queen Air B80.
2 Cessna 180.
12 Cessna 182N.
1 Cessna 500.
Helicopters:
15 Aérospatiale Alouette III.
6(?) Bell 47G.
12 Bell UH–1D and UH–1H.
Trainers:
approx 65 aircraft, inc 12 BAC Jet Provost T.52, 25 Beechcraft T–34, 24 Rockwell (North American) T–2D.

Programme
Formation of further transport squadrons with 12 CASA C.212. Phasing out of Bell 47G helicopters and BAC Jet Provost T.52 trainers.

Army 28,000 men.
Army aviation
approx 20 helicopters: 15 Aérospatiale Alouette III, some (3?) Bell 47G.
Navy 8,000 men.
Naval aviation
– men.
1 squadron.
12 operational aircraft.
2 helicopters.
Organization
1 maritime-reconnaissance and ASW squadron with S–2E.

Equipment
Maritime-reconnaissance and ASW aircraft:
4 Grumman HU–16.
6(?) Grumman S–2E.
Transports:
2 Douglas C–47.
Liaison and AOP aircraft:
2(?) Cessna 337.
Helicopters:
2 Bell 47J.

Vietnam
Air force
men 12,000.
squadrons 19.
operational aircraft 210.
helicopters 30.
Organization
4 fighter squadrons with MiG–21.
2 fighter squadrons with F–6 (MiG–19).
6 strike-fighter squadrons with MiG–17F and PF, plus Su–7.
1 bomber squadron with Il–28.
1 transport squadron with An–2.
2 transport squadrons with Il–12, Il–14 and Li–2.
2 helicopter squadrons with Mi–4.
1 helicopter squadron with Mi–6.
– trainer squadrons with Yak–11.
– trainer squadrons with MiG–15UTI.
Fighter and strike-fighter squadrons each with 10–12 aircraft.
Bases
Bai Thuong, Bien Hoa, Binh Thuy, Cam Ranh Bay, Chulai, Dalat, Da Nang, Dien Bien Phu, Dong Hoi, Gia Lam, Hoa Lac, Kep Na San, Nha Trang, Phan Rang, Phuc Yen, Pleiku, Quang Lang, Qui Nhon, Tanh Sonh Nhut (Saigon), Vinh.
Military training aid from
Soviet Union.
Equipment
Fighters and strike-fighters:
70 Mikoyan MiG–17F and PF.
50 Mikoyan MiG–21 and MiG–21U.
25 Shenyang F–8 (Mikoyan MiG–19).
Bombers:
8 Ilyushin Il–28.
Transports:
20 Antonov An–2.
4 Antonov An–24.
some Ilyushin Il–12.
12 Ilyushin Il–14.
some Lisunov Li–2.
1 Ilyushin Il–18.
Helicopters:
some Mil Mi–1.
20 Mil Mi–4.
5 Mil Mi–6.
Trainers:
approx 30(40?) aircraft, inc 10(?) Mikoyan MiG–15UTI, Yakovlev Yak–11, Yakovlev Yak–18.
In addition, there are the aircraft captured from the former South Vietnamese Air Force in April 1975, inc
Fighters and strike-fighters:
51(37?) Northrop F–5A and B.
27 Northrop F–5E.
Ground-attack aircraft:
76(113?) Cessna A–37A and B.
26 Douglas A–1E, G, H and J.
Night ground-support aircraft:
10(?) Douglas AC–47.
37 Fairchild AC–119G and K.
Reconnaissance and ECM aircraft:
some (5?) Douglas EC–47.
9 Northrop RF–5A.
Transports:
32 de Havilland Canada DHC–4.
13(20?) Douglas C–47.
8 Fairchild C–119G.
23(10?) Lockheed C–130A.
Liaison and AOP aircraft:
183 aircraft, inc 111(114?) Cessna O–1, Cessna O–2, Cessna T–41, Cessna U–17, 33 de Havilland Canada DHC–2.
Helicopters:
approx 400(430?) Bell UH–1B, D and H.
29(32?) Boeing-Vertol CH–47C.
It is uncertain how many of these aircraft can be put into service.

Yemen Arab Republic (North)
Air force
men 1,600.
squadrons 2.
operational aircraft 25(?).
helicopters 10(?).
Organization
1 strike-fighter squadron with MiG–17F.
1 bomber squadron with Il–28.
Bases
Hodeida, Sana, Taiz.
Military training aid from
Egypt, Soviet Union.
Equipment
Fighters and strike-fighters:
10–12 Mikoyan MiG–17F.
Bombers:
6–8 Ilyushin Il–28.
Transports:
some Douglas C–47 and Ilyushin Il–14.
2 Short Skyvan 3M.
Helicopters:
some Agusta-Bell AB.205(?), Mil Mi–1 and Mil Mi–4.
Trainers:
some Yakovlev Yak–11 and 4(?) Mikoyan MiG–15UTI.
Programme
Replacement of Mikoyan MiG–17 strike-fighters by Mikoyan MiG–21?
Army 15,000 men.
Navy 300 men.

Yugoslavia
Air force (Jugoslovensko Ratno Vazduhoplovstvo)
men 20,000.
squadrons 25.
operational aircraft 350.
helicopters 70.
Organization
6 fighter squadrons with MiG–21F and MiG–21PF.
2 fighter squadrons with F–86D and F–86E(M).
1 strike-fighter squadron with F–84G.
6 ground-attack squadrons with Jastreb.
2 ground-attack squadrons with Kraguj.
2 reconnaissance squadrons with RT–33A and Jastreb.
1 transport squadron with C–47.
1 transport squadron with Il–14.
– liaison squadrons with UTVA–60 and UTVA–66.
1 helicopter squadron with Alouette III.
1 helicopter squadron with S.A.341.
1 helicopter squadron with Mi–4.
1(2?) helicopter squadron with Mi–8.
– trainer squadrons with Aero 2 and Aero 3.

– trainer squadrons with Galeb and T–33A.
Fighter, strike-fighter, ground-attack and reconnaissance
  squadrons each with 12–15 aircraft.
Major bases
Agram, Batajnica (Belgrade), Cattaro, Cerklje, Laibach,
  Mostar, Neusatz, Niksic, Nish, Pleso, Pola, Salusani,
  Sarajevo, Skopje, Sombor, Titograd, Tuzla, Vrsac (Werschitz),
  Zemun.
Military training aid from
Soviet Union(?).
Equipment
Fighters and strike-fighters:
80(100?) Mikoyan MiG–21F and MiG–21PF.
some Mikoyan MiG–21U.
30(?) North American F–86D and F–86E(M).
some (10?) Republic F–84G.
Ground-attack aircraft:
95 Soko J–1 Jastreb.
20(15?) Soko P–2 Kraguj.
Reconnaissance aircraft:
15 Lockheed RT–33A.
some North American RF–86F.
20 Soko J–2 Jastreb.
Transports:
1 Aérospatiale S.E.210 Caravelle.
15 Douglas C–47.
4 Douglas DC–6B.
12 Ilyushin Il–14.
1 Ilyushin Il–18.
some Li–2(?).
3 Yakovlev Yak–40.
Liaison and AOP aircraft:
some Cijan Kurir, de Havilland Canada DHC–2, L–60,
  UTVA–60 and UTVA–66, Yakovlev Yak–12A.
Helicopters:
20 Aérospatiale Alouette III.
20 Aérospatiale S.A.341H.
15 Mil Mi–4.
12(25?) Mil Mi–8.
some (10?) Westland Whirlwind 2.
Trainers:
approx 150 aircraft, inc Aero 2, 40(?) Aero 3, 30 Lockheed
  T–33A, 60 Soko G–2A Galeb and some Type 214–D.
Programme
Replacement of North American F–86D and F–86E(M)
  fighters by Mikoyan MiG–21. Phasing out of Republic
  F–84G strike-fighters and introduction of the joint
  Romanian–Yugoslav developed Orao (Jurom) trainer and
  ground-attack aircraft from 1977–78. Formation of further
  helicopter squadrons with Aérospatiale S.A.341H (112
  Yugoslav licence-built aircraft (by Soko) delivered or on order
  from 1974/75).
Army 190,000 men.
Navy 20,000 men.
Naval aviation
some Kamov Ka–25 and Mil Mi–8 helicopters.
Aircraft factories
Soko (Preduzece Soko), UTVA (Fabrika Aviona UTVA).

Zaire
Air force (Force Aérienne Zaïroise)
men 3,000.
squadrons 9.
operational aircraft 64.
helicopters 45.
Organization
1 strike-fighter squadron with Mirage 5–Z.
1 ground-attack squadron with MB.326GB.

1 transport squadron with C–47.
1 transport squadron with DHC–5D.
1 transport squadron with C–54 and C–130H.
1 helicopter squadron with Alouette III.
2 helicopter squadrons with S.A.330.
1 trainer squadron with T–6G and T–28D.
1 trainer squadron with Cessna 150.
2 trainer squadrons with SF.260MC.
Major bases
Kamina, Kinshasa, Kinsangani, Kolwezi.
Military training aid from
Italy.
Equipment
Fighters and strike-fighters:
15 Dassault Mirage 5–Z.
2 Dassault Mirage 5–ZD.
Ground-attack aircraft:
20(17?) Aermacchi MB.326GB.
Transports:
6 de Havilland Canada DHC–5D.
9 Douglas C–47.
4 Douglas C–54.
1 Douglas DC–6.
5 Lockheed C–130H.
2 Mitsubishi MU–2J.
Liaison and AOP aircraft:
2 Dornier Do–27.
15 Cessna 310R.
Helicopters:
15 Aérospatiale Alouette III.
23 Aérospatiale S.A.330.
some Bell 47G.
Trainers:
15 Cessna 150 Aerobat.
6 North American T–6G.
5 North American T–28D.
20 SIAI-Marchetti SF.260MC.
Army 40,000 men.
Navy 400 men.

Zambia
Air force (Zambia Air Force)
men 1,000.
squadrons 7.
operational aircraft 56.
helicopters 32.
Organization
2 ground-attack squadrons with MB.326GB.
1 ground-attack squadron with Jastreb.
1 transport squadron with Do–28D.
1 transport squadron with DHC–4 and C–47.
1 liaison squadron with DHC–2 and Pembroke C.1.
2 helicopter squadrons with AB.205.
1 trainer squadron with SF.260MZ.
Bases
Balovale, Lusaka, Mbala (Abercorn), Mumbwa, Siluwe.
Military training aid from
Italy.
Equipment
Ground-attack aircraft:
18 Aermacchi MB.326GB.
4 Soko J–1 Jastreb.
Transports:
4 de Havilland Canada DHC–4.
6 de Havilland Canada DHC–5.
10 Dornier Do–28D.
10 Douglas C–47.

1 Hawker Siddeley H.S.748.
2 Hunting Pembroke C.1.
Liaison and AOP aircraft:
5 de Havilland Canada DHC–2.
Helicopters:
25 Agusta-Bell AB.205.

1 Agusta-Bell AB.212.
6(?) Mil Mi–6.
Trainers:
8 SIAI-Marchetti SF.260MZ.
2 Soko G–2A Galeb.
Army 5,000 men.

Aircraft

FMA I.A.35 'Huanquero'.

Type: Navigation trainer (Type IA).
Weights:
empty 7,716lb (3,500kg).
normal 12,566lb (5,700kg).
Performance:
maximum speed at 9,843ft (3,000m)
  225mph (362km/hr).
maximum cruising speed at 9,843ft
  (3,000m) 217mph (350km/hr).
range 975 miles (1,570km).
ferry range 1,317 miles (2,120km).
initial rate of climb 16.4ft/sec
  (5.0m/sec).
service ceiling 20,998ft (6,400m).
Dimensions:
wing span 64ft 3in (19.60m).
length overall 45ft 10¼in (13.98m).
height overall 12ft 1½in (3.70m).
wing area 452.1sq ft (42.00sq m).
Power plant: Two 620hp I.A.19R El
  Indio piston engines.
Armament:
Type IB: Two 12.7mm machine-guns,

max underwing weapon load 440lb
  (200kg) e.g. four 110lb (50kg) bombs
  or rockets.
Payload:
Type IA: 3 man crew, 4 trainees and 1
  instructor.
Type II: 3 man crew and 7 troops or
  freight.
Variants:
Type IB: Bombing/gunnery trainer with
  uprated (750hp) engines.
Type IV: Photo-reconnaissance aircraft.
First flights:
Prototype: 21 September 1953.
First production model: 27 March 1957.
Production: 31 built of all variants
  1956–65.
In service: Argentina.

FMA I.A.50 'Guarani II'.
Type: Light transport.
Weights:
empty 8,650lb (3,924kg).
maximum 17,085lb (7,750kg).

Performance:
maximum speed at sea level 310mph
  (500km/h).
maximum cruising speed 305mph
  (491km/h).
range w.m.p. 1,240 miles (1,995km).
ferry range 1,600 miles (2,575km).
initial rate of climb 43.9ft/sec
  (13.4m/sec).
service ceiling 41,000ft (12,500m).
Dimensions:
wing span 64ft 3¼in (19.59m).
length overall 50ft 2¼in (15.30m).
height overall 18ft 5in (5.61m).
wing area 450sq ft (41.81sq m).
Power plant: Two 930hp Turboméca
  Bastan VI–A turboprops.
Payload: 2 man crew and 10–15
  troops or max 3,300lb (1,500kg)
  freight.
First flights:
Prototype: 23 April 1963.
Production: 2 prototypes, 1
  pre-production and 28(38?) production

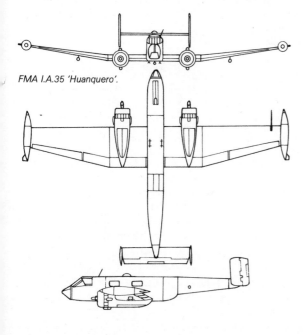

FMA I.A.35 'Huanquero'.

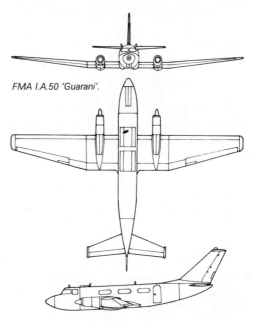

FMA I.A.50 'Guarani'.

models 1966–71.

In service: Argentina.

FMA I.A.58 'Pucara'.

Type: Two-seat light ground-attack aircraft.

Weights:
empty 7,826lb (3,550kg).
maximum 13,668lb (6,200kg).

Performance:
maximum speed at 9,840ft (3,000m) 323mph (520km/hr).
maximum cruising speed at 9,840ft (3,000m) 300mph (485km/hr).
ferry range 1,890 miles (3,040km).
initial rate of climb 59.1ft/sec (18.0m/sec).
service ceiling 27,170ft (8,280m).

Dimensions:
wing span 47ft 6¾in (14.50m).
length overall 45ft 7½in (13.90m).
height overall 17ft 2¼in (5.24m).
wing area 326.1sq ft (30.30sq m).

Power plant: Two 1,022hp Turboméca Astazou XVIG turboprops.

Armament: Two 20mm Hispano cannon and four 7.62mm FN machine-guns and max 2,200lb (1,000kg) weapon load on 3 hard points.

First flights:
Prototype: 20 August 1969.

Production: 2 prototypes, series production from 1973, over 80 delivered or on order to date.

In service: Argentina.

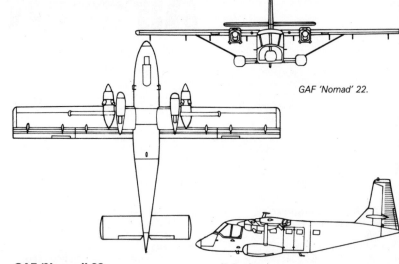

GAF 'Nomad' 22.

GAF 'Nomad' 22.

Type: Light transport.

Weights:
empty 4,360lb (2,100kg).
maximum 8,000lb (3,629kg).

Performance:
maximum speed at sea level 213mph (341km/hr).
maximum cruising speed at 10,000ft (3,050m) 200mph (322km/hr).
range with 1,600lb (726kg) payload 200mph (322km/hr).
initial rate of climb 25.0ft/sec

(7.6m/sec).
service ceiling 24,000ft (7,315m).

Dimensions:
wing span 54ft 0in (16.46m).
length overall 41ft 2½in (12.56m).
height overall 17ft 11¼in (5.47m).
wing area 320.0sq ft (29.70sq m).

Power plant: Two 416hp Allison 250–B17 turboprops.

Armament: Weapon load on 4 hard points, e.g. two-four weapon packs each containing one 7.62mm Minigun with 1,500rpg or four rocket launchers

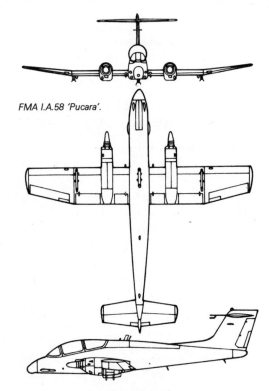

FMA I.A.58 'Pucara'.

Aerotec 122 'Uirapuru' (T–23).

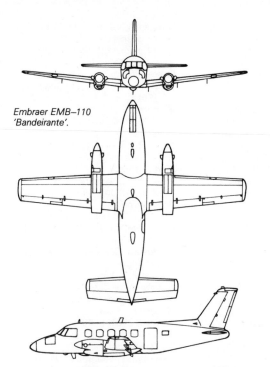

Embraer EMB–110 'Bandeirante'.

Neiva C–42 'Regente'.

each containing seven 70mm rockets or two rocket launchers each containing nineteen 70mm rockets.
Payload: 2 man crew and 13 troops or max 3,110lb (1,410kg) freight.
Variants:
Nomad 24: Civil variant with lengthened fuselage.
Nomad Mission Master: Maritime-reconnaissance aircraft.
First flights:
Prototype: 23 July 1971.
Production:
2 prototypes, series production from 1973, 20 delivered or on order to date.
Nomad Mission Master: 6 built 1975.
In service: Australia, Peru, Philippines. Mission Master: Indonesia.

Aerotec 122 'Uirapuru' (T–23).
Type: Two-seat trainer.
Weights:
empty 1,190lb (540kg).
maximum 1,852lb (840kg).
Performance:
maximum speed at sea level 140mph (225km/hr).
maximum cruising speed at 4,987ft (1,520m) 115mph (185km/hr).
ferry range 497 miles (800km).
initial rate of climb 13.1ft/sec (4.0m/sec).
service ceiling 14,763ft (4,500m).
Dimensions:
wing span 27ft 10¾in (8.50m).
length overall 21ft 7¾in (6.60m).
height overall 8ft 10¼in (2.70m).
wing area 145sq ft (13.50sq m).
Power plant: One 160hp Lycoming O–320–B2B piston engine.

First flights:
Prototype: 2 June 1965.
Production: Series production from 1968, 110 delivered or on order.
In service: Bolivia, Brazil, Paraguay.

Embraer EMB–110 'Bandeirante'.
Type: Light transport.
Weights:
empty 7,054lb (3,200kg).
maximum 11,680lb (5,300kg).
Performance:
maximum speed at 9,840ft (3,000m) 282mph (454km/h).
maximum cruising speed at 9,840ft (3,000m) 260mph (418km/h).
ferry range 1,275 miles (2,050km).
initial rate of climb 32.8ft/sec (10.0m/sec).
service ceiling 24,930ft (7,600m).
Dimensions:
wing span 50ft 2¼in (15.30m).
length overall 46ft 8½in (14.22m).
height overall 15ft 6in (4.73m).
wing area 312.13sq ft (29.00sq m).
Power plant: Two 680hp Pratt & Whitney PT6A–27 turboprops.
Payload: 2 man crew and 12 troops or 4 stretcher cases and 2 medics.
Variants:
EMB–110B: Photographic survey aircraft (RC–95).
EMB–110K: Later series with fuselage lengthened by 2ft 7½in (0.80m).
EMB–111: Maritime-reconnaissance version, two 750hp Pratt & Whitney PT6A–34 turboprops, range 1,750 miles (2,815km).
EMB–120: Planned further development, transport.

First flights:
Prototype: 26 October 1968.
First production model: 15 August 1972.
Production:
3 prototypes; series production from 1972, 115 delivered or on order to date, further 70 planned.
EMB–111: 16 from 1978.
In service:
EMB–110: Brazil (C–95), Chile, Uruguay.
EMB–111: Brazil.

Neiva C–42 'Regente'.
Type: Liaison aircraft.
Weights:
empty 1,410lb (640kg).
maximum 2,293lb (1,040kg).
Performance:
maximum speed at sea level 137mph (220km/hr).
maximum cruising speed at 5,000ft (1,500m) 132mph (212km/hr).
ferry range 576 miles (928km).
initial rate of climb 11.5ft/sec (3.5m/sec).
service ceiling 11,812ft (3,600m).
Dimensions:
wing span 29ft 11½in (9.13m).
length overall 23ft 3in (7.21m).
height overall 9ft 7¼in (2.93m).
wing area 144.8sq ft (13.45sq m).
Power plant: One 210hp Continental IO–360–D piston engine.
Payload: 1 man crew and 3 troops.
First flights:
Prototype: 7 September 1961.
C–42: February 1965.
Production: 80 built 1965–68.
In service: Brazil.

Neiva L–42 'Regente'.
Type: AOP aircraft.
Details as for C–42 with the following
 exceptions:
Weights:
empty 1,623lb (736kg).
Performance:
maximum speed at sea level 153mph
 (246km/hr).
maximum cruising speed at 5,000ft
 (1,500m) 142mph (229km/hr).
ferry range 590 miles (950km).
initial rate of climb 15.4ft/sec
 (4.7m/sec).
service ceiling 15,750ft (4,800m).
Power plant: One 180hp Lycoming
 O–360–A1D piston engine.
Payload: 2 crew (and 1 casualty).
First flights: October 1967.
Production: 40 built 1967–70.
In service: Brazil.

Neiva T–25 'Universal'.
Type: Two/three-seat trainer.
Weights:
empty 2,425lb (1,100kg).
normal 3,085lb (1,400kg).
maximum 3,750lb (1,700kg).
Performance:
maximum speed at 5,000ft (1,500m)
 190mph (306km/h).
maximum speed at sea level 184mph
 (296km/h).
radius of action 447 miles (720km).
ferry range 930 miles (1,500km).
initial rate of climb 17.4ft/sec
 (5.3m/sec).
service ceiling 16,400ft (5,000m).
Dimensions:
wing span 36ft 1in (11.00m).
length overall 28ft 2½in (8.60m).
height overall 10ft 2in (3.10m).
wing area 183sq ft (17.00sq m).
Power plant: One 300hp Lycoming
 IO–540–K1D5 piston engine.
Variants:
Universal II: Light trainer and
 ground-support aircraft; 150 planned.
First flights:
Prototype: 29 April 1966.
Production: 142(132?) built 1970–75.
In service: Brazil, Chile.

Canadair CL–28 'Argus' Mk. 2.
Type: Maritime-reconnaissance and
 ASW aircraft, 15 man crew.
Weights:
empty 81,000lb (36,742kg).
normal 148,000lb (67,133kg).
Performance:
maximum speed at 20,000ft (6,100m)
 317mph (507km/hr).
patrol speed under 985ft (300m)
 190mph (305km/hr).
maximum cruising speed at 5,000ft
 (1,525m) 230mph (370km/hr).
range 4,040 miles (6,500km).
ferry range 5,900 miles (9,500km).
initial rate of climb 28.2ft/sec

(8.6m/sec).
service ceiling 20,000ft (6,100m).
Dimensions:
wing span 142ft 3½in (43.37m).
length overall 128ft 2¾in (39.09m).
height overall 36ft 8½in (11.19m).
wing area 2,075sq ft (192.77sq m).
Power plant: Four 3,700hp Wright
 R–3350TC981–EA–1 piston engines.
Armament: Max 7,990lb (3,630kg)
 weapon load in two fuselage bays;
 e.g. depth-charges, homing torpedoes
 and mines plus max 7,600lb (3,447kg)
 weapon load on underwing hard
 points; e.g. homing torpedoes, rockets
 and bombs.
Variants: Argus Mk.1: Earlier version.
First flights:
Prototype: 28 March 1957.
Production:
Series production 1958–60;
Argus Mk.1: 13 built.
Argus Mk.2: 20 built.
In service: Canada (CP–107).

Canadair CL–41A 'Tutor'.
Type: Two-seat trainer.
Weights:
empty 4,872lb (2,210kg).
normal 7,397lb (3,355kg).
Performance:
maximum speed at 28,500ft (8,700m)
 498mph (801km/hr).
range 945 miles (1,520km).
ferry range 1,342 miles (2,160km).
initial rate of climb 70.5ft/sec
 (21.5m/sec).
time to 15,000ft (4,570m) 4min 33sec.
service ceiling 43,000ft (13,100m).
Dimensions:

wing span 36ft 5½in (11.11m).
length overall 32ft 0¼in (9.76m).
height overall 8ft 9½in (2.86m).
wing area 220sq ft (20.44sq m).
Power plant: One Orenda
 J85–Can–40 turbojet rated at 2,635lb
 (1,195kg) st.
Variants:
CL–41G: Trainer and light ground-attack
 aircraft.
CL–41R: CL–41A fitted with
 nose-section of CF–104 strike-fighter.
First flights:
CL–41A: 13 January 1960.
CL–41R: 13 July 1962.
Production:
CL–41A: 190 built 1962–66.
In service: CL–41A: Canada (CT–114).

Canadair CL–41G.
Type: Trainer and light ground-support
 aircraft.
Details as for CL–41A with the
 following exceptions:
Weights:
empty 5,290lb (2,400kg).
maximum 11,312lb (5,131kg).
Performance:
maximum speed at 28,500ft (8,700m)
 480mph (774km/h).
service ceiling 52,000ft (12,800m).
Power plant: One General Electric
 J85–J4 turbojet rated at 2,950lb
 (1,340kg) st.
Armament: Max 3,500lb (1,588kg)
 weapon load on 6 hard points, e.g.
 weapon packs and bombs.
First flights: CL–41G: June 1964.
Production: 20 built 1967–69.
In service: Malaysia (Tebuan).

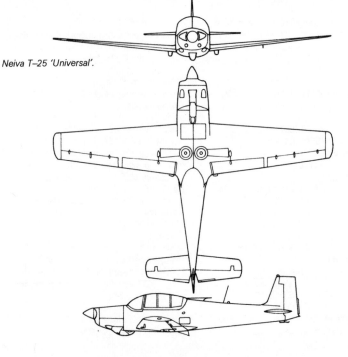

Neiva T–25 'Universal'.

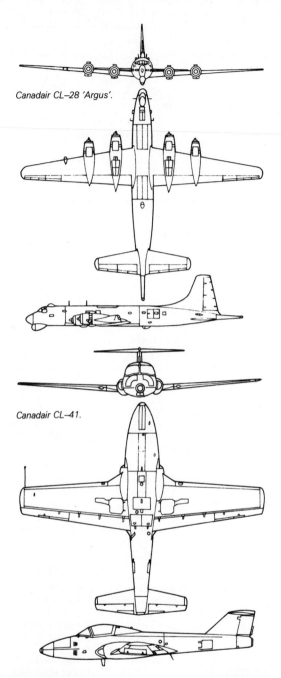

Canadair CL–28 'Argus'.

Canadair CL–215.

Canadair CL–41.

De Havilland Canada
DHC–1 'Chipmunk'.

Canadair CL–215.
Type: ASR, fire-fighting, light transport amphibian.
Weights:
empty 27,660lb (12,587kg).
normal 37,700lb (17,100kg).
maximum 43,500lb (19,731kg).
Performance:
maximum cruising speed at 10,000ft (3,050m) 180 mph (291km/h).
range 1,150 miles (1,850km).
ferry range 1,395 miles (2,260km).
initial rate of climb 16.67ft/sec (5.08m/sec).

Dimensions:
wing span 93ft 10in (28.60m).
length overall 65ft 0½in (19.82m).
height overall 29ft 2⅜in (8.91m).
wing area 1,076.4sq ft (100.00sq m).
Power plant: Two 2,100/1,800hp Pratt & Whitney R–2800 piston engines.
Payload: 2 man crew and 36 troops or 12 stretcher cases or max 1,200gals (5,443l) water or max 6,800lb (3,085kg) freight.
First flights:
Prototype: 23 October 1967.
Production: Series production from

1968, over 65 delivered or on order to date.
In service: Algeria, Canada, France, Greece, Spain.

De Havilland Canada DHC–1 'Chipmunk'.
Type: Two-seat trainer.
Weights:
empty 1,425lb (647kg).
normal 2,015lb (914kg).
maximum 2,100lb (953kg).
Performance:
maximum speed at sea level 125mph

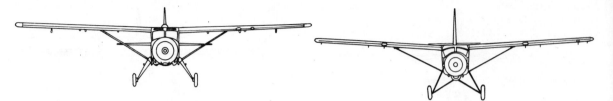

De Havilland Canada DHC–2 Beaver'.　　　　　　　De Havilland Canada DHC–3 'Otter'.

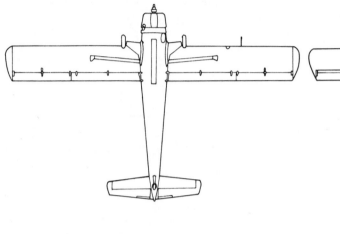

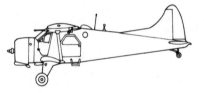

(222km/hr).
maximum cruising speed 120mph
  (192km/hr).
ferry range 490 miles (780km)(?).
initial rate of climb 14.1ft/sec
  (4.3m/sec).
service ceiling 15,810ft (4,820m).
Dimensions:
wing span 34ft 4½in (10.47m).
length overall 25ft 5in (7.75m).
height overall 7ft 0in (2.13m).
wing area 173.2sq ft (16.10sq m).
Power plant: One 145hp Bristol
  Siddeley (D.H.) Gipsy Major 8 piston
  engine.
First flights:
Prototype: 22 May 1946.
Production: 1,292 built 1946–59, inc
  218 licence-built in Canada and 60
  Portuguese licence-built by OGMA
  1955–59.
In service: Burma(?), Great Britain
  (T.10, T.20), Eire, Lebanon, Portugal,
  Sri Lanka.

**De Havilland Canada DHC–2
'Beaver'.**

Type: Liaison aircraft.
Weights:
empty 2,850lb (1,293kg).
maximum 5,100lb (2,313kg).
Performance:
maximum speed at sea level 140mph
  (225km/hr).
maximum speed at 5,000ft (1,530m)
  163mph (262km/hr).
maximum cruising speed at 5,000ft
  (1,530m) 143mph (230km/hr).
range 453 miles (730km).
ferry range 733 miles (1,180km).
initial rate of climb 17.0ft/sec
  (5.2m/sec).
service ceiling 18,000ft (5,490m).
Dimensions:
wing span 47ft 11½in (14.63m).
length overall 30ft 3in (9.22m).
height overall 8ft 11¾in (2.74m).
wing area 250sq ft (23.20sq m).
Power plant: One 450hp Pratt &
  Whitney R–985–AN–1 or –3 Wasp
  piston engine.
Payload: 1–2 man crew and 4 troops.
Variants: Floatplane version: DHC–2
  Mk.II Turbo-Beaver. Further

development with one 578hp Pratt &
  Whitney turboprop.
First flights:
Prototype: 16 August 1947.
Turbo-Beaver: 30 December 1963.
Production: 1,657 built 1954–67, inc
  968 U–6A (new designation for
  L–20A).
Turbo-Beaver: Limited number 1964.
In service: Argentina, Austria, Canada,
  Colombia, Dominican Republic, Great
  Britain (Beaver AL.1), Iran, Kenya,
  Laos, Pakistan, South Yemen, Turkey,
  USA (U–6A), Uruguay, Yugoslavia,
  Zambia.

**De Havilland Canada DHC–3
'Otter'.**
Type: Light transport.
Weights:
empty 4,431lb (2,010kg).
maximum 8,000lb (3,629kg).
Performance:
maximum speed at 5,000ft (1,530m)
  160mph (257km/hr).
maximum cruising speed at 5,000ft
  (1,530m) 138mph (222km/hr).

range 944 miles (1,520km).
initial rate of climb 12.1ft/sec
(3.7m/sec).
service ceiling 18,800ft (5,730m).
Dimensions:
wing span 18ft 1½in (17.69m).
length overall 41ft 10in (12.75m).
height overall 12ft 7in (3.84m).
wing area 374.5sq ft (34.80sq m).
Power plant: One 600hp Pratt &
Whitney R–1340–S1H1–G or
R–1340–S3H1–G piston engine.
Payload: 2 man crew and 10 troops or
6 stretcher cases and 4 medics.
Variants:
Ski- or floatplane versions.
First flights:
Prototype: 12 December 1951.
Production: 460 built 1955–66, inc 176
U–1A and 17 U–1B.
In service: Australia, Bangladesh(?),
Burma, Cambodia, Canada, Colombia,
India, Indonesia, Panama, Paraguay,
USA (U–1A, U–1B).

De Havilland Canada DHC–4A 'Caribou'.
Type: Light STOL transport.
Weights:
empty 16,976lb (7,700kg).
normal 28,500lb (12,928kg).
maximum 31,300lb (14,197kg).
Performance:
maximum speed at 6,500ft (1,980m)

216mph (347km/hr).
maximum cruising speed at 7,500ft
(2,285m) 182mph (293km/hr).
range w.m.p. 242 miles (390km).
ferry range 1,307 miles (2,103km).
initial rate of climb 22.6ft/sec
(6.9m/sec).
service ceiling 24,800ft (7,560m).
Dimensions:
wing span 95ft 7½in (29.15m).
length overall 72ft 7in (22.13m).
height overall 31ft 9in (9.70m).
wing area 912sq ft (84.72sq m).
Power plant: Two 1,450hp Pratt &
Whitney R–2000–7M2 piston engines.
Payload: 2–3 man crew and 32 troops
or 26 paratroops or 22 stretcher cases
and 8 medics or max 8,818lb (4,000kg)
freight.
First flights:
Prototype: 30 July 1958.
Production: 307 built 1959–73.
In service: Abu Dhabi, Australia,
Cameroun, Canada (CC–108), India,
Kenya, Kuwait, Malaysia, Spain (T–9),
Tanzania, Taiwan, Uganda, USA
(CV–2A, B; now C–7A, B), Vietnam(?),
Zambia.

De Havilland Canada DHC–5 'Buffalo'.
Type: Medium STOL transport.
Weights:
empty 22,899lb (10,387kg).

normal 41,000lb (18,597kg).
maximum 45,100lb (20,457kg).
Performance:
maximum speed at 10,000ft (3,050m)
282mph (454km/hr).
maximum cruising speed 253mph
(407km/hr).
range w.m.p. 518 miles (834km).
range with 7,900lb (3,600kg) payload
1,600 miles (2,575km).
ferry range 2,218 miles
(3,570km).
initial rate of climb 34.8ft/sec
(10.6m/sec).
service ceiling 31,500ft (9,600m).
Dimensions:
wing span 96ft 0in (29.26m).
length overall 79ft 0in (24.08m).
height overall 28ft 8in (8.73m).
wing area 945sq ft (87.80sq m).
Power plant: Two 3,055hp General
Electric CT64–820–1 turboprops.
Payload: 3 man crew and 41 troops or
35 paratroops or 24 stretcher cases
and 6 medics or max 14,109lb
(6,400kg) freight.
Variants:
DHC–5D: Later, improved series, max
18,000lb (8,165kg) freight.
First flights:
Prototype: 9 April 1964.
Production: 59 built 1967–71.
In service: Brazil, Canada, (CC–115),
Peru, Spain, USA (C–8A).

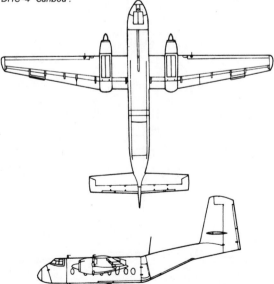

*De Havilland Canada
DHC–4 'Caribou'.*

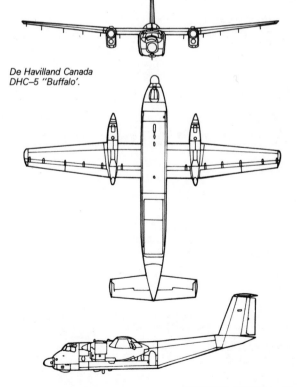

*De Havilland Canada
DHC–5 "Buffalo".*

De Havilland Canada DHC–5D.

Type: Medium STOL transport.
Details as for DHC–5 with the following exceptions:
Weights:
empty 24,800lb (11,249kg).
maximum 49,200lb (22,317kg).
Performance:
maximum speed at 10,000ft (3,050m) 288mph (463km/hr).
range w.m.p. 400 miles (648km).
ferry range 2,040 miles (3,280km).
initial rate of climb 36.7ft/sec (11.2m/sec).
Power plant: Two 3,095hp General Electric CT64–820–1 turboprops.
Production: 19 built 1974–76.
In service: Congo, Ecuador, Togo, Zambia.

De Havilland Canada DHC–6 'Twin Otter' Series 300.

Type: Light transport.
Weights:
empty 7,230lb (3,180kg).
maximum 12,500lb (5,670kg).
Performance:
maximum cruising speed at 10,000ft (3,050m) 210mph (338km/hr).

range with 3,220lb (1,474kg) payload 744 miles (1,198km).
initial rate of climb 26.6ft/sec (8.1m/sec).
service ceiling 26,700ft (8,138m).
Dimensions:
wing span 65ft 0in (19.81m).
length overall 51ft 9in (15.77m).
height overall 18ft 7in (5.66m).
wing area 420sq ft (39.02sq m).
Power plant: Two 652hp Pratt & Whitney PT6A–27 turboprops.
Payload: 1–2 man crew and 20 troops or 9 stretcher cases and 3 medics.
Variants:
Twin Otter Series 100 and Series 200: Earlier versions, inc floatplane variants.
First flights:
Prototype: 20 May 1965.
Production:
5 prototypes; over 500 built to date, inc only 50 military variants.
Series 100: 115 built 1966–68.
Series 200: 115 built 1968–69.
Series 300: over 270 built from 1969.
In service:
Series 100: Chile, Norway, Paraguay, Peru.
Series 300: Canada (CC–138), Ecuador,

Panama, Peru, Sudan, Uganda, USA (UV–18A).

De Havilland Canada DHC–6 'Twin Otter' Series 200.

Type: Light transport.
Details as for Series 300 with the following exceptions:
Weights:
empty 6,500lb (2,950kg).
maximum 11,580lb (5,252kg).
Performance:
maximum cruising speed at 10,000ft (3,050m) 190mph (306km/hr).
ferry range 945 miles (1,520km).
initial rate of climb 21.3ft/sec (6.5m/sec).
service ceiling 24,300ft (7,400m).
Power plant: Two 579hp Pratt & Whitney PT6A–20 turboprops.
Payload: 1–2 man crew and 19 troops or 9 stretcher cases and 3 medics or max 4,000lb (1,815kg) freight.
In service:
Series 200: Argentina, Jamaica, Nepal.

Shenyang F–9.

Type: Single-seat fighter and strike-fighter.

Shenyang F–9.

De Havilland Canada DHC–6 'Twin Otter' Series 300.

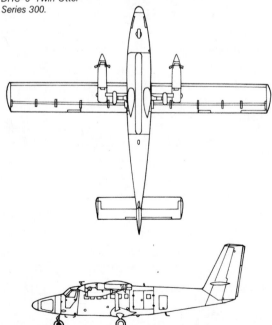

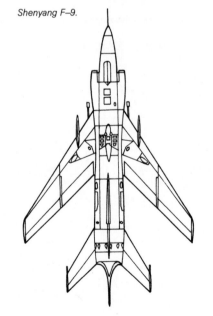

Weights:
empty 13,670lb (6,200kg).
normal 20,280lb (9,200kg).
maximum 23,590lb (10,700kg).
Performance:
maximum speed (Mach 1.56).
maximum speed at sea level (Mach 1.0).
radius of action 210–490 miles (340–790km).
initial rate of climb 590.5ft/sec (180.0m/sec).
time to 36,000ft (11,000m) 1min 30sec.
service ceiling 52,490ft (16,000m).
Dimensions:
wing span 29ft 10¼in (9.10m).
length overall 46ft 3in (14.10m).
wing area 269.1sq ft (25.00sq m).
Power plant: Two RD–9B–811 mod turbojets each rated at 5,732/8,267lb (2,600/3,750kg) st.
Armament: Two 30mm NR–30 cannon with 70rpg and max 2,205(3,307?)lb

(1,000(1,500?)kg) weapon load, e.g. (as fighter) two Atoll AAMs or (as strike-fighter) four 550lb (250kg) bombs or four rocket launchers each containing eight 57mm S–5 rockets.
Production: Series production from 1973(?).
In service: China (People's Republic).

Aero L–29 'Delfin' (Maya).
Type: Two-seat trainer.
Weights:
empty 5,027lb (2,280kg).
normal 7,231lb (3,280kg).
maximum 7,804lb (3,540kg).
Performance:
maximum speed at sea level 382mph (615km/hr).
maximum speed at 16,400ft (5,000m) 407mph (655km/hr).
maximum cruising speed at sea level 359mph (575km/hr).
ferry range 592 miles (900km).

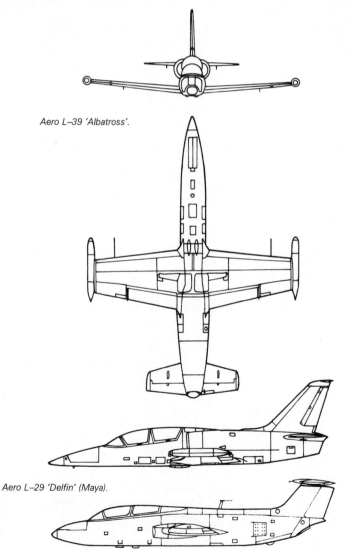

Aero L–39 'Albatross'.

Aero L–29 'Delfin' (Maya).

initial rate of climb 45.9ft/sec (14.0m/sec).
time to 20,000ft (6,100m) 12min 0sec.
service ceiling 36,100ft (11,000m).
Dimensions:
wing span 33ft 9in (10.29m).
length overall 35ft 5½in (10.81m).
height overall 10ft 3in (3.13m).
wing area 213.1sq ft (19.80sq m).
Power plant: One M–701 turbojet rated at 1,960kg (890kg) st.
Armament: Two 220lb (100kg) bombs or 4 unguided rockets or two 7.62mm machine-guns in underwing pods.
Variants:
L–29A Delfin-Akrobat: Aerobatic aircraft.
First flights:
Prototype: 5 April 1959.
First production model: April 1963.
Production:
Approx 3,600 built 1962–73/74.
In service: Bulgaria, Czechoslovakia (C–29), Egypt (UAR), Germany (East), Guinea, Hungary, Iraq, Nigeria, Romania, Syria, Uganda, USSR.

Aero L–39 'Albatross'.
Type: Two-seat trainer.
Weights:
empty 7,440lb (3,375kg).
normal 9,260lb (4,200kg).
maximum 32,187lb (14,600kg).
Performance:
maximum speed at 16,400ft (5,000m) 470mph (757km/hr).
maximum speed at sea level 438mph (705km/hr).
range 565 miles (910km).
ferry range 930 miles (1,500km).
initial rate of climb 72.2ft/sec (22.0m/sec).
time to 16,400ft (5,000m) 5min 0sec.
service ceiling 37,250ft (11,350m).
Dimensions:
wing span 31ft 0½in (9.46m).
length overall 40ft 5in (12.32m).
height overall 15ft 5¾in (4.72m).
wing area 202.36sq ft (18.80sq m).
Power plant: One Walter Titan (Ivchenko AI–25TL) turbofan rated at 3,790lb (1,720kg) st.
Armament: Max –lb weapon load on 2 underwing hard points, e.g. weapon packs with cannon or rockets.
Variants:
L–39Z: Single–seat light ground-support aircraft, under development; max 2,200lb (1,000kg)(?) on 4 hard points, e.g. weapon pods with 20mm cannon, or rockets, or bombs.
First flights:
Prototype: 4 November 1968.
First pre-production model: 1971.
Production: 5 prototypes, 10 pre-production models, series production 1973–74, over 700 delivered or on order to date.
In service: Czechoslovakia, Iraq, USSR.

L–60 'Brigadýr'.

Type: Liaison and AOP aircraft.
Weights:
empty 2,138lb (970kg).
normal 3,219lb (1,460kg).
maximum 3,439lb (1,560kg).
Performance:
maximum speed 120mph (193km/hr).
maximum cruising speed 109mph
 (175km/hr).
range 447 miles (720km).
initial rate of climb 14.4ft/sec
 (4.4m/sec).
time to 3,280ft (1,000m) 4min 20sec.
service ceiling 13,775ft (4,200m).
Dimensions:
wing span 45ft 9½in (13.96m).
length overall 27ft 8⅔in (8.45m).
height overall 8ft 11in (2.72m).
wing area 261.6sq ft (24.30sq m).
Power plant: One 220hp Praga Doris
 M–208B piston engine.
Armament: One machine-gun optional.
Payload: 1 man crew and 3 troops or 2
 stretcher cases.
Variants:
Agricola: Agricultural crop-dusting
 aircraft.
First flights:
Prototype: 1955.

Production: Approx 400 built 1956–60,
 majority as civil crop-dusters.
In service: Czechoslovakia, Germany
 (East), Romania, Yugoslavia.

Zlin Z–526 'Trenér'.

Type: Two-seat trainer.
Weights:
empty 1,468lb (666kg).
normal 2,149lb (975kg).
Performance:
maximum speed at sea level 151mph
 (243km/hr).
maximum cruising speed 132mph
 (212km/hr).
range 360 miles (580km).
ferry range 640 miles (1,030km).
initial rate of climb 18.0ft/sec
 (5.5m/sec).
service ceiling 15,750ft (4,800m).
Dimensions:
wing span 34ft 9in (10.60m).
length overall 25ft 8¼in (7.83m).
height overall 6ft 9in (2.06m).
wing area 166.3sq ft (15.45sq m).
Power plant: One 160hp Walter Minor
 6–III piston engine.
Variants:
Z–26, Z–126: earlier versions.
Z–226: Further development of Z–126.

Z–326: Further development of Z–226
 with retractable undercarriage.
Z–726: Further development of Z–526.
First flights: Prototype Z–26: 1947.
Z–326: 1957.
Z–526: 1965.
Z–726: 1973.
Production: Series production of
 Zlin–Trenér from 1947, over 1,700 of
 all variants built to date.
In service: Cuba, Czechoslovakia,
 Egypt (UAR), Germany (East).

Zlin Z–226 'Trenér'.

Type: Two-seat trainer.
Details as for Z–526 'Trenér' with the
 following exceptions:
Weights:
empty 1,257lb (570kg).
normal 1,808lb (820kg).
Performance:
maximum speed at sea level 137mph
 (220km/hr).
maximum cruising speed 121mph
 (195km/hr).
ferry range 522 miles (840km).
initial rate of climb 15.7ft/sec
 (4.8m/sec).
Dimensions:
wing span 33ft 8⅔in (10.28m).

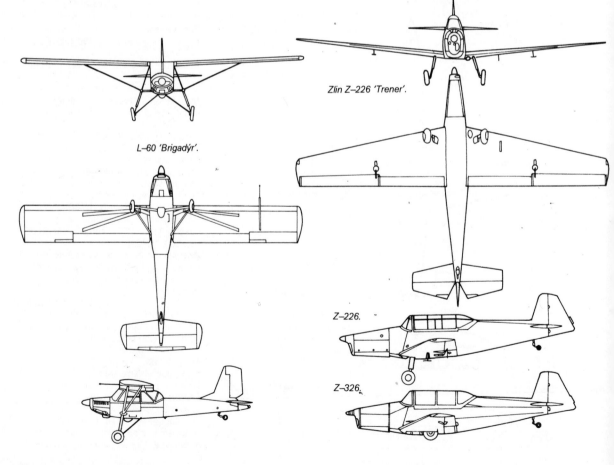

Zlin Z–226 'Trener'.

L–60 'Brigadýr'.

Z–226.

Z–326.

wing area 160.4sq ft (14.90sq m).
First flights:
Z–226: 1955.

Aérospatiale N.262D 'Frégate'.
Type: Light transport.
Weights:
empty 15,287lb (6,934kg).
normal 15,873lb (7,200kg).
maximum 23,369lb (10,600kg).
Performance:
maximum speed at sea level 260mph
  (418km/hr).
cruising speed at 15,090ft (4,600m)
  254mph (408km/hr).
range w.m.p. 652 miles (1,050km).
ferry range 1,491 miles (2,400km).
initial rate of climb 24.9ft/sec
  (7.6m/sec).
service ceiling 26,247ft (8,000m).
Dimensions:
wing span 74ft 1¾in (22.60m).
length overall 63ft 3in (19.28m).
height overall 20ft 4in (6.21m).
wing area 592sq ft (55.00sq m).
Power plant: Two 1,360hp Turboméca
  Bastan VIIA turboprops.
Payload:
2–3 man crew and 29 troops or 18
  paratroops or 12 stretcher cases and 2

medics or max 6,834lb (3,100kg) freight.
Variants:
N.262A, B: earlier versions, N.262C:
  civil variant of N.262D.
First flights:
Prototype: 24 December 1962.
Production:
N.262A: 67 built, inc 21 military,
  1965–69.
N.262B: 4 built (civil).
N.262C: 7 built from 1970.
N.262D: 30 built from 1970.
N.262E: 1 built.
In service:
N.262A, D: France, Upper Volta.
N.262C: Gabon.

Aérospatiale S.E.313B.
Type: Light helicopter.
Weights:
empty 1,984lb (900kg).
maximum 3,527lb (1,600kg).
Performance:
maximum speed at sea level 115mph
  (185km/hr).
maximum cruising speed 106mph
  (170km/hr).
range with 827lb (375kg) payload 186
  miles (300km).
ferry range 351 miles (565km).

initial rate of climb 14.8ft/sec (4.5m/sec).
service ceiling 10,172ft (3,100m).
hovering ceiling in ground effect 5,085ft
  (1,550m).
hovering ceiling out of ground effect
  2,950ft (900m).
Dimensions:
main rotor diameter 33ft 5¾in (10.20m).
length of fuselage 31ft 9¾in (9.70m).
height 9ft 0in (2.75m).
Power plant: One 360hp Turboméca
  Artouste IIC6 turboshaft.
Armament: Optional: Two-four A.S.10
  or A.S.11 ASMs.
Payload: 1 man crew and 4 troops or
  max 1,323lb (600kg) freight or 2
  stretcher cases and 1 medic.
Variants:
S.A.315B Lama: Uprated engine (870hp
  Artouste IIIB).
S.A.318C: Further development.
First flights:
Prototype: 12 March 1955.
Production:
2 prototypes and 3 pre-production
  models.
S.E.313B: 923 built 1957–65.
S.A.315B: over 191 built from 1969; inc
  100 licence-built in India by HAL from
  1972.

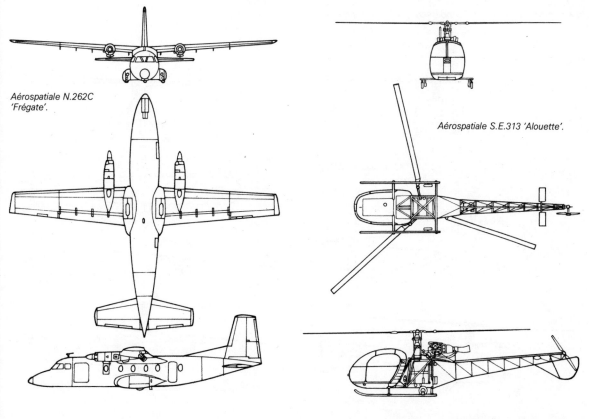

Aérospatiale N.262C
'Frégate'.

Aérospatiale S.E.313 'Alouette'.

In service:

S.E.313B: Belgium, Cambodia,
Cameroun, Central African Republic,
Chad, Congo (Brazzaville), Dominican
Republic, Finland(?), France, Germany
(West), Great Britain (Alouette AH.2),
India, Indonesia, Israel, Ivory Coast,
Kenya, Lebanon, Libya, Madagascar
(Malagasy), Mexico, Morocco,
Portugal, Senegal, South Africa,
Sweden (SKP–2), Switzerland, Togo,
Tunisia.

S.A.315B: Argentina, Ecuador, India
(Cheetah).

Aérospatiale S.A.318C 'Alouette' II.

Type: Light helicopter.
Details as for the S.E.313B with the
following exceptions:

Weights:
empty 1,961lb (890kg).
maximum 3,630lb (1,650kg).

Performance:
maximum speed at sea level 127mph
(205km/hr).
maximum cruising speed 112mph
(180km/hr).
range with 827lb (375kg) payload 62
miles (100km).
ferry range 466 miles (720km).
initial rate of climb 21.7ft/sec
(6.6m/sec).
service ceiling 10,800 ft (3,300m).

Dimensions:
length of fuselage 31ft 11¾in (9.75).

Power plant: One 523hp Turboméca
Astazou IIA turboshaft.

First flights: 31 January 1961.

Production: Series production from
1964, over 370 delivered or on order
to date.

In service: France, Germany (West).

Aérospatiale S.A.316A 'Alouette' III.

Type: Light transport helicopter.

Weights:
empty 2,447lb (1,100kg).
normal 4,189lb (1,900kg).
maximum 4,630lb (2,100kg).

Performance:
maximum speed at sea level 131mph
(210km/hr).
maximum cruising speed 118mph
(190km/hr).
range 62–310 miles (100–500km).
ferry range 341 miles (550km).
initial rate of climb 18.0ft/sec
(5.5m/sec).
service ceiling 10,670ft (3,250m).
hovering ceiling in ground effect 5,578ft
(1,700m).
hovering ceiling out of ground effect
1,804ft (550m).

Dimensions:
main rotor diameter 36ft 1in (11.00m).
length of fuselage 32ft 10¾in (10.03m).
height 10ft 1¼in (3.09m).

Power plant: One 550hp Turboméca
Artouste IIIB turboshaft.

Armament: As armed helicopter:
one-two free-mounted 7.62mm
machine-guns or 20mm cannon, four

A.S.11 or two A.S.12 ASMs or two
rocket launchers each containing
either eighteen or thirty-six 37mm
unguided rockets.

Payload: 1 man crew and 6 troops or 2
stretcher cases and 2 medics or max
1,807lb (820kg) freight.

Variants:
S.A.316B, S.A.316C, S.A.319: Further
developments.

First flights:
Prototype: 28 February 1959.

Production:
2 prototypes and 2 pre-production models.
S.A.316A: 981 built 1961–71; Licence-
built in India (160 built by HAL
1965–75), Switzerland (60 Al.IIIS built
by F & W 1970–74), Romania (50 built
by IAR, inc assembly, from 1973).
S.A.316B: – built: S.A.316C, S.A.319
Series production from 1971.

In service:
S.A.316: Argentina, Austria, Belgium,
Burma, Burundi, Cameroun, Chad,
Chile, Congo, Dahomey, Denmark,
Dominican Republic, Ecuador, Eire,
Ethiopia, France, Gabon, Hongkong,
India, Iraq, Ivory Coast, Jordan,
Lebanon, Libya, Madagascar
(Malagasy), Malaysia, Mexico,
Morocco, Mozambique, Nepal,
Netherlands, Pakistan, Peru, Portugal,
Rhodesia, Rwanda, Romania, Saudi
Arabia, Singapore, South Africa,
Switzerland, Tunisia, Venezuela,
Yugoslavia.
S.A.319: Abu Dhabi, France.

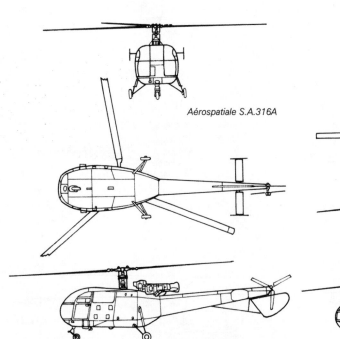

Aérospatiale S.A.316A

Aérospatiale S.A.321 'Super Frelon'.

Aérospatiale S.A.321 'Super Frelon'.

Type: Medium transport helicopter.
Weights:
empty 14,420lb (6,540kg).
normal 24,471lb (11,100kg).
maximum 27,557lb (12,500kg).
Performance:
maximum speed at sea level 149mph (240km/hr).
maximum cruising speed 143mph (230km/hr).
range with 5,512lb (2,500kg) payload 404 miles (650km).
ferry range 672 miles (1,080km).
initial rate of climb 24.9ft/sec (7.6m/sec).
service ceiling 11,475ft (3,500m).
hovering ceiling in ground effect 7,400ft (2,250m).
hovering ceiling out of ground effect 1,822ft (550m).
Dimensions:
main rotor diameter 62ft 0in (18.90m).
length of fuselage 63ft 7¾in (19.40m).
height 21ft 10¼in (6.66m).
Power plant: Three 1,550hp Turboméca Turmo IIIC6 turboshafts.
Payload: 2 man crew and 27–30 troops or 15 stretcher cases or max 9,921lb (4,500kg) freight.
Variants:
S.A.321G: ASW helicopter with up to 2 homing torpedoes or 2 ASM.
S.A.321F, J: Civil variants.

First flights:
Prototype: 7 December 1962.
First production model: 30 November 1965.
Production: 2 prototypes and 4 pre-production models; over 100 built 1965–77.
In service: China (People's Republic) (S.A.321J), France (S.A.321G), Iran, Iraq (S.A.321K), Israel (S.A.321K), Libya, South Africa (S.A.321L).

Aérospatiale/Westland S.A.330 'Puma'.

Type: Medium transport helicopter.
Weights:
empty 7,562lb (3,430kg).
maximum 14,770lb (6,700kg).
Performance:
maximum speed at sea level 174mph (280km/hr).
maximum cruising speed 164mph (265km/hr).
range 373 miles (600km).
ferry range 870 miles (1,400km).
initial rate of climb 23.3ft/sec (7.1m/sec).
service ceiling 15,090ft (4,600m).
hovering ceiling in ground effect 9,187ft (2,800m).
hovering ceiling out of ground effect 6,324ft (1,900m).
Dimensions:
main rotor diameter 49ft 2½in (15.00m).
length of fuselage 46ft 1½in (14.06m).

height 13ft 8½in (4.18m).
Power plant: Two 1,320hp Turboméca Turmo IIIC4 turboshafts.
Payload: 2 man crew and 16–20 troops or 6 stretcher cases and 4 medics or max 5,512lb (2,500kg) freight.
Variants:
S.A.330F: Civil variant.
First flights:
Prototype: 15 April 1965.
Production:
2 prototypes and 6 pre-production models, series production from 1968, over 280 delivered or on order to date. Licence-production (100?) planned in Romania (IAR330?).
In service: Abu Dhabi, Algeria, Belgium, Cameroun, Chile, Congo, Ecuador, France, Gabon, Great Britain (Puma HC.1), Ivory Coast, Kuwait,. Mexico, Morocco, Nepal, Pakistan, Portugal, South Africa, Togo.

Aérospatiale/Westland S.A.341 'Gazelle'.

Type: Light helicopter.
Weights:
empty 1,875lb (850kg).
maximum 3,750lb (1,700kg).
Performance:
maximum speed at sea level 165mph (265km/hr).
maximum cruising speed 149mph (240km/hr).

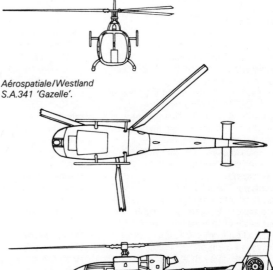

Aérospatiale/Westland S.A.330 'Puma'.

Aérospatiale/Westland S.A.341 'Gazelle'.

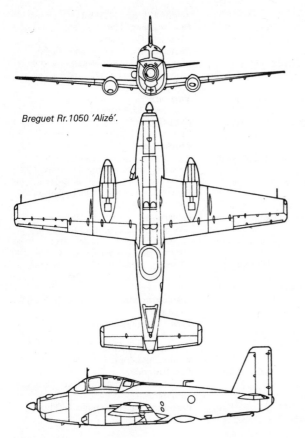

Breguet Rr.1050 'Alizé'.

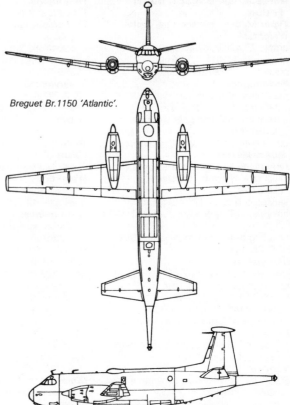

Breguet Br.1150 'Atlantic'.

range 404 miles (650km).
initial rate of climb 20.3ft/sec
  (6.2m/sec).
service ceiling 16,400ft (5,000m).
hovering ceiling in ground effect
  10,170ft (3,100m).
hovering ceiling out of ground effect
  8,530ft (2,600m).
Dimensions:
main rotor diameter 34ft 6in (10.50m).
length of fuselage 31ft 3 in (9.52m).
height 10ft 3½in (3.14m).
Power plant: One 592hp Turboméca
  Astazou IIIN turboshaft.
Payload: 1 man crew and 4 troops or
  max 1,323lb (600kg) freight.
Variants: S.A.341G: Civil variant.
  S.A.341H: Military export versions.
  S.A.342: Improved series.
  S.A.360 Dauphin, S.A.365, S.A.366:
  Further civil developments.
First flights:
Prototype: 7 April 1967.
First production model: 6 August 1971.
Production: 2 prototypes and 6
  pre-production models, series
  production from 1971; 715 currently
  delivered or on order; 112 licence-built
  in Yugoslavia by SOKO from 1973.
In service: Egypt (UAR), France
  (S.A.341F), Great Britain (S.A.341B, C,
  D, E = Gazelle AH.1, HT.2, HT.3,
  HCC.4), Kuwait, Qatar, Senegal,

Trinidad and Tobago, Yugoslavia
(S.A.341

Breguet Br.1050 'Alizé'.
Type: Shipboard ASW aircraft, 3 man
  crew.
Weights:
empty 12,544lb (5,690kg).
normal 18,078lb (8,200kg).
Performance:
maximum speed at 9,840ft (3,000m)
  292mph (470km/hr).
maximum cruising speed 205mph
  (330km/hr).
patrol speed at 1,480ft (450m): 143mph
  (230km/hr).
range 745 miles (1,200km).
ferry range 1,783 miles (2,870km).
initial rate of climb 22.9ft/sec
  (7.0m/sec.)
service ceiling 20,510ft (6,250m).
Dimensions:
wing span 51ft 2in (15.60m).
length overall 45ft 6in (13.87m).
height overall 15ft 7in (4.75m).
wing area 387.5sq ft (36.00sq m).
Power plant: One 1,950hp Rolls-Royce
  Dart R.Da 21 turboprop.
Armament: Max 2,150lb (975kg)
  weapon load, e.g. one homing torpedo
  or three 353lb (160kg) depth-charges
  in fuselage bay and two 330lb (150kg)
  or 385lb (175kg) depth-charges and six

127mm rockets or two A.S.12 ASMs
  underwing.
First flights:
Prototype: 6 October 1956.
First production model: 26 March 1959.
Production: 2 prototypes; 3
  pre-production and 87 production
  models 1958–61.
In service: France, India.

Breguet Br.1150 'Atlantic'.
Type: Maritime-reconnaissance and
  ASW aircraft, 12 man crew.
Weights:
empty 52,911lb (24,000kg).
maximum 95,900lb (43,500kg).
Performance:
maximum speed at 19,685ft (6,000m)
  409mph (658km/hr).
patrol speed at 984ft (300m) 199mph
  (320km/hr).
maximum cruising speed at 26,247ft
  (8,000m) 363mph (584km/hr).
radius of action 620 miles (1,000km).
ferry range 4,950 miles (7,970km).
initial rate of climb 40.7ft/sec
  (12.4m/sec.)
service ceiling 32,809ft (10,000m).
Dimensions:
wing span 119ft 1in (36.30m).
length overall 104ft 2in (31.75m).
height overall 37ft 2in (11.33m).
wing area 1,295sq ft (120.34sq m).

Power plant: Two 6,105hp Rolls-Royce Tyne Mk.21 turboprops.
Armament: Eight 434lb (197kg) homing torpedoes or four 1,124lb (510kg) homing torpedoes, plus four A.S.12 ASMs underwing.
Variants:
Atlantic Mk.2: Planned further development.
First flights:
Prototype: 21 October 1961.
Production:
3 prototypes and 87 production models 1965–73.
In service: France, Germany (West), Italy, Netherlands (SP–13A), Pakistan.

Dassault 'Etendard' IVM.

Type: Single-seat shipboard strike-fighter.
Weights:
empty 12,787lb (5,800kg).
normal 19,400lb (8,800kg).
maximum 22,650lb (10,275kg).
Performance:
maximum speed at sea level (Mach 0.9) 684mph (1,100km/hr).
maximum speed at 36,000ft (11,000m) (Mach 1.02) 674mph (1,085km/hr).
maximum cruising speed at 36,000ft (11,000m) 510mph (820km/hr).
radius of action 220–435 miles (320–700km).

ferry range 1,740 miles (2,800km).
initial rate of climb 328.1ft/sec (100m/sec).
time to 42,000ft (12,800m) 6min 0sec.
service ceiling 50,900ft (15,500m).
Dimensions:
wing span 31ft 6in (9.60m).
length overall 47ft 3in (14.40m).
height overall 12ft 7¾in (3.85m).
wing area 312sq ft (29.00sq m).
Power plant: One SNECMA Atar 8B turbojet rated at 9,700lb (4,400kg) st.
Armament: One–two 30mm DEFA 552 cannon, two Sidewinder AAMs or max 3,000lb (1,350kg) weapon load, e.g. two A.S.30 ASMs and unguided rockets or two 882lb (400kg) bombs.
Variants:
Etendard IVP: Strike-fighter and reconnaissance aircraft with 3 cameras.
Super Etendard: Further development with uprated engines (Atar 8K–50 rated at 10,913lb (4,950kg) st).
First flights:
Prototype: 21 May 1958.
First production model: 1 July 1961.
Super Etendard: 28 October 1974.
Production: 6 pre-production models:
IVM: 69 built 1961–65.
IVP: 21 built 1962–65.
Super Etendard: 60(80?) 1975–76 delivered or on order.
In service: France.

Dassault (Fan Jet) 'Falcon' 20 ('Mystère' 20).

Type: Light transport and trainer.
Weights:
empty 15,430lb (7,000kg).
normal 22,818lb (10,350kg).
maximum 28,660lb (13,000kg).
Performance:
maximum speed at 25,000ft (7,620m) 533mph (859km/hr).
maximum cruising speed at 40,000ft (12,200m) 466mph (750km/hr).
range with 1,600lb (725kg) payload 1,864 miles (3,000km).
ferry range 2,274 miles (3,595km).
service ceiling 42,656ft (13,000m).
Dimensions:
wing span 53ft 6in (16.30m).
length overall 56ft 3in (17.15m).
height overall 17ft 5in (5.32m).
wing area 440sq ft (41.00sq m).
Power plant: Two General Electric CF–700–2D–2 turbofans each rated at 4,320lb (1,960kg) st.
Payload: 2 man crew and 8–14 troops or max 3,042lb (1,380kg) freight.
Variants: Civil variants.
Falcon 20G: Improved series with more powerful Garrett ATF3s.
Falcon 10: Light transport and trainer.
Falcon 30: Enlarged version.
First flights:
Prototype: 4 May 1963.

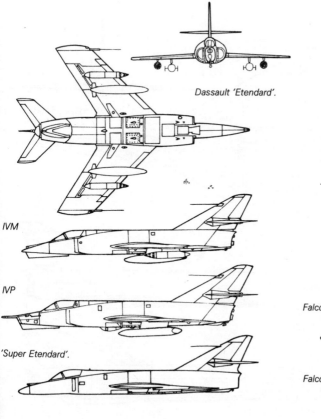

Dassault 'Etendard'.

IVM

IVP

'Super Etendard'.

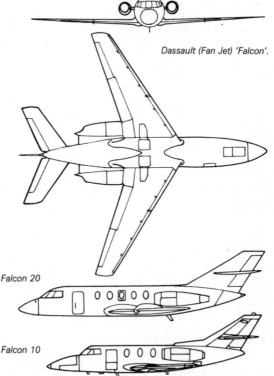

Dassault (Fan Jet) 'Falcon'.

Falcon 20

Falcon 10

First production model: 1 January 1965.

Production: Series production from
  1964; over 360 delivered or on order
  to date, of which only 30 military
  variants.
Falcon 20G: 41 to be built from 1977.
Falcon 10: 86 built.

In service: Australia, Belgium, Canada
  (CC–117)(?), Central African Republic,
  Egypt (UAR), France, Gabon, Iran,
  Ivory Coast, Jordan, Libya, Norway,
  Oman, Pakistan, Spain (T–11).
Falcon 20G: USA.

Dassault 'Mirage' IIIC.

Type: Single-seat fighter and
  strike-fighter.

Weights:
empty 13,820lb (6,270kg).
normal 18,636lb (8,453kg).
maximum 26,455lb (12,000kg).

Performance:
maximum speed at sea level 926mph
  (1,490km/hr).
maximum speed at 36,000ft (11,000m)
  (Mach 2.15). 1,429mph (2,300km/hr)
maximum cruising speed at 36,000ft
  (11,000m) (Mach 0.9) 593mph
  (954km/hr).
radius of action 180–478 miles
  (290–770km).
ferry range 1,429 miles (2,300km).
time to 36,000ft (11,000m) 6min 30sec.
service ceiling 54,100ft (16,500m).

Dimensions:
wing span 27ft 0in (8.22m).
length overall 45ft 1¼in (13.75m).
length overall (IIIB): 45ft 8¼in (13.93m).
height overall 13ft 9½in (4.20m).
wing area 365.9sq ft (34.0sq m).

Power plant: One SNECMA Atar 09B
  turbojet rated at 9,370lb
  (4,250kg)/13,228lb (6,000kg) st.

Armament: Two 30mm DEFA 552
  cannon with 125rpg and (as fighter)
  two AIM–9 Sidewinder AAMs and one
  Matra R.530 AAM or (as strike-fighter)
  max 3,968lb (1,800kg) weapon load.

Variants:
Mirage IIIA: Earlier version.
Mirage IIIB, IIID: Two-seat
  strike-trainers.
Barak: Improved Israeli development of
  Mirage IIIC.

First flights:
Prototype: 17 November 1956.
Mirage IIIC: 9 October 1960.

Production:
Mirage IIIB: 73 built 1962–64.
Mirage IIIC: 244 built 1961–64.
Mirage IIID: Series production from
  1966.

In service: Fighter and strike-fighter:
  France (IIIC), Israel (IICJ and Barak),
  South Africa (IIICZ).
Strike-trainer: Argentina (IIIDA),
  Australia (IIIDO), Brazil (IIIDBR = F–
  103D), France (IIIB, BE), Israel (IIIBJ),
  Lebanon (IIIBL), Pakistan (IIIDP), Saudi

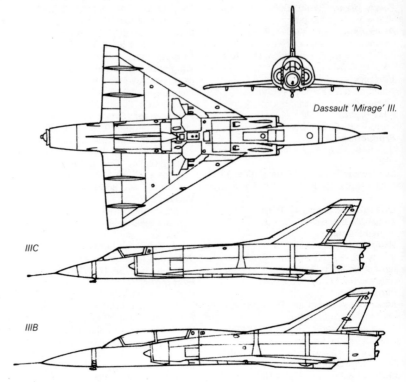

Dassault 'Mirage' III.

IIIC

IIIB

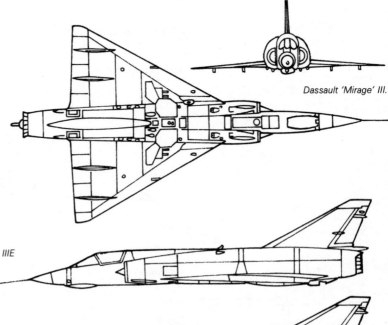

Dassault 'Mirage' III.

IIIE

IIIR

Arabia (IIISDD), South Africa (IIIBZ, DZ), Spain (IIIDE = CE–11), Switzerland (IIIBS).

Dassault 'Mirage' IIIE.
Type: Single-seat strike-fighter.
Weights:
empty 15,540lb (7,050kg).
normal 21,164lb (9,600kg).
maximum 29,760lb (13,500kg).
Performance:
maximum speed at sea level 850mph (1,370km/hr).
maximum speed at 40,000ft (12,200m) (Mach 2.2) 1,462mph (2,350km/hr).
maximum cruising speed at 36,000ft (11,000m) (Mach 0.9) 593mph (954km/hr).
radius of action 180–373 miles (290–600km).
ferry range 1,430 miles (2,300km).
time to 49,210ft (15,000m) 6min 50sec.
service ceiling 55,773ft (17,000m).
Dimensions:
wing span 27ft 0in (8.22m).
length overall 49ft 3½in (15.03m).
height overall 13ft 11½in (4.25m).
wing area 375sq ft (34.85sq m).
Power plant: One SNECMA Atar 09C turbojet rated at 9,435lb (4,280kg)/13,671lb (6,200kg) st, plus optional SEPR 844 rocket motor rated at 3,307lb (1,500kg) st.
Armament: Two 30mm DEFA 552 cannon with 125rpg and (as fighter) two AIM–9 Sidewinder AAMs and one Matra R.530 AAM or (as strike-fighter) max 3,968lb (1,800kg) weapon load, e.g. four 882lb (400kg) bombs or two 882lb (400kg) bombs plus one A.S.30 ASM.
Variants: Mirage IIIEA, IIIEBR, IIIEE, IIIEL, IIIEP, IIIEV, IIIEZ, IIISDE: export versions.
Mirage IIIO, IIIS: Australian and Swiss licence-built.
First flights:
Mirage IIIE: 5 April 1961.
Production: Series production from 1963; over 455 delivered to date; Australian licence-production by GAF (48 Mirage IIIOF fighters, 50 IIIOA strike-fighters, and 10 IIIDO strike-trainers from 1963–68; 8 further trainers 1972–73).
In service: Argentina (IIIEA), Australia (IIIO), Brazil (IIIEBR = F–103E), France (IIIE), Lebanon (IIIEL), Pakistan (IIIEP), Saudi Arabia (IIISDE), South Africa (IIIEZ), Spain (IIIEE = C–11), Switzerland (IIIS), Venezuela (IIIEV).

Dassault 'Mirage' IIIR.
Type: Single-seat reconnaissance aircraft.
Details as for 'Mirage' IIIE with the following exceptions:
Weights:
empty 14,550lb (6,600kg).

Dimensions:
length overall 50ft 10¼in (15.50m).
Variants:
Mirage IIIR, IIIRD: Single-seat reconnaissance aircraft.
Mirage IIIRP, IIIRS, IIIRZ: Export versions of IIIR.
First flights:
Mirage IIIR: November 1961.
Production: Series production from 1963; over 105 delivered to date.
In service: France (IIIR, IIIRD), Pakistan (IIIRP), South Africa (IIIRZ), Switzerland (IIIRS).

Dassault 'Mirage' IVA.
Type: Two-seat bomber.
Weights:
Empty 31,965lb (14,500kg).
normal 69,665lb (31,600kg).
maximum 73,855lb (33,500kg).
Performance:
maximum speed at 39,375ft (12,000m) (Mach 2.2) 1,454mph (2,340km/hr).
maximum cruising speed at 40,000ft (12,200m) (Mach 0.9) 596mph (960km/hr).
radius of action 777–994 miles (1,250–1,600km).
ferry range 2,485 miles (4,000km).
time to 36,000ft (11,000m) 4min 15sec.
service ceiling 65,600ft (20,000m).
Dimensions:
wing span 38ft 10½in (11.85m).
length overall 27ft 1in (23.50m).
height overall 17ft 8½in (5.40m).
wing area 840sq ft (78.00sq m).
Power plant: Two SNECMA Atar 09K turbojets each rated at 10,360lb (4,700kg)/15,400lb (7,000kg) st.
Armament: Max 14,110lb (6,400kg)

weapon load, e.g. one 50kiloton nuclear bomb or sixteen 882lb (400kg) bombs or four A.S.37 Martel ASMs.
First flights:
Prototype: 17 June 1959.
First production model: 7 December 1963.
Production: 1 prototype, 3 pre-production and 62 production models 1964–67.
In service: France.

Dassault 'Mirage' 5.
Type: Single-seat strike-fighter.
Weights:
empty 14,550lb (6,600kg).
maximum 29,752lb (13,500kg).
Performance:
maximum speed at sea level (Mach 1.1) 830mph (1,335km/hr).
maximum speed at 39,375ft (12,000m) (Mach 2.1) 1,386mph (2,230km/hr).
maximum cruising speed at 36,000ft (11,000m) 594mph (956km/hr).
radius of action 400–745 miles (650–1,200km).
ferry range 2,485 miles (4,000km).
time to 36,000ft (11,000m) 3min 0sec.
service ceiling 59,060ft (18,000m).
Dimensions:
wing span 27ft 0in (8.22m).
length overall 51ft 0¼in (15.55m).
height overall 13ft 11½in (4.25m).
wing area 375sq ft (34.85sq m).
Power plant: One SNECMA Atar 9C turbojet rated at 9,436lb (4,280kg)/13,670lb (6,200kg) st.
Armament: Two 30mm DEFA 552 cannon with 125rpg and max 8,944lb (4,200kg) weapon load on 7 hard points, e.g. two 882lb (400kg) bombs, ten 500lb (227kg) and two 250lb (113kg) bombs plus two auxiliary tanks

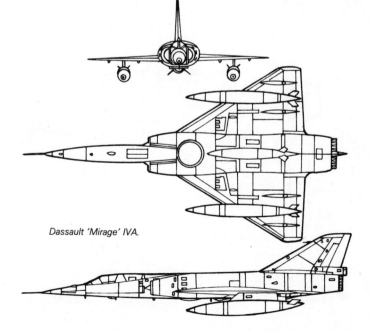

Dassault 'Mirage' IVA.

or one R.530 AAM and AIM–9 Sidewinder AAMs or rocket launchers and one A.S.30 ASM.

Variants:
Mirage, 5–BR, 5–COR, 5–DR, 5–RAD, 5–RG: single-seat reconnaissance aircraft.
Mirage 5–BD, 5–COD, 5–DAD, 5–DD, 5–DV, 5–PD: Two-seat strike-trainers.
Mirage Milan: Further development with more powerful engine and retractable foreplanes (Moustaches).

First flights:
Prototype: 19 May 1967.
First production model: May 1968.

Production: Series production from 1968. Approx. 420 currently delivered or on order, inc 8 Mirage 5–AD, 63 Mirage 5–BA, 16 Mirage 5–BD, 27 Mirage 5–BR, 14 Mirage 5–COA, 2 Mirage 5–COD, 2 Mirage 5–COR, 58 Mirage 5–D, 2 Mirage 5–DAD, 10 Mirage 5–DD, 32 Mirage 5–DE, 10 Mirage 5–DR, 50 Mirage 5–F (previously 5–J), 3 Mirage 5–G, 28 Mirage 5–PA, 20 Mirage 5–P, 2 Mirage 5–PD, 2 Mirage 5–RAD, 2 Mirage 5–RG, 4 Mirage 5–V, 2 Mirage 5–DV.

In service: Abu Dhabi (5–AD, 5–DAD, 5–RAD), Belgium (5–BA, 5–BD, 5–BR), Colombia (5–COA, 5–COD, 5–COR), Congo (5–Z), Egypt (UAR), France (5–F), Gabon (5–G, 5–RG), Libya (5–D, 5–DD, 5–DE, 5–DR), Pakistan (5–PA), Peru (5–P, 5–PD), Venezuela (5–V, 5–DV).

Dassault 'Mirage' F1C.

Type: Single-seat fighter and strike-fighter.

Weights:
empty 17,110lb (7,760kg).
normal 24,970lb (11,325kg).
maximum 33,510lb (15,200kg).

Performance:
maximum speed at sea level (Mach 1.2) 905mph (1,472km/hr).
maximum speed at 39,375ft (12,000m) (Mach 2.2) 1,450mph (2,335km/hr).
maximum cruising speed at 29,530ft (9,000m) 550mph (885km/hr).
radius of action 447–760 miles (720–1,220km).
ferry range 2,050 miles (3,300km).
initial rate of climb 700ft/sec (213.0m/sec).
service ceiling 60,700ft (18,500m).

Dimensions:
wing span 27ft 7½in (8.42m).
length overall 49ft 7in (15.12m).
height overall 14ft 8½in (4.49m).
wing area 269sq ft (25.00sq m).

Power plant: One SNECMA Atar 9K–50 turbojet rated at 11,067lb (5,020kg)/15,873lb (7,200kg) st.

Armament:
Two 30mm DEFA 553 cannon with 135rpg.
Fighter: 1–2 Matra 530 or Matra 550 Magic AAMs and two A1M–9 Side-winder AAMs.
Strike-fighter: Max 8,050lb (3,650kg) weapon load, e.g. eight 882lb (400kg) bombs or six 80 US gall (300l) napalm tanks or five rocket launchers each containing eighteen 70mm rockets.

Variants:
Planned models: F–1A: strike-fighter; F–1B: Two-seat strike-trainer; F–1E: Fighter and strike-fighter; F–1R: strike-fighter and reconnaissance aircraft Mirage F1 International (=Super Mirage): planned further development, abandoned 1975.

First flights:
Prototype: 23 December 1966.
First production model: 15 February 1973.
F1B: 26 May 1976.

Production: 1 prototype, 3 pre-production models, series production 1972–73, over 360 delivered or on order to date, plus 150 Egyptian assemblies from 1980 and 32(50?) licence-built in South Africa by Atlas from 1976(?).

In service: Egypt (UAR), France (F1CG), Iraq(?), Kuwait (F1CK, F1BK), Libya(?) (F1C), Morocco (F1CH), South Africa (F1CZ, F1AZ), Spain (F1CE = C–14).

Dassault 'Super Mystère' B2.

Type: Single-seat fighter and strike-fighter.

Weights:
empty 15,400lb (6,985kg).
normal 19,840lb (9,000kg).
maximum 22,046lb (10,000kg).

Performance:
maximum speed at sea level (Mach 0.94).

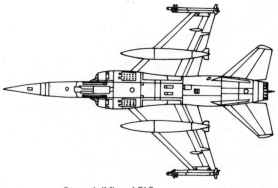

Dassault 'Mirage' 5.

Dassault 'Mirage' F1C.

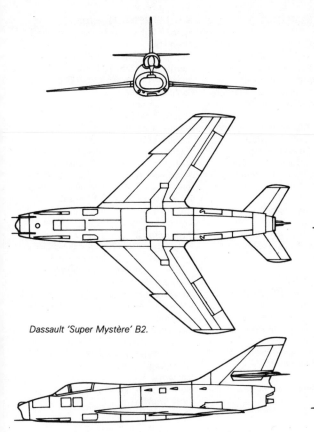

Dassault 'Super Mystère' B2.

Dassault-Breguet/Dornier 'Alphajet'.

Maximum speed at 36,000ft (11,000m) (Mach 1.13) 744mph (1,196km/hr). maximum cruising speed at 39,375ft (12,000m) 620mph (1,000km/hr). radius of action 273 miles (440km). ferry range 730miles (1,175km). initial rate of climb 291.3ft/sec (88.8m/sec). time to 40,000ft (12,200m) 5min 0sec. service ceiling 55,775ft (17,000m).

Dimensions:
wing span 34ft 5½in (10.50m). length overall 46ft 0¾in (14.04m). height overall 14ft 10½in (4.53m). wing area 376.9sq ft (35.02sq m).

Power plant: One SNECMA Atar 101G–2 turbojet rated at 7,495lb (3,400kg)/9,700lb (4,400kg) st.

Armament: Two 30mm cannon and max 2,200lb (1,000kg) weapon load, e.g. fifty-five 68mm rockets or two rocket launchers each containing 19 rockets, two 1,100lb (500kg) bombs or napalm tanks or twelve ASMs.

First flights:
Prototype: 2 March 1955.
First production model: 26 February 1957.

Production: 5 pre-production models; 180 built 1956–59.

In service:
France, Honduras, Israel.

Dassault-Breguet/Dornier 'Alphajet'.

Type: Two-seat trainer and ground-attack aircraft.

Weights:
empty 6,725lb (3,150kg). normal 10,780lb (4,890kg). maximum 15,430lb (7,000kg).

Performance:
maximum speed at 40,000ft (12,190m) (Mach 0.85). 560mph (901km/hr). maximum speed at sea level 616mph (991km/hr). radius of action 160–390 miles (260–630km). ferry range 1,900 miles (3,050km). initial rate of climb 193.6ft/sec (59.0m/sec). service ceiling 44,950ft (13,700m).

Dimensions:
wing span 29ft 10½in (9.11m). length overall 40ft 3¾in (12.29m). height overall 13ft 9in (4.19m). wing area 188.36 sq ft (17.50sq m).

Power plant: Two SNECMA-Turboméca Larzac 04 turbofans each rated at 2,315lb (1,350kg) st.

Armament: One 30mm DEFA 533 cannon with 150rpg in weapon pod and max 4,850lb (2,200kg) weapon load on 4 underwing hard points.

First flights:
Prototype: 26 October 1973.

Production: 4 Prototypes 1973–74; series production 1977–78; over 433 delivered or on order to date.

In service: Belgium, France, Germany (West), Turkey(?).

Max Holste M.H.1521M 'Broussard'.

Type: Liaison and AOP aircraft.

Weights:
empty 3,373lb (1,530kg). normal 5,511lb (2,500kg). maximum 5,953lb (2,700kg).

Performance:
maximum speed at 3,280ft (1,000m) 168mph (270km/hr). maximum cruising speed at 3,280ft (1,000m) 152mph (245km/hr). range 746 miles (1,200km). initial rate of climb 18.0ft/sec (5.5m/sec). time to 5,500ft (1,500m) 5min. service ceiling 18,050ft (5,500m).

Dimensions:
wing span 45ft 1in (13.75m). length overall 28ft 2½in (8.60m). height overall 12ft 1in (2.79m). wing area 271.3sq ft (25.20sq m).

Power plant: One 450hp Pratt & Whitney R–985–AN–1 Wasp piston engine.

Payload: 1 man crew and 5 troops or 2 stretcher cases and 2 medics.

First flights:
Prototype: 17 November 1952.
First production model: 16 June 1954.

Production:
2 prototypes; 27 pre-production and 335 production models from 1953–59.

In service: Central African Republic, Chad, Congo (Brazzaville), Dahomey, France, Ivory Coast, Mauritania, Senegal, Togo, Upper Volta.

Morane-Saulnier M.S.760A 'Paris' I.

Type: Two-seat trainer and four-seat liaison aircraft.

Weights:
empty 4,272lb (1,941kg).
normal 7,441lb (3,375kg).
maximum 7,658lb (3, 474kg).

Performance:
maximum speed at sea level 405mph (652km/hr).
maximum speed at 23,016ft (7,015m) 345mph (555km/hr).
maximum cruising speed at 16,400ft (5,000m) 350mph (563km/hr).
range 932 miles (1,500km).
initial rate of climb 38.1ft/sec (11.6 m/sec).

service ceiling 32,800ft (10,000m).

Dimensions:
wing span 33ft 3in (10.13m).
length overall 32ft 11in (10.03m).
height overall 8ft 10in (2.69m).
wing area 193.7sq ft (18.00sq m).

Power plant: Two Turboméca Marboré IIC turbojets each rated at 880lb (400kg) st.

Armament: Two 7.5mm machine-guns plus (on some aircraft) one 30mm cannon and max 882lb (400kg) weapon load, e.g. eight 110lb (50kg) bombs or twelve 75mm unguided rockets.

Variants:
M.S.706B: Trainer and liaison aircraft with more powerful engines (two Marboré II each rated at 1,058lb (480kg) st); some converted up from M.S.760A standard.

First flights:
Prototype: 29 July 1954.
First production model: 27 July 1958.

Production:
1 prototype, series production 1958–64.
M.S.760A: 150 built, inc 48 Argentinian licence-built by FMA.
M.S.760B: 63 built, inc 48 Brazilian licence-built (by Embraer?).

In service:
M.S.760A: Argentina, France.
M.S.760B: Brazil, France.

Nord N.2501 'Noratlas'.

Type: Medium transport.

Weights:
empty 29,325lb (13,302kg).
normal 45,410lb (20,600kg).
maximum 48,500lb (22,000kg).

Performance:
maximum speed at 5,000ft (1,524m) 250mph (402km/hr).
maximum cruising speed at 4,920ft (1,500m) 201mph (324km/hr).
maximum cruising speed at 9,840ft (3,000m) 208mph (335km/hr).
range w.m.p. 1,550 miles (2,500km).
ferry range 2,485 miles (4,000km).
initial rate of climb 19.4ft/sec (5.9m/sec).
service ceiling 23,290ft (7,100m).

Dimensions:
wing span 106ft 7in (32.50m).
length overall 72ft 0in (21.96m).
height overall 19ft 8in (6.00m).
wing area 1,089.3sq ft (101.20sq m).

Power plant: Two 2,090hp SNECMA (Bristol) Hercules 738 or 758 piston engines.

Payload: 4–5 man crew and 45 troops or 36 paratroops or 18 stretcher cases and several medics or max 12,125lb (5,500kg) payload.

Variants:
Nord N.2504: ASW trainer.

First flight:

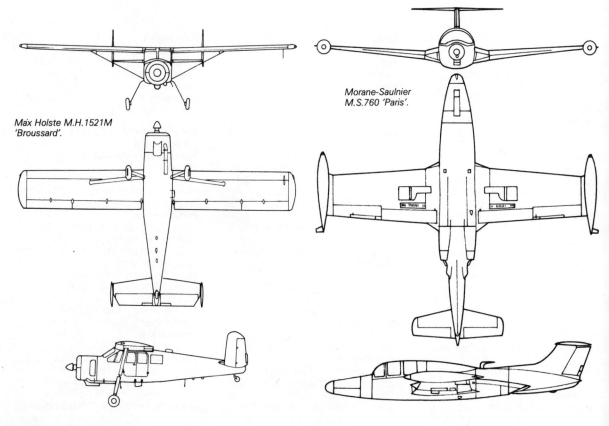

Max Holste M.H.1521M 'Broussard'.

Morane-Saulnier M.S.760 'Paris'.

Prototype: 27 November 1950.

Production:
N.2501: 428 built 1951–61, inc 161
  German licence-built 1958–61.
N.2504: 5 built.

In service:
N.2501: Angola(?), France, Greece,
  Israel, Mozambique, Niger, Portugal.

Potez-Air Fouga C.M.170 'Magister'.

Type: Two-seat trainer.

Weights:
empty 4,740lb (2,150kg).
normal 6,835lb (3,100kg).

Performance:
maximum speed at sea level 403mph
  (648km/hr).
maximum speed at 30,000ft (9,140m)
  444mph (715km/hr).
ferry range 733 miles (1,180km).
initial rate of climb 49.2ft/sec
  (15m/sec).
service ceiling 36,000ft (11,000m).

Dimensions:
wing span 37ft 1¼in (11.30m).
length overall 33ft 5½in (10.20m).
height overall 9ft 2in (2.80m).
wing area 184.6sq ft (17.15sq m).

Power plant: Two Turboméca Marboré
  IIA turbojets each rated at 882lb
  (400kg) st.

Armament: Two 7.5 or 7.62mm

machine-guns, four 55lb (25kg)
unguided rockets or two rocket
launchers each containing either seven
68mm or eighteen 37mm rockets or
two 110lb (50kg) bombs or two A.S.11
ASMs.

Variants:
C.M.175 Zephyr: Naval variant of
  C.M.170.

First flights:
Prototype: 23 July 1952.
First production model: 29 February
  1956.

Production:
3 prototypes and 10 pre-production
  models.
C.M.170: 726 built from 1952–63, inc
  licence-production in Germany (188 by
  Flugzeug-Union-Süd), Finland (62 by
  Valmet), Israel (36 by IAI).
C.M.175: 32 built from 1959–61.

In service:
C.M.170: Algeria, Belgium, Cameroun,
  El Salvador, Finland, France, Israel,
  Libya, Morocco, Netherlands, Nigeria,
  Rwanda(?), Togo, Uganda.
C.M.175: France.

Potez-Air Fouga C.M.170–2 'Super-Magister'.

Type: Two-seat trainer.
Details as for C.M.170 'Magister' with

the following exceptions:

Weights:
empty 5,093lb (2,310kg).
normal 7,187lb (3,260kg).

Performance:
maximum speed at sea level 435mph
  (700km/hr).
maximum speed at 463mph
  (745km/hr).
ferry range 780 miles (1,250km).
initial rate of climb 59.1ft/sec
  (18.0m/sec).
time to 29,500ft (9,000m) 14min 30sec.
service ceiling 39,375ft (12,000m).

Dimensions:
wing span 39ft (12.15m).
length overall 32ft 9¾in (10.00m).
wing area 186.1sq ft (17.30sq m).

Power plant: Two Turboméca Marboré
  VIC turbojets each rated at 1,058lb
  (480kg) st.

Production: 137 built 1963–68.

In service: Eire, France, Lebanon.

SEPECAT 'Jaguar' A.

Type: Single-seat strike-fighter
  (A = Appui Tactique).

Weights:
empty 14,900lb (6,800kg).
normal 23,000lb (10,430kg).
maximum 32,600lb (14,790kg).

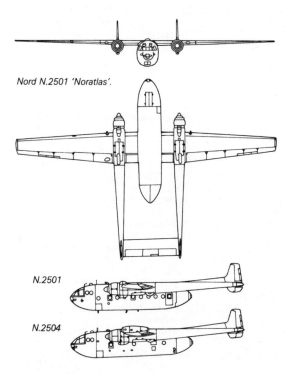

Nord N.2501 'Noratlas'.

N.2501

N.2504

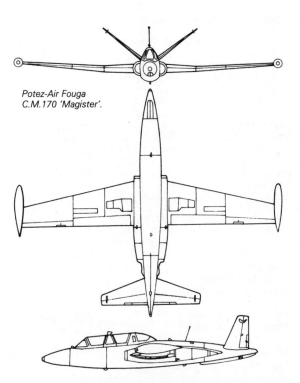

Potez-Air Fouga
C.M.170 'Magister'.

Performance:
maximum speed at 32,800ft (10,000m)
  (Mach 1.6) 1,057mph (1,700km/hr).
maximum speed at 980ft (300m) (Mach
  1.1) 820mph (1,320km/hr).
maximum cruising speed at 39,375ft
  (12,000m) (Mach 0.65) 429mph
  (690km/hr).
radius of action 373–710 miles
  (600–1,140km).
ferry range 2,270 miles (3,650km).
service ceiling 45,930ft (14,000m).
Dimensions:
wing span 28ft 6in (8.69m).
length overall (A.M.S.) 50ft 11in
  (15.52m).
length overall (B.E.) 53ft 10in (16.42m).
height overall 16ft 0½in (4.89m).
wing area 260.3sq ft (24.18sq m).
Power plant:
Two Rolls-Royce/Turboméca RT.172
  Adour 102 turbofans each rated at
  4,620lb (2,095kg)/7,140ft (3,240kg) st.
Armament: Two 30mm DEFA 553
  cannon with 150rpg and max 8,900lb
  (4,540kg) weapon load on 5 hard
  points, e.g. eight 880lb (400kg) or
  eleven 550lb (250kg) bombs or fifteen
  225lb (125kg) bombs or two A.S.37
  Martel ASMs and two 264gal (1,200l)
  auxiliary tanks or two Matra Magic
  AAMs.
Jaguar S: Two 30mm Aden cannon,
  otherwise as Jaguar A.
Jaguar B: One 30mm Aden cannon,
  otherwise as Jaguar A.
Variants:
Jaguar M(=Marine): Single-seat
  shipboard strike-fighter, not built.
Jaguar S(=Strike): Single-seat
  strike-fighter.
Jaguar B, Jaguar E(=Ecole): Two-seat
  strike-trainers.
Jaguar S(E).1, Jaguar S(O).1: Export
  versions with uprated power plants
  (Rolls-Royce/Turboméca Adour
  Mk.804 each rated at 5,370lb
  (2,436kg)/8,000lb (3,629kg) st).
First flights:
Prototype: 8 September 1968.
First production model (Jaguar E): 2
  November 1971.
Production:
8 prototypes.
Jaguar A.E.: total 200 to be built
  1971–80.
Jaguar B: 37 to be built 1972–77.
Jaguar S: 165 to be built 1972–77.
Jaguar S(E).1: 12 to be built 1974–77.
Jaguar S(O).1: 12 to be built 1975–77.
In service:
Jaguar A.E.: France.
Jaguar B.S: Great Britain (Jaguar GR.1,
  T.2).
Jaguar S(E).1: Ecuador.
Jaguar S(O).1: Oman.

Transall C.160.
Type: Medium transport.

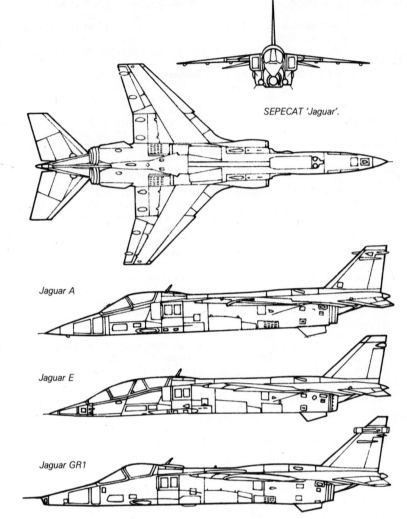

SEPECAT 'Jaguar'.

Jaguar A

Jaguar E

Jaguar GR1

Weights:
empty 63,400lb (28,758kg).
normal 97,450lb (44,200kg).
maximum 108,250lb (49,100kg).
Performance:
Maximum speed at 14,760ft (4,500m)
  333mph (536km/hr).
maximum cruising speed at 18,050ft
  (5,500m) 319mph (513km/hr).
range with 17,635lb (8,000kg) payload
  2,832 miles (4,558km).
ferry range w.m.p. with 35,270lb
  (16,000kg) payload 730 miles (1,175km).
  initial rate of climb 24 ft/sec
  (7.3m/sec).
service ceiling 27,900ft (8,500m).
Dimensions:
wing span 131ft 3in (40.00m).
length overall 106ft 3½in (32.40m).
height overall 38ft 5in (11.65m).
wing area 1,722.7sq ft (160.10sq m).

Power plant: Two 5,665hp Rolls-Royce
  Tyne R.Ty.20 Mk.22 turboprops.
Payload: 4 man crew and 93 troops or
  81 paratroops or 62 stretcher cases
  and 4 medics or max 35,270lb
  (16,000kg) freight.
First flights:
Prototype: 25 February 1963.
First production model: 21 May 1965.
Production:
3 prototypes, 6 pre-production and 169
  production models (C.160F: 50 built,
  C.160D: 110 built, C.160Z: 9 built)
  1965–72.
C.160P: Conversion of 4 C.160F for the
  French civil Postal Service 1973: 75
  re-ordered from 1978(?).
In service:
C.160D: Germany (West), Turkey.
C.160F: France.
C.160Z: South Africa.

Dornier DO–27A–4.

Type: Liaison and AOP aircraft.
Weights:
empty 2,368lb (1,074kg).
normal 4,070lb (1,850kg).
Performance:
maximum speed at 3,280ft (1,000m)
  140mph (227km/hr).
maximum cruising speed 130mph
  (209km/hr).
ferry range 684 miles (1,100km).
initial rate of climb 10.8ft/sec
  (3.3m/sec).
service ceiling 10,825ft (3,300m).
Dimensions:
wing span 39ft 4½in (12.00m).
length overall 31ft 6in (9.60m).
height overall 9ft 2¼in (2.80m).
wing area 208.8sq ft (19.45sq m).
Power plant: One 270hp Lycoming
  GO–480–B1A6 piston engine.
Payload: 2 man crew and 4 troops.

Variants:
Do–25, Do–27A–1, A–3: Earlier
  versions.
Do–27B–1, B–2: Trainers.
Do–27H: More powerful (340hp)
  engine.
Do–27Q: Civil variant.
CASA C.127: Spanish licence-built.
First flights:
Prototype: 27 June 1955.
Do–27A: 17 October 1956.
Production:
3 prototypes, 621 of all versions built
  1956–65; inc 428 Do–27A and 50
  Spanish (CASA) licence-built.
In service: Belgium, Congo, Germany
  (West), Israel, Malta, Nigeria, Portugal,
  Spain (L–9, LD–9), Sweden,
  Switzerland, Turkey.

Dornier Do–28D 'Skyservant'.

Type: Light transport and utility aircraft.

Weights:
empty 4,775lb (2,166kg).
maximum 8,380lb (3,800kg).
Performance:
maximum speed at 10,000ft (3,050m)
  199mph (320km/hr).
maximum cruising speed at 10,000ft
  (3,050m) 178mph (286km/hr).
ferry range 1,142 miles (1,837km).
initial rate of climb 19.7ft/sec
  (6.0m/sec).
service ceiling 24,300ft (7,400m).
Dimensions:
wing span 50ft 10¼in (15.50m).
length overall 37ft 5in (11.40m).
height overall 13ft 2in (4.01m).
wing area 308.9sq ft (28.70sq m).
Power plant: Two 380hp Lycoming
  IGSO–540–A1E piston engines.
Payload: 1–2 man crew and 8–12
  troops or 5 stretcher cases and 5
  seated wounded.

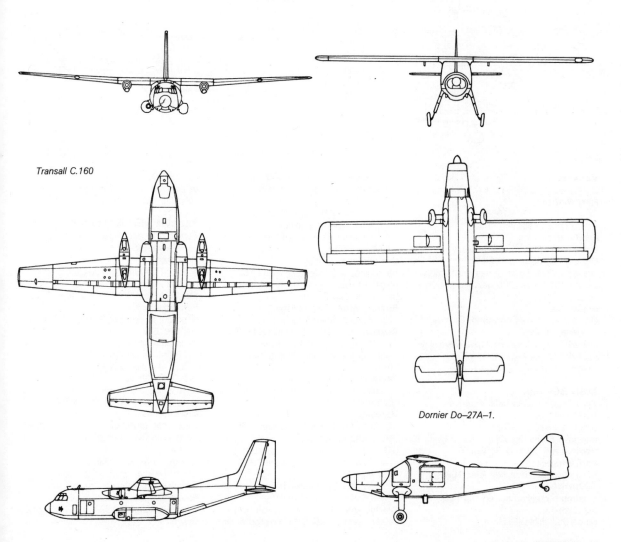

Transall C.160

Dornier Do–27A–1.

MBB BO–105.

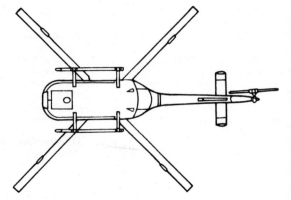

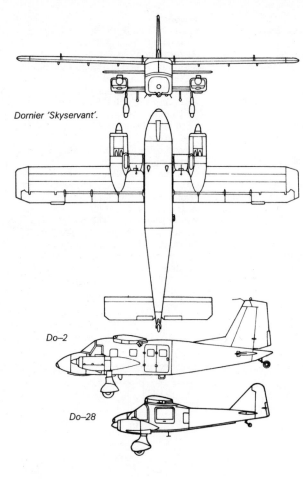

Dornier 'Skyservant'.

Do–2

Do–28

Variants:
Do–28A–1, Do–28B–1: Civil variants.
First flights:
Prototype: 29 April 1959.
Do–28D: 23 February 1966.
Production:
Do–28A–1: 60 built 1961–66.
Do–28B–1: 60 built 1964–71.
Do–28D, D–1, D–2: Series production
  since 1967, over 220 delivered or on
  order to date.
In service:
Do–28A–1, B–1: Cameroun, Greece,
  Nigeria, Turkey.
Do–28D, D–1, D–2: Ethiopia, Germany
  (West), Israel, Nigeria, Somali,
  Thailand, Turkey, Zambia.

MBB BO–105.
Type: Light liaison helicopter.
Weights:
empty 2,369lb (1,070kg).
normal 4,630lb (2,100kg).
maximum 5,070lb (2,300kg).
Performance:
maximum speed at sea level 168mph
  (270km/hr).
maximum cruising speed 144mph
  (232km/hr).
range 357 miles (575km).

ferry range 640 miles (1,030km).
initial rate of climb 31.17ft/sec
  (9.5m/sec).
service ceiling 16,503ft (5,030m).
maximum hovering ceiling in/out of
  ground effect 7,612/5,823ft
  2,320/1,775m.
Dimensions:
main rotor diameter 32ft 2½in (9.82m).
length of fuselage 28ft 0½in (8.55m).
height 9ft 9¼in (2.98m).
Power plant: Two 405hp Allison
  250–C20 turboshafts.
Armament: Optional: e.g. six HOT or
  TOW anti-tank ASMs; or two rocket
  launchers each with twelve 80mm
  rockets.
Payload: 2 man crew and 4 troops, or
  3 stretcher cases or max 1,918lb
  (870kg) freight.
Variants:
BO–106: Further development with
  increased dimensions.
BO–115: Two-seat strike-helicopter,
  termination of development 1976.
First flights:
Prototype: 16 February 1967.
BO–106: 25 September 1973.
Production: Series production from
  1971; over 350(580?) delivered or on

order to date.
In service: Germany, Netherlands,
  Nigeria, Spain (Z–15?).

Panavia MRCA 'Tornado'.
Type: Two-seat fighter and
  strike-fighter.
Weights:
empty 28,000lb (12,700kg).
normal 39,680lb (18,000kg).
maximum 55,120lb (25,000kg).
Performance:
maximum speed at 36,090ft (11,000m)
  (Mach 2.0) 1,320mph (2,125km/hr).
maximum speed at sea level (Mach 1.1)
  839mph (1,350km/hr).
radius of action 230–745 miles
  (370–1,200km).
ferry range 2,500 miles (4,830km).
service ceiling 50,030ft (15,250m).
Dimensions:
wing span (spread) 45ft 7¼in (13.90m).
wing span (fully swept) 28ft 2½in
  (8.60m).
length overall 53ft 9½in (16.70m).
height overall 18ft 8¼in (5.70m).
wing area 322.9sq ft (30.0sq m).
Power plant: Two Rolls-Royce
  Turbo-Union RB.199–34R–4 turbofans
  each rated at 8,510lb

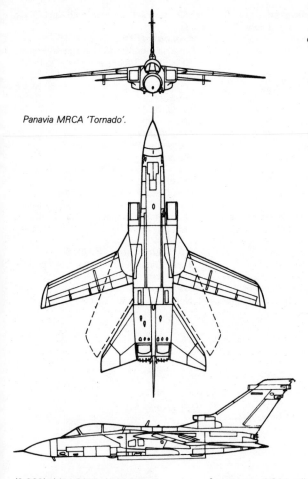

Panavia MRCA 'Tornado'.

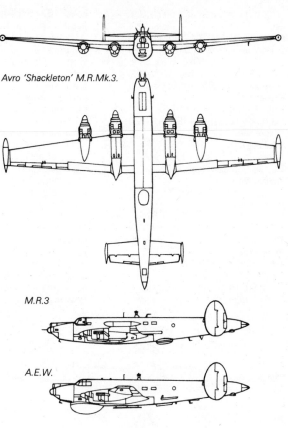

Avro 'Shackleton' M.R.Mk.3.

M.R.3

A.E.W.

(3,860kg)/14,990lb (6,800kg) st.
Armament: Two 27mm Mauser
cannon each with 125rpg and max
14,330lb (6,500kg) weapon load on 7
hard points.
First flights: Prototype: 14 August
1974.
Production: 9 prototypes and 6
pre-production models; series
production from 1977; 807 planned
(Germany 322, Great Britain 385, Italy
100).
In service: Germany, Great Britain,
Italy.

Avro 'Shackleton' M.R.Mk.3, Phase 3.

Type: Maritime-reconnaissance and
ASW aircraft, 10 man crew.
Weights:
empty 57,798lb (26,217kg).
normal 85,000lb (38,555kg).
maximum 100,000lb (45,359kg).
Performance:
maximum speed at 12,000ft (3,650m)
302mph (486km/hr).
maximum cruising speed at 9,840ft
(3,000m) 253mph (407km/hr).
patrol speed at 1,500ft (460m) 200mph
(322km/hr).

ferry range 4,214 miles (6,783km).
initial rate of climb 14.1ft/sec
(4.3m/sec).
service ceiling 19,200ft (5,850m).
Dimensions:
wing span 119ft 9½in (36.52m).
length overall 92ft 6in (28.19m).
height overall 23ft 4in (7.11m).
wing area 1,458 sq ft (135.44sq m).
Power plant: Four 2,450hp
Rolls-Royce Griffon 57A piston
engines plus two auxiliary Rolls-Royce
Bristol Viper 203 turbojets each rated
at 2,500lb (1,134kg) st.
Armament: Two 20mm Hispano Mk.V
cannon in nose and max 12,000lb
(5,443kg) weapon load in fuselage
bay; e.g. 3 homing torpedoes and 9
depth-charges or twelve 1,000lb
(454kg) bombs or mines or 29 troops
(as auxiliary transport).
Variants:
MR.1, MR.2: Earlier versions.
T.4: Trainer.
AEW.2: Early-warning aircraft.
First flights:
Prototype: 9 March 1949.
MR.3: 2 September 1955.
Production:
3 prototypes;

MR.1: 77 built 1950–52, some
converted to T.4.
MR.2: 69 built 1952–55, 12 converted
to AEW.2 in 1971–72.
MR.3: 38(?) built 1956–59.
In service:
AEW.2, MR.2, T.4: Great Britain.
MR.3: South Africa.

BAC 145 'Jet Provost' T.Mk.5.
Type: Two-seat trainer.
Weights:
empty 5,490lb (2,490kg).
normal 7,629lb (3,460kg).
maximum 9,200lb (4,173kg).
Performance:
maximum speed at sea level 409mph
(658km/hr).
maximum speed at 25,000ft (7,620m)
440mph (708km/hr).
ferry range 900 miles (1,448km).
initial rate of climb 59.1ft/sec
(18.0m/sec).
service ceiling 34,450ft (10,500m).
Dimensions:
wing span 35ft 4in (10.77m).
length overall 33ft 8½in (10.27m).
height overall 10ft 2in (3.10m).
wing area 213.7sq ft (19.80sq m).
Power plant: One Rolls-Royce Viper

202 turbojet rated at 2,500lb (1,134kg) st.

Armament: Two 7.62mm FN machine-guns with 550rpg and (T.55) max 2,200lb (1,000kg) weapon load on 4 hard points, e.g. two 500lb (227kg) and six 200lb (90.7kg) bombs.

Variants:
T.55: Export version of T.5.
T.3 (Export T.51), T.4 (Export T.52): Earlier versions.

First flights:
Prototype: 26 June 1954.
T.5: 28 February 1967.

Production:
T.3: 201 built 1958–62; T.51: 22 built from 1961; T.52: 43 built.
T.4: 198 built from 1961; T.52: 43 built.
T.5: 115 built from 1968–1972/73.
T.55: 5 built.

In service:
T.4, T.5: Great Britain.
T.51: Sri Lanka, Sudan.
T.52: Sudan, South Yemen, Venezuela.
T.55: Sudan.

BAC 167 'Strikemaster'.

Type: Two-seat trainer and light ground-attack aircraft.

Weights:
empty 5,960lb (2,653kg).
normal 8,353lb (3,789kg).
maximum 11,500lb (5,216kg).

Performance:
maximum speed at sea level 450mph (724km/hr).
maximum speed at 20,000ft (6,100m) 472mph (760km/hr).
radius of action 145–250 miles (230–400km).
ferry range 1,680 miles (2,700km).
initial rate of climb 85.3ft/sec (26.0m/sec).
time to 30,000ft (9,150m) 8min 45sec.
service ceiling 40,000ft (12,200m).

Dimensions:
wing span 35ft 4in (10.77m).
length overall 33ft 8¼in (10.27m).
height overall 10ft 2in (3.10m).
wing area 213.7sq ft (19.80sq m).

Power plant: One Rolls-Royce Viper

535 turbojet rated at 3,420lb (1,547kg) st.

Armament: Two 7.62mm FN machine-guns with 550rpg and max 3,000lb (1,360kg) weapon load on 8 hard points, e.g. two 500lb (227kg) bombs and up to sixteen R–80 SURA rockets.

Variants:
Mk. 80–Mk. 89: Export versions.

First flights:
Prototype: 26 October 1967.

Production:
Over 145 built 1968–77.

In service:
Mk.80 and Mk.80A: Saudi Arabia, Mk.82: Oman, Mk.83: Kuwait, Mk.81 and Mk.84: Singapore, Mk 87: Kenya, Mk 88: New Zealand, Mk.89: Ecuador.

BAC 'Lightning' F.Mk.6.

Type: Single-seat all-weather fighter and strike-fighter.

Weights:
Normal 40,000lb (18,144kg).

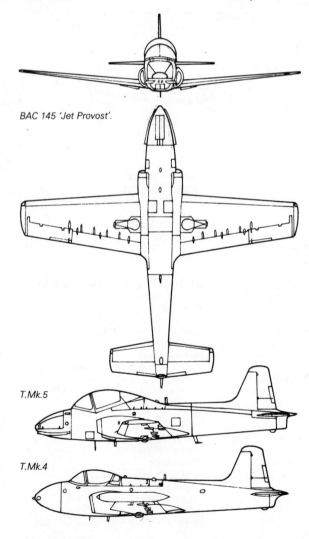

BAC 145 'Jet Provost'.

T.Mk.5

T.Mk.4

BAC 167 'Strikemaster'.

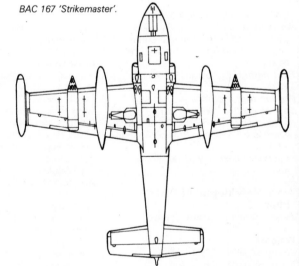

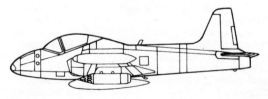

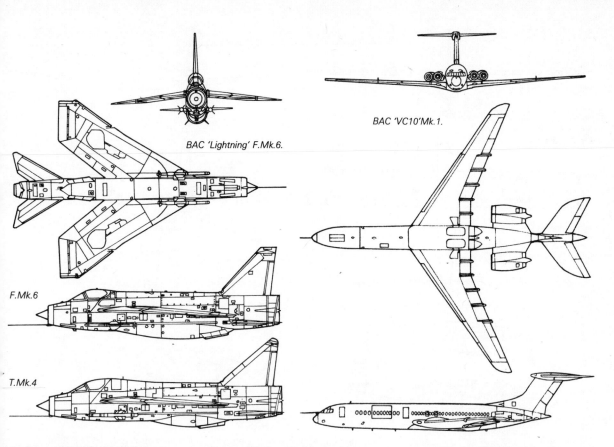

BAC 'Lightning' F.Mk.6.

BAC 'VC10' Mk.1.

F.Mk.6

T.Mk.4

maximum 47,995lb (21,770kg).
Performance:
maximum speed at 36,000ft (11,000m)
(Mach 2.2) 1,450mph (2,335km/hr).
maximum cruising speed at 36,000ft
(11,000m)–39,000ft (12,000m)
595mph (957km/hr).
range 746 miles (1,200km).
initial rate of climb 833ft/sec
(254.0m/sec).
time to 40,000ft (12,200m) 2min 30sec.
service ceiling 60,000ft (18,300m).
Dimensions:
wing span 34ft 10in (10.61m).
length overall 55ft 3in (16.84m).
height overall 19ft 7in (5.97m).
wing area 474.4sq ft (44.08sq m).
Power plant: Two Rolls-Royce RB.146
Avon 301 turbojets each rated at
11,100lb (5,035kg)/16,300lb (7,393kg)
st.
Armament: F.6: Two Red Top or
Firestreak AAMs or forty-four 51mm
rockets and (F.53) two weapon packs
each containing one 30mm Adem
cannon with 120rpg and two 1,000lb
(454kg) bombs or eighteen 68mm
SNEB rockets.
Variants: F.1, F.1A, F.2 (Export version
F.52), F.3: Earlier versions T.4 (Export
version T.54), T.5 (Export version
T.55): Two-seat strike-trainers.
First flights:
Prototype: 4 April 1957.

First production model: April 1958.
F.6: 16 June 1965.
Production:
5 prototypes, 20 pre-production
models; series production from
1958–70; F.1: 20 built; F.1A: 28 built;
F.2: 44 built, of which 30 converted to
F.2A and 5 to F.52; F.3: 58 built; F.6:
67 built, of which 24 modernized to
F.6A; F.53: 47 built; T.4: 20 built, of
which 2 converted to T.54; T.5: 22
built; T.55: 8 built.
In service:
F.1, F.1A, F.2, F.2A, F.3, F.6, F.6A, T.4,
T.5: Great Britain.
F.52, F.53, T.54, T.55: Saudi Arabia.

BAC 'VC10' C.Mk.1.
Type: Strategic support.
Weights:
empty 146,979lb (66,226kg).
maximum 321,995lb (146,059kg).
Performance:
maximum speed at 30,000ft (9,140m)
(Mach 0.86) 580mph (933km/hr).
maximum cruising speed at 38,000ft
(11,600m) 550mph (886km/hr).
range w.m.p. 3,899 miles (6,275km).
range with 24,000lb (10,886kg) payload
5,370 miles (8,642km).
Dimensions:
Wing span 146ft 2in (44.55m).
length overall 165ft 11½in (50.60m).

height overall 40ft 0in (12.20m).
wing area 2,932sq ft (272.40sq m).
Power plant: Four Rolls-Royce
Conway R.Co.43 turbofans each rated
at 22,500lb (10,206kg) st.
Payload: 4–5 man crew and 150
troops and max 19,057lb (8,644kg)
freight or 78 stretcher cases and 8
medics or max 57,386lb (26,030kg)
payload.
Variants:
VC10 (Series 1100), Super VC10: Civil
versions.
First flights:
Prototype: 29 July 1962.
VC10C.1: 26 November 1965.
Production:
1 prototype, series production
1962–70; VC10C.1: 14 built 1965–68.
VC10 (Series 1100): 17 built.
Super VC10: 22 built.
In service:
VC10C.1: Great Britain.
VC10 (Series 1100): Abu Dhabi, Oman.

Britten-Norman (Fairey) BN–2A
'Islander' 'Defender'.
Type: Light transport.
Weights:
empty 3,587lb (1,627kg).
normal 6,000lb (2,722kg).
maximum 6,300lb (2,857kg).
Performance:
maximum speed at sea level 170mph

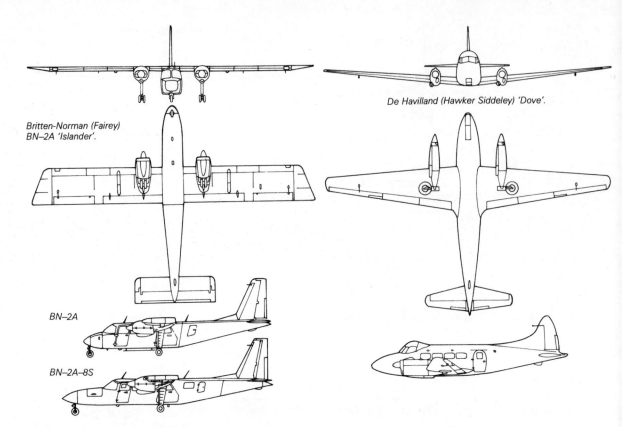

Britten-Norman (Fairey) BN–2A 'Islander'.

De Havilland (Hawker Siddeley) 'Dove'.

BN–2A

BN–2A–8S

(273km/hr).
maximum cruising speed at 7,000ft
(2,140m) 160mph (257km/hr).
range 717 miles (1,154km).
ferry range 1,264 miles (2,035km).
initial rate of climb 17.4ft/sec
(5.3m/sec).
service ceiling 14,600ft (4,450m).
Dimensions:
wing span 49ft 0in (14.94m).
length overall 35ft 8in (10.87m).
height overall 13ft 8in (4.16m).
wing area 325sq ft (30.20sq m).
Power plant: Two 260hp Lycoming
O–540–E4C5 piston engines.
Payload: 1–2 man crew and 8–9
troops or 2 stretcher cases and 2
medics.
Variants:
Defender: Max 23,000lb (1,043kg)
weapon load on 4 underwing hard
points, e.g. 2 weapon packs containing
7.62mm machine-guns and 2 rocket
launchers containing 68mm rockets or
two 500lb (227kg) bombs.
BN–2A–8S: With lengthened fuselage
(length 39ft 5¼in (12.02m)).
First flights:
Prototype: 12 June 1956.
First production model: 24 August
1967.
Defender: 20 May 1971.
BN–2A–8S: 22 August 1972.
Production:
2 prototypes; series production from

1966, transferred to Fairey in Belgium
since 1973.
Islander: Over 725 delivered or on
order up to end of 1975;
licence-assembled in Romania by
IRMA (215 fuselages?) from 1969;
completion of 20 and licence-assembly
of 60 aircraft in the Philippines.
Defender: 18 built from 1974–77.
In service:
Islander: Abu Dhabi, Belgium, Ghana,
Guyana, Hong Kong, Iraq, Israel,
Jamaica, Mexico, Panama, Philippines,
Rhodesia, Rwanda, Thailand, Turkey.
Defender: India, Madagascar,
Mauritania (Malagasy), Oman.

De Havilland (Hawker Siddeley) D.H.104 'Dove'.
Type: Light transport and trainer.
Weights:
empty 6,325lb (2,869kg).
maximum 8,950lb (4,060kg).
Performance:
maximum speed at 8,500ft (2,590m)
230mph (370km/hr).
maximum cruising speed at 8,000ft
(2,440m) 210mph (338km/hr).
range 385 miles (620km).
ferry range 880 miles (1,416km).
initial rate of climb 18.7ft/sec
(5.7m/sec).
service ceiling 21,720ft (6.620m).
Dimensions:
wing span 57ft 0in (17.37m).

length overall 39ft 3in (11.96m).
height overall 13ft 4½in (4.08m).
wing area 334.7sq ft (31.10sq m).
Power plant: Two 380hp Bristol
Siddeley Gipsy Queen 70 Mk.3 piston
engines.
Payload: 2 man crew and 5–11 troops.
Variants:
Devon C.1 and C.2, Sea Devon C.20:
Military variants of 'Dove' for Great
Britain.
First flights:
Prototype: 25 September 1945.
Production:
544 built 1946–64, inc over 30 Devon
C.1 and 13 Sea Devon C.20; Devon
C.1 subsequently converted to Devon
C.2 with more powerful engines
(Gipsy Queen 175).
In service: Argentina(?), Eire, Ethiopia,
Great Britain (Devon C.1, C.2, Sea
Devon C.20), India (Devon), Jordan,
Lebanon, Malaysia, New Zealand
(Devon C.1), Sri Lanka.

De Havilland D.H.115 'Vampire' T.Mk.11.
Type: Two-seat trainer.
Weights:
empty 7,380lb (3,347kg).
normal 11,155lb (5,060kg).
maximum 12,920lb (5,860kg).
Performance:
maximum speed at sea level (Mach 0.7)
538mph (866km/hr).

maximum speed at 20,000ft (6,100m)
(Mach 0.77) 549mph (883km/hr).
maximum cruising speed at 40,000ft
(12,200m) 403mph (650km/hr).
ferry range 850 miles (1,370km).
initial rate of climb 74.8ft/sec
(22.8m/sec).
service ceiling 40,000ft (12,200m)

Dimensions:
wing span 38ft 0½in (11.59m).
length overall 34ft 5¾in (10.51m).
height overall 7ft 3¾in (2.23m).
wing area 261.0sq ft (24.25sq m).
Power plant: One de Havilland Goblin
35 turbojet rated at 3,500lb (1,588kg)
st.

Armament:
T.11: Two 20mm Hispano 404 cannon,
two 500lb (227kg) bombs and eight
unguided rockets.
T.55: Four 20mm cannon and max
1,477lb (670kg) weapon load.

Variants:
Vampire T.55: Export version of T.11.
Sea Vampire T.22: Shipboard trainer.
Vampire T.33, T.34, T.35: Australian
licence-built T.11.
Vampire F.1, F.3, FB.5, FB.6, FB.9,
FB.50: Single-seat strike-fighters, four
20mm cannon and max 2,000lb
(908kg) weapon load.

First flights:
Prototype: 15 November 1950.

Production:
Series production 1951–58, 2
prototypes.
T.11 and T.55: 731 built, inc 60 Indian
(HAL) licence-built T.55.
T.22: 73 built.
T.33, T.34 and T.35: 109 built.

In service:
T.11: Mexico, Rhodesia, South Africa.
T.22: Chile.
T.55: Burma, Chile, South Africa,
Switzerland.
Vampire–strike-fighter: Dominican
Republic (F.1, FB.50), Mexico (F.3),
Rhodesia (FB.9), South Africa (FB.6,
FB.9).

De Havilland 'Venom' F.B.Mk.50.
Type: Single-seat strike-fighter.
Weights:
normal 13,650lb (6,192kg).
maximum 15,700lb (7,122kg).
Performance:
maximum speed at sea level 597mph
(961km/hr).
maximum speed at 20,000ft (6,100m)
(Mach 0.805) 560mph (901km/hr).
maximum cruising speed 390mph
(629km/hr).
ferry range 1,000 miles (1,610km).
initial rate of climb 120.4ft/sec
(36.7m/sec).
service ceiling 50,850ft (15,500m).

Dimensions:
wing span 41ft 9in (12.70m).
length overall 31ft 10in (9.70m).
height overall 6ft 2in (1.88m).
wing area 279.8sq ft (26.00sq m).
Power plant: One de Havilland Ghost
103 turbojet rated at 4,850lb (2,200kg)
st.

Armament: Four 20mm Hispano 804
cannon and max 2,000lb (908kg)
weapon load.

Variants:
Venom FB.1, FB.4: Single-seat
strike-fighters.
Venom NF.2 and 3: Two-seat
night-fighters.
Sea Venom F.(AW)20, 21, 22:
Shipboard strike fighters (Export version
FAW.53).
Aquilon: French licence-built version of
Sea Venom by Sud Aviation.

First flights:
Prototype Venom: 2 September 1949.

Production:
Venom: 887 built 1950–57.
Venom FB.50: 250 licence-built in
Switzerland by FFA 1951–54.
Sea Venom: 5 prototypes, 256(295?)
built 1952–58.
Aquilon: 94(117?) built
1952–58(?).

In service:
F.B.50: Switzerland.

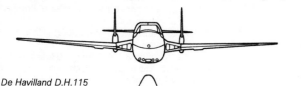

*De Havilland D.H.115
'Vampire' T.Mk.11.*

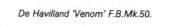

De Havilland 'Venom' F.B.Mk.50.

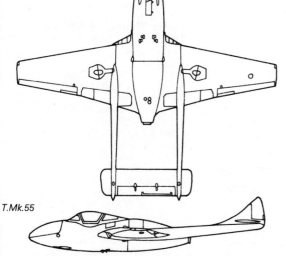

T.Mk.55

F.B.Mk.6

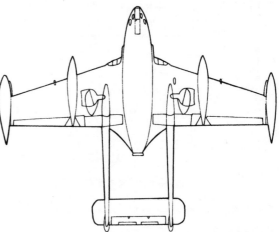

English Electric 'Canberra' B.(I)Mk.8.

Type: Two- to three-seat bomber and reconnaissance aircraft.

Weights:
empty 23,170lb (10,510kg).
normal 47,000lb (21,319kg).
maximum 51,000lb (23,134kg).

Performance:
maximum speed at sea level (Mach 0.68) 510mph (821km/hr).
maximum speed at 40,000ft (12,200m) (Mach 0.83) 560mph (901km/hr).
maximum cruising speed 404mph (650km/hr).
range 808 miles (1,300km).
ferry range 3,600 miles (5,792km).
initial rate of climb 60ft/sec (18.3m/sec).
service ceiling 48,000ft (14,630m).

Dimensions:
wing span 63ft 4½in (19.31m).
length overall 65ft 5¾in (19.96m).
height overall 15ft 6½in (4.74m).
wing area 963.2sq ft (89.50sq m).

Power plant: Two Rolls-Royce Avon 109 turbojets each rated at 7,500lb (3,402kg) st.

Armament:
B.8: Four 20mm Hispano Mk.V cannon, max 3,000lb (1,362kg) weapon load in fuselage bay plus 2,000lb (908kg) weapon load underwing, e.g. five 1,000lb (454kg) bombs.

Variants:
B.(I)12, B.(I)58: Export versions of B.(I)8.
B.2: Earlier version.
B.15: Conversion of B.6.
B.20: Australian licence-built B.2.
E.15: ECM aircraft.
PR.3, 7, 9 and 57: Reconnaissance aircraft.
T.4, 13, 21 and 22: Strike-trainers.
T.11 and 17: Radar-trainers.
TT.18: Target-towing aircraft.

First flights:
Prototype: 13 May 1949.
B.(I)8: 23 July 1954.

Production: 4 prototypes; 954 built 1949–61; numerous conversions by 1975; B.2: 418 built; B.6: 99 built; B.(I)6: 22 built; B.(I)8: 57 built; B.(I)12: 16 built; B.20: 49 built; B.(I)58: 71 built; PR.3: 36 built; PR.7: 74 built; PR.9: 23 built; PR.57: 10 built; T.4: 58 built; T.21: 7 built.

In service:
Argentina (B.62, T.64), Australia (B.20), Ecuador (B.6), Ethiopia (B.52), Great Britain (B.2, B.6, B.15, E.15, PR.7, PR.9, T.4, T.11, T.17, T.19, T.22, TT.18), India (B.(I)58, B.66, Pr.57, T.4, T.67), Peru (B.72, B(I)78, T.74), Rhodesia (B.2, T.4), South Africa (B(I)12, T.4), Venezuela (B.82, B.(I)88, PR.83, T.84).

English Electric 'Canberra' B.15.

Type: Light bomber.
Details as for B.(I)Mk.8 with the following exceptions.

Weights:
empty 21,760lb (9,870kg).
normal 46,000lb (20,866kg).
maximum 49,000lb (22,226kg).

Performance:
maximum speed at sea level 518mph (834km/hr).
maximum speed at 40,000ft (12,200m) 570mph (917km/hr).
ferry range 3,100 miles (4,988km).
initial rate of climb 61.7ft/sec (18.8m/sec).

Armament: Max 8,000lb (3,632kg) weapon load, e.g. eight 1,000lb (454kg) bombs.

Fairey 'Gannet' A.E.W.Mk.3.

Type: Shipboard early-warning aircraft, 3 man crew.

Weights:
normal 21,000lb (9,525kg).
maximum 24,967lb (11,325kg).

Performance:
maximum speed at 5,000ft (1,525m) 250mph (402km/hr).
patrol speed 130–40mph (210–25km/hr).
range 800 miles (1,290km).
service ceiling 25,000ft (7,620m).

Dimensions:
wing span 54ft 6¾in (16.61m).
length overall 44ft 0in (13.41m).
height overall 6ft 10in (5.13m).
wing area 490sq ft (45.52sq m).

Power plant: One 3,875hp Bristol Siddeley Double Mamba 102 turboprop.

Variants:
Gannet COD.4: Shipboard liaison aircraft.
Gannet AS.1, AS.4: ASW aircraft

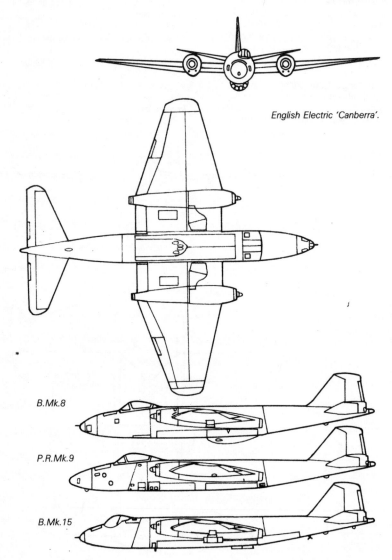

English Electric 'Canberra'.

B.Mk.8

P.R.Mk.9

B.Mk.15

(export version Gannet Mk.1).
Gannet T.2, T.5: ASW trainers (export versions Gannet Mk.2, Mk.5).

First flights:
Gannet prototype: 19 September 1949.
Gannet AEW.3 prototype: 20 August 1958.

Production:
3 prototypes; series production 1952–61. AS.1: 181 built; AEW.3: 44(38?) built; AS.4: 75 built; T.2: 38 built; T.5: 8 built.
5 AS.4 conversions to Gannet COD.4.
In service: Gannet AEW.3, COD.4: Great Britain.

Handley Page 'Jetstream' T.Mk.1.
Type: Trainer and light transport.
Weights:
empty 8,760lb (3,973kg).
maximum 12,520lb (5,680kg).
Performance:
maximum speed at 12,000ft (3,660m) 285mph (459km/hr).
maximum cruising speed at 12,000ft (3,660m) 278mph (448km/hr).
ferry range 1,350 miles (2,170km).

initial rate of climb 38.4ft/sec (11.7m/sec).
service ceiling 26,100ft (7,955m).
Dimensions:
wing span 52ft 0in (15.85m).
length overall 47ft 1¼in (14.36m).
height overall 17ft 5½in (5.32m).
wing area 269.69sq ft (25.08sq m).
Power plant: Two 996hp Turboméca/Rolls-Royce Astazou XVI turboprops.
Payload: 2 man crew and 8–12 troops.
Variants:
Jetstream 100: Civil passenger transport.
First flights:
Prototype: 18 August 1967.
Jetstream T.1: 13 April 1973.
Production:
5 prototypes.
Jetstream 100: 36 built 1968–72(?).
Jetstream T.1: 26 built 1973–74.
In service: Great Britain.

Handley Page 'Victor' K.Mk.2.
Type: Heavy tanker, 5 man crew.

Weights:
empty 73,965lb (33,550kg).
maximum 226,800lb (101,242kg).
Performance:
maximum speed at 40,000ft (12,200m) (Mach 0.92) 600mph (966km/hr).
radius of action 2,000 miles (3,220km).
ferry range 4,600 miles (7,400km).
service ceiling 55,000ft (16,800m).
Dimensions:
wing span 117ft 1in (35.69m).
length overall 114ft 11in (35.05m).
height overall 28ft 1¾in (8.58m).
wing area 2,199.29sq ft (204.38sq m).
Power plant: Four Rolls-Royce Conway 201 (R.Co.17) turbojets each rated at 20,618lb (9,352kg) st.
Armament:
Bomber: Max 35,032lb (15,890kg) weapon load; e.g. thirty-five 1,000lb (454kg) bombs.
Payload: – gal transferable fuel capacity.
Variants:
B.1, B.1A: Heavy bombers, converted to tankers; B.(K)1A, K.1 and K.1A; K.1A converted to K.2.

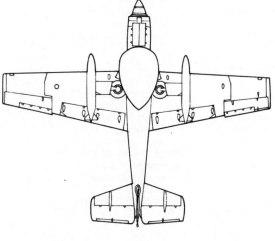
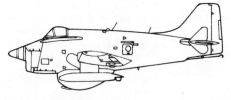

Fairey 'Gannet' A.E.W.Mk.3.

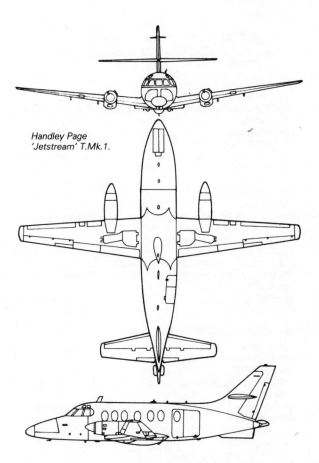

Handley Page 'Jetstream' T.Mk.1.

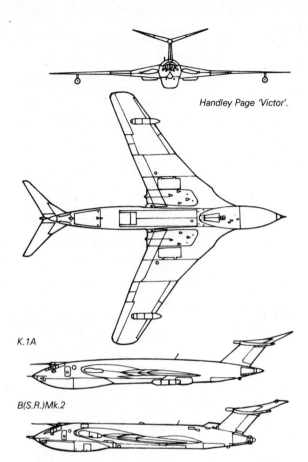

Handley Page 'Victor'.

K.1A

B(S.R.)Mk.2

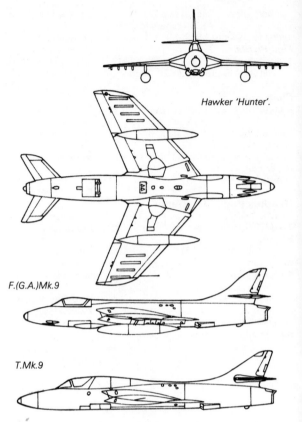

Hawker 'Hunter'.

F.(G.A.)Mk.9

T.Mk.9

B.2: Heavy bomber, converted to B.(SR)2 reconnaissance aircraft and K.2 tankers.

First flights:
Prototype: 24 December 1952.
B.1: 1 February 1956.
B.2: 20 February 1959.
B.(K)1A: 28 April 1965.
K.2: 1 March 1972.

Production:
B.1: 50 built 1956–58. 24 conversions to B.1A, 6 conversions to B.(K)1A, 10 conversions to K.1, and 14 to K.1A 1965–70.
B.2: 34 built 1960–64. 21 conversions to B.2R; 9 conversions to B.(SR)2, and 24 to K.2 1971–73/74.

In service:
K.1A, K.2: Great Britain.

Hawker 'Hunter' F.(G.A.)Mk.9.

Type: Single-seat fighter and strike-fighter.

Weights:
empty 13,270lb (6,020kg).
normal 18,386lb (8,340kg).
maximum 24,000lb (10,885kg).

Performance:
maximum speed at sea level (Mach 0.94) 710mph (1,144km/hr).
maximum speed at 36,000ft (11,000m)

608mph (978km/hr).
maximum cruising speed 460mph (740km/hr).
radius of action 217–354 miles (350–570km).
ferry range 1,840 miles (2,965km).
initial rate of climb 133.5ft/sec (40.7m/sec).
time to 45,930ft (14,000m) 6min 45sec.
service ceiling 50,000ft (15,250m).

Dimensions:
wing span 33ft 8in (10.26m).
length overall 45ft 10½in (13.98m).
height overall 13ft 1¾in (4.01m).
wing area 349sq ft (32.42sq m).

Power plant: One Rolls-Royce Avon 207 or Avon 203 turbojet rated at 10,150lb (4,604kg) st.

Armament: Four 30mm Aden cannon and max 3,000lb (1,816kg) weapon load, e.g. 1,000lb (454kg) or 2,000lb (908kg) bombs or twenty-four 76.2mm rockets.

Variants:
F.1, F.2, F.4 (export versions F.50, F.51, F.52), GA.11, F.5, F.6 (Export versions F.56, Mk.58): Earlier versions.
FGA.9, FR.10: Strike-fighter and reconnaissance aircraft, F.6 conversions.
T.7, T.8, T.53, T.66: Two-seat

strike-trainers.

First flights:
Prototype: 20 July 1951.
F.6: 25 March 1955.
T.7: 11 October 1957.

Production: Series production 1954–61(?): 1,426 fighters and strike-fighters (inc 383 Hunter F.6) and 101 strike-trainers built in Great Britain; over 600 Hunters of various series modernized or converted to date. 208 Hunter F.4 and 237 Hunter F.6 built in Belgium and the Netherlands (common licence-assembly by Avions Fairey and Fokker 1954–60/61).

In service: F.6 and FGA.9 strike-fighters and T.7 strike-trainer: Abu Dhabi (FGA.76, FR.76A, T.77), Chile (FGA.71, FR.10, T.72), Great Britain (F.6, F.6A, FGA.9, FR.10, GA.11, T.7, T.7A, T.8), India (FGA.56, T.66), Iraq (F.6, FGA.59, T.69), Kenya (FGA.9), Kuwait (FGA.57, T.67), Lebanon (F.6, F.70, FGA.9, T.69), Oman (FGA.9, FGA.73, T.66B), Peru (F.52, T.62), Qatar (FGA.78, T.79), Rhodesia (FGA.57, T.52), Singapore (Mk.74, Mk.74B, FR.74, T.75, T.75A), Switzerland (Mk.58, Mk.58A, T.68).

Hawker Siddeley 'Andover'.

Hawker Siddeley 'Buccaneer' S.Mk.2B.

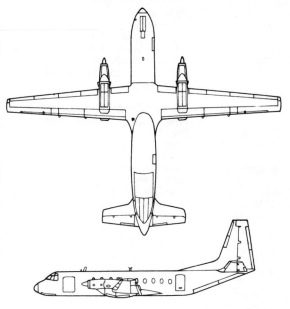

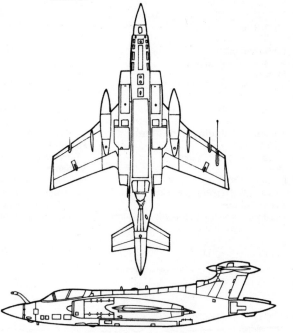

Hawker Siddeley 'Andover' C.Mk.1.

Type: Medium transport.
Weights:
empty 26,616lb (12,073kg).
maximum 50,001lb (22,680kg).
Performance:
maximum speed at 15,000ft (4,570m) 301mph (485km/hr).
maximum cruising speed at 15,000ft (4,570m) 265mph (426km/hr).
range/w.m.p. 282 miles (454km).
range with 10,000lb (4,536kg) payload 1,160miles (1,865km).
initial rate of climb 19.7ft/sec (6.0m/sec).
service ceiling 24,020ft (7,320m).
Dimensions:
wing span 98ft 3in (29.95m).
length overall 77ft 11½in (23.77m).
height overall 30ft 0in (9.15m).
wing area 829sq ft (77.20sq m).
Power plant: Two 3,245hp Rolls-Royce Dart R.Da.12. Mk.301C turboprops.
Payload: 4 man crew and 32–44 troops or 26 paratroops and 2 dispatchers or 18 stretcher cases, 5 seated wounded and 3 medics or max 14,750lb (6,691kg) freight.
Variants:
H.S.748 series 2 and 2A: Civil airliners

and special military VIP and command transports.
H.S.748 series 1: Earlier civil variant.
H.S.748 Coastguarder: Planned maritime-reconnaissance variant.
First flights:
Prototype: 24 June 1960: Andover C.1: 9 July 1965.
Production:
Andover C.1: 31 built 1965–67, converted to ECM aircraft 1977.
H.S.748 series 1: 18 built 1961–62.
H.S.748 series 2 and 2A: Over 315 built from 1962 (inc only a few as military VIP transports) plus 79 Indian licence-built by HAL from 1961–74.
In service:
Andover C.1: Great Britain, New Zealand.
H.S.748 series 2 and 2A: Argentina, Australia (C.2, T.4), Belgium, Brazil (C–11), Brunei, Cameroun, Colombia, Ecuador, Great Britain (Andover CC.2), India, Korea (South), Nepal, Tanzania, Thailand, Venezuela, Zambia.

Hawker Siddeley 'Buccaneer' S.Mk.2B.

Type: Two-seat bomber and reconnaissance aircraft.

Weights:
Normal 46,000lb (20,865kg).
maximum 62,000lb (28,123kg).
Performance:
maximum speed at 29,860ft (9,100m) (Mach 0.92) 620mph (998km/hr).
maximum speed at 250ft (75m) (Mach 0.85) 646mph (1,040km/hr).
maximum cruising speed at 3,000ft (915m) (Mach 0.75) 570mph (917km/hr).
radius of action 500–600 miles (805–965km).
ferry range 4,000 miles (6,400km).
Dimensions:
wing span 44ft 0in (13.41m).
length overall 63ft 5in (19.33m).
height overall 16ft 3in (4.95m).
wing area 514.7sq ft (47.82sq m).
Power plant: Two Rolls-Royce RB.168–1A Spey Mk.101 turbofans each rated at 11,100lb (5,035kg) st.
Armament: Max 16,000lb (7,257kg) weapon load, e.g. four 500lb (227kg) or 540lb (245kg) or 1,000lb (454kg) bombs in fuselage weapons bay and up to three 1,000lb (454kg) or six 550lb (227kg) bombs on each of the 4 hard points or three A.S.37 Martel ASMs.
Variants: S.1, S.2, S.2A: Earlier

versions.
S.50: Export version of S.2.

First flights:
Prototype: 30 April 1958.
S.1: January 1962.
S.2: 17 May 1963.
S.2B: 8 January 1970.

Production:
S.1: 60 built 1958–63.
S.2: 84 built 1963–68, approx 80 converted to S.2A, S.2B, S.2C and S.2D.
S.50: 16 built.
S.2B: 45 built 1970–75.

In service:
S.2, S.2A, S.2B, S.2C, S.2D: Great Britain.
S.50: South Africa.

Hawker Siddeley 'Dominie' T.Mk.1.

Type: Navigation trainer.
Weights:
empty 11,402lb (5,172kg).
maximum 21,198lb (9,615kg).
Performance:
maximum speed at 25,000ft (7,620m)

472mph (760km/hr).
maximum speed at 30,000ft (9,150m) (Mach 0.735) 500mph (805km/hr).
maximum cruising speed at 38,000ft (11,600m) 420mph (676km/hr).
range 1,330 miles (2,150km).
ferry range 1,700 miles (2,736km).
initial rate of climb 66.6ft/sec (203m/sec).
time to 25,000ft (7,620m) 13min 0sec.
service ceiling 41,000ft (12,500m).

Dimensions:
wing span 47ft 0in (14.33m).
length overall 47ft 5in (14.45m).
height overall 16ft 6in (5.03m).
wing area 353sq ft (32.79sq m).

Power plant:
Two Bristol Siddeley Viper 301 turbojets each rated at 2,998lb (1,360kg) st.
Payload: 2 man crew, 2–3 trainees and 1 instructor.

Variants:
H.S.125: Light (6–8 passenger) executive transport.
H.S.125–400, H.S.125–600: Further developments for 12 and 16

passengers resp.

First flights:
H.S.125: 13 August 1962.
Dominie: 30 December 1964.

Production:
Dominie: 20 built 1965–66.
H.S.125: Over 130 built 1962–68.
H.S.125–400: 101 built 1968–73.
H.S.125–600: Series production from 1973, over 120 delivered or on order to date.

In service:
Dominie: Great Britain.
H.S.125: Argentina, Brazil, Ghana, Malaysia, South Africa (Mercurius).
H.S.124–400, H.S.125–600: Great Britain (H.S.125, CC.1, CC.2).

Hawker Siddeley 'Gnat' Mk.1.

Type: Single-seat strike-fighter.
Weights:
empty 4,850lb (2,200kg).
normal 6,650lb (3,020kg).
maximum 8,885lb (4,030kg).
Performance:
maximum speed at 20,000ft (6,100m) 695mph (1,118km/hr).

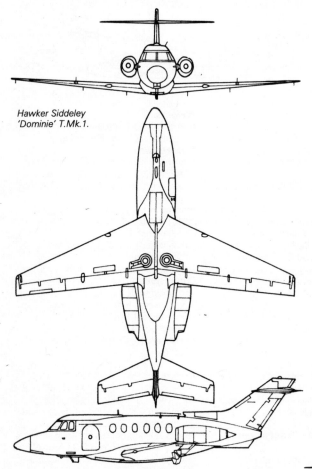

Hawker Siddeley 'Dominie' T.Mk.1.

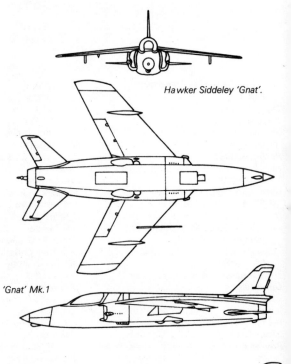

Hawker Siddeley 'Gnat'.

'Gnat' Mk.1

'Gnat' T.Mk.1

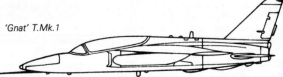

maximum speed at 36,000ft (11,000m)
(Mach 0.98) 646mph (1,040km/hr).
maximum cruising speed 400mph
(645km/hr).
radius of action 500 miles (805km).
initial rate of climb 334.6 ft/sec
(102.0m/sec).
time to 45,000ft (13,700m) 5min 15sec.
service ceiling 50,000ft (15,240m).
Dimensions:
wing span 22ft 2in (6,76m).
length overall 29ft 9in (9.07m).
height overall 8ft 10in (2.69m).
wing area 136.6sq ft (12.69sq m).
Power plant: One Bristol Siddeley
Orpheus 701 turbojet rated at 4,700lb
(2,132kg) st.
Armament: Two 30mm Aden cannon
with 115rpg and max 2,000lb (908kg)
weapon load, e.g. two 500lb (227kg)
or 1,000lb (454kg) bombs or twelve
76mm rockets.
Variants:
Gnat T.1: Two-seat strike-trainer.
HAL Gnat: Indian licence-built Gnat
Mk.1.
Gnat Mk.2: Indian development (Ajit).
First flights:
Prototype: 18 July 1955.
T.1: 31 August 1959.
Ajit: 6 March 1975.
Production:
Mk.1: 45 built 1956–59, plus 215(236?)
Indian licence-built from 1962–74.
T.1: 105 built 1962–64.
Ajit: 2 prototypes, series production
from 1976, 100 planned.
In service:
Mk.1 and Ajit: India (HAL Gnat).
T.1: Great Britain.

Hawker Siddeley 'Harrier' G.R. Mk.3.

Type: Single-seat V/STOL
strike-fighter.
Weights:
empty 12,400lb (5,624kg).
normal 18,000lb (8,165kg).
maximum 26,000lb (11,793kg).
Performance:
maximum speed at 1,000ft (305m)
(Mach 0.95) 720mph (1,160km/hr).
maximum speed with weapon load at
1,000ft (305m) (Mach 0.85) 640mph
(1,030km/hr).
maximum cruising speed at 20,000ft
(6,100m) (Mach 0.8) 560mph
(900km/hr).
tactical radius with two 100gal (455l)
drop tanks 260–400 miles
(420–640km).
ferry range 2,070 miles (3,330km).
initial rate of climb 590.6(?)ft/sec
(180(?)m/sec).
service ceiling 49,900ft (15,250m).
Dimensions:
wing span 25ft 3in (7.70m).
length overall 45ft 7¾in (13.91m).
length overall (T.4) 55ft 9in (17.00m).

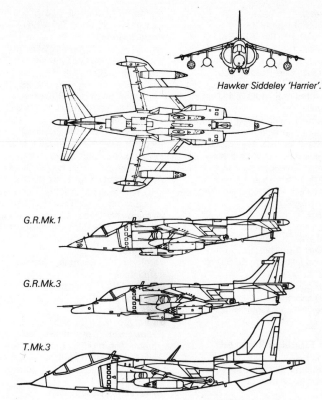

Hawker Siddeley 'Harrier'.

G.R.Mk.1

G.R.Mk.3

T.Mk.3

height overall 11ft 3in (3.43m).
wing area 201.1sq ft (18.68sq m).
Power plant: One Rolls-Royce Bristol
Pegasus 103 turbofan rated at
21,500lb (9,752kg) st.
Armament:
GR.3: Two 30mm Aden cannon with
130rpg in weapon pods and max
5,000lb (2,268kg) weapon load on 5
hard points; e.g. three 1,000lb (454kg)
bombs and two launchers each with
nineteen 68mm rockets.
AV–8A (as fighter): Two AIM–9
Sidewinder AAMs.
Variants:
P.1127 Kestrel: Pre-production model.
Harrier GR.1: Earlier series with less
powerful engine (Pegasus 101 rated at
19,200lb (8,710kg) st), converted to
Harrier GR.1A (with Pegasus 102 rated
20,000lb (9,071kg) st) or to Harrier
GR.3.
Harrier T.2: Two-seat strike-trainer with
Pegasus 101, converted to Harrier
T.2A (Pegasus 102) or to Harrier T.4
(Pegasus 103).
Harrier Mk.50, Mk.51: Export versions
of GR.3 and T.4 resp.
Harrier Mk.52: Further development.
Sea Harrier FSR.1: Improved naval
version.
AV–8B: Further development, 336 to
be built from 1981.
First flights:
P.1127 Kestrel: 31 August 1966.

Gr.1: 28 December 1967.
T.2: 24 April 1967.
Mk.50: 20 November 1970.
Mk.52: 16 September 1971.
Production:
6 pre-production models.
GR.1: 77 built 1968–71.
GR.3: 15 built 1973–75.
T.2: 13 built 1969–72.
Mk.50: 108 built 1970–76.
Mk.51: 10 built 1973–76.
Mk.52: 1 built.
FSR.1: 25 built 1976–77.
In service:
GR.3, T.4: Great Britain.
Mk.50, Mk.51: Spain (Matador), United
States (AV–8A, TAV–8A).

Hawker Siddeley 'Hawk' T.Mk.1.

Type: Two-seat trainer and light
ground-attack aircraft.
Weights:
empty 7,449lb (3,379kg).
normal 10,250lb (4,649kg).
maximum 16,270lb (7,375kg).
Performance:
maximum speed Mach 1.16.
maximum speed at sea level (Mach
0.87) 647mph (1,041km/hr).
cruising speed (Mach 0.8).
radius of action with 4,410lb (2,000kg)
weapon load 320 miies (515km).
ferry range 1,950 miles (3,150km).
range 1,500 miles (2,415km).
time to 30,000ft (9,150m) 6min 20sec.
service ceiling 48,000ft (14,630m).

Dimensions:
wing span 30ft 9¾in (9.39m).
length overall 36ft 8in (11.17m).
height overall 13ft 5in (4.09m).
wing area 179.6sq ft (16.69sq m).
Power plant: One Rolls-Royce
Turboméca RT.172–06–11 Adour 151
turbojet rated at 5,340lb (2,422kg) st.
Armament:
Trainer: Max 1,500lb (680kg) weapon
load on 3 hard points.
Ground-attack aircraft: Max 5,000lb
(2,268kg) weapon load on 5 hard
points, e.g. 1 weapon pack with one
30mm Aden cannon and 2 rocket
launchers each with eighteen 70mm
rockets or eight bombs.
First flights:
Prototype (= pre-production model): 21
August 1974.
Production: 1 pre-production model,
series production from 1975, 175
delivered or on order;
licence-production planned in Finland
(up to 50 aircraft).
In service: Finland, Great Britain (Hawk
T.1).

Hawker Siddeley 'Nimrod' M.R.Mk.1.

Type: Maritime-reconnaissance and
ASW aircraft, 12 man crew.
Weights:

normal 177,500lb (80,510kg).
maximum 192,000lb (87,090kg).
Performance:
patrol speed 210mph (338km/hr).
maximum speed at 32,800ft (10,000m)
575mph (926km/hr).
maximum cruising speed at 29,530ft
(9,000m) 547mph (880km/hr).
ferry range 5,180 miles (8,340km).
Dimensions:
wing span 114ft 10in (35.00m).
length overall 126ft 9in (38.63m).
height overall 29ft 6in (9.01m).
wing area 2,121.0sq ft (197.05sq m).
Power plant: Four Rolls-Royce
RB.168–20 Spey Mk.250 turbofans
each rated at 12,160lb (5,515kg) st.
Armament: Depth-charges, torpedoes,
bombs. Convertible to transport for 45
troops.
Variants:
Nimrod R.1: Electronic reconnaissance
aircraft.
Nimrod MR.2: Planned further
development.
First flights:
Prototype: 23 May 1967.
Production: 2 prototypes; 38
production models 1968–71 plus 3
additional Nimrod R.1, as electronic
reconnaissance aircraft, 8 further
M.R.1 1972–73.
In service: Great Britain.

Hawker Siddeley 'Vulcan' B.Mk.2.

Type: Heavy bomber, 5 man crew.
Weights:
normal 179,898lb (81,600kg).
maximum 200,180lb (90,800kg).
Performance:
maximum speed at sea level (Mach
0.75) 528mph (850km/hr).
maximum speed at 39,375ft (12,000m)
(Mach 0.96) 645mph (1,038km/hr).
maximum cruising speed at 55,100ft
(16,800m) (Mach 0.95) 627mph
(1,009km/hr).
radius of action 1,710–2,300 miles
(2,750–3,700km).
ferry range 4,750 miles (7,650km).
service ceiling 64,960ft (19,800m).
Dimensions:
wing span 111ft 0in (33.83m).
length overall 99ft 11in (30.45m).
height overall 27ft 2in (8.28m).
wing area 3,964sq ft (368.30sq m).
Power plant: Four Bristol Siddeley (RR)
Olympus 301 turbojets each rated at
20,000lb (9,072kg) st.
Armament:
Twenty-one 1,000lb (454kg) bombs in
fuselage bay.
Variants:
B.1, B.1A: Earlier versions, some
converted to reconnaissance aircraft.
Vulcan SR.2: B.2 bomber conversions

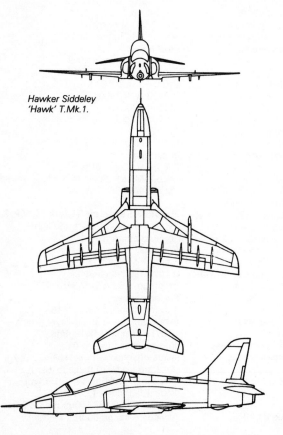

Hawker Siddeley
'Hawk' T.Mk.1.

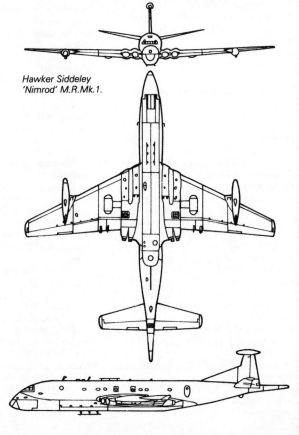

Hawker Siddeley
'Nimrod' M.R.Mk.1.

to reconnaissance aircraft 1974–75.
First flights:
Prototype: 30 August 1952.
B.1: 4 February 1955.
B.2: 19 August 1958.
Production
2 prototypes:
B.1: 42 built 1955–57.
B.2: 76 built 1958–64.
In service: Great Britain (B.2, S.R.2).

Hunting 'Pembroke' C.Mk.1.
Type: Light transport.
Weights:
empty 9,178lb (4,163kg).
normal 13,500lb (6,124kg).
Performance:
maximum speed at 2,000ft (610m)
  224mph (360km/hr).
maximum cruising speed at 8,000ft
  (2,440m) 155mph (249km/hr).
range 1,150 miles (1,850km).
initial rate of climb 17.7ft/sec
  (5.4m/sec).
service ceiling 21,980ft (6,700m).
Dimensions:
wing span 64ft 6in (19.66m).
length overall 45ft 11¾in (14.02m).
height overall 16ft 1in (4.90m).
wing area 400sq ft (37.20sq m).
Power plant: Two 540hp Alvis
  Leonides 127 piston engines.

Payload: 2 man crew and 8 troops.
Variants:
Pembroke C.52, C.53, C.54, C.55:
  Export versions of C.1.
Sea Prince C.1, C.2: Light transports.
Sea Prince T.1: Radar and navigation
  trainer.
First flights:
Prototype: 20 November 1952.
Production:
Pembroke: ? built from 1953, inc 46
  Pembroke (C.1), some of which were
  modernized from 1969–71.
Sea Prince C.1: 3 built.
C.2: 4 built.
T.1: 41 built.
In service:
Pembroke: Great Britain (C.1), Malawi,
  Sudan (C.54), Zambia (C.1).
Sea Prince: Great Britain (C.1, C.2, T.1).

Scottish Aviation 'Bulldog' Series 120.
Type: Two-seat trainer.
Weights:
empty 1,431lb (649kg).
maximum 2,348lb (1,066kg).
Performance:
maximum speed at sea level 150mph
  (241km/hr).
maximum cruising speed at 4,000ft
  (1,220m) 145mph (222km/hr).
ferry range 600 miles (1,000km).

initial rate of climb 17.4ft/sec (5.3m/sec).
service ceiling 16,000ft (4,880m).
Dimensions:
wing span 33ft 0in (10.06m).
length overall 23ft 2in (7.08m).
height overall 7ft 6in (2.28m).
wing area 129.4sq ft (12.02sq m).
Power plant: One 200hp Lycoming
  IO–360–A1B6 piston engine.
Variants:
Bulldog 200 (civil version Bullfinch):
  Further development with retractable
  undercarriage.
First flights:
Prototype: 19 May 1969.
Production: Series production from
  1971, over 290 delivered or on order.
In service: Ghana, Great Britain
  (Bulldog T.1), Jordan, Kenya, Lebanon,
  Malaysia, Nigeria, Sweden (Sk.61).

Short 'Skyvan' 3M.
Type: Light transport.
Weights:
empty 7,400lb (3,356kg).
maximum 14,500lb (6,577kg).
Performance:
maximum speed at 10,000ft (3,050m)
  200mph (323km/hr).
maximum cruising speed at 10,000ft
  (3,050m) 172mph (278km/hr).
range w.m.p. 165 miles (267km).
ferry range 660 miles (1,062km).

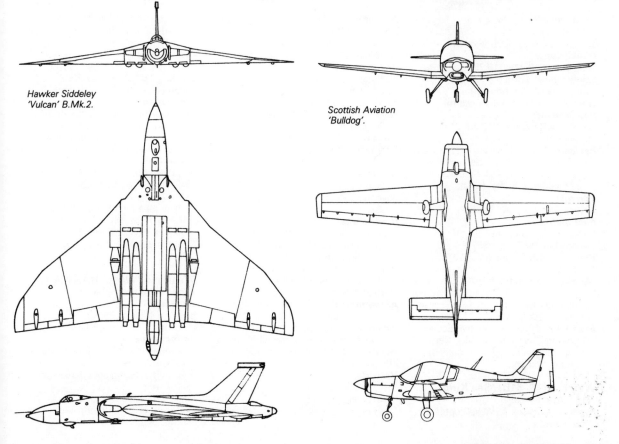

Hawker Siddeley
'Vulcan' B.Mk.2.

Scottish Aviation
'Bulldog'.

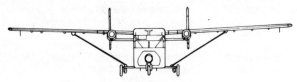

Short 'Skyvan' 3M.

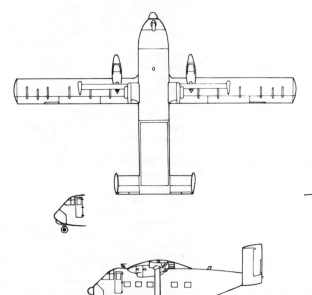

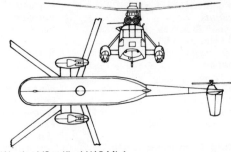

Westland 'Sea King' HAS.Mk.1.

H.A.S.Mk.1.

Commando

initial rate of climb 24.9ft/sec
  (7.6m/sec).
service ceiling 21,000ft (6,400m).
Dimensions:
wing span 64ft 11in (19.79m).
length overall 41ft 4in (12.60m).
height overall 15ft 1in (4.60m).
wing area 372.9sq ft (34.65sq m).
Power plant: Two 715hp
  Garrett-AiResearch TPE331–201
  turboprops.
Payload: 1–2 man crew and 22 troops
  or 16 paratroops and 1 dispatcher or
  12 stretcher cases and 2 medics or
  max 5,000lb (2,268kg) freight.
Variants:
Skyvan Series 3: Civil variant.
First flights:
Prototype Skyvan Series 3A: 15
  December 1967.
Prototype 3M: Beginning of 1970.
Production
Series production from 1970. Over 50
  Skyvan 3M and 65 Skyvan 3 delivered
  or on order by end of 1976. 1 Skyvan
  produced per month.
In service: Argentina, Austria, Ecuador,
  Ghana, Indonesia, Mauritania, Nepal,
  Oman, Singapore, South Yemen(?),
  Thailand, Yemen.

Westland (S–61B) 'Sea King' HAS.Mk.1.
Type: Amphibious ASW helicopter, 4
man crew.

Weights:
empty 12,975lb (5,885kg).
normal 15,474lb (7,019kg).
maximum 21,500lb (9,751kg).
Performance:
maximum speed at sea level 143mph
  (230km/hr).
patrol speed 86mph (138km/hr).
radius of action 95–320 miles
  (150–510km).
range 690 miles (1,110km).
ferry range 1,012 miles (1,630km).
initial rate of climb 29.5ft/sec
  (9.0m/sec).
service ceiling 10,000ft (3,050m).
hovering ceiling in ground effect 5,000ft
  (1,525m).
Dimensions:
main rotor diameter 62ft 0in (18.90m).
length of fuselage 54ft 9in (16.69m).
height 15ft 17in (4.85m).
Power plant: Two 1,500 hp
  Rolls-Royce Gnome H.1400
  turboshafts.
Armament: Four homing torpedoes,
  bombs or four depth-charges.
Payload: As transport: 2 man crew and
  25–27 troops or 9–12 stretcher cases
  and 2 medics or max 6,000lb (2,720kg)
  freight.
Variants:
SH–3D: Basic American model of
  Westland Sea King.
Sea King HAS.2, HAR.3: Improved
  series.

Westland Commando Mk.1, Mk.2:
  Medium transport helicopters for 25
  and 34 troops resp.
First flights:
Prototype: 8 September 1967.
Sea King HAS.1: 7 May 1969.
Commando Mk.1: 12 September 1973.
Production:
Sea King: Series production from 1969:
  197 delivered or on order to date.
Commando: series production from
  1973, 30 delivered or on order to date.
In service:
Sea King: Australia (Mk.50), Belgium
  (Mk.48), Egypt (UAR) (Sea King
  Mk.47), Germany (Mk.41), Great
  Britain (Sea King HAS.1, HAS.2,
  HAR.3), India (Mk.42), Norway
  (Mk.43), Pakistan (Mk.45).
Commando Mk.1, Mk.2: Egypt (UAR),
  Qatar.

Westland 'Wasp' HAS.Mk.1.
Type: ASW helicopter.
Weights:
empty 3,455lb (1,567kg).
maximum 5,500lb (2,495kg).
Performance:
maximum speed at sea level 120mph
  (193km/hr).
maximum cruising speed 109mph
  (176km/hr).
range 270 miles (435km).
initial rate of climb 23.9ft/sec
  (7.3m/sec).

service ceiling 12,200ft (3,720m).
hovering ceiling in ground effect
  12,500ft (3,810m).
hovering ceiling out of ground effect
  8,800ft (2,680m).
Dimensions:
main rotor diameter 32ft 3in (9.83m).
length of fuselage 30ft 3½in (9.25m).
height 8ft 8in (2.64m).
Power plant: One 710hp Rolls-Royce
  Bristol Nimbus 503 turboshaft.
Armament: Max 538lb (244kg) weapon
  load, e.g. 2 homing torpedoes or
  depth-charges or bombs.
Payload: 1–2 man crew.
First flights:
Prototype P.531: 9 August 1959.
Wasp: 28 October 1962.
Production: Series production from
  1963.
In service: Brazil, Great Britain,
  Netherlands (AH–12A), New Zealand,
  South Africa.

Westland 'Scout' AH.Mk.1.

Type: Light AOP helicopter.
Details as for 'Wasp' HAS.Mk.1 with
  the following exceptions.:
Weights:
empty 3,084lb (1,399kg).
maximum 5,300lb (2,404kg).

Performance:
maximum speed at sea level 131mph
  (211km/hr).
maximum cruising speed 122mph
  (196km/hr).
ferry range 315 miles (507km).
initial rate of climb 27.6ft/sec
  (8.4m/sec).
service ceiling 13,400ft (4,085m).
Dimensions:
main rotor diameter 32ft 3in (9.83m).
length of fuselage 30ft 4in (9.24m).
height 8ft 11in (2.72m).
Power plant: One 685hp Rolls-Royce
  Nimbus 101 or 102 turboshaft.
Payload: 2 man crew and 3 troops or 2
  stretcher cases and 1 medic.
First flights: Scout: 4 August 1960.
Production: Over 150 built from
  1961–70.
In service: Bahrain, Great Britain,
  Uganda(?).

Westland 'Wessex' HAS.Mk.3.

Type: ASW helicopter.
Weights:
empty 8,909lb (4,041kg).
maximum 14,013lb (6,356kg).
Performance:
maximum speed at sea level 127mph
  (204km/hr).
maximum cruising speed 121mph
  (195km/hr).
range 300 miles (483km).
initial rate of climb 25.6ft/sec
  (7.8m/sec).
service ceiling 12,000ft (3,660m).
hovering ceiling in ground effect 5,500ft

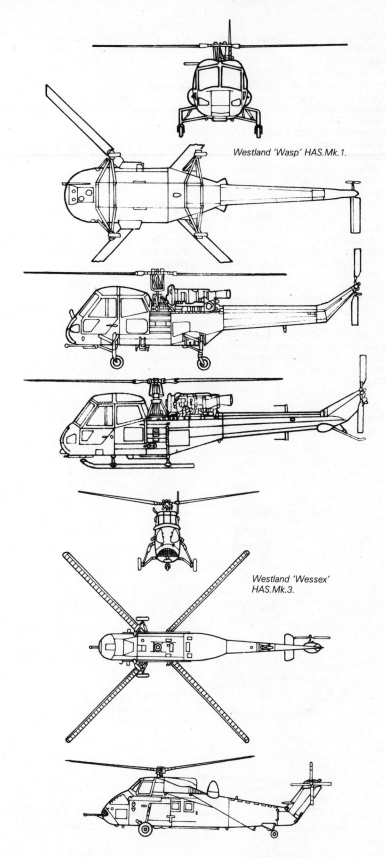

Westland 'Wasp' HAS.Mk.1.

Westland 'Wessex'
HAS.Mk.3.

(1,680m).

hovering ceiling out of ground effect 4,000ft (1,220m).

Dimensions:

main rotor diameter 50ft 0½in (17.08m). length of fuselage 48ft 4½in (14.74m). height 16ft 2in (4.93m).

Power plant: One 1,600hp Rolls-Royce Gazelle 165 turboshaft.

Armament: 2 homing torpedoes.

Payload: 4 man crew.

Variants:

Wessex HAS.1: ASW helicopter.
Wessex HC.2: Transport helicopter.
Wessex Mk.52, Mk.53, Mk.54: Export versions of HC.2.
Wessex HAS.31: ASW helicopter for Australia.

First flights:

Prototype: 17 May 1957.

Production: 376 built of all variants 1958–72.

In service:

HAS.1, HC.2, HAS.3: Great Britain.
HC.2: Oman(?).

Westland 'Wessex' HU.Mk.5.

Type: Medium transport helicopter. Details as for HAS.Mk.3 with the following exceptions.

Weights:

empty 8,664lb (3,930kg).
maximum 13,500lb (6,124kg).

Performance:

maximum speed at sea level 132mph

(212km/hr).
range 270 miles (435km).
ferry range 480 miles (770km).
initial rate of climb 27.6ft/sec (8.4m/sec).

Dimensions:

height 14ft 5in (4.39m).

Power plant: Two coupled 1,550hp Rolls-Royce Gnome 112 and 113 turboshafts.

Payload: 2–3 man crew and 16 troops or 7 stretcher cases or max 4,000lb (1,816kg) freight.

First flights:

HU.5: 31 May 1963.

In service:

HU.5: Bangladesh, Great Britain.

Westland WG.13 'Lynx' AH.Mk.1.

Type: Light transport helicopter.

Weights:

empty 5,530lb (2,509kg).
maximum 9,105lb (4,130kg).

Performance:

maximum speed at sea level 207mph (333km/hr).
maximum cruising speed at sea level 184mph (296km/hr).
range 173–490 miles (278–788km).
ferry range 1,150 miles (1,850km).
initial rate of climb 46.6ft/sec (14.2m/sec).
maximum hovering ceiling out of ground effect 11,975ft (3,650m).

Dimensions:

main rotor diameter 42ft 0in (12.80m). length of fuselage 38ft 3in (11.66m). height 11ft 3in (3.43m).

Power plant: Two 900hp Rolls-Royce BS.360–07–26 turboshafts.

Armament:

HR.2 (ASW version): 2–4 homing torpedoes, or depth-charges or rockets.

Payload: 2 man crew and 9–12 troops or 3 stretcher cases and 1 medic or max 2,738lb (1,242kg) freight.

Variants:

Lynx HR.2: ASW helicopter.
Lynx HT.3: Training helicopter.
HC.4: Liaison helicopter.
Westland 606: Civil variant, 2 man crew and 12 passengers.

First flights:

Prototype: 21 March 1971.
First production model: 6 July 1973.

Production: 6 prototypes, 7 pre-production models, series production from 1973, over 500 delivered or on order to date.

In service:

Lynx AH.1, HC.4, HT.3: Egypt (UAR), Great Britain, Qatar.
Lynx HR.2: Brazil, Egypt (UAR), France, Great Britain, Netherlands (AH–14).

HAL HF–24 'Marut' Mk.1A.

Type: Single-seat fighter and strike-fighter.

Weights:

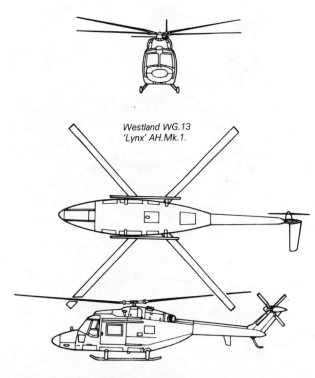

Westland WG.13 'Lynx' AH.Mk.1.

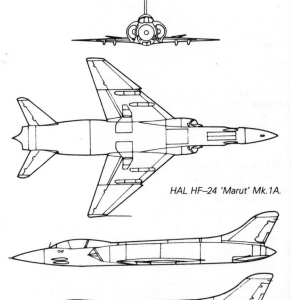

HAL HF–24 'Marut' Mk.1A.

empty 13,658lb (6,195kg).
normal 19,734lb (8,951kg).
maximum 24,048lb (10,908kg).
Performance:
maximum speed at 40,000ft (12,200m) (Mach 1.02) 673mph (1,083km/hr).
maximum speed at 3,280ft (1,000m) 745mph (1,200km/hr).
maximum cruising speed at 36,000ft (11,000m) 559mph (900km/hr).
radius of action 373–423 miles (600–680km).
time to 39,375ft (12,000m) 7min 9sec.
service ceiling 45,932ft (14,000m).
Dimensions:
wing span 29ft 6¼in (9.00m).
length overall 52ft 0¾in (15.87m).
height overall 11ft 9¾in (3.60m).
wing area 306.8sq ft (28.50sq m).
Power plant: Two Rolls-Royce Bristol Orpheus 703 turbojets each rated at 4,850lb (2,200kg) st.
Armament: Four 30mm Aden Mk.2 cannon with 130rpg, 50 unguided 68mm rockets or four 1,000lb (454kg) bombs.
Variants:
HF–24 'Marut' Mk.1T: Two-seat strike-trainer.
HF–24 'Marut' Mk.1A, Mk.1R, Mk.2, Mk.3: Later series with more powerful engines.
First flights:
Prototype: 17 June 1961.
First production model: March 1963.

Prototype HF–24 Mk.1T: 30 April 1970.
Production:
'Marut' Mk.1: 2 prototypes, 15(18?) pre-production and 107 production models from 1965–76.
'Marut' Mk.1T: 2 prototypes, 10 production models from 1971–72.
'Marut' Mk.1R: 4 built 1973–74(?).
In service: India.

HAL HJT–16 Mk.2. 'Kiran'.
Type: Two-seat trainer.
Weights:
empty 5,644lb (2,560kg).
normal 7,940lb (3,600kg).
maximum 9,260lb (4,200kg).
Performance:
maximum speed at 30,000ft (9,150m) 428mph (688km/hr).
maximum speed at sea level 432mph (695km/hr).
maximum cruising speed at 30,000ft (9,150m) 265mph (426km/hr).
range 465 miles (748km).
ferry range 620 miles (1,000km).
initial rate of climb 79.1ft/sec (24.1m/sec).
time to 30,180ft (9,200m) 10min 30sec.
service ceiling 42,200ft (12,800m).
Dimensions
wing span 35ft 1¾in (10.71m).
length overall 34ft 9in (10.60m).
height overall 11ft 11½in (3.64m).
wing area 204.5sq ft (19.00sq m).
Power plant: One Rolls-Royce Viper

ASV.11 turbojet rated at 2,500lb (1,134kg) st.
Armament: Two 7.62mm machine-guns and four 29lb (13kg) practice bombs or twelve 68mm rockets.
First flights:
Prototype: 4 September 1964.
Production: 2 prototypes, 24 pre-production models from 1966–70, 36 production models from 1969–70, further 100 planned.
In service: India.

HAL HT–2.
Type: Two-seat trainer.
Weights:
empty 1,533lb (699kg).
normal 2,236lb (1,016kg).
Performance:
maximum speed 130mph (209km/hr).
maximum cruising speed 115mph (185km/hr).
range 350 miles (563km).
initial rate of climb 13.1ft/sec (4.0m/sec).
service ceiling 14,500ft (4,420m).
Dimensions:
wing span 35ft 3in (10.74m).
length overall 24ft 8½in (7.53m).
height overall 8ft 11in (2.72m).
wing area 173.3sq ft (16.10sq m).
Power plant: One 155hp Blackburn Cirrus Major III piston engine.
First flights:

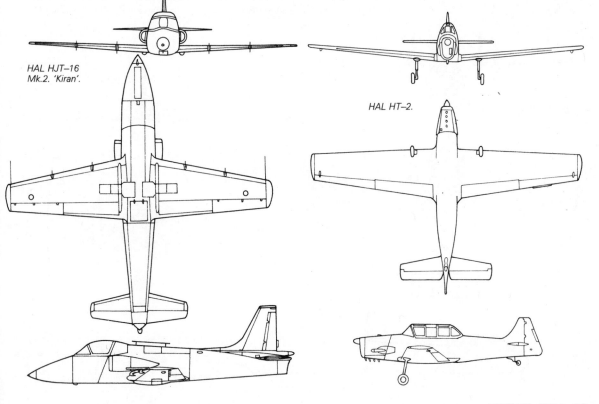

HAL HJT–16 Mk.2. 'Kiran'.

HAL HT–2.

Prototype: 5 August 1951.
Production: 169 built from 1952–58.
In service: India.

IAI–201 'Arava'.
Type: Light transport.
Weights:
empty 7,787lb (3,532kg).
maximum 14,998lb (6,803kg).
Performance:
maximum speed at 10,000ft (3,050m) 203mph (326km/hr).
maximum cruising speed at 10,000ft (3,050m) 193mph (310km/hr).
range 200 miles (323km).
ferry range 800 miles (1,300km).
initial rate of climb 25.9ft/sec (7.9m/sec).
service ceiling 24,000ft (7,315m).
Dimensions:
wing span 68ft 6in (20.88m).
length overall 42ft 7½in (12.99m).
height overall 17ft 1in (5.21m).
wing area 470.17sq ft (43.68sq m).
Power plant: Two 783hp Pratt & Whitney PT6A–34 turboprops.
Armament: Optional: Two 12.7mm machine-guns with 250rpg in weapon fuselage weapon pods and one 12.7mm machine-gun in tail position plus max 1,213lb (550kg) weapon load on two fuselage hard points, e.g. sixteen 82mm rockets.
Payload: 2 man crew and 23 troops or 16 paratroops or 8 stretcher cases and 2 medics or max 5,510lb (2,500kg) freight.
First flights:

Prototype IAI–101: 27 November 1970.
Prototype IAI–201: 1971.
Production: 2 prototypes, series production from 1972, over 80 delivered or on order to date.
In service: Bolivia, Ecuador, El Salvador, Guatemala, Honduras, Israel, Mexico, Nicaragua.

IAI 'Kfir'. C2.
Type: Single-seat fighter and strike-fighter.
Weights:
empty 16,072lb (7,290kg).
normal 20,700lb (9,390kg).
maximum 32,190lb (14,600kg).
Performance:
maximum speed at 36,090ft (11,000m) (Mach 2.34).
maximum speed at sea level (Mach 1.11).
radius of action 217–746 miles (350–1,200km).
initial rate of climb 787.4ft/sec (240.0m/sec).
time to 36,090ft (11,000m) 1min 45sec.
service ceiling 55,775ft (17,000m).
Dimensions:
wing span 26ft 11½in (8.22m).
length overall 51ft 0in (15.55m).
height overall 13ft 11¼in (4.25m).
wing area 375.12sq ft (34.85sq m).
Power plant: One General Electric J79–GE–17 turbojet rated at 11,872/17,900lb (5,385/8,120kg) st.
Armament: Two 30mm DEFA cannon with 180rpg and (fighter version) two or four Shafrir AAMs or (strike-fighter

version) max 8,819(?)lb (4,000(?)kg) weapon load on 7 hard points.
Variants:
Kfir: Earlier version without foreplanes.
Dassault 'Mirage' IIIC: Single-seat fighter and strike-fighter.
'Barak': Initial designation of 'Kfir'.
First flights:
Prototype: September 1971.
Production: series production from 1973; 40 delivered up to end 1975.
In service: Israel.

Aeritalia-Aermacchi AM.3C.
Type: Liaison and AOP aircraft.
Weights:
empty 2,533lb (1,149kg).
normal 3,307lb (1,500kg).
maximum 3,858lb (1,750kg).
Performance:
maximum speed at sea level 162mph (260km/hr).
maximum speed at 8,000ft (2,440m) 173mph (278km/hr).
maximum cruising speed at 8,000ft (2,440m) 153mph (246km/hr).
ferry range 615 miles (990km).
initial rate of climb 22.9ft/sec (7.0m/sec).
time to 9,840ft (3,000m) 7min 30sec.
service ceiling 27,560ft (8,400m).
Dimensions:
wing span 41ft 5¾in (12,64m).
length overall 29ft 10in (9.09m).
height overall 8ft 11in (2.72m).
wing area 219.1sq ft (20.36sq m).
Power plant: One 340hp Piaggio Lycoming GSO–480–B1B6 piston

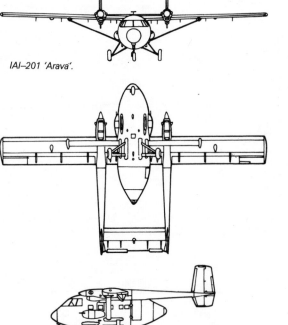

IAI–201 'Arava'.

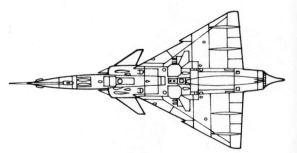

IAI 'Kfir'.

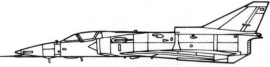

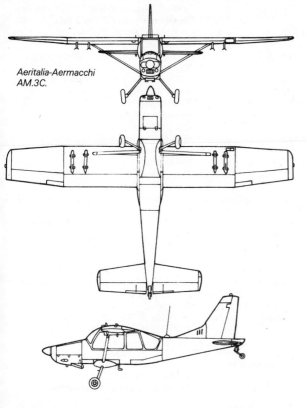

Aeritalia-Aermacchi AM.3C.

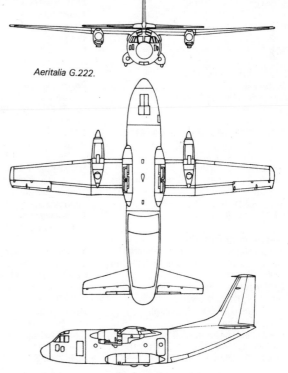

Aeritalia G.222.

engine.

Armament: Max 1,150lb (522kg)
weapon load on 4 hard points, e.g.
two weapon packs each containing
two 7.62mm machine-guns with
1,000rpg or one Minigun or two Matra
rocket launchers each containing six
70mm rockets or two 250lb (113kg) or
200lb (91kg) bombs.

Variants:
Kudu: South African further
development by Atlas.

Payload: 1 man crew and 2 troops.

First flights:
Prototype: 12 May 1967.

Production: 2 Prototypes, series
production from 1972, 63 delivered or
on order to date.

In service: Italy, Rwanda, South Africa
(Bosbok).

Aeritalia G.222.

Type: Medium transport.

Weights:
empty 32,166lb (14,590kg).
normal 54,013lb (24,500kg).
maximum 58,422lb (26,500kg).

Performance:
maximum speed at 15,500ft (4,575m)
335mph (540km/hr).
maximum speed at sea level 329mph
(530km/hr).
maximum cruising speed at 14,750ft
(4,500m) 273mph (440km/hr).
range 3,262 miles (5,250km).

ferry range with 11,020lb (5,000kg)
payload 2,030 miles (3,250km).
initial rate of climb 31.5ft/sec
(9.6m/sec).
service ceiling 25,000ft (7,620m).

Dimensions:
wing span 94ft 6¼in (28.80m).
length overall 74ft 5½in (22.70m).
height overall 32ft 1¾in (9.80m).
wing area 970.9sq ft (90.20sq m).

Power plant: Two 3,400hp General
Electric T64–P4D turboprops.

Payload: 3–4 man crew and 44 troops
or 32 paratroops or 36 stretcher cases
and 8 medics or max 19,840lb
(9,000kg) payload.

First flights:
Prototype: 18 July 1970.

Production: 2 prototypes, 6
pre-production models, series
production 1972–73; 48 delivered or
on order to date.

In service: Argentina, Dubai, Italy.

Aermacchi MB.326G.

Type: Two-seat trainer.

Weights:
empty 5,920lb (2,685kg).
maximum 10,090lb (4,577kg).

Performance:
maximum speed at 20,000ft (6,100m)
(Mach 0.82) 524mph (843km/hr).
maximum cruising speed 495mph
(797km/hr).
ferry range 1,520 miles (2,445km).

initial rate of climb 101ft/sec
(30.8m/sec).
time to 20,000ft (6,100m) 4min 10sec.
Service ceiling 39,050ft (11,900m).

Dimensions:
wing span 33ft 3¾in (10.15m).
length overall 34ft 11¼in (10.65m).
height overall 12ft 2½in (3.72m).
wing area 208.3sq ft (19.35sq m).

Power plant: One Rolls-Royce Viper
20 Mk.540 turbojet rated at 3,410lb
(1,547kg) st.

Armament: Max 4,000lb (1,814kg)
weapon load on 6 hard points, e.g.
bombs and rockets.

Variants:
MB.326, MB.326B, MB.326E,
MB.326F: Earlier versions.
MB.326GB: Export version of
MB.326G, licence-built in Australia by
GAF (MB.326H), in Brazil by Embraer
(AT–26 Xavante), and in South Africa
by Atlas (MB.326M).
MB.326K: Single-seat light
ground-attack aircraft, licence-built in
South Africa.

First flights:
Prototype MB.326: 10 December 1957.
MB.326G: 9 May 1967.
MB.326K: 22 August 1970.

Production
Series production from 1959.
MB.326: 100 built.
MB.326B: 8 built.
MB.326E: 12 built.

MB.326F: 7 built.
MB.326G: – built.
MB.326GB: 206(?) built
(inc 155 AT–26 Xavante).
MB.326H: 108 built.
MB.326K: 46 built.
MB.326KD: 7 built.
MB.326L: 1 built.
MB.326M: 160 built.
In service:
MB.326, MB.326G: Italy.
MB.326B: Tunisia.
MB.326F: Ghana.
MB.326GB: Argentina, Brazil (AT–26
Xavante), Bolivia, Congo, Togo
(AT–26), Zambia.
MB.326H: Australia.
MB.326K: Argentina, Ghana, South
Africa.
MB.326KD, MB.326L: Dubai.
MB.326M: South Africa (Impala).

Aermacchi MB.326K.
Type: Light ground-attack aircraft.
Details as for trainer with the following
exceptions:
Weights:
empty 5,920lb (2,558kg).
maximum 11,500lb (5,216kg).
Performance:
maximum speed at 20,000ft (6,100m)
(Mach 0.75) 483mph (778km/hr).
radius of action 80–404 miles

(130–650km).

Fiat G.91R.1 and R.3.
Type: Single-seat strike-fighter and
reconnaissance aircraft.
Weights:
empty 6,834lb (3,100kg).
normal 11,750lb (5,330kg).
maximum 12,522lb (5,680kg).
Performance:
maximum speed at sea level (Mach
0.88) 668mph (1,075km/hr).
maximum speed at 5,000ft (1.500m)
(Mach 0.9) 674mph (1,085km/hr).
radius of action 195–373 miles
(315–600km).
ferry range 1,150 miles (1,850km).
initial rate of climb 98.4ft/sec
(30.0m/sec).
service ceiling 39,375ft (12,000m).
Dimensions:
wing span 28ft 1in (8.56m).
length overall 33ft 9½in (10.30m).
height overall 31ft 1in (4.00m).
wing area 176.6sq ft (16.43sq m).
Power plant: One Bristol Siddeley
Orpheus 803 turbojet rated at 5,000lb
(2,270kg) st.
Armament:
R.1, R.4: Four 12.7mm machine-guns
with 300rpg and max 1,000lb (454kg)
weapon load.
R.3: Two 30mm DEFA 552 cannon

with 125rpg and max 1,000lb (454kg)
weapon load, e.g. two 500lb (227kg)
bombs or two A.S.20 ASMs or rocket
launchers.
R.1, R.3, R.4: 1–3 cameras.
Variants:
G.91T.1, T.4: Two-seat strike-trainer.
G.91PAN: Aerobatic machine.
First flights:
Prototype: 9 August 1956.
G.91T: 31 May 1960.
First G.91 completed in Germany: 20
July 1961.
Production
Series production from 1958–66; 3
prototypes and 27 pre-production
models inc 16 converted to G.91PAN.
G.91R.1: 98 built.
G.91R.3: 344 built, inc 294 licence-built
by Dornier.
G.91R.4: 50 built.
G.91T.1: 76 built, plus 25(?) repeat
orders from 1971.
G.91T.3: 44 built, plus 22 repeat orders
from 1969–71.
In service:
G.91R.1, G.91T.1, G.91PAN: Italy.
G.91R.3, G.91T.3: Germany (West),
Portugal.
G.91R.4: Portugal.

Fiat G.91Y.
Type: Single-seat strike-fighter and

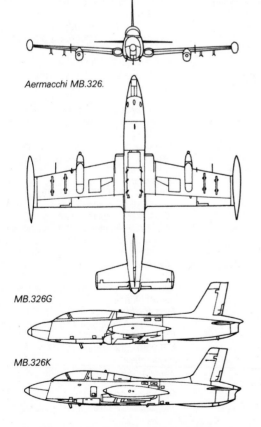

Aermacchi MB.326.

MB.326G

MB.326K

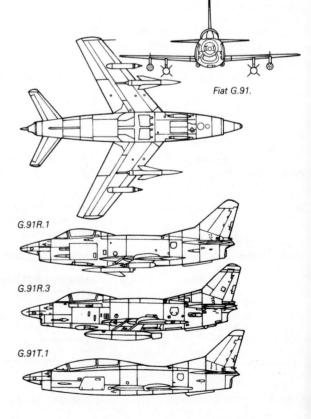

Fiat G.91.

G.91R.1

G.91R.3

G.91T.1

reconnaissance aircraft.

Weights:
empty 8,598lb (3,900kg).
normal 17,196lb (7,800kg).
maximum 19,180lb (8,700kg).

Performance:
maximum speed at sea level (Mach 0.9)
690mph (1,110km/hr).
maximum speed at 32,810ft (10,000m)
(Mach 0.95) 671mph (1,080km/hr).
maximum cruising speed at 492ft
(150m) 391mph (630km/hr).
radius of action 239–466 miles
(385–750km).
ferry range 2,110 miles (3,400km).
initial rate of climb 283.5ft/sec
(86.4m/sec).
time to 40,000ft (12,200m) 4min 30sec.
service ceiling 41,000ft (12,500m).

Dimensions:
wing span 29ft 6½in (9.01m).
length overall 38ft 3½in (11.67m).
height overall 14ft 6in (4.43m).
wing area 195.15sq ft (18.13sq m).

Power plant: Two General Electric
J85–GE–13A turbojets each rated at
2,720lb (1,236kg)/4,080lb (1,850kg) st.

Armament: Two 30mm DEFA 552
cannon and max 4,000lb (1,814kg)
weapon load on 4 hard points.

Variants:
G.91YT: Planned two-seat strike-trainer.

First flights:

Prototype: 27 December 1966.

Production
2 prototypes.
20 pre-production models from
1968–71, delivery of 55 production
models from 1971–73.

In service: Italy.

Piaggio P.166M.

Type: Light transport.

Weights:
empty 5,181lb (2,350kg).
maximum 8,115lb (3,681kg).

Performance:
maximum speed at 9,500ft (2,900m)
222mph (357km/hr).
maximum cruising speed at 12,800ft
(3,900m) 207mph (333km/hr).
range 801 miles (1,290km).
ferry range 1,199 miles (1,930km).
initial rate of climb 20.7ft/sec
(6.3m/sec).
service ceiling 25,527ft (7,780m).

Dimensions:
wing span 45ft 9in (14.25m).
length overall 38ft 0½in (11.60m).
height overall 16ft 5in (5.00m).
wing area 285.9sq ft (26.56sq m).

Power plant: Two 340hp Lycoming
GSO–480–B–1C6 piston engines.

Payload: 1 man crew and max 10
troops.

Variants:

P.166, P.166B Portofino, P.166C: Civil
variants.
P.166S: Maritime-reconnaissance
variant for South Africa.
P.166–DL3: Improved variant, two
587hp Arco Lycoming LTP–101–600
turboprops.

First flights:
Prototype: 26 November 1957.
P166B: March 1962.
P166C: 1964.
P.166–DL3: 3 July 1976.

Production:
P.166, P.166B, P.166C: Approx 50 built.
P.166M: 51 built from 1961–1963.
P.166S: 9 built 1968/69.

In service:
P.166M: Italy.
P.166S: South Africa (Albatross).

Siai-Marchetti S.208M.

Type: Liaison aircraft.

Weights:
empty 1,823lb (827kg).
maximum 3,310lb (1,502kg).

Performance:
maximum speed at sea level 177mph
(285km/hr).
maximum cruising speed at 6,560ft
(2,000m) 161mph (260km/hr).
range 746 miles (1,200km).
ferry range 1,118 miles (1,800km).
service ceiling 21,000ft (6,400m).

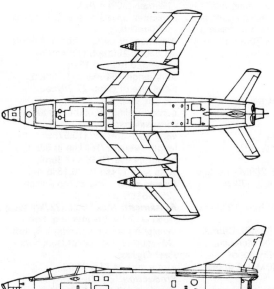

Fiat G.91Y.

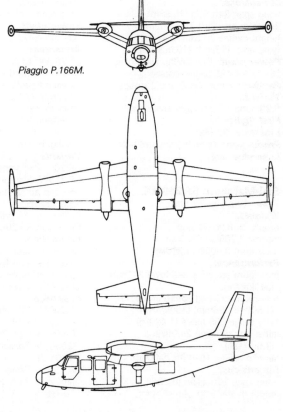

Piaggio P.166M.

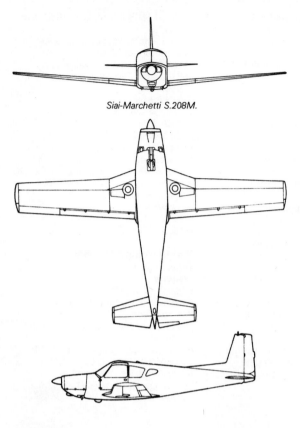

Siai-Marchetti S.208M.

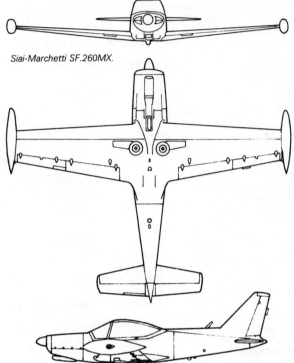

Siai-Marchetti SF.260MX.

Dimensions:
wing span 34ft 8½in (10.88m).
length overall 26ft 7in (8.09m).
height overall 9ft 5¾in (2.89m).
wing area 173sq ft (16.09sq m).
Power plant: One 260hp Lycoming
O–540–E4A5 piston engine.
Payload: 2 man crew and 3 troops.
Variants:
S.205 and S.208: Light civil aircraft.
First flights:
Prototype: 22 May 1967.
Production: 44 built from 1968–74.
In service: Italy.

Siai-Marchetti SF.260MX.
Type: Two-seat trainer.
Weights:
empty 1,587lb (720kg).
normal 2,205lb (1,000kg).
maximum 3,000lb (1,360kg).
Performance:
maximum speed at sea level 211mph
(340km/hr).
maximum cruising speed at 4,920ft
(1,500m) 186mph (300km/hr).
ferry range 895 miles (1,440kg).
initial rate of climb 24.9ft/sec
(7.6m/sec).
service ceiling 16,400ft (5,000m).
Dimensions:
wing span 26ft 11¾in (8.25m).
length overall 23ft 3½in (7.10m).

height overall 7ft 11in (2.41m).
wing area 108.5sq ft (10.10sq m).
Power plant: One 260hp Lycoming
O–540–E4A5 piston engine.
Armament:
SF.260W: Max 661lb (300kg) weapon
load on 2 hard points, e.g. two Matra
weapon packs each containing two
7.62mm MAC AAF1 machine-guns or
two rocket launchers each containing
eighteen 50mm or nine 70mm rockets
or two 265lb (120kg) or two 110lb
(50kg) bombs.
Variants:
SF.260: Civil variant.
SF.260W Warrior: Light trainer and
ground-attack aircraft.
First flights:
Prototype: 15 July 1964.
Prototype SF.206W: May 1972.
Production:
Series production of SF.260MX military
export variant from 1969, 173(?)
delivered or on order.
SF.260W: Over 40 built from 1973–74.
In service:
SF.260MX: Belgium (260MB), Burma,
Congo (260MC), Italy(?), Morocco,
Philippines (260MP), Singapore
(260MS), Thailand (260MT), Zambia
(260MZ).
SF.260W: Congo (260WC), Dubai
(260WD), Eire, Philippines (260WP),
Tunisia (260WT).

Siai-Marchetti SM.1019A.
Type: Liaison and AOP aircraft.
Weights:
empty 1,500lb (680kg).
maximum 2,800lb (1,270kg).
Performance:
maximum speed at 6,000ft (1,830m)
188mph (302km/hr).
maximum speed at sea level 182mph
(293km/hr).
maximum cruising speed at 6,000ft
(1,830m) 155mph (250km/hr).
range 320 miles (515km).
ferry range 764 miles (1,230km).
initial rate of climb 27.2ft/sec
(8.3m/sec).
service ceiling 19,680ft (6,000m).
Dimensions:
wing span 36ft 0in (10.97m).
length overall 27ft 11½in (8.52m).
height overall 7ft 9¾in (2.38m).
wing area 174sq ft (16.16sq m).
Power plant: One 317hp Allison
250–B15G turboprop.
Armament: Max 500lb (227kg) weapon
load on 2 hard points, e.g. two
weapon packs containing 7.62mm
Minigun or two rocket launchers.
First flights:
Prototype: 24 May 1969.
Production: 2 prototypes, series
production from 1972/73–76, 100
delivered or on order to date.
In service: Italy.

Fuji KM–2.

Type: Two-seat trainer.
Weights:
empty 2,386lb (1,083kg).
maximum 3,286lb (1,495kg).
Performance:
maximum speed at sea level 201mph
  (323km/hr).
maximum speed at 16,400ft (5,000m)
  227mph (365km/hr).
maximum cruising speed 183mph
  (295km/hr).
ferry range 767 miles (1,235km).
initial rate of climb 25.9ft/sec
  (7.9m/sec).
service ceiling 29,200ft (8.900m).
Dimensions:
wing span 32ft 10in (10.00m).
length overall 26ft 1in (7.95m).
height overall 9ft 7in (2.92m).
wing area 177.6sq ft (16.49sq m).
Power plant: One 340hp Lycoming
  IGSO–480–A1C6 piston engine.
Variants:
Fuji LM–1 and LM–2 Nikko: Four-seat
  liaison aircraft and trainers.
KM–2B: Further development.
First flights:
LM–1: 6 June 1955.
Production:
LM–1: 27 built 1956–57, some
  converted to LM–2 with more
  powerful engine.
LM–2: ? built.
KM–2: 28 built 1963–69.
KM–2B: 60(?) built from 1976–77.
In service: Japan.

Fuji T–1A 'Hatsutaka'.

Type: Two-seat trainer.
Weights:
empty 6,088lb (2,757kg).
normal 9,500lb (4,310kg).
maximum 11,000lb (4,993kg).
Performance:
maximum speed at 20,000ft (6,100m)
  576mph (927km/hr).
maximum cruising speed at 30,000ft
  (9,150m) 404mph (650km/hr).
range 652 miles (1050km).
ferry range 1,210 miles (1,950km).
initial rate of climb 108.3ft/sec (33.0m/sec).
service ceiling 45,930ft (14,000m).
Dimensions:
wing span 34ft 5in (10.50m).
length overall 39ft 9in (12.12m).
height overall 13ft 4½in (4.07m).
wing area 239.2sq ft (22.22sq m).
Power plant: One Bristol Siddeley
  Orpheus 805 turbojet rated at 4,000lb
  (1,810kg) st.
Armament:
One 12.7mm machine-gun and max
  1,500lb (680kg) weapon load, e.g. two
  12.7mm machine-guns in weapon
  packs, two Sidewinder AAMs, two
  rocket launchers or two bombs.
First flights:
Prototype: 19 January 1958.

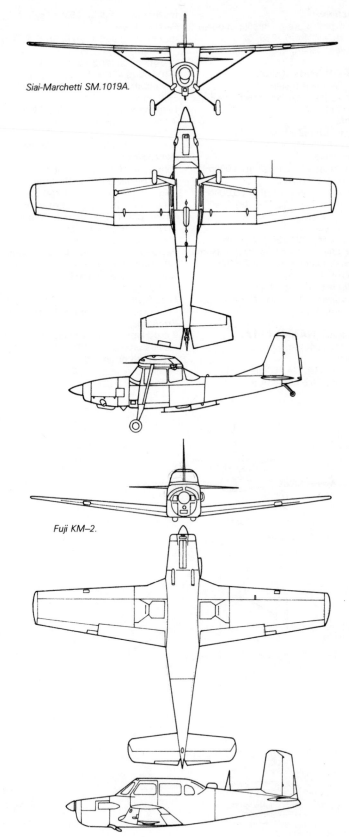

Siai-Marchetti SM.1019A.

Fuji KM–2.

Production:
2 prototypes, 4 pre-production models.
T–1A: 40 built from 1959–62.
In service: Japan.

Fuji T–1B 'Hatsutaka'.
Type: Two-seat trainer.
Details as for T–1A with the following
  exceptions:
Weights:
empty 6,261lb (2,840kg).
normal 9,680lb (4,390kg).
Performance:
maximum speed at 19,685ft (6,000m)
  518mph (834km/hr).
maximum cruising speed at 30,000ft
  (9,150m) 357mph (575km/hr).
initial rate of climb 78.7ft/sec
  (24.0m/sec).
service ceiling 39,370ft (12,000m).
Power plant: One Ishikawajima-Harima
  J3–IHI–3 turbojet rated at 2,646lb
  (1,200kg) st.
First flights: 17 May 1960.
Production: T–1B: 20 built 1961–63.
In service: Japan.

Kawasaki (NAMC) C–1A.
Type: Medium transport.
Weights:
empty 53,130lb (24,100kg).
normal 85,980lb (39,000kg).

maximum 99,200lb (45,000kg).
Performance:
maximum speed at 25,000ft (7,620m)
  489mph (787km/hr).
maximum cruising speed at 34,800ft
  (10,600m) 426mph (685km/hr).
range with 17,640lb (8,000kg) payload
  865 miles (1,295km).
ferry range 2,072 miles (3,335km).
initial rate of climb 66.6ft/sec
  (20.3m/sec).
service ceiling 39,375ft (12,000m).
Dimensions:
wing span 100ft 4½in (30.60m).
length overall 95ft 1⅞in (29.00m).
height overall 32ft 9¾in (10.00m).
wing area 1,297.0sq ft (120.50sq m).
Power plant: Two Pratt & Whitney
  JT8D–9 turbofans each rated at
  14,500lb (6,575kg) st.
Payload: 5 man crew and 60 troops or
  45 paratroops or 36 stretcher cases
  and medics or max 17,637lb
  (8,000kg(?) freight.
First flights:
Prototype: 12 November 1970.
Production:
2 prototypes, 2 pre-production models,
  series production 1972–73, 24
  delivered or on order to date, 10
  additional orders likely.
In service: Japan.

Mitsubishi MU–2C.
Type: Liaison and reconnaissance
  aircraft.
Weights:
empty 5,340lb (2,422kg).
maximum 8,929lb (4,050kg).
Performance:
maximum cruising speed at 10,000ft
  (3,050m) 310mph (500km/hr).
ferry range 1,200 miles (1,930km).
initial rate of climb 35.4ft/sec (10.8
  m/sec).
service ceiling 26,080ft (7,950m).
Dimensions:
wing span 39ft 2in (11.94m).
length overall 33ft 2⅜in (10.13m).
height overall 12ft 11¼in (3.94m).
wing area 177.6sq ft (16.50sq m).
Power plant: Two 605hp
  Garrett-AiResearch TPE–331–25A
  turboprops.
Armament:
MU–2C: Two 12.7mm machine-guns,
  practice bombs, rockets, 2 cameras.
Payload: 1 man crew and 6–8 troops.
Variants:
MU–2E: ASR aircraft.
MU–2G, MU–2J, MU–2K, MU–2L.
MU–2M: Further developments.
First flights:
Prototype: 14 September 1963.
Production:

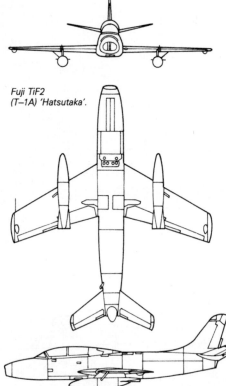

Fuji TiF2
(T–1A) 'Hatsutaka'.

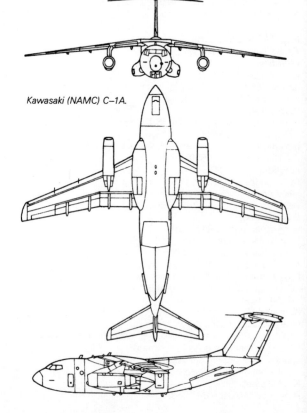

Kawasaki (NAMC) C–1A.

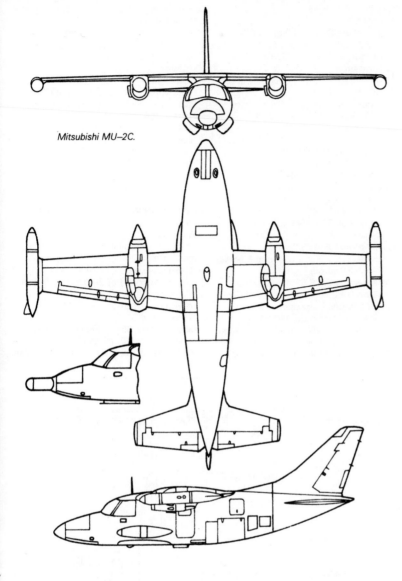

Mitsubishi MU–2C.

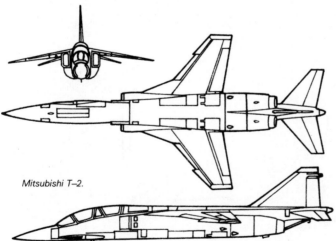

Mitsubishi T–2.

Series production from 1966, over 415 delivered or on order by 1975, inc 48 military variants: 10 MU–2C, 19 MU–2E, 4 MU–2G, 7 MU–2J, 18 MU–2K.

In service:
MU–2C: Japan (LR–1); MU–2E: Japan (MU–2S); MU–2G, MU–2K: Japan, MU–2J: Congo, Japan, Mexico.

Mitsubishi T–2.
Type: Two-seat strike-trainer.
Weights:
empty 13,660lb (6,197kg).
normal 21,330lb (9,675kg).
maximum 28,220lb (12,801kg).
Performance:
maximum speed at 40,000ft (12,000m) (Mach 1.6) 1,056mph (1,700km/hr).
radius of action 340(?) miles (565(?) km).
ferry range 1,600 miles (2,575km).
initial rate of climb 583.3ft/sec (177.8m/sec).
service ceiling 50,000ft (15,240m).
Dimensions:
wing span 25ft 10¼in (7.88m).
length overall 58ft 6¾in (17.85m).
height overall 14ft 3¼in (4.45m).
wing area 228.2sq ft (21.20sq m).
Power plant: Two Ishikawajima-Harima TF40–iHi–801A (Rolls-Royce Turboméca Rb.172–T.260 Adour) turbofans each rated at 3,810/7,070lb (1,728/3,207kg) st.
Armament:
T–2: One 20mm M–61A1 cannon with 750rpg and max – weapon load on 5 hard points, e.g. two AAMs or bombs or ASMs.
FS–T2kai: One 20mm M–61A1 cannon with 750rpg and max 6,000lb (2,722kg) weapon load on 7 hard points, e.g. (as fighter) 2 or 4 AAMs or (as strike-fighter) eight 500lb (227kg) bombs and 2 ASMs.
Variants:
Mitsubishi FS–T2kai: Single-seat strike-fighter, redesignated F–1.
First flights:
Prototype T–2: 20 July 1971.
Prototype FS–T2kai: 3 June 1975.
Production:
4 prototypes; series production from 1973, 42 T–2 delivered or on order to date, a further 17 planned.
FS–T2kai: 2 prototypes, 18 delivered or on order, a further 50 planned.
In service: Japan.

NAMC YS–11A.
Type: Medium transport.
Weights:
empty 33,942lb (15,396kg).
maximum 54,010lb (24,500kg).
Performance:
maximum speed at 15,000ft (4,575m). 291mph (469km/hr).
maximum cruising speed at 20,000ft (6,100m) 281mph (452km/hr).

range w.m.p. 680miles (1,090km).
ferry range 1,998 miles (3,215km).
initial rate of climb 20.3ft/sec
(6.2m/sec).
service ceiling 22,900ft (6,980m).

Dimensions:
wing span 104ft 11¾in (32.00m).
length overall 86ft 3½in (26.30m).
height overall 29ft 5½in (8.98m).
wing area 1,020.4sq ft (94.80sq m).

Power plant: Two 3,060hp Rolls-Royce
Dart Mk.542–10K turboprops.

Payload: 2 man crew and 32–48
troops or max 13,228lb (6,000kg)
payload.

Variants:
YS–11A–206: ASW trainer.
YS–11A–207: ASR aircraft.

First flights:
Prototype: 30 August 1962.

Production:
2 prototypes, 182 built 1963–72, 20 of
which delivered to Japanese air arms
(16 as transports and 4 as ASW
trainers).

In service: Gabon, Japan, Philippines.

Shin Meiwa PS–1.
Type: Amphibious
maritime-reconnaissance and ASW
aircraft, 10 man crew.

Weights:
empty 58,000lb (26,300kg).
normal 79,366lb (36,000kg).
maximum 99,208lb (45,000kg).

Performance:
maximum speed at 5,000ft (1,520m)
340mph (547km/hr).
maximum cruising speed at 5,000ft
(1,520m) 265mph (426km/hr).
range 1,346 miles (2,167km).
ferry range 2,948 miles (4,745km).
initial rate of climb 22.8ft/sec
(6.9m/sec).
service ceiling 29,500ft (9,000m).

Dimensions:
wing span 108ft 8¾in (33.14m).
length overall 109ft 11¼in (33.50m).
height overall 31ft 10in (9.71m).
wing area 1,453.1sq ft (135.80sq m).

Power plant: Four 3,060hp
Ishikawajima-Harima (General Electric)
T64–IHI–10 turboprops.

Armament: Max 8,820lb (4,000kg)
weapon load, e.g. four 330lb (150kg)
depth-charges in weapons bay, two
underwing pods mounted between
each pair of engine nacelles and each
containing two homing torpedoes, and
one launcher beneath each wingtip
each containing three 127mm rockets.

Variants:
US–1: Further developments as ASR
aircraft (old designation SS–2A), 8 man
crew, 36 stretcher cases and 5
medics.

First flights:
Prototypes SS–2: 5 October 1967.
Prototype US–1: 16 October 1974.

Production:
PS–1: 2 prototypes SS–2, 2
pre-production models 1972, 14
production models 1972–76; further
orders planned.

In service:
PS–1, US–1: Japan.

Fokker-VFW F.27M 'Troopship'.
Type: Medium transport.

Weights:
empty 23,200lb (10,524kg).
maximum 42,000lb (19,051kg).

Performance:
maximum speed at 20,000ft (6,100m)
305mph (491km/hr).
maximum cruising speed 282mph
(454km/hr).
range w.m.p. 656 miles (1,056km).
ferry range 1,285 miles (2,068km).
initial rate of climb 23.3ft/sec (7.1m/sec).

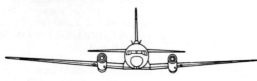

NAMC YS–11A.

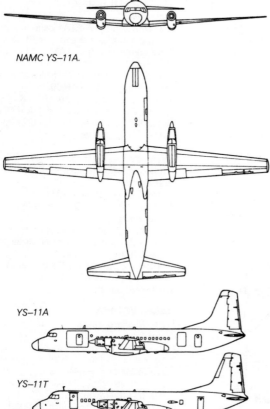

Shin Meiwa Ps–1.

YS–11A

YS–11T

service ceiling 30,184ft (9,200m)
Dimensions:
wing span 95ft 2in (29.00m).
length overall 17ft 3½in (23.56m).
height overall 27ft 6¾in (8.40m).
wing area 754sq ft (70.00sq m).
Power plant: Two 2,210hp Rolls-Royce Dart R.Da.7 Mk.532–7 turboprops.
Payload: 2–3 man crew and 45 paratroops or 24 stretcher cases and 7 medics or max 10,000lb (4,536kg) freight.
Variants:
F.27 Friendship Srs.100, 200: Civil airliners for 40–52 passengers.
F.27 Friendship Srs.300, 400, 500, 600: Civil transports for freight or 56 passengers.
F.27 Friendship Srs.400M: Military version of Srs.400.
F.27 Maritime: Maritime-reconnaissance aircraft.
First flights:
Prototype: 24 November 1955.
Srs.500: 15 October 1967.
Prototype F.27 Maritime: 25 March 1976.
Production:
Series production from 1958, over 650 of all variants delivered or on order tq

date, inc 9 F.27M, 40 F.27 Srs.400M and 205 American licence-built FH–227B by Fairchild-Hiller.
F.27 Maritime: 2 built 1977.
In service:
F.27M: Netherlands.
F.27 Srs.400M: Argentina, Ghana, Iran, Ivory Coast, Nigeria, Senegal, Sudan.
F.27 (all series): Algeria, Argentina, Ghana, Iceland, Indonesia, Iran, Italy, Ivory Coast, Mexico, Netherlands, Nigeria, New Zealand, Pakistan, Philippines, Sudan, Uruguay.
F.27 Maritime: Peru.

NZAI CT–4 'Airtrainer'.
Type: Two-seat trainer.
Weights:
empty 1,460lb (662kg).
maximum 2,400lb (1,088kg).
Performance:
maximum speed at 5,265ft (1,605m) 173mph (278km/hr).
maximum speed at sea level 178mph (286km/hr).
maximum cruising speed at sea level 160mph (259km/hr).
range 800 miles (1,270km).
ferry range 1,400 miles (2,250km).
time to 5,000ft (1,525m) 4min 36sec.

inital rate of climb 22.31ft/sec (6.8m/sec).
Dimensions:
wing span 25ft 11¾in (7.92m).
length overall 23ft 2in (7.06m).
height overall 8ft 6in (2.59m).
wing area 128.95sq ft (11.98sq m).
Power plant: One 210hp Continental IO–360–H piston engine.
Armament: Optional: Max 500lb (227kg) weapon load, e.g. one 500lb (227kg) bomb under fuselage or two 250lb (113kg) bombs, or two weapon pods each containing two 7.62mm machine-guns (with 1,200rpg) or two underwing rocket launchers each with seven 70mm rockets.
Variants:
Airtourer T.6: Earlier version.
First flights:
Prototype: 21 February 1972.
Production: 91 from 1973–76.
In service:
CT–4 Airtrainer: Australia, Hong Kong, New Zealand, Thailand.
Airtourer T.6: New Zealand, Singapore, Thailand.

PZL–104 'Wilga' 35AD.
Type: Liaison and AOP aircraft.

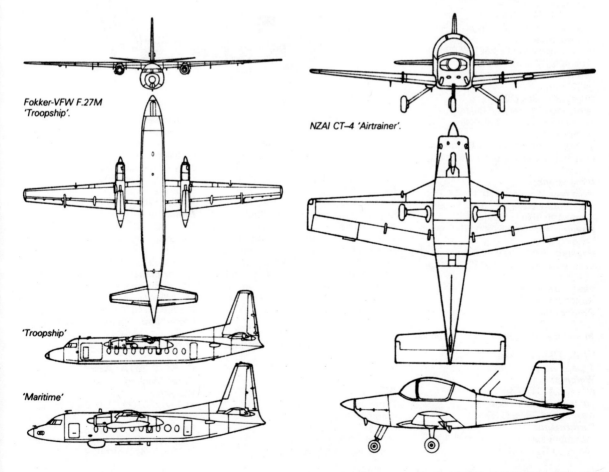

Fokker-VFW F.27M 'Troopship'.

NZAI CT–4 'Airtrainer'.

'Troopship'

'Maritime'

Weights:
empty 1,874lb (850kg).
maximum 2,711lb (1,230kg).
Performance:
maximum speed 130mph (210km/hr).
maximum cruising speed 120mph
  (193km/hr).
ferry range 422 miles (680km).
initial rate of climb 21.0ft/sec (8.0m/sec).
service ceiling 15,025ft (4,580m).
Dimensions:
wing span 36ft 6½in (11.14m).
length overall 26ft 6¾in (8.10m).
height overall 9ft 8in (2.94m).
wing area 166.8sq ft (15.50sq m).
Power plant: One 260hp Ivchenko
  AI–14RA piston engine.
Payload: 1 man crew and 3 troops or 1
  stretcher case and 1 medic.
First flights:
Prototype: 24 April 1962.
Production: Series production from
  1963, 56 Indonesian licence-built by
  Lipnur.
In service: Bulgaria, Czechoslovakia,
  Germany (East), Indonesia (Gelatik),
  Korea (North), Mongolia (People's
  Republic), Poland, USSR.

WSK SM–2.
Type: Light helicopter.
Weights:
empty 4,167lb (1,890kg).
maximum 5,500lb (2,495kg).
Performance:
maximum speed at 6,560ft (2,000m)
  105mph (170km/hr).
maximum cruising speed 81mph
  (130km/hr).
range 190 miles (305km).
ferry range 310 miles (500km).
initial rate of climb 14.8ft/sec
  (4.5m/sec).
service ceiling 13,120ft (4,000m).
hovering ceiling in ground effect 6,103ft
  (1,860m).
Dimensions:
main rotor diameter 47ft 1in (14.35m).
length of fuselage 39ft 8½in (12.09m).
height 10ft 10in (3.30m).
Power plant: One 575hp LiT–3 piston
  engine.
Payload: 1 man crew and 4 troops or 3
  stretcher cases or max 705lb (320kg)
  freight.
First flights:
Prototype: 1960.
Production: Series production
  1961–66(?).
In service: Hungary, Poland, Romania.

WSK TS–11 'Iskra'.
Type: Two-seat trainer.
Weights:
empty 5,423lb (2,460kg).
normal 8,070lb (3,660kg).
maximum 8,380lb (3,800kg).
Performance:
maximum speed at 16,400ft (5,000m)
  447mph (720km/hr).

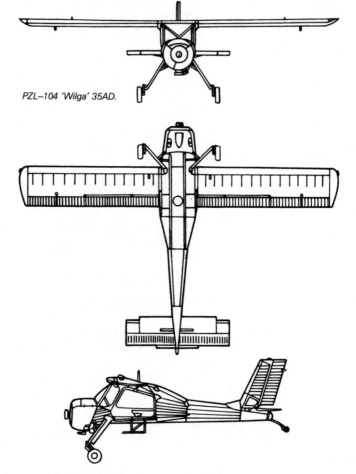

PZL–104 'Wilga' 35AD.

maximum cruising speed 373mph
  (600km/hr).
ferry range 910 miles (1,460km).
initial rate of climb 52.5ft/sec (16.0m/sec).
time to 19,700ft (6,000m) 9min 40sec.
service ceiling 41,010ft (12,500m).
Dimensions:
wing span 33ft 0½in (10.07m).
length overall 36ft 11in (11.25m).
height overall 10ft 8in (3.25m).
wing area 188.37sq ft (17.50sq m).
Power plant: One OKL 50–3 turbojet
  rated at 2,205lb (1,000kg) st.
Armament: One 23mm cannon and
  max 441lb (200kg) weapon load on 4
  hard points, e.g. practice bombs and
  unguided rockets.
First flights:
Prototype: 5 February 1960.
Production: 4 prototypes, 700(?) built
  from 1963.
In service: India(?), Poland.

AISA I–115.
Type: Two-seat trainer.
Weights:
empty 2,001lb (610kg).
normal 1,980lb (900kg).
maximum 2,183lb (990kg).

Performance:
maximum speed 143mph (230km/hr).
maximum cruising speed126mph
  (204km/hr).
ferry range 620 miles (1,000km).
initial rate of climb12.5ft/sec
  (3.8m/sec).
service ceiling 14,110ft (4,300km).
Dimensions:
wing span 31ft 3¼in (9.53m).
length overall 24ft 1in (7.34m).
height overall 6ft 10in (2.08m).
wing area 150.6sq ft (14.00sq m).
Power plant: One 150hp ENMA Tigre
  G–IV–B piston engine.
First flights:
Prototype: 16 July 1952.
Production: Approx 450 built from
  1954.
In service: Spain (E–9).

CASA C.207A 'Azor'.
Type: Medium transport.
Weights:
empty 23,370lb (10,600kg).
maximum 35,270lb (16,000kg).
Performance:
maximum speed at 4,920ft (1,500m)
  261mph (420km/hr).

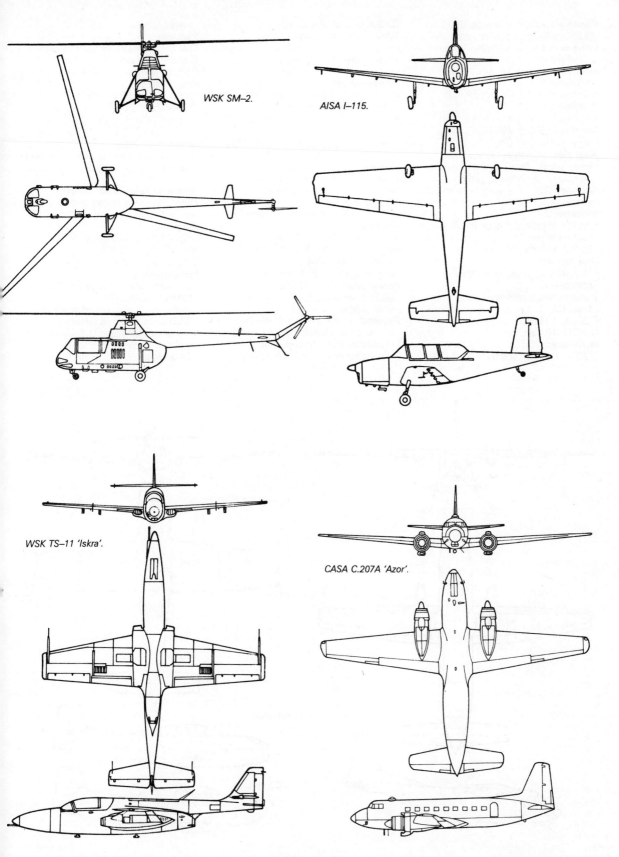

WSK SM–2.

AISA I–115.

WSK TS–11 'Iskra'.

CASA C.207A 'Azor'.

maximum cruising speed at 10,000ft
(3,050m) 222mph (357km/hr).
range with 6,610lb (3,000kg) payload
1,460 miles (2,350km).
initial rate of climb 18.04ft/sec
(5.5m/sec).
service ceiling 27,890ft (8,500m).
Dimensions:
wing span 91ft 2½in (27.80m).
length overall 68ft 4¾in (20.85m).
height overall 25ft 5in (7.75m).
wing area 923.6sq ft (85.80sq m).
Power plant: Two 2,040hp Bristol
Hercules 730 piston engines.
Payload: C.207A: 4 man crew and 38
troops.
Variants:
C.207C: Improved production model; 4
man crew and 37 paratroops or max
7,385lb (3,350kg) freight.
First flights:
Prototype: 28 September 1955.
Production:
2 prototypes, series production from
1956–68.
C.207A: 10 built.
C.207C: 10 built.
In service:
C.207A, C.207C: Spain (T–7A, T–7B).

CASA C.212 'Aviocar'.
Type: Light transport.
Weights:
empty 8,045lb (3,650kg).
maximum 13,890lb (6,300kg).
Performance:
maximum speed at 12,000ft (3,660m)
249mph (400km/hr).
maximum speed at sea level 227mph
(365km/hr).
maximum cruising speed at 12,000ft
(3,660m) 243mph (391km/hr).
range 445 miles (720km).
ferry range 1,198 miles (1,927km).
initial rate of climb 27.9ft/sec
(8.5m/sec).
service ceiling 24,606ft (7,500m).
Dimensions:
wing span 62ft 4in (19.00m).
length overall 49ft 10½in (15.20m).
height overall 20ft 8in (6.30m).
wing area 430.56sq ft (40.00sq m).
Power plant: Two 776hp
Garrett-AiResearch TPE–331–5–251C
turboprops.
Payload: 2 man crew and 18–21
troops or 10 stretcher cases and 3
medics or 15 paratroops and 1
dispatcher or max 4,410lb (2,000kg)

freight.
Variants:
C.212B: Photographic survey aircraft.
C.212C: Civil airliner.
C.212E: Navigational trainer.
First flights:
Prototype: 26 March 1971.
Production: 2 prototypes, 12
pre-production models 1973; series
production 1973–74, 78 delivered or
on order to date.
In service: Indonesia, Jordan, Portugal,
Spain (T–12), Venezuela.

Hispano HA–200D 'Saeta'.
Type: Two-seat trainer and light
ground-attack aircraft.
Weights:
empty 4,233lb (1,920kg).
normal 5,842lb (2,650kg).
maximum 7,617lb (3,455kg).
Performance:
maximum speed at 22,965ft (7,000m)
404mph (650km/hr).
maximum cruising speed at 9,840ft
(3,000m) 329mph (530km/hr).
ferry range 930 miles (1,500km).
initial rate of climb 45.9ft/sec
(14.0m/sec).

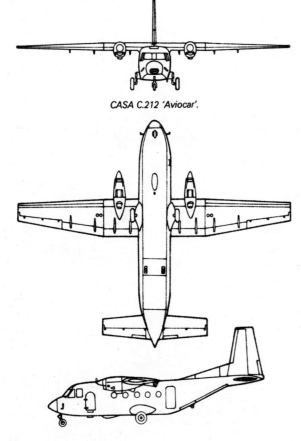

CASA C.212 'Aviocar'.

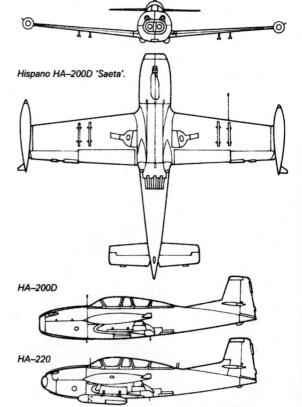

Hispano HA–200D 'Saeta'.

HA–200D

HA–220

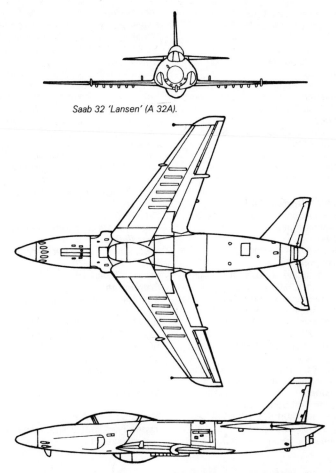

Saab 32 'Lansen' (A 32A).

service ceiling 39,370ft (12,000m).
Dimensions:
wing span 35ft 10¼in (10.93m).
length overall 29ft 5in (8.97m).
height overall 9ft 4¼in (2.85m).
wing area 187.4sq ft (17.42sq m).
Power plant: Two Turboméca Marboré
IIA turbojets each rated at 882lb
(400kg) st.
Armament: Two 7.7mm Breda
machine-guns, four 110lb (50kg)
bombs or four 22lb (10kg) unguided
rockets.
Variants:
HA–200, HA–200A: Earlier versions.
HA–200B: Egyptian licence-built.
First flights:
Prototype HA–200: 12 August 1955.
HA–200A: 11 October 1962.
HA–200D: April 1965.
Production:
2 prototypes, series production from
1962–72.
HA–200: 10 built.
HA–200A: 30 built.
HA–200B: 90 built.
HA–200D: 55 built.
In service:
HA–200A, D: Spain (E–14A, C–10B).
HA–200B: Egypt (UAR) (Al Kahira).

Hispano HA–220 'Super-Saeta'.
Type: Single-seat light ground-attack
aircraft.
Details as for HA–200D 'Saeta' with the
following exceptions:
Weights:
empty 4,894lb (2,220kg).
maximum 8,160lb (3,700kg).
Performance:
maximum speed at 22,965ft (7,000m)
435mph (700km/hr).
maximum cruising speed at 19,685ft
(6,000m) 354mph (570km/hr).
ferry range 1,056 miles (1,700km).
initial rate of climb 55.77ft/sec
(17.0m/sec).
service ceiling 42,650ft (13,000m).
Dimensions:
wing span 35ft 10¼in (10.93m).
length overall 29ft 5in (8.97m).
height overall 9ft 4¼in (2.85m).
wing area 187.5sq ft (17.42sq m).
Power plant: Two Turboméca Marboré
VI turbojets each rated at 1,058lb
(480kg) st.
Armament: Two 7.7mm Breda
machine-guns and max 2,954lb
(1,340kg) weapon load on 6 hard
points.
First flights: 25 April 1970.

Production: 25 built.
In service: Spain (C–10C).

Saab 32 'Lansen' (A 32A).
Type: Two-seat strike-fighter.
Weights:
empty 16,402lb (7,440kg).
normal 22,950lb (10,410kg).
maximum 28,660lb (13,000kg).
Performance:
maximum speed at sea level (Mach 0.9)
692mph (1,114km/hr).
maximum speed at 36,000ft (11,000m)
627mph (1,009km/hr).
maximum cruising speed at 36,000ft
(11,000m) (Mach 0.8) 608mph
(978km/hr).
radius of action 404–746 miles
(650–1,200km).
ferry range 2,000 miles (3,220km).
initial rate of climb 196.9ft/sec
(60.0m/sec).
service ceiling 49,200ft (15,000m).
Dimensions:
wing span 42ft 8in (13.00m).
length overall 48ft 0in (14.65m).
height overall 15ft 6in (4.75m).
wing area 402.6sq ft (37.40sq m).
Power plant: One Svenska Flygmotor
RM5A2 turbojet rated at 7,628lb
(3,460kg)/10,362lb (4,700kg) st.
Armament: Four 20mm Hispano
cannon, max 2,645lb (1,200kg)
weapon load, e.g. two Rb 04C ASMs
or four 550lb (250kg) or two 1,100lb
(500kg) or twelve 220lb (100kg)
bombs or max twenty-four 135mm or
150mm rockets.
Variants:
J 32B: Two-seat all-weather fighter
(four 30mm cannon and 2–4
Sidewinder AAMs).
S 32C: Two-seat reconnaissance
aircraft.
First flights:
Prototype: 3 November 1952.
J 32B: 7 January 1957.
S 32C: 26 March 1957.
Production:
A 32A: 285 built 1955–58.
J 32B: 120 built 1958–60.
S 32C: 45 built 1959–60.
In service: A 32A, J 32B, S 32C:
Sweden.

Saab 35 'Draken' (J 35F).
Type: Single-seat fighter and
strike-fighter.
Weights:
empty 16,815lb (7,627kg).
normal 25,130lb (11,400kg).
maximum 33,070lb (15,000kg).
Performance:
maximum speed at 36,000ft (11,000m)
(Mach 2.0) 1,320mph (2,125km/hr).
maximum speed with 4 AAMs at
36,000ft (11,000m) (Mach 1.4)
926mph (1,490km/hr).
maximum cruising speed 590mph

(950km/hr).
radius of action 348–684 miles
(560–1,100km).
ferry range 1,760 miles (2,840km).
initial rate of climb 574ft/sec
(175m/sec).
time to 36,000ft (11,000m) 2min 36sec.
service ceiling 60,040ft (18,300m).
Dimensions:
wing span 30ft 9½in (9.38m).
length overall 46ft 10¼in (14.28m).
height overall 12ft 9in (3.89m).
wing area 529.6sq ft (49.20sq m).
Power plant: One Svenska Flygmotor
RM6C turbojet rated at 12,710lb
(5,765kg)/17,262lb (7,830kg) st.
Armament:
One 30mm Aden M/55 cannon with
90rpg.
Fighter: Two Rb27 and two Rb28
(Falcon) AAMs.
Strike-fighter: Max 2,205lb (1,000kg)
weapon load; e.g. twelve 135mm
Bofors unguided rockets or two
1,102lb (500kg) bombs or nine 220lb
(100kg) bombs or two rocket
launchers each containing nineteen
75mm rockets.
Variants:
J 35A, J 35B, J 35D: Earlier versions.
S 35E: Single-seat reconnaissance
aircraft.
Sk 35C: Two-seat strike trainer.
Saab 35X: Export version of J 35F.
Saab 35XT: Two-seat strike trainer.
First flights:
Prototype: 25 October 1955.

J 35A: 15 February 1958.
Sk 35C: 30 December 1959.
J 35F: 1961.
S 35E: 27 June 1963.
Saab 35X: 29 January 1970.
Production:
3 prototypes, approx 550 of all versions
for Sweden built 1957–71, 65 export
versions built 1970–74/75.
In service:
J 35A, J 35B, J 35D, J 35F, S 35E, Sk
35C: Sweden.
Saab 35D and XT: Denmark (F–35,
TF–35).
Saab 35BS, Saab 35XS: Finland.

Saab 37 'Viggen' (AJ 37).
Type: Single-seat strike-fighter and
all-weather fighter.
Weights:
normal 35,275lb (16,000kg).
Performance:
maximum speed at 36,000ft (11,000m)
(Mach 2.0) 1,320mph (2,125km/hr).
maximum speed at 360ft (100m) (Mach
1.15) 876mph (1,410km/hr).
radius of action 310–620 miles
(500–1,000km).
initial rate of climb 300.3ft/sec
(91.5m/sec).
time to 36,000ft (11,000m) 2min 0sec.
service ceiling 60,000ft (18,300m).
Dimensions:
wing span 34ft 9¼in (10.60m).
length overall 50ft 8¼in (15.45m).
height overall 18ft 4½in (5.60m).
wing area (inc foreplanes) 567.3sq ft

(52.7sq m).
Power plant: One Svenska Flygmotor
RM8 turbofan rated at 14,705lb
(6,670kg)/26,455lb (12,000kg) st.
Armament:
Max 13,230lb (6,000kg)(?) weapon load
on 7 hard points.
Strike-fighter: Bombs, rockets and
three Rb 04C or Rb 05A ASMs.
Fighter: Rb 24 (Sidewinder) or Rb 27
and Rb 28 (Falcon) AAMs.
Variants:
Sk 37: Two-seat strike-trainer.
JA 37: Single-seat interceptor with one
30mm Oerlikon KCA cannon.
SF 37: Single-seat reconnaissance
aircraft.
SH 37: Single-seat
maritime-reconnaissance aircraft.
First flights:
Prototype AJ 37: 8 February 1967.
Sk 37: 2 July 1970.
SF 37: 21 May 1973.
Production:
7 prototypes and pre-production
models.
AJ 37: 150 built 1971–75/76.
Sk 37: 25 built 1972–75/76.
SF 37, SH 37: – built 1973–74.
JA 37: 4 prototypes, 1 pre-production
model, 30 production models
1976–77.
In service: Sweden.

Saab 91D 'Safir'.
Type: Two- to four-seat trainer and
liaison aircraft.

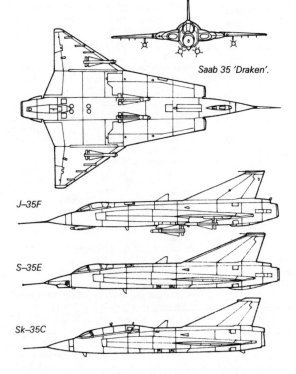

Saab 35 'Draken'.

J–35F

S–35E

Sk–35C

Saab 37 'Viggen'.

S–37

Sk–37

Saab 91D 'Safir'.

Saab 105.

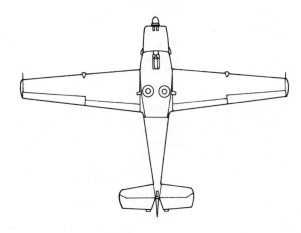

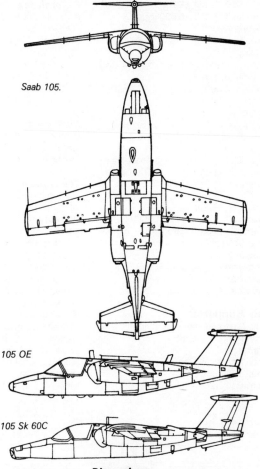

105 OE

105 Sk 60C

Weights:
empty 1,565lb (710kg).
maximum 2,657lb (1,205kg).
Performance:
maximum speed at sea level 165mph
(265km/hr).
maximum cruising speed 136mph
(220km/hr).
ferry range 660 miles (1,060km).
initial rate of climb 13.4ft/sec
(4.1m/sec).
service ceiling 16,400ft (5,000m).
Dimensions:
wing span 34ft 9in (10.60m).
length overall 26ft 4in (8.03m).
height overall 7ft 2in (2.20m).
wing area 146.3sq ft (13.60sq m).
Power plant: One 180hp Lycoming
O–360–A1A piston engine.
Variants:
Saab 91A, 91B: Two- to three-seat
trainers.
Saab 91C: Two- to four-seat trainer and
liaison aircraft.
First flights:
Prototype Saab 91: 20 November 1945.
Saab 91D: 1957.
Production:
Saab 91A: 49 built from 1946.
Saab 91B: 135 built from 1951.

Saab 91C: 39 built.
Saab 91D: 100 built.
In service:
Saab 91B: Ethiopia, Norway, Sweden
(Sk 50B, Tp91).
Saab 91C: Ethiopia, Sweden (Sk 50C).
Saab 91D: Austria, Finland, Tunisia.

Saab 105 (Sk 60).
Type: Two-seat trainer and light
ground-attack aircraft.
Weights:
empty 5,534lb (2,510kg).
normal 8,930lb (4,050kg).
maximum 9,920lb (4,500kg).
Performance:
maximum speed at sea level 447mph
(720km/hr).
maximum speed at 20,000ft (6,000m)
478mph (770km/hr).
maximum cruising speed at 20,000ft
(6,000m) 441mph (710km/hr).
radius of action with 1,543lb (700kg)
weapon load 196 miles (315km).
ferry range 680 miles (1,940km).
initial rate of climb 65.6ft/sec
(20.0m/sec).
time to 32,800ft (10,000m) 17min
30sec.
service ceiling 41,667ft (12,700m).

Dimensions:
wing span 31ft 2in (9.50m).
length overall 34ft 5in (10.50m).
height overall 8ft 10½in (2.70m).
wing area 175.45sq ft (16.30sq m).
Power plant: Two Turboméca
Aubisque turbojets each rated at
1,638lb (743kg) st.
Armament: Max 1,653lb (750kg)
weapon load on 6 hard points.
Variants:
Sk 60B: Two-seat trainer and light
ground-attack aircraft.
Sk 60C: Two-seat trainer and light
reconnaissance aircraft.
Saab 105XT: Export version of Saab
105 with more powerful engines.
First flights:
Prototype: 29 June 1963.
Production: 150 built 1965–70.
In service: Sweden (Sk 60A, Sk 60B,
Sk 60C).

Saab 105XT.
Type: Two-seat trainer and light
ground-attack aircraft.
Details as for Saab 105 (Sk 60) with the
following exceptions:
Weights:
empty 5,988lb (2,720kg).

normal 10,258lb (4,653kg).
maximum 14,330lb (6,500kg).
Performance:
maximum speed at sea level 603mph
(970km/hr).
maximum speed at 32,800ft (10,000m)
543mph (875km/hr).
maximum cruising speed at 42,650ft
(13,000m) 435mph (700km/hr).
radius of action 528 miles (850km).
ferry range 1,373 miles (2,225km).
initial rate of climb 213.3ft/sec
(65.0m/sec).
time to 32,800ft (10,000m) 4min 30sec.
service ceiling 44,950ft (13,700m).
Power plant: Two General Electric
J85–GE–17B turbojets each rated at
2,850lb (1,293kg) st.
Armament: Max 4,400lb (2,000kg)
weapon load on 6 hard points, e.g. six
500lb (227kg) bombs or two
Sidewinder AAMs.
First flights: 29 April 1967.
Production: 40 built 1970–72.
In service: Austria (Saab 105OE).

Saab 'Supporter'.
Type: Two-seat trainer and light
ground-attack aircraft.
Weights:
empty 1,415lb (642kg).
normal 1,984lb (900kg).
maximum 2,425lb (1,100kg).

Performance:
maximum speed at sea level 155mph
(250km/hr).
maximum cruising speed at sea level
138mph (222km/hr).
range 580 miles (933km).
initial rate of climb 18.04ft/sec
(5.5m/sec).
time to 6,562ft (2,000m) 6min 0sec.
service ceiling 21,330ft (6,500m).
Dimensions:
wing span 29ft 0½in (8.85m).
length overall 22ft 11½in (7.00m).
height overall 8ft 6¼in (2.60m).
wing area 128.09sq ft (11.9sq m).
Power plant: One 200hp Avco
Lycoming IO–360–A1B6 piston
engine.
Armament: Max 661lb (300kg) weapon
load on 6 hard points; e.g. two 330lb
(150kg) bombs or six Bantam anti-tank
missiles or fourteen 75mm rockets or
two weapon pods each with one
7.62mm machine-gun or four rocket
containers each with seven 68mm
rockets.
Variants:
Malmö-Flygindustrie MFI–9: Civil
predecessor, German licence-built by
Bölkow (BO–208 Junior).
Safari (original designation MFI–15):
Civil version.
MFI–17: Earlier designation for

Supporter.
First flights:
Prototype MFI–15: 11 July 1969.
Prototype MFI–17: 6 July 1972.
Production:
2 prototypes.
Safari: 12 built from 1973.
Supporter: Over 77 delivered or on
order from 1974.
In service:
Safari: Sierra Leone.
Supporter: Denmark (T–17), Pakistan.

Pilatus P–3.
Type: Two-seat trainer.
Weights:
empty 2,447lb (1,110kg).
normal 3,120lb (1,415kg).
maximum 3,307lb (1,500kg).
Performance:
maximum speed at sea level 192mph
(309km/hr).
maximum cruising speed 171mph
(275km/hr).
ferry range 466 miles (750km).
initial rate of climb 23.3ft/sec
(7.1m/sec).
service ceiling 18,045ft (5,500m).
Dimensions:
wing span 34ft 1in (10.40m).
length overall 28ft 8in (8.75m).
height overall 10ft 0in (3.05m).
wing area 177.1sq ft (16.45sq m).

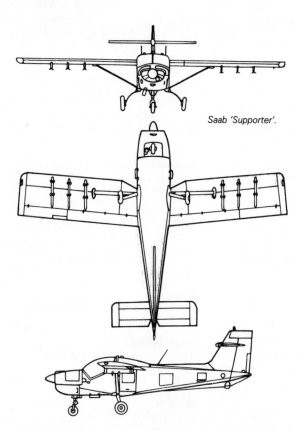

Saab 'Supporter'.

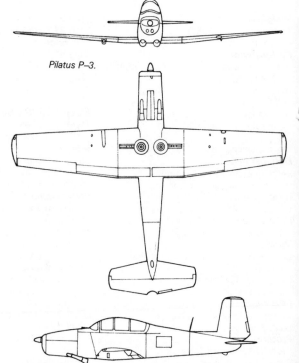

Pilatus P–3.

Power plant: One 260hp Lycoming GO–435–C2A.

Armament: One weapon pack containing one 7.92mm machine-gun with 180 rounds plus two 50mm rockets or four 25lb (12kg) practice bombs.

Variants:
PC–7 Turbo Trainer: Further development, one 550hp Pratt & Whitney PT–6A–25 turboprop.

First flights:
Prototype: 3 September 1953.
Prototype PC–7: 12 April 1966.

Production:
P–3: 2 prototypes, 78 built from 1956.
PC–7: 2 prototypes, planned series production from 1977.

In service: Switzerland.

Pilatus PC–6 'Porter'.

Type: Liaison aircraft.

Weights:
empty 2,359lb (1,070kg).
maximum 4,321lb (1,960kg).

Performance:
maximum speed 144mph (233km/hr).
maximum cruising speed at 7,875ft (2,400m) 135mph (217km/hr).
range 398 miles (640km).
ferry range 746 miles (1,200km).
initial rate of climb 17.1ft/sec (5.2m/sec).
service ceiling 23,950ft (7,300m).

Dimensions:
wing span 49ft 10½in (15.20m).
length overall 33ft 5½in (10.20m).

height overall 10ft 6in (3.20m).
wing area 310sq ft (28.80sq m).

Power plant: One 340hp Lycoming GSO–480–B1A6 piston engine.

Payload: 1 man crew and 7 troops.

First flights:
Prototype PC–6: May 1959.

Production:
PC–6: 59 built 1959–68.

In service: Brazil, Colombia.

Pilatus PC–6A, B, C 'Turbo-Porter'.

Type: Liaison aircraft.

Details as for PC–6 with the following exceptions. Figures below refer specifically to PC–6B:

Weights:
empty 2,401lb (1,089kg).
maximum 4,850lb (2,205kg).

Performance:
maximum speed 175mph (282km/hr).
maximum cruising speed at 10,000ft (3,050m) 158mph (254km/hr).
ferry range 584 miles (940km).
initial rate of climb 23.6ft/sec (7.2m/sec).
service ceiling 25,918ft (7,900m).

Dimensions:
wing span 36ft 1½in (11.00m).

Power plant: One 550hp Pratt & Whitney PTA6A–6 or PT6A–20 turboprop.

Variants:
PC–6A: Variant with one 523hp Turboméca Astazou IIE or IIG turboprop.

PC–6C: Variant with one 575hp Garret–AiResearch TPE–331–25D turboprop.

Fairchild-Hiller Porter: American licence-built PC–6B and PC–6C by Fairchild-Hiller.

Fairchild AU–23A 'Peacemaker': light night ground-support aircraft with two 7.62mm machine-guns or one 20mm XM–197 cannon and max 2,000lb (907kg) weapon load on 4 hard points, e.g. rockets or bombs.

First flights:
PC–6A: 2 May 1961.
PC–6B: 1 May 1964.

Production:
PC–6A, B, C: Approx 255 built from 1961–76.
FH Porter: Approx 75 built from 1964-75.
AU–23A: 22(42?) built from 1972–76.

In service:
PC–6A, B, C: Angola, Australia, Austria, Bolivia, Burma, Colombia, Ecuador, Israel, Oman, Peru, Sudan, Switzerland. AU–23A: Thailand.

Pazmany/Caf PL–1B 'Chienshou'.

Type: Two-seat trainer.

Weights:
empty 950lb (431kg).
maximum 1,437lb (635kg).

Performance:
maximum speed at sea level 150mph (241km/hr).
cruising speed at sea level 115mph (185km/hr).

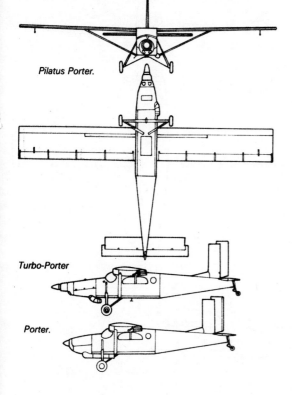

Pilatus Porter.

Turbo-Porter

Porter.

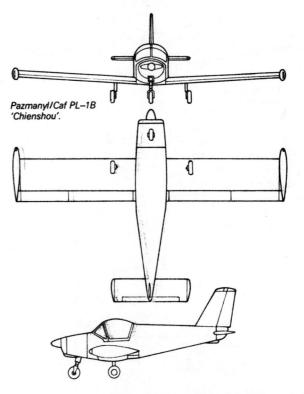

Pazmanyl/Caf PL–1B 'Chienshou'.

ferry range 405 miles (651km).
initial rate of climb 26.9 ft/sec
  (8.2m/sec).
service ceiling 18,000ft (5,500m).
Dimensions:
wing span 28ft 0in (8.53m).
length overall 19ft 7½in (5.99m).
height overall 7ft 4¼in (2.24m).
wing area 116sq ft (10.78sq m).
Power plant: One 150hp Lycoming
  O–320–E2A piston engine.
Variants: PL–2: Later series.
First flights:
Prototype: PL–1A: 26 October 1968.
Production:
3 prototypes, PL–1A.
PL–1B: 50 built 1969/70–72.
PL–2: 7 built 1972–73.
In service: PL–1A, B: Taiwan.
PL–2: Korea (South), Thailand.

Beechcraft C–45G 'Expeditor'.
Type: Light transport.
Weights:
empty 5,613lb (2,546kg).
normal 8,510lb (3,860kg).
maximum 9,000lb (4,082kg).
Performance:
maximum speed at sea level 225mph
  (362km/hr).
maximum cruising speed at 5,000ft
  (1,520m) 211mph (340km/hr).
range 1,200 miles (1,930km).
ferry range 1,530 miles (2,460km)(?).

initial rate of climb 21.3ft/sec
  (6.5m/sec).
service ceiling 21,980ft (6,700m).
Dimensions:
wing span 47ft 6¾in (14.50m).
length overall 43ft 11½in (13.40m).
height overall 9ft 2½in (2.81m).
wing area 345sq ft (32.50sq m).
Power plant: Two 450hp Pratt &
  Whitney R–985–AN–3 or –B5 piston
  engines.
Payload: 2 man crew and 6 troops.
Variants:
C–45H: Later series.
RC–45H: Photographic aircraft.
TC–45H: Trainer.
T–7: Navigation trainer.
T–11 Kansan: Trainer.
Super 18 and Model 18: Civil series.
First flights:
Civil prototype: 15 January 1937.
Military variant: 1941.
Production:
5,204 military variants built 1941–45.
1,887 civil variants (C–18 and D–18)
  built 1937–69.
In service:
C–45: Argentina, Bolivia, Brazil, Burma,
  Canada, Chile, Colombia, Costa Rica,
  Ecuador, Haiti, Mexico, Nicaragua,
  Paraguay, Thailand, Turkey, USA,
  Uruguay.
T–11: Argentina, Dominican Republic,
  El Salvador, Honduras, Mexico,
  Nicaragua.

Beechcraft 'Musketeer Sport'.
Type: Two-seat trainer.
Weights:
empty 1,349lb (612kg).
maximum 2,249lb (1,020kg).
Performance:
maximum speed at sea level 140mph
  (225km/hr).
maximum cruising speed at 7,000ft
  (2,135m) 131mph (211km/hr).
ferry range 767 miles (1,235km).
initial rate of climb 11.5ft/sec
  (3.5m/sec).
service ceiling 11,100ft (3,380m).
Dimensions:
wing span 32ft 9in (9.98m).
length overall 25ft 0in (7.62m).
height overall 8ft 3in (2.51m).
wing area 146sq ft (13.57sq m).
Power plant: One 150hp Lycoming
  O–320–E2C piston engine.
Payload: As liaison aircraft: 1 man
  crew and 3 troops.
Variants:
Sundowner (formerly Musketeer
  Custom), Sierra (formerly Musketeer
  Super R), Musketeer Super.
Other series, Sierra with retractable
  undercarriage.
Production: Series production from
  1962, over 2,000 delivered to date,
  almost all as civil models.
In service: Canada (CT–134), Hong
  Kong, Indonesia, Mexico.

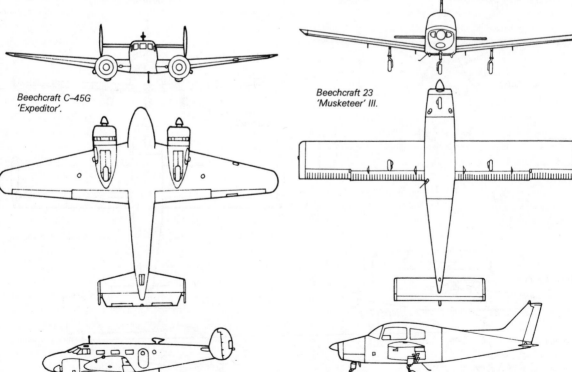

Beechcraft C–45G
'Expeditor'.

Beechcraft 23
'Musketeer' III.

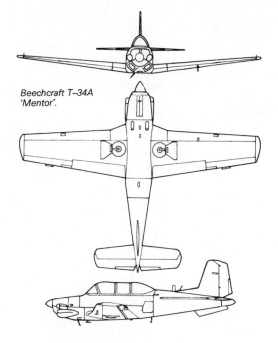

Beechcraft T–34A
'Mentor'.

Beechcraft Model
B55 Baron
(T–42A 'Cochise').

Beechcraft T–34A 'Mentor'.
Type: Two-seat trainer.
Weights:
empty 2,155lb (978kg).
maximum 2,950lb (1,338kg).
Performance:
maximum speed at sea level 189mph
(304km/hr).
maximum speed at 7,550ft (2,300m)
184mph (297km/hr).
maximum cruising speed at 10,000ft
(3,050m) 173mph (278km/hr).
range 735 miles (1,183km).
initial rate of climb 18.7ft/sec
(5.7m/sec).
time to 5,020ft (1,530m) 4min 54sec.
service ceiling 18,210ft (5,550m).
Dimensions:
wing span 32ft 10in (10.00m).
length overall 25ft 11½in (7.91m).
height overall 9ft 7in (2.92m).
wing area 177.6sq ft (16.49sq m).
Power plant: One 225hp Continental
O–470–13 piston engine.
Variants:
T–34: Naval version of T–34A.
Beech Model B45: Export version of
T–34A.
Beech Bonanza: Civil series.
First flights:
Prototype: 2 December 1948.
Production: 3 prototypes, 1,149 built
1953–57, inc 475 T–34A, 423 T–34B,
75 Argentinian and 176 Japanese
licence-built by FMA and Fuji resp.
In service:
T–34A, T–34B, Model B45: Argentina,
Chile, Colombia, El Salvador, Japan,
Mexico, Peru, Philippines, Spain
(E–17), Turkey, USA (T–34A, T–34B),

Uruguay, Venezuela.
Bonanza: Iran (Series F32C, F33A,
F33C), Mexico (F33C), Spain
(F33A = E–21, F33C = E21B).

Beechcraft T–34C 'Mentor'.
Type: Two-seat trainer.
Details as for T–34A with the following
exceptions:
Weights:
empty 2,632lb (1,194kg).
maximum 4,270lb (1,940kg).
Performance:
maximum cruising speed at 17,500ft
(5,340m) 247mph (397km/hr).
range 750 miles (1,207km).
initial rate of climb 21.3ft/sec
(6.5m/sec).
Dimensions:
wing span 33ft 4¼in (10.17m).
length overall 28ft 8½in (8.75m).
height overall 9ft 10in (3.00m).
wing area 179.9sq ft (16.71sq m).
Power plant: One 400hp Pratt &
Whitney PT6A–45 turboprop.
First flights:
Prototype: 21 September 1973.
Production: 2 prototypes; 280 (over
300?) to be built 1974–78.
In service: Ecuador, Morocco, USA.

Beechcraft T–42A 'Cochise'.
Type: Four- to six-seat trainer and
liaison aircraft.
Weights:
empty 3,071lb (1,393kg).
maximum 5,100lb (2,313kg).
Performance:
maximum speed at sea level 236mph

(380km/hr).
maximum cruising speed at 10,000ft
(3,050m) 195mph (314km/hr).
ferry range 1,225 miles (1,970km).
initial rate of climb 27.9ft/sec
(8.5m/sec).
service ceiling 19,700ft (6,000m).
Dimensions:
wing span 37ft 10in (11.53m).
length overall 27ft 3in (8.31m).
height overall 9ft 7in (2.92m).
wing area 199.2sq ft (18.50sq m).
Power plant: Two 260hp Continental
IO–470–L piston engines.
Variants:
Beechcraft Model 55 Baron, Model 58
Baron: Civil variants.
First flight:
Prototype: 24 February 1960.
Production:
Model 55: 2,650 built 1960–74, inc only
65 T–42A models 1965–66.
Model 58: 455 built from 1969.
In service:
T–42A: Peru(?), Turkey, USA.
Baron: Rhodesia, Spain (E–20).

Beechcraft U–8F 'Seminole'.
Type: Liaison aircraft.
Weights:
empty 4,641lb (2,105kg).
maximum 7,700lb (3,493kg).
Performance:
maximum speed at 12,000ft (3,600m)
239mph (385km/hr).
maximum cruising speed at 15,000ft
(4,600m) 214mph (344km/hr).
ferry range 1,590 miles (2,558km).
initial rate of climb 21.7ft/sec
(6.6m/sec).

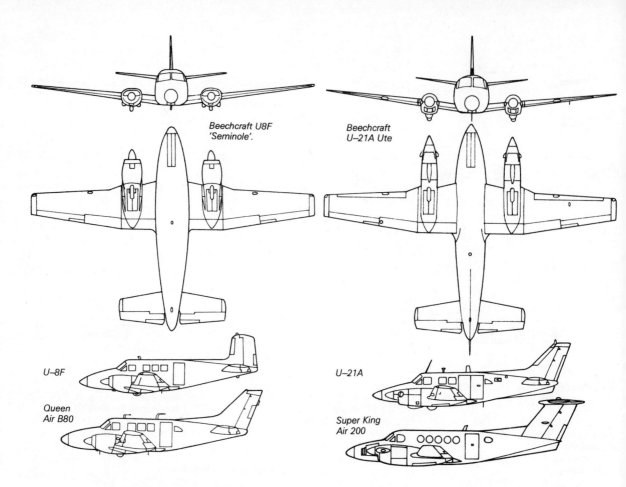

Beechcraft U8F 'Seminole'.

Beechcraft U–21A Ute

U–8F

Queen Air B80

U–21A

Super King Air 200

service ceiling 31,300ft (9,540m).
Dimensions:
wing span 45ft 10½in (13.98m).
length overall 33ft 4½in (10.17m).
height overall 14ft 2in (4.32m).
wing area 277.06sq ft (25.73sq m).
Power plant: Two 340hp Lycoming
IGSO–480–A1A6 piston engines.
Payload: 1–2 man crew and 6 troops.
Variants:
Queen Air: Civil light aircraft.
U–8D, E: Earlier versions.
Model 150 Twin-Bonanza: Earlier (civil)
version.
First flights:
Prototype Queen Air: 28 August 1958.
Production:
Series production from 1959.
U–8F: 3 pre-production and 68
production models.
Queen Air: Over 770 of all versions
delivered or on order up to 1974.
In service:
U–8D, U–8F: USA.
Queen Air: Cameroun, Israel, Japan,
Peru, Uruguay, Venezuela.
Twin-Bonanza: Chile, Morocco,
Pakistan, Switzerland.

Beechcraft U–21A 'Ute'.
Type: Liaison aircraft.
Weights:
empty 5,463lb (2,478kg).
maximum 9,650lb (4,377kg).
Performance:
maximum speed at 11,000ft (3,350m)
250mph (401km/hr).
maximum cruising speed at 10,000ft
(3,050m) 245mph (395km/hr).
range 1,170 miles (1,880km).
ferry range 1,676 miles (2,697km).
initial rate of climb 33.1ft/sec
(10.1m/sec).
service ceiling 25,590ft (7,800m).
Dimensions:
wing span 45ft 10½in (13.98m).
length overall 35ft 6in (10.82m).
height overall 14ft 2½in (4.33m).
wing area 279.65sq ft (25.98sq m).
Power plant: Two 550hp Pratt &
Whitney T74–CP–700 turboprops.
Payload: 2 man crew and 6–10 troops
or 3 stretcher cases and 3 seated
wounded or max 3,000lb (1,360kg)
freight.
Variants:
RU–21A, B, C, D, E, F, J:

Electronic-reconnaissance aircraft.
VC–6A: Command transport.
T–44A: Trainer.
King Air Model 90, Model 100: Civil
versions.
Super King Air: Improved series.
C–12a, U2SA Huron: Military versions
of Super King Air A200.
First flights:
Prototype U–21: March 1967.
Prototype King Air: 20 January 1964.
Super King Air: 27 October 1972.
Production:
King Air Model 90: 729 built 1964–70,
inc approx 160(162?) U–21 1967–70
and 61 T–44A 1977–79.
King Air Model 100: 191 built from
1969, inc 5 U–21F.
Super King Air: Series production
1973–74, inc 40 U–25A and 50
C–12A.
In service:
T–44A, U–21, RU–21: Korea (South),
USA.
King Air: Bolivia, Jamaica, Japan,
Morocco, Spain (E–22, E–23).
C–12A, U–25A: USA.
Super King Air: Argentina, Bolivia,

Indonesia, Iran, Pakistan, Saudi Arabia.

Bell 47G–3B–2 'Trooper' (OH–13H 'Sioux').
Type: Light helicopter.
Weights:
empty 1,794lb (814kg).
maximum 2,950lb (1,338kg).
Performance:
maximum speed at sea level 105mph (169km/hr).
maximum cruising speed 87mph (140km/hr).
range 315 miles (507km).
initial rate of climb 22.6ft/sec (6.9m/sec).
service ceiling 20,000ft (6,100m).
hovering ceiling in ground effect 18,000ft (5,486m).
hovering ceiling out of ground effect 15,000ft (4,572m).
Dimensions:
main rotor diameter 37ft 2in (11.32m).
length of fuselage 31ft 7in (9.63m).
height 9ft 2¾in (2.83m).
Power plant: One 240hp Lycoming TVO–435–A1B piston engine.
Payload: 1 man crew and 1–2 troops or 2 stretcher cases.
Variants:
Bell 47D: Earlier version.
Bell 47G–3B (OH–13S): Later and more powerful (260hp) series.
AB.47G: Italian licence-built by Agusta.
KH–4: Japanese licence-built by Kawasaki.
Westland Sioux: British licence-built.
TH–13M, TH–13T: Helicopter trainers.
First flights:
Prototype: 8 December 1945.

Production:
Series production from 1947, Model 47G from 1953; over 5,000 built 1953–73, licence-built in Great Britain, Italy and Japan.
AB.47: Over 1,000 built.
KH–4: 423 built from 1954.
Sioux: 250 built.
In service:
Bell 47D: Argentina, Colombia, Spain.
Bell 47G: Argentina, Australia, Brazil, Burma, Chile, Colombia, Congo, Ecuador, Greece, Guinea, Indonesia, Israel(?), Jamaica, Kenya, Madagascar (Malagasy), Malaysia, Malta, Mexico, Morocco, New Zealand, Pakistan, Paraguay, Peru, Sri Lanka, Turkey(?), Tanzania, USA (OH–13G, OH–13H, OH–13S, TH–13M, TH–13S), Uruguay, Venezuela.
AB.47G: Italy, Libya, Senegal, Spain (Z–7A).
KH–4: Taiwan, Japan, Korea (South), Thailand.
Sioux: Great Britain (Sioux AH.1).

Bell 47J–2 'Ranger' (UH–13).
Type: Light helicopter.
Weights:
empty 1,731lb (785 kg).
normal 2,851lb (1,293kg).
maximum 2,950lb (1,338kg).
Performance:
maximum speed at sea level 105mph (169km/hr).
maximum cruising speed 93mph (150km/hr).
range 258 miles (415km).
initial rate of climb 13.5ft/sec (4.1m/sec).

service ceiling 10,982ft (3,353m).
hovering ceiling in ground effect 9,203ft (2,805m).
Dimensions:
main rotor diameter 37ft 2in (11.32m).
length of fuselage 32ft 5in (9.87m).
height 9ft 2¾in (2.83m).
Power plant: One 260hp Lycoming VO–540–B1B piston engine.
Payload: 1 man crew and 3–4 troops or 2 stretcher cases.
Variants:
AB.47J: Italian licence-built by Agusta; some with uprated power plants.
AB.47J–3: ASW helicopter.
First flights:
Prototype: 1954.
Bell 47J–2: 1960.
Production:
Series production 1955–66, majority as civil models; licence-built in Italy and Japan (122 built by Kawasaki?).
In service:
Bell 47J: Argentina, Brazil, Colombia, Iceland, Mexico, USA (UH–13J, UH–13P), Venezuela(?).
AB.47J: Cyprus, Italy.

Bell 204B (UH–1B 'Iroquois').
Type: Transport helicopter.
Weights:
empty 4,599lb (2,086kg).
normal 8,499lb (3,855kg).
maximum 9,500lb (4,309kg).
Performance:
maximum speed at sea level 120mph (193km/hr).
maximum cruising speed 110mph (177km/hr).

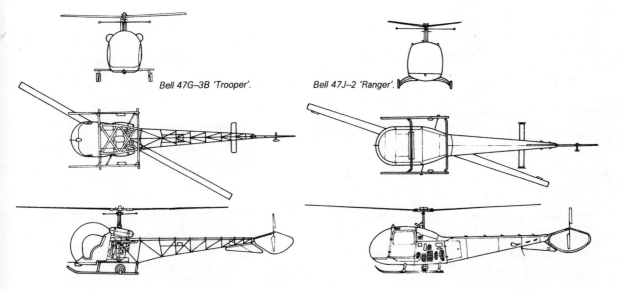

Bell 47G–3B 'Trooper'.   Bell 47J–2 'Ranger'.

ferry range 390 miles (630km).
initial rate of climb 23.3ft/sec
  (7.1m/sec).
service ceiling 15,810ft (4,820m).
hovering ceiling in ground effect
  10,000ft (3,050m).
hovering ceiling out of ground effect
  4,300ft (1,370m).
Dimensions:
main rotor diameter 48ft 0in (14.63m).
length of fuselage 40ft 4¾in (12.31m).
height 12ft 8½in (3.87m).
Power plant: One 1,100hp Lycoming
  T53–L–11A turboshaft.
Armament: Optional.
Payload: 2 man crew and 7 troops or 3
  stretcher cases and 1 medic or max
  3,000lb (1,360kg) freight.
Variants:
AB.204B: Italian licence-built UH–1B by
  Agusta.
UH–1C, E, F, L: Later series, majority
  with uprated power plants.
HH–1K: ASR helicopter.
TH–1F, TH–1L Seawolf: Training
helicopters.
AB.204ASW: ASW helicopter, 3 man
  crew, 2 homing torpedoes.
First flights:
Prototype: 22 October 1956.
Production: Several thousand built
  1961–70(?); licence-built in Italy (by
  Agusta) and Japan (102 built by Fuji
  1962–71).
In service:
Bell 204B: Argentina, Australia,
  Colombia, Indonesia, Japan, Panama,
  Peru, Spain, Thailand, USA (UH–1B, C,
  E, F, L; HH–1K; TH–1F, L), Vietnam(?).
AB.204B: Austria, Greece, Italy,
  Netherlands, Norway, Sweden
  (HKP–3), Spain (Z–8), Turkey.
AB.204ASW: Italy, Spain.

Bell 205A (UH–1H 'Iroquois').
Type: Transport helicopter.
Weights:
empty 5,082lb (2,305kg).
maximum 9,500lb (4,309kg).
Performance:
maximum speed at sea level 127mph
  (204km/hr).
maximum cruising speed at 5,380ft
  (2,440m) 111mph (179km/hr).
range 344 miles (553km).
ferry range 404(?) miles (650(?)km).
initial rate of climb 27.9ft/sec
  (8.5m/sec).
service ceiling 12,600ft (3,840m).
hovering ceiling in ground effect
  10,400ft (3,170m).
hovering ceiling out of ground effect
  6,000ft (1,830m).
Dimensions:
main rotor diameter 48ft 0in (14.63m).
length of fuselage 41ft 6in (12.65m).
height 14ft 6in (4.42m).
Power plant: One 1,400hp Lycoming
  T53–L–13 turboshaft.
Armament: Optional.
Payload: 2 man crew and 12 troops or
  6 stretcher cases and 1 medic or max
  3,880lb (1,759kg) freight.
Variants:
UH–1D: Earlier version with less
  powerful engine (1,100hp Lycoming
  T53–L–11).
AB.205: Italian licence-built UH–1D and
  UH–1H by Agusta.
HH–1H: Rescue helicopter.
Bell 214A: Further development of
  UH–1H.
Bell 212 (UH–1N): Further
  development,
  Italian licence-built AB.212.
First flights:
Prototype: 16 August 1961.

Production:
Bell 205A (UH–1D, UH–1H): Series
  production from 1963, over 6,000(?)
  delivered or on order to date;
  licence-built in Taiwan (118 UH–1H),
  Germany (West) (352 UH–1D by
  Dornier), Italy (AB.205 by Agusta) and
  Japan (81 UH–1H by Fuji from 1972).
Bell 214A: 287 (299?) built from 1974.
In service:
Bell 205A (UH–1D): Australia, Brazil,
  Brunei, Cambodia, Chile, Colombia(?),
  Ethiopia, Germany (West), Greece,
  Guatemala, Israel, Korea (South), Laos,
  New Zealand, Panama, Peru,
  Philippines, Spain (Z–14), Thailand,
  Turkey, Uganda, USA, Venezuela(?),
  Vietnam(?).
Bell 205A (UH–1H): Brazil, Burma,
  Cambodia(?), Canada (CH–118), Chile,
  Dubai, Greece, Japan, Kuwait, Mexico,
  New Zealand, Philippines, Spain
  (Z–10B), Taiwan, Thailand, USA (also
  HH–1H), Venezuela, Vietnam(?).
AB.205: Greece, Iran, Israel, Italy,
  Kuwait, Morocco, Oman, Saudi Arabia,
  Spain, Turkey, Uganda, Yemen(?),
  Zambia.
Bell 214A: Iran, Oman(?).

Bell 206A 'JetRanger' (OH–58A 'Kiowa').
Type: Light helicopter.
Weights:
empty 1,424lb (646kg).
normal 2,000lb (953kg).
maximum 3,000lb (1,360kg).
Performance:
maximum speed at sea level 150mph
  (241km/hr).
maximum cruising speed 131 mph
  (211km/hr).
range 392 miles (630km).

Bell UH–1H 'Iroquois'.

Bell UH–1B 'Iroquois'.

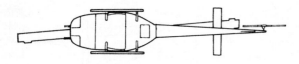

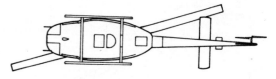

ferry range 460 miles (740km).
initial rate of climb 24.3ft/sec
 (7.4m/sec).
service ceiling 17,700ft (5,395m).
hovering ceiling in ground effect 9,700ft
 (2,410m).
hovering ceiling out of ground effect
 3,350ft (1,020m).
Dimensions:
main rotor diameter 33ft 4in (10.16m).
length of fuselage 31ft 2in (9.50m).
height 9ft 6½in (2.91m).
Power plant: One 317hp Allison
 250–C18A turboshaft.
Armament: Optional, e.g. two weapon
 packs each with one 7.62mm Minigun
 with 1,500rpg.
Payload: 1 man crew and 4 troops or
 max 250lb (113kg)(?) freight.
Variants:
TH–57A SeaRanger: Training helicopter.
AB.206A, AB.206A–1, AB.206B: Italian
 licence-built by Agusta.
Bell 206B JetRanger II: Later series
 with uprated turboshaft (400hp Allison
 250–C20).
Bell 206L LongRanger: Enlarged further
 (civil) development for 6 passengers.
First flights:
Prototype: 10 January 1966.
Bell 206B: 1971.
Bell 206L: 1973.
Production:
Series production from 1967, over
 4,000 delivered or on order to date,
 inc OH–58A: over 2,200 built
 1967–72.
TH–57A: 40 built, licence-built in
 Australia (191 1973–74 by CAC), and
 Italy (by Agusta).
In service:
Bell 206A: Austria, Brazil, Brunei,
 Canada (CH–136), Chile, Dubai,

Indonesia, Israel, Jamaica, Japan,
 Mexico, Peru, Spain (Z–12), Sri Lanka,
 Thailand, Uganda, USA (OH–58A,
 TH–57A).
AB.206A: Finland, Greece, Iran, Italy,
 Libya, Malta, Morocco, Oman, Saudi
 Arabia, Spain (Z–12), Sweden
 (HKP–6A), Turkey.
Bell 206B: Australia, Austria, Brazil,
 Malaysia, USA (OH–58B).
AB.206B: Sweden (HKP–6B).

Bell 212 Twin Two-Twelve (UH–1N 'Twin-Huey').

Type: Transport helicopter.
Weights:
empty 5,500lb (2,495kg).
maximum 10,000lb (4,535kg).
Performance:
maximum speed at sea level 120mph
 (194km/hr).
ferry range 295 miles (476km).
initial rate of climb 243ft/sec
 (7.4m/sec).
maximum hovering ceiling in ground
 effect 17,100ft (5,210m).
maximum hovering ceiling out of
 ground effect 9,900ft (3,020m).
Dimensions:
main rotor diameter 48ft 2⅓ in (14.69m).
length of fuselage 42ft 10½in (13.07m).
height 14ft 5in (4.39m).
Power plant: One 1,800hp Pratt &
 Whitney PT6T–3 Twin Pac turboshaft.
Armament: AB.212 AS: Two homing
 torpedoes or two A.S.12 ASMs.
Payload: 2 man crew and 12–14
 troops or 6 stretcher cases and 1
 medic or max –lb freight.
Variants:
AB.212: Italian licence-built by Agusta.
AB.212 AS: ASW helicopter.

VH–1N: American Presidential VIP
 transport helicopter.
Production: Series production
 1969–70.
In service:
Bell 212 (UH–1N): Argentina, Brunei,
 Canada (CH–135), Colombia, Dubai,
 Ghana, Jamaica, Korea (South),
 Mexico, Morocco, Oman, Panama,
 Peru, Uganda, USA (also VH–1N).
AB.212: Iran, Lebanon, Malaysia,
 Zambia.
AB.212 AS: Italy, Peru(?), Spain,
 Turkey.

Bell AH–1G 'Huey Cobra'.

Type: Two-seat attack helicopter.
Weights:
empty 6,096lb (2,765kg).
maximum 9,500lb (4,309kg).
Performance:
maximum speed at sea level 219mph
 (352km/hr).
radius of action 230 miles (370km).
range 386 miles (622km).
initial rate of climb 26.5ft/sec
 (8.0m/sec).
service ceiling 12,697ft (3,870m).
hovering ceiling in ground effect 9,892ft
 (3,015m).
Dimensions:
main rotor diameter 44ft 0in (13.41m).
length of fuselage 44ft 5in (13.54m).
height 13ft 5¾in (4.10m).
Power plant: One 1,400hp Lycoming
 T53–L–13 turboshaft.
Armament:
Two 7.62mm Miniguns with 4,000rpg
 or two 40mm grenade launchers, each
 with 300 rounds, or one Minigun and
 one 40mm grenade launcher in
 rotating turret and max 1,653lb (750kg)

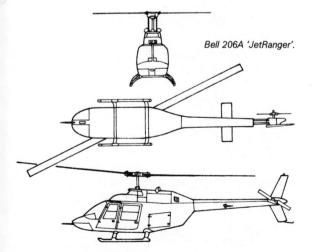

Bell 206A 'JetRanger'.

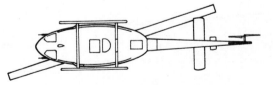

Bell 212 UH–1N
'Twin Huey'.

weapon load on 4 hard points, e.g. 2–4 rocket launchers each containing nineteen 70mm FFAR rockets or 2 rocket launchers each containing seven 70mm FFAR rockets plus 2 weapon packs each containing one 7.62mm Minigun with 1,500rpg.

Variants:
King Cobra: Further development.
AH–1Q: Conversion of 290 AH–1G to anti-tank helicopters with six Tow ASMs from 1975–77.
AH–1S and AH–1T: Further developments of AH–1G and AH–1J resp.

First flights:
Prototype: 7 September 1965.
King Cobra: 10 September 1971.

Production:
1 prototype and 2 pre-production models.
AH–1G: 1,078(1,500?) built 1966–71/72(–1978/79?).
AH–1S: 148 built from 1974–75.
AH–1T: 57 built from 1977.

In service:
AH–1G: Israel, Saudi Arabia, Spain (Z–16), USA.
AH–1Q, S, T: USA.
AH–1S: Japan.

Bell AH–1J 'Sea Cobra'.
Type: Two-seat attack helicopter.
Details as for AH–1G with the following exceptions:

Weights:
empty 6,618lb (3,002kg).
normal 6,825lb (3,096kg).
maximum 10,000lb (4,535kg).

Performance:
maximum speed at sea level 208mph (333km/hr).

maximum cruising speed 185mph (298km/hr).
range 358 miles (577km).
initial rate of climb 18.0ft/sec (5.5m/sec).
service ceiling 10,548ft (3,215m).
hovering ceiling in ground effect 9,892ft (3,794m).
hovering ceiling out of ground effect 3,498ft (1,066m).

Dimensions:
main rotor diameter 44ft 0in (13.41m).
length of fuselage 44ft 7in (13.59m).
height 13ft 7½in (4.15m).

Power plant: One 1,800hp Pratt & Whitney T400–CP–400 coupled turboshaft.

Armament: One 20mm cannon in rotating turret and max 1,653lb (750kg) weapon load on 4 hard points.

Production:
AH–1J: 291 built from 1969–77.
AH–1T: 72(?) built from 1977.

In service: Iran, Israel, USA.

Boeing 707–320C.
Type: Long-range transport.
Weights:
empty 138,323lb (62,742kg).
maximum 328,000lb (148,780kg).

Performance:
maximum speed 627mph (1,010km/hr).
maximum cruising speed at 25,000ft (7,620m) 600mph (966km/hr).
range w.m.p. 3,400 miles (5,470km).
ferry range 7,475 miles (12,030km).
initial rate of climb 66.6ft/sec (20.3m/sec).

Dimensions:
wing span 145ft 9in (44.42m).
length overall 152ft 11in (46.61m).
height overall 42ft 4¾in (12.94m).

wing area 3,010sq ft (279.64sq m).

Power plant: Four Pratt & Whitney JT4A–11 turbojets each rated at 18,000lb (8,165kg) st.

Payload: 4 man crew and up to 199 troops or max 80,000lb (36,285kg) freight.

Variants:
Boeing 707, Boeing 720: Civil airliners and freighters, numerous series.
E–3A: Airborne HQ command post (original designation EC–137D).

First flights:
Prototype: 15 July 1954.

Production:
707 and 720: Series production from 1958; over 920 aircraft of all variants delivered by 1975.

In service:
707–120: USA (VC–137B).
707–320B: Argentina, USA (VC–137C).
707–320C: Canada (CC–137), Egypt (UAR), Germany (West), Iran, Israel, Portugal, Saudi Arabia.

Boeing E–3A (AWACS).
Type: Airborne HQ command post.
Details as for Boeing 707–320C with the following exceptions:

Weights:
maximum 330,700lb (150,000kg).

Performance:
radius of action 310 miles (500km).

Power plant: Four Pratt & Whitney TF33 PW 100/100A turbofans each rated at 21,000lb (9,525kg) st.

Payload: 17 man crew.

First flights:
Prototype: 9 September 1972.

Production: 2 EC–137D prototypes, 3 pre-production and 31 production models from 1975; a further 27

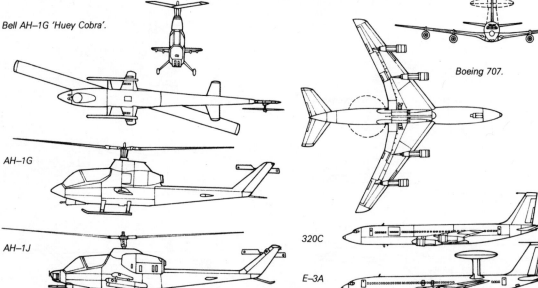

Bell AH–1G 'Huey Cobra'.

AH–1G

AH–1J

Boeing 707.

320C

E–3A

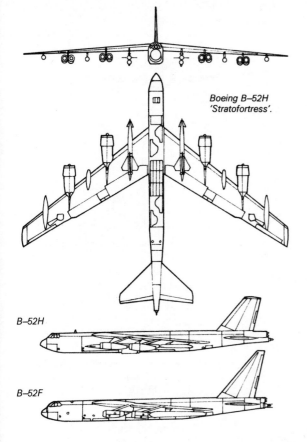

Boeing B–52H 'Stratofortress'.

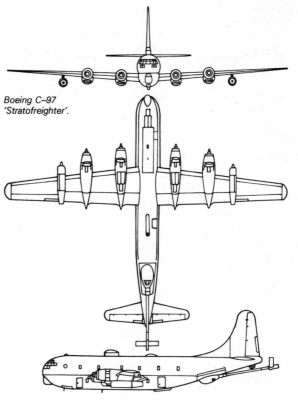

Boeing C–97 'Stratofreighter'.

B–52H

B–52F

planned for NATO.
In service: USA.

Boeing B–52H 'Stratofortress'.

Type: Strategic heavy bomber, 6 man
crew.
Weights:
empty 225,484lb (111,350kg).
maximum 488,000lb (221,357kg).
Performance:
maximum speed at 39,375ft (12,000m)
 (Mach 0.95) 630mph (1,014km/hr).
maximum speed at 20,000ft (6,100m)
 (Mach 0.95) 665mph (1,070km/hr).
maximum cruising speed at 36,000ft
 (11,000m) 565mph (909km/hr).
ferry range 12,500 miles (20,120km).
service ceiling 60,040ft (18,300m).
Dimensions:
wing span 185ft 0in (56.39m).
length overall 157ft 7in (48.03m).
height overall 40ft 8¼in (12.40m).
wing area 4,000sq ft (371.60sq m).
Power plant: Eight Pratt & Whitney
 TF33–P–3 turbofans each rated at
 17,015lb (7,718kg) st.
Armament:
B–52D: Four 12.7mm machine-guns in
 tail position, max 60,000lb (27,216kg)
 weapon load, e.g. eighty-four 500lb

(227kg) bombs in fuselage bay and
twenty-four 750lb (340kg) bombs
underwing.
B–52H: One 20mm ASG–21 cannon in
 tail position, max –lb weapon load,
 e.g. 2 AGM–28B Hound Dog ASMs
 and ALE–25 packs with diversionary
 missiles underwing, twenty-seven
 750lb (340kg) bombs and ADM–20
 Quail diversionary missiles in fuselage
 bay or max 20 AGM–69A SRAM
 ASMs (8 in fuselage bay, 12 on 2
 underwing hard points).
Variants:
B–52B, RB–52B, B–52C, D, E, F, G:
 Earlier versions.
First flights:
Prototype: 2 October 1952.
B–52H: 6 March 1961.
Production:
2 prototypes, 3 pre-production models;
 series production 1954–62. B–52B: 23
 built; RB–52B: 27 built; B–52C: 35
 built; B–52D: 170 built; B–52E: 100
 built; B–52F: 89 built; B–52G: 193
 built; B–52H: 102 built; modernization
 of 96 B–52G and B–52H for
 AGM–69A SRAM operations from
 1972, and of 80 B–52D likewise from
 1973.
In service: B–52D, F, G, H: USA.

Boeing KC–97L 'Stratofreighter'.

Type: Heavy tanker and transport.
Weights:
normal 153,000lb (69,400kg).
maximum 175,000lb (79,380kg).
Performance:
maximum speed at 25,000ft (7,620m)
 (Mach 0.62) 425mph (684km/hr).
maximum cruising speed 301mph
 (485km/hr).
ferry range 4,300miles (6,920km).
service ceiling 35,100ft (10,700m).
Dimensions:
wing span 141ft 3in (43,05m).
length overall 117ft 5in (35.79m).
height overall 38ft 3in (11.66m).
wing area 1,719sq ft (159.70sq m).
Power plant: Four 3,500hp Pratt &
 Whitney R–4360–59B piston engines
 and two General Electric J47–GE–23
 turbojets each rated at 5,880lb
 (2,667kg) st.
Payload:
As tanker: 10,825gal (49,210 l)
 transferable fuel capacity or 65 troops
 or 49 stretcher cases.
As transport: 5 man crew and 96
 troops or 69 stretcher cases and –
 medics or max 68,500lb (31,072kg)
 freight.

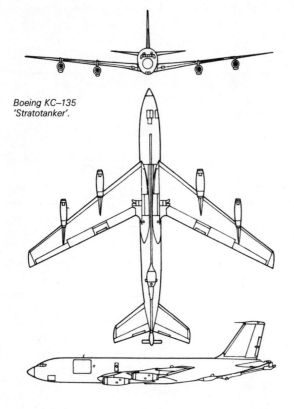

Boeing KC–135 'Stratotanker'.

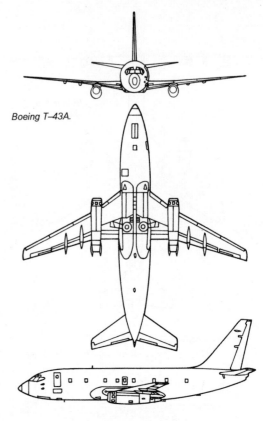

Boeing T–43A.

Variants:
KC–97G: Tanker, without auxiliary turbojets under wings.
C–97G, C–97K: Freight and passenger versions resp.
HC–97G: Search and rescue aircraft.

First flights:
Prototype XC–97: 15 November 1944.
Prototype KC–97A: December 1950.

Production: 888 of all series built from 1945–56, inc 3 KC–97A, 60 KC–97E, 159 KC–97F and 592 KC–97G; various conversions of KC–97G: to KC–97L, C–97G (135), C–97K (26), and HC–97G.

In service:
KC–97G: Israel, USA.
KC–97L: Spain (TK–1), USA.

Boeing KC–135A 'Stratotanker'.
Type: Heavy tanker-transport.
Weights:
empty 98,465lb (44,664kg).
normal 245,000lb (111,123kg).
maximum 297,000lb (134,719kg).
Performance:
maximum speed at 25,000ft (7,600m) 624mph (1,004km/hr).
maximum cruising speed at 35,000ft (10,700m) 592mph (953km/hr).
radius of action 1,150 miles (1,850km).
initial rate of climb 21.6ft/sec (6.6m/sec).

Dimensions:
wing span 130ft 10in (39.88m).
length overall 136ft 3in (41.53m).
height overall 38ft 4in (11.68m).
wing area 2,433.1sq ft (226.04sq m).
Power plant: Four Pratt & Whitney J57–P–59W turbojets each rated at 13,750lb (6,237kg) st.
Payload: 4 man crew, 26,060gal (118,470l) transferable fuel capacity or 80 troops or max 50,000lb (22,680kg) freight.
Variants:
KC–135F: Tanker for France.
EC–135C, G, H, J, K, L, N, P: Flying command posts.
RC–135A, B, C, D, E, M, S, U: Electronic-reconnaissance aircraft.
VC–135B: VIP and command transport.
WC–135B: Weather-reconnaissance aircraft.
KC–135Q, R, T: KC–135A conversions.
First flights:
KC–135A: 31 August 1956.
C–135A: 19 May 1961.
Production:
KC–135A: 732 built from 1957–65, inc a number converted to EC–135, RC–135 and WC–135.
KC–135B (later EC–135B): 17 built;
KC–135F: 12 built. C–135A: 15 built;
RC–135A: 4 built; RC–135B: 10 built.
In service:
KC–135, C–135B, EC–135, RC–135,

VC–135, WC–135: USA.
KC–135F: France.

Boeing C–135B 'Stratolifter'.
Type: Heavy transport.
Details as for KC–135A with the following exceptions:
Weights:
empty 106,472lb (48,295kg).
normal 275,500lb (124,967kg).
maximum 292,000lb (132,451kg).
Performance:
maximum speed at 36,000ft (11,000m) 638mph (1,027km/hr).
maximum cruising speed at 40,000ft (12,200m) 604mph (972km/hr).
range 2,993 miles (4,817km).
Dimensions:
length overall 134ft 6in (41.00m).
height overall 41ft 8in (12.70m).
Power plant: Four Pratt & Whitney TF33–P–5 turbofans each rated at 18,000lb (8,165kg) st.
Payload: 6 man crew and 126 troops or 44 stretcher cases and 54 seated wounded or max 87,100lb (39,545kg) freight.
Production: 30 built.

Boeing T–43A.
Type: Navigation trainer.
Weights:
empty 68,450lb (31,050kg).
normal 106,167lb (48,157kg).

maximum 115,500lb (52,390kg).
Performance:
maximum speed at 23,000ft (7,010m)
576mph (927km/hr).
ferry range 3,225 miles (5,190km).
initial rate of climb 62.66ft/sec
(19.1m/sec).
Dimensions:
wing span 93ft 0in (28.35m).
length overall 100ft 0in (30.48m).
height overall 37ft 0in (11.28m).
wing area 980.1sq ft (91.05sq m).
Power plant: Two Pratt & Whitney
JT8D–9 turbofans each rated at
14,500lb (6,577kg) st.
Payload: 2 man crew, 3 instructors and
16 pupils.
Variants:
Boeing 737–200: Civil airliner for up to
130 passengers.
Boeing 737–100: Earlier (civil) version
for up to 115 passengers.
First flights:
T–43: 10 April 1973.
Boeing 737–100: 9 April 1967.
737–200: 8 August 1967.
Production:
T–43A: 19 built 1973–74.
Boeing 737: Series production from
1967, over 500 built.
In service:
T–43A: USA.
Boeing 737–200: Brazil.

Boeing-Vertol 107–II (CH–46D 'Sea-Knight').
Type: Medium transport helicopter.
Weights:
empty 13,067lb (5,927kg).
maximum 23,000lb (10,433kg).

Performance:
maximum speed at sea level 166mph
(267km/hr).
maximum cruising speed 143–61mph
(246–59km/hr).
range 239 miles (385km).
initial rate of climb 21.0ft/sec
(6.4m/sec).
service ceiling 14,000ft (4,265m).
hovering ceiling in ground effect 9,500ft
(2,895m).
hovering ceiling out of ground effect
5,750ft (1,753m).
Dimensions:
main rotor diameter 51ft 0¼in (15.55m).
length of fuselage 44ft 9½in (13.67m).
height 16ft 11¾in (5.18m).
Power plant: Two 1,400hp General
Electric T58–GE–10 turboshafts.
Armament: Optional.
Payload: 2–3 man crew and 25 troops
or 15 stretcher cases and 2 medics or
max 7,136lb (3,237kg) freight.
Variants:
CH–46A, UH–46A: Earlier versions with
less powerful engines.
HH–46A: Conversions of 61 CH–46A to
rescue helicopters.
CH–46F: Later series.
CH–46E: Modernization of 292 CH–46D
and CH–46E (two 1,870hp General
Electric T58–GE–16 turboshafts).
Kawasaki-Vertol KV–107: Japanese
licence-built by Kawasaki.
First flights:
Prototype: 22 April 1958.
CH–46D: September 1966.
Production:
Series production 1961–73:
CH–46A: 159 built.
UH–46A: 14 built.

CH–46D: 297 built.
UH–46D: 10 built.
CH–46F: 174 built.
Model 107: 149 built, plus 91
licence-built in Japan.
In service: Burma (KV–107), Canada
(CH–113), Labrador, Japan
(KV–107/II–3, –4, –5), Sweden (HKP–4
and HKP–7 = KV–107), Thailand
(KV–107), USA (CH–46D, CH–46E,
CH–46F, HH–46A, UH–46D).

Boeing-Vertol CH–47C 'Chinook'.
Type: Medium transport helicopter.
Weights:
empty 20,873lb (9,468kg).
normal 33,000lb (14,970kg).
maximum 46,000lb (20,865kg).
Performance:
maximum speed at sea level 190mph
(306km/hr).
maximum cruising speed 158mph
(254km/hr).
radius of action 115 miles (185km).
ferry range 311 miles (500km).
initial rate of climb 47.9ft/sec
(14.6m/sec).
service ceiling 19,521ft (5,950m).
hovering ceiling in ground effect
15,000ft (4,570m).
hovering ceiling out of ground effect
9,596ft (2,925m).
Dimensions:
main rotor diameter 60ft 0in (18.29m).
length of fuselage 51ft 0in (15.54m).
height 18ft 6½in (5.65m).
Power plant: Two 3,750hp Lycoming
T55–L–11 turboshafts.
Payload: 2–3 man crew and 33–44
troops or 27 paratroops or 24
stretcher cases and 2 medics or
max 22,000lb

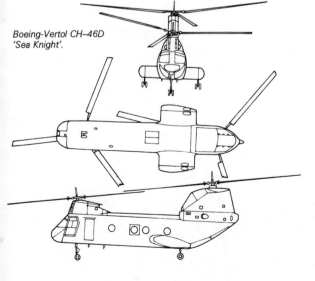

Boeing-Vertol CH–46D 'Sea Knight'.

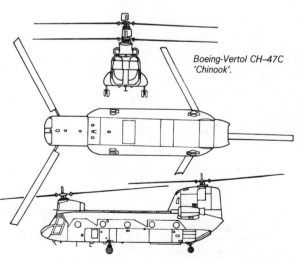

Boeing-Vertol CH–47C 'Chinook'.

(10,000kg) freight.

Variants:
C–47A, CH–47B: Earlier versions, from 1973 conversions to CH–47C.

First flights:
Prototype: 21 September 1961.
CH–47C: 14 October 1967.

Production: Series production from 1962, over 739 of all series (inc 376 CH–47A) delivered or on order to date, plus 52(56?) Italian licence-built by Agusta (Elicotteri Meridionali).

In service:
CH–47A: USA, Vietnam(?).
CH–47B: USA.
CH–47C: Australia, Canada (CH–147), Iran, Israel, Italy, Libya, Spain (Z–16), Thailand, USA, Vietnam(?).

Cessna A–37B 'Dragonfly'.

Type: Two-seat light ground-attack aircraft.

Weights:
empty 5,886lb (2,670kg).
maximum 15,000lb (6,804kg).

Performance:
maximum speed at sea level 458mph (746km/hr).
maximum speed at 14,990ft (4,570m) 475mph (769km/hr).
radius of action with 4,100lb (1,860kg) weapon load 249 miles (400km).
ferry range 1,012 miles (1,628km).
initial rate of climb 116.5ft/sec (35.5m/sec).
service ceiling 32,150ft (9,800m).

Dimensions:
wing span 35ft 10½in (10.93m).
length overall 29ft 3½in (8.93m).
height overall 9ft 2in (2.79m).
wing area 183.9sq ft (17.09sq m).

Power plant: Two General Electric J85–GE–17A turbojets each rated at 2,850lb (1,293kg) st.

Armament: One 7.62mm GAU–2B/A Minigun with 1,500rpg and max 4,100lb (1,860kg) weapon load on 8 hard points.

Variants:
T–37A, T–37B, T–37C: Two-seat trainers.

First flights:
Yat–37D: 22 October 1963.
A–37B: May 1968.

Production:
A–37A: 3 prototypes and 39 production models built May–September 1967.
A–37B: 416 (over 500?) built 1968–75.

In service:
A–37A: Vietnam(?).
A–37B: Chile, Guatemala, Peru, USA, Vietnam(?).

Cessna O–1E 'Birddog'.

Type: Liaison and AOP aircraft.

Weights:
empty 1,613lb (732kg).
normal 2,400lb (1,090kg).

Performance:
maximum speed at sea level 115mph (184km/hr).
maximum cruising speed at 5,000ft (1,530m) 104mph (167km/hr).
ferry range 530 miles (850km).
initial rate of climb 19.0ft/sec (5.8m/sec).
service ceiling 18,500ft (5,640m).

Dimensions:
wing span 36ft 0in (10.97m).
length overall 25ft 10½in (7.89m).
height overall 7ft 4in (2.23m).
wing area 173.5sq ft (16.15sq m).

Power plant: One 213hp Continental O–470–11 piston engine.

Payload: 2 man crew.

Variants:
O–1A, O–1B, O–1C: Earlier versions (original designation L–19).
O–1F, O–1G: Conversions of previous series.
L–19A–1T, TO–1D: Instrument trainers.

First flights:
Prototype: January 1950.
O–1A: November 1950.

Production:
Series production 1950–64.
O–1A: 2,499 built.
O–1B: 62 built.
O–1C: 25 built.
O–1E: 494 built, plus approx 100 Japanese licence-built by Fuji and under production in Pakistan from

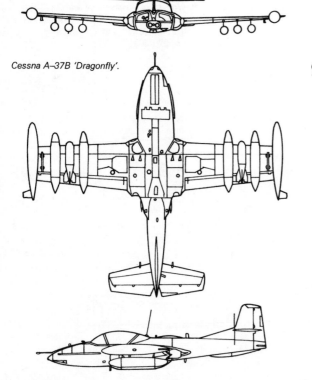

Cessna A–37B 'Dragonfly'.

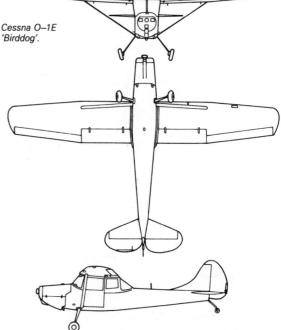

Cessna O–1E 'Birddog'.

1972.
L–19A–1T: 66 built.
TO–1D: 307 built.
In service: Austria, Brazil, Cambodia(?),
Chile, France, Italy, Japan, Korea
(South), Laos, Norway, Pakistan, Spain
(L–12), Thailand, USA (O–1E, F, G,
TO–1D), Vietnam(?).

Cessna O–2A.
Type: AOP aircraft.
Weights:
empty 2,848lb (1,292kg).
normal 4,630lb (2,100kg).
maximum 5,400lb (2,450kg).
Performance:
maximum speed at sea level 200mph
(322km/hr).
maximum cruising speed at 5,480ft
(1,670m) 192mph (309km/hr).
range 800 miles (1,255km).
ferry range 1,290 miles (2,075km).
initial rate of climb 18.4ft/sec
(5.6m/sec).
service ceiling 19,300ft (5,880m).
Dimensions:
wing span 38ft 2in (11.63m).
length overall 29ft 9in (9.07m).
height overall 9ft 3in (2.82m).
wing area 202sq ft (18.81sq m).
Power plant: Two 210hp Continental
IO–360–D piston engines.
Armament: Max 1,400lb (635kg)

weapon load on 4 hard points, e.g.
two 7.62mm Minigun machine-guns
and two rocket launchers each
containing seven 70mm rockets.
Payload: 1 man crew and 3 troops.
Variants:
O–2B: Special loudspeaker-equipped
version for psychological warfare
duties.
Cessna 337 Super Skymaster: Civil
variant, licence-built in France by
Reims-Aviation (F.337).
First flights:
Prototype Super Skymaster: 28
February 1961.
O–2: 1967.
Production:
O–2A and O–2B: 510 built 1967–70.
Super Skymaster: Over 1,700 built
1964–65.
In service:
O–2A: Iran, USA (also O–2B),
Vietnam(?).
Super Skymaster: Dahomey, Ecuador,
Ghana, Haiti, Niger, Sri Lanka, Togo,
Trinidad & Tobago, Upper Volta,
Venezuela.
F.337: Chad, Gabon, Hungary, Ivory
Coast, Madagascar (Malagasy),
Mauritania, Niger, Portugal, Senegal,
Togo, Upper Volta.

Cessna T–37B.
Type: Two-seat trainer.

Weights:
empty 3,800lb (1,724kg).
normal 6,572lb (2,982kg).
Performance:
maximum speed at 20,000ft (6,100m)
425mph (686km/hr).
maximum cruising speed at 35,000ft
(10,700m) 360mph (580km/hr).
range 932 miles (1,500km).
ferry range 1,324 miles (2,130km).
initial rate of climb 56.1ft/sec
(17.1m/sec).
service ceiling 38,700ft (11,800m).
Dimensions:
wing span 33ft 9¼in (10.30m).
length overall 29ft 3in (8.93m).
height overall 9ft 4¼in (2.85m).
wing area 183.9sq ft (17.09sq m).
Power plant: Two Continental
J69–T–25 turbojets each rated at
1,025lb (465kg) st.
Armament:
T–37C: Max 500lb (226kg) weapon load
on 2 hard points, e.g. two weapon
packs each containing one 12.7mm
machine-gun or four Sidewinder AAMs
or four 70mm rockets or two 250lb
(113kg) bombs.
Variants:
T–37C: Two-seat trainer and light
ground-attack aircraft.
A–37B: Light ground-attack aircraft.
First flights:
Prototype: 12 October 1954.

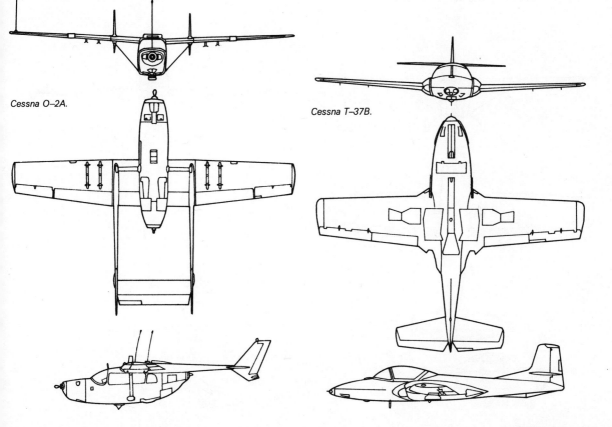

Cessna O–2A.

Cessna T–37B.

T–37A: 27 September 1955.
Production: 3 prototypes, 12
  pre-production models T–37.
T–37A: 537 built 1954–59.
T–37B: 447 built 1959–67.
T–37C: Over 252 built 1964–72.
In service:
T–37B: Cambodia, Chile, Germany
  (West), Greece, Jordan(?), Pakistan,
  Peru, Thailand, Turkey, USA,
  Vietnam(?).
T–37C: Brazil, Cambodia, Chile,
  Colombia, Guatemala, Portugal, USA,
  Vietnam(?).

Cessna T–41B 'Mescalero'.

Type: Two-/four-seat trainer and liaison
  aircraft.
Weights:
empty 1,404lb (637kg).
maximum 2,460lb (1,115kg).
Performance:
maximum speed 153mph (246km/hr).
maximum cruising speed at 10,000ft
  (3,050m) 105mph (169km/hr).
range 1,010 miles (1,625km).
initial rate of climb 14.76ft/sec
  (4.5m/sec).
service ceiling 17,000ft (5,180m).
Dimensions:
wing span 35ft 10in (10.92m).
length overall 26ft 10¾in (8.20m).
height overall 8ft 9½in (2.68m).
wing area 174sq ft (16.16sq m).

Power plant: One 210hp Continental
  IO–360–D piston engine.
Payload: 2 man crew and 2 troops.
Variants:
Cessna 170 and 172: Earlier (civil)
  variants.
Cessna 175, Cessna Skyhawk:
  Improved civil series.
F 172, FR 172 Reims Rocket: French
  licence-production by Reims Aviation
  from 1963.
Cessna 182 and Cessna Skylane:
  Further developments, Argentinian
  licence-production by FMA from 1966.
First flights:
Prototype Cessna 172: November
  1955.
T–41A: 1964
Production:
Cessna 170: 5,136 built 1948–57.
Cessna 172 and Skyhawk: Over 20,500
  built up to mid-1975.
T–41A: 237 built 1964–65.
T–41B: 255 built 1966–67.
T–41C: 52 built 1967–68.
T–41D: Over 260 built and – Pakistan
  licence-built.
F 172: Over 947 built.
FR 172 Rocket: 447 built.
Cessna 182 and Skylane: Over 14,000
  built up to mid-1975.
In service:
T–41A: Ecuador, Greece, Peru, Saudi
  Arabia, USA.
F–41B: Laos, USA.

T–41C: USA.
T–41D: Argentina, Bolivia, Cambodia(?),
  Colombia, Dominican Republic,
  Greece, Honduras, Iran, Korea (South),
  Laos, Liberia, Pakistan, Philippines,
  Turkey.
Cessna 172: Bolivia, Ecuador, Eire,
  Guatemala, Iran, Madagascar
  (Malagasy), Pakistan, Saudi Arabia.
Cessna 182: Canada (L–19L), Dubai, El
  Salvador, Guatemala, Uruguay,
  Venezuela.

Cessna U–3A 'Blue Canoe'.

Type: Liaison aircraft.
Weights:
empty 3,065lb (1,381kg).
normal 4,751lb (2,155kg).
maximum 4,989lb (2,263kg).
Performance:
maximum speed at sea level 240mph
  (386km/hr).
maximum cruising speed at 6,500ft
  (1,980m) 223mph (359km/hr).
range 963 miles (1,550km).
ferry range 1,725 miles (2,780km).
initial rate of climb 28.9ft/sec
  (8.8m/sec).
service ceiling 21,500ft (6,550m).
Dimensions:
wing span 36ft 11in (11.25m).
length overall 29ft 7in (9.02m).
height overall 9ft 11in (3.02m).
wing area 181.1sq ft (16.83sq m).

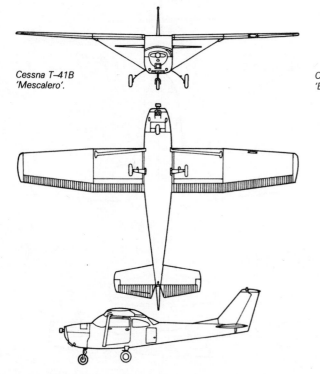

Cessna T–41B
'Mescalero'.

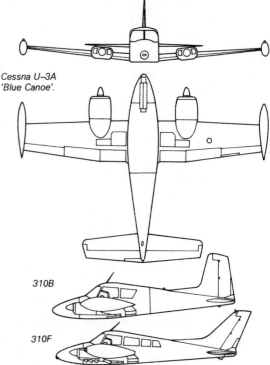

Cessna U–3A
'Blue Canoe'.

310B

310F

Power plant: Two 260hp Continental
IO–470–D piston engines.
Payload: 1 man crew and 5 troops or
max 595lb (270kg) freight.
Variants:
U–3B: All-weather version.
Cessna 310, 320 Skynight: Civil
variants, some with different power
plants.
Cessna 401, 402, 411, 414, 421: Other
series.
First flights:
Prototype: 3 January 1953.
Production:
Over 3,000 civil and military variants
built 1954–74/75, inc 160 U–3A and
35 U–3B.
In service:
Cessna 310: Argentina, Bolivia, Congo,
France, Haiti, Indonesia, Iran, Saudi
Arabia, Tanzania, USA (U–3A, U–3B).
Cessna 320: Argentina.
Cessna 411: France.
Cessna 402, 414, 421: Bolivia.

Cessna U–17A and B.
Type: Liaison aircraft.
Weights:
empty 1,585lb (719kg).
maximum 3,349lb (1,519kg).
Performance:
maximum speed at sea level 178mph
(286km/hr).
maximum cruising speed at 7,545ft

(2,300m) 169mph (272km/hr)
range 660 miles (1,062km).
ferry range 1,075 miles (1,730km).
initial rate of climb 16.7ft/sec
(5.1m/sec).
service ceiling 17,160ft (5,230m).
Dimensions:
wing span 35ft 10in (10.92m).
length overall 25ft 9in (7.85m).
height overall 7ft 9in (2.36m).
wing area 174sq ft (16.16sq m).
Power plant: One 300hp Continental
IO–520–D piston engine.
Payload: 1 man crew and 5 troops or
max 397lb (180kg)(?) freight.
Variants:
Cessna 180 and 185 Skywagon: Earlier
(civil) variants.
First flights:
Prototype Cessna 180: 1952.
Prototype Cessna 185: July 1960.
U–17A: 1963.
Production:
Cessna 180: Series production from
1952, over 5,500 delivered or on order
by 1974.
Cessna 185: Series production
1960–61, over 2,400 delivered or on
order by 1974, inc 169 U–17A, 136
U–17B and some U–17C.
In service:
U–17: Argentina, Costa Rica, Greece,
Korea (South), Laos(?), Nicaragua,
Panama, Turkey, Uruguay, Vietnam(?).
Cessna 180 Skywagon: Argentina,

Burma, Chile, Ecuador, El Salvador,
Guatemala, Honduras, Iran, Liberia,
Mexico, Nicaragua, Uganda,
Venezuela.
Cessna 185 Skywagon: Bolivia,
Ecuador, El Salvador, Honduras, Iran,
Jamaica, Paraguay, Peru, Portugal,
Rhodesia, South Africa.

Convair F–102A 'Delta Dagger'.
Type: Single-seat all-weather fighter.
Weights:
normal 27,701lb (12,565kg).
maximum 31,526lb (14,300kg).
Performance:
maximum speed at 39,375ft (12,000m)
(Mach 1.25) 825mph (1,328km/hr).
TF–102A: maximum speed at 39,375ft
(12,000m) 645mph (1,038km/hr).
maximum speed at 36,000ft (11,000m)
with two auxiliary tanks (Mach 0.95)
631mph (1,015km/hr).
maximum cruising speed at 34,400ft
(10,500m) 540mph (869km/hr).
radius of action 497 miles (800km).
ferry range 1,352 miles (2,175km).
initial rate of climb 216.9ft/sec
(66.1m/sec).
time to 32,808ft (10,000m) 4min 15sec.
service ceiling 54,000ft (16,460m).
Dimensions:
wing span 38ft 1½in (11.62m).
length overall 68ft 4½in (20.84m).
height overall 21ft 2½in (6.46m).

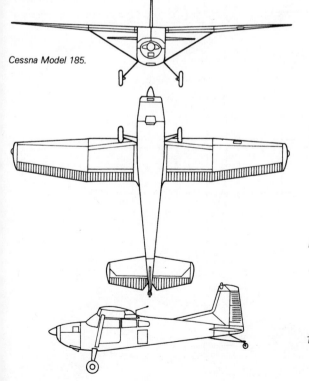

Cessna Model 185.

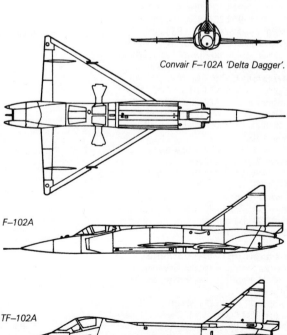

Convair F–102A 'Delta Dagger'.

F–102A

TF–102A

wing area 695sq ft (64.57sq m).
Power plant: One Pratt & Whitney
  J57–P–23 turbojet rated at 11,700lb
  (5,307kg)/17,200lb (7,802kg) st.
Armament: Three AIM–4C or AIM–4D
  Falcon AAMs and one AIM–26A or
  AIM–26B Falcon AAM in fuselage bay.
Variants:
TF–102A: Two-seat strike-trainer.
QF–102A, PQM–102A: Conversion of 2
  and 68 F–102A resp to drone aircraft
  from 1973.
First flights:
YF–102: 24 October 1953.
YF–102A: 20 December 1954.
TF–102A: 8 November 1955.
Production:
14 prototypes and trial models.
F–102A: 975 built 1954–58.
TF–102A: 63 built.
In service: Greece(?), Turkey, USA.

Convair F–106A 'Delta Dart'.

Type: Single-seat all-weather fighter.
Weights:
empty 23,655lb (10,730kg).
normal 35,500lb (16,103kg).
maximum 38,250lb (17,350kg).
Performance:
maximum speed at 41,000ft (12,500m)
  (Mach 2.31) 1,525mph (2,455km/hr).
maximum cruising speed at 41,000ft
  (12,500m) (Mach 0.92) 609mph
  (980km/hr).
radius of action 575 miles (925km).
ferry range 1,500 miles (2,415km).
service ceiling 57,100ft (17,400m).
Dimensions:
wing span 38ft 3½in (11.67m).
length overall 70ft 3¾in (21.56m).
height overall 20ft 3¼in (6.18m).
wing area 687sq ft (63.83sq m).
Power plant: One Pratt & Whitney
  J75–P–17 turbojet rated at 17,200lb
  (7,802kg)/24,500lb (11,113kg) st.
Armament: One 20mm M–61 Vulcan
  cannon, two AIM–4F or AIM–4G
  Super Falcon AAMs and one AIR–2A
  Genie or AIR–2B Super Genie AAM
  with nuclear warhead in fuselage bay.
Variants:
F–106B: Two-seat strike-trainer.
First flights:
F–106A: 26 December 1956.
F–106B: 9 April 1958.
Production:
F–106A: 277 built 1956–60.
F–106B: 63 built.
In service: USA.

Convair PBY–5A 'Catalina'.

Type: Maritime reconnaissance and
  ASW amphibian, 7–9 man crew.
Weights:
empty 17,564lb (7,967kg).
normal 34,000lb (15,422kg).
maximum 35,453lb (16,081).
Performance:
maximum speed at sea level 169mph

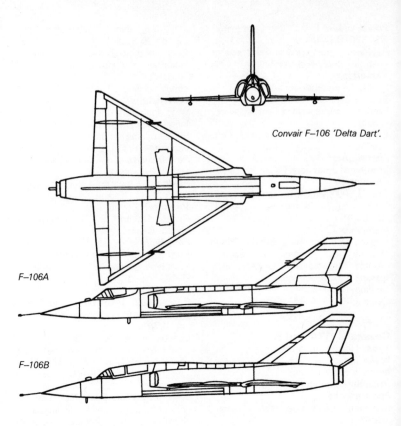

Convair F–106 'Delta Dart'.

F–106A

F–106B

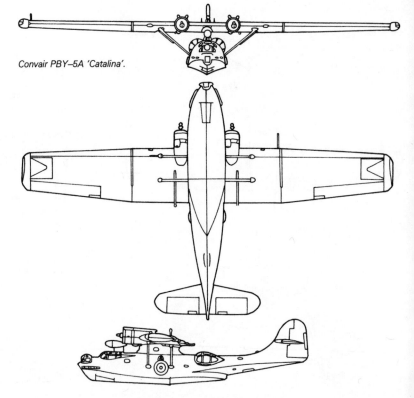

Convair PBY–5A 'Catalina'.

(272km/hr).
maximum speed at 6,560ft (2,000m) 195mph (315km/hr).
ferry range 2,520 miles (4,055km).
time to 10,000ft (3,050m) 19min 20sec.
service ceiling 14,700ft (4,480m).

Dimensions:
wing span 104ft 0in (31.70m).
length overall 63ft 10¼in (19.46m).
height overall 18ft 10in (5.74m).
wing area 1,400sq ft (130.06sq m).

Power plant: Two 1,200hp Pratt & Whitney R–1930–92 piston engines.

Armament: Two 7.62mm machine-guns in nose turret, one 7.62mm machine-gun in dorsal position, one 12.7mm machine-gun in each side blister, max 3,993lb (1,816kg) weapon load, e.g. four 1,000lb (454kg) bombs or twelve 100lb (45kg) bombs and four 650lb (295kg) depth-charges or two torpedoes.

Variants:
PBY–6A: Further development.
GST (Mop): Soviet licence-built.

First flights:
Prototype XPBY–5A: 22 November 1939.

Production: 3,290 of all variants built from 1939–45, excluding Soviet licence-built.

In service: Brazil, Chile(?), Colombia, Dominican Republic, Indonesia, Mexico.

Curtiss-Wright C–46D 'Commando'.

Type: Medium transport.

Weights:
empty 27,480lb (13,372kg).
maximum 45,000lb (20,412kg).

Performance:
maximum speed at 13,120ft (4,000m) 140mph (388km/hr).
maximum cruising speed 226mph (365km/hr).
radius of action 900 miles (1,450km).
ferry range 2,995 miles (4,820km).
initial rate of climb 21.6ft/sec (6.6m/sec).
service ceiling 27,560ft (8,400m).

Dimensions:
wing span 108ft 1in (32.94m).
length overall 76ft 4in (23.27m).
height overall 21ft 9in (6.63m).
wing area 1,361sq ft (126.50sq m).

Power plant: Two 2,000hp Pratt & Whitney R–2800–51 or –75 piston engines.

Payload: 4 man crew and 50 troops or max 16,000lb (7,258kg) freight.

Variants:
C–46A, C–46E, C–46F: Other series.

First flights:
Prototype: 26 March 1940.

Production:
3,180 built 1941–45, inc C–46A: 1,491 built, C–46D: 1,410 built, C–46F: 234 built.

In service: Dominican Republic, Korea (South), Taiwan.

Douglas A–3B 'Skywarrior'.

Type: Three-seat shipboard bomber.

Weights:
empty 39,408lb (17,875kg).
normal 73,000lb (33,113kg).
maximum 81,000lb (37,195kg).

Performance:
maximum speed at 10,000ft (3,050m) (Mach 0.83) 610mph (982km/hr).
maximum speed at 36,000ft (11,000m) (Mach 0.85) 560mph (901km/hr).
maximum cruising speed at 36,000ft (11,000m) (Mach 0.72) 475mph (765km/hr).
radius of action 1,050 miles (1,690km).
ferry range 2,900 miles (4,666km).
time to 20,000ft (6,000m) 5min 0sec.
service ceiling 41,000ft (12,500m).

Dimensions:
wing span 72ft 6in (22.10m).
length overall 76ft 4½in (23.27m).
height overall 22ft 9¾in (6.95m).
wing area 815.9sq ft (75.80sq m).

Power plant: Two Pratt & Whitney J57–P–10 turbojets each rated at 10,500lb (4,763kg)/12,400lb (5,624kg) st.

Armament: Max 12,000lb (5,443kg) weapon load plus (some aircraft) two 20mm cannon in tail barbette, tankers and reconnaissance aircraft unarmed.

Variants:
A–3A: Earlier version.
RA–3B: Photo-reconnaissance aircraft.
EA–3B: ECM aircraft with 7 man crew.

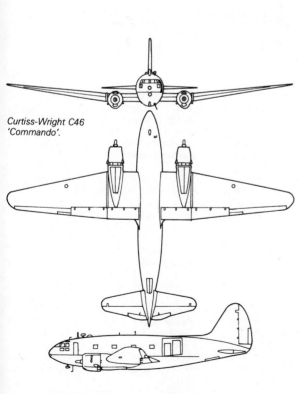

Curtiss-Wright C46 'Commando'.

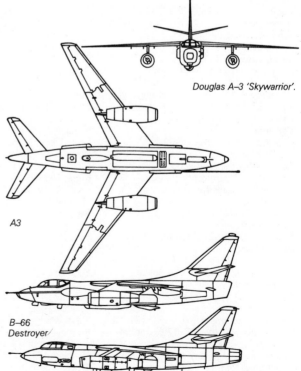

Douglas A–3 'Skywarrior'.

A3

B–66 Destroyer

TA–3B: Radar trainer.
KA–3B: Tanker with 1,084gal (4,925l)
 disposable fuel.
EKA–3B: Tanker and ECM aircraft.
B–66 Destroyer: Bomber.
RB–66A, B, C: Photo- and
 electronic-reconnaissance aircraft.
EB–66B, C, F: Reconnaissance and
 ECM aircraft.
First flights:
Prototype: 28 October 1952.
A–3A: 16 September 1953.
Production:
2 prototypes, series production
 1953–61.
A–3A: 50 built (inc 5 converted to
 EA–3A), EA–3B: 5 built, A–3B: 164
 built, RA–3B: 30 built, EA–3B: 25
 built, TA–3B: 12 built; aircraft of
 various series converted to 50 KA–3B
 and 39 EKA–3B.
In service: TA–3B, KA–3B, EKA–3B:
 USA.

Douglas C–47 'Skytrain' (Dakota).
Type: Transport.
Weights:
empty 16,971lb (7,698kg).
maximum 26,000lb (11,794kg).
Performance:
maximum speed at 7,550ft (2,300m)
 228mph (368km/hr).
maximum cruising speed at 9,840ft
 (3,000m) 185mph (298km/hr).
range 1,500 miles (2,414km).
initial rate of climb 18.7ft/sec
 (5.7m/sec).
service ceiling 23,950ft (7,300m).
Dimensions:
wing span 95ft 0½in (28.96m).
length overall 64ft 5½in (19.65m).
height overall 16ft 11¾in (5.18m).
wing area 977sq ft (91.70sq m).
Power plant: Two 1,200hp Pratt &
 Whitney R–1830–90C piston engines.
Payload: 2 man crew and 28 troops or
 max 7,495lb (3,400kg) freight.
Variants:
Li–2 (Cab): Soviet licence-built.
DC–3: Airliner.
AC–47: Night ground-support aircraft
 with three 7.62mm Miniguns.
EC–47: Electronic-reconnaissance
 aircraft.
C–117D: Further development.
First flights:
Prototype DC–3: 22 December 1935.
Production:
C–47: 10,926 built 1941–45; numerous
 conversions; approx 2,000 Soviet
 licence-built by Lisunov.
C–117D: 101 built 1950–51.
In service:
Argentina, Australia, Bolivia, Burma,
Cambodia, Canada (CC–129), Central
African Republic, Chad, Chile,
Colombia, Congo, Congo (Brazzaville),
Dahomey, Denmark, Dominican

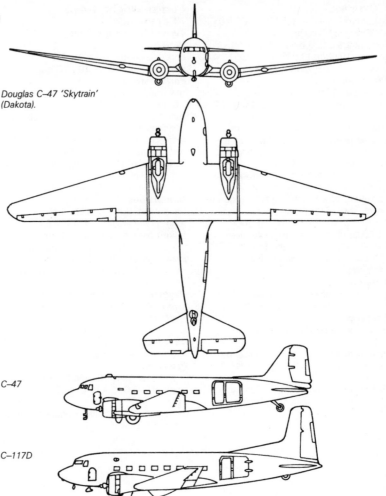

Douglas C–47 'Skytrain'
(Dakota).

C–47

C–117D

Republic, Ecuador, El Salvador,
Ethiopia, Finland, Greece, Guatemala,
Haiti, Honduras, India, Indonesia,
Israel, Italy, Ivory Coast, Korea (South),
Laos, Libya, Madagascar (Malagasy),
Malawi, Mali, Mauritania, Mexico,
Morocco, Mozambique, Nicaragua,
Niger, Nigeria, Pakistan, Panama,
Papua-New Guinea, Paraguay, Peru,
Philippines, Portugal(?), Rhodesia,
Rwanda, Senegal, Somali, South
Africa, Spain (T–3), Sweden, Syria,
Taiwan, Thailand, Togo, Turkey,
Uganda, USA, Upper Volta, Uruguay,
Venezuela, Vietnam(?), Yemen,
Yugoslavia, Zambia.
C–117D: USA.
Li–2: Bulgaria, China (People's
 Republic), Czechoslovakia, Germany
 (East), Hungary, Korea (North), Poland,
 Romania, Vietnam, Yugoslavia(?).
AC–47: Cambodia, Laos, Philippines,
 Thailand, USA, Vietnam(?).
EC–47: Brazil, Italy, USA, Vietnam(?).

Douglas C–54 'Skymaster'.
Type: Medium transport.
Weights (applicable for C–54D):
empty 38,201lb (17,328kg).
maximum 73,000lb (33,113kg).
Performance:
maximum speed at 14,100ft (4,300m)
 275mph (441km/hr).
maximum cruising speed at 15,160ft
 (4,620m) 239mph (385km/hr).
range 1,500 miles (2,414km).
ferry range 3,900 miles (6,275km).
initial rate of climb 17.7ft/sec
 (5.4m/sec).
Dimensions:
wing span 117ft 6in (35.81m).
length overall 93ft 11½in (28.63m).
height overall 27ft 6¼in (8.39m).
wing area 1,462.9sq ft (135.91sq m).
Power plant: Four 1,350hp Pratt &
 Whitney R–2000–7 or –11 piston
 engines.
Payload: 4–5 man crew and 50 troops
 or max 32,000lb (14,515kg) freight.

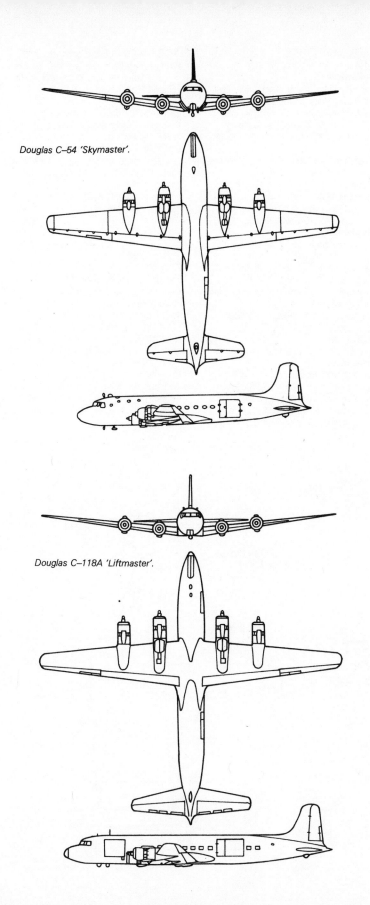

Douglas C–54 'Skymaster'.

Douglas C–118A 'Liftmaster'.

Variants:
C–54A, B, E, G and R5D (later
redesignated C–54M): Other series.
DC–4: Airliner.
HC–54D: Rescue aircraft.
First flights:
Prototype: 26 March 1942.
Production: 1,088 of all military
variants built 1942–45, inc 24 C–54,
207 C–54A, 220 C–54B, 350 C–54D,
75 C–54E, 76 C–54G and 211 R5D.
DC–4: 154 built.
In service: Argentina, Bolivia(?),
Cambodia(?), Central African Republic,
Colombia, Congo, Denmark, El
Salvador, Ethiopia, Guatemala,
Honduras, Madagascar (Malagasy),
Mexico, Niger, Paraguay, Peru,
Rhodesia(?), South Africa, Spain (T–4),
Thailand, USA, Venezuela.

Douglas C–118A 'Liftmaster'.
Type: Long-range transport.
Weights:
empty 49,763lb (22,572kg).
maximum 107,000lb (48,535kg).
Performance:
maximum speed at 17,880ft (5,450m)
370mph (598km/hr).
maximum cruising speed at 22,300ft
(6,800m) 307mph (494km/hr).
range 3,859 miles (6,211km).
ferry range 4,909 miles (7,900km).
initial rate of climb 18.7ft/sec
(5.7m/sec).
Dimensions:
wing span 117ft 6in (35.81m).
length overall 105ft 7in (32.18m).
height overall 28ft 5in (8.66m).
wing area 1,463sq ft (136.00sq m).
Power plant: Four 2,500hp Pratt &
Whitney R–2800–52W piston engines.
Payload: 5 man crew and 76 troops or
60 stretcher cases or max 27,000lb
(12,247kg) freight.
Variants:
C–118B: Transport.
VC–118A, B: VIP and command
transports.
DC–6A, B, C: Civil airliners.
First flights:
Prototype DC–6: 15 February 1946.
C–118A: September 1949.
Production:
Series production of military variants
1950–55.
C–118A: 100 built; C–118B: 61 built;
VC–118: 1 built; VC–118B: 4 built.
In service:
C–118A, B: Argentina, Chile, Mexico,
USA.
DC–6: Argentina, Bolivia (B)(?), Chile (A,
B), Congo, Ecuador (B), France (B),
Guatemala (B), Paraguay (B), Portugal
(A, B), Taiwan, Zambia (B).

Fairchild A–10A.
Type: Single-seat ground-attack
aircraft.

Weights:
empty 18,788lb (8,522kg).
normal 28,650lb (12,995kg).
maximum 45,203lb (20,504kg).

Performance:
maximum speed 518mph (883km/hr).
maximum speed at sea level 461mph (742km/hr).
maximum cruising speed at 25,000ft (7,620m) 357mph (574km/hr).
radius of action with 9,500lb (4,309kg) weapon load 285–472 miles (460–760km).
ferry range 2,650 miles (4,265km).
initial rate of climb 101.38ft/sec (30.9m/sec).

Dimensions:
wing span 55ft 0in (16.76m).
length overall 52ft 7in (16.03m).
height overall 14ft 5½in (4.41m).
wing area 488sq ft (45.13sq m).

Power plant: Two General Electric TF34–GE–100 turbofans each rated at 9,275lb (4,207kg) st.

Armament: One 30mm GAU–8/A cannon with 1,350rpg and max 18,500lb (8,392kg) weapon load on 11 hard points, e.g. twenty-four 500lb (227kg) bombs or sixteen 750lb (340kg) bombs or four 2,000lb (907kg) bombs or nine AGM–65 Maverick ASMs.

First flights:
Prototype: 10 May 1972.

Production:
2 prototypes, 10 pre-production models. Series production from 1975: production of 733 aircraft planned up to 1979, 396 on order to date.

In service: USA.

Fairchild C–119G 'Flying Boxcar'.

Type: Medium transport.

Weights:
empty 39,983lb (18,136kg).
normal 46,000lb (29,030kg).
maximum 74,470lb (33,778kg).

Performance:
maximum speed at 17,000ft (5,200m) 295mph (476km/hr).
maximum cruising speed at 14,760ft (4,500m) 200mph (322km/hr).
range with 10,000lb (4,536kg) payload 2,000 miles (3,220km).
ferry range 2,267 miles (3,648km).
initial rate of climb 10.8ft/sec (3.3m/sec).
service ceiling 21.980ft (6,700m).

Dimensions:
wing span 109ft 3¾in (33.32m).
length overall 86ft 6in (26.36m).
height overall 26ft 5½in (8.07m).
wing area 1,447sq ft (134.43sq m).

Power plant: Two 2,500hp Wright R–3350–89A piston engines.

Payload: 4–5 man crew and 62 troops or 35 stretcher cases or max 30,000lb (13,608kg) freight.

Variants:
C–119B, C, F: Earlier versions.
C–119J: Conversions of 68 C–119G, new tail doors.
C–119K: C–119G with two auxiliary underwing turbojets (General Electric J85–GE–17 rated at 2,850lb (1,293kg) st).
AC–119G Shadow, AC–119K Stinger: Conversions to night ground-support aircraft with four 7.62mm Miniguns and (K) two 20mm cannon.
EC–119J: Conversion of C–119J to ECM aircraft.

First flights:
Prototype: November 1947.
C–119G: 28 October 1952.

Production:
1,112 of all series built 1948–55; C–119B: 55 built; C–119C: 347 built; C–119F: 210 built; C–119G: 480 built, inc 26 each converted to AC–119G and AC–119K.

In service:
C–119F, G: Ethiopia, India (some with additional turbojet mounted above fuselage), Italy, Morocco, Taiwan, Vietnam(?).

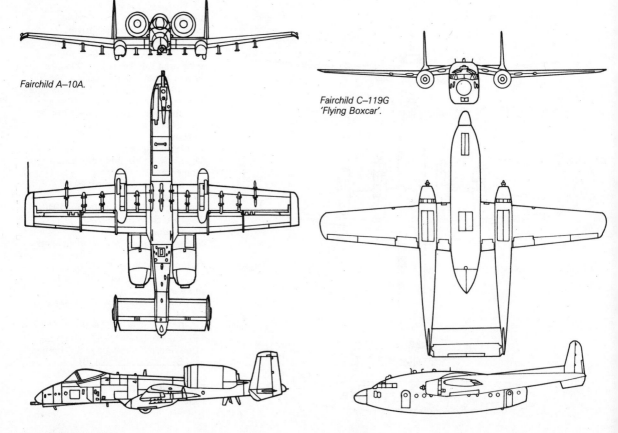

Fairchild A–10A.

Fairchild C–119G 'Flying Boxcar'.

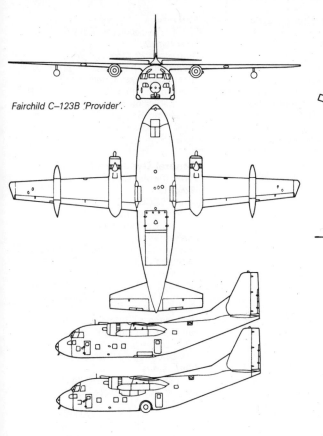

Fairchild C–123B 'Provider'.

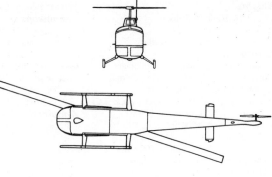

Fairchild-Hiller FH–1100.

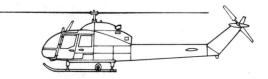

C–119J: Italy.
C–119K: Ethiopia, USA.
AC–119G, K: Vietnam(?).
EC–119J: Italy.

Fairchild C–123B 'Provider'.
Type: Medium transport.
Weights:
empty 31,378lb (14,233kg).
normal 56,500lb (25,628kg).
maximum 60,000lb (27,216kg).
Performance:
maximum speed at 9,840ft (3,000m)
  253mph (407km/hr).
maximum cruising speed 186mph
  (299km/hr).
range with 19,000lb (8,618kg) payload
  1,350 miles (2,156km).
range with 4,753lb (2,156kg) payload
  2,440 miles (3,927km).
initial rate of climb 19.0ft/sec
  (5.8m/sec).
service ceiling 23,000ft (7,000m).
Dimensions:
wing span 110ft 0in (33.55m).
length overall 75ft 3in (23.24m).
height overall 34ft 1in (10.38m).
wing area 1,223.2sq ft (113.64sq m).
Power plant: Two 2,500lb Pratt &
  Whitney R–2800–99W piston engines.
Payload: Two man crew and 60 troops
  or 50 stretcher cases and 12 medics
  or max 24,000lb (10,886kg) freight.

Variants:
C–123K: With two auxiliary underwing
  J85–GE–17 turbojets each rated at
  2,850lb (1,293kg) st, max 26,900lb
  (12,200kg) freight.
C–123H: With two auxiliary wingtip
  turbojets.
UC–123B: With defoliation and
  insecticide spray equipment under
  wings and tail.
First flights:
Prototype: 14 October 1949.
C–123B: 1 September 1954.
C–123K: 27 May 1966.
Production:
5 pre-production and 300 production
  models built from 1954–58, inc 183
  converted to C–123K 1966–69 and 10
  to C–123H in 1973.
In service:
C–123B: Cambodia(?), Thailand, USA,
  Venezuela.
C–123K: Korea (South), Philippines,
  Taiwan, USA.
C–123H, UH–123B: USA.

Fairchild-Hiller FH–1100.
Type: Light helicopter.
Weights:
empty 1,396lb (633kg).
maximum 2,750lb (1,247kg).
Performance:
maximum speed at sea level 127mph

(204km/hr).
maximum cruising speed 122mph
  (196km/hr).
range 348 miles (560km).
initial rate of climb 26.6ft/sec
  (8.1m/sec).
service ceiling 14,200ft (4,325m).
hovering ceiling in ground effect
  13,400ft (4,085m).
hovering ceiling out of ground effect
  8,400ft (2,560m).
Dimensions:
main rotor diameter 35ft 4¾in (10.79m).
length of fuselage 29ft 9½in (9.08m).
height 9ft 3½in (2.83m).
Power plant: One 317hp Allison
  250–C18 turboshaft.
Payload: 1 man crew and 4 troops or 2
  stretcher cases and 1 medic.
First flights:
Prototype: 26 January 1963.
First production model: 3 June 1966.
Production: Series production from
  1965, over 250 delivered or on order
  to date, approx only 30 as military
  variants.
In service: Argentina, Cyprus, Ecuador,
  El Salvador, Panama, Philippines,
  Thailand.

General Dynamics F–16.
Type: Single-seat fighter and
  strike-fighter.

Weights:
empty 14,100lb (6,395kg).
normal 22,000lb (10,070kg).
maximum 33,000lb (14,969kg).
Performance:
maximum speed with 2 Sidewinder
 AAMs at 36,000ft (10,970m) (Mach
 1.95) 1,255mph (2,020km/hr).
maximum speed at sea level (Mach 1.2)
 915mph (1,472km/hr).
radius of action 340–550 miles
 (550–885km).
ferry range 2,300 miles (3,700km).
initial rate of climb 1,033.4ft/sec
 (315.0m/sec).

service ceiling 52,000ft (15,850m).
Dimensions:
wing span 31ft 0in (9.45m).
length overall 47ft 7½in (14.52m).
height overall 16ft 5¼in (5.01m).
wing area 300sq ft (27.87sq m).
Power plant: One Pratt & Whitney
 F–100–PW–100(3) turbofan rated at
 –/25,000lb (–/11,340kg) st.
Armament: One 20mm M–61A–1
 Vulcan cannon with 500rpg and (as
 fighter) two–six AIM–9J or AIM–9L
 Sidewinder AAMs or (as strike-fighter)
 max 11,000lb (4,990kg) weapon load
 on 9 hard points.

Variants:
F–16B: Two-seat strike-trainer.
First flights:
Prototype: 20 January 1974.
Production: 2 prototypes, 8 YF–16
 pre-production models.
Series production 1978–79, over 1,158
 planned or on order to date.
In service: Belgium, Denmark, Iran,
 Netherlands, Norway, USA.

General Dynamics F–111E.
Type: Two-seat strike-fighter.
Weights:
empty 51,864lb (23,525kg).
normal 74,000lb (33,566kg).
maximum 91,501lb (41,504kg).
Performance:
maximum speed at sea level (Mach 1.2)
 864mph (1,390km/hr).
maximum speed at 40,000ft (12,200m)
 (Mach 2.5) 1,650mph (2,655km/hr).
radius of action with 16,000lb (7,257kg)
 weapon load 1,500 miles (2,415km).
ferry range 3,800 miles (6,115km).
initial rate of climb 666.7ft/sec
 (203.2m/sec).
service ceiling 60,000ft (18,300m)
Dimensions:
wing span (spread) 63ft 0in (19.20m).
wing span (fully swept) 31ft 11½in
 (9.74m).
length overall 73ft 6in (22.40m).
height overall 17ft 1½in (5.22m).
Power plant: Two Pratt & Whitney
 TF30–P–9 turbofans each rated at
 11,993lb (5,440kg)/19,600lb (8,890kg)
 st.
Armament: One 20mm M–61A
 cannon with 2,000rpg or two 750lb
 (340kg) bombs in fuselage
 weapon-bay and max 30,000lb
 (13,608kg) weapon load on 8 hard
 points.
Variants:
F–111A: Earlier version.
F–111C: 24 built for Australia.
F–111D: Strike-fighter with improved
 avionics.
F–111F: Strike-fighter with more
 powerful (24,912lb (11,300kg) st)
 engines and simplified avionics.
EF–111A: ECM aircraft.
RF–111A: Reconnaissance and
 strike-fighter, prototypes only.
First flights:
F–111A: 21 December 1964.
Production:
28 evaluation aircraft.
F–111A: 141 built 1965–73, inc 2
 converted to EF–111A 1973–74.
F–111C: 24 built; F–111E: 94 built
 1969–70.
F–111D: 96 built 1970/71–73.
F–111F: 118 built 1971/72–75.
In service:
F–111A, E, D, F: USA.
F–111C: Australia.

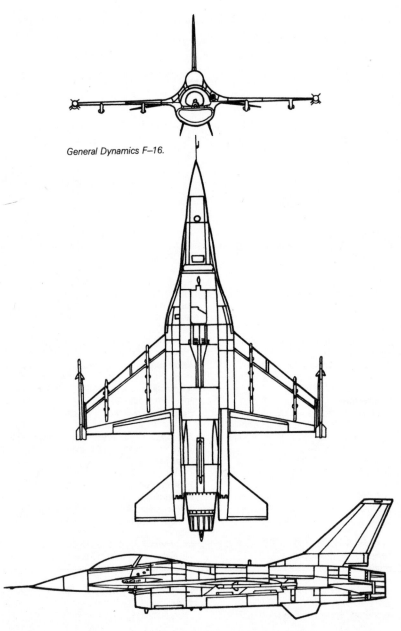

General Dynamics F–16.

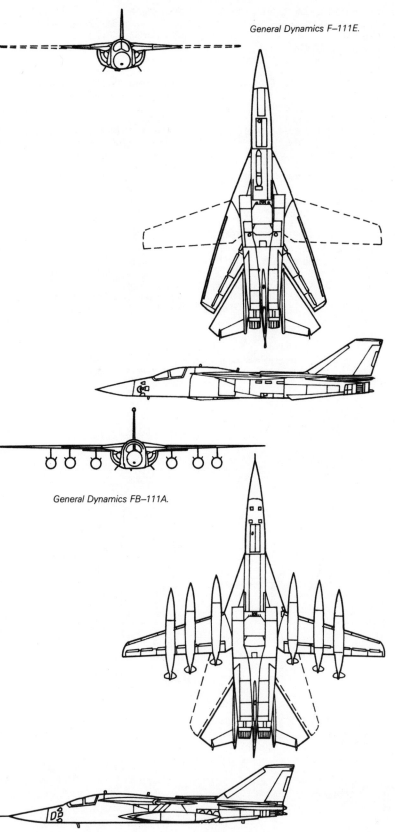

General Dynamics F–111E.

General Dynamics FB–111A.

General Dynamics FB–111A.
Type: Two-seat strategic bomber.
Weights:
maximum 100,002lb (45,360kg).
Performance:
maximum speed at sea level (Mach 1.2) 913mph (1,470km/hr).
maximum speed at 36,000ft (11,000m) (Mach 2.5) 1,450mph (2,334km/hr).
radius of action with four SRAM ASMs 1,200 miles (1,930km).
ferry range 4,101 miles (6,600km).
service ceiling 65,000ft (19,810m).
Dimensions:
wing span (spread) 70ft 0in (21.34m).
wing span (fully swept) 33ft 11in (10.34m).
length overall 73ft 6in (22.40m).
height overall 17ft 1½in (5.22m).
Power plant: Two Pratt & Whitney TF30–P–7 turbofans each rated at 12,500/20,350lb (5,670/9,230kg) st.
Armament:
Strategic operations: Max six 2,200lb (998kg) Boeing AGM–69A SRAM missiles.
Conventional operations: Max 37,480lb (17,000kg) weapon load, e.g. fifty 750lb (340kg) bombs (wings spread), reducing to twenty 750lb (340kg) bombs (wings fully swept).
First flights:
Prototype: 30 July 1967.
Production: 77 built 1968–71.
In service: USA.

Grumman A–6E 'Intruder'.
Type: Two-seat shipboard bomber.
Weights:
empty 26,000lb (11,795kg).
normal 37,147lb (16,836kg).
maximum 60,450lb (27,420kg).
Performance:
maximum speed at 36,000ft (11,000m) (Mach 0.94) 625mph (1,006km/hr).
maximum speed at sea level (Mach 0.86) 655mph (1,052km/hr).
maximum cruising speed at 36,000ft (11,000m) 654mph (776km/hr).
radius of action 370–1,125 miles (595–1,810km).
range with four Bullpup ASMs 1,920 miles (3,090km).
ferry range 2,990 miles (4,890km).
initial rate of climb 143.4ft/sec (43.7m/sec).
time to 30,000ft (9,150m) 4min 36sec.
service ceiling 44,600ft (13,600m).
Dimensions:
wing span 13ft 0in (16.15m).
length overall 54ft 7in (16.64m).
height overall 16ft 2in (4.93m).
wing area 529sq ft (49.15sq m).
Power plant: Two Pratt & Whitney J52–P–8A/B turbojets rated at 9,300lb (4,218kg) st.
Armament: Max 15,000lb (6,804kg) weapon load on 5 hard points, e.g. thirty 500lb (227kg) bombs or two

AGM–12 Bullpup ASMs and three 2,000lb (907kg) bombs or two 1,000lb (454kg) bombs and three 80gal (359l) auxiliary tanks.

Variants:

A–6B: Conversions of 19 A–6A to provide AGM–78A anti-radar missile capability.

A–6C: Conversion of 12 A–6A.

A–6E: Improved series.

EA–6A: Conversion of 27 A–6A to ECM aircraft.

EA–6B 'Prowler': Four-seat ECM aircraft.

KA–6D: Conversion of 70 A–6A to flight-refuelling tanker aircraft up to 1975.

First flights:

Prototype: 19 April 1960.

First production model: delivered 1963. A–6E: 27 February 1970.

Production: 8 evaluation aircraft; series production from 1963: 488 A–6A (inc 228 converted to A–6A from 1974), 94 A–6E, 90 EA–6B up to 1980.

In service: USA.

Grumman C–2A 'Greyhound'.

Type: Shipboard transport.

Weights:

empty 31,674lb (14,367kg).

maximum 54,807lb (24,860kg).

Performance:

maximum speed at 11,500ft (3,500m) 352mph (567km/hr).

maximum cruising speed at 27,300ft (8,320m) 297mph (478km/hr).

range with 10,000lb (4,536kg) payload 1,500 miles (2,414km).

initial rate of climb 38.7ft/sec (11.8m/sec).

service ceiling 28,800ft (8,780m).

Dimensions:

wing span 80ft 7in (24.56m).

length overall 56ft 8in (17.2m).

height overall 15ft 11in (4.85m).

wing area 700sq ft (65.03sq m).

Power plant: Two 4,050hp Allison T–56–A–8A turboprops.

Payload: 2 man crew and 39–42 troops or 20 stretcher cases and 4 medics or max 15,000lb (6,804kg) freight.

First flights:

Prototype: 18 November 1964.

Production: 17 built 1966–68, plus 8 further C–2A built 1970–71.

In service: USA.

Grumman E–2C 'Hawkeye'.

Type: Shipboard early-warning and maritime patrol aircraft, 5 man crew.

Weights:

empty 38,050lb (17,256kg).

normal 51,900lb (23,540kg).

maximum 59,880lb (27,160kg).

Performance:

maximum speed at sea level 348mph (560km/hr).

maximum cruising speed 309mph (498km/hr).

ferry range 1,600 miles (2,580km).

time to 20,000ft (6,100m) 13min 0sec.

initial rate of climb 42.0ft/sec (12.3m/sec).

service ceiling 30,840ft (9,400m).

Dimensions:

wing span 80ft 7in (24.56m).

length overall 57ft 7in (17.55m).

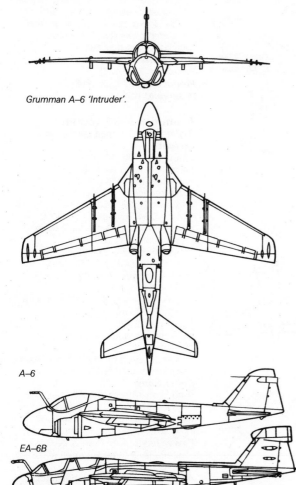

Grumman A–6 'Intruder'.

A–6

EA–6B

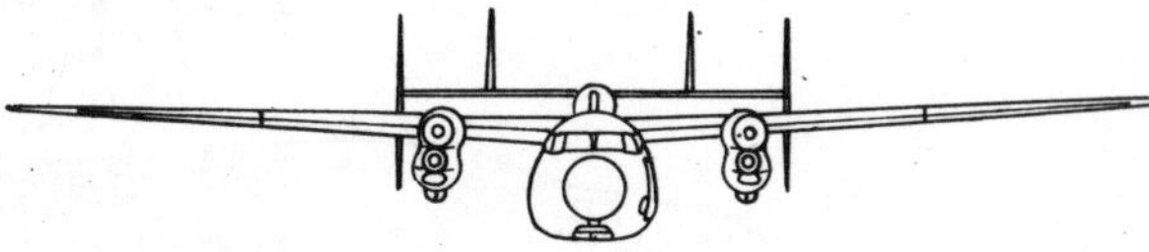

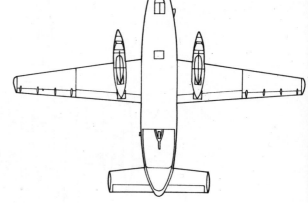

Grumman C–2A 'Greyhound'.

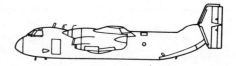

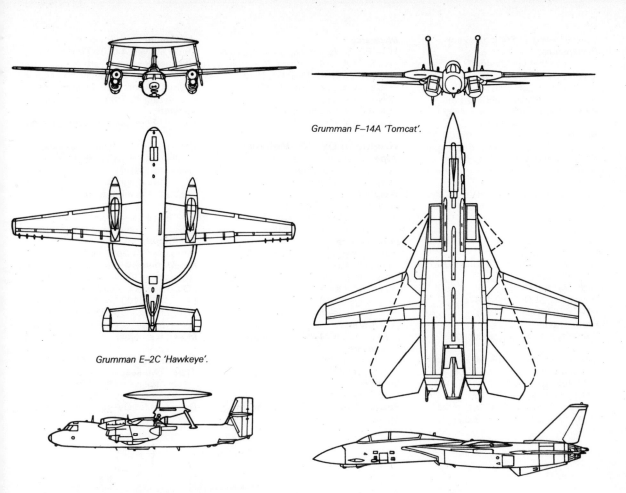

Grumman F–14A 'Tomcat'.

Grumman E–2C 'Hawkeye'.

height overall 18ft 4in (5.59m).
wing area 700sq ft (65.03sq m).
Power plant: Two 4,910hp Allison
T56–A–425 turboprops.
Variants:
E–2B: 52 E2A with new electronic
computer installation.
E–2C: Further development.
TE–2A: Trainer.
First flights:
Prototype: 21 October 1960.
E–2C: 20 January 1971.
Production:
E–2A: 59 built 1964–67.
E–2C: 67(71?) built 1971–80.
TE–2A: 2 built.
In service: Israel, USA.

Grumman F–14A 'Tomcat'.
Type: Two-seat shipboard fighter and
strike-fighter.
Weights:
empty 40,070lb (18,176kg).
normal 55,000lb (24,948kg).
maximum 68,565lb (31,101kg).
Performance:
maximum speed at 40,000ft (12,200m)
(Mach 2.34) 1,565mph (2,486km/hr).
maximum speed at sea level (Mach 1.2)

915mph (1,470km/hr).
radius of action with four AIM–7 AAMs
450 miles (725km).
time to 60,000ft (18,300m) 2min 6sec.
Dimensions:
wing span (spread) 64ft 1½in (19.54m).
wing span (fully swept) 33ft 3½in
(10.15m).
length overall 61ft 11½in (18.89m).
height overall 16ft 0in (4.88m).
wing area 565.11sq ft (52.50sq m).
Power plant: Two Pratt & Whitney
TF30–P–412 turbofans each rated at
–/20,900lb (–/9,480kg) st.
Armament: One 20mm M–61A1
cannon with 675rpg and (as fighter) six
AIM–7E/F Sparrow and four
AIM–9G/H Sidewinder AAMs, or six
AIM–54A Phoenix and two AIM–9G/H
Sidewinder AAMs or (as strike-fighter)
max 14,500lb (6,577kg) weapon load.
Variants:
F–14B: Improved version with uprated
engines (two Pratt & Whitney
F401–PW–40 each rated at –/28,098lb
(–/12,745kg)) st and more
sophisticated avionics.
F–14D: Planned further development
with simplified avionics.

First flights:
Prototype: 21 December 1970.
F–14B: 12 September 1973.
Production:
12(20?) pre-production models; series
production from 1972.
F–14A: 509(589) built.
F–14B: 2 prototypes 1973–74.
In service:
F–14A: Iran, USA.

Grumman HU–16B 'Albatross'.
Type: Maritime-reconnaissance, ASW
and ASR amphibian 3–6 man crew.
Weights:
empty 22,883lb (10,379kg).
normal 29,500lb (13,381kg).
maximum 37,500lb (17,010kg).
Performance:
maximum speed at sea level 236mph
(380km/hr).
maximum speed at 18,700ft (5,700m)
295mph (416km/hr).
maximum cruising speed 224mph
(361km/hr).
range 1,770 miles (2,850km).
ferry range 2,850 miles (4,585km).
initial rate of climb 24.3ft/sec
(7.4m/sec).

service ceiling 21,500ft (6,550m).
Dimensions:
wing span 96ft 8in (29.46m).
length overall 62ft 11in (19.18m).
height overall 25ft 10in (7.87m).
wing area 1,035sq ft (96.20sq m).
Power plant: Two 1,425hp Wright
R–1820–76A piston engines.
Armament: ASW version: max 5,200lb
(2,358kg) weapon load underwing and
in fuselage bay, e.g. four homing
torpedoes, depth-charges, rockets or
mines.
Payload: 3 man crew and 10–22
troops or 12 stretcher cases or max
6,610lb (3,000kg) freight.
Variants:
HU–16A: Basic model.
HU–16C: Naval version.
HU–16E: Version for US Coastguard.
TU–16C: Trainer.
First flights:
Prototype: 24 October 1947.
HU–16B: 16 January 1956.
Production:
7 prototypes and pre-production
models.
Series production 1949–54. HU–16A:
305 built, majority converted to
HU–16B from 1957. HU–16C: 112
built, converted to HU–16D. HU–16E:
approx 35 built, plus 37 converted
from HU–16A. TU–16C: 5 built.

In service:
HU–16A, B: Argentina, Brazil, Canada
(CSR–110), Chile, Greece (ASW), Italy,
Mexico, Norway, Pakistan, Peru,
Philippines, Spain (AD–1, ASW:
AN–1), Taiwan, Thailand, USA.
HU–16C, D: Indonesia, USA,
Venezuela(?).

Grumman OV–1D 'Mohawk'.
Type: Two-seat reconnaissance aircraft
with SLAR (Side-Looking Airborne Radar)
and infra-red surveillance equipment.
Weights:
empty 12,053lb (5,467kg).
normal 15,545lb (7,051kg).
maximum 18,110lb (8,214kg).
Performance:
maximum speed at 10,000ft (3,050m)
305mph (491km/hr).
maximum cruising speed at 10,000ft
(3,050m) 290mph (465km/hr).
ferry range 1,010 miles (1,625km).
initial rate of climb 60.0ft/sec
(18.3m/sec).
service ceiling 24,950ft (7,600m).
Dimensions:
wing span 48ft 0in (14.63m).
length overall 43ft 8in (13.31m).
height overall 12ft 8in (3.86m).
wing area 360sq ft (33.45sq m).
Power plant: Two 1,400hp Lycoming
T53–L–702 turboprops.

Armament:
Optional: Max 4,000lb (1,814kg)
weapon load on 6 hard points; e.g.
rocket launchers containing unguided
70mm rockets and weapon pods
containing 12.7mm machine-guns.
Variants:
OV–1A: Photographic-reconnaissance
aircraft.
OV–1B: Electronic-reconnaissance
aircraft with SLAR (Side-Looking
Airborne Radar).
OV–1C: Photographic-reconnaissance
aircraft with infra-red surveillance
equipment.
EV–1E: 16 OV–1B with new
electronic-surveillance equipment.
First flights:
Prototype: 14 April 1959.
Production 9 evaluation aircraft, series
production 1960–70: 64 OV–1A, 101
OV–1B, 133 OV–1C, 37 OV–1D.
From 1974: 108 OV–1B and OV–1C
converted to OV–1D with new
photographic-surveillance equipment.
In service: Israel (EV–1 only), USA.

Grumman OV–1C 'Mohawk'.
Type: Two-seat AOP and
reconnaissance aircraft with infra-red
surveillance equipment.
Details as for OV–1D with the following
exceptions:

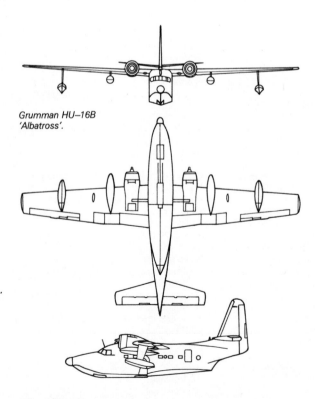

Grumman HU–16B
'Albatross'.

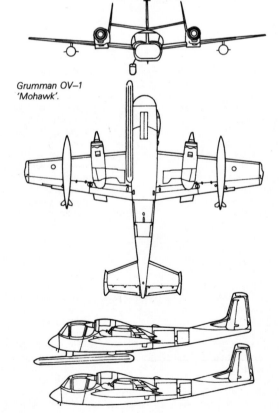

Grumman OV–1
'Mohawk'.

Grumman S2–E 'Tracker'.

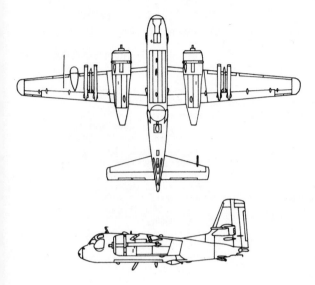

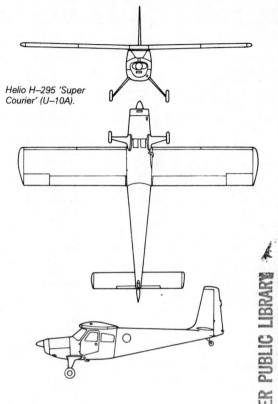

Helio H–295 'Super Courier' (U–10A).

Weights:
empty 10,311lb (4,704kg).
normal 13,040lb (5,915kg).
maximum 15,400lb (6,985kg).
Performance:
maximum speed at 5,000ft (1,520m)
  308mph (496km/hr).
maximum cruising speed 279mph
  (478km/hr).
range 441 miles (710km).
ferry range 1,330 miles (2,140km).
initial rate of climb 44.6ft/sec
  (13.6m/sec).
service ceiling 30,000ft (9,150m).
Dimensions:
wing span 42ft 0in (12.80m).
length overall 41ft 0in (12.50m).
height overall 12ft 8in (3.86m).
wing area 330sq ft (30.65sq m).
Power plant: Two 1,150hp Lycoming
T53–L–7 or L–15 turboprops.

Grumman S–2E 'Tracker'.

Type: Shipboard ASW aircraft, 4 man
  crew.
Weights:
empty 18,750lb (8,505kg).
normal 26,147lb (11,860kg).
maximum 29,150lb (13,222kg).
Performance:
maximum speed at sea level 268mph

(431km/hr).
maximum speed 265mph (426km/hr).
maximum cruising speed at 5,000ft
  (1,524m) 170mph (273km/hr).
patrol speed at 1,500ft (457m) 150mph
  (241km/hr).
ferry range 1,300 miles (2,095km).
initial rate of climb 22.97ft/sec
  (7.0m/sec).
service ceiling 21,000ft (6,400m).
Dimensions:
wing span 72ft 7in (22.13m).
length overall 43ft 6in (13.26m).
height overall 16ft 7in (5.06m).
wing area 496sq ft (46.08sq m).
Power plant: Two 1,525hp Wright
R–1820–82WA piston engines.
Armament: Fuselage bay: two homing
  torpedoes, two nuclear depth-charges
  or four 386lb (174.5kg) depth-charges.
  Underwing attachments for six 250lb
  (113.4kg) bombs or six unguided
  127mm rockets or Zuni rockets or
  torpedoes.
Variants:
S–2A, S–2C, S–2D: Earlier versions.
S–2B, S–2F, S–2N: Conversions of
  S–2A.
S–2G: Conversions of fifty S–2E.
CS2F–1 and 2: Canadian licence-built
  S–2A.

TS–2A: Trainer, 207 converted from
  S–2A.
First flights:
Prototype: 4 December 1952.
S–2D: 20 May 1959.
Production: Series production from
  1953–68.
S–2A: 655 built.
S–2C: 60 built.
S–2D: 119 built.
S–2E: 252 built from 1962–68.
CS2F–1 and –2: 100 built.
In service:
S–2A: Argentina, Brazil, Taiwan,
  Uruguay.
S–2D: Turkey.
S–2E: Australia, Brazil, Peru, Turkey,
  USA.
S–2F: Italy, Japan, Thailand.
S–2G: USA.
CS2F–1 and –2: Brazil, Canada,
  Netherlands.
TS–2A: Turkey, USA.

Helio U–10A 'Courier'.

Type: Liaison aircraft.
Weights:
empty 2,079lb (943kg).
normal 3,000lb (1,360kg).
maximum 3,400lb (1,542kg).

Performance:
maximum speed at sea level 167mph (269km/hr).
maximum cruising speed 150mph (241km/hr).
range 659 miles (1,060km).
ferry range 1,380 miles (2,220km).
initial rate of climb 19.03ft/sec (5.8m/sec).
service ceiling 20,510ft (6,250m).

Dimensions:
wing span 39ft 0in (11.89m).
length overall 31ft 0in (9.45m).
height overall 8ft 10in (2.69m).
wing area 231sq ft (21.46sq m).

Power plant: One 295hp Lycoming GO–480–G1D6 piston engine.

Payload: 1 man crew and 4 troops.

Variants:
U–10B, U–10D: Further developments.
H–250 Courier, H–295 Super Courier: Civil variants.
H–390 Courier: Initial civil variant.

First flights:
Prototype: 8 April 1949.
Courier H–390: 1953.
U–10: 1962.
Courier H–250: May 1964.
Super Courier H–295: 24 February 1965.

Production: Over 450 built of all variants from 1954, inc over 130 U–10.

In service:
U–10A, B, D: Thailand, USA.
H–295 Super Courier: Guyana.
H–250 Courier: Peru, Somali.

Hiller 12E (OH–23G 'Raven').
Type: Light AOP helicopter.
Weights:
empty 1,750lb (794kg).

normal 2,800lb (1,270kg).
maximum 3,303lb (1,498kg).

Performance:
maximum speed at sea level 96mph (154km/hr).
maximum cruising speed 90mph (145km/hr).
range 250 miles (400km).
ferry range 500 miles (805km).
initial rate of climb 21.3ft/sec (6.5m/sec).
service ceiling 15,200ft (4,640m).
hovering ceiling in ground effect 9,500ft (2,895m).
hovering ceiling out of ground effect 5,800ft (1,768m).

Dimensions:
main rotor diameter 35ft 4¾in (10.79m).
length of fuselage 28ft 6in (8.69m).
height 9ft 3½in (2.83m).

Power plant: One 305hp Lycoming VO–540–A1B piston engine.

Payload: 1 man crew and 2 troops.

Variants:
Hiller 12: Civil variant.
OH–23A, B, C, D: Earlier versions.
OH–23F: Four-seat further development.

First flights:
Prototype: 1949.
OH–23G: 1958.
OH–23F: 1960.

Production:
Over 2,000 built of all versions 1950–66, inc OH–23A: 82 built; OH–23B: 289 built; OH–23C: 143 built; OH–23D: 484 built; OH–23F: 22 built; OH–23G: 347(?) built.

In service:
OH–23G: Argentina, Chile, Colombia, Guatemala, Mexico, Netherlands, Paraguay, Thailand, Uruguay.

Hughes 269A (TH–55A 'Osage').
Type: Training helicopter.
Weights:
empty 1,010lb (458kg).
normal 1,598lb (725kg).

Performance:
maximum speed at sea level 86mph (138km/hr).
maximum cruising speed 70mph (113km/hr).
range 198 miles (320km).
initial rate of climb 19.0ft/sec (5.8m/sec).
service ceiling 11,900ft (3,625m).
hovering ceiling in ground effect 5,500ft (1,675m).
hovering ceiling out of ground effect 3,750ft (1,145m).

Dimensions:
main rotor diameter 25ft 3½in (7.71m).
length of fuselage 22ft 3¾in (6.80m).
height 8ft 3in (2.51m).

Power plant: One 180hp Lycoming HIO–360–B1A piston engine.

Payload: 2 man crew.

Variants:
Hughes 300: Three-seat civil variant.

First flights:
Prototype: October 1956.
First production model: October 1961.

Production:
Series production from 1961, over 1,175 civil variants built by mid-1968.
TH–55A: 792 built from 1964–68.
TH–55J: 48 Japanese licence-built by Kawasaki.

In service:
Hughes 269: Algeria, Ghana(?), Guyana, Nicaragua, Sierra Leone, Sweden.
TH–55A: Colombia, USA.
TH–55J: Japan.
Hughes 300: India.

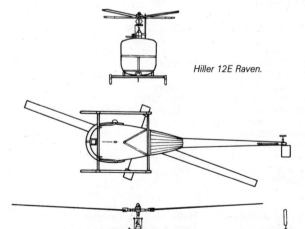

Hiller 12E Raven.

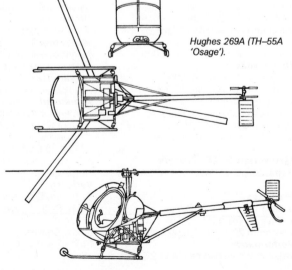

Hughes 269A (TH–55A 'Osage').

Hughes OH–6A 'Cayuse'.

Type: Light helicopter.

Weights:
empty 1,157lb (525kg).
normal 2,400lb (1,089kg).
maximum 2,700lb (1,225kg).

Performance:
maximum speed at sea level 150mph (241km/hr).
maximum cruising speed at 5,000ft (1,500m) 134mph (216km/hr).
range 379 miles (610km).
initial rate of climb 25.9ft/sec (7.9m/sec).
service ceiling 15,800ft (4,815m).
hovering ceiling in ground effect 11,800ft (3,595m).
hovering ceiling out of ground effect 7,300ft (2,225m).

Dimensions:
main rotor diameter 26ft 3in (8.00m).
length of fuselage 23ft 0in (7.01m).
height 8ft 1½in (2.48m).

Power plant: One 252hp Allison T63–A–5A turboshaft.

Armament: Hughes 500M–D: one weapon pod containing one 7.62mm Minigun machine-gun or one 30mm cannon and four TOW ASMs or two rocket launchers each containing seven 70mm rockets.

Payload: 2 man crew and 4 troops or max 950lb (431kg) freight.

Variants:
Hughes 500: Civil variant.
Hughes 500M: Export version of OH–6A.

KH–369: Japanese licence-built by Kawasaki (OH–6J).
Hughes 500 M–D Defender: Attack helicopter, one 420hp Allison 250–C20B turboshaft.
Hughes 500 ASW: ASW helicopter with 2 homing torpedoes.

First flights:
Prototype: 27 February 1963.

Production:
OH–6A: 1,434(1,415?) built 1964–70, licence-built in Argentina (120 built from 1974 by RACA?) and Italy (by Nardi).
OH–6J: 122(137?) built from 1969.
Hughes 500M: Over 80 built by end 1975 and licence-built in Pakistan.
Hughes 500M–D: 34 built and 66 licence-built in Korea (South).
Hughes 500 ASW: 12 built 1972–73.

In service:
OH–6A: USA.
OH–6J: Japan.
Hughes 500M: Argentina, Bolivia, Colombia, Denmark, Dominican Republic, Finland, Nicaragua, Pakistan, Taiwan.
Hughes 500 M–D: Korea (South).
Hughes 500 ASW: Spain (Z–13).

Kaman HH–43B 'Huskie'.

Type: Fire-fighting and transport helicopter.

Weights:
empty 4,469lb (2,027kg).
normal 5,969lb (2,707kg).
maximum 9,150lb (4,155kg).

Performance:
maximum speed at sea level 120mph (193km/hr).
maximum cruising speed 110mph (177km/hr).
range 236 miles (380km).
ferry range 277 miles (445km).
initial rate of climb 33.1ft/sec (10.1m/sec).
service ceiling 25,000ft (7,620m).
hovering ceiling in ground effect 20,000ft (6,100m).
hovering ceiling out of ground effect 16,000ft (4,880m).

Dimensions:
main rotor diameter 47ft 0in (14.33m).
length of fuselage 25ft 2in (7.67m).
height 15ft 6in (4.73m).

Power plant: One 860hp Lycoming T53–L–1B turboshaft.

Payload: 1 man crew and 8 troops or 2 fire-fighters and 1,000lb (454kg) fire-fighting equipment.

Variants:
HH–43A: Earlier version.
UH–43C, OH–43D: Transport helicopters.

First flights:
Prototype: 27 September 1956.
HH–43B: 13 December 1958.

Production:
Series production 1958–65; HH–43A: 18 built; HH–43B: 193 built; UH–43C: 24 built; OH–43D: 81 built.

In service:
HH–43B: Burma, Colombia, Pakistan, USA.
UH–43C: USA.

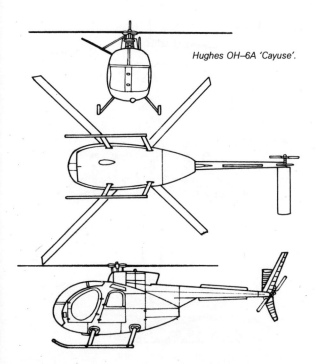

Hughes OH–6A 'Cayuse'.

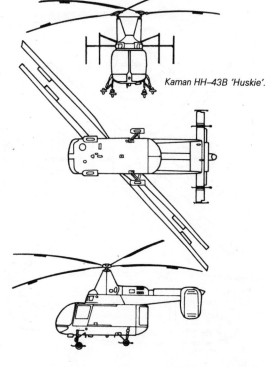

Kaman HH–43B 'Huskie'.

Kaman HH–43F 'Huskie'.

Type: Fire-fighting and transport helicopter.

Details as for HH–43B with the following exceptions:

Weights:
empty 4,620lb (2,096kg).
normal 6,500lb (2,948kg).

Performance:
ferry range 504 miles (810km).
initial rate of climb 30.2ft/sec (9.2m/sec).
service ceiling 23,000ft (7,010m).

Power plant: One 1,100hp Lycoming T53–L–11A turboshaft.

Payload: 1 man crew and 11 troops or 2 fire-fighters and 1,000lb (454kg) fire-fighting equipment.

First flights: HH–43F: August 1964.

Production: HH–43F: 40 built.

In service: HH–43F: Iran, USA.

Kaman SH–2F 'Seasprite'.

Type: ASW helicopter, 3 man crew.

Weights:
empty 6,704lb (3,041kg).
normal 12,200lb (5,805kg).
maximum 13,300lb (6,032kg).

Performance:
maximum speed 168mph (270km/hr).
maximum cruising speed 150mph (241km/hr).
ferry range 445 miles (716km).

initial rate of climb 40.7ft/sec (12.4m/sec).
service ceiling 22,500ft (6,858m).
hovering ceiling in ground effect 19,260ft (5,670m).
hovering ceiling out of ground effect 15,400ft (4,695m).

Dimensions:
main rotor diameter 44ft 0in (13.41m).
length of fuselage 40ft 4¼in (12.30m).
height 15ft 6in (4.72m).

Power plant: Two 1,350hp General Electric T58–GE–8F turboshafts.

Armament: HH–2C: One 7.62mm Minigun machine-gun in turret and two 7.62mm M–60 machine-guns. SH–2D, SH–2F: Two Mk.46 homing torpedoes.

Variants:
UH–2A, UH–2B: Transport helicopters, 42 converted to UH–2C from 1966–68.
HH–2C: Conversion of six UH–2B to armed rescue helicopters 1969.
HH–2D: Conversion of 67 UH–2B to unarmed rescue helicopters from 1969–71.
SH–2D, SH–2F: Conversion of 105 UH–2 and HH–2 of various series to ASW helicopters from 1971–75/76 (20 SH–2D, 85 SH–2F).

First flights: Prototype: 2 July 1959.

Production:
Series production 1961–66.

UH–2A: 88 built.
UH–2B: 102 built.
Conversions to UH–2C, HH–2C, HH–2D, SH–2D and SH–2F from 1966.

In service: USA.

Lockheed C–5A 'Galaxy'.

Type: Strategic transport.

Weights:
empty 325,244lb (147,528kg).
maximum 764,500lb (346,770kg).

Performance:
maximum speed at 25,000ft (7,620m) 571mph (919km/hr).
maximum cruising speed at 30,000ft (9,150m) 541mph (871km/hr).
range with 80,000lb (36,287kg) payload 6,500 miles (10,460km).
range with 220,462lb (100,000kg) payload 2,950 miles (4,745km).
initial rate of climb 38.4ft/sec (11.7m/sec).
service ceiling 34,000ft (10,360m).

Dimensions:
wing span 222ft 8in (67.88m).
length overall 247ft 10in (75.54m).
height overall 65ft 1½in (19.85m).
wing area 6,200sq ft (576.00sq m).

Power plant: Four General Electric TF–39–GE–1 turbofans each rated at 41,000lb (18,598kg) st.

Payload: 5 man crew and 10 seats for relief crew and couriers, 75 troops on

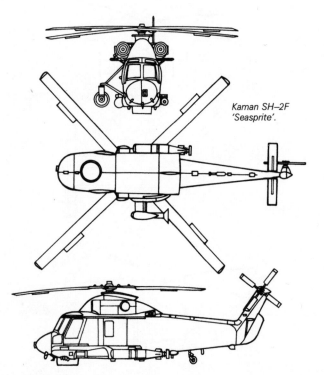

Kaman SH–2F 'Seasprite'.

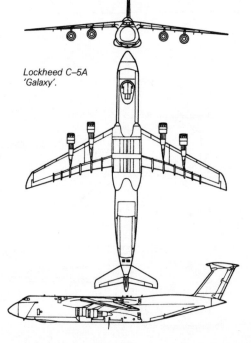

Lockheed C–5A 'Galaxy'.

the upper and 270 troops on the lower deck, or max 264,550lb (120,000kg) freight, e.g. 2 M–60 tanks or 5 M–113 personnel carriers or 10 Pershing missiles with tow and launch vehicles.
First flights: Prototype: 20 June 1968.
Production: 8 evaluation aircraft: 81 built 1969–73.
In service: USA.

Lockheed C–121G 'Constellation'.
Type: Long-range transport.
Weights:
empty 75,130lb (34,080kg).
normal 133,000lb (60,329kg).
maximum 145,000lb (65,770kg).
Performance:
maximum speed at 20,000ft (6,100m) 368mph (593km/hr).
maximum cruising speed at 23,000ft (7,000m) 331mph (533km/hr).
range 2,210 miles (3,555km).
ferry range 4,330 miles (6,970km).
initial rate of climb 18.37ft/sec (5.6m/sec).
service ceiling 22,300ft (6,800m)
Dimensions:
wing span 123ft 0$\frac{1}{4}$in (37.50m).
length overall 116ft 2in (35.41m).
height overall 24ft 8in (7.52m).
wing area 1,757.8sq ft (153.30sq m).
Power plant: Four 3,250hp Wright R–3350–91 piston engines.
Payload: 5 man crew and 72 troops or 47 stretcher cases and 2 medics or max 40,000lb (18,144kg) freight.
Variants:
L.749 Constellation, L.1049 Super Constellation: Civil airliners.
EC–121C, D, H, K, P, Q, R, S, T: Electronic-reconnaissance aircraft.
C–121A, C, J: Transports.
WC–121N: Weather-reconnaissance aircraft.
First flights:
Prototype L.1049: 13 October 1950.
Prototype C–121: 1951.
Production:
169 of all military variants built 1951–55, numerous conversions up to 1969(?), inc 142 to EC–121K.
L.749: 478 built.
L.1049: 606 built.
In service:
C–121A, G, J and WC–121N: USA.
L.749A: France.
L.1049: India, Indonesia.

Lockheed EC–121 'Warning Star'.
Type: Electronic-reconnaissance aircraft.
Details as for C–121G with the following exceptions:
Weights:
empty 80,612lb (36,565kg).
normal 143,600lb (67,137kg).
Performance:

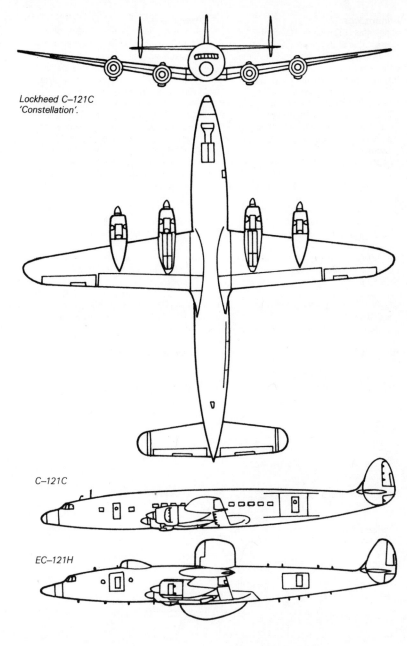

Lockheed C–121C 'Constellation'.

C–121C

EC–121H

maximum speed at 20,000ft (6,100m) 321mph (517km/hr).
patrol speed 240mph (386km/hr).
radius of action 4,600 miles (7,400km).
initial rate of climb 14.1ft/sec (4.3m/sec).
service ceiling 20,670ft (6,300m).
Dimensions:
wing span 126ft 1$\frac{3}{4}$in (38.45m).
length overall 116ft 2in (35.41m).
height overall 27ft 0in (8.23m).
Power plant: Four 3,650hp Wright R–3350–93 piston engines.
Payload: 27–31 man crew.
In service: USA.

Lockheed C–130H 'Hercules'.
Type: Medium transport.
Weights:
empty 72,890lb (33,063kg).
normal 155,000lb (70,310kg).
maximum 175,000lb (79,380kg).
Performance:
maximum speed 384mph (618km/hr).
maximum cruising speed at 20,000ft (6,100m) 375mph (603km/hr).
range w.m.p. 2,590 miles (4,170km).
ferry range 17,950 miles (8,150km).
initial rate of climb 31.82ft/sec (9.7m/sec).
service ceiling 26,500ft (8,075m).

Dimensions:
wing span 132ft 0½in (40.25m).
length overall 97ft 8½in (29.78m).
height overall 38ft 3in (11.66m).
wing area 1,745sq ft (162.12sq m).
Power plant: Four 4,910hp Allison
T56–A–15 turboprops.
Payload: 4 man crew and 92 troops or
64 paratroops or 74 stretcher cases
and 2 medics or max 45,000lb
(20,412kg) freight.
Variants:
C–130A, B, C, D, F: Earlier versions.
C–130K: Version for Great Britain.
HC–130B, E, H, N, P: Rescue aircraft.
KC–130F, H,R: Tankers.
EC–130E, G, Q, RC–130A:
Reconnaissance aircraft.
WC–130B, E: Weather-reconnaissance
aircraft.
JC–130A, B: Research aircraft.
LC–130F, R: Ski planes.
DC–130A, E: Target drone control
aircraft.
AC–130 Gunship: Night ground-support
aircraft.
Lockheed L–100, L–382: Civil versions
of C–130.
First flights:
Prototype: 23 August 1954.
C–130E: 25 August 1961.
HC–130H: 8 December 1964.

Production:
Series production from 1954, over
1,720 of all variants delivered to date.
In service:
C–130A: Australia, USA, Vietnam(?).
C–130B: Colombia, Indonesia, Iran,
Pakistan, South Africa, USA.
C–130E: Argentina, Australia, Brazil,
Canada (CC–130), Colombia, Iran,
Israel, Libya, Pakistan(?), Peru, Saudi
Arabia, Sweden, Turkey, USA.
C–130H: Abu Dhabi, Argentina,
Belgium, Bolivia, Brazil, Canada,
Cameroun, Chile, Congo, Denmark,
Egypt (UAR), Greece, Iran, Israel, Italy,
Malaysia, Morocco, New Zealand,
Norway, Peru(?), Portugal, Saudi
Arabia, Spain (T–10), USA, Venezuela.
C–130K: Great Britain (Hercules C.1,
W.2).
KC–130H: Brazil, Israel, Saudi Arabia,
Spain (TK–10), KC–130R: USA.
C–130D, F; AC–130; DC–130; EC–130;
HC–130; JC–130; KC–130F; LC–130;
RC–130; WC–130: USA.
L–100–20: Kuwait, Philippines.
L–100–30: Gabon, Iraq, Syria.

Lockheed C–140B 'JetStar'.
Type: Light transport.
Weights:
empty 22,074lb (10,012kg).

normal 37,997lb (17,235kg).
maximum 42,000lb (19,051kg).
Performance:
maximum speed at 21,200ft (6,460m)
566mph (911km/hr).
maximum cruising speed at 23,000ft
(7,010m) 570mph (917km/hr).
ferry range 2,237 miles (3,600km).
initial rate of climb 86.6ft/sec
(26.4km/sec).
service ceiling 37,400ft (11,400m).
Dimensions:
wing span 54ft 5in (16.60m).
length overall 60ft 5in (18.42m).
height overall 20ft 5in (6.23m).
wing area 542.5sq ft (50.40sq m).
Power plant: Four Pratt & Whitney
JT12A–8 turbojets each rated at
3,300lb (1,497kg) st.
Payload:
2 man crew and 8–12 troops.
Variants:
JetStar I: Basic civil version.
JetStar II: Further development with
more powerful engines (four
Garrett-AiResearch TFE731–3 rated at
3,700lb (1,678kg) st).
First flights:
Prototype: 4 September 1957.
JetStar II: 10 July 1974.
Production: 2 prototypes, JetStar I:
162 built from 1961–73, inc 24 military

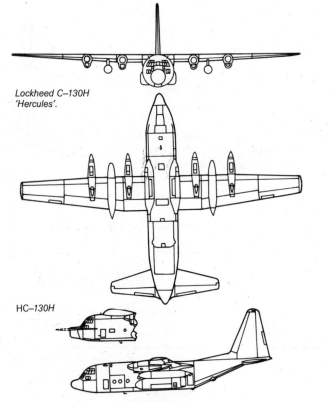

Lockheed C–130H
'Hercules'.

HC–130H

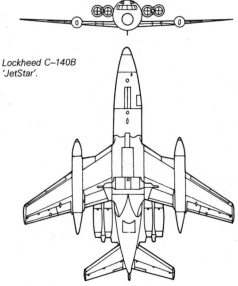

Lockheed C–140B
'JetStar'.

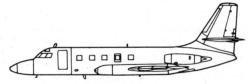

Lockheed F–104 'Starfighter'.

Lockheed C–141A 'Starlifter'.

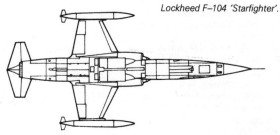

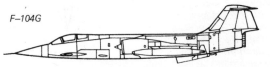

F–104G

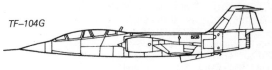

TF–104G

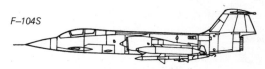

F–104S

configuration.

In service: Germany (West), Indonesia, Libya, Mexico, Saudi Arabia, USA (C–140A, VC–140B).

Lockheed C–141A 'Starlifter'.

Type: Strategic transport.
Weights:
empty 133,770lb (60,678kg).
maximum 316,580lb (143,600kg).
Performance:
maximum speed at 25,000ft (7,620m) 571mph (919km/hr).
maximum cruising speed 564mph (908km/hr).
range with 70,550lb (32,000kg) payload 3,970 miles (6,390km).
ferry range 6,140 miles (9,880km).
initial rate of climb 51.18ft/sec (15.6m/sec).
service ceiling 41,600ft (12,680m).
Dimensions:
wing span 159ft 10¾in (48.74m).
length overall 145ft 0¼in (44.20m).
height overall 39ft 3in (11.96m).
wing area 3,228sq ft (299.90sq m).

Power plant: Four Pratt & Whitney TF33–P–7 turbofans each rated at 21,000lb (9,526kg) st.
Payload: 4 man crew and 154 troops or 123 paratroops or 80 stretcher cases and 8 medics or max 70,850lb (32,136kg) freight.
Similar:
Ilyushin Il–76 (Candid): Soviet strategic transport, first appeared at 1971 Paris Air Show.
Variants:
C–141B: Planned conversion of C–141A; lengthened fuselage 168ft 5¼in (51.34m), max 89,180lb (40,450kg) freight.
First flights: No prototypes, first C–141A: 17 December 1963.
Production: 285 built 1964–68.
In service: USA.

Lockheed F–104G 'Starfighter'.

Type: Single-seat fighter and strike-fighter.
Weights:
empty 14,088lb (6,390kg).
normal 19,842lb (9,000kg).

maximum 28,770lb (13,050kg).
Performance:
maximum speed at sea level (Mach 1.2) 913mph (1,470km/hr).
maximum speed at 39,375ft (12,000m) (Mach 2.0) 1,324mph (2,130km/hr).
maximum cruising speed at 36,000ft (11,000m) (Mach 0.95) 609mph (980km/hr).
radius of action 684–808 miles (1,100–1,300km).
ferry range 2,180 miles (3,510km).
initial rate of climb 833ft/sec (254m/sec).
service ceiling 58,000ft (17,680m).
Dimensions:
wing span 21ft 11in (6.68m).
length overall 54ft 9in (16.69m).
height overall 13ft 6in (4.11m).
wing area 196.1sq ft (18.22sq m).
Power plant: One General Electric J79–11A turbojet rated at 10,000lb (4,536kg)/15,800lb (7,167kg) st.
Armament: One 20mm M–61 Vulcan cannon and (as fighter) two-four A1M–9 Sidewinder AAMs or (as strike-fighter) max 3,970lb (1,800kg)

weapon load; e.g. two Bullpup ASMs
and three 1,000lb (454kg) bombs or
one nuclear bomb.

Variants:
F–104A, C: Earlier versions.
F–104B, D, DJ, F, CF–104D: Two-seat
strike trainers.
CF–104: Canadian licence-built F–104G.
RF–104G: Single-seat reconnaissance
aircraft.
TF–104G: Two-seat strike-trainer.
F–104J: Version of F–104G for Japan.
F–104S: Further development of
F–104G for Italy, with more powerful
engine (General Electric) J79–GE–19
turbojet rated at 11,872lb
(5,385kg)/17,902lb (8,120kg) st, and
two AIM–7E Sparrow and two AIM–9
Sidewinder AAMs.

First flights:
Prototype: 7 February 1954.
F–104G: 5 October 1960.
TF–104G: October 1962.
F–104S: December 1966.

Production: 17 evaluation models;
series production from 1955; F–104A:
153 built; F–104B: 26 built; F–104C:
77 built; F–104D: 21 built; F–104F: 30
built; F–104G and RF–104G: 1,156
built (1960–65, plus 50 German
re-orders 1970–73); TF–104G:
158(181?) built (1962–65); CF–104:
340 built (1961–64); CF–104D: 38
built (1962–64); F–104J: 210 built
(1963–68); F–104DJ: 20 built
(1963–64); F–104S: 245 built
(1968–77).

In service:
F–104A, F–104B: Jordan, Pakistan,
Taiwan.
F–104G, TF–104G: Belgium, Denmark,
Germany (West), Greece, Italy,
Netherlands, Norway, Taiwan, Turkey.
RF–104G: Netherlands, Taiwan.
CF–104, CF104D: Canada, Denmark.
F–104J, F–104DJ: Japan.
F–104S: Italy, Turkey.

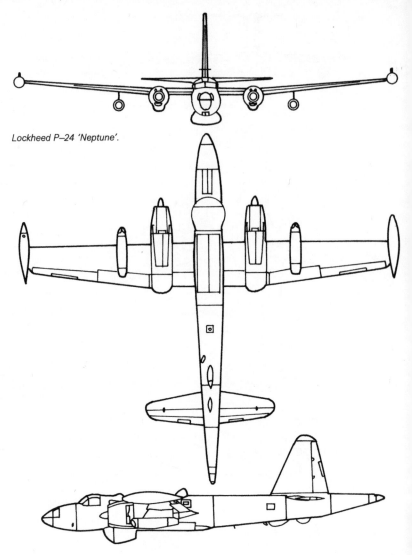

Lockheed P–24 'Neptune'.

Lockheed P–2H 'Neptune'.

Type: Maritime-reconnaissance and
ASW aircraft, 6–7 man crew.

Weights:
empty 49,935lb (22,650kg).
normal 76,456lb (34,680kg).
maximum 80,071lb (36,320kg).

Performance:
maximum speed with auxiliary turbojets
403mph (648km/hr).
maximum speed without auxiliary
turbojets 356mph (573km/hr).
maximum cruising speed at 8,500ft
(2,590m) 305mph (490km/hr).
patrol speed at 980ft (300m) 173mph
(278km/hr).
range 2,200 miles (3,540km).
ferry range 3,685 miles (5,930km).
initial rate of climb 34.4ft/sec
(10.5m/sec).

time to 9,840ft (3,000m) 4min 0sec.
service ceiling 22,000ft (6,700m).

Dimensions:
wing span 103ft 10¾in (31.67m).
length overall 91ft 8in (27.94m).
height overall 29ft 4in (8.94m).
wing area 999.9sq ft (920.90sq m).

Power plant: Two 3,500hp Wright
R–3350–32W piston engines plus two
auxiliary Westinghouse J34–WE–36
turbojets each rated at 3,400lb
(1,542kg) st.

Armament: Max 8,000lb (3,630kg)
weapon load in fuselage bay and
underwing, e.g. two homing torpedoes
or two 2,000lb (907kg) mines or eight
1,000lb (454kg) bombs or mines or
twelve 325lb (147kg) depth-charges or
one nuclear weapon in fuselage bay

and sixteen 127mm rockets
underwing.

Variants:
P–2E, J–2F: Earlier versions.
SP–2H: 154 P–2Hs with more modern
search equipment.
Kawasaki P–21: Japanese further
development.
AP–2H: Conversion of four P–2Hs to
night ground-support aircraft.

First flights:
Prototype: 17 May 1945.
P–2E: 29 December 1950.
P–2F: 16 October 1952.
P–2H: 26 April 1954.
P–2J: 21 July 1966.

Production:
Series production from 1945–62: Total
of 1,195 built in 8 different versions,

inc P–2E: 424 built from 1950–54.
P–2F: 83 built from 1952–54.
P–2H: 359 built from 1954–62, plus 48
 Japanese licence-built from 1960–62.
P–2J: 89(91?) built from 1969–77.
In service: P–2E: Brazil (P–15),
 Portugal.
P–2H: France, Japan.
SP–2H: Argentina, Australia, Chile,
 Netherlands.
P–2J: Japan.

Lockheed P–3C 'Orion'.
Type: Maritime-reconnaissance and
 ASW aircraft, 10 man crew.
Weights:
empty 61,486lb (27,890kg).
normal 135,000lb (61,235kg).
maximum 142,000lb (64,410kg).
Performance:
maximum speed at 15,000ft (4,570m)
 473mph (761km/hr).
patrol speed at 1,500ft (457m) 237mph
 (381km/hr).
maximum cruising speed at 25,000ft
 (7,620m) 397mph (639km/hr).
radius of action 1,555 miles (2,500km).
ferry range 4,770 miles (7,670km).
initial rate of climb 48.0ft/sec
 (14.6m/sec).
service ceiling 28,300ft (8,625m).

Dimensions:
wing span 99ft 8in (30.37m).
length overall 116ft 10in (35.61m).
height overall 33ft 8½in (10.29m).
wing area 1,300sq ft (120.77sq m).
Power plant: Four 4,910hp Allison
 T56–A–14 turboprops.
Armament: Max 7,250lb (3,240kg)
 weapon load in fuselage bay, e.g. two
 nuclear depth-charges and four
 torpedoes or eight bombs and (as
 delivery transport only) max 6,000lb
 (2,720kg) weapon load on 10 hard
 points under fuselage and underwing,
 e.g. bombs, rockets or torpedoes.
Payload: As auxiliary transport: 50
 troops and max 4,000lb (1,814kg)
 freight.
Variants:
P–3A, P–3B: Earlier versions.
EP–3E: Electronic-reconnaissance
 aircraft.
WP–3A: Weather-reconnaissance
 aircraft.
P–3F: Simplified export version of
 P–3C.
RP–3D: Specialized long-range version
 for mapping earth's magnetic field.
First flights:
Prototype: 25 November 1959.
P–3C: 18 September 1968.

Production:
P–3A: 157 built 1960–66, 12 converted
 to EP–3E.
P–3B: 144 built 1966–69.
P–3C: 220 built 1968–80, 1 converted
 to RP–3D.
P–3F: 6 built 1973–76.
In service:
P–3A: Spain (AN–2), USA.
P–3B: Australia, New Zealand, Norway,
 USA.
P–3C: Australia, Canada (CP–140
 Aurora), Iran, USA.
P–3F: Iran.
EP–3E, RP–3D, WP–3A: USA.

Lockheed S–3A 'Viking'.
Type: Shipboard ASW aircraft, 4 man
 crew.
Weights:
empty 26,600lb (12,065kg).
normal 42,000lb (19,050kg).
maximum 52,530lb (23,831kg).
Performance:
maximum speed at sea level 507mph
 (816km/hr).
maximum cruising speed 403mph
 (649km/hr).
patrol speed 184mph (257km/hr).
radius of action 528–2,300 miles
 (850–3,700km).

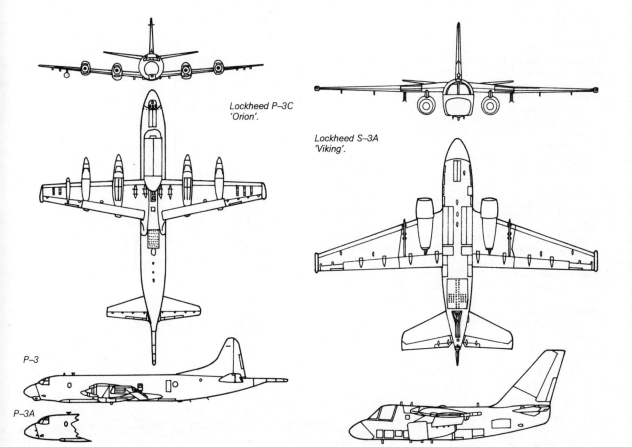

Lockheed P–3C
'Orion'.

Lockheed S–3A
'Viking'.

P–3

P–3A

ferry range 3,455 miles (5,560km).
initial rate of climb 70.0ft/sec
  (21.3m/sec).
service ceiling 40,000ft (12.200m).
Dimensions:
wing span 68ft 8in (20.93m).
length overall 53ft 4in (16.26m)
height overall 22ft 9in (6.93m).
wing area 598sq ft (55.56sq m).
Power plant: Two General Electric
  TF–34–GE–2 turbofans each rated at
  9,275lb (4,207kg) st.
Armament: Max 7,716lb (3,500kg)
  weapon load, e.g. four homing
  torpedoes or four bombs or two
  depth-charges and four mines in two
  fuselage bays plus bombs, rockets and
  ASMs underwing.
Variants:
US–3A COD: Shipboard transport, 2
  man crew and 6 troops or max 7,507lb
  (3,000kg) freight; range 3,340 miles
  (5,370km).
First flights:
Prototype: 21 January 1972.
US–3A COD: July 1976.
Production:
8 prototypes and pre-production
  models.
S–3A: Series production 1973–77; 187
  delivered or on order to date.
US–3A COD: Production of 30 planned
  1977–78.
In service: USA.

Lockheed SR–71A.
Type: Two-seat
  strategic-reconnaissance aircraft.
Weights:
normal 140,000–145,500lb
  (63,500–66,000kg).
maximum 170,000lb (77,110kg).
Performance:
maximum speed at 78,740ft (24,000m)
  (Mach 3.0+) 2,000mph (3,220km/hr).
maximum cruising speed (Mach 3.0)
  1,980mph (3,186km/hr).
ferry range 2,980 miles (4,800km).
service ceiling 80,000ft (27,450m).
Dimensions:
wing span 55ft 7in (16.95m).
length overall 107ft 4in (32.74m).
height overall 18ft 6in (5.64m).
Power plant: Two Pratt & Whitney J58
  (JT11D–20B) turbojets each rated at
  32,450lb (14,740kg) st.
Armament:
YF–12A: Eight AIM–47A AAMs.
Variants:
A–11: Earlier version, three converted
  to VF–12.
YF–12: Experimental fighter with eight
  (four?) AIM–47A AAMs, one YF–12
  converted to SR–71C.
SR–71C: Strike-trainer.
First flights:
A–11: 26 April 1962.
YF–12: 1964.

SR–71A: 22 December 1964.
Production:
A–11: 3 built.
SR–71A: Approx 24(27?) built 1964–68.
In service: USA.

Lockheed T–33 'T–Bird'.
Type: Two-seat trainer.
Weights:
empty 8,400lb (3,810kg).
normal 11,967lb (5,428kg).
maximum 13,007lb (5,900kg).
Performance:
maximum speed at sea level (Mach
  0.78) 600mph (996km/hr).
maximum speed at 25,000ft (7,620m)
  543mph (874km/hr).
ferry range 1,345 miles (2,165km).

initial rate of climb 91.2ft/sec
  (27.8m/sec).
time to 25,000ft (7,620m) 6min 30sec.
service ceiling 47,500ft (14,480m).
Dimensions:
wing span 38ft 10½in (11.85m).
length overall 37ft 9¼in (11.51m).
height overall 11ft 8in (3.55m.)
wing area 237sq ft (22.02sq m).
Power plant: One Allison J33–A–35
  turbojet rated at 4,600lb (2,087kg)
  /5,400lb (2,449kg) st (with water
  injection) (CL–30: Rolls-Royce Nene
  10 rated at 5,100lb (2,313kg) st).
Armament: Two 12.7mm M–3
  machine-guns.
Variants:
T–33A–N: Canadian licence-built
  (CL–30 Silver Star).

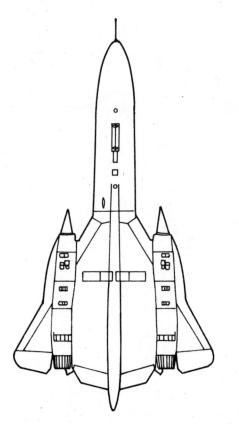

Lockheed SR–71.

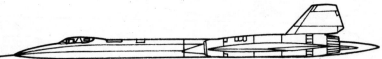

Lockheed T–33.

Lockheed U–2.

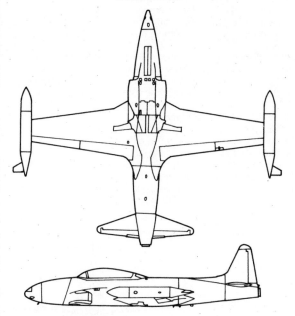

T–33B and naval version TV–2: Later
 series.
RT–33A: Single-seat reconnaissance
 aircraft.
WT–33A: Weather-reconnaissance
 aircraft. .
DT–33A: Target aircraft.
T–1A SeaStar: Further development,
 naval trainer.
First flights:
Prototype: 22 March 1948.
T–1A: 15 December 1953.
Production:
T–33A, B: 5,691 built 1948–59,
 additional 210 Japanese licence-built
 1956–58.
CL–30: 656 built.
T–1A: 271 built 1954–58.
In service:
T–33: Belgium(?), Brazil, Burma, Chile,
 Colombia, Denmark, Ecuador, Ethiopia,
 France, Germany (West), Greece,
 Guatemala, Honduras, Indonesia, Iran,
 Italy, Japan, Korea (South), Libya,
 Mexico, Nicaragua, Norway, Pakistan,
 Peru, Philippines, Portugal, Saudi
 Arabia, Spain (E–15), Taiwan, Thailand,
 USA, Uruguay, Yugoslavia.
T–33A–N: Bolivia, Canada (CT–133),
 Greece, Turkey.
T–1A: USA.
RT–33A: Iran, Thailand, Yugoslavia.

Lockheed U–2C.
Type: Single-seat strategic high-altitude

reconnaissance aircraft.
Weights:
normal 15,850lb (7,190kg).
maximum 17,273lb (7.835kg).
Performance:
maximum speed at 39,375ft (12,000m)
 528mph (850km/hr).
maximum cruising speed 460mph
 (740km/hr).
range 4,000 miles (6,440km).
service ceiling 80,050ft (24,400m).
Dimensions:
wing span 80ft 0in (24.38m).
length overall 49ft 6¾in (15.11m).
height overall 13ft 0in (3.96m).
wing area 365.11sq ft (52.50sq m).
Power plant: One Pratt & Whitney
 J75–P–13 turbojet rated at 17,000lb
 (7,710kg) st.
Variants:
U–2A: Earlier version with less
 powerful engine (Pratt & Whitney
 J57–P–13A turbojet rated at 11,200lb
 (5,080kg) st).
U–2B: As U–2A, but with equipment
 modifications.
U–2D: Two-seat variant.
First flights:
Prototype: 1 August 1955.
Production:
2(?) prototypes: series production from
 1955–58.
U–2A, B and C: 48 built.
U–2D: 5 built.
In service: USA.

Martin B–57B.
Type: Two-seat bomber and
 reconnaissance aircraft.
Weights:
empty 30,000lb (13,608kg).
normal 49,500lb (22,453kg).
maximum 54,500lb (24,721kg).
Performance:
maximum speed at sea level 520mph
 (837km/hr).
maximum speed at 39,375ft (12,000m)
 (Mach 0.88) 581mph (936km/hr).
maximum cruising speed 478mph
 (770km/hr).
radius of action 1,100 miles (1,770km).
ferry range 2,650 miles (4,264km).
initial rate of climb 58.4ft/sec
 (17.8m/sec).
service ceiling 48,000ft (14,630m).
Dimensions:
wing span 63ft 11¼in (19.49m).
length overall 65ft 5¾in (19.96m).
height overall 15ft 7in (4.75m).
wing area 959.3sq ft (89.19sq m).
Power plant: Two Wright J65–W–5
 turbojets each rated at 7,200lb
 (3,275kg) st.
Armament: Eight 12.7mm Colt
 Browning machine-guns, max 8,000lb
 (3,629kg) weapon load in fuselage bay
 and underwing.
Variants:
B–57A, C, E: Other series.
RB–57A, D: Reconnaissance aircraft
 and bombers.

RB–57F: Conversion of 17 B–57B and 4 RB–57D to strategic high-altitude reconnaissance aircraft.
B–57G: Conversions of 16 B–57Bs to night ground-support aircraft.
EB–57A, D, E: Conversion to ECM aircraft.
WB–57F: RB–57F conversions to weather reconnaissance aircraft.

First flights:
B–57A: 20 July 1953.
B–57B: 28 June 1954.

Production:
Series production 1952–56, conversions 1964–70; B–57A: 8 built; RB–57A: 67 built; B–57B: 202 built; B–57C: 38 built; RB–57D: 20 built; B–57E: 68 built.

In service:
B–57B: Pakistan, USA.
B–57G, EB–57, WB–57F: USA.

Martin RB–57F.

Type: Strategic high-altitude reconnaissance aircraft.
Details as for B–57B with the following exceptions:

Weights:
normal 63,000lb (28,576kg).

Performance:
maximum speed at 39,375ft (12,000m) 500mph (805km/hr).
maximum cruising speed at 60,000ft (18,300m) 460mph (740km/hr).
range 3,000 miles (4,800km).
time to 60,000ft (18,300m) 35–40min.
service ceiling 69,900ft (21,300m).

Dimensions:
wing span 122ft 5¼in (37.32m).
length overall 69ft 0in (21.03m).
height overall 19ft 0in (5.79m).
wing area 2,000sq ft (185.80sq m).

Power plant: Two Pratt & Whitney TF–33–P–11 turbofans each rated at 18,000lb (8,165kg) st and two Pratt & Whitney J60–P–9 turbojets each rated at 3,300lb (1,497kg) st.

In service: Pakistan.

McDonnell Douglas A–4F 'Skyhawk'.

Type: Single-seat shipboard strike-fighter.

Weights:
empty 9,998lb (4,535kg).
normal 16,301lb (7,394kg).
maximum 24,500lb (11,113kg).

Performance:
maximum speed at sea level (Mach 0.88) 674mph (1,086km/hr).
maximum speed at 35,000ft (10,700m) (Mach 0.92) 612mph (985km/hr).
radius of action 341 miles (550km).
ferry range 2,436 miles (3,920km).
service ceiling 57,570ft (14,500m).

Dimensions:
wing span 27ft 6in (8.38m).
length overall 40ft 1in (12.22m).
height overall 15ft 0in (4.57m).
wing area 260sq ft (24.16sq m).

Power plant: One Pratt & Whitney J52–P–8A turbojet rated at 9,300lb (4,218kg) st.

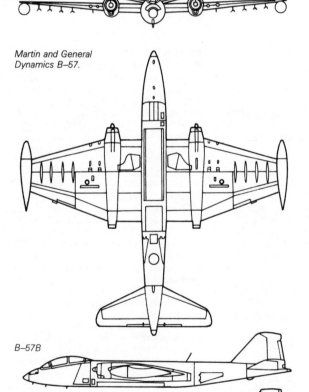

Martin and General Dynamics B–57.

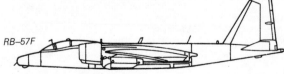

B–57B

RB–57F

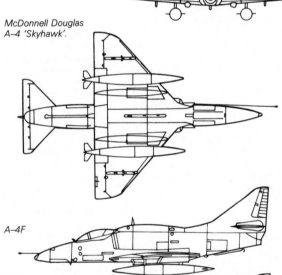

McDonnell Douglas A–4 'Skyhawk'.

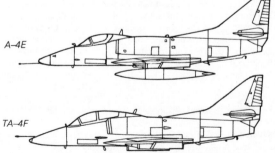

A–4F

A–4E

TA–4F

Armament: Two 20mm Mk.12 cannon with 100rpg and max 8,200lb (3,720kg) weapon load; e.g. two Bullpup ASMs or bombs and rockets.

Variants:
A–4A, B, C, E: Earlier versions.
A–4G, H, K, M, N: Later series.
A–4L: Conversion of A–4C; now as A–4F.
A–4P, Q, S and TA–4S: Conversions of 112 A–4B.
TA–4F, G, H, J, K, S: Two-seat strike-trainers.

First flights:
Prototype: 22 June 1954.
A–4F: 31 August 1966.
A–4N: 12 June 1972.

Production: 2,966 built from 1954–78; over 2,800 delivered or on order to date, inc 166 A–4A, 542 A–4B, 638 A–4C, 449 A–4E, 154 A–4F, 16 A–4G, 108 A–4H, 10 A–4K, 30 A–KU, 50 A–4M, 104 A–4N, 200 TA–4F, 4 TA–4G, 10(13?) TA–4H, 185 TA–4J, 4 TA–4K, 6 TA–4KU.

In service: Argentina (A–4B, F, P, Q), Australia (A–4G, TA–4G), Brazil (A–4F), Israel (A–4E, H, N, TA–4H), Kuwait (A–4KU, TA–4KU), New Zealand (A–4K, TA–4K), Singapore (A–4S, TA–4S), USA (A–4E, F, L and TA–4F, J).

McDonnell Douglas A–4M.
Type: Single-seat shipboard strike-fighter.
Details as for A–4F with the following exceptions.
Weights:
empty 10,465lb (4,747kg).

normal 12,280lb (5,570kg).
maximum 24,500lb (11,113kg).
Performance:
maximum speed at 25,000ft (7,620m) (Mach 0.94) 640mph (1,030km/hr).
maximum speed at sea level 700mph (1,078km/hr).
ferry range 2,055 miles (3,307km).
initial rate of climb 264.1ft/sec (80.5m/sec).
Dimensions:
length overall 40ft 3in (12.27m).
Power plant: One Pratt & Whitney J52–P–408A turbojet rated at 11,200lb (5,080kg) st.
Armament: Two 20mm Mk.12 cannon with 200rpg and max 9,155lb (4,153kg) weapon load, e.g. two Bullpup ASMs or bombs or rockets.
First flights: A–4M: 10 April 1970.
Production: Over 170 built.
In service: Kuwait, USA.

McDonnell Douglas C–9A 'Nightingale'.
Type: Aeromedical transport.
Weights:
empty 59,214lb (26,859kg).
normal 98,000lb (44,450kg).
maximum 108,000lb (48,988kg).
Performance:
maximum cruising speed at 25,000ft (7,620m) 565mph (909km/hr).
ferry range 2,800 miles (4,505km).
Dimensions:
wing span 93ft 5in (28.47m).
length overall 119ft 4in (36.37m).
height overall 27ft 6in (8.38m).
wing area 1,000.7sq ft (92.97sq m).

Power plant: Two Pratt & Whitney JT8D–9 turbofans each rated at 14,495lb (6,575kg) st.
Payload: 3 man crew and over 40 troops or 30–40 stretcher cases and 4–6 medics.
Variants:
McDonnell Douglas C–9B 'Skytrain II': Transport.
VC–9C: Staff transport.
McDonnell Douglas DC–9: Civil airliner.
First flights:
Prototype DC–9: February 1965.
C–9A: June 1968.
Production:
DC–9: Series production from 1965, over 900 built.
C–9A: 21 built 1968–72.
C–9B: 14 built from 1972–75.
VC–9C: 3 built 1975.
In service:
C–9A, C–9B, VC–9C: USA.
DC–9–32: Italy.
DC–9CF: Kuwait.

McDonnell Douglas F–4B, C, D and RF–4B, C 'Phantom II'.
Type: Two-seat fighter and strike-fighter (F–4B, C, D) or reconnaissance aircraft (RF–4B, C).
Weights:
empty 27,998lb (12,700kg).
normal 46,000lb (20,865kg).
maximum 54,598lb (24,765kg).
Performance:
maximum speed at sea level (Mach 1.2) 915mph (1,472km/hr).
maximum speed at 48,200ft (14,700m) (Mach 2.4) 1,583mph (2,548km/hr).
maximum cruising speed at 40,000ft

McDonnell Douglas C–9A 'Nightingale'.

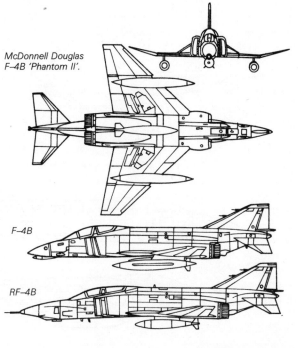

McDonnell Douglas F–4B 'Phantom II'.

F–4B

RF–4B

(12,200m) 575mph (925km/hr).
radius of action 404–900 miles
(650–1,450km).
ferry range 2,300 miles (3,700km).
initial rate of climb 469ft/sec
(143.0m/sec).
time to 49,200ft (15,000m) 2min 0sec.
service ceiling 71,000ft (21,640m).
Dimensions:
wing span 38ft 5in (11.70m).
length overall 58ft 3in (17.76m).
length overall RF–4B, C: 62ft 9¾in
(19.15m).
height overall 16ft 3in (4.96m).
wing area 530.1sq ft (49.24sq m).
Power plant: Two General Electric
J79–GE–8 or –15 turbojets each rated
at 10,913lb (4,950kg)/16,000lb
(7,711kg) st.
Armament:
F–4B, C, D: (as fighter) four AIM–7E
Sparrow III and four AIM–9
Sidewinder AAMs or (as strike-fighter)
max 15,984lb (7,250kg) weapon load;
e.g. fifteen 1,000lb (454kg) bombs.
RF–4B, C: Cameras and SLAR
(Side-looking Airborne Radar).
Variants:
F–4A: Pre-production model.
F–4G, F–4J, F–4E: Further
developments.

F–4K, F–4M: Fighter and strike-fighter
for Great Britain with British engines.
F–4N: Conversion of 228 F–4B from
1972–75.
F–4S: Updating of 302 F–4J from 1976.
First flights:
Prototype: 27 May 1958; F–4B: 1961;
F–4C: 27 May 1963; F–4D: 8
December 1965; RF–4B: 12 March
1965; RF–4C: 9 August 1963; F–4J:
27 May 1966; F–4N: June 1972.
Production: Series production from
1960–72: F–4A: 47 built; F–4B: 635
built; F–4C: 583 built; F–4D: 825
built; RF–4B: 46 built; RF–4C: 495
built; F–4G: 12 built; F–4K: 52 built;
F–4M: 118 built; F–4J: 522 built.
In service:
F–4B, RF–4B, RF–4C, F–4J, F–4N:
USA.
F–4C: Spain (C–12), USA.
F–4D: Iran, Korea (South), USA.
F–4K, M: Great Britain (Phantom FG.1,
Phantom FGR.2).

McDonnell Douglas F–4E 'Phantom'.
Type: Two-seat fighter and
strike-fighter.
Weights:
empty 30,423lb (13,800kg).

normal 47,400lb (21,500kg).
maximum 60,630lb (27,502kg).
Performance:
maximum speed at 40,000ft (12,200m)
(Mach 2.27) 1,500mph (2,414km/hr).
maximum speed at 985ft (300m) (Mach
1.2) 900mph (1,464km/hr).
maximum cruising speed at 40,000ft
(12,200m) 575mph (925km/hr).
radius of action 155–660 miles
(250–1,060km).
ferry range 2,300 miles (3,700km).
initial rate of climb 498.7ft/sec
(152.0m/sec).
service ceiling 64,630ft (19,700m).
Dimensions:
wing span 38ft 5in (11.70m).
length overall 62ft 11¾in (19.20m).
height overall 16ft 3in (4.96m).
wing area 530sq ft (49.20sq m).
Power plant: Two General Electric
J79–GE–17 turbojets each rated at
11,872lb (5,385kg)/17,902lb (8,120kg)
st.
Armament: One 20mm M–61A1
cannon with 639rpg and (as fighter)
four–six AIM–7E Sparrow IIIB AAMs
and four AIM–9D Sidewinder 1C
AAMs and (as strike-fighter) max
16,000lb (7,257kg) weapon load.
Variants:
F–4EJ: Japanese licence-built F–4E by
Mitsubishi.
F–4F: Strike-fighter with simplified
avionics.
F–4G: Conversion of 116 F–4E to ECM
aircraft from 1977.
First flights:
F–4E: 30 June 1967.
F–4EJ: 14 January 1971.
F–4F: 24 May 1973.
Production:
F–4E: Series production since 1967,
over 1,200 delivered or on order to
date.
F–4FJ: 142 built from 1971.
F–4F: 185 built 1973–77.
In service:
F–4E: Greece, Iran, Israel, Korea
(South), Turkey, USA.
F–4EJ: Japan.
F–4F: Germany (West).
F–4G: USA.

McDonnell Douglas RF–4E 'Phantom'.
Type: Two-seat reconnaissance
aircraft.
Details as for F–4E with the following
exceptions:
Weights:
normal 46,077lb (20,900kg).
maximum 57,320lb (26,000kg).
Performance:
radius of action 684 miles (1,100km).
Armament: One 20mm M–61A1
cannon with 639rpg: Infra-red, radar
and photographic reconnaissance
equipment.

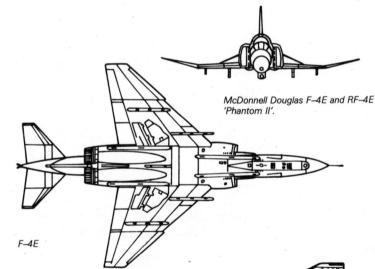

*McDonnell Douglas F–4E and RF–4E
'Phantom II'.*

F–4E

RF–4E

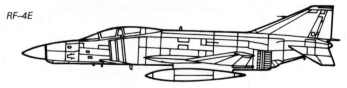

Production: Series production from 1967, over 150 delivered or on order to date.

In service: Germany (West), Greece, Iran, Israel, Japan, Turkey.

McDonnell Douglas F–15A 'Eagle'.

Type: Single-seat fighter and strike-fighter.

Weights:
empty 26,145lb (11,860kg).
normal 38,250lb (17,350kg).
maximum 56,000lb (25,400kg).

Performance:
maximum speed at 36,000ft (11,000m) (Mach 2.3) 1,520mph (2,446km/hr).
maximum speed at 980ft (300m) (Mach 1.2) 913mph (1,470km/hr).
radius of action 685–1,120 miles (1,100–1,800km).
ferry range 2,980 miles (4,800km).
time to 40,000ft (12,000m) 1min 0sec.
service ceiling 66,900ft (20,390m).

Dimensions:
wing span 42ft 9½in (13.04m).
length overall 36ft 9½in (19.44m).
height overall 18ft 7¼in (5.67m).
wing area 611.4sq ft (56.80sq m).

Power plant: Two Pratt & Whitney F100–PW–100 turbofans each rated at 19,000/27,000lb (8,620/12,247kg) st.

Armament: One 20mm M–61A–1 Vulcan Cannon with 960(680?)rpg and (as fighter) four AIM–7F Sparrow and AIM–9L Sidewinder AAMs or (as strike-fighter) max 12,000lb (5,440kg) weapon load on 5 hard points, e.g. eighteen 500lb (227kg) bombs.

Variants: TF–15: Two-seat strike-trainer.
RF–15C: Planned two-seat reconnaissance aircraft.

First flights:
Prototype: 27 July 1972.
Prototype TF–15: 7 July 1973.

Production: 20 prototypes and pre-production models, series production from 1973, 431 delivered or on order to date; 754 aircraft to be built by 1978.

In service: Israel, USA.

McDonnell Douglas/Northrop F–18 'Hornet'.

Type: Single-seat shipboard fighter and strike-fighter.

Weights:
empty 20,635lb (9,360kg).
normal 33,000lb (14,970kg).
maximum 44,000lb (19,960kg).

Performance:
maximum speed at 39,470ft (12,000m) (Mach 1.8).
maximum speed at sea level (Mach 1.2).
radius of action 460–840 miles (740–1,350km).
ferry range 2,300 miles (3,700km).
service ceiling 49,850ft (15,200m).

Dimensions:
wing span 40ft 8½in (12.41m).
length overall 56ft 4in (17.17m).
height overall 14ft 10½in (4.52m).
wing area 414.41sq ft (38.50sq m).

Power plant: Two General Electric F–404–GE–400 turbofans each rated at –/16,030lb (–/7,270kg) st.

Armament: One 20mm M–G1A–1 Vulcan cannon with 500(450?)rpg and (as fighter) two AIM–7 Sparrow AAMs and two AIM–9E Sidewinder AAMs or (as strike-fighter) max 13,000lb (5,900kg) weapon load on 5 hard points.

Variants:
Northrop YF–17: Single-seat strike-fighter, only 2 prototypes converted in 1975.
F–18L Cobra: Single-seat fighter and strike-fighter.

First flights:
YF–17: 9 July 1974.
Prototype F–18: July 1978(?).

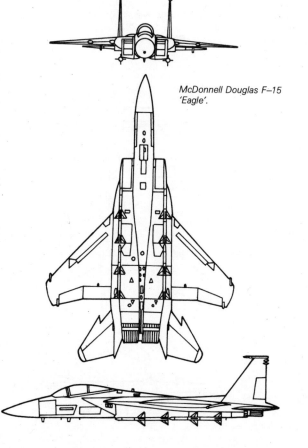

McDonnell Douglas F–15 'Eagle'.

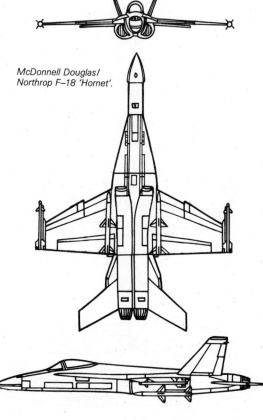

McDonnell Douglas/ Northrop F–18 'Hornet'.

Production:
11 evaluation models from 1976.
F–18L: Approx 2,000 planned from 1981–82.
F–18: Series production from 1979–80(?), approx 800 (500 fighters, 300 strike-fighters) planned.
In service: USA.

McDonnell F–101B 'Voodoo'.
Type: Two-seat all-weather fighter.
Weights:
empty 27,954lb (12,680kg).
normal 39,802lb (18,054kg).
maximum 46,672lb (21,170kg).
Performance:
maximum speed at sea level (Mach 0.94) 716mph (1,152km/hr).
maximum speed at 40,000ft (12,200m) (Mach 1.85) 1,220mph (1,963km/hr).
maximum cruising speed at 36,000ft (11,000m) 590mph (950km/hr).
range 1,553 miles (2,500km).
ferry range 2,200 miles (3,540km).
initial rate of climb 283.5ft/sec (86.4m/sec).
service ceiling 52,000ft (15,850m).
Dimensions:
wing span 39ft 8in (12.09m).
length overall 67ft 4½in (20.54m).
height overall 18ft 0in (5.49m).
wing area 358sq ft (34.19sq m).
Power plant: Two Pratt & Whitney J57–P–55 turbojets each rated at 11,989lb (5,438kg)/14,782lb (6,705kg) st.
Armament: Three AIM–4E or –4F

Super Falcon AAMs in fuselage bay and two underwing AIR–2A Genie AAMs.
Variants:
F–101A, F–101C: Fighter and strike-fighter; numerous conversions to RF–101G and RF–101H reconnaissance aircraft.
RF–101A: Reconnaissance aircraft.
TF–101B: Two-seat fighter and strike-trainer.
F–101F, TF–101F: Updating of 56 F–101B and 10 TF–101B.
First flights:
Prototype: 29 September 1954.
F–101B: 27 March 1957.
Production: Series production 1957–61; F–101A: 79 built; RF–101A: 35 built; F–101C: 47 built; F–101B and TF–101B: 478 built.
In service:
F–101F, TF–101F: Canada (CF–101B, CF–101F).
RF–101G, H: USA.

McDonnell RF–101C 'Voodoo'.
Type: Single-seat reconnaissance aircraft.
Details as for the F–101B with the following exceptions:
Weights:
normal 40,345lb (18,300kg).
maximum 48,722lb (22,100kg).
Performance:
maximum speed at 37,700ft (11,500m) (Mach 1.58) 1,040mph (1,673km/hr).
range 1,678 miles (2,700km).

initial rate of climb 232.9ft/sec (71.0m/sec).
Dimensions:
length overall 69ft 3in (21.11m).
Power plant: Two Pratt & Whitney J57–P–13 turbojets each rated at 10,099lb (4,581kg)/14,880lb (6,750kg) st.
Armament: Five cameras.
First flights: 12 July 1957.
Production: 166 built.

North American F–86D(L) 'Sabre'.
Type: Single-seat all-weather fighter.
Weights:
empty 13,500lb (6,123kg).
normal 18,160lb (8,237kg).
maximum 19,952lb (9,050kg).
Performance:
maximum speed at sea level (Mach 0.9) 693mph (1,115km/hr).
maximum speed at 40,000ft (12,200m) (Mach 0.93) 616mph (991km/hr).
maximum cruising speed 547mph (880km/hr).
radius of action 270 miles (435km).
ferry range 767 miles (1,235km).
initial rate of climb 200ft/sec (61.0m/sec).
service ceiling 49,375ft (15,050m).
Dimensions:
wing span 37ft 2in (11.32m).
length overall 40ft 3in (12.27m).
height overall 14ft 11¾in (4.57m).
wing area 289.6sq ft (26.90sq m).
Power plant: One General Electric

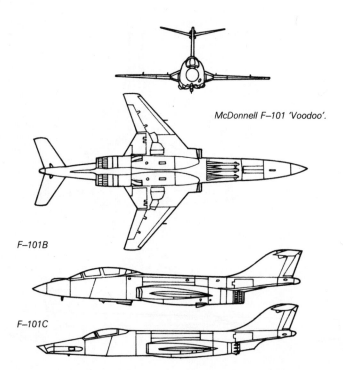

McDonnell F–101 'Voodoo'.

F–101B

F–101C

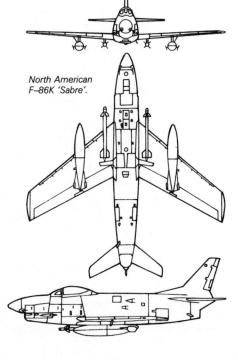

North American F–86K 'Sabre'.

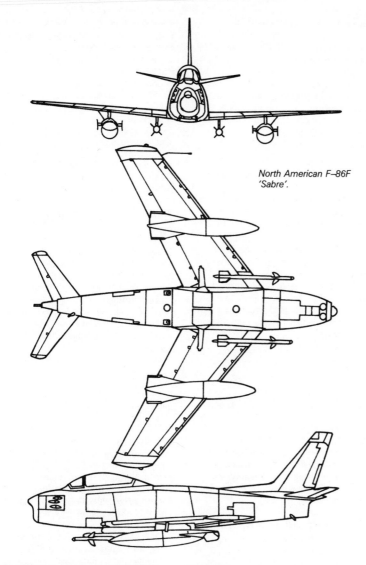

North American F–86F 'Sabre'.

North American F–86F 'Sabre'.
Type: Single-seat fighter and
strike-fighter.
Weights:
empty 11,122lb (5,045kg).
normal 15,200lb (6,895kg).
maximum 20,610lb (9,350kg).
Performance:
maximum speed at 36,000ft (11,000m)
(Mach 0.9) 599mph (964km/hr).
maximum speed at sea level (Mach
0.98) 677mph (1,090km/hr).
maximum cruising speed 528mph
(850km/hr).
radius of action 460 miles (745km).
ferry range 1,525 miles (2,455km).
initial rate of climb 166.6ft/sec
(50.8m/sec).
time to 30,200ft (9,200m) 5min 12sec.
service ceiling 50,000ft (15,250m).
Dimensions:
wing span 39ft 0in (11.91m).
length overall 37ft 0in (11.43m).
height overall 14ft 8in (4.47m).
wing area 313.0sq ft (29.08sq m).
Power plant: One General Electric
J47–GE–27 turbojet rated at 5,970lb
(2,708kg) st.
Armament: Six 12.7mm M–3
machine-guns and (as fighter) two
AIM–9B Sidewinder AAMs or (as
strike-fighter) max 2,000lb (908kg)
weapon load, e.g. two 1,000lb (454kg)
bombs or eight rockets.
Variants:
F–86E: Earlier version (Canadian
licence-built CL–13 Sabre Mk.2 and 4).
CA–27 Sabre Mk.30, 31, 32: Australian
licence-built with Avon engine.
CL–13B Sabre Mk.6: Canadian
licence-built with Orenda engine.
RF–86F: Single-seat reconnaissance
aircraft.
FJ–2, FJ–3, FJ–4, FJ–4B Fury: Naval
variants.
First flights:
Prototype: 1 October 1947; F–86F: 19
March 1952.
Prototype Fury: 27 December 1951.
Production: Series production
1950–56; F–86E: 456 built (inc 120
Canadian assembled by Canadair),
F–86F: 1,794 built, F–86F–40: 300
built (Japanese assembled by
Mitsubishi 1956–61), F–86H: 475 built,
CL–13 Sabre Mk.2: 350 built, CL–13
Mk.4: 438 built, CL–13 Mk.5: 370
built, CL–13B Sabre Mk.6: 655 built,
CA–27: 112 built, Fury: 1,115 built.
In service:
F–86F: Argentina, Bolivia, Burma,
Colombia, Ethiopia, Japan, Korea
(South), Pakistan, Peru, Philippines,
Portugal(?), Thailand(?), Tunisia.
CA–27: Indonesia, Malaysia.

J47–GE–33 turbojet rated at 5,500lb
(2,495kg)/7,650lb (3,470kg) st.
Armament:
F–86D: Twenty-four 70mm unguided
rockets in weapon tray and two
AIM–9B Sidewinder AAMs.
F–86L: Four 20mm M–24A–1 cannon
and two AIM–9B Sidewinder AAMs.
Variants:
F–86K: Further development of F–86D.
F–86L: 981 converted F–86Ds with
more modern electronics.
First flights:
YF–86D: 22 December 1949.
Production:
F–86D: 2,504 built 1950–55.
In service:
F–86D: Philippines, Yugoslavia.

North American F–86K 'Sabre'.
Type: Single-seat all-weather fighter.
Details as for F–86D with the following
exceptions:

Weights:
empty 13,367lb (6,063kg).
normal 18,377lb (8,335kg).
maximum 20,772lb (9,150kg).
Performance:
maximum speed at 40,000ft (12,200m)
512mph (985km/hr).
ferry range 746 miles (1,200km).
initial rate of climb 169.9ft/sec
(51.8m/sec).
Dimensions:
wing span 39ft 1½in (11.92m).
length overall 40ft 11in (12.47m).
wing area 314.3sq ft (29.20sq m).
Power plant: One General Electric
J47–GE–17B turbojet rated at 5,423lb
(2,460kg)/7,500lb (3,402kg) st.
Armament: Four 20mm M–24A–1
cannon and two AIM–9B Sidewinder
AAMs.
First flights:
YF–86K: 15 July 1954.
Production:

CL–13B: Colombia, Pakistan, South
, Africa.
RF–86F: Korea (South), Yugoslavia.

North American F–100D 'Super Sabre'.
Type: Single-seat strike-fighter.
Weights:
empty 21,000lb (9,526kg).
normal 29,762lb (13,500kg).
maximum 34,831lb (15,799kg)
Performance:
maximum speed at 35,000ft (10,680m)
  (Mach 1.3) 862mph (1,388km/hr).
maximum speed at 8,000ft (2,440m)
  (Mach 1.1) 810mph (1,304km/hr).
maximum cruising speed at 36,000ft
  (11,000m)–46,000ft (14,000m) (Mach
  0.86) 565mph (910km/hr).
radius of action 550 miles (885km).
ferry range 1,500 miles (2,415km).
initial rate of climb 267.4ft/sec
  (81.5m/sec).
time to 32,800ft (10,000m) 2min 30sec.
service ceiling 50,000ft (15,240m).
Dimensions:
wing span 36ft 9¾in (11.82m).
length overall 49ft 6in (15.09m).
height overall 16ft 2½in (4.94m).
wing area 385.1sq ft (35.78sq m).
Power plant: One Pratt & Whitney
  J57–P–21A turbojet rated at 11,700lb
  (5,307kg)/16,950lb (7,688kg) st.
Armament: Four 20mm M–39E
  cannon and max 7,500lb (3,402kg)
  weapon load on 6 hard points, e.g.
  four Sidewinder AAMs and two
  Bullpup ASMs, bombs and rockets.
Variants:
F–100A, F–100C: Earlier versions.
First flights:
Prototype YF–100A: 25 May 1953.
F–100D: 24 January 1956.
Production:
Series production 1953–59.
F–100A: 203 built; F–100C: 476 built;
  F–100D: 1,274 built.
In service:
F–100C: USA.
F–100D, F: Denmark, France, Taiwan,
  Turkey, USA.

North American F–100F 'Super Sabre'.
Type: Two-seat strike-fighter and
  trainer.
Details as for F–100D with the
  following exceptions:
Weights:
empty 22,300lb (10,115kg).
normal 30,700lb (13,926kg).
maximum 40,000lb (18,143kg).
Dimensions:
length overall 52ft 5¼in (16.00m).
Armament: Two 20mm M–39E
  cannon and max 6,000lb (2,772kg)
  weapon load, e.g. rockets, napalm
  tanks and bombs.
First flights: F–100F: 7 March 1957.

Production: F–100F: 333 built.

North American T–6G 'Texan'.
Type: Two-seat trainer.
Weights:
empty 4,270lb (1,937kg).
maximum 5,618lb (2,548kg).
Performance:
maximum speed at 5,000ft (1,524m)
  211mph (341km/hr).
maximum cruising speed 170mph
  (274km/hr).
ferry range 870 miles (1,400km).
initial rate of climb 27.2ft/sec
  (8.3m/sec).
service ceiling 24,080ft (7,340m).
Dimensions:
wing span 42ft 0½in (12.81m).
length overall 29ft 6in (8.99m).
height overall 11ft 8¼in (3.56m).
wing area 253.5sq ft (23.56sq m).
Power plant: One 550hp Pratt &
  Whitney R–1340–AN–1 piston engine.
Variants:
BC–1, AT–6, T–6: Earlier versions.
Harvard: Canadian licence-built T–6.
First flights:
Prototype NA–26: 1937.
BC–1: 1938.
Production:
T–6: 15,094 built 1940–45.
Harvard: 555 built 1940–54.
T–6G: Conversion of 2,068 T–6 and
  Harvards 1949–50.
In service: Argentina, Bolivia, Chile(?),
  Colombia(?), Congo, Dominican
  Republic, El Salvador, Guatemala,
  Haiti, Italy(?), Mexico, Morocco,
  Nicaragua, Pakistan, Paraguay, Peru,
  Portugal, South Africa, Taiwan,
  Uruguay.

North American T–28A 'Trojan'.
Type: Two-seat trainer.
Weights:
empty 5,107lb (2,318kg).
normal 6,365lb (2,887kg).
maximum 7,462lb (3,385kg).
Performance:
maximum speed at 5,900ft (1,800m)
  285mph (455km/hr).
maximum cruising speed 191mph
  (306km/hr).
ferry range 1,056 miles (1,700km).
initial rate of climb 31.2ft/sec
  (9.5m/sec).
service ceiling 24,020ft (7,320m).
Dimensions:
wing span 40ft 1in (12.22m).
length overall 32ft 0¼in (9.76m).
height overall 12ft 8in (3.86m).
wing area 268sq ft (24.89sq m).
Power plant: One 800hp Wright
  R–1300–1A piston engine.
Variants:
T–28B, C: Naval versions of T–28.
T–28D, AT–28D and Fennec:
  Conversions of T–28 to light
  ground-attack aircraft.

First flights:
Prototype XT–28: 26 September 1949.
T–28B: 6 April 1953.
T–28C: 19 September 1955.
Production:
T–28A: 1,193 built 1949–53.
T–28B: 492 built 1953–55.
T–28C: 301 built 1955–57.
In service:
T–28A: Argentina, Bolivia, Congo,
  Dominican Republic, Ecuador, Ethiopia,
  Haiti, Korea (South), Laos, Mexico,
  Nicaragua, Philippines, Taiwan,
  Thailand.
T–28B, C: USA.

North American T–28D 'Trojan'.
Type: Two-seat light ground-attack
  aircraft.
Weights:
empty 6,510lb (2,953kg).
normal 8,120lb (3,682kg).
maximum 12,100?lb (5,490?kg).
Performance:
maximum speed at 3,770ft (1,150m)
  352mph (566km/hr).
maximum speed at sea level 298mph
  (480km/hr).
maximum cruising speed 191mph
  (326km/hr).
radius of action 220? miles (350?km).
ferry range 1,130 miles (1,820km).
initial rate of climb 31.2ft/sec
  (19.2m/sec).
service ceiling 37,100ft (11,300m).
Dimensions:
wing span 40ft 7in (12.37m).
length overall 32ft 9in (9.98m).
height overall 12ft 7in (3.84m).
wing area 217.0sq ft (25.18sq m).
Power plant: One 1,300hp Wright
  R–1820–56S piston engine.
Armament:
T–28D: Max 3,000lb (1,360kg) weapon
  load on 6 hard points, e.g. two
  weapon packs each containing
  12.7mm M–3 machine-guns, two
  500lb (227kg) bombs, two rocket
  launchers each with eight 70mm
  rockets and thirty-six 19lb (8.26kg)
  fragmentation bombs.
Fennec: Four 12.7mm machine-guns
  and four 330lb (150kg) bombs.
Variants:
T–28A, B and C: Trainers.
AT–28D: Light ground-attack aircraft.
First flights:
Prototype T–28D: 1961.
Production:
358 T–28 converted to T–28D 1961–67.
245 T–28A converted to Fennec in
  France 1960–61.
– T–28 converted to AT–28D in 1973.
In service:
T–28D: Bolivia, Cambodia(?), Congo,
  Dominican Republic, Ethiopia,
  Honduras, Laos, Morocco, Philippines,
  Thailand, USA.
Fennec: Argentina.

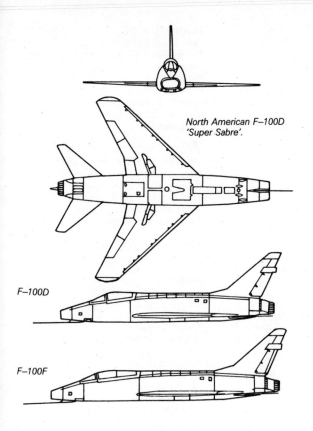

North American F–100D 'Super Sabre'.

F–100D

F–100F

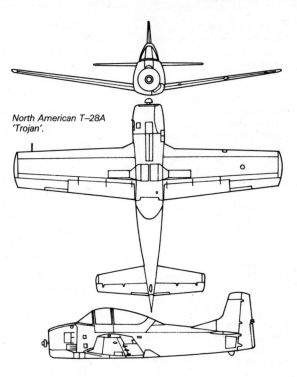

North American T–28A 'Trojan'.

North American T–6G 'Texan'.

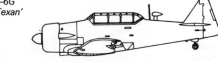

T–6G 'Texan'

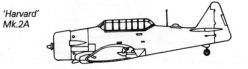

'Harvard' Mk.2A

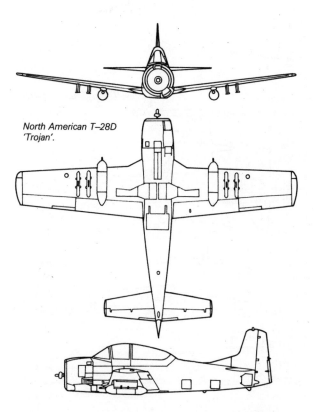

North American T–28D 'Trojan'.

Northrop F–5A.

Type: Single-seat fighter and strike-fighter.

Weights:
empty 8,085lb (3,667kg).
normal 14,212lb (6,446kg).
maximum 20,576lb (933kg).

Performance:
maximum speed at sea level (Mach 0.96) 745mph (1,199km/hr).
maximum speed at 36,000ft (11,000m) (Mach 1.4) 924mph (1,487km/hr).
maximum cruising speed at 36.000ft (11,000m) 553mph (890km/hr).
radius of action 215–550 miles (346–885km).
ferry range 1,565 miles (2,518km).
initial rate of climb 478.4ft/sec (145.8m/sec).
service ceiling 50,000ft (15,250m).

Dimensions:
wing span 25ft 3in (7.70m).
length overall 47ft 2in (14.38m).
height overall 13ft 2in (4.01m).
wing area 170sq ft (15.79sq m).

Power plant: Two General Electric J85–GE–13 turbojets each rated at 2,720lb (1,234kg)/4,081lb (1,851kg) st.

Armament: Two 20mm M–39 cannon with 280rpg and max 6,200lb (2,812kg) weapon load on 7 hard points, e.g. four Bullpup ASMs or bombs, Napalm tanks, rockets and two AIM–9 Sidewinder AAMs.

Variants:
CF–5A, CF–5D, NF–5A, NF–5B: Canadian licence-built by Canadair.
SF–5A, B: Spanish licence-built by CASA.
RF–5A: Single-seat reconnaissance aircraft with 4 cameras.
F–5E Tiger II: Further development with uprated 3,500lb (1,588kg)/5,000lb (2,268kg) st engines.

First flights:
Prototype: 3 July 1959.
F–5A: October 1963.
F–5E: 28 March 1969.

Production:
Series production 1963–72. F–5A: 621(755?) built; licence-built in Canada (89 CF–5A, 46 CF–5D, 75 NF–5A, 30 NF–5B) and Spain (36 SF–5A, 34 SF–5B).
F–5E: Series production from 1972; over 1,000 on order to date.

In service:
F–5A, B: Brazil (B only), Ethiopia, Greece, Iran, Korea (South), Morocco, Norway, Philippines, Saudi Arabia (B only), Taiwan, Thailand, Turkey, USA, Vietnam(?).
RF–5A: Greece, Iran, Morocco, Norway, Thailand, Turkey, Vietnam(?).
CF–5A, D: Canada, Venezuela.
NF–5A, B: Netherlands.
SF–5A, B: Spain (C–9, CE–9, Cr–9).

Northrop F–5B.

Type: Two-seat strike-trainer.
Details as for F–5A with the following exceptions:

Weights:
empty 8,361lb (3,792kg).
normal 13,752lb (6,237kg).
maximum 20,116lb (9,124kg).

Performance:
maximum speed at 36,000ft (11,000m) (Mach 1.34) 884mph (1,422km/hr).
ferry range 1,570 miles (2,525km).

Dimensions:
length overall 46ft 4in (14.12m).
height overall 13ft 1in (3.99m).

First flights: February 1964.

Production: 134 built.

Northrop F–5E 'Tiger' II.

Type: Single-seat fighter and strike-fighter.

Weights:
empty 9,588lb (4,349kg).
normal 15,400lb (6,985kg).
maximum 24,083lb (10,924kg).

Performance:
maximum speed at sea level (Mach 1.0) 760mph (1,223km/hr).
maximum speed at 36,090ft (11,000m) (Mach 1.6) 1,056mph (1,700km/hr) (F–5F: Mach 1.54).
maximum cruising speed (Mach 1.45) 957mph (1,540km/hr).
radius of action 173–426 miles

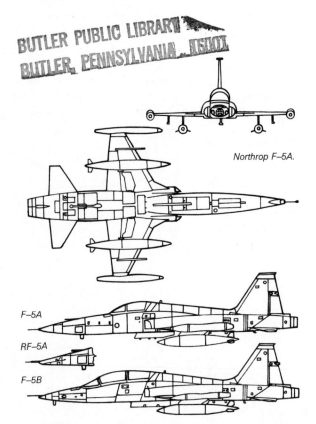

Northrop F–5A.

F–5A

RF–5A

F–5B

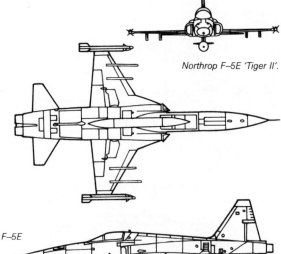

Northrop F–5E 'Tiger II'.

F–5E

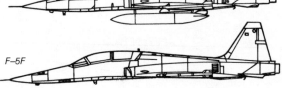

F–5F

Northrop T–38A 'Talon'.

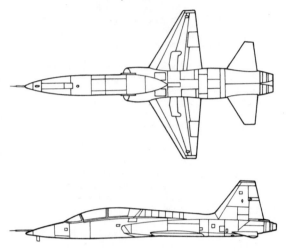

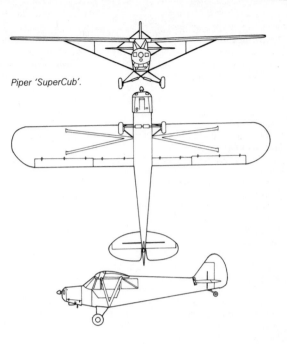

Piper 'SuperCub'.

(278–686km).
ferry range 1,595 miles (2,567km).
initial rate of climb 526.9ft/sec
  (160.6m/sec).
service ceiling 53,500ft (16,305m).
Dimensions:
wing span 26ft 8½in (8.14m).
length overall 48ft 2½in (14.69m) (F–5F:
  51ft 8½in (15.76m).
height overall 13ft 4in (4.06m).
wing area 186.2sq ft (17.29sq m).
Power plant: Two General Electric
  J85–GE–21 turbojets each rated at
  3,500lb (1,588kg)/5,000lb (2,268kg) st.
Armament: Two 20mm M–39 cannon
  with 280rpg and (as fighter) two
  AIM–9 Sidewinder AAMs or (as
  strike-fighter) max 7,000lb (3,175kg)
  weapon load on 5 hard points.
Variants:
F–5A, F–5B: Single-seat strike-fighter
  and two-seat trainer.
F–5F: Two-seat strike-trainer.
RF–5E: Single-seat reconnaissance
  aircraft.
First flights:
Prototype: 11 August 1972.
F–5F: 25 September 1974.
Production:
6 prototypes and pre-production models;
  series production from 1973, over 1,000
  delivered or on order to date.
Licence-production of components for
  100 aircraft in Taiwan 1974–75.
In service: Brazil, Chile, Ethiopia, Iran,
  Jordan, Korea (South), Malaysia,
  Philippines, Saudi Arabia, Singapore,
  Switzerland, Taiwan, Thailand,
  Tunisia(?), Turkey, USA, Vietnam(?).

Northrop T–38A 'Talon'.
Type: Two-seat trainer.
Weights:
empty 7,628lb (3,460kg).
maximum 12,090lb (5,485kg).
Performance:
maximum speed at 36,000ft (11,000m)
  (Mach 1.23) 820mph (1,320km/hr).
maximum cruising speed at 40,000ft
  (12,200m) 686mph (1,104km/hr).
range 1,095 miles (1,760km).
ferry range 1,320 miles (2,125km).
initial rate of climb 506.6ft/sec
  (154.4m/sec).
service ceiling 53,600ft (16,335m).
Dimensions:
wing span 25ft 3in (7.70m).
length overall 46ft 4½in (14.13m).
height overall 12ft 10½in (3.92m).
wing area 170sq ft (15.79sq m).
Power plant: Two General Electric
  J85–GE–5 turbojets each rated at
  2,680/3,850lb (1,216/1,748kg) st.
First flights:
Prototype: 10 April 1959.
T–38A: May 1960.
Production: 2 prototypes, 4
  pre-production models and 1,187
  production models 1960–72.
In service: Germany (West), USA.

Piper U–7A 'SuperCub'.
Type: Liaison and AOP aircraft.
Weights:
empty 930lb (422kg).
maximum 1,750lb (794kg).
Performance:
maximum speed at sea level 130mph
  (209km/hr).

maximum cruising speed 115mph
  (185km/hr).
ferry range 460 miles (740km).
initial rate of climb 16.1ft/sec
  (4.9m/sec).
service ceiling 18,996ft (5,790m).
Dimensions:
wing span 35ft 4in (10.77m).
length overall 22ft 6½in (6.86m).
height overall 6ft 7¾in (2.03m).
wing area 178.5sq ft (16.58sq m).
Power plant: One 135hp Lycoming
  O–290–D2 piston engine.
Payload: 1 man crew and 1 observer.
Variants:
PA–18–150 SuperCub: Civil variant.
U–7B: Later series.
L–4 (J–3 Cub), L–18 (PA–18–95
  SuperCub): Earlier versions.
First flights:
Prototype: 1949.
PA–18–150: 1955.
Production: Over 9,000 of all series
  built from 1951 in both civil and
  military variants, inc 105 L–18B, 838
  L–18C, 150 U–7A, 582 U–7B.
In service:
L–4: Paraguay; L–18B: Turkey.
L–18C: Denmark, France, Israel, Italy,
  Netherlands(?), Norway, Thailand,
  Uganda.
U–7A, U–7B (earlier designations
  L–21A, L–21B): Argentina, Greece,
  Italy, USA.

Piper U–11A 'Aztec'.
Type: Liaison aircraft.
Weights:
empty 3,080lb (1,397kg).

maximum 5,200lb (2,360kg).
Performance:
maximum speed 218mph (351km/hr).
maximum cruising speed at 7,500ft
  (2,300m) 210mph (338km/hr).
range 830 miles (1,335km).
ferry range 1,210 miles (1,950km).
initial rate of climb 24.93ft/sec
  (7.6m/sec).
service ceiling 21,000ft (6,400m).
Dimensions:
wing span 37ft 2½in (11.34m).
length overall 31ft 2¾in (9.52m).
height overall 10ft 4in (3.15m).
wing area 207.53sq ft (19.28sq m).
Power plant: Two 250hp Lycoming
  IO–540–C4B5 piston engines.
Payload: 2 man crew and 3 troops.
Variants:
PA–23–150 Apache, PA–23–160
  Apache, PA–23–235 Apache: Earlier
  versions (150hp or 160hp Lycoming
  O–320 or O–320B piston engines
  resp) and their subsequent
  development (235hp Lycoming O–540
  piston engines).
PA–23–250 Aztec: Civil light aircraft.
PA–E23–250 Turbo-Aztec: Improved
  series.
First flights:
Prototype Twin Stinton: 2 March 1952.
PA–23–150: 29 January 1954.
PA–23–250: 18 September 1959.

U–11A: 1960.
PA–23–235: 22 January 1962.
PA–E23–250: 21 June 1965.
Production: Series production from
  1954, over 3,000 Apache, Aztec and
  Turbo-Aztec delivered or on order to
  date, inc 20 U–11A.
In service:
Aztec: Argentina, France, Madagascar
  (Malagasy), Spain, Uganda, USA
  (U–11A).
Turbo-Aztec: Spain (E–19).

Rockwell B–1A.
Type: Heavy strategic bomber, 5 man
  crew.
Weights:
Maximum 389,800lb (176,822kg).
Performance:
maximum speed at 40,000ft (12,200m)
  (Mach 2.2) 1,450mph (2,335km/hr).
radius of action 3,600 miles (5,800km).
ferry range 6,100 miles (9,800km).
Dimensions:
wing span (spread) 136ft 8in (41.66m).
wing span (fully swept) 78ft 2in
  (23.83m).
length overall 150ft 3in (45.80m).
height overall 33ft 7in (10.24m).
Power plant: Four General Electric
  F101–GE–100 turbofans each rated at
  30,000lb (13,610kg) st.
Armament: Max 73,850lb (33,500kg)

weapon load in three fuselage bays,
  e.g. twenty-four AGM–69A SRAM
  ASMs and max 40,000?lb (18,000?kg)
  weapon load on hard points
  underwing, e.g. eight AGM–69A
  SRAM ASMs.
First flights:
Prototype: 23 December 1974.
Production: 3 prototypes; series
  production 1976–77, 244 planned.
In service: USA.

Rockwell 'Shrike Commander'.
Type: Light transport.
Weights:
empty 4,635lb (2,102kg).
maximum 6,750lb (3,062kg).
Performance:
maximum speed at sea level 228mph
  (367km/hr).
maximum cruising speed at 9,000ft
  (2,750m) 203mph (326km/hr).
range 750 miles (1,205km).
ferry range 920 miles (1,480km).
initial rate of climb 22.31ft/sec
  (6.8m/sec).
service ceiling 19,350ft (5,900m).
Dimensions:
wing span 49ft 0½in (14.95m).
length overall 36ft 7in (11.15m).
height overall 14ft 6in (4.42m).
wing area 255sq ft (23.69sq m).
Power plant: Two 290hp Lycoming

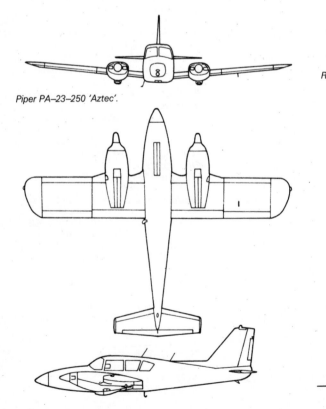

Piper PA–23–250 'Aztec'.

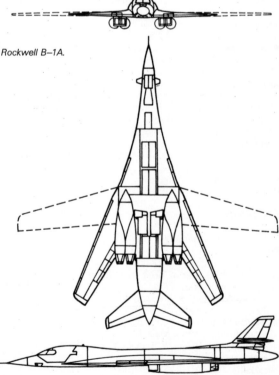

Rockwell B–1A.

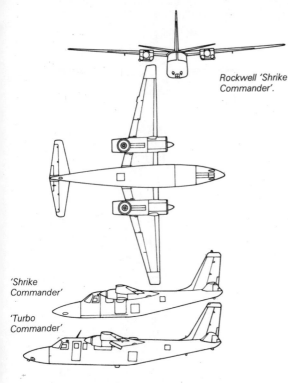

Rockwell 'Shrike Commander'.

'Shrike Commander'

'Turbo Commander'

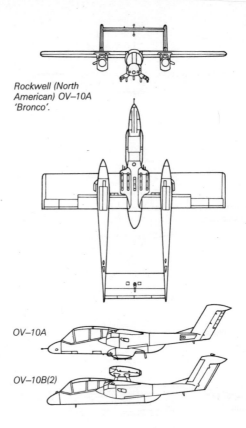

Rockwell (North American) OV–10A 'Bronco'.

OV–10A

OV–10B(2)

IO–540–E1B5 piston engines.
Payload: 1–2 man crew and 5–7 troops.
Variants:
Commander 520, 560, 500B: Earlier versions.
Commander 500U: Former designation for Shrike Commander.
Commander 680, 720, Courser Commander (new designation for Grand Commander), Commander 685: Later, improved series.
Turbo Commander 680T, 680V, 681 (new designation for Hawk Commander), 681A, 681B, 690, 690A: Further developments.
First flights:
Prototype: 23 April 1948.
Shrike Commander: 24 July 1958.
Production: Over 2,000 built of all variants from 1951.
In service:
Commander 520: Dominican Republic, Korea (South), Philippines.
560: Korea (South), USA (U–4A).
500B: Colombia, Dahomey, Ivory Coast, Niger, Upper Volta.
Shrike Commander: Argentina, Iran.
Commander 680: Argentina, Greece, Guatemala, Iran, Pakistan, USA (U–9C, U–9D).

Rockwell 'Turbo Commander 680'.
Type: Light transport.

Details as for 'Shrike Commander' with the following exceptions:
Performance:
maximum cruising speed 285mph (459km/hr).
ferry range 1,000 miles (1,610km).
initial rate of climb 35.43ft/sec (10.8m/sec).
service ceiling 27,890ft (8,500m).
Dimensions:
wing span 44ft 0¾in (13.43m).
length overall 41ft 3¼in (12.58m).
height overall 14ft 6in (4.42m).
wing area 242.51sq ft (22.53sq m).
Power plant: Two 605hp Garrett-AiResearch TPE–331–43 turboprops.
Payload: 1–2 man crew and 7–9 troops.
First flights:
Turbo Commander 680: 31 December 1964.
In service:
Turbo Commander 680V: Argentina.
681, 681B: Iran.
690: Guatemala, Iran.
690A: Iran.

Rockwell (North American) OV–10A 'Bronco'.
Type: Two-seat AOP and light ground-support aircraft.
Weights:
empty 7,190lb (3,260kg).
normal 12,500lb (5,670kg).

maximum 14,445lb (6,552kg).
Performance:
maximum speed at 10,000ft (3,050m) 280mph (452km/hr).
maximum speed at sea level 279mph (449km/hr).
maximum cruising speed 244mph (361km/hr).
radius of action 170 miles (270km).
radius of action with 2,800lb (1,270kg) weapon load 200 miles (310km).
ferry range 1,430 miles (2,300km).
initial rate of climb 46.59ft/sec (14.2m/sec).
service ceiling 27,000ft (8,230m).
Dimensions:
wing span 40ft 0in (12.19m).
length overall 39ft 9in (12.12m).
height overall 15ft 2in (4.62m).
wing area 291sq ft (27.03sq m).
Power plant: Two 715hp Garrett-AiResearch T–76–G–10/12 turboprops.
Armament: Four 7.62mm M–60C machine-guns with 500rpg and max 3,600lb (1,633kg) weapon load on 5 hard points.
Variants:
OV–10B: Target-tug.
OV–10C, E, F: Export versions of OV–10A.
OV–10B(Z): Target-tug with one additional General Electric J85–GE–4 turbojet rated at 2,950lb (1,339kg) st, max speed 393mph (632km/hr).

North American
T–2B 'Buckeye'.

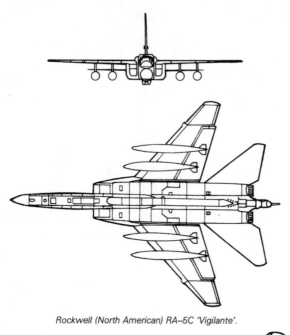

Rockwell (North American) RA–5C 'Vigilante'.

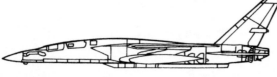

OV–10D: Night-AOP aircraft (two
1,040hp Garrett-AiResearch
T–76–G–420/21 turboprops; one
20mm cannon).
First flights:
Prototype: 16 July 1965.
OV–10B: 21 September 1970.
Production:
OV–10A: 7 prototypes and 271
production models 1966–69.
OV–10B: 17 built 1969–71.
OV–10B(Z): 1 built 1970.
OV–10C: 32 built 1970–75.
OV–10D: 2 evaluation models 1976.
OV–10E: 16 built 1972–73.
OV–10F: 16 built 1975–77.
OV–10G: 24 built 1977–78.
In service:
OV–10A: USA.
OV–10B, OV–10B(Z): Germany (West).
OV–10C: Thailand.
OV–10E: Venezuela.
OV–10F: Indonesia.
OV–10G: Korea (South).

Rockwell (North American) RA–5C 'Vigilante'.
Type: Two-seat shipboard
reconnaissance aircraft and bomber.
Weights:
normal 66,820lb (30,310kg).
maximum 79,998lb (36,285kg).
Performance:
maximum speed at sea level (Mach

0.95) 684mph (1,103km/hr).
maximum speed at 40,000ft (12,200m)
(Mach 2.1) 1,386mph (2,230km/hr).
maximum cruising speed at 40,000ft
(12,200m) (Mach 0.85) (559mph
(900km/hr).
range with four 333gal (1,514l) auxiliary
fuel tanks 3,000 miles (4,830km).
radius of action 995 miles (1,600km).
service ceiling 64,000ft (19,500m).
Dimensions:
wing span 53ft 0in (16.15m).
length overall 75ft 10in (23.11m).
height overall 19ft 5in (5.92m).
wing area 769sq ft (71.44sq m).
Power plant: Two General Electric
J79–GE–10 turbojets each rated at
11,894lb (5,395kg)/17,902lb (8,120kg)
st.
Armament: Max 8,000lb (3,630kg)
weapon load on 4 underwing hard
points, e.g. two 1,000lb (454kg) or
2,000lb (908kg) bombs, two napalm
tanks or two Bullpup ASMs.
Variants:
A–5A, A–5B: Shipboard bombers.
First flights:
Prototype YA–5A: 31 August 1958.
RA–5C: 30 June 1962.
Production:
YA–5A: 2 built; A–5A: 57 built
1959–63; A–6B: 6 built; RA–5C: 91
built 1963–71; in addition 43 A–5A
and all 6 A–6B since modified to

RA–5C standard.
In service: USA.

Rockwell (North American) T–2C 'Buckeye'.
Type: Two-seat shipboard trainer.
Weights:
empty 8,113lb (3,680kg).
maximum 13,177lb (5,977kg).
Performance:
maximum speed at 25,000ft (7,620m)
520mph (838km/hr).
ferry range 1,050 miles (1,685km).
initial rate of climb 103.3ft/sec
(31.5m/sec).
service ceiling 40,400ft (12,320m).
Dimensions:
wing span 38ft 2in (11.63m).
length overall 38ft 8in (11.79m).
height overall 15ft 0in (4.57m).
wing area 257.26sq ft (23.69sq m).
Power plant: Two Pratt & Whitney
J85–GE–4 turbojets each rated at
2,950lb (1,339kg) st.
Armament: Max 640lb (290kg) weapon
load on 2 hard points underwing, e.g.
two 100lb (45kg) practice bombs or
two weapon packs each containing
one 12.7mm machine-gun with 100rpg
or two rocket launchers containing
seven 70mm rockets each.
Variants:
T–2A: Earlier version with one
Westinghouse J34–WE–36 turbojet

rated at 3,400lb (1,540kg) st.
T–2B: As T–2C but different power plant (two General Electric J60–P–6 turbojets each rated at 2,950lb (1,339kg) st.
T–2D, T–2E: Export versions of T–2C.

First flights:
T–2A: 31 January 1958.
T–2B: 30 August 1962.
T–2C: 10 December 1968.

Production:
T–2A: 217 built 1958–61.
T–2B: 97 built 1965–68.
T–2C: 231(243?) built 1968–74.
T–2D: 12 built 1973–76.
T–2E: 60 built from 1974.

In service:
T–2B, C: USA.
T–2D: Venezuela.
T–2E: Greece, Morocco.

Rockwell (North American) T–39A 'Sabreliner'.
Type: Trainer and light transport.
Weights:
empty 10,250lb (4,649kg).
normal 16,700lb (7,575kg).
maximum 17,758lb (8,055kg).
Performance:
maximum speed at 36,000ft (11,000m (Mach 0.82) 540mph (869km/hr).
maximum cruising speed at 43,300ft (13,200m) (Mach 0.7) 502mph (808km/hr).
ferry range 1,950 miles (3,130km).
time to 35,100ft (10,700m) 18min 0sec.
service ceiling 45,275ft (13,800m).

Dimensions:
wing span 44ft 3¾in (13.53m).
length overall 43ft 8¾in (13.33m).
height overall 16ft 0in (4.88m).
wing area 342.4sq ft (31.82sq m).
Power plant: Two Pratt & Whitney J60–P–3A turbojets each rated at 3,000lb (1,361kg) st.
Payload:
Trainer: 2 man crew.
Transport: 2 man crew and 4–8 troops.
Variants:
T–39B, T–39F: Radar trainers.
T–39D, CT–39E: Naval trainers.
Sabreliner Series 40 and Series 60; Sabre 75 and 75A: Civil variants.
First flights:
Prototype: 16 September 1958.
Production:
T–39A: 143 built 1960–63, inc 3 converted to T–39F; T–39B: 6 built; T–39D: 42 built; CT–39E: 7 built; CT–39G: 5 built 1973.
Sabreliner and Sabre: Over 245 of all variants delivered or on order by beginning of 1975.
In service:
T–39: USA.
Sabreliner: Argentina.

Sikorsky S–55 (H–19 'Chickasaw').
Type: Transport helicopter.
Weights:
empty 5,260lb (2,386kg).
normal 7,500lb (3,402kg).
maximum 7,900lb (3,583kg).

Performance:
maximum speed at sea level 112mph (180km/hr).
maximum cruising speed 92mph (148km/hr).
range 360 miles (580km).
initial rate of climb 17.1ft/sec (5.2m/sec).
hovering ceiling in ground effect 5,800ft (1,770m).
hovering ceiling out of ground effect 2,300ft (700m).
Dimensions:
main rotor diameter 52ft 11¾in (16.15m).
length of fuselage 42ft 3in (12.88m).
height 14ft 0in (4.06m).
Power plant: One 800hp Wright R–1300–3 piston engine.
Payload: 2 man crew and 10 troops or 6 stretcher cases and 1 medic or freight.
Variants:
Whirlwind: British (Westland) licence-built.
First flights:
Prototype: 9 November 1949.
Production:
S–55: 1,281 built 1950–59, plus 44 Japanese and French licence-built 1961–62.
Whirlwind: Over 435 built 1952–64.
In service:
S–55: Dominican Republic, Guatemala, Haiti, Honduras, Korea (South), Turkey, USA (UH–19B, UH–19D, UH–19F).
Whirlwind 2: Nigeria, Yugoslavia.

North American T–39.

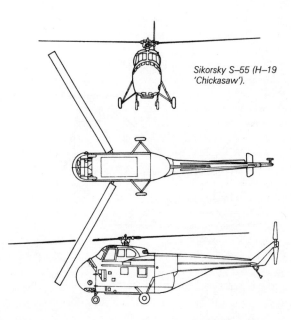

Sikorsky S–55 (H–19 'Chickasaw').

Whirlwind 3: Brazil, Great Britain (HAR.10, HCC.10), Nigeria, Qatar.

Sikorsky S–58 (CH–34A 'Choctaw', UH–D 'Sea Horse').

Type: Medium transport helicopter.
Weights (apply specifically to CH–34A):
empty 7,750lb (3,515kg).
normal 12,993lb (5,897kg).
maximum 14,000lb (6,350kg).
Performance:
maximum speed at sea level 122mph (196km/hr).
maximum cruising speed 97mph (156km/hr).
range 245 miles (397km).
initial rate of climb 18.5ft/sec (5.6m/sec).
service ceiling 9,500ft (2,900m).
hovering ceiling in ground effect 4,916ft (1,495m).
hovering ceiling out of ground effect 2,407ft (732m).
Dimensions:
main rotor diameter 56ft 0in (17.07m).
length of fuselage 46ft 9in (14.25m).
height 15ft 11in (4.85m).
Power plant: One 1,525hp Wright R–1820–84B or D piston engine.
Payload: 2 man crew and 16–18 troops or 8 stretcher cases.
Variants:
SH–34G Seabat, SH–34J, LH–34D: ASW helicopters, 4 man crew, homing torpedoes, mines, depth-charges.
Wessex: British licence-built S–58 by Westland.
S–58B, S–58D: Civil versions.
S–58T: Installation of 1,525hp Pratt &

Whitney PT6 T–3 Twin Pac turbine power plant into old S–58 models.
First flights:
Prototype: 8 March 1954.
S–58T: 19 August 1970.
Production:
1,821 of all variants built 1954–69, plus 166 licence-built in France by Sud-Aviation and 40(?) Japanese licence-built by Mitsubishi.
S–58T: Over 100 built by 1974.
In service:
CH–34A: Belgium(?), Chad, Haiti, Nicaragua, Thailand.
SH–34J: Brazil, Central African Republic, France, Germany (West), Uruguay.
S–58C: Belgium(?).
S–58T: Argentina, Chile.
UH–34D: Indonesia, Laos, USA(?).
CH–34C, LH–34D, UH–34E, VH–34D: USA.

Sikorsky S–61B (SH–3D 'Sea King').

Type: Amphibious ASW and transport helicopter, 4 man crew.
Weights:
empty 12,083lb (5,381kg).
normal 18,626lb (8,449kg).
maximum 20,500lb (9,297kg).
Performance:
maximum speed at sea level 166mph (267km/hr).
maximum cruising speed 148mph (238km/hr).
ferry range 625 miles (1,004km).
initial rate of climb 40.0ft/sec (11.2m/sec).

service ceiling 14,700ft (4,480m).
hovering ceiling out of ground effect 8,200ft (2,500m).
Dimensions:
main rotor diameter 62ft 0in (18.90m).
length of fuselage 54ft 9in (16.69m).
height 15ft 6in (4.72m).
Power plant: Two 1,400hp General Electric T58–GE–10 turboshafts.
Armament: Max 840lb (381kg) weapon load, e.g. 2 homing torpedoes or depth-charges.
Payload:
S–61A: 2–3 man crew and 26 troops or 15 stretcher cases.
Variants:
S–61B, SH–3A: Earlier versions, 11 converted to SH–3G and 105 to SH–3H, plus 9 converted to RH–3A mine-sweeping helicopters.
Sea King: British licence-built SH–3D by Westland.
First flights:
Prototype: 11 March 1959.
Production:
SH–3A: 255 built 1961–65, plus 57(61?) Japanese licence-built by Mitsubishi from 1964.
SH–3D: 90 built from 1965, plus 34 Italian licence-built by Agusta.
CH–3B: 6 built; VH–3A: 10 built; HH–3A: 12 built.
In service:
SH–3A: Canada (CH–124), Japan, USA.
SH–3D: Brazil, Iran, Italy, Spain (Z–9), USA.
S–61A: Denmark, Malaysia (Nuri).
CH–3B, HH–3A, RH–3A, SH–3G, SH–3H, VH–3A, VH–3D: USA.
S–61D–4: Argentina.

Sikorsky S–61B.

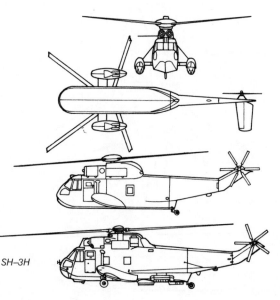

Sikorsky S–58.

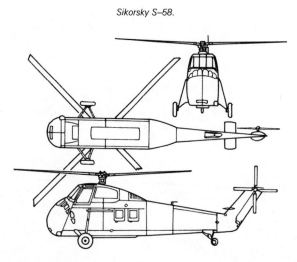

SH–3H

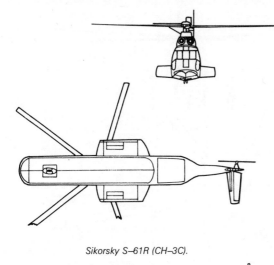

Sikorsky S–61R (CH–3C).

Sikorsky S–62A.

Sikorsky S–61R (CH–3E).
Type: Amphibious transport and rescue helicopter.
Weights:
empty 13,250lb (6,010kg).
normal 21,242lb (9,635kg).
maximum 22,050lb (10,000kg).
Performance:
maximum speed at sea level 163mph (261km/hr).
maximum cruising speed 144mph (232km/hr).
range 465 miles (748km).
ferry range 780 miles (1,255km).
initial rate of climb 21.7ft/sec (6.6m/sec).
service ceiling 12,205ft (3,720m).
hovering ceiling in ground effect 4,101ft (1,250m).
Dimensions:
main rotor diameter 62ft 0in (18.90m).
length of fuselage 57ft 3in (17.45m).
height 18ft 1in (5.51m).
Power plant: Two 1,500hp General Electric T–58–GE–5 turboshafts.
Armament: Optional: Two weapon pods each containing one 7.62mm Minigun.
Payload: 2–3 man crew and 25–30 troops or 15 stretcher cases or max 5,000lb (2,270kg) freight.
Variants:
CH–3C: Earlier version (with less powerful engines); all modified to CH–3E standard.
HH–3E, HH–3F Pelican: Rescue

helicopters.
S–61L, S–61N: Earlier civil variants (L = Land, N = Naval amphibian).
First flights:
S–61L: 2 November 1961.
S–61N: 7 August 1962.
S–61R: 17 June 1963.
Production:
Series production from 1962: 41 CH–3C, 42 CH–3E (from 1966), 50 HH–3E, 40 HH–3F (plus over 25 Italian licence-built by Agusta from 1974–75), and (up to 1974) over 70 S–61L and S–61N.
In service: Argentina (S–61NR), Israel (CH–3C), Italy (HH–3F), Iran (AS–61A–4), Libya (AS–61A–4), USA (CH–3E, HH–3E, HH–3F).

Sikorsky S–62A.
Type: Amphibious transport helicopter.
Weights:
empty 4,957lb (2,248kg).
maximum 7,900lb (3,583kg).
Performance:
maximum speed at sea level 101mph (163km/hr).
maximum cruising speed 92mph (148km/hr).
range 462 miles (743km).
initial rate of climb 19.0ft/sec (5.8m/sec).
service ceiling 6,600ft (2,010m).
hovering ceiling in ground effect 12,200ft (3,720m).
hovering ceiling out of ground effect

1,700ft (520m).
Dimensions:
main rotor diameter 53ft 0in (16.16m).
length of fuselage 44ft 6½in (13.58m).
height 16ft 0in (4.88m).
Power plant: One 1,250hp General Electric CT58–110–1 turboshaft.
Payload: 2 man crew and 12 troops or max 3,017lb (1,368kg) freight.
Variants:
S–62C: Military export and civil version.
First flights: Prototype: 14 May 1958.
Production: Series production from 1960: 26 licence-built in Japan by Mitsubishi from 1963.
In service: Iceland, India, Japan, Philippines, Thailand.

Sikorsky HH–52A.
Type: Amphibious transport helicopter.
Details as for S–62A with the following exceptions:
Weights:
empty 5,053lb (2,306kg).
normal 8,100lb (3,674kg).
Performance:
maximum speed at sea level 109mph (175km/hr).
maximum cruising speed 98mph (158km/hr).
range 475 miles (765km).
initial rate of climb 18.0ft/sec (5.5m/sec).
service ceiling 11,200ft (3,410m).
hovering ceiling in ground effect 14,100ft (4,295m).

hovering ceiling out of ground effect
4,600ft (1,400m).
Power plant: One 1,250hp General
Electric T58–GE–8 turboshaft.
Production: 99 built.
In service: USA.

Sikorsky S–64 'Skycrane' (CH–54A 'Tarhe').

Type: Heavy flying-crane helicopter.
Weights:
empty 19,234lb (8,724kg).
normal 38,000lb (17,237kg).
maximum 42,000lb (19,050kg).
Performance:
maximum speed at sea level 127mph
(204km/hr).
maximum cruising speed 109mph
(175km/hr).
range 253 miles (407km).
initial rate of climb 28.2ft/sec
(8.6m/sec).
service ceiling 13,000ft (3,960m).
hovering ceiling in ground effect
10,600ft (3,230m).
hovering ceiling out of ground effect
6,900ft (2,100m).
Dimensions:
main rotor diameter 72ft 0in (21.95m).
length of fuselage 70ft 3in (21.41m).
height 25ft 5in (7.75m).
Power plant: One 4,500hp Pratt &
Whitney T73–P–1 turboshaft.
Payload: 2–3 man crew and
interchangeable pod with
accommodation for 45 troops or 24
stretcher cases or max 15,000lb
(6,800kg) external freight load.
Variants:
S–64E: Civil variant of CH–54A.
CH–54B (S–64F): Further development
with uprated (4,800hp Pratt & Whitney
T73–P–700) power plant.
First flights:
Prototype: 9 May 1962.
CH–54B: 30 June 1969.
Production:
CH54A: 3 prototypes, 6 pre-production
models; 60 built 1965–68.
CH–54B: 20(?) built from 1969.
S–64E: 7 built.
In service: USA (CH–54A, B).

Sikorsky S–65A (CH–53A 'Sea Stallion').

Type: Heavy transport helicopter.
Weights (apply specifically to CH–53D):
empty 23,485lb (10,653kg).
normal 36,400lb (16,510kg).
maximum 42,000lb (19,050kg).
Performance:
maximum speed at sea level 195mph
(315km/hr).
maximum cruising speed 173mph
(278km/hr).
range 257 miles (413km).
ferry range 806 miles (1,297km).
initial rate of climb 36.5ft/sec

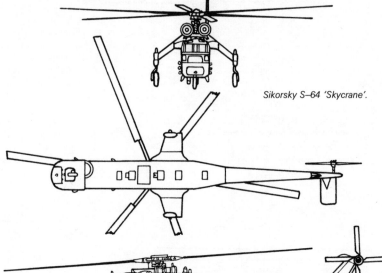

Sikorsky S–64 'Skycrane'.

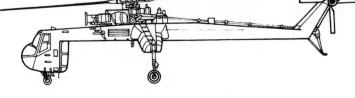

Sikorsky S–65A (Ch–53A 'Sea Stallion'.

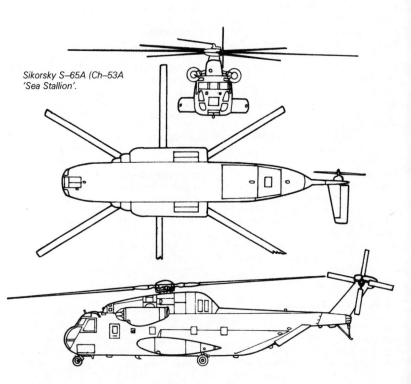

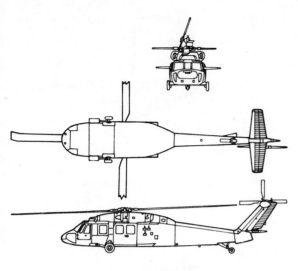

Vought A–7D 'Corsair' II.

Sikorsky S–70 (UH–60A).

TA–7C

(11.1m/sec).
service ceiling 21,000ft (6,400m).
hovering ceiling in ground effect
  13,400ft (4,080m).
hovering ceiling out of ground effect
  6,500ft (1,980m).
Dimensions:
main rotor diameter 72ft 3in (22.02m).
length of fuselage 67ft 2in (20.47m).
height 24ft 9in (7.55m).
Power plant: Two 3,925hp General
  Electric T–64–GE–413 turboshafts.
Payload: 3 man crew and 38–64
  troops or 24 stretcher cases and 4
  medics or max 24,000lb (10,886kg)(?)
  freight.
Variants:
CH–53A: Earlier version.
CH–53DG: Export version of CH–53D
  for Germany (West).
HH–53B, HH–53C: Armed rescue and
  recovery helicopters, three 7.62mm
  Miniguns.
RH–53D: Minesweeping helicopter.
S–65C: Export version for Austria.
CH–53–E: Further development with
  three 4,380hp General Electric
  T64–GE–415 turboprops.
VH–3D: Transport helicopter for
  American president.
First flights:
Prototype: 14 October 1964.
HH–53B: 15 March 1967.
YCH–53E: 1 March 1974.

Production:
Series production from 1966.
CH–53A: 106 built.
CH–53D: 159 built 1969–72.
CH–53DG: 110 built, partly under
  licence in Germany by VFW-Fokker
  (1971–75).
HH–53B: 8 built 1967.
HH–53C: 64(72?) built 1968/69–74.
RH–53D: 36 built 1972–73.
S–65C: 2 built 1969–70.
CH–53E: 76(?) built from 1975.
VH–3D: 6 built 1972.
In service:
CH–53A Sea Stallion, HH–53B,
  HH–53C, VH–3D: USA.
CH–53DG: Germany (West).
CH–53D: Israel, USA.
S–65C: Austria (S–650E).
S–65A: Iran(?).
CH–53E: USA.
RH–53D: Iran, USA.

Sikorsky S–70 (UH–60A).
Type: Medium transport helicopter.
Weights:
normal 16,810lb (7,485kg).
maximum 22,000lb (9,979kg).
Performance:
maximum speed at sea level 200mph
  (322km/hr).
range 460 miles (740km).
maximum hovering ceiling in ground
  effect 10,000ft (3,048m).

maximum hovering ceiling out of
  ground effect 5,800ft (1,768m).
Dimensions:
rotor diameter 52ft 11¾in (16.15m).
length of fuselage 50ft 11½in (15,53m).
height 16ft 1½in (4.91m).
Power plant: Two 1,536hp General
  Electric YT700–GE–700 turboshafts.
Payload: 2–3 man crew and 11 troops.
Variants:
S–78–20: Civil variant for 20
  passengers.
First flights:
Prototype YUH–60A: 17 October 1974.
Production:
4 prototypes, series production
  1977–78, seventy-one machines on
  order to date (1,107 planned).
In service: USA.

Vought A–7D 'Corsair' II.
Type: Single-seat strike-fighter.
Weights:
empty 19,275lb (8,743kg).
normal 30,000lb (13,608kg).
maximum 43,722lb (19,832kg).
Performance:
maximum speed at sea level (Mach
  0.92) 706mph (1,125km/hr).
radius of action 528 miles (850km).
ferry range 3,879 miles (6,243km).
initial rate of climb 225.7ft/sec
  (68.8m/sec).
service ceiling 52,500ft (16,000m).

Dimensions:
wing span 38ft 8½in (11.79m).
length overall 14ft 1½in (14.06m).
height overall 16ft 0in (4.88m).
wing area 375sq ft (34.84sq m).
Power plant: One Allison TF41–A–1
turbofan rated at 14,250lb (6,463kg) st.
Armament: One 20mm M–61A–1
cannon with 1,000rpg and max
15,000lb (6,804kg) weapon load on 8
hard points.
Variants:
A–7A, A–7B, A–7C: Earlier versions.
A–7H: Simplified export version of
A–7E.
TA–7C: Conversion of 40 A–7B and 41
A–7C to two-seat strike-trainers
1975–79.
First flights:
Prototype: 27 September 1965.
A–7D: 6 April 1968.
Production:
Series production from 1966.
A–7A: 199 built 1966–68.
A–7B: 196 built 1968–69.
A–7C: 67 built 1969–71.
A–7D: 459(669?) built from 1969.
A–7H: 60 built 1974–77.
In service:
A–7A, B, C, D, E; TA–7C: USA.
A–7H: Greece.

Vought A–7E 'Corsair' II.

Type: Single-seat shipboard
strike-fighter.
Details as for A–7D with the following
exceptions:
Weights:
empty 17,571lb (7,969kg).
maximum 42,000lb (19,050kg).
Performance:
ferry range 2,775 miles (4,465km).
Power plant: One TF–41–A–Z (R.R. RB
168–62 Spey) turbofan rated at
15,000lb (6,804kg) st.
Armament: Max 20,000lb (9,072kg)
weapon load.
First flights:
A–7E: 25 November 1968.
Production: 542(692?) delivered or on
order from 1969.

Vought F–8E and F–8J 'Crusader'.

Type: Single-seat shipboard fighter and
strike-fighter.
Weights:
normal 29,000lb (13,155kg).
maximum 34,000lb (15,422kg).
Performance:
maximum speed at 40,000ft (12,200m)
(Mach 1.7) 1,120mph (1,802km/hr).
maximum cruising speed at 36,000ft
(11,000m) 560mph (900km/hr).
radius of action 600 miles (965km).
ferry range 1,400 miles (2,253km).
time to 40,000ft (12,200m) 5min 0sec.
service ceiling 35,327ft (17,675m).

Vought F–8E 'Crusader'.

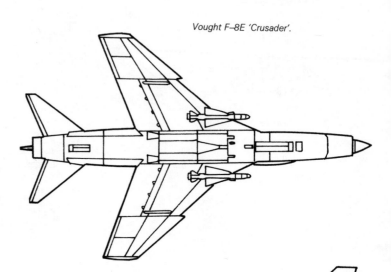

F–8E

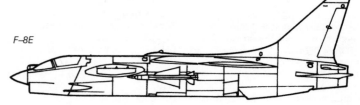

RF–8G

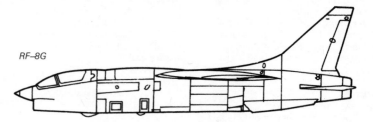

Dimensions:
wing span 35ft 8in (10.87m).
length overall 54ft 6in (16.61m)
(RF–8G: 54ft 3in (16.54m).
height overall 15ft 9in (4.80m).
wing area 375sq ft (34.84sq m).
Power plant: One Pratt & Whitney
J57–P–20/22 turbojet rated at
10,700lb (4,853kg)/18,000lb (8,165kg)
st.
Armament: Four 20mm Mk.12 cannon
with 84rpg and (as fighter) two–four
Sidewinder AAMs or (as strike-fighter)

max 5,000lb (2,270kg) weapon load,
e.g. two AGM–12 Bullpup ASMs or
bombs and rockets; RF–8: five
cameras.
Variants:
F–8A, B, C, D: Earlier versions.
F–8E(FN): Shipboard strike fighter for
France, after modernization similar to
F–BH, J, K, L.
F–8H, J, K, L: Updated versions
modified from 89 F–8D, 136 F–8E, 87
F–8C and 63 F–8B.
RF–8A: Reconnaissance aircraft, 73

converted to RF–8G.

First flights:
Prototype: 25 March 1955.
F–8E: 30 June 1961.

Production:
Series production from 1957–65,
  conversions 1966–70; F–8A: 318
  built; F–8B: 130 built; F–8C: 187
  built; F–8D: 152 built; F–8E: 286
  built; F–8E(FN): 42 built; RF–8A: 144
  built.

In service:
F–8E(FN): France.
F–8H, J, K, L, RF–8G: USA.

Antonov An–2 (Colt).

Type: Light transport.
Weights:
empty 7,396lb (3,355kg).
normal 11,574lb (5,250kg).
maximum 12,125lb (5,500kg).

Performance:
maximum speed at 5,750ft (1,750m)
  159mph (256km/hr).
maximum cruising speed at 3,820ft
  (1,000m) 137mph (220km/hr).
range w.m.p. 466 miles (750km).
ferry range 745 miles (1,200km).
time to 6,560ft (2,000m) 8min 6sec.
initial rate of climb 9.2ft/sec
  (2.8m/sec).

service ceiling 14,760ft (4,500m).

Dimensions:
wing span (upper) 59ft 7in (18.17m).
wing span (lower) 46ft 8in (14.23m).
length overall 41ft 9¼in (12.73m).
height overall 13ft 6½in (4.13m).
wing area 767.43sq ft (71.30sq m).

Power plant: One 1,000hp Shvetsov
  ASh–62–IR piston engine.

Payload: 2 man crew and 10–12
  troops or 14 paratroops or 6 stretcher
  cases and 2 medics or max 3,340lb
  (1,515kg) freight.

Variants:
Over 18 variants, inc An–2P, An–2S,
  An–2Sa and An–2W.
Fongshu–2: Chinese licence-built An–2.
An–2M: Further development.

First flights:
Prototype: 1947.

Production: An–2: Series production
  from 1949, over 5,000 delivered up to
  1962. Licence-built in Poland by WSK
  (from 1960) and China (from 1957).
An–2M: Series production from 1964;
  over 5,000 delivered to date.

In service:
Afghanistan, Albania, Bulgaria, China
  (People's Republic) (Fongshu–2), Cuba,
  Czechoslovakia, Germany (East),
  Hungary, Iraq, Korea (North), Mali(?),
  Mongolia (People's Republic), Poland,

Romania, Somali, Tanzania, USSR
  (SS–1), Vietnam.

Antonov An–12 (Cub).

Type: Medium transport.
Weights:
empty 61,700lb (28,000kg).
normal 119,000lb (54,000kg).
maximum 134,500lb (61,000kg).

Performance:
maximum speed 444mph (715km/hr).
maximum cruising speed at 24,600ft
  (7,500m) 342mph (550km/hr).
range with 44,100lb (20,000kg) payload
  350miles (5,550km).
ferry range 3,420 miles (5,000km).
initial rate of climb 32.8ft/sec
  (10.0m/sec).
service ceiling 33,465ft (10,200m).

Dimensions:
wing span 124ft 8in (38.00m).
length overall 121ft 4¾in (37.00m).
height overall 32ft 3in (9.83m).
wing area 1,286.3sq ft (119.50sq m).

Power plant: Four 4,000hp Ivchenko
  AI–20K turboprops.

Armament: Two 23mm NR–23 cannon
  in tail position.

Payload: 5–6 man crew and 105
  troops or 60 paratroops or max
  44,100lb (20,000kg) freight.

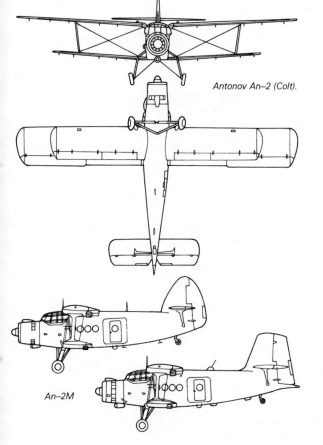

Antonov An–2 (Colt).

Antonov An–12 (Cub).

An–2M

Variants:
An–10A (Cat): Civil airliner.
An–12B: Civil transport.
An–12 (Cub–C): ECM aircraft.
First flights: Prototype: 1957.
Production:
Series production from 1958, over 900
  built to date.
In service: Algeria, Bulgaria, Cuba,
  Egypt (UAR), India, Indonesia, Iraq,
  Poland, Sudan, USSR.

Antonov An–14 'Pchelka' (Clod).

Type: Light transport and liaison
  aircraft.
Weights:
empty 4,410lb (2,000kg).
maximum 7,935lb (3,600kg).
Performance:
maximum speed at 3,280ft (1,000m)
  138mph (222km/hr).
maximum cruising speed at 6,560ft
  (2,000m) 109mph (175km/hr).
range w.m.p. 404 miles (650km).
range with 1,290lb (630kg) payload 422

miles (680km).
initial rate of climb 16.7ft/sec
  (5.1m/sec).
time to 6,560ft (2,000m) 8min 0sec.
service ceiling 17,100ft (5,200m).
Dimensions:
wing span 72ft 2½in (22.00m).
length overall 37ft 6½in (11.44m).
height overall 15ft 2½in (4.63m).
wing area 427.5sq ft (39.72sq m).
Power plant: Two 300hp Ivchenko
  AI–14RF piston engines.
Payload: 1–2 man crew and 7–9
  troops or 8 paratroops or 6 stretcher
  cases and 2 medics or max 1,590lb
  (720kg) freight.
Variants:
Also civil versions.
Capital No. 1 Shat-Tu: Scaled-down
  Chinese version of An–14 licence-built
  from 1958–59.
First flights:
Prototype: 15 March 1958.
Production: Series production from
  1965.

In service: China (People's Republic),
  Germany (East), Guinea, USSR.

Antonov An–28.

Type: Light transport and liaison
  aircraft.
Details as for An–14 with the following
  exceptions:
Weights:
empty 7,716lb (3,500kg).
normal 12,570lb (5,700kg).
Performance:
maximum speed at 3,820ft (1,000m)
  205mph (330km/hr).
maximum cruising speed at 6,560ft
  (2,000m) 217mph (356km/hr).
range with 2,870lb (1,300kg) payload
  620 miles (1,000km).
ferry range 715 miles (1,150km).
time to 6,560ft (2,000m) 8min 0sec.
service ceiling 19,685ft (6,000m).
Dimensions:
wing span 72ft 2½in (22.0m).
length overall 42ft 7in (12.98m).

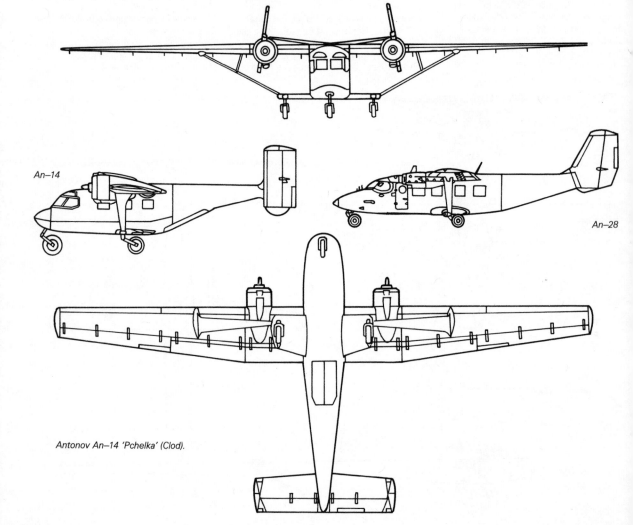

An–14

An–28

Antonov An–14 'Pchelka' (Clod).

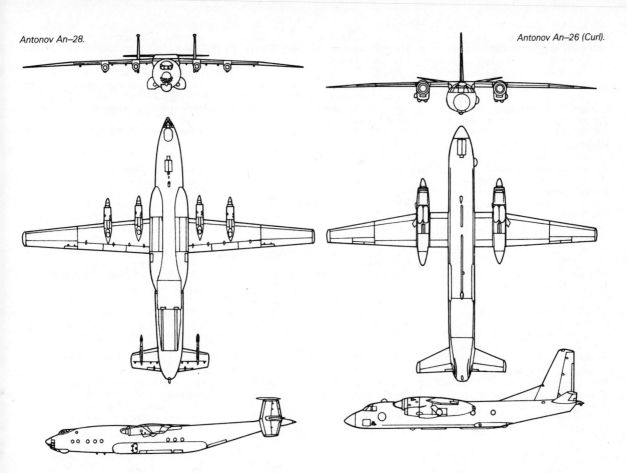

Antonov An–28.

height overall 15ft 1in (4.60m).
Power plant: One 960hp Isotov
 Glushenkov TWD–10A turboprop.
Payload: 2 man crew and 15 troops or
 8 paratroops or 6 stretcher cases and
 2 medics or max 3,310lb (1,500kg)
 freight.
First flights:
Prototype An–28 (original designation
 An–14M): September 1969.
Production:
Series production from 1974.
In service: USSR.

Antonov An–22 'Antheus' (Cock).
Type: Strategic transport.
Weights:
empty 25,600lb (116,000kg).
maximum 551,200lb (250,000kg).
Performance:
maximum speed at 26,250ft
 (8,000m)–32,800ft (10,000m) 460mph
 (740km/hr).
maximum cruising speed at 26,250ft
 (8,000m)–32,800ft (10,000m) 423mph
 (679km/hr).
range with 176,370lb (80,000kg)
 payload 3,110 miles (5,000km).
ferry range 6,800 miles (10,950km).
service ceiling 26,250–32,800ft
 (8,000–10,000m).

Dimensions:
wing span 211ft 4in (64.40m).
length overall 189ft 7in (57.80m).
height overall 41ft 1½in (12.53m).
wing area 3,713sq ft (345.00sq m).
Power plant: Four 15,000hp Kusnetsov
 NK–12MV turboprops.
Payload: 5–6 man crew and 28–29
 troops plus max 176,370lb (80,000kg)
 freight.
Variants:
Civil version for 330–350 passengers.
First flights:
Prototype: 27 February 1965.
Production model: 1967.
Production:
3 prototypes, series production from
 1967, approx 60 delivered up to end
 1974.
In service: USSR.

Antonov An–26 (Curl).
Type: Medium transport.
Weights:
empty 37,300lb (16,914kg).
maximum 52,910lb (24,000kg).
Performance:
maximum speed at 19,700ft (6,000m)
 311mph (500km/hr).
maximum cruising speed at 19,700ft
 (6,000m) 270mph (435km/hr).
range w.m.p. 610 miles (980km).

ferry range 1,820 miles (2,930km).
initial rate of climb 26.25ft/sec
 (8.0m/sec).
service ceiling 24,600ft (7,500m).
Dimensions:
wing span 95ft 9½in (29.20m).
length overall 78ft 1in (23.80m).
height overall 28ft 1½in (8.57m).
wing area 867.08sq ft (74.98sq m).
Power plant: Two 2,820hp Ivchenko
 AI–24WT turboprops plus one
 Tumansky RU–19–300 auxiliary
 turbojet rated at 1,985lb (900kg) st in
 starboard nacelle.
Payload: 2–5 man crew and 38 troops
 or 24 stretcher cases and – medics or
 max 12,100lb (5,500kg) freight.
Variants:
An–24 (Coke): Civil airliner.
An–30 (Clank): Photographic and survey
 aircraft.
First flights:
Prototype An–24: 1959.
Prototype An–26: 1968.
Production:
An–24: Series production from 1961;
 over 500 delivered to date.
An–26: Series production from 1969;
 over 400(350?) delivered to date.
In service:
An–24, An–26: Bangladesh, Congo
 (Brazzaville), Cuba, Czechoslovakia,

Egypt (UAR), Germany (East), Hungary, Iraq, Korea (North), Laos, Mongolia (People's Republic), Poland, Somali, South Yemen, Sudan, USSR, Vietnam.

Beriev Be–6 (Madge).
Type: Maritime-reconnaissance and ASW flying-boat, 8 man crew.
Weights:
empty 41,505lb (18,827kg).
normal 51,590lb (23,400kg).
maximum 55,120lb (25,000kg).
Performance:
maximum speed at sea level 234mph (377km/hr).
maximum speed at 7,870ft (2,400m) 258mph (415km/hr).
maximum cruising speed 211mph (340km/hr).
ferry range 2,800 miles (4,500km).
service ceiling 21,325ft (6,500m).
Dimensions:
wing span 108ft 3¼in (33.00m).
length overall 77ft 3½in (23.56m).
height overall 225ft 0¾in (7.64m).
wing area 1,291.7sq ft (120.00sq m).
Power plant: Two 2,400hp Shvetsov ASh–73TK piston engines.
Armament: Three–four 23mm cannon, mines, bombs and torpedoes in fuselage bay, rockets and bombs underwing.
Variants:

4 variants: Maritime-reconnaissance aircraft with tail armament: ASW aircraft with MAD (magnetic anomaly detection) search equipment in tail 'sting'; ASW aircraft with ECM direction-finding equipment; rescue and transport aircraft.
First flights: Prototype: 1947.
Production: Series production from 1949–.
In service: China (People's Republic), USSR(?).

Beriev Be–12 'Tchaika' (Mail).
Type: Maritime-reconnaissance amphibian, 6–10 man crew.
Weights:
maximum 65,035lb (29,500kg).
Performance:
maximum speed at 10,000ft (3,050m) 379mph (610km/hr).
maximum cruising speed at 15,000ft (4,570m) 340mph (547km/hr).
patrol speed at 1,000ft (300m) 199mph (320km/hr).
ferry range 2,500 miles (4,000km).
initial rate of climb 49.9ft/sec (15.2m/sec).
service ceiling 37,075ft (11,300m).
Dimensions:
wing span 107ft 11½in (32.90m).
length overall 97ft 5½in (29.70m).
height overall 22ft 11½in (7.00m).

wing area 1,027.9sq ft (95.70sq m).
Power plant: Two 4,190hp Ivchenko A1–20D turboprops.
Armament: Homing torpedoes, depth-charges, mines, rockets, bombs.
First flights: Prototype: 1960.
Production: Series production from 1964.
In service: USSR (M–12).

Ilyushin Il–14M (Crate).
Type: Medium transport.
Weights:
empty 27,998lb (12,700kg).
maximum 38,580lb (17,500kg).
Performance:
maximum speed at 7,875ft (2,400m) 268mph (431km/hr).
maximum cruising speed at 8,200–9,850ft (2,500–3,000m) 199mph (320km/hr).
range with 3,527lb (1,600kg) payload 1,087 miles (1,750km).
ferry range 1,990 miles (3,200km).
initial rate of climb 20.0ft/sec (6.1m/sec).
service ceiling 24,280ft (7,400m).
Dimensions:
wing span 104ft 0½in (31.70m).
length overall 73ft 2½in (22.31m).
height overall 25ft 7¼in (7.80m).
wing area 1,076sq ft (100sq m).
Power plant: Two 1,900hp Shvetsov

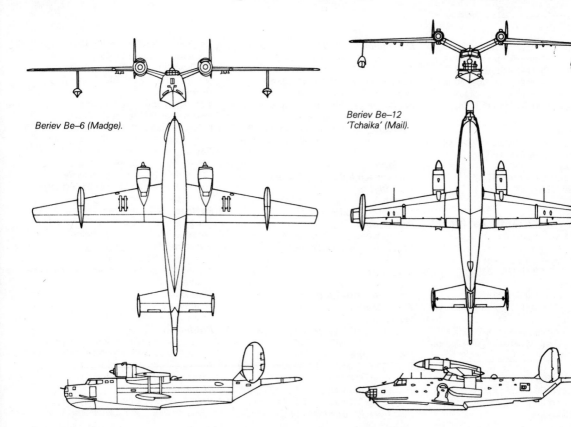

Beriev Be–6 (Madge).

Beriev Be–12 'Tchaika' (Mail).

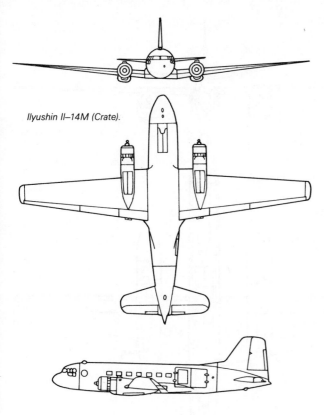

Ilyushin Il–14M (Crate).

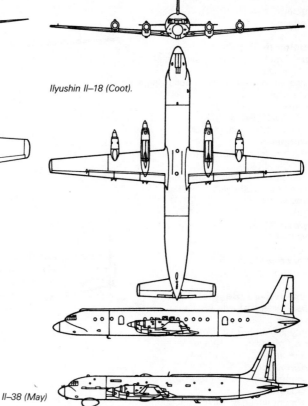

Ilyushin Il–18 (Coot).

Il–38 (May)

ASh–82T–7 piston engines.
Payload: 3 man crew and 30–32
troops or 24 paratroops or max
7,275lb (3,300kg) freight.
Variants:
Il–14ECM: Conversions to ECM aircraft.
First flights:
Il–14: 1953.
Il–14M: 1956.
Production:
Il–14: Approx 3,500 built from 1954;
licence-built in East Germany as Il–14P
1956–59; Czech licence-built as
Avia–14.
In service:
Il–14: Afghanistan, Albania, Algeria,
Bulgaria, China (People's Republic),
Congo (Brazzaville), Cuba,
Czechoslovakia, Egypt, Ethiopia,
Germany (East), Guinea, Hungary,
India, Indonesia, Iraq, Korea (North),
Mongolia (People's Republic), Poland,
Romania, Syria, USSR, Vietnam,
Yemen, Yugoslavia.
Il–14ECM: USSR.

Ilyushin Il–12 (Coach).
Type: Medium transport.
Details as for Il–14M with the following
exceptions:

Weights:
empty 26,675lb (12,100kg).
maximum 38,030lb (17,250kg).
Performance:
maximum speed at 8,200ft (2,500m)
253mph (407km/hr).
maximum cruising speed at
8,200–9,850ft (2,500–3,000m) 205mph
(330km/hr).
range with 3,527lb (1,600kg) payload
777 miles (1,250km).
ferry range 1,243 miles (2,000km).
initial rate of climb 15.1ft/sec
(4.6m/sec).
service ceiling 21,980ft (6,700m).
Dimensions:
length overall 69ft 11in (21.30m).
height overall 26ft 0in (8.07m).
wing area 1,108.7sq ft (103,0sq m).
Power plant: Two 1,775hp Shvetsov
ASh–82FNV piston engines.
Payload: 4 man crew and 26 troops or
20 paratroops or max 6,614lb
(3,000kg) freight.
First flights: Il–12: 1945.
Production:
Il–12: Approx 3,000 built from 1947.
In service: Bulgaria, China (People's
Republic), Korea (North), Mongolia
(People's Republic), Poland, Romania,
USSR, Vietnam.

Ilyushin Il–18 (Coot).
Type: Medium transport.
Weights:
empty 69,000lb (31,300kg).
normal 99,870lb (45,300kg).
maximum 141,100lb (64,000kg).
Performance:
maximum speed 400mph (675km/hr).
maximum cruising speed at 26,250ft
(8,000m) 388mph (625km/hr).
range with 29,760lb (13,500kg) payload
2,300 miles (3,700km).
ferry range 4,038 miles (6,500km).
service ceiling 31,170ft (9,500m).
Dimensions:
wing span 122ft 9in (37.40m).
length overall 117ft 1½in (35.70m).
height overall 33ft 5½in (10.20m).
wing area 1,507sq ft (140.00sq m).
Power plant: Four 4,250hp Ivchenko
AI–20M turboprops.
Payload: 5 man crew and 80 troops or
max 29,760lb (13,500kg) freight.
Variants:
Il–38 (May): Conversion of Il–18 to
maritime-reconnaissance and ASW
aircraft with 12 man crew.
First flights:
Prototype Il–18: 4 July 1957.
Production: Over 700(?) built 1957–67.
In service: Afghanistan, Algeria,

Bulgaria(?), China (People's Republic), Czechoslovakia, Germany (East), Guinea, Korea (North), Poland, Romania, Syria(?), USSR, Yugoslavia, Vietnam.

Ilyushin Il–38 (May).

Type: Maritime-reconnaissance and ASW aircraft.

Details as for Il–18 with the following exceptions:

Weights:
empty 80,000lb (36,287kg).
maximum 140,000lb (63,500kg).

Performance:
maximum speed 400mph (645km/hr) at 15,090ft (4,600m).
patrol speed 370mph (595km/hr).
ferry range 4,500 miles (7,250km).

Dimensions:
length overall 131ft 3in (40.0m).

Payload: 12 man crew.

First flights:
Prototype Il–38: 1968.

Production: From 1969.

In service: India, USSR.

Ilyushin Il–28 (Beagle).

Type: Three-seat light bomber.

Weights:
empty 28,417lb (12,890kg).
normal 40,565lb (18,400kg).
maximum 46,300lb (21,000kg).

Performance:
maximum speed at sea level 497mph (800km/hr).
maximum speed at 14,765ft (4,500m) 559mph (900km/hr).
maximum cruising speed at 32,800ft (10,000m) 478mph (770km/hr).
radius of action 590 miles (950km).
ferry range 2,144 miles (3,450km).
initial rate of climb 49.2ft/sec (15.0m/sec).
time to 32,800ft (10.000m) 18min.
service ceiling 40,355ft (12,300m).

Dimensions:
wing span 70ft 4¾in (21.45m).
length overall 57ft 10¾in (17.65m).
height overall 20ft 4¼in (6.20m).
wing area 654.44sq ft (60.80sq m).

Power plant: Two Klimov VK–1 turbojets each rated at 5,952lb (2,700kg) st.

Armament: Two 23mm NR–23 cannon with 85rpg in fuselage nose and two 23mm NR–23 cannon with 225rpg in tail position; max 4,409lb (2,000kg) weapon load, e.g. bombs, torpedoes, mines.

Variants:
Il–28T: Torpedo bomber.
Il–28R: Reconnaissance aircraft with 3–5 cameras.
Il–28U (MASCOT): Bomber trainer.
Il–20: Civil transport version.

First flights:
Prototype: 8 August 1948.

Production: Several thousand built

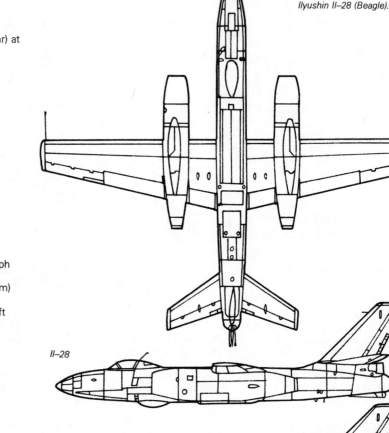

Ilyushin Il–28 (Beagle).

Il–28

Il–28U

1949–61; licence-built in Czechoslovakia, version also built in China (People's Republic). Conversion from ECM aircraft 1965–66.

In service: Afghanistan, Algeria, Bulgaria, China (People's Republic), Czechoslovakia (B228), Finland(?), Indonesia, Iraq, Korea (North), Morocco, Nigeria, Poland, Romania, Somali, South Yemen, Syria, USSR, Vietnam, Yemen.

Ilyushin Il–76 (Candid).

Type: Heavy transport.

Weights:
maximum 235,900lb (157,000kg).

Performance:
maximum speed 560(?)mph (900(?)km/hr).
maximum cruising speed at 42,650ft (13,000m) 528mph (850km/hr).
range w.m.p. 3,110 miles (5,000km).
service ceiling 42,650ft (13,000m).

Dimensions:
wing span 165ft 11½in (50.50m).
length overall 152ft 8½in (46.55m).
height overall 48ft 5in (14.76m).
wing area 3,229.20sq ft (300.00sq m).
Power plant: Four Soloviev D–30–KP
 turbofans each rated at 26,455lb
 (12,000kg) st.
Payload: 3–5 man crew or max
 88,185lb (40,000kg) freight.
First flights:
Prototype: 25 March 1971.
Production: Series production
 1974–75; over 100 delivered to date.
In service: USSR.

Kamov Ka–25 (Hormone–A).
Type: Shipboard ASW helicopter, 3–4
 man crew.
Weights:
empty 10,472lb (4,750kg).
maximum 16,530lb (7,500kg).
Performance:
maximum speed at sea level 130mph
 (210km/hr).
maximum cruising speed 120mph
 (195km/hr).
range 250 miles (400km).
ferry range 405 miles (650km).
service ceiling 11,500ft (3,500m).
Dimensions:
main rotor diameter 51ft 8in (15.75m).
length of fuselage 35ft 5in (10.8m).
height 17ft 8in (5.35m).
Powerplant: Two 900hp Glushenkov
 GTD–3 turboshafts.
Armament: Two homing torpedoes or
 bombs and mines.
Variants: Ka–20 (Harp): Earlier version.
Ka–25K (Hormone–A): Civil version.
First flights:
Prototype: 1961.
Ka–25K: 1965.
Production: Series production from
 1962.
In service: Syria, USSR, Yugoslavia.

**Mikoyan-Gurevich MiG–15UTI
 (Midget).**
Type: Two-seat trainer.
Weights:
empty 8,818lb (4,000kg).
normal 10,692lb (4,850kg).
maximum 11,905lb (5,400kg).
Performance:
maximum speed at sea level 628mph
 (1,010km/hr).
maximum cruising speed at 16,400ft
 (5,000m) 423mph (680km/hr).
ferry range with two 55gal (250l)
 auxiliary tanks 833 miles (1,340km).
initial rate of climb 126.3ft/sec
 (38.5m/sec).
service ceiling 48,637ft (14,825m).
Dimensions:
wing span 36ft 1in (11.00m).
length overall 33ft 1¾in (10.10m).
height overall 12ft 2in (3.70m).

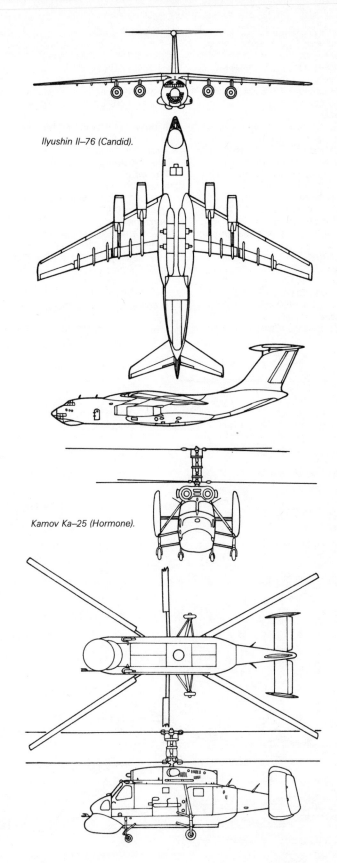

Ilyushin Il–76 (Candid).

Kamov Ka–25 (Hormone).

wing area 222.8sq ft (20.70sq m).
Power plant: One RD–45F turbojet
rated at 5,005lb (2,270kg) st.
Armament: One 12.7mm UBK–E
machine-gun with 150rpg; one 23mm
NR–23 cannon with 80rpg; two 220lb
(100kg) bombs.
Variants:
CS–102: Czechoslovakian licence-built.
Lim–3: Polish licence-built.
MiG–15 and MiG–15bis (Fagot):
Single-seat strike-fighters.
Lim–1, Lim–2, S–102, S–103: Polish
and Czech licence-built MiG–15 and
MiG–15bis resp.
CS–102, Lim–3: Czech and Polish
licence-built MiG–15UTI resp.
Shenyang F–2: Chinese licence-built
MiG–15 from 1956.
First flights:
Prototype MiG–15: 30 December 1947.
MiG–15UTI: 1949–50(?).
Production: approx 15,000 of all
variants built 1950–58(1960?).
In service: Afghanistan, Albania,
Angola, Bulgaria, China (People's
Republic), Cuba, Czechoslovakia,
Finland, Germany (East), Hungary, Iraq,
Korea (North), Mali, Mongolia
(People's Republic), Morocco,
Nigeria(?), Poland, Romania, Somali,
South Yemen, Syria, Uganda(?), Sri
Lanka, USSR, Vietnam, Yemen.

Mikoyan-Gurevich MiG–17F (Fresco–C).

Type: Single-seat fighter and
strike-fighter.
Weights:
empty 8,664lb (3,930kg).
normal 11,785lb (5,345kg).
maximum 13,393lb (6,075kg).
Performance:
maximum speed at 9,840ft (3,000m)
(Mach 0.98) 682mph (1,097km/hr).
maximum speed at sea level (Mach
0.92) 699mph (1,125km/hr).
maximum cruising speed at 32,800ft
(10,000m) 485mph (780km/hr).
radius of action 360 miles (580km).
ferry range 1,230 miles (1,980km).
time to 32,800ft (10,000m) 5min 48sec.
initial rate of climb 164.0ft/sec
(50.0m/sec).
service ceiling 54,500ft (16,600m).
Dimensions:
wing span 31ft 7in (9.63m).
length overall 36ft 11¼in (11.26m).
height overall 12ft 5⅜in (3.80m).
wing area 243.26sq ft (22.60sq m).
Power plant: One Klimov VK–1A
turbojet rated at 5,953/7,055lb
(2,700/3,200kg) st.
Armament:
MiG–17, MiG–17P: Two 23mm NR–23
cannon with 80rpg, one 37mm N5–37
cannon with 40rpg.
MiG–17F, MiG–17PF: Three 23mm
NR–23 cannon, two 550lb (250kg)
bombs or four rocket launchers each
containing eight 55mm rockets or four
unguided rockets.
MiG–17PFU: Four Alkali AAMs.
Variants:
MiG–17 (Fresco–A), MiG–17P
(Fresco–B): Earlier versions.
MiG–17PF (Fresco–D), MiG–17PFU
(Fresco–E): Later series.

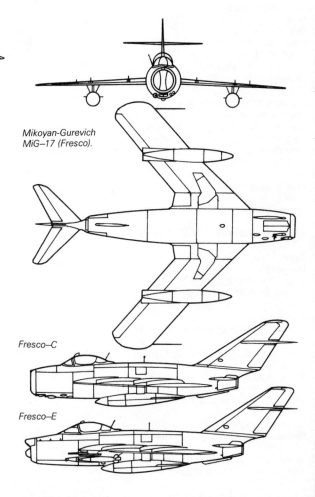

Mikoyan-Gurevich
MiG–15 (Midget).

MiG–15UTI

MiG–15

Mikoyan-Gurevich
MiG–17 (Fresco).

Fresco–C

Fresco–E

Lim–5P, S–104: Polish and Czech
licence-built MiG–17F resp.
Shenyang F–4: Chinese licence-built
MiG–17F.
Lim–6: Single-seat Polish ground-attack
aircraft.
First flights: Prototype: January 1950.
Production: Approx 9,000 built
1952–60; licence-built in China (over
1,000 up to 1965), Poland,
Czechoslovakia.
In service:
MiG–17P: Albania(?).
MiG–17F: Afghanistan, Algeria,
Bulgaria, Cuba, Czechoslovakia, Egypt
(UAR), Guinea, Hungary, Indonesia,
Iraq, Korea (North), Mali, Morocco,
Nigeria, Romania, Somali, South
Yemen, Sudan, Syria, Uganda, USSR,
Vietnam, Yemen.
F–4: Albania, China, Korea (North),
Sudan, Sri Lanka, Tanzania.

Mikoyan-Gurevich MiG–17PF (Fresco–D).

Type: Single-seat all-weather fighter.
Details as for Fresco–C with the
following exceptions:
Weights:
empty 9,920lb (4,182kg).
normal 12,345lb (5,600kg).
maximum 13,955lb (6,330kg).
Performance:
maximum speed at 13,150ft (4,000m)
667mph (1,074km/hr).
ferry range 1,200 miles (1,930km).
time to 32,800ft (10,000m) 7min 36sec.
service ceiling 52,000ft (15,850m).
Dimensions:
wing span 31ft 7in (9.63m).
length overall 38ft 4in (11.68m).
height overall 12ft 5¾in (3.80m).
wing area 243.26sq ft (22.60sq m).
Power plant: One Klimov VK–1FA
turbojet rated at 5,952/7,452lb
(2/700/3,380kg) st.
In service:
MiG–17PF: Algeria, Bulgaria, Cuba,
Czechoslovakia, Egypt (UAR), Hungary,
Indonesia, Iraq, Korea (North),
Romania, Syria, Tanzania, USSR,
Vietnam.

Mikoyan MiG–19S (Farmer C).

Type: Single-seat fighter and
strike-fighter.
Weights:
empty 11,402lb (5,172kg).
normal 16,310lb (7,400kg).
maximum 19,620lb (8,900kg).
Performance:
maximum speed at 32,800ft (10,000m)
(Mach 1.33) 901mph (1,450km/hr).
maximum speed at sea level (Mach
0.95) 684mph (1,100km/hr).
maximum cruising speed 590mph
(950km/hr).
radius of action 280–425 miles
(450–685km).

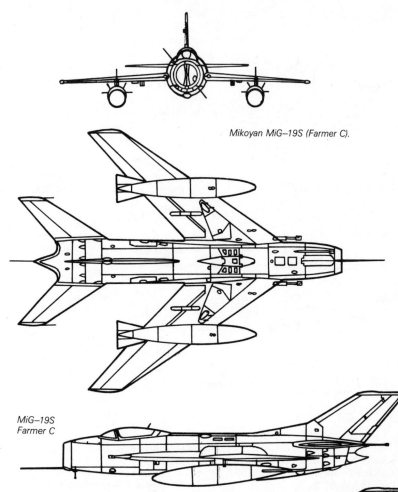

Mikoyan MiG–19S (Farmer C).

*MiG–19S
Farmer C*

*MiG–19PM
Farmer D*

ferry range 1,370 miles (2,200km).
time to 32,800ft (10,000m) 1min 6sec.
initial rate of climb 377.3ft/sec
(115.0m/sec).
service ceiling 57,410ft (17.500m).
Dimensions:
wing span 29ft 6⅓in (9.00m).
length overall 41ft 4in (12.60m).
height overall 12ft 9½in (3.90m).
wing area 269.1sq ft (25.00sq m).
Power plant: Two Klimov RD–9B
turbojets each rated at 5,732/7,165lb
(2,600/3,250kg) st.
Armament: One 30mm NR–30 cannon
with 55rpg in fuselage, two 30mm
NR–30 cannon with 73rpg in wings
and two Atoll AAMs or four rocket
launchers each containing eight 55mm

rockets or two 550lb (250kg) bombs.
Variants:
MiG–19F (Farmer–A): Pre-production
model, two 23mm and one 37mm
cannon.
MiG–19P (Farmer–B): Initial production
model with limited all-weather
capability, two 23mm and one 37mm
cannon.
MiG–19PM (Farmer–D): All-weather
fighter, four Alkali AAMs.
Shenyang F–6 and F–7: Chinese
licence-built MiG–19S and MiG–19P
resp.
First flights: Prototype: 1953.
Production:
MiG–19F: Approx 60 built.
MiG–19S: Series production

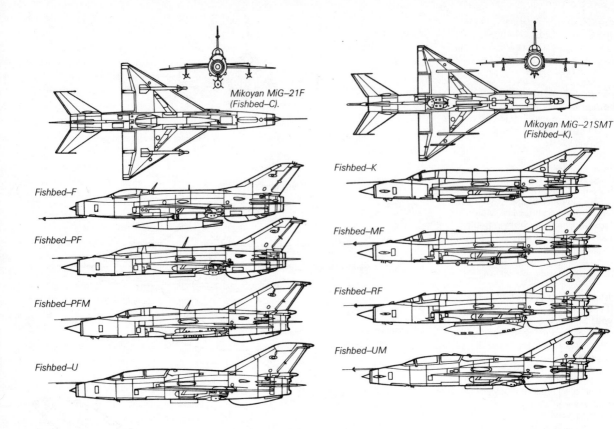

Mikoyan MiG–21F
(Fishbed–C).

Mikoyan MiG–21SMT
(Fishbed–K).

Fishbed–F

Fishbed–PF

Fishbed–PFM

Fishbed–U

Fishbed–K

Fishbed–MF

Fishbed–RF

Fishbed–UM

1955–62/63; licence-built in China (over 2,600 F–6 from 1961) and Czechoslovakia (approx 850 S–105 1958–61 by Aero).

In service:
MiG–19S: Afghanistan, Cuba, Indonesia, Korea (North), Syria, USSR.
F–6: Albania, China (People's Republic), Pakistan, Tanzania, Vietnam.

Mikoyan MiG–21F (Fishbed–C).
Type: Single-seat fighter and strike-fighter.
Weights:
empty 12,015lb (5,450kg).
normal 15,543lb (7,050kg).
maximum 17,086lb (7,750kg).
Performance:
maximum speed at 36,000ft (11,000m) (Mach 2.0) 1,317mph (2,120km/hr).
radius of action 375 miles (600km).
ferry range 1,150 miles (1,850km).
initial rate of climb 492.1ft/sec (150.0m/sec).
time to 39,375ft (12,000m) 4min 30sec.
service ceiling 59,420ft (17,500m).
Dimensions:
wing span 23ft 5½in (7.15m).
length overall 44ft 2in (13.46m).
height overall 14ft 9in (4.50m).
wing area 347.57sq ft (23.00sq m).
Power plant: One Tumansky R–11 turbojet rated at 9,920lb

(4,500kg)/12,676lb (5,750kg) st.
Armament:
MiG–21F: One 30mm NR–30 cannon and two Atoll AAMs or two rocket launchers each containing nineteen 55mm rockets or two 550lb (250kg) bombs.
MiG–21FL: Two 23mm GSh–23 cannon in GP–9 weapon pods.
Variants:
MiG–21FL: Export version.
MiG–21 (Fishbed–A and B): Earlier versions.
MiG–21 (Fishbed–G): Single-seat VTOL strike-fighter, experimental model only, two lift-jet engines in fuselage.
MiG–21U (Mongol–A): Two-seat strike-trainer.
Shenyang F–8: Chinese built MiG–21.
First flights: Prototype: 1955.
Production:
Over 20,000 of all series built from 1959, licence-built in China, Czechoslovakia and India (196 built by HAL 1966/67–73).
In service:
MiG–21F, PF and U: Afghanistan, Algeria, Angola, Bangladesh, Bulgaria, Cuba, Czechoslovakia, Egypt (UAR), Finland, Germany (East), Hungary, India, (Type 74, Type 77, Type 66), Indonesia, Iraq, Korea (North), Poland, Romania, Somali, South Yemen,

Sudan, Syria, Uganda, USSR, Vietnam, Yugoslavia.
F–8: Albania, China (People's Republic), Tanzania.

Mikoyan MiG–21PF (Fishbed–D).
Type: Single-seat fighter and strike-fighter.
Details as for MiG–21F with the following exceptions:
Weights:
normal 17,637lb (8,000kg).
maximum 19,511lb (8,850kg).
Dimensions:
length overall 45ft 11in (14.00m).
Power plant:
One Tumansky R–11–F2S–300 turbojet rated at 8,598/13,670lb (3,900/6,200kg) st.
Armament:
As for MiG–21F, but without cannon.

Mikoyan MiG–21SMT (Fishbed–K).
Type: Single-seat fighter and strike-fighter.
Weights:
empty 12,350lb (5,600kg).
normal 18,520lb (8,400kg).
maximum 20,945lb (9,500kg).
Performance:
maximum speed at 39,375ft (12,000m) (Mach 2.1) 1,386mph (2,230km/hr).

maximum speed at sea level (Mach
1.06) 808mph (1,300km/hr).
radius of action 310 miles (500km).
ferry range 5,900 miles (1,800km).
service ceiling 59,060ft (18,000m).
Dimensions:
wing span 23ft 5½in (7.15m).
length overall 44ft 2in (13.46m).
height overall 14ft 9in (4.50m).
wing area 247.59sq ft (23.00sq m).
Power plant: 0ne Tumansky R–13
turbojet rated at 11,244/14,550lb
(5,100/6,600kg) st.
Armament: Two 23mm GSh–23
cannon with 100rpg and (as fighter)
2–4 Atoll AAMs or (as strike-fighter)
max 2,200lb(?) (1,000kg(?) weapon
load; e.g. four 550lb (250kg) or four
rocket launchers each with sixteen
55mm rockets or four 220mm or
325mm rockets.
Variants:
MiG–21PFM (Fishbed–F), MiG–21MF
(Fishbed–J): Earlier series.
MiG–21R (Fishbed–G), MiG–21RF
(Fishbed–H): Single-seat
reconnaissance aircraft.
MiG–21UM (Mongol–B): Two-seat
strike-trainer.
First flights: MiG–21MF: 1968.
Production:
Series production from 1968;
licence-built in India by HAL (150 from
1973–80?).
In service:
MiG–21PFM, MF and UM: Bulgaria,
Cuba, Czechoslovakia (MiG–21SPS),
Egypt (UAR), Germany (East),
Hungary, India, Poland, Romania,
Syria, USSR.
MiG–21SMT: USSR.

Mikoyan MiG–23S (Flogger–B).
Type: Single-seat fighter.
Weights:
empty 22,050lb (10,000kg).
normal 30,870lb (14,000kg).
maximum 37,480lb (17,000kg).
Performance:
maximum speed at 36,000ft (11,000m)
(Mach 2.2).
maximum speed at sea level (Mach
1.1).
maximum cruising speed at sea level
(Mach 0.8) 609mph (980km/hr).
radius of action 217–620 miles
(350–1,000km).
ferry range 1,370 miles (2,200km).
time to 36,000ft (11,000m) 8min 0sec.
service ceiling 50,030ft (15,250m).
Dimensions:
wing span (spread) 47ft 3in (14.40m).
wing span (fully swept) 28ft 6½in
(8.70m).
length overall 53ft 7⅞in (16.35m).
height overall 12ft 11½in (3.95m).
wing area 387.50sq ft (36.00sq m).
Power plant: One Tumansky turbojet

rated at 14,109/24,250lb
(6,400/11,000kg) st.
Armament: One 23mm GSh–23
cannon plus two Apex and two Aphid
AAMs.
Variants:
MiG–23U (Flogger–C): Two-seat
strike-trainer.
MiG–27(?) (Flogger–D): Single-seat
strike-fighter.
MiG–23 (Flogger–E) and MiG–27
(Flogger–F): Simplified export versions
of MiG–23S (Flogger–B) and MiG–27
(Flogger–D) resp.
First flights: Prototype: 1967.
Production: Series production from
1971; over 1,000 delivered to date.
In service: Egypt (UAR), Iraq, Libya,
Syria, USSR.

Mikoyan MiG–27 (Flogger–D).
Type: Single-seat strike-fighter.
Details as for Flogger–B with the
following exceptions:
Weights:
empty 17,640lb (8,000kg).
normal 35,270lb (16,000kg).
Performance:
maximum speed at 36,000ft (11,000m)
(Mach 1.6).
ferry range 2,550 miles (4,100km).
Power plant: One Tumansky jet
engine rated at 14,990/19,840lb
(6,800/9,000kg) st.
Armament: One 23mm cannon and
max 6,614lb (3,000kg) weapon load on
4 hard points; e.g. four 550lb (250kg)
bombs.

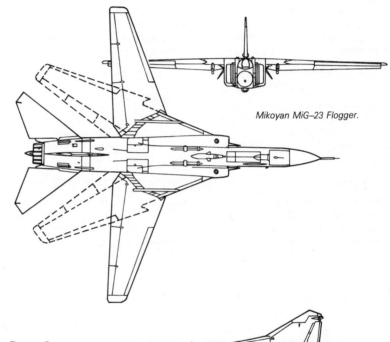

Mikoyan MiG–23 Flogger.

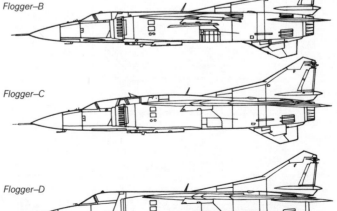

Flogger–B

Flogger–C

Flogger–D

Mikoyan MiG–25 (Foxbat–A).

Type: Single-seat all-weather fighter.
Weights:
empty 44,100lb (20,000kg).
maximum 77,160lb (35,000kg).
Performance:
maximum speed at 39,375ft (12,000m)
 (Mach 2.8).
maximum speed at 5,000ft (1,500m)
 (Mach 1.3).
range 1,240 miles (2,000km).
time to 36,000ft (11,000m) 2min 30sec.
service ceiling 72,180ft (22,000m).
Dimensions:
wing span 45ft 11¼in (14.00m).
length overall 73ft 2in (22.30m).
height overall 18ft 4½in (5.60m).
wing area 602.8sq ft (56.00sq m).
Power plant: Two Tumansky R–266
 turbojets each rated at
 16,755/24,250lb (7,600/11,000kg) st.
Armament: Two or four Anab AAMs
 and one weapon pod with one 23mm
 GSh–23 cannon under fuselage.
Variants:
MiG–25R (Foxbat–B): Single-seat
 unarmed reconnaissance aircraft, max
 speed at 39,375ft (12,000m) Mach
 3.2.
MiG–25U (Foxbat–C): Two-seat
 strike-trainer.
E–266: Speed-record aircraft.
First flights: Prototype: 1963–64.
Production: Approx 400 built
 1970/71–75.
In service: USSR.

Mil MI–1 and Mi–3 (Hare).

Type: Light AOP and transport
 helicopter.
Weights:
empty 4,107lb (1,863kg).
normal 5,200lb (2,358kg).
maximum 5,622lb (2,550kg).
Performance:
maximum speed at sea level 105mph
 (170km/hr).
maximum speed at 6,560ft (2,000m)
 96mph (155km/hr).
maximum cruising speed up to 3,280ft
 (1,000m) 84mph (135km/hr).
range 217 miles (350km).
ferry range 360 miles (580km).
initial rate of climb 21.3ft/sec
 (6.5m/sec).
service ceiling 14,765ft (4,500m).
hovering ceiling in ground effect
 10,830ft (3,300m).
hovering ceiling out of ground effect
 6,560ft (2,000m).
Dimensions:
main rotor diameter 46ft 0½in (14.34m).
length of fuselage 39ft 9in (12.11m).
height 10ft 9¾in (3.30m).
Power plant: One 575hp Ivchenko
 AI–26V piston engine.
Payload: 1 man crew and 3 troops or 2
 stretcher cases and 1 medic or max
 397lb (180kg) freight.
Variants:
Mi–1U: Training helicopter.
Mi–1T, Mi–1NCH and Mi–1 Moskvich:
 Civil variants.
Mi–3: Further development of Mi–1.
SM–1: Polish licence-built Mi–1.
SM–2: Polish further development.
First flights: Prototype: September
 1948.
Production:
Mi–1: Series production from 1950–63.
SM–1: Series production from
 1957–63.

SM–2: Series production from 1964–.
In service: Afghanistan, Albania,
 Algeria(?), Bulgaria, China (People's
 Republic), Cuba, Czechoslovaka, Egypt
 (UAR), Germany (East), Hungary, Iraq,
 Korea (North), Mongolia (People's
 Republic), Poland (also SM–1, SM–2),
 Romania, USSR, Vietnam, Yemen.

Mil Mi–2 (Hoplite).

Type: Light transport helicopter.
Weights:
empty 5,180lb (2,350kg).
normal 7,826lb (3,550kg).
maximum 8,157lb (3,700kg).
Performance:
maximum speed at 1,640ft (500m)
 130mph (210km/hr).
maximum cruising speed 124mph
 (200km/hr).
range w.m.p. 105 miles (170km).
ferry range 360 miles (580km).
initial rate of climb 14.8ft/sec
 (4.5m/sec).
service ceiling 13,120ft (4,000m).
hovering ceiling in ground effect 6,560ft
 (2,000m).
hovering ceiling out of ground effect
 3,280ft (1,000m).
Dimensions:
main rotor diameter 47ft 6¾in (14.50m).
length of fuselage 37ft 4¾in (11.40m).
height 11ft 4in (3.45m).
Power plant: Two 400hp Isotov
 GTD–350 turboshafts.
Armament: Optional: four Sagger
 ASMs.
Payload: 1 man crew and 6–8 troops
 or 4 stretcher cases and 1 medic or
 max 1,543lb (700kg) freight.
Variants: Civil versions.

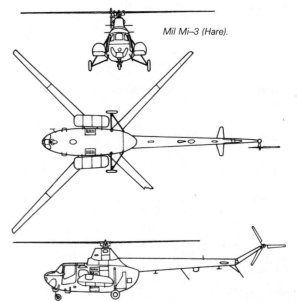

Mil Mi–3 (Hare).

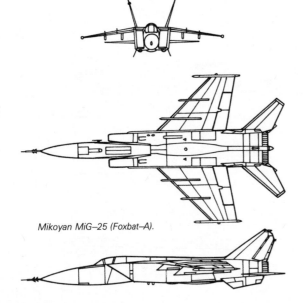

Mikoyan MiG–25 (Foxbat–A).

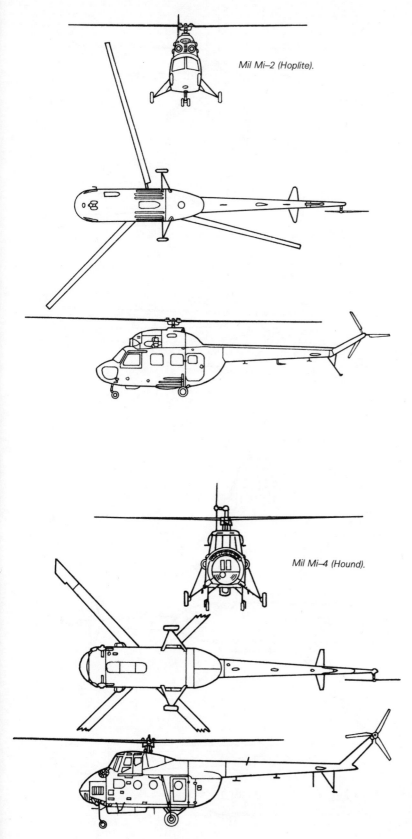

Mil Mi–2 (Hoplite).

Mil Mi–4 (Hound).

First flights: Prototype: 1961.
Production: Series production from 1963; licence-built in Poland (WSK/Mil Mi–2) from 1965.
In service: Bulgaria, Czechoslovakia, Germany (East), Hungary, Poland, Romania, Somali, Soviet Union, Syria.

Mil Mi–4 (Hound).
Type: Medium transport and ASW helicopter.
Weights:
empty 10,803lb (4,900kg).
normal 15,763lb (7,150kg).
maximum 16,645lb (7,550kg).
Performance:
maximum speed at sea level 115mph (185km/hr).
maximum cruising speed 99mph (160km/hr).
range w.m.p. 124 miles (200km).
ferry range 255 miles (410km).
initial rate of climb 16.4ft/sec (5.0m/sec).
service ceiling 16,400ft (5,000m).
hovering ceiling in ground effect 5,578ft (1,700m).
Dimensions:
main rotor diameter 68ft 11in (21.00m).
length of fuselage 55ft 1in (16.79m).
height 17ft 0in (5.18m).
Power plant: One 1,700hp Shvetsov ASh–82V piston engine.
Armament: Optional: One 12.7mm TKP machine-gun in under-fuselage gondola.
Payload: 2–3 man crew and 8–14 troops or 8 stretcher cases and 1 medic or max 2,650lb (1,200kg) freight.
Variants:
Mi–4A, Mi–4P, Mi–4S: Civil versions.
First flights: Prototype: August 1952.
Production: Over 3,000 built 1953–64, licence-built in China from 1958–59.
In service: Afghanistan, Albania, Algeria, Bulgaria, Burma, China (People's Republic), Cuba, Czechoslovakia, Egypt (UAR), Finland, Germany (East), Hungary, India, Indonesia, Iraq, Korea (North), Mali(?), Mongolia (People's Republic), Poland, Romania, Somali, South Yemen(?), Sudan, Syria, USSR, Vietnam, Yemen, Yugoslavia.

Mil Mi–6 (Hook).
Type: Heavy transport helicopter.
Weights:
empty 60,055lb (27,240kg).
normal 85,675lb (40,500kg).
maximum 93,500lb (42,500kg).
Performance:
maximum speed at 3,280ft (1,000m) 186mph (300km/hr).
maximum cruising speed 155mph (250km/hr).

range with 17,640lb (8,000kg) payload
385 miles (620km).
range with 9,920lb (4,500kg) payload
620 miles (1,000km).
ferry range 900 miles (1,450km).
service ceiling 14,750ft (4,500m).
Dimensions:
main rotor diameter 114ft 10in
(35.00m).
length of fuselage 108ft 9½in (33.16m).
height 32ft 4in (9.86m).
Power plant: Two 5,500hp Soloview
D–25V turboshafts.
Payload: 5 man crew and 65–70
troops or 41 stretcher cases and 2
medics or max 26,450lb (12,000kg)
freight.
Variants: Mi–6P: Civil version.
First flights: Prototype: 1957.
Production: 5 prototypes and 30
pre-production models, over 500(?)
production models built 1959–60.
In service: Egypt (UAR), Indonesia,
USSR, Vietnam, Zambia(?).

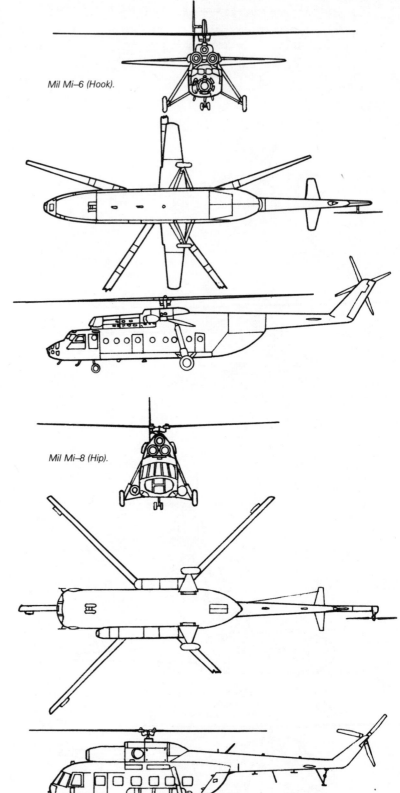

Mil Mi–6 (Hook).

Mil Mi–8 (Hip).

Mil Mi–8 (Hip).
Type: Medium transport helicopter.
Weights:
empty 15,829lb (7,180kg).
normal 24,470lb (11,100kg).
maximum 26,455lb (12,000kg).
Performance:
maximum speed at sea level 155mph
(250km/hr).
maximum cruising speed 140mph
(225km/hr).
range with 6,615lb (3,000kg) payload
264 miles (425km).
ferry range 590 miles (950km).
service ceiling 14,760ft (4,500m).
hovering ceiling in ground effect 5,900ft
(1,800m).
hovering ceiling out of ground effect
2,625ft (800m).
Dimensions:
main rotor diameter 69ft 10½in (21.29m).
length of fuselage 60ft 0¾in (18.31m).
height 18ft 4½in (5.60m).
Power plant: Two 1,500hp Isotov
TB–2–117A turboshafts.
Armament: Optional four rocket
launchers each containing eight 55mm
rockets.
Payload: 2–3 man crew and 28 troops
or 12 stretcher cases and 1 medic or
max 8,820lb (4,000kg) freight.
Variants: Civil versions.
V–14: Float version.
First flights:
Prototype: 1961 (1 power plant only).
Production: Series production from
1964, over 1,200 delivered up to end
1975.
In service: Afghanistan, Algeria,
Bangladesh, Bulgaria, Cuba,
Czechoslovakia, Egypt (UAR), Ethiopia,

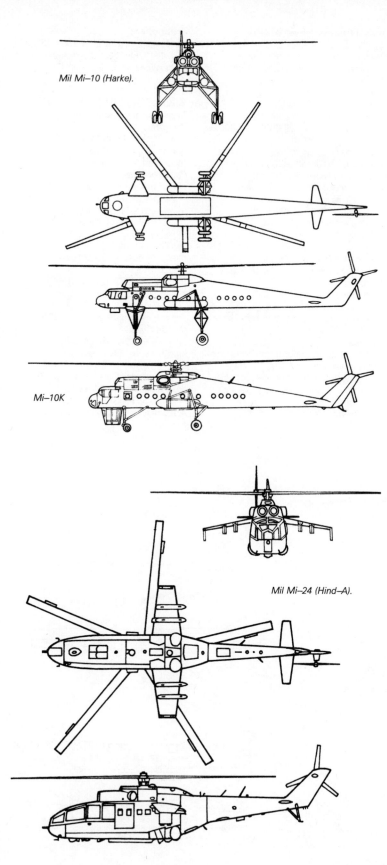

Mil Mi–10 (Harke).

Mi–10K

Mil Mi–24 (Hind–A).

Finland, Germany (East), Hungary, Iraq, Korea (North), Libya, Laos, Pakistan, Peru, Poland, Romania, Somali, South Yemen, Sudan, Syria, USSR, Yugoslavia.

Mil Mi–10 (Harke).

Type: Heavy flying-crane helicopter.
Weights:
empty 60,186lb (27,300kg).
maximum 95,790lb (43,450kg).
Performance:
maximum speed at sea level 124mph (200km/hr).
maximum cruising speed 112mph (180km/hr).
range with 26,455lb (12,000kg) payload 155 miles (250km).
ferry range 391 miles (630km).
service ceiling 9,850ft (3,000m).
Dimensions:
main rotor diameter 114ft 10in (35.00m).
length of fuselage 10ft 9¾in (32.86m).
height 32ft 6in (9.90m).
Power plant: Two 5,500hp Soloview D–25V turboshafts.
Payload: 2–3 man crew and 28 troops or max 33,070lb (15,000kg) external freight.
Variants: Mi–10K: Further development.
First flights: Prototype: 1960.
Production:
Mi–10: Series production 1960–61.
In service: USSR.

Mil Mi–10K (Harke).

Type: Heavy flying-crane helicopter.
Details as for Mi–10 (Harke) with the following exceptions:
Weights:
empty 54,410lb (24,680kg).
maximum 83,776lb (38,000kg).
Performance:
maximum speed at sea level 155mph (250km/hr).
maximum cruising speed 124mph (200km/hr).
ferry range 494 miles (795(?)km).
Dimensions:
height overall 25ft 7in (7.80m).
Payload: 2–3 man crew and 28 troops or max 24,250lb (11,000kg) external freight.
First flights: Mi–10K: 1965.
Production: Series production from 1969.

Mil Mi–24 (Hind–A).

Type: Attack helicopter.
Weights:
empty 10,360lb (4,700kg).
maximum 18,520lb (8,400kg).

Performance:
maximum speed 193mph (310km/hr).
maximum cruising speed 183mph (295km/hr).
radius of action 56–225 miles (90–360km).
range 310 miles (500km).
initial rate of climb 28.87ft/sec (8.8m/sec).
hovering ceiling in ground effect 14,760ft (4,500m).
hovering ceiling out of ground effect 72,180ft (2,200m).
Dimensions:
main rotor diameter 55ft 11½in (17.05m).
length of fuselage 63ft 3¾in (19.30m).
height 13ft 11¼in (20ft 6in?) (4.25m) (6.25m?).
Power plant: Two 1,500hp Gluchenko GTD–3F mod turboshafts.
Armament: One 127mm UBK machine-gun with 250rpg in nose, four Sagger or Swatter anti-tank guided missiles and four rocket launchers each containing thirty-two 57mm rockets.
Payload: 2 man crew and 8–12 troops or max 6,393lb (2,900kg) freight.
First flights: Prototype: 1970(?).
Production:
Series production from 1972.
In service: USSR.

Myasishchev M–4 'Molot' (Bison).
Type: Strategic heavy bomber and reconnaissance aircraft, 6–8 man crew.
Weights:
maximum 352,740lb (160,000kg).
Performance:
maximum speed at 36,000ft (11,000m) 559mph (900km/hr).
maximum cruising speed at 36,000ft (11,000m) 519mph (835km/hr).
range 6,990 miles (11,250km).
service ceiling 44,950ft (13,700m).
Dimensions:
wing span 167ft 3¾in (51.00m).
length overall 159ft 1¼in (48.50m).
height overall 42ft 0in (12.80m).
wing area 3,229.2sq ft (300.00sq m).
Power plant: Four Mikulin AM–3D turbojets each rated at 19,180lb (8,700kg) st.
Armament: Six 23mm NR–23 cannon set in pairs, max 26,455lb (12,000kg) weapon load, e.g. bombs, rockets or ASMs.
Variants:
Tanker transport variants (conversions of bombers from 1963).
201–M Molot: Further development with more powerful D–15 engines (each of 28,660lb (13,000kg) st).
First flights: Prototype: 1953.

Production:
M–4: Approx 150 built 1954–56.
201–M: Only a limited number built?
In service: M–4, 201–M: USSR.

Sukhoi Su–7BM (Fitter–A).
Type: Single-seat strike-fighter.
Weights:
empty 19,004lb (8,620kg).
normal 26,450lb (12,000kg).
maximum 29,797lb (13,425kg).
Performance:
maximum speed at 39,375ft (12,000m) (Mach 1.7) (1,700km/hr).
maximum speed at 980ft (300m) (Mach 0.95) 720mph (1,160km/hr).
maximum cruising speed at 985ft (300m) 528mph (850km/hr).
radius of action 120–285 miles (320–460km).
ferry range 900 miles (1,450km).
initial rate of climb 492.1ft/sec (150.0m/sec).
service ceiling 49,210ft (15,000m).
Dimensions:
wing span 29ft 3½in (8.93m).
length overall 56ft 0in (17.00m).
height overall 15ft 5in (4.70m).
Power plant: One Lyulka AL–7F–1 turbojet rated at 14,198lb (6,440kg)/22,046lb (10,000kg) st.
Armament: Two 30mm NR–30 cannon

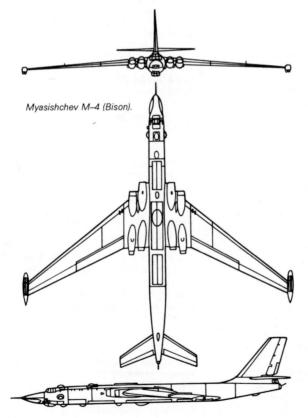

Myasishchev M–4 (Bison).

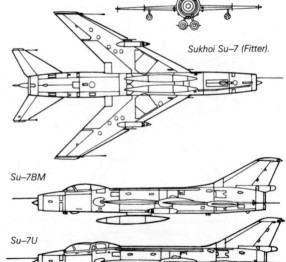

Sukhoi Su–7 (Fitter).

Su–7BM

Su–7U

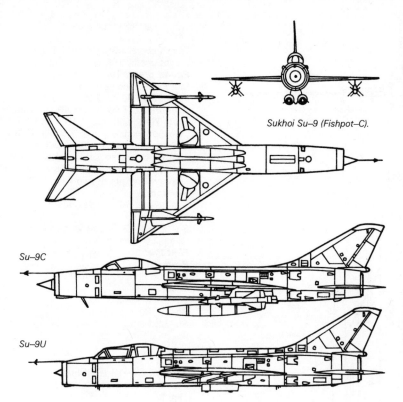

Sukhoi Su–9 (Fishpot–C).

Su–9C

Su–9U

Sukhoi Su–15 (Flagon–A).

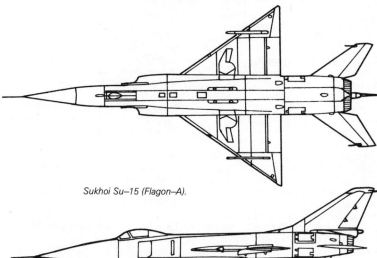

with 70rpg and max 2,200lb (1,000kg) weapon load on 4 hard points, e.g. two 1,100lb (500kg) or 550lb (250kg) bombs and two rocket launchers each containing sixteen 55mm unguided rockets.

Variants:
Su–7U (Moujik): Two-seat strike-fighter.
Su–17 (Fitter–C): Single-seat strike-fighter with variable geometry wings.

First flights:
Prototype: 1955.

Production: Series production from 1958.

In service: Afghanistan, Algeria, Cuba, Czechoslovakia, Egypt (UAR), Germany (East), Hungary, India (Su–7BMK), Iraq, Korea (North), Poland, Romania, Syria, USSR, Vietnam(?).

Sukhoi Su–9 (Fishpot–C).

Type: Single-seat all-weather fighter.
Weights:
normal 25,353lb (11,500kg).
maximum 28,660–29,983lb (13,000–13,600kg).

Performance:
maximum speed at 39,375ft (12,000m) (Mach 1.8) 1,190mph (1,915km/hr).
maximum cruising speed at 36,000ft (11,000m) 571mph (920km/hr).
radius of action 310 miles (500km).
initial rate of climb 449.4ft/sec (137.0m/sec).
time to 39,375ft (12,000m) 4min 30sec.
service ceiling 55,770ft (17,000m).

Dimensions:
wing span 27ft 8¾in (9.45m).
length overall 54ft 11¾in (16.76m).
height overall 16ft 0¼in (4.88m).
wing area 425.1sq ft (39.50sq m).

Power plant: One Tumansky TRD–31 turbojet rated at 14,198lb (6,440kg)/22,046lb (10,000kg) st.

Armament: Four Alkali AAMs or two Anab AAMs.

Variants:
Su–9UTI (Maiden): Two-seat strike-trainer.

First flights: Prototype: 1955.

Production: Series production 1959–69/70, several series.

In service: USSR.

Sukhoi Su–15 (Flagon–A).

Type: Single-seat all-weather fighter.
Weights:
normal 35,270–39,680lb (16,000–18,000kg).

Performance:
maximum speed at 39,375ft (12,000m) (Mach 2.5) 1,650mph (2,655km/hr).
maximum speed at 980ft (300m) (Mach 1.2) 910mph (1,465km/hr).
ferry range 1,490 miles (2,400km).
service ceiling: 65,000ft (19,800m).

Dimensions:
wing span 31ft 2in (9.50m).

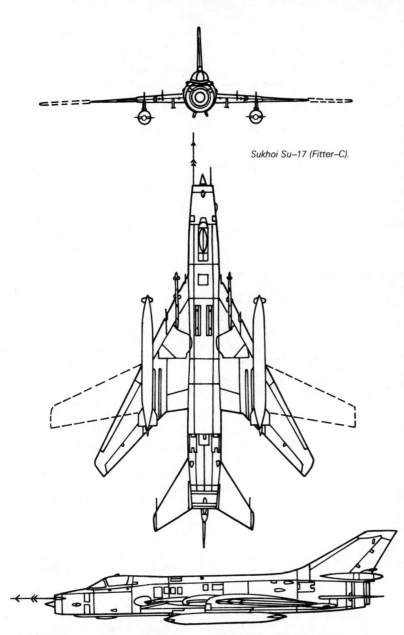

Sukhoi Su–17 (Fitter–C).

length overall 70ft 6¼in (21.50m).
height overall 16ft 5in (5.00m).
Power plant: Two Lyulka AL–21F
turbojets each rated at
17,195/24,690lb (7,800/11,200kg) st.
Armament: Two Anab AAMs.
Variants:
Flagon–B: STOL fighter with three
additional lift-jet engines in fuselage
(experimental model?).
Flagon–C: Two-seat strike-trainer.
Flagon–D, E: Improved series.
First flights: Prototype: 1964–65.
Production: Series production from
1968(?), over 400(?) delivered to date,
monthly production of 15(?) aircraft.

In service: USSR.

Sukhoi Su–17 (Fitter–C).
Type: Single-seat strike-fighter.
Weights:
empty 19,840lb (9,000kg).
normal 32,630lb (14,800kg).
maximum 39,020lb (17,700kg).
Performance:
maximum speed at 39,375ft (12,000m)
(Mach 2.17) 1,430mph (2,300km/hr).
maximum speed at sea level (Mach
1.06) 808mph (1,300km/hr).
radius of action 260–370 miles
(420–600km).
ferry range 1,420 miles (2,280km).
time to 36,000ft (11,000m) 12min 0sec.
service ceiling 10,874ft (17,500m).
Dimensions:
wing span (spread) 44ft 11½in (13.70m).

wing span (fully swept) 32ft 5¾in
(9.90m).
length overall 43ft 10¼in (13.37m).
height overall 15ft 5in (4.70m).
Power plant: Two Lyulka Al–21–F3
turbojets each rated at
17,196/24,690lb (7,800/11,200kg) st.
Armament: Two 30mm NR–30 cannon
with 70rpg and max 7,720lb (3,500kg)
weapon load, e.g. two 1,653lb (750kg)
bombs and four 1,100lb (500kg)
bombs or two rocket launchers each
with sixteen 55mm or 160mm, or four
240mm rockets or two Kerry ASMs.
Variants:
Su–7 (Fitter–A): Single-seat
strike-fighter.
Su–20, Su–22: Export versions with
simplified electronics.
First flights: Prototype: 1966(?).
Production:
Series production from 1971.
In service:
Su–17: USSR.
Su–20: Poland, Syria.
Su–22: Peru.

Sukhoi Su–19 (Fencer).
Type: Two-seat strike-fighter and
fighter.
Weights:
empty 35,270lb (16,000kg).
maximum 68,340lb (31,000kg).
Performance:
maximum speed at 36,000ft (11,000m)
(Mach 2.3) 1,525mph (2,455km/hr).
maximum speed at sea level (Mach 1.1)
830mph (1,335km/hr).
maximum cruising speed at sea level
(Mach 0.85) 650mph (1,045km/hr).
radius of action 155–250 miles
(250–400km).
range 810 miles (1,300km).
service ceiling 52,500ft (16,000m).
Dimensions:
wing span (spread) 65ft 7½in (20.00m).
wing span (fully swept) 39ft 4½in
(12.00m).
length overall 73ft 0in (22.50m).
height overall 15ft 1in (4.60m).
Power plant: Two jet engines each
rated at 33,950/49,383lb
(15,400/22,400kg) st.
Armament: One 23mm GSh–23
cannon and (as fighter) max 9,920lb
(4,500kg) weapon load on 6 hard
points, e.g. four ASMs, or (as fighter)
four AAMs.
First flights: Prototype: 1968(?).
Production:
Series production from 1974(?).
In service: USSR.

Tupolev Tu–16 (Badger–A).
Type: Medium bomber and
reconnaissance aircraft, 7 man crew.
Weights:

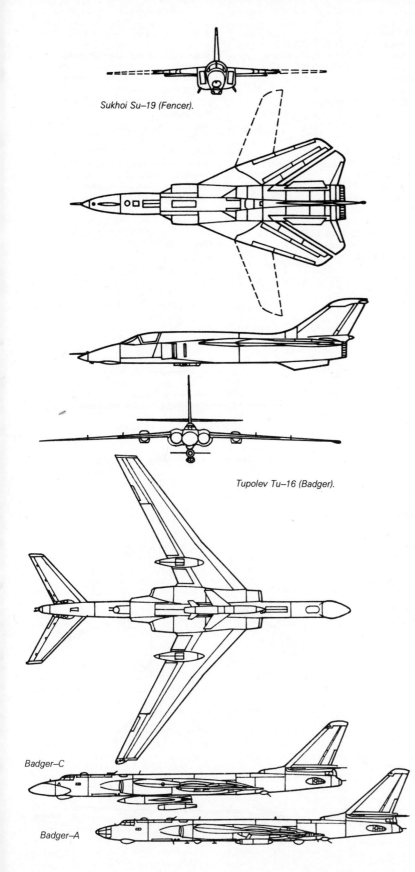

Sukhoi Su–19 (Fencer).

Tupolev Tu–16 (Badger).

Badger–C

Badger–A

empty 115,740lb (52,500kg).
normal 149,910lb (68,000kg).
maximum 169,757lb (77,000kg).
Performance:
maximum speed at 35,000ft (10,700m)
 (Mach 0.87) 587mph (945km/hr).
maximum cruising speed at 32,800ft
 (10,000m) 490mph (790km/hr).
range with 6,600lb (3,000kg) payload
 4,000 miles (6,400km).
range w.m.p. 3,000 miles (4,800km).
service ceiling 42,650ft (13,000m).
Dimensions:
wing span 110ft 0in (33.50m).
length overall 119ft 9in (36.50m).
height overall 35ft 6in (10.80m).
wing area 1,814sq ft (168.60sq m).
Power plant: Two Mikulin AM–3M
 turbojets each rated at 20,950lb
 (9,500kg) st.
Armament: Six flexible 23mm cannon
 in turrets, one fixed 23mm cannon in
 fuselage, and (Badger–A) max
 19,800lb (9,000kg) weapon load (e.g.
 bombs), or (Badger–B, G): two Kennel
 or Kelt ASMs underwing; or
 (Badger–C): one Kipper ASM stand-off
 bomb mounted beneath the fuselage.
Variants:
Badger–B, C and G: with ASMs.
Badger–D, E, F: with additional
 electronic equipment, mounted partly
 in underwing pods.
First flights: Prototype: 1954.
Production: Over 2,000 built from
 1955; approx 60 manufactured in
 China (People's Republic) 1968–74/75.
In service: China (People's Republic),
 Egypt (UAR), Indonesia, Iraq, USSR.

Tupolev Tu–20 (Bear–A).
Type: Strategic heavy bomber and
 reconnaissance aircraft, 6–8 man
 crew.
Weights:
empty 198,416lb (90,000kg).
maximum 339,500lb (154,000kg).
Performance:
maximum speed at 41,000ft (12,500m)
 (Mach 0.76) 500mph (805km/hr).
maximum speed at 11,480ft (3,500m)
 (Mach 0.83) 540mph (870km/hr).
maximum cruising speed at 32,800ft
 (10,000m) 470mph (756km/hr).
range 7,800 miles (12,550km).
ferry range 9,320 miles (15,000km).
initial rate of climb 137.8ft/sec
 (42.0m/sec).
service ceiling 44,300ft (13,500m).
Dimensions:
wing span 159ft 1½in (48.50m).
length overall 155ft 10in (47.50m).
height overall 44ft 0in (13.50m).
wing area 3,149.5sq ft (292.60sq m).
Power plant: Four 14,750hp Kusnetsov
 NK–12M turboprops.
Armament:
Bear–A: One fixed 23mm cannon in

starboard nose, two fuselage turrets and one tail position each with two 23mm NR–23 cannon and max 26,500lb (12,000kg) weapon load.

Variants:
Bear–B: Strategic bomber with one Kangaroo ASM.
Bear–C, D, E, F: Strategic maritime-reconnaissance aircraft.
Tu–114 (Cleat): Airliner.

First flights: Prototype: 1954.

Production:
Bear–A: Approx 300 built 1956–60, from 1961 conversions to Bear–B, from 1964 to Bear–C and 1966–67 to Bear–D, E and F.
Tu–114: Over 31 built(?).

In service: USSR.

Tupolev Tu–126 (Moss).

Type: Early warning and reconnaissance aircraft, over 20 man crew.

Weights:
empty 253,532lb (115,000kg).
normal 360,000lb (163,300kg).
maximum 174,800lb (170,000kg).

Performance:
patrol speed at 19,685ft (6,000m) 404mph (650km/hr).
ferry range 3,980 miles (6,400km).
time to 36,090ft (11,000m) 35min 0sec.
initial rate of climb 36.1ft/sec (11.00m/sec).
service ceiling 39,040ft (11,900m).

Dimensions:
wing span 168ft 0in (51.20m).
length overall 188ft 0in (57.30m).
height overall 51ft 0in (15.50m).
wing area 3,349sq ft (311.10sq m).

Power plant: Four 14,795hp Kusnetsov NK–12MV turboprops.

First flights: Prototype: 1966(?).

Production: Series production from 1968(?), over 20(40?) delivered from 1970(?).

In service: USSR.

Tupolev Tu–22 (Blinder–A).

Type: Medium bomber and reconnaissance aircraft, 3 man crew.

Weights:
maximum 185,188lb (84,000kg).

Performance:
maximum speed at 39,375ft (12,000m) (Mach 1.5) 988mph (1,590km/hr).
maximum speed at 1,000ft (300m) (Mach 0.95) 720mph (1,160km/hr).
maximum cruising speed at 39,375ft (12,000m) (Mach 0.9) 596mph (960km/hr).
radius of action 696 miles (1,120km).
ferry range 4,850 miles (7,800km).
service ceiling 60,000ft (18,300m).

Dimensions:
wing span 91ft 0in (27.74m).
length overall 132ft 10½in (40.50m).
height overall 17ft 0in (5.18m).
wing area 2,030sq ft (188.60sq m).

Power plant: Two turbojets each rated

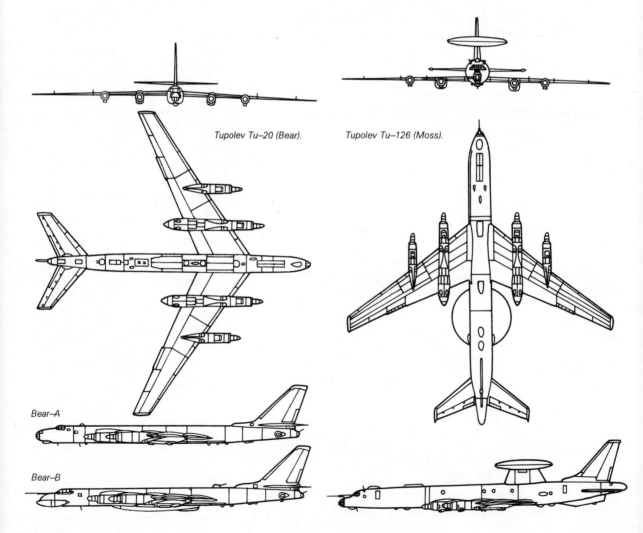

Tupolev Tu–20 (Bear).

Tupolev Tu–126 (Moss).

Bear–A

Bear–B

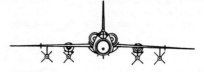

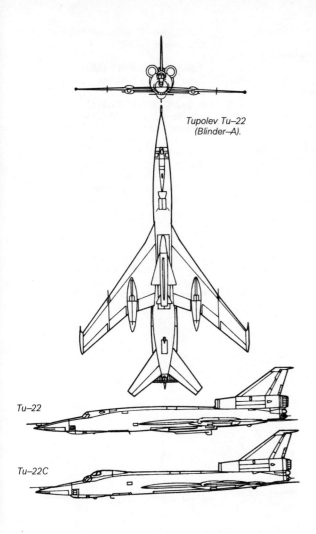

Tupolev Tu–22
(Blinder–A).

Tupolev Tu–28P
(Fiddler).

Tu–22

Tu–22C

at 27,006lb (12,250kg) st.

Armament: One 23mm cannon in tail
position, bombs and ASMs of max
22,000lb (10,000kg).

Variants:
Blinder–B: Bomber with Kitchen ASMs.
Blinder–C: Maritime-reconnaissance
and ECM aircraft.
Tu–22U (Blinder–D): Bomber trainer.
First flights: Prototype: 1960.
Production: 200(250?) built
1963/64–75(?).
In service: Libya, USSR (from 1965).

Tupolev Tu–28P (Fiddler).
Type: Two-seat all-weather fighter and
reconnaissance aircraft.
Weights:
normal 78,044lb (35,400kg).
maximum 96,011lb (43,550kg).

Performance:
maximum speed at 39,375ft (12,000m)
(Mach 1.65) 1,084mph (1,745km/hr).
radius of action 900–1,100 miles
(1,450–1,770km).
ferry range 3,107 miles (5,000km).
service ceiling 52,490ft
(16,000m).
Dimensions:
wing span 64ft 11½in (19.80m).
length overall 90ft 0in (27.43m).
height overall 22ft 11½in (7.00m).
wing area 807.3sq ft (75.00sq m).
Power plant: Two turbojets each rated
at 24,251lb (11,000kg) st.
Armament: Four Ash AAMs.
First flights: Prototype: 1957.
Production:
Series production 1959–68/69.
In service: USSR.

Tupolev Tu–124 (Cookpot).
Type: Medium transport.
Weights:
empty 50,485lb (22,500kg).
normal 80,470lb (36,500kg).
maximum 83,775lb (38,000kg).
Performance:
maximum speed at 26,250ft (8,000m)
603mph (970km/hr).
maximum cruising speed at 32,800ft
(10,000m) 540mph (870km/hr).
range w.m.p. 746 miles (1,200km).
ferry range 1,305 miles (2,100km).
service ceiling 38,390ft (11,700m).
Dimensions:
wing span 83ft 9½in (25.55m).
length overall 100ft 4in (30.58m).
height overall 26ft 6in (8.08m).
wing area 1,281sq ft (119.00sq m).
Power plant:

Two Soloviev D–20P turbojets each
rated at 11,905lb (5,400kg) st.
Payload: 3–4 man crew and 44–56
troops or max 13,290lb (6,000kg)
freight.
Variants: Civil versions.
First flights: Prototype: June 1960.
Production: Approx 120 built 1961–66,
nearly all as civil versions.
In service: Germany (East), India, Iraq,
USSR.

Tupolev Tu–26(?) (Backfire–B).
Type: Heavy bomber, 3 man crew.
Weights:
empty 114,640lb (52,000kg).
maximum 286,600lb (130,000kg).
Performance:
maximum speed at 36,000ft (11,000m)
(Mach 2.0) 1,320mph (2,125km/hr).
maximum speed at sea level (Mach 0.9)
700mph (1,125km/hr).
maximum cruising speed (Mach 0.82).
radius of action 1,555 miles (2,500km).

ferry range 4,470–6,910 miles (?)
(7,200–11,120km)(?).
initial rate of climb 459.3ft/sec
(140.0m/sec).
time to 36,000ft (11,000m) 22min 0sec.
service ceiling 59,050ft (18,000m).
Dimensions:
wing span (spread) 113ft 2¼in (34.50m).
wing span (fully swept) 90ft 2½in
(27.50m).
length overall 139ft 5¼in (42.50m).
height overall 28ft 10½in (8.80m).
wing area 1,447.76/1,808.35sq ft
(134.5/168.0sq m).
Power plant: Two Kusnetsov NK–144
turbojets each rated at
33,070/46,300lb (15,000/21,000kg) st.
Armament: One 30mm cannon in tail
position and max 22,050lb (10,000kg)
weapon load in fuselage bay, e.g.
fifteen 1,102lb (500kg) bombs or two
ASM–6 ASMs.
First flights: Prototype: 1969(1970?).
Production: Series production from

1972, over 80 delivered to date.
In service: USSR.

Yakovlev Yak–11 (Moose).
Type: Two-seat trainer.
Weights:
empty 4,190lb (1,900kg).
maximum 5,290lb (2,400kg).
Performance:
maximum speed at sea level 262mph
(423km/hr).
maximum speed at 7,380ft (2,250m)
286mph (460km/hr).
maximum cruising speed 205mph
(330km/hr).
ferry range 795 miles (1,280km).
service ceiling 23,300ft (7,100m).
Dimensions:
wing span 30ft 10in (9.40m).
length overall 27ft 10¾in (8.50m).
height overall 10ft 9¼in (3.28m).
wing area 166sq ft (15.40sq m).
Power plant: One 730hp Shvetsov
ASh–21 piston engine.

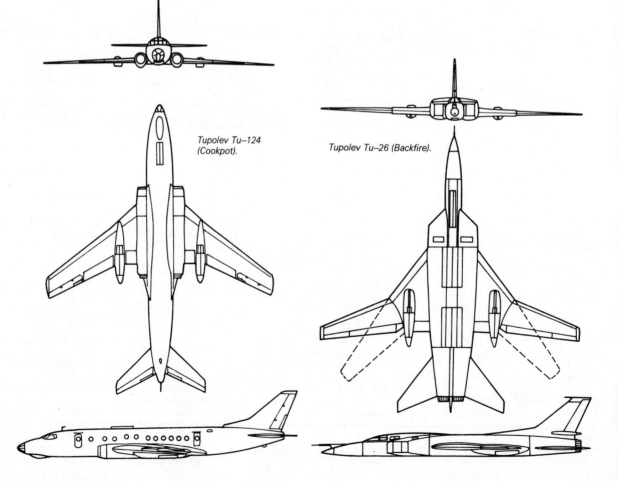

Tupolev Tu–124
(Cookpot).

Tupolev Tu–26 (Backfire).

Yakovlev Yak–11 (Moose).

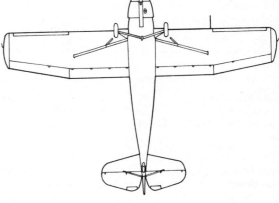

Yakovlev Yak–12A (Creek–D).

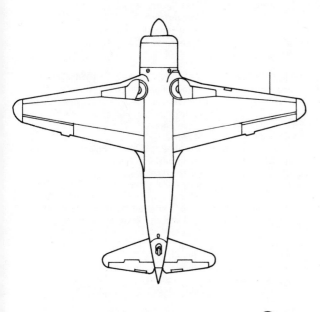

Armament: One 7.62mm or 12.7mm
  UBS machine-gun and two 112lb
  (50kg) practice bombs underwing.

Variants:
C.11U: Czechoslovakian licence-built by
  Let, with tricycle undercarriage.
First flights: Prototype: 1946.
Production: 3,859 built from 1946,
  licence-built in Czechoslovakia (approx
  700 1952–56).
In service: Afghanistan, Albania,
  Algeria, Bulgaria, China (People's
  Republic), Czechoslovakia (C.11U),
  Egypt (UAR), Germany (East),
  Hungary, Iraq, Korea (North), Mongolia
  (People's Republic), Poland, Romania,
  Somali, Syria, USSR, Vietnam,
  Yemen.

Yakovlev Yak–12A (Creek–D).
Type: Liaison and AOP aircraft.
Weights:
empty 2,330lb (1,059kg).
maximum 3,494lb (1,588kg).
Performance:
maximum speed 133mph (214km/hr).
maximum cruising speed 112mph
  (180km/hr).
range 472 miles (760km).
ferry range 688 miles (1,070km).
initial rate of climb 11.8ft/sec
  (3.6m/sec).
service ceiling 15,090ft (4,600m).
Dimensions:
wing span 41ft 4in (12.60m).
length overall 29ft 6in (9.00m).
height overall 10ft 3in (3.12m).
wing area 233.6sq ft (21.70sq m).

Power plant:
One 240hp Ivchenko AI–14R piston
  engine.
Payload: 1 man crew and 2–3 troops
  or 1 stretcher case and 1 seated
  casualty plus 1 medic or max 660lb
  (300kg) freight.
Variants:
Yak–12 (Creek–A), Yak–12R (Creek–B),
  Yak–12M (Creek–C): Earlier versions.
PZL–101 'Gawron': Further
  development in Poland.
First flights:
Prototype Yak–12: 1944.
Yak–12A: 1957.
Prototype PZL–101: 1958.
Production:
Series production 1946–61, licence-built
  in Poland by PZL 1959–61.
PZL101: Series production from 1962.

In service: Germany (East), Mali(?), USSR, Yugoslavia(?).

Yakovlev Yak–18A.

Type: Two-seat trainer.
Weights:
empty 2,259lb (1,025kg).
normal 2,910lb (1,316kg).
Performance:
maximum speed 162mph (260km/hr).
ferry range 466 miles (705km).
initial rate of climb 17.4ft/sec
  (5.3m/sec).
service ceiling 16,601ft (5,060m).
Dimensions:
wing span 34ft 9¼in (10.60m).
length overall 27ft 4¾in (8.53m).
height overall 11ft 0in (3.35m).
wing area 183sq ft (17.00sq m).
Power plant: One 260hp Ivchenko
  AI–14R piston engine.
Variants:
Yak–18 (Max), Yak–18U: Earlier
  versions.
Yak–18 P and PM: Single-seat
  aerobatic versions.
Yak–18T: Further development.
First flights:
Prototype Yak–18: 1945.
Yak–18T: 1974.
Production:
Yak–18: from 1946–55.
Yak–18U: from 1955–57.
Yak–18A: from 1957–.

Yak–18T: from 1974–.
6,670 built of all variants.
In service: Afghanistan, Albania,
  Algeria, Bulgaria, China (People's
  Republic), Egypt (UAR), Germany
  (East), Guinea, Hungary, Iraq, Korea
  (North), Mali(?), Mongolia (People's
  Republic), Poland, Romania, Somali,
  Syria, USSR, Vietnam.

Yakovlev Yak–25F (Flashlight–A).

Type: Two-seat fighter.
Weights:
normal 20,280lb (9,200kg).
maximum 33,350lb (10,500kg).
Performance:
maximum speed at 36,000ft (11,00m)
  (Mach 0.09) 593mph (956km/hr).
maximum speed at sea level (Mach
  0.83) 630mph (1,015km/hr).
maximum cruising speed at 36,000ft
  (11,000m) (Mach 0.75) 497mph
  (800km/hr).
radius of action 600 miles (965km).
ferry range 1,864 miles (3,000km).
initial rate of climb 163.4ft/sec
  (49.8m/sec).
service ceiling 50,900ft (15,500m).
Dimensions:
wing span 36ft 1in (11.00m).
length overall 51ft 4½in (15.66m).
height overall 12ft 5¾in (3.80m).
wing area 311.49sq ft (28.94sq m).
Power plant: Two Tumansky RD–9
  turbojets each rated at 5,732/7,275lb

(2,600/3,300kg) st.
Armament: Two 37mm NS–37 cannon
  and two (four?) AAMs or four rocket
  launchers with 55mm rockets.
Variants:
Yak–25R (Flashlight–B): Two-seat
  reconnaissance aircraft.
Yak–27P (Flashlight–C): Further
  development of Yak–25F, limited
  numbers only.
First flights: Prototype: 1953.
Production:
Series production from 1954.
In service: USSR.

Yakovlev Yak–27R (Mangrove).

Type: Two-seat reconnaissance
  aircraft.
Details as Yak–25F with the following
  exceptions:
Weights:
normal 22,000lb (9,980kg).
maximum 25,000lb (11,340kg).
Performance:
maximum speed at 36,000ft (11,000m)
  (Mach 0.95) 685mph (1,104km/hr).
maximum cruising speed at 36,000ft
  (11,000m) 600mph (917km/hr).
radius of action 500 miles (805km).
initial rate of climb 299.9ft/sec
  (91.4m/sec).
service ceiling 50,000ft (15,250m).
Dimensions:
wing span 36ft 1in (11.00m).

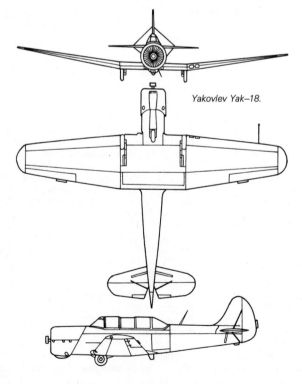

Yakovlev Yak–18.

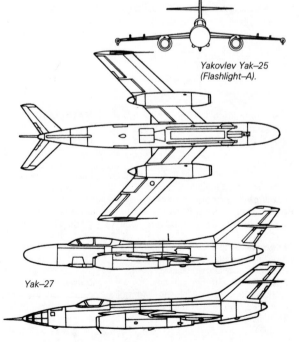

Yakovlev Yak–25
(Flashlight–A).

Yak–27

length overall 54ft 11¾in (16.76m).
height overall 12ft 5¾in (3.80m).
wing area 322.9sq ft (30.00sq m).
Power plant: Two Tumansky RD–9
turbojets each rated at 5,732/7,275lb
(2,600/3,300kg) st.
Armament:
One 30mm NR–30 cannon.
First flights: Prototype: 1956–57.
Production: Series production from
1959–, limited numbers only.
In service: USSR.

Yakovlev Yak–28 (Brewer).
Type: Two-seat light bomber and
reconnaissance aircraft.
Weights:
normal 35,270lb (16,000kg).
maximum 41,890lb (19,000kg).
Performance:
maximum speed at 39,370ft (12,000m)
(Mach 1.15) 761mph (1,225km/hr).
maximum speed at sea level (Mach
0.95) 725mph (1,167km/hr).
maximum cruising speed at 36,100ft
(11,00m) (Mach 0.9) 572mph
(920km/hr).
radius of action 230–310 miles
(370–500km).
ferry range 1,550 miles (2,500km).
initial rate of climb 466ft/sec
(142.0m/sec).
service ceiling 55,120ft (16,800m).

Dimensions:
wing span 41ft 0in (12.50m).
length overall 70ft 0in (21.34m).
height overall 13ft 0in (3.96m).
wing area 403.65sq ft (37.50sq m).
Power plant: Two Tumansky R–11
turbojets each rated at 10,141lb
(4,600kg) st.
Armament: One 30mm NR–30
cannon, max 4,410lb (2,000kg)
weapon load, e.g. two 1,100lb (500kg)
bombs in fuselage bomb bay and two
ASMs or bombs or four rocket
launchers each containing sixteen
55mm rockets underwing.
Variants:
Yak–28P (Firebar): Two-seat all-weather
fighter.
Yak–28R(Brewer–E): Two-seat
reconnaissance aircraft,
electronic-reconnaissance equipment
and auxiliary tanks in fuselage bay.
Yak–28U (Maestro): Two-seat bomber
trainer.
First flights: Prototype: 1960.
Production: Series production
1963/64–69/70(?).
In service: USSR.

Yakovlev Yak–28P (Firebar).
Type: Two-seat all-weather fighter.
Details as for Yak–28 with the following
exceptions:
Weights:

normal 37,480lb (17,000kg).
maximum 40,786lb (18,500kg).
Performance:
maximum speed with two Anab AAMs
696mph (1,220km/hr).
maximum cruising speed 559mph
(900km/hr).
radius of action 550 miles (885km).
Dimensions:
length overall 72ft 2in (22.00m).
Power plant: Two Tumansky R–11
turbojets each rated at 13,669lb
(6,200kg) st.
Armament: Two ANAB AAMs and (on
some aircraft) two Atoll AAMs.
In service: USSR.

Yakovlev Yak–36 (Forger).
Type: Single-seat ship-borne V/STOL
strike-fighter.
Weights:
empty 14,990lb (6,800kg).
with four Atoll AAMs 22,000lb
(9,980kg).
maximum 24,000lb (10,890kg).
Performance:
maximum speed at sea level (Mach
1.05).
radius of action 230–520 miles
(370–835km).
Dimensions:
wing span 22ft 11¾in (7.00m).
length overall 54ft 11½in (16.75m).
wing area 69.00sq ft (19.23sq m).
Power plant: One jet engine of

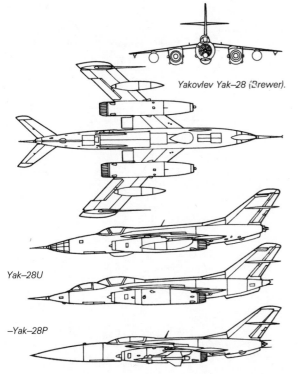

Yakovlev Yak–28 (Brewer).

Yak–28U

–Yak–28P

Yakovlev Yak–36 (Forger).

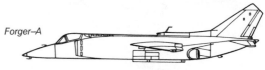

Forger–A

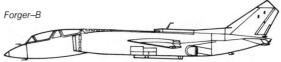

Forger–B

15,430lb (7,000kg) st, plus two lift engines each of 6,613lb (3,000kg) st.

Armament: Two 23mm GSh–23 cannon in external pods, plus max 3,000lb (1,360kg) weapon load; e.g. bombs and rockets, or (as fighter) four Atoll or Aphid AAMs.

Variants:
Forger–B: Two-seat strike-trainer; length 55ft 9½in in (17.00m).
First flights: –.
Production: Series production from 1976(?).
In service: USSR.

Yakovlev Yak–40 (Codling).

Type: Light transport.
Weights:
empty 19,864–21,715lb (9,010–9,850kg).
normal 27,250–34,170lb (12,360–15,500kg).
maximum 36,375lb (16,500kg).
Performance:
maximum speed at 17,060ft (5,200m) 466mph (750km/hr).
maximum speed at sea level 373mph (600km/hr).
maximum cruising speed at 19,685ft (6,000m) 342mph (550km/hr).
range 620–920 miles (1,000–1,480km).
initial rate of climb 33.33ft/sec (10.16m/sec).
service ceiling 38,710ft (11,800m).

Dimensions:
wing span 82ft 0¼in (25.00m).
length overall 66ft 10in (20.36m).
height overall 21ft 4in (6.50m).
wing area 753.48sq ft (70.00sq m).
Power plant: Three Ivchenko IA–25 turbofans each rated at 3,307lb (1,500kg) st.
Payload: 2–3 man crew and 27–40 troops or max 6,000lb (2,720kg) freight.
First flights:
Prototype: 21 October 1966.
Production: 5 prototypes, series production from 1968 to end of 1975, over 600 delivered.
In service: Poland, USSR, Yugoslavia.

Aero 3.

Type: Two-seat trainer.
Weights:
maximum 2,647lb (1,200kg).
Performance:
maximum speed at sea level 143mph (230km/hr).
maximum cruising speed at 2,953ft (900m) 112mph (180km/hr).
ferry range 423 miles (680km).
service ceiling 14,100ft (4,300m).
Dimensions:
wing span 34ft 5in (10.50m).
length overall 28ft 1in (8.58m).
height overall 8ft 10in (2.69m).

Power plant: One 185(190?)hp Lycoming O–435–A piston engine.
Variants: Aero 2: Earlier version.
Production Series production from 1957.
In service: Yugoslavia.

Jurom (Soko–Iar) 'Orao'.

Type: Single-seat light ground-attack aircraft.
Weights:
empty 9,700lb (4,400kg).
maximum 19,842lb (9,000kg).
Performance:
maximum speed at 39,995ft (12,190m) (Mach 0.95) 628mph (1,010km/hr).
maximum speed at sea level (Mach 0.92) 700mph (1,126km/hr).
maximum cruising speed at 435–560mph (700–900km/hr).
radius of action 125–284 miles (200–400km).
initial rate of climb 301.9ft/sec (92.0m/sec).
time to 36,090ft (11,000m) 5min 0sec.
service ceiling 44,290ft (13,500m).
Dimensions:
wing span 24ft 9½in (7.56m).
length overall 42ft 3¾in (12.90m).
height overall 12ft 5in (3.78m).
wing area 193.8sq ft (18.00sq m).
Power plant: Two Rolls-Royce Viper 632 turbojets rated at 4,000lb (1,814kg) st.

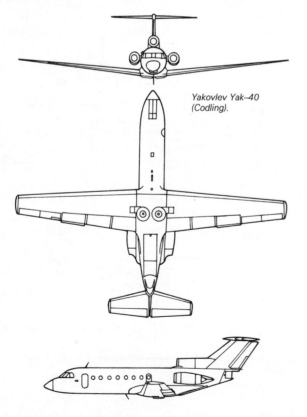

Yakovlev Yak–40 (Codling).

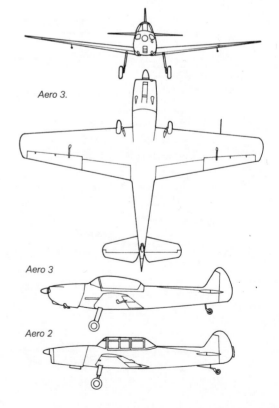

Aero 3.

Aero 3

Aero 2

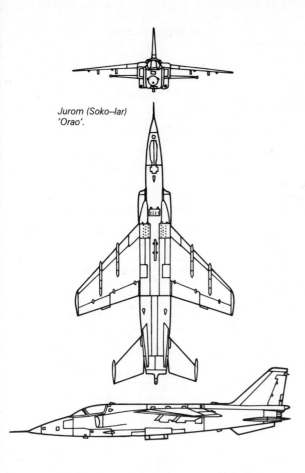

Jurom (Soko–Iar) 'Orao'.

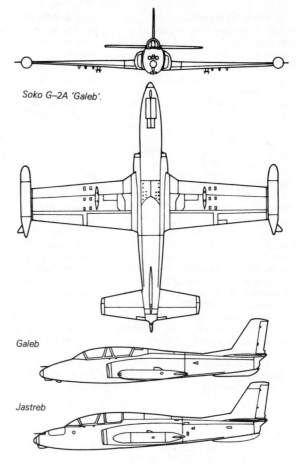

Soko G–2A 'Galeb'.

Galeb

Jastreb

Armament: Two 30mm cannon and max 4,409lb (2,000kg) weapon load on 5 hard points, e.g. bombs and rockets.

Variants: Developments planned for single-seat reconnaissance and two-seat strike-trainer versions.

First flights: Prototype: August 1974.

Production:
2 prototypes; a number of pre-production models from 1976; series production of up to 400 planned 1977–78.

In service: Romania, Yugoslavia.

Soko G–2A 'Galeb'.

Type: Two-seat trainer.

Weights:
empty 5,485lb (2,488kg).
normal 7,690lb (3,488kg).
maximum 9,211lb (4,178kg).

Performance:
maximum speed at sea level 470mph (756km/hr).
maximum speed at 20,340ft (6,200m) 505mph (812km/hr).
ferry range 770 miles (1,240km).
initial rate of climb 74.8ft/sec (22.8m/sec).
time to 19,680ft (6,000m) 5min 30sec.
service ceiling 39,375ft (12,000m).

Dimensions:
wing span 5ft 4in (10.47m).
length overall 33ft 11in (10.34m).
height overall 10ft 8¾in (3.28m).
wing area 209.1sq ft (19.43sq m).

Power plant: One Rolls-Royce Bristol Viper 11 Mk.22–6 turbojet rated at 2,500lb (1,134kg) st.

Armament: Two 12.7mm machine-guns with 160rpg and max 440lb (200kg) weapon load, e.g. two or four 110lb (50kg) bombs, or four 57mm rockets or two 127mm rockets.

Variants:
G–3A Galeb: Further development of G–2A.

First flights:
Prototype: May 1961.
First production model G–2A: February 1963.
G–3A: 19 August 1970.

Production: Approx 150 built 1963–70.

In service: Libya(?), Yugoslavia, Zambia.

Soko J–1 'Jastreb'.

Type: Single-seat light ground-attack aircraft.
Details as for G–2A with the following exceptions:

Weights:

empty 5,759lb (2,612kg).
normal 8,757lb (3,972kg).
maximum 9,859lb (4,472kg).

Performance:
maximum speed at 19,680ft (6,000m) 510mph (820km/hr).
maximum cruising speed at 16,400ft (5,000m) 460mph (740km/hr).
ferry range 777 miles (1,250kg).
initial rate of climb 68.9ft/sec (21.0m/sec).

Dimensions:
wing span 5ft 8in (10.56m).
length overall 35ft 1in (10.71m).
height overall 11ft 11in (3.64m).
wing area 204.5sq ft (19.00sq m).

Power plant: One Rolls-Royce Viper 531 turbojet rated at 3,000lb (1,360kg) st.

Armament: Two 12.7mm machine-guns with 135rpg and max 1,100lb (500kg) weapon load on 8 hard points, e.g. two 550lb (250kg) bombs or six 57mm or 127mm rockets or two 33gal (150l) napalm.

Variants:
J–2 Jastreb: Light reconnaissance aircraft with 3–5 cameras.

Production:
J–1, J–2: Series production from 1968.

In service:
J–1, J–2: Yugoslavia, Zambia.

Soko P–2 'Kraguj'.

Type: Single-seat light ground-attack aircraft.

Weights:
empty 2,491lb (1,130kg).
maximum 3,580lb (1,624kg).

Performance:
maximum speed at sea level 171mph (275km/hr).
maxlmum speed at 5,000ft (1,500m) 183mph (295km/hr).
maximum cruising speed at 5,000ft (1,500m) 174mph (280km/hr).
ferry range 497 miles (800km).
initial rate of climb 22.3ft/sec (6.8m/sec).

Dimensions:
wing span 34ft 11in (10.64m).
length overall 26ft 10in (7.93m).
height overall 9ft 10in (3.00m).
wing area 183sq ft (17.00sq m).

Power plant: One 340hp Lycoming GSO–480–B1A6 piston engine.

Armament: Two 7.62mm machine-guns with 325rpg, two 220lb (100kg) bombs or two 33gal (150 l) napalm tanks or two rocket launchers each containing twelve 55mm unguided rockets.

First flights: Prototype: 1966.

Production: 30(40?) built 1958–71/72.

In service: Yugoslavia.

UTVA–60AT1.

Type: Liaison and reconnaissance aircraft.

Weights:
empty 2,100lb (952kg).
normal 3,192lb (1,448kg).
maximum 3,571lb (1,620kg).

Performance:
maximum speed at sea level 157mph (252km/hr).
maximum cruising speed 143mph (230km/hr).
range 485 miles (780km).
ferry range 590 miles (950km).
initial rate of climb 21ft/sec (6.4m/sec).
service ceiling 17,000ft (5,200m).

Dimensions:
wing span 37ft 5in (11.40m).
length overall 26ft 11½in (8.22m).
height overall 8ft 11in (2.72m).
wing area 194.5sq ft (18.08sq m).

Power plant: One 270hp Lycoming GO–480–B1A6 piston engine.

Payload: 1 man crew and 3 troops or (U–60AM) 2 stretcher cases and 1 medic or max 908lb (412kg) freight.

Variants: U–60H: Floatplane.

First flights:
Prototype: UTVA–56: 22 April 1959.
UTVA–60: 1960.

Production: Series production 1960–67(?).

In service: Yugoslavia.

UTVA–66.

Type: Liaison and reconnaissance aircraft.

Details as for UTVA–60 with the following exceptions:

Weights:
empty 2,756lb (1,250kg).
maximum 4,000lb (1,814kg).

Performance:
maximum speed at sea level 155mph (250km/hr).
maximum cruising speed 143mph (230km/hr).
range 466 miles (750km).
initial rate of climb 14.76ft/sec (4.5m/sec).
service ceiling 22,080ft (6,700m).

Dimensions:
wing span 37ft 5in (11.40m).
length overall 27ft 6in (8.38m).
height overall 10ft 6in (3.20m).
wing area 194.5sq ft (18.08sq m).

Power plant: One 270hp Lycoming GSO–480–B1J6 piston engine.

First flights: UTVA–66:1966.

Production: Series production from 1967(?).

In service: Yugoslavia.

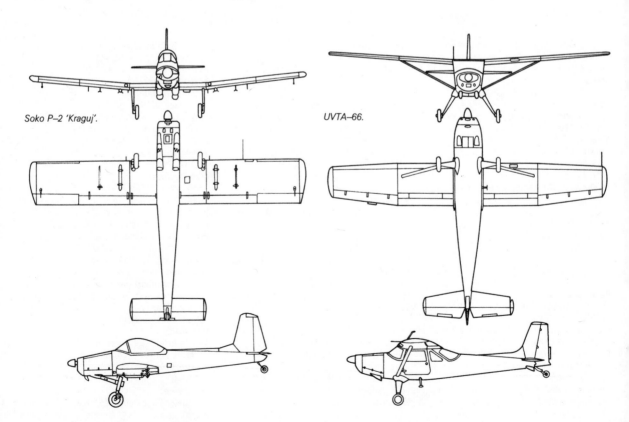

Soko P–2 'Kraguj'.

UVTA–66.

Weaponry

Abbreviations

CAL	Calibre
GW	Gun weight
L	Length
LW	Launch weight
M	Mach
R	Range
RF	Rate of fire
RW	Round weight (machine-gun)
s/min	Shots/minute
SW	Shell weight (cannon)
Vo	Muzzle velocity

Guns

The difference between machine-guns and cannon lies not in the weapons themselves, but in the ammunition they use. While machine-guns fire metal-cased bullets, cannon employ shells fitted with rotating rings.

Aircraft of the Western powers are armed with machine-guns as well as cannon. The advent of the armed helicopter and, in part, the counter-insurgency (COIN) ground-attack aircraft has given a new lease of life to the machine-gun. For fighters and fighter-bombers, special emphasis is placed upon high rates of fire and muzzle velocity. For helicopters, a greater emphasis is sometimes put upon the efficiency of single-round fire against living targets. Cannon calibres are generally in the 20 to 30mm range. The United States keeps to a standard 20mm calibre.

In contrast, the USSR first introduced larger calibres; cannon of 23 and 37mm calibre, which were not replaced by 30mm weapons until much later. Machine-guns are only occasionally to be found in older types of aircraft, and recently, in armed helicopters. The Soviet emphasis was laid upon shell weight, with a limited overall weapon weight being achieved at the expense of rate of fire and muzzle velocity.

France

7.5mm A–52 machine-gun: GW 24.31lb (11kg), RW 9.0g, Vo 2,707ft/sec (825m/sec), RF 700s/min. Army weapon, employed in helicopters, and armed trainers.

20mm MG 151 cannon: GW 92.6lb (42kg), SW 90g, Vo 2,362ft/sec (720m/sec), RF 780s/min. German Second World War design, employed in helicopters.

20mm M 621 cannon: GW 127.8lb (58kg), SW 100g, Vo 3,379ft/sec (1,030m/sec), RF 300 and 740s/min. Army weapon, equips helicopters.

30mm DEFA 552 cannon: GW 176.4lb (80kg), SW 224g, Vo 2,674ft/sec (815m/sec), RF 1,100–1,500s/min. Equips older French aircraft and G.91R.3.

30mm DEFA 553 cannon: GW 187.4lb (85kg), SW 244g, Vo 2,674ft/sec (815m/sec), RF 1,200–1,300s/min. Equips latest French aircraft, A–4H and A–4N.

Germany

27mm Mauser cannon: RF 1,000 and 1,700s/min. Under development for MRCA Tornado.

Great Britain

20mm Mk.5 cannon: GW 99.2lb (45kg), SW 122g, Vo 2,789ft/sec (850m/sec), RF 800s/min. Hispano-Suiza design licence-built since beginning of the Second World War, equips Canberra, phased out in Great Britain.

30mm Aden Mk.4 cannon: GW 198.4lb (90kg), SW 226g, Vo 2,680ft/sec (815m/sec), RF 1,200s/min. Equips British fighters and strike-fighters.

Netherlands

7.62mm FN machine-gun: GW 99.2lb (45kg), RW 9.5g, Vo 2,559ft/sec (780m/sec), RF 1,000s/min. Equips BAC 167, also in weapon packs.

Switzerland

20mm HS–804 cannon: GW 99.2lb (45kg), SW 120g, Vo 2,723ft/sec (830m/sec), RF 750–800s/min. Equips A 32A Lansen and Venom FB.50.

30mm KCA cannon: GW 794lb (360kg), SW 360g, Vo 3,379ft/sec (1,030m/sec), RF 1,350s/min. Equips JA37 Viggen.

USA

7.62mm M–60C, D machine-gun: GW 22lb (10kg), RW 9.5g, Vo 2,799ft/sec 853m/sec), RF 550s/min. Derivative of army weapon, employed in helicopters and ground-attack aircraft.

7.62mm M–37C machine-gun: GW 30.9lb (14kg), RW 9.5g, Vo 2,799ft/sec (853m/sec), RF 550s/min. Derivative of tank machine-gun, employed in helicopters.

7.62mm Heligun machine-gun: RW 9.5g, Vo 2,799ft/sec (853m/sec), RF 4,000s/min. Twin-barrelled rotating machine-gun, employed in helicopters.

7.62mm M–134 Minigun: GW 48.5lb (22kg), RW 9.5g, Vo 2,799ft/sec (853m/sec), RF 3,000 or 6,000s/min. Six-barrelled rotating machine-gun, employed in helicopters, 'Gun Ships' and weapon packs.

12.7mm M–2 machine-gun: GW 83.8lb (38kg), RW 45g, Vo 2,930ft/sec (893m/sec), RF 500–650s/min. Army weapon, employed in helicopters.

12.7mm M–3 machine-gun: GW 68lb (31kg), RW 45g, Vo 2,841ft/sec (866m/sec), RF 1,200s/min. Equips F–84, F–86, G.91R.1, also in weapon packs.

20mm M–11 cannon: GW 229.3lb (104kg), SW 110g, Vo 3.199ft/sec (975m/sec), RF 700 or 4,200s/min. Naval weapon, twin-barrelled, in weapon packs for strike-fighters.

20mm M–24A1 cannon: GW 114.6lb (52kg), SW 130g, Vo 2,749ft/sec (838m/sec), RF 750–850s/min. Licence-built Hispano-Suiza design. Equips F–86K.

20mm M–39 cannon: GW 179lb (81kg), SW 104g, V_0 3,400ft/sec (1,036m/sec), RF 1,200–1,500s/min. Equips F–100, F–5.

20mm M–61, M–61A, M–61A1 Vulcan cannon: GW 200–211lb (114–120kg), SW 104g, V_0 3,400ft/sec (1,036m/sec), RF 6,000–7,200s/min. Six-barrelled rotating cannon, equips F–104, F–4E, F–14, or in weapon packs in weapon pods.

20mm M–12 cannon.

USSR

12.7mm UB machine-gun: GW 48.5lb (22kg), RW 48g, V_0 2,776ft/sec (860m/sec), RF 1,000s/min. Equips trainers and armed helicopters. Derivatives UBS and UBK.

20mm B–20 cannon: GW 55.1lb (25kg), SW 96g, V_0 2,625ft/sec (800m/sec), RF 800s/min. Equips maritime-reconnaissance aircraft.

23mm NR–23 cannon: GW 86lb (39kg), SW 196g, V_0 2,264ft/sec (690m/sec), RF 850 (650)'s/min. Nudelmann–Richter design. Equips fighters, strike-fighters, bombers and transports.

23mm GSh–23 cannon: RF 1,800s/min. Twin-barrelled, equips later MiG–21 and MiG–23 series, also in GP–9 weapon packs.

23mm cannon: RF 5,500s/min. Six-barrelled rotating cannon, equips Su–19 and MiG–23S.

30mm NR–30 cannon: GW 145.5lb (66kg), SW 410g, V_0 2,559ft/sec (780m/sec), RF 900s/min. Equips all cannon-armed aircraft entering service after 1955.

37mm NS–37 cannon: GW 227lb (103kg), SW 735g, V_0 2,264ft/sec (690m/sec), RF 400 (450)'s/min. Nudelmann–Suranov design. Equips older-type fighters and strike-fighters.

20mm M–12 cannon: GW 101.4lb (46kg), SW 110g, V_0 3,199ft/sec (975m/sec), RF 1,000s/min. Equips only carrier-borne aircraft.

20mm XM–197 cannon: GW 146lb (66kg), RF 400 and 1,500s/min. Equips Huey Cobra helicopter.

30mm XM–188 cannon: GW 150lb (68kg), V_0 2,198ft/sec (670m/sec), RF 500 and 2,000s/min. Three-barrelled rotating cannon, equips YAH–63.

30mm GAU–8/A cannon: GW 619.5lb (281kg), SW 369g, V_0 3,399–3,451ft/sec (1,036–1,052m/sec), RF 2,100 and 4,200s/min. Seven-barrelled rotating cannon, equips A–10A.

40mm M–5 automatic grenade-launcher: SW 170g, RF 250s/min. Equips helicopters.

Trials are currently being carried out with a large number of machine-gun, cannon and grenade-launcher prototypes for helicopter employment. The French 30mm DEFA 553 cannon is being produced under licence and used to equip various production models of the A–4 series.

Air-to-Air Missiles (AAM)

AAMs equipped with an infra-red homing head necessitate orthodox fighter tactics; the attacking aircraft must close in on the enemy from the rear. This position is particularly difficult to achieve if the attacker has only marginal advantage in speed. In addition, this homing head possesses disadvantages in bad weather (rain and fog), however, it cannot be affected by enemy action.

With AAMs equipped with radar-guidance attacks, can also be mounted along an intersecting course; beam attacks are also possible. They can be carried by attacking aircraft which are slower than their target. But this method of guidance is affected by ground-echo at low altitude.

The majority of AAMs are fitted with either proximity-fuses or proximity and contact-fuses.

¹ theoretical (figure obtained from practical tests).

France

Matra R.511: L 10.14ft (3.09m), LW 397lb (180kg), M 1.8, R 4.4 miles (7km), radar.

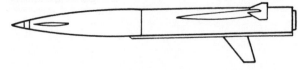

Matra R.530: L 10.76ft (3.28m), LW 430lb (195kg), M 2.7, R 11.2 miles (18km), radar or infra-red.

Matra R.530

Matra R.550 Magic: L 9.19ft (2.80m), LW 194lb (88kg), R 6.2 miles (10km), infra-red.

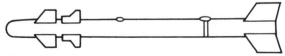

Matra R.550

Development: Matra Super 530.

Germany
Development: FK–80 Viper.

Great Britain
Firestreak: L 10.47ft (3.19m), LW 300lb (136kg), M 2+, R 5.0 miles (8km), infra-red.

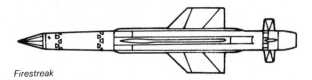

Firestreak

Red Top: L 10.76ft (3,28m), LW 300lb (136kg), M 3, R 6.8 miles (11km), infra-red.

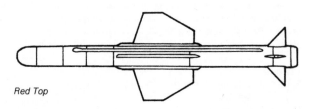

Red Top

Development: SRAAM.

Israel
Shafrir: L 8.1ft (2.47m), LW 205lb (93kg), M 2.5, R 3.1 miles, infra-red.

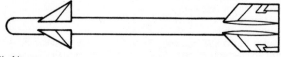

Shafrir

Italy
Development: Aspide 1A.

Japan
AAM 1: L 8.2ft (2.50m), LW 167.6lb (76kg), M 2.5, R 4.4 miles (7km), infra-red.
AAM 2: L 7.22ft (2.20m) LW 163.1lb (74kg), M 3.5, R 3.1 miles (5km), infra-red.

South Africa
Whiplash

Sweden
Rb 24: L 9.19ft (2.8m), LW 159lb (72kg), M 2.5, R 4.4 miles (7km), infra-red. Licence-built Sidewinder.

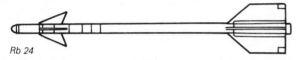

Rb 24

Rb 27 (HM–55): L 7.15ft (2.18m), LW 150lb (68kg), M 2.5, R 5.6 miles (9km), radar. Licence-built AIM–26B Falcon.

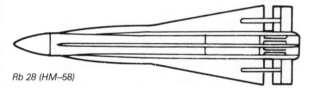

Rb 27 (HM–55)

RB 28 (HM–58): L 6.73ft (2.05m), LW 145.5lb (66kg), M 2.5, R 6.8 miles (11km), infra-red. Licence-built AIM–4D Falcon.

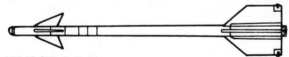

Rb 28 (HM–58)

United States
AIM–9B Sidewinder 1A: L 9.32ft (2.84m), LW 185lb (84kg), M 2, R 6.8 miles (11km), infra-red. Licence-built in Germany.

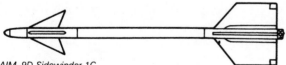

AIM–9B Sidewinder 1A

AIM–9C Sidewinder 1B: L 9.32ft (2.84m), LW 159lb (72kg), M 2.5, R 6.2 miles (10km), radar.
AIM–9D Sidewinder 1C: L 9.51ft (2.90m), LW 185lb (84kg), M 2.5, R 6.2 miles (10km), infra-red.

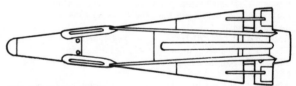

AIM–9D Sidewinder 1C

AIM–9E Sidewinder: Converted AIM–9B.
AIM–9G Sidewinder: Converted AIM–9D.
AIM–9H Sidewinder: Improved AIM–9G.
AIM–9J Sidewinder: Converted AIM–9B.
AIM–9K Sidewinder: Earlier version of AIM–9L.
AIM–9L Super Sidewinder: L 9.35ft (2.85m), LW 187lb (85kg), M 2.5, R 9.3 miles (15km), infra-red.

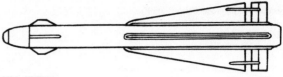

AIM–4C Falcon

AIM–4A Falcon: L 6.5ft (1.98m), LW 110lb (50kg), M 2, R 5.0 miles (8km), radar.
AIM–4C Falcon: L 6.5ft (1.98m), LW 110lb (50kg), M 2, R 5.0 miles (8km), infra-red.
AIM–4D Falcon: L 6.63ft (2.02m), LW 134lb (61kg), M 3.2, R 5.6 miles (9km), infra-red. Licence-built in Great Britain and Sweden.
AIM–4E Super Falcon: L 7.15ft (2.18m), LW 141lb (64kg), M 3, R 5.6 miles (9km), radar.
AIM–4F Super Falcon: L 7.15 ft (2.18m), LW 150lb (68kg), M 3, R 6.8 miles (11km), radar.
AIM–4G Super Falcon: L 6.76ft (2.06m), LW 146lb (66kg), M 3, R 6.8 miles (11km), radar.

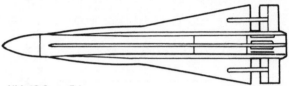

AIM–4G Super Falcon

AIM–26A Nuclear Falcon: L 6.99ft (2.13m), LW 201lb (91kg), M 2, R 5.6 miles (9km), radar. Nuclear warhead.

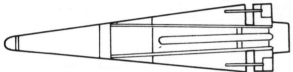

AIM–26A Nuclear Falcon

AIM–26B Falcon: L 7.12ft (2.17m), LW 249lb (113kg), M 2, R 5 miles (8km), radar.
AIM–47A Falcon: L 12.01ft (3.66m), LW 800lb (363kg), M 5, R 46.6 miles (75km), infra-red or radar.

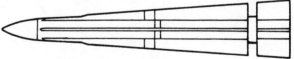

AIM–47A Falcon

AIM–7E Sparrow IIIB: L 12.01ft (3.66m), LW 452lb (205kg), M 4, R 31 miles (50km), radar.

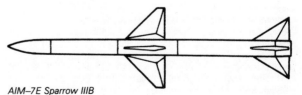

AIM–7E Sparrow IIIB

AIM–7F Sparrow III: L 11.98ft (3.65m), LW 502lb (228kg), M 4, R 62.5 miles (100km), radar.
AIM–54A Phoenix: L 12.99ft (3.96m), LW 836lb (380kg), M 5, R 124 miles (200km), radar.

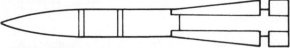

AIM–54A Phoenix

AIR–2A Genie: L 7.51ft (2.29m), LW 820lb (372kg), M 3, R 6.8 miles (11km), unguided. Nuclear warhead.

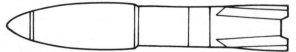

AIR–2A Genie

AIR–2B Super Genie: As AIR–2A with improved power plant.
Development: Agile. Brazo: Aircraft-radar homing. Claw: Light close combat ('dogfight') AAM. XAIM–97A Seek Bat: From AGM–78. BMD: Bomber defence missile. Night-attack missile.

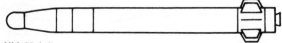

AIM–95 Agile

USSR

While nearly all Western fighters and strike-fighters are built to carry various types of AAMs, in the Eastern bloc almost every aircraft type is equipped with a different missile. The names quoted below are the official NATO code designations.

Acrid AA–6: (a) L 20.18ft (6.15m), LW 1,874lb (850kg), M 4.5, R 28 miles (45km), radar. (b) L 19.03ft (5.80m), LW 1,874lb (850kg), M 4.5, R 12.4 miles (20km), infra-red; for MiG–25.
Alkali AA–1: L 6.17ft (1.88m), LW 201lb (91kg), M 1.5+, R 3.7 miles (6km), radar; for MiG–17, MiG–19, Su–11, Yak–25.

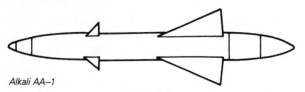

Alkali AA–1

Anab AA–3: L 11.81–13.12ft (3.60–4.0m), LW 500lb (227kg), R 6.2 miles (10km), infra-red or radar; for Su–11, Yak–28P.

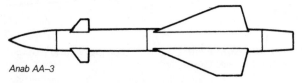

Anab AA–3

Advanced Anab: For Su–11, MiG–23, Su–15.
Apex AA–7: (a) L 14.76ft (4.5m), LW 705lb (320kg), M 3.5, R 20.5 miles (33km), Radar. (b) L 13.85ft (4.22m), LW 705lb (320kg), M 3.5, R 9.3 miles (15km), infra-red; for MiG–23.
Aphid AA–8: (a) L 7.05ft (2.15m), LW 121.3lb (55kg), M 3, R 9.3 miles (15km), radar. (b) L 6.56ft (2.0m), LW 121.3lb (55kg), M 3, R 4.35 miles (7km), infra-red; for MiG–23.

Ash AA–5: L 17–18ft (5.20–5.50m), LW 441lb (200kg), R 7.46 miles (12km), infra-red or radar; for Tu–28.

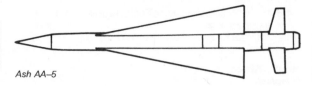

Ash AA–5

Atoll AA–2 (USSR designation K–13): L 9.15ft (2.79m), LW 154lb (70kg), M 2.5, R 1.8 miles (3km), infra-red; for MiG–19, MiG–21. Licence-built in India.

Atoll AA–2

Advanced Atoll: L 9.84ft (3.0m), M 2.5, R 4.4 miles (7km), radar; for MiG–21.
Awl AA–4: L 15.09ft (4.6m), R 5 miles (8km), infra-red; for MiG–25.

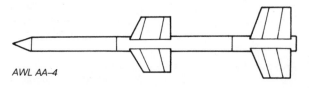

AWL AA–4

Air-to-Surface Missiles (ASM)

ASMs constitute the main armament of strike-fighters and bombers to an ever-increasing degree. They can be launched during the approach to the target while still out of range of the defences. Some are also used as decoys (to simulate an aircraft target). Other types are intended specifically to destroy radar installations. They home automatically on to the transmitter. More and more ASMs are being employed, especially in the anti-shipping role.

France

Nord A.S.12: L 6.14ft (1.87m), LW 165lb (75kg), R 3.7 miles (6km), wire-guidance.

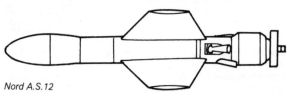

Nord A.S.12

Nord A.S.20: L 8.53ft (2.60m), LW 315lb (143kg), R 4.4 miles (7km), radio-guidance. Licence-built in Germany.

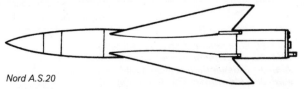

Nord A.S.20

Nord A.S.30: L 12.43ft (3.79m), LW 1,146lb (520kg), R 7.5 miles (12km), radio-guidance.

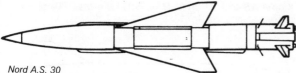

Nord A.S. 30

Nord A.S.30L: L 11.81ft (3.60m), LW 838lb (380kg), R 6.8 miles (11km), radio-guidance.
Matra Martel A.S.37: L 13.58ft (4.14m), LW 1,168lb (530kg), R 24.9 miles (40km), radio and radar-guidance.

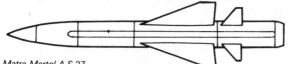

Matra Martel A.S.37

Development: AM–39: Sub-variant of the ship-to-ship guided missile, for use by aircraft and helicopters.

Germany
Kormoran: L 14.44ft (4.40m), LW 1,323lb (600kg), R 23 miles (37km), inertia navigation.

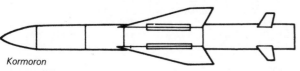

Kormoron

Development: Jumbo.

Great Britain
Martel AJ 168: L 12.73ft (3.88m), LW 1,213lb (550kg), R 24.9 miles (40km), radio and television-guidance.
Development: Sea Skua (CL–834).

Italy
Development: Aitos, Marte.

Japan
Development: ASM–1.

Sweden
Robot Rb04C: L 14.6ft (4.45m), LW 1,323lb (600kg), autopilot-control.

Robot Rb04C

Robot Rb04D: Similar.
Robot Rb04E: Improved version of Rb04C, radio-guidance.
Robot Rb05A: L 11.77ft (3.75m), LW 672lb (305kg), R 6.21 miles (10km), radio-guidance.

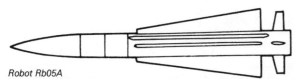

Robot Rb05A

United States
AGM–12A Bullpup: L 10.5ft (3.2m), LW 571lb (259kg), R 5.6 miles (9km), radio guidance.
AGM–12B Bullpup A: L 10.5ft (3.2m), LW 571lb (259kg), R 6.8 miles (11km), radio-guidance.

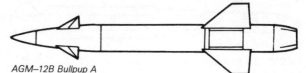

AGM–12B Bullpup A

AGM–12C Bullpup B: L 13.58ft (4.14m), LW 1,786lb (810kg), R 9.9 miles (16km), radio-guidance. AGM–12D with nuclear warhead, but otherwise similar.

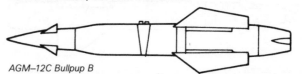

AGM–12C Bullpup B

AGM–28B Hound Dog: L 42.03ft (12.81m), LW 10,145lb (4,602kg), R 786 miles (1,265km), inertia navigation. Nuclear warhead.

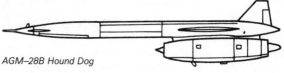

AGM–28B Hound Dog

AGM–45A Shrike: L 10.01ft (3.05m), LW 390lb (177kg), R 9.9 miles (16km), radar-guidance.

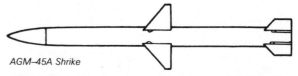

AGM–45A Shrike

AGM–53A Condor: L 13.81ft (4.21m), LW 2,112lb (958kg), R 68.4 miles (110km), television and automatic-guidance.

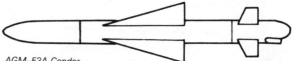

AGM–53A Condor

AGM–65A Maverick: L 8.07ft (2.46m), LW 474lb (215kg), R 13.7 miles (22km), television and automatic-guidance.

AGM–65A Maverick

AGM–69A SRAM[1]: L 14.01ft (4.27m), LW 2,240lb (1,016kg), R 138 miles (222km), inertia navigation. Nuclear warhead.

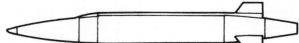

AGM–69A SRAM

ADAM–20C (previously GAM–72A) Quail: L 12.83ft (3.91m), LW 1,230lb (5.58kg), R 400 miles (649km), inertia guidance. Anti-radar-device.
AGM–78A Standard ARM[2]: L 15.0ft (4.57m), LW 1,800lb (816kg), R 15.5 miles (25km), radar-guidance. Also AGM–78C and D.

[1]SRAM = Short-Range-Attack-Missile.
[2]ARM =Anti-Radar-Missile.

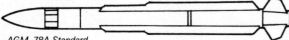

AGM–78A Standard

AGM–83A Bulldog: L 9.75ft (2.98m), LW 600lb (272kg), R 6.2 miles (10km), laser-guidance.

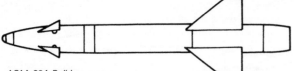

AGM–83A Bulldog

AGM–84A Harpoon: L 12.6ft (3.84m), LW 1,151lb (522kg), R 68.4 miles (110km), radio or radar-guidance.

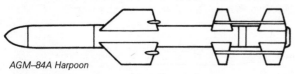

AGM–84A Harpoon

Development: ADSM: radar-guidance. Harm: radar-guidance. Hellfire: anti-tank missile. Hornet, Turbo Condor: Improved AGM–53A with increased range.

USSR

The names quoted below are the official NATO code-designations. The majority of the missiles are intended for the anti-shipping role.
Performance details are estimated.
AS–6: L 29.53ft (9.0m), LW 10,582lb (4,800kg), inertia navigation with radar-homing device; for Backfire.
Kangaroo AS–3: L 49.9ft (15.2m), R 298.3 miles (480km), radio-guidance; for Tu–20, Tu–22.

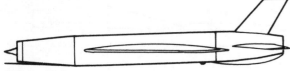

Kangaroo AS–3

Kelt AS–5: L 31.0ft (9.45m), R 99.4 miles (160km), radar-guidance; for Tu–16.

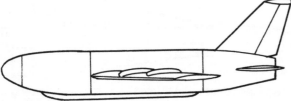

Kelt AS–5

Kennel AS–1: L 25.92ft (7.9m), LW 6,610lb (3,000kg), R 56 miles (90km), radio and radar-guidance; for Tu–16.

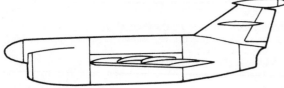

Kennel AS–1

Kerry AS–7: Radio guidance; for Su–17.

Kipper AS–2: L 31.0ft (9.45m), R 111.8 miles (180km), radio-guidance; for Tu–16.

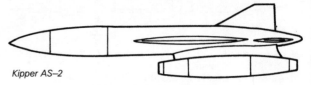

Kipper AS–2

Kitchen AS–4: L 35.99ft (10.97m), R 198.8 miles (320km), radar-guidance; for Tu–22.

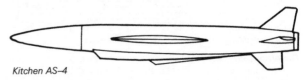

Kitchen AS–4

Unguided Rockets

The advantages of rockets over guns are twofold – their simpler method of firing, and their larger calibre. This means that a bigger warhead can be delivered on target. To compensate the spreading effect, use is made of high speeds, stabilizing fins, and the firing of rockets in salvoes. The line of flight of unguided rockets is governed by the direction of the whole aircraft at the moment of launching.

Brazil
37mm SBAT–37 Rocket: LW 37lb (17kg).
127mm SBAT–127 Rocket: LW 110lb (50kg).

France
37mm SNEB Rocket: LW 2.21lb (1.0kg). In packs of 16 and 36 rockets, sometimes also housed in nose of auxiliary fuel tanks.
68mm SNEB22 Rocket: LW 11.2–13.9lb (5.1–6.3kg). In packs of 19 or 36 rockets, sometimes also housed in nose of auxiliary fuel tanks.
120mm Rocket: LW 60lb (27.2kg). Obsolescent.

Great Britain
51mm Rocket (2"): In packs of 12, 19, 24, 31 and 37 rockets. Also integral launching trays.
76.2mm Rocket (3"): LW 81.6lb (37kg), in packs of 6 rockets or individually mounted.

Israel
82mm Rocket: In packs of 6 rockets.

Italy
50mm 2ARF/8M2 Rocket: LW 7.9lb (3.6kg).

Spain
37mm INTA S9 Rocket: In packs of 18 and launchers of 54 rockets.
57mm Rocket.
70mm Rocket: In packs of 6 and 18 rockets.
100mm INTA S–12: In packs of 6 rockets.

Sweden
75mm M55 and M57 Rocket: LW 15.4lb (7.0kg). In packs of 7 and 19 rockets or individually mounted.
135mm M56 and M60 Rocket: LW 92.6lb (42.0kg). Individually mounted.
135mm M70 Rocket: LW 96.1lb (43.5kg). In packs of 6 rockets.

145mm Rocket: Obsolescent.
180mm Rocket: Obsolescent.

Switzerland
80mm R–80 SURA Rocket: LW 26.2lb (11.9kg). Individually mounted.

United States
70mm FFAR[1] Mighty Mouse (2.75") Rocket: LW 18.7lb (8.5kg). In packs of 7, 16 and 19 rockets.
127mm ZUNI (5") Rocket: LW 106.9lb (48.5kg). In packs of 4 and 7 rockets, also individually mounted.
127mm HVAR[2] (5") Rocket: LW 136.7lb (62kg). Obsolescent.

USSR
55mm RS–55 Rocket: In packs of 8, 16, 19 and 32 rockets.
137mm M100 Rocket: LW 34.4lb (15.6kg). Individually mounted.
160mm Rocket.
190mm TRS–190 Rocket: LW 101.4lb (46.0kg). Individually mounted.
212mm ARS–121 Rocket: LW 256lb (116kg). Individually mounted.
240mm S–24 Rocket: Individually mounted.

Bombs
Only the more important of the numerous types of bombs currently in service are listed below. Other than the weights, little is known of the types employed by the Eastern bloc, but it is safe to assume that they correspond in the main to those of the West.
General Purpose Bomb (GP): Because of the ratio of explosive to overall weight (approx 50%), also known as 50% bomb. Employed in many roles in the 100lb (45kg) to 4,000lb (1,800kg) weight range, fitted with nose- and tail-fuses, some also with time-fuses.
Armour Piercing Bomb (AP): Also known as 15% bomb. Employed against targets protected by armour or concrete, tail-fuse only.
Semi-Armour Piercing Bomb (SAP): Also known as 30% bomb. Employed against targets protected by medium-thickness armour, mainly tail-fuses.
Light Case Bomb (LC): No fragmentation effect, increased explosives content.
Fragmentation Bomb (FRAG): Increased fragmentation effect, employed on anti-personnel operations. Also as cluster ('ripple') bombs in canisters.
Incendiary Bomb (INC).
Fire Bomb (Napalm): Employed against combustible targets, tanks and fieldworks. As an anti-personnel weapon, its effect is achieved by the removal of oxygen from the air. The very thin-walled bomb is normally first attached to the aircraft's bomb-pylon and then filled. The mixture is composed of petrol, to which is added napalm-powder. In emergencies, auxiliary fuel tanks can also be employed as fire-bombs.
Flare, Photoflash or Target Identification Bomb.
Practice Bomb.
Delayed Descent (Retarded) Bomb: To prevent damage to aircraft during low-level attack, rate of fall is reduced by means of either a tail-brake (Great Britain), a parachute (France), or a braking balloon (USA).
Guided Bomb ('Smart Bomb'): For increased accuracy, these bombs are either guided after launch from the parent

[1] FFAR = Folding-Fin Aerial Rocket
[2] HVAR = High-Velocity-Aircraft-Rocket

aircraft by means of a TV camera in the nose of the weapon, or steered independently to a target illuminated by laser beam from elsewhere.
Walleye II (GW Mk.5 Mod.4): L 13.25ft (4.04m), LW 2,339lb (1,061kg), warhead 2,000lb (907kg), television-guidance.

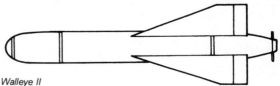

Walleye II

Walleye I: With 850lb (386kg), warhead.
Paveway: Laser-guidance. Modified bombs of 500lb (227kg) to 3,000lb (1,361kg). Without propulsion.
KMU–351/B: L 14ft (4.27m), LW 2,057lb (931kg).
Cluster (Ripple) Bomb: This bomb disperses a large number of smaller bombs. Primarily used against personnel and area targets.
Nuclear Weapons: Obviously no specific details are available about these bombs. In recent years it has often been possible to decrease the overall weight of this type of bomb while retaining, or even increasing, their destructive effect.
Depth-charge: Serves in the ASW role. Known types include those of the United States, 325lb (147.5kg); France, 353lb (160kg); and France/United States, 386lb (175kg). The American Mk.101 Lulu nuclear depth-charge is a special case.
Aircraft Torpedoes: Despite the introduction of new and improved models after the Second World War, the importance of the torpedo as an anti-surface-vessel weapon has waned drastically. Although the height of release has now risen to above 328ft (100m) and speeds too have increased, modern anti-aircraft defences have rendered the conventional torpedo attack, with its requisite straight and level approach flight, all but impossible. For operations against surface vessels, most countries have replaced the torpedo by the ASM.

But homing torpedoes are still in general use in the ASW role. They are fitted with search equipment with a range of up to 1,094yds (1,000m) and are designed for use in depths of up to 985ft (300m). Here too, only limited information has been made available.

France
L4 Homing Torpedo: Calibre 533mm, weight 1,190lb (540kg).

Great Britain
Mk.30 Homing Torpedo.

Italy
A.244 Homing Torpedo: Calibre 324mm, weight 507lb (230kg).

United States
Mk.34 Homing Torpedo: Calibre 483mm, weight 1,387lb (629kg). Obsolescent.
Mk.43 Homing Torpedo: Calibre 254mm, weight 320lb (145kg).
Mk.44 Homing Torpedo: Calibre 324mm, weight: Model 0 507lb (230kg). Model 1 520lb (236kg).
Mk.46 Homing Torpedo: Calibre 324mm, weight 570lb (258kg).
Anti-surface-vessel Torpedo: Calibre 583mm, weight 2,150lb (975kg).

Index
to the Aircraft section

A–3B 'Skywarrior' (Douglas), 151
A–4F 'Skyhawk' (McDonnell Douglas), 172
A–4M (McDonnell Douglas), 173
A–6E 'Intruder' (Grumman), 157
A–10A (Fairchild), 153
A 32A (Saab 32 'Lansen'), 131
A–37B 'Dragonfly' (Cessna), 146
Aeritalia-Aermacchi AM.3C., 118
Aeritalia G.222, 119
Aermacchi MB.326G, 119
  MB.326K., 120
Aero 3, 216
  L–29 'Delfin' (Maya), 85
  L–39 'Albatross', 85
Aérospatiale N.262D 'Frégote', 87
  S.A.316A 'Alouette' III, 88
  S.A.318C 'Alouette' II, 88
  S.A.321 'Super Frelon', 89
  S.E.313B, 87
Aérospatiale/Westland S.A.330 'Puma', 89
  S.A.341 'Gazelle', 89
Aerotec 122 'Uirapuru' (T–23), 79
A.E.W.Mk.3 (Fairey 'Gannet'), 106
AH–1G 'Huey Cobra' (Bell), 141
AH–1J 'Sea Cobra' (Bell), 142
'Airtrainer' (NZAI CT–4), 127
AISA I–115, 128
AJ 37 (Saab 37 'Viggen'), 132
'Albatross' (Aero L–39), 85
'Albatross' (Grumman HU–16B), 159
'Alizé' (Breguet Br.1050), 90
'Alouette' II (Aérospatiale S.A.318C), 88
'Alouette' III (Aérospatiale S.A.316A), 88
'Alphajet' (Dassault-Breguet/Dornier), 95
A.M.3C. (Aeritalia-Aermacchi), 118
An–2 (Colt) (Antonov), 191
An–12 (Cub) (Antonov), 191
An–14 'Pchelka' (Clod) (Antonov), 192
An–22 'Antheus' (Cock) (Antonov), 193
AN–26 (Curl) (Antonov), 193
An–28 (Antonov), 192
'Andover' C.Mk.1 (Hawker Siddeley), 109
'Antheus' (Cock) (Antonov An–22), 193
Antonov An–2 (Colt), 191
An–12 (Cub), 191
An–14 'Pchelka' (Clod), 192
An–22 'Antheus' (Cock), 193

An–26 (Curl), 193
An–28, 192
'Arava' (IAI–201), 118
'Argus' Mk.2. (Canadair CL–28), 80
A. (SEPECAT 'Jaguar'), 97
'Atlantic' (Breguet Br.1150), 90
'Aviocar' (CASA C.212), 130
Avro 'Shackleton' M.R.Mk.3, Phase 3, 101
AWACS (Boeing E–3A), 142
'Azor' (CASA C.207A), 128
'Aztec' (Piper U–11A), 181

B–1A (Rockwell), 182
B.(1)Mk.8 (English Electric 'Canberra'), 106
B2 (Dassault 'Super Mystère'), 94
B–52H 'Stratofortress' (Boeing), 143
B–57B (Martin), 171
BAC 145 'Jet Provost' T.Mk.5, 101
BAC 167 'Strikemaster', 102
BAC 'Lightning' F.Mk.6., 102
  'VC10'C.Mk.1., 103
Backfire–B (Tupolev Tu–26(?)), 212
'Bandeirante' (Embraer EMB–110), 79
Be–6 (Madge) (Beriev), 194
Be–12 'Tchaika' (Mail) (Beriev), 194
Beagle (Ilyushin Il–28), 196
Bear–A (Tupolev Tu–20), 209
'Beaver' (De Havilland Canada DHC–2), 82
Beechcraft C45G 'Expeditor', 136
  'Musketeer Sport', 136
  T–34A 'Mentor', 137
  T–34C 'Mentor', 137
  U–8F 'Seminole', 137
  U–21A 'Ute', 138
Bell 47G–3B–2 'Trooper' (OH–13H 'Sioux'), 139
  47J–2 'Ranger' (UK–13), 139
  204B (UH–1B 'Iroquois'), 139
  205A (UH–1H 'Iroquois'), 140
  206A 'JetRanger' (OH–58A 'Kiowa'), 140
  212 Twin Two-Twelve (UH–1N 'Twin-Huey'), 141
  AH–1G 'Huey Cobra', 141
  AH–1J 'Sea Cobra', 142
Beriev Be–6 (Madge), 194
  Be–12 'Tchaita' (Mail), 194
'Birddog' (Cessna O–1E), 146
Bison (Myasishchev M–4 'Molot'), 206

Blinder–A (Tupolev Tu–22), 210
'Blue Canoe' (Cessna U–3A), 148
BN–2A 'Islander' (Britten-Norman (Fairey)), 103
BO–105 (MBB), 100
Boeing 707–320C. 142
  B–52H 'Stratofortress', 143
  C–135B 'Stratolifter', 144
  E–3A (AWACS), 142
  KC–97L 'Stratofighter', 143
  KC–135A 'Stratotanker', 144
  T–43A, 144
Boeing-Vertol 107–N (CH–46D 'Sea Knight'), 145
  CH–47C 'Chinook', 145
Br.1050 'Alizé' (Breguet), 90
Br.1150 'Atlantic' (Breguet), 90
Breguet Br.1050 'Alizé', 90
  Br.1150 'Atlantic', 90
Breguet/Dornier 'Alphajet' (Dassault), 95
Brewer (Yakolev Yak–28), 215
'Brigadýr' (L–60), 86
Britten-Norman (Fairey) BN–2A 'Islander', 103
'Bronco' (Rockwell (North American) OV–10A), 183
'Broussard' (Max Holste M.H.1521M), 95
'Buccaneer' S.Mk.2B (Hawker Siddeley), 109
'Buckeye' (Rockwell (North American) T–2C), 184
'Buffalo' (De Havilland Canada DHC–5), 83
'Bulldog' Series 120 (Scottish Aviation), 113

C–1A (Kawasaki (NAMC)), 124
C–2A 'Greyhound' (Grumman), 158
C–5A 'Galaxy' (Lockheed), 164
C–9A 'Nightingale' (McDonnell Douglas), 173
C–42 'Regente' (Neiva), 79
C–45G 'Expeditor' (Beechcraft), 136
C–46D 'Commando' (Curtiss-Wright), 151
C–47 'Skytrain' (Dakota) (Douglas), 152
C–54 'Skymaster' (Douglas), 152
C–118A 'Liftmaster' (Douglas), 153
C–119G 'Flying Boxcar' (Fairchild), 154
C–121G 'Constellation' (Lockheed). 165

C–123B 'Provider' (Fairchild), 155
C–130H 'Hercules' (Lockheed), 165
C–135B 'Stratolifter' (Boeing), 144
C–140B 'JetStar' (Lockheed), 166
C–141A 'StarLifter' (Lockheed), 167
C.160 (Transall), 98
C.207A 'Azor' (CASA), 128
C.212 'Aviocar' (CASA), 130
Canadair CL–28 'Argus' Mk.2., 80
  CL–41A 'Tutor', 80
  CL–41G, 80
  CL–215, 81
'Canberra' B.(1)Mk.8 (English Electric),
  106
  B.15 (English Electric), 106
Candid (Ilyushin Il–76), 196
'Caribou' (De Havilland Canada
  DHC–4A), 83
Casa C.212 'Aviocar', 130
  C.207A 'Azor', 128
'Catalina' (Convair PBY–5A), 150
'Cayuse' (Hughes OH–6A), 163
Cessna A–37B 'Dragonfly', 146
  O–1E 'Birddog', 146
  O–2A, 147
  T–37B, 147
  T–41B 'Mescalero', 148
  U–3A 'Blue Canoe', 148
  U–17A and B, 149
Ch–3E (Sikorsky S–61R), 187
CH–34A 'Choctaw' (Sikorsky S–58), 186
CH–46D 'Sea Knight' (Boeing-Vertol
  107–ll), 145C
CH–47C 'Chinook' (Boeing-Vertol), 145
CH–53A 'Sea Stallion' (Sikorsky S–65A),
  188
CH–54A 'Tarhe' (Sikorsky S–64
  'Skycrane'), 188
'Chienshou' (Pazmany/Caf PL–1B), 135
'Chinook' (Boeing-Vertol CH–47C), 145
'Chipmunk'(De Havilland Canada
  DHC–1), 81
CL–28 'Argus' Mk.2. (Canadair), 80
CL–41G (Canadair), 80
CL–41A 'Tutor' (Canadair), 80
CL–215 (Canadair), 81
C.M.170 'Magister' (Potez-Air Fouga),
  97
C.M.170–2 'Super-Magister' (Potez-Air
  Fouga), 97
Coach (Ilyushin Il–12), 195
Codling (Yakovel Yak–40), 216
Colt (Antonov An–2), 191
'Commando' (Curtiss-Wright C–46D),
  151
'Constellation' (Lockheed C–121G), 165
Convair F–102A 'Delta Dagger', 149
  F–106A 'Delta Dart', 150
  PBY–5A 'Catalina', 150
Cookpot (Tupolev Tu–124), 211
Coot (Ilyushin Il–18), 195
'Corsair' II (Vought A–7D), 189
'Courier' (Helio U–10A), 161
Crate (Ilyushin Il–14M), 194
Creek–D (Yakovel Yak–12A), 213
'Crusader' (Vought F–8E and F–8J),
  190
CT–4 'Airtrainer' (NZAI), 127
Cub (Antonov An–12), 191

Curtiss-Wright C–46D 'Commando',
  151
Dakota (Douglas C–47 'Skytrain'), 152
Dassault 'Etendard' IVM, 91
  (Fan Jet) 'Falcon' 20 ('Mysteré 20), 91
  'Mirage' IIIC, 92
  'Mirage' IIIE, 93
  'Mirage' IIIR, 93
  'Mirage' IVA, 93
  'Mirage' 5, 93
  'Mirage' F1C, 94
  'Super Mystère' B2, 94
Dassault-Breguet/Dornier 'Alphajet', 95
De Havilland (Hawker Siddeley) D.H.104
  'Dove', 104
  D.H.115 'Vampire' T.Mk.11, 104
  'Venom' F.B.Mk.50., 105
De Havilland Canada DHC–1
  'Chipmunk', 81
  DHC–2 'Beaver', 82
  DHC–3 'Otter', 82
  DHC–4A 'Caribou', 83
  DHC–5 'Buffalo', 83
  DHC–5D, 84
  DHC–6 'Twin Otter' Series 200, 84
  DHC–6 'Twin Otter' Series 300, 84
'Delfin' (Maya) (Aero L–29), 85
'Delta Dagger' (Convair F–102A), 149
'Delta Dart' (Convair F–106A), 150
D.H.104 'Dove' (De Havilland) (Hawker
  Siddeley), 104
D.H.115 'Vampire' T.Mk.11 (De
  Havilland), 104
DHC–1 'Chipmunk' (De Havilland
  Canada), 81
DHC–2 'Beaver' (De Havilland Canada),
  82
DHC–3 'Otter' (De Havilland Canada),
  82
DHC–4A 'Caribou' (De Havilland
  Canada), 83
DHC–5 'Buffalo' (De Havilland Canada),
  83
DHC–5D (De Havilland Canada), 84
DHC–6 'Twin Otter' Series 200, (De
  Havilland Canada), 84
DHC–6 'Twin Otter' Series 300 (De
  Havilland Canada), 84
Do–27A–4 (Dornier), 99
Do–28D 'Skyservant' (Dornier), 99
'Dominie' T.Mk.1. (Hawker Siddeley),
  110
Dornier 'Alphajet' (Dassault-Breguet),
  95
  Do–27A–4, 99
  Do–28D 'Skyservant', 99
Douglas A–3B 'Skywarrior', 151
  C–47 'Skytrain' (Dakota), 152
  C–54 'Skymaster', 152
  C–118A 'Liftmaster', 153
'Dove' (De Havilland (Hawker Siddeley)
  D.H.104, 104
'Dragonfly' (Cessna A–37B), 146
'Draken' (J35F) (Saab 35), 131

E–2C 'Hawkeye' (Grumman), 158
E–3A (AWACS) (Boeing), 142
'Eagle' (McDonnell Douglas F–15A),
  175

EC–121 'Warning Star' (Lockheed, 165
EMB–110 'Bandeirante' (Embraer), 79
Embraer EMB–110 'Bandeirante', 79
English Electric 'Canberra' B.(I)Mk.8.,
  106
  'Canberra' B.15, 106
'Etendard' IV.M (Dassault), 91
'Expeditor' (Beechcraft C–45G), 136

F1C (Dassault 'Mirage'), 94
F–4E 'Phantom' (McDonnell Douglas),
  174
F–5A (Northrop), 180
F–5B (Northrop), 180
F–5E 'Tiger' II (Northrop), 180
F–9 (Shenyang), 84
F–14A 'Tomcat' (Grumman), 159
F–15A 'Eagle' (McDonnell Douglas),
  175
F–16 (General Dynamics), 155
F.27M 'Troopship' (Fokker), 126
F–86D(L) 'Sabre' (North American), 176
F–86F 'Sabre' (North American), 177
F–86K 'Sabre' (North American), 177
F–100D 'Super Sabre' (North
  American), 178
F–100F 'Super Sabre' (North American),
  178
F–101B 'Voodoo' (McDonnell), 176
F–102A 'Delta Dagger' (Convair), 149
F–104G 'Starfighter' (Lockheed), 167
F–106A 'Delta Dart' (Convair), 150
F–111E (General Dynamics), 156
Fairchild A–10A, 153
  C–119G 'Flying Boxcar', 154
  C–123B 'Provider', 155
Fairchild-Hiller FH–1100, 155
Fairey BN–2A 'Islander'
  (Britten-Norman), 103
  'Gannet' A.E.W.Mk.3, 106
'Falcon' 20 ('Mystère' 20) (Dassault
  (Fan Jet)), 91
(Fan Jet) 'Falcon' 20 ('Mystère' 20)
  (Dassault), 91
Farmer C (Mikoyan MiG–195), 199
FB–11A (General Dynamics), 157
F.(G.A.) Mk.9 (Hawker 'Hunter'), 108
Fencer (Sukhoi Su–19), 208
FH–1100 (Fairchild-Hiller), 155
Fiat G.91R.1 and R.3, 120
  G.91Y., 121
Fiddler (Tupolev Tu–28P), 211
Firebar (Yakovel Yak–28P), 215
Fishbed–C (Mikoyan MiG–21F), 200
  –D (Mikoyan MiG–21PF), 200
  –K (Mikoyan MiG–21SMT), 200
Fishpot–C (Sukhoi Su–11), 207
Fitter–A (Sukhoi Su–7BM), 206
  C (Sukhoi Su–17), 208
Flagon–A (Sukhoi Su–15), 207
Flashlight–A (Yakovel Yak–25F), 214
Flogger–B (Mikoyan MiG–23S), 201
  D (Mikoyan MiG–23), 201
'Flying Boxcar' (Fairchild C–119G), 154
FMA I.A.35 'Huanquero', 77
  I.A.50 'Guarani II', 77
  I.A.58 'Pucara', 78
F.Mk.6 (BAC 'Lightning'), 102
T.Mk.5. (BAC 145 'Jet Provost'), 101

Fokker-VFW F.27M 'Troopship', 126
Forger (Yakovlev Yak–36), 215
Fouga C.M.170 'Magister' (Potez-Air), 97
  C.M.170–2 'Super-Magister' (Potez-Air), 97
Foxbat–A (Mikoyan MiG–25), 202
'Frégate' (Aérospatiale N.262D), 87
Fresco–C (Mikoyan-Gurevich MiG–17F), 198
  –D (Mikoyan-Gurevich MiG–17PF), 199
Fuji KM–2., 123
  T–1A 'Hatsutaka', 123
  T–1B 'Hatsutaka', 124

G–2A 'Galeb' (Soko), 217
G.222 (Aeritalia), 119
G.91R.1 and R.3 (Fiat), 120
G.91Y. (Fiat), 121
GAF 'Nomad' 22., 78
'Galaxy' (Lockheed C–5A), 164
'Galeb' (Soko G–2A), 217
'Gannet' A.E.W.Mk.3 (Fairey), 106
'Gazelle' (Aérospatiale/Westland S.A.341), 89
General Dynamics F–16, 155
  F–111E, 156
  FB–111A, 157
'Gnat' Mk.1. (Hawker Siddeley), 110
'Greyhound' (Grumman C–2A), 158
Grumman A–6E 'Intruder', 157
  C–2A 'Greyhound', 158
  E–2C 'Hawkeye', 158
  F–14A 'Tomcat', 159
  HU–16B 'Albatross', 159
  OV–1C 'Mohawk', 160
  OV–1D 'Mohawk', 160
  S–2E 'Tracker', 161
'Guarani II' (FMA I.A.50), 77

H–19 'Chickawa' (Sikorsky S–55), 185
HA–200D 'Saeta' (Hispano), 130
HA–220 'Super-Saeta' (Hispano), 131
HAL HF–24 'Marut' Mk.1A., 116
  HJT–16 Mk.2. 'Kiran', 117
  HT–2, 117
Handley Page 'Jetstream' T.Mk.1, 106
Handley Page 'Victor' K.Mk.2, 107
Hare (Mil MI–1 and Mi–3), 202
Harke (Mil Mi–10), 205
  (Mil Mi–10K), 205
'Harrier' G.R.Mk.3. (Hawker Siddeley), 111
'Hatsutaka' (Fuji T–1A), 123
  (Fuji T–1B), 124
'Hawk' T.Mk.1. (Hawker Siddeley), 111
Hawker 'Hunter' F.(G.A.) Mk.9, 108
Hawker Siddeley 'Andover' C.Mk.1., 109
  'Buccaneer' S.Mk.2B, 109
  D.H.104 'Dove' (De Havilland), 104
  'Dominie' T.Mk.1., 110
  'Gnat' Mk.1., 110
  'Harrier' G.R.Mk.3., 111
  'Hawk' T.Mk.1., 111
  'Nimrod' M.R.Mk.1., 112
  'Vulcan' B.Mk.2., 112
'Hawkeye' (Grumman E–2C), 158

Helio U–10A 'Courier', 161
'Hercules' (Lockheed C–130H), 165
HF–24 'Marut' Mk.1A. (HAL), 116
HH–43B 'Huskie' (Kaman), 163
HH–43F 'Huskie' (Kaman), 164
Hiller 12E (OH–23G 'Raven'), 162
Hind A (Mil Mi–24), 205
Hip (Mil Mi–8), 204
Hispano HA–200D 'Saeta', 130
  HA–220 'Super-Saeta', 131
HJT–16 Mk.2. 'Kiran' (HAL), 117
HT–2 (HAL), 117
Holste M.H.1521M 'Broussard' (Max), 95
Hook (Mil Mi–6), 203
Hoplite (Mil Mi–2), 202
Hormone–A (Kamov Ka–25), 197
Hound (Mil Mi–4), 203
HU–16B 'Albatross' (Grumman), 159
'Huanquero' (FMA I.A.35), 77
'Huey Cobra' (Bell AH–1G), 141
Hughes 269A (TH–55A 'Osage'), 162
  OH–6A 'Cayuse', 163
'Hunter' F.(G.A.)Mk.9 (Hawker), 108
Hunting 'Pembroke' C.Mk.1., 113
'Huskie' (Kaman HH–43B), 163
  (Kaman HH–43F), 164

I. (Morane Saulnier M.S.760A 'Paris'), 96
I–115 (AISA), 128
I.A.35 'Huanquero' (FMA), 77
I.A.50 'Guarani II' (FMA), 77
I.A.58 'Pucara' (FMA), 78
IAI–201 'Arava', 118
IAI 'Kfir'. C2, 118
Il–12 (Coach) (Ilyushin), 195
Il–14M (Crate) (Ilyushin), 194
Il–18 (Coot) (Ilyushin), 195
Ilyushin Il–12 (Coach), 195
  Il–14M (Crate), 194
  Il–18 (Coot), 195
  Il–28 (Beagle), 196
  Il–38 (May), 196
  Il–76 (Candid), 196
'Intruder' (Grumman A–6E), 157
'Iskra' (WSK TS–11), 128
'Islander' (Britten-Norman (Fairey) BN–2A), 103

J–1 'Jastreb' (Soko), 217
J 35F (Saab 35 'Draken'), 131
'Jaguar' A. (SEPECAT), 97
'Jastreb' (Soko J–1), 217
'Jet Provost' T.Mk.5. (BAC 145), 101
'JetRanger' (OH–58A 'Kiowa') (Bell 206A), 140
'JetStar' (Lockheed C–140B), 166
'Jetstream' T.Mk.1. (Handley Page), 107
Jurom (Soko–Iar) 'Orao', 216

Kaman HH–43B 'Huskie', 163
  HH–43F 'Huskie', 164
  SH–2F 'Seasprite', 164
Kamov Ka–25 (Hormone–A), 197
Kawasaki (NAMC) C–1A, 124
KC–135A 'Stratotanker' (Boeing), 144
KC–97L 'Stratofighter' (Boeing), 143
'Kfir'. C2. (IAI), 118

'Kiran' (HAL HJT–16 Mk.2., 117
KM–2 (Fuji), 123
'Kraguj' (Soko P–2), 218

L–29 'Delfin' (Maya) (Aero), 85
L–39 'Albatross' (Aero), 85
L–42 'Regente' (Neiva), 80
L–60 'Brigadýr', 86
'Lansen' (A32A) (Saab 32), 131
'Liftmaster' (Douglas C–118A), 153
'Lightning' F.Mk.6. (BAC), 102
Lockheed C–5A 'Galaxy', 164
  C–121G 'Constellation', 165
  C–130H 'Hercules', 165
  C–140B 'JetStar', 166
  C–141A 'Starlifter', 167
  EC–121 'Warning Star', 165
  F–104G 'Starfighter', 167
  P–2H 'Neptune', 168
  P–3C 'Orion', 169
  S–3A 'Viking', 169
  SR–71A, 170
  T–33 'T–Bird', 170
  U–2C, 171
'Lynz' AH.Mk.1. (Westland WG.13), 116

M–4 'Molot' (Bison) (Myasishchev), 206
Madge (Beriev Be–6), 194
'Magister' (Potez-Air Fouga C.M.170), 97
Mail (Beriev Be–12 'Tchaika'), 194
Mangrove (Yakovlev Yak–27R), 214
Martin B–57B, 171
  RB–57F, 172
'Marut' Mk.1A. (HAL HF–24), 116
Max Holste M.H.1521M 'Broussard', 95
May (Ilyushin Il–38), 196
Maya (Aero L–29 'Delfin'), 85
MB.326G (Aermacchi), 119
MB.326K (Aermacchi), 120
MBB BO–105, 100
McDonnell F–101B 'Voodoo', 176
  RF–101C 'Voodoo', 176
McDonnell Douglas A–4F 'Skyhawk', 172
  A–4M, 173
  C–9A 'Nightingale', 173
  F–4B, C, D and RF–4B, C 'Phantom II', 173
  F–4E 'Phantom', 174
  F–15A 'Eagle', 175
  RF–4E 'Phantom', 174
McDonnell Douglas/Northrop F–18, 175
Meiwa PS–1 (Shin), 126
'Mentor' (Beechcraft T–34A), 137
'Mentor' (Beechcraft T–34C), 137
'Mescalero' (Cessna T–41B), 148
M.H.1521M 'Broussard' (Max Holste), 95
Mi–8 (Hip)., 204
Mi–10 (Harke), (Mil), 205
Mi–10K (Harke) (Mil), 205
Mi–24 (Hind–A) (Mil), 205
Midget (Mikoyan-Gurevich MiG–15UTI), 197
MiG–15UTI (Midget) (Mikoyan-Gurevich), 197
MiG–17F (Fresco–C) (Mikoyan-Gurevich), 198

MiG–17PF (Fresco–D)
  (Mikoyan-Gurevich), 199
MiG–19S (Farmer C) (Mikoyan), 199
MiG–21F (Fishbed–C) (Mikoyan), 200
MiG–21PF (Fishbed–D) (Mikoyan), 200
MiG–21SMT (Fishbed–K) (Mikoyan),
  200
MiG–23 (Flogger–D) (Mikoyan), 201
MiG–23S (Flogger–B) (Mikoyan), 201
Mikoyan MiG–19S (Farmer C), 199
  MiG–21F (Fishbed–C), 200
  MiG–21PF (Fishbed–D), 200
  MiG–21SMT (Fishbed–K), 200
  MiG–23 (Flogger–D), 201
  MiG–23S (Flogger–B), 201
  MiG–25 (Foxbat–A), 202
Mikoyan-Gurevich MiG–15UTI (Midget),
  197
  MiG–17F (Fresco–C), 198
  MiG–17PF (Fresco–D), 199
Mil MI–1 and Mi–3 (Hare), 202
  Mi–2 (Hoplite), 202
  Mi–4 (Hound), 203
  Mi–6 (Hook), 203
  Mi–8 (Hip)., 204
  Mi–10 (Harke), 205
  Mi–10K (Harke), 205
  Mi–24 (Hind–A), 205
'Mirage' IIIC (Dassault), 92
  IIIE (Dassault), 93
  IIIR (Dassault), 93
  IVA (Dassault), 93
  5 (Dassault), 93
  FIC (Dassault), 94
Mitsubishi MU–2C, 124
  T–2, 125
'Mohawk' (Grumman OV–1C), 160
  (Grumman OV–1D), 160
'Molot' (Bison) (Myasishchev M–4), 206
Moose (Yakolev Yat–11), 212
Morane-Saulnier M.S.760A 'Paris' I.,
  96
Moss (Tupolev Tu–126), 210
M.R.Mk.3, Phase 3 (Avro 'Shackleton'),
  101
MRCA 'Tornado' (Panavia), 100
M.S.760A 'Paris' I. (Morane-Saulnier),
  96
MU–2C (Mitsubishi), 124
'Musketeer Sport' (Beechcraft), 136
Myasishchev M–4 'Molot' (Bison), 206
'Mystere' 20 (Dassault (Fan Jet)
  'Falcon' 20), 91

N.2501 'Noratlas (Nord), 96
N.262D 'Fregate' (Aérospatiale), 87
NAMC C–1A (Kawasaki), 124
NAMC YS–11A, 125
Neiva C–42 'Regente', 79
  L–42 'Regente', 80
  T–25 'Universal', 80
'Neptune' (Lockheed P–2H), 168
'Nightingale' (McDonnell Douglas
  C–9A), 173
'Nimrod' M.R.Mk.1 (Hawker Siddeley),
  112
'Nomad' 22 (GAF), 78
'Noratlas' (Nord N.2501), 96
Nord N.2501 'Noratlas', 96

North American F–86D(L) 'Sabre', 176
  F–86F 'Sabre', 177
  F–86K 'Sabre', 177
  F–100D 'Super Sabre', 178
  F–100F 'Super Sabre', 178
  OV–10A 'Bronco' (Rockwell), 183
RA–5C 'Vigilante' (Rockwell), 184
  T–2C 'Buckeye' (Rockwell), 184
  T–6G 'Texan', 178
  T–28A 'Trojan', 178
  T–28D 'Trojan', 178
  T–39A 'Sabreliner' (Rockwell), 185
Northrop F–5A, 180
  F–5B, 180
  F–5E 'Tiger' II, 180
  F–18 (McDonnell Douglas), 175
  T–38A 'Talon', 181
NZAI CT–4 'Airtrainer', 127

O–1E 'Birddog' (Cessna), 146
O–2A (Cessna), 147
OH–6A 'Cayuse' (Hughes), 163
OH–13H 'Sioux' (Bell 47G–3B–2
  'Trooper'), 139
OH–23G 'Raven' (Hiller 12E), 162
OH–58A 'Kiowa' (Bell 206A
  'JetRanger'), 140
'Orao' (Jurom (Soko-Iar)), 216
'Orion' (Lockheed P–3C), 169
'Otter' (De Havilland Canada DHC–3),
  82
OV–1C 'Mohawk' (Grumman), 160
OV–1D 'Mohawk' (Grumman), 160

P–2 'Kraguj' (Soko), 218
P–2H 'Neptune' (Lockheed), 168
P–3 (Pilatus), 134
P–3C 'Orion' (Lockheed), 169
P.166M (Piaggio), 121
Panavia MRCA 'Tornado', 100
'Paris' I (Morane-Saulnier M.S.760A),
  96
Pazmany/Caf PL–1B 'Chienshou', 135
PBY–5A 'Catalina' (Convair), 150
PC–6 'Porter' (Pilatus), 135
PC–6A, B, C 'Turbo-Porter' (Pilatus),
  135
'Pchelka' (Clod). (Antonov An–14), 192
'Pembroke' C.Mk.1. (Hunting), 113
'Phantom' (McDonnell Douglas F–4E),
  174
  (McDonnell Douglas RF–4E), 174
  II (McDonnell Douglas F–4B, C, D and
  RF–4B, C), 173
Piaggio P.166M., 121
Pilatus P–3, 134
Pilatus PC–6 'Porter', 135
Pilatus PC–6A, B, C 'Turbo-Porter', 135
Piper U–7A 'SuperCub', 181
Piper U–11A 'Aztec', 181
'Porter' (Pilatus PC–6), 135
Potez-Air Fouga C.M.170 'Magister', 97
  C.M.170–2 'Super-Magister', 97
'Provider' (Fairchild C–123B), 155
PS–1 (Shin Meiwa), 126
'Pucara' (FMA I.A.58),78
'Puma' (Aérospatiale/Westland
  S.A.330), 89
PZL–104 'Wilga' 35AD, 127

'Ranger' (UK–13) (Bell 47J–2), 139
RB–57F (Martin), 172
'Regente' (Neiva C–42), 79
  (Neiva L–42), 80
RF–4E 'Phantom' (McDonnell Douglas),
  174
RF–101C 'Voodoo' (McDonnell), 176
Rockwell B–1A, 182
Rockwell 'Shrike Commander', 182
Rockwell 'Turbo Commander 680', 183
Rockwell (North American) OV–10A
  'Bronco', 183
  (North American) RA–5C 'Vigilante',
  184
  (North American) T–2C 'Buckeye', 184
  (North American) T–39A 'Sabreliner',
  185

S–2E 'Tracker' (Grumman), 161
S–3A 'Viking' (Lockheed), 169
S–61B 'Sea King' HAS.Mk.1.
  (Westland), 114
S.A.316A 'Alouette' III (Aérospatiale),
  88
S.A.318C 'Alouette' II (Aérospatiale), 88
S.A.321 'Super Frelon' (Aérospatiale),
  89
S.A.330 'Puma'
  (Aérospatiale/Westland), 89
S.A.341 'Gazelle'
  (Aérospatiale/Westland), 89
Saab 32 'Lansen' (A 32A), 131
  35 'Draken' (J 35F), 131
  37 'Viggen' (AJ37), 132
  91D 'Sarif', 132
  105 (Sk 60), 133
  105XT, 133
  'Supporter', 134
'Sabreliner' (Rockwell (North American)
  T–39A), 185
'Sabre' (North American F–86D(L)), 176
  (North American F–86F), 177
  (North American F–86K), 177
'Saeta' (Hispano HA–200D), 130
'Sarif' (Saab 91D), 132
Scottish Aviation 'Bulldog Series 120,
  113
'Scout' AHMk.1. (Westland), 115
S.E.313B (Aérospatiale), 87
'Sea Cobra' (Bell AH–1J), 142
'Sea King' HAS.Mk.1. (Westland
  (S–61B)), 114
'Seasprite' (Kaman SH–2F), 164
'Seminole' (Beechcraft U–8F), 137
SEPECAT 'Jaguar' A, 97
SH–2F 'Seasprite' (Kaman), 164
SH–3D 'Sea King' (Sikorsky) S–61B,
  186
'Shackleton' M.R.Mk. 3, Phase 3 (Avro),
  101
Shenyang F–9, 84
Shin Meiwa PS–1, 126
Short 'Skyvan' 3M., 113
'Shrike Commander' (Rockwell), 182
SIAI–Marchetti S.208M., 121
  SF.260MX., 122
  SM–1019A, 122
Sikorsky HH–52A, 187
  S–55 (H–19 'Chickawa'), 185

S–58 (CH–34A 'Choctaw', UH–D 'Sea Horse'), 186
S–61B (SH–3D 'Sea King'), 186
S–61R (CH–3E), 187
S–62A, 187
S–64 'Skycrane' (CH–54A 'Tarhe'), 188
S–65A (CH–53A 'Sea Stallion'), 188
S–70 (UH–60A), 189
(Sk 60) (Saab 105), 133
'Skyhawk' (McDonnell Douglas A–4F), 172
'Skymaster' (Douglas C–54), 152
'Skyservant' (Dornier Do–28D), 99
'Skytrain' (Dakota) (Douglas C–47), 152
'Skyvan' 3M (Short), 113
'Skywarrior (Douglas A–3B), 151
S.208M. (SIAI-Marchetti), 121
SF.260MX. (SIAI-Marchetti), 122
SM–2 (WSK), 128
SM.1019A. (SIAI-Marchetti), 122
Soko G–2A 'Galeb', 217
 J–1 'Jastreb', 217
 P–2 'Kraguj', 218
Soko-lar 'Orao' (Jurom), 216
SR–71A (Lockheed), 170
'Starfighter' (Lockheed F–104G), 167
'Starlifter' (Lockheed C–141A), 167
'Stratofighter' (Boeing KC–97L), 143
'Stratofortress' (Boeing B–52H), 143
'Stratolifter' (Boeing C–135B), 144
'Stratotanker' (Boeing KC–135A), 144
'Strikemaster' (BAC 167), 102
Sukhoi Su–7BM (Fitter–A), 206
 Su–11 (Fishpot–C), 207
 Su–15 (Flagon–A), 207
 Su–17 (Fitter–C), 208
 Su–19 (Fencer), 208
'SuperCub' (Piper U–7A), 181
'Super Frelon' (Aérospatiale S.A.321), 89
'Super-Magister' (Potez-Air Fouga C.M.170–2), 97
'Super Mystère' B2 (Dassault), 94
'Super Sabre' (North American F–100D), 178
'Super Sabre' (North American F–100F), 178
'Super-Saeta' (Hispano HA–220), 131
'Supporter' (Saab), 134

T–1A 'Hatsutaka' (Fuji), 123
T–1B 'Hatsutaka' (Fuji), 124
T–2 (Mitsubishi), 125
T–6G 'Texan' (North American), 178
T–23 (Aerotec 122) 'Uirapuru', 79
T–25 'Universal' (Neiva), 80

T–28A 'Trojan' (North American), 178
T–28D 'Trojan' (North American), 178
T–33 'T–Bird' (Lockheed), 170
T–34A 'Mentor' (Beechcraft), 137
T–34C 'Mentor' (Beechcraft), 137
T–37B (Cessna), 147
T–38A 'Talon' (Northrop), 181
T–41B 'Mescalero' (Cessna), 148
T–43A (Boeing), 144
'Talon' (Northrop T–38A), 181
'T–Bird' (Lockheed T–33), 170
'Tchaika' (Mail) (Beriev Be–12), 194
'Texan' (North American T–6G), 178
TH–55A 'Osage' (Hughes 269A), 162
'Tiger' II (Northrop F–5E), 180
'Tomcat' (Grumman F–14A), 159
'Tornado' (Panavia MRCA), 100
'Tracker' (Grumman S–2E), 161
Transall C.160., 98
'Trenér' (Zlin Z–226), 86
 (Zlin Z–526), 86
'Trojan' (North American T–28A), 178
'Trojan' (North American T–28D), 178
'Troopship' (Fokker-VFW F.27M), 126
TS–11 'Iskra' (WSK), 128
'Trooper' (OH–13H 'Sioux') (Bell 47G–3B–2), 139
Tupolev Tu–20 (Bear A), 209
 Tu–22 (Blinder–A), 210
 Tu–26(?) (Backfire–B), 212
 Tu–28P (Fiddler), 211
 Tu–124 (Cookpot), 211
 Tu–126 (Moss), 210
'Turbo Commander 680' (Rockwell), 183
'Turbo-Porter' (Pilatus PC–6A, B, C), 135
'Tutor' (Canadair CL–41A), 80
'Twin Otter' Series 200 (De Havilland Canada DHC–6), 84
 Series 300 (De Havilland Canada DHC–6),84
Twin Two-Twelve (UH–1N 'Twin-Huey') (Bell 212), 141

U–2C (Lockheed), 171
U–3A 'Blue Canoe' (Cessna), 148
U–7A 'Super Cub' (Piper), 181
U–8F 'Seminole' (Beechcraft), 137
U–10A 'Courier' (Helio), 161
U–11A 'Aztec' (Piper), 181
U–17A and B (Cessna), 149
U–21A 'Ute' (Beechcraft), 138
UH–1B 'Iroquois', (Bell 204B), 139
UH–1H 'Iroquois' (Bell 205A), 140

UH–1N 'Twin-Huey' (Bell 212 Twin Two-Twelve), 141
UH–60A (Sikorsky S–70), 189
UH–D 'Sea Horse' (Sikorsky S–58), 186
UK–13 (Bell 47J–2 'Ranger'), 139
'Uirapuru' (T–23) (Aerotec 122), 79
'Universal' (Neiva T–25), 80
'Ute' (Beechcraft U–21A), 138
UTVA–60ATI, 218
 –66, 218

'Vampire' T.Mk.11 (De Havilland D.H.115), 104
'VC10'C.Mk.1. (BAC), 103
'Venom' F.B.Mk.50. (De Havilland), 105
'Victor' K.Mk.2 (Handley Page), 107
'Viggen' (AJ37) (Saab 37), 132
'Vigilante' (Rockwell (North American) RA–5C), 184
'Viking' (Lockheed S–3A), 169
'Voodoo' (McDonnell F–101B), 176
 (McDonnell RF–101C), 176
Vought A–7D 'Corsair' II, 189
 F–8E and F–8J 'Crusader', 190
'Vulcan' B.Mk.2. (Hawker Siddeley), 112

'Warning Star' (Lockheed EC–21), 165
'Wasp' HAS.Mk.1. (Westland), 114
'Wessex' HAS.Mk.3. (Westland), 115
 HU.Mk.5. (Westland), 116
Westland (S–61B) 'Sea King' HAS.Mk.1., 114
 'Scout' AH.Mk.1., 115
 'Wasp' HAS.Mk.1., 114
 'Wessex' HAS.Mk.3., 115
 'Wessex' HU.Mk.5., 116
 WG.13 'Lynx' AH.Mk.1., 116
'Wilga' 35AD (PZL–104), 127
WSK SM–2, 128
 TS–11 'Iskra', 128

Yakolev Yak–11 (Moose), 212
 Yak–12A (Creek–D), 213
 Yak–18A, 214
 Yak–25F (Flashlight–A), 214
 Yak–27R (Mangrove), 214
 Yak–28 (Brewer), 215
 Yak–28P (Firebar), 215
 Yak–36 (Forger), 215
 Yak–40 (Codling), 216
Ys–11A (NAMC), 125

Z–226 'Trenér' (Zlin), 86
Z–526 'Trenér' (Zlin), 86
Zlin Z–226 'Trenér', 86
 Z–526 'Trenér', 86